A Couple in the Corps:

*A Peace Corps Journey
from a Couple's Perspective*

By Eric Starr

Cover Design by
Christine Charboneau

Book Layout by
Brushy Mountain Publishing

Table of Contents

1. Peace Corps.. 1

2. Background On Who We Are....................................... 3

3. Why We Joined The Peace Corps............................... 10

4. Placement Process.. 17

5. Staging In Miami For Three Days............................... 22

6. Arrival In Managua and Training For Three Days in Granada. 25

7. History of Nicaragua.. 32

8. Hurricane Mitch.. 57

9. Separation And Departure To Our Training Towns.......... 62

10. Training Week 1: Training Begins, A Period of Adjustment..... 72

11. Training Week 2: Spanish Classes and Animal Brutality.......... 118

12. Training Week 3: Language Humor, Learning About
    Dengue Fever and Malaria.. 121

13. Training Week 4: Applied Spanish, Middle of the Night
    "Wake Up" Call, Learning About Volunteer Sexual Assault...... 126

14. Training Week 5: Volunteer Visit, Folkloric Dance,
    Adventurous Hike... 135

15. Training Week 6: Routine, Unique Businessman,
    Language Exam.. 141

16. Training Week 7: Teaching, Health Issue, Mystery Solved,
    Site Placement.. 143

17. Training Week 8: Trainee Assault, Counterpart Day, Site Visit 149

18. Training Week 9: Site Visit, Negotiating Rent, Surfboard Deal,
    Baseball Arrives... 155

19. Training Week 10: Personal Spanish Classes, Community Bank
    Priority, Coping with Stress....................................... 168

20. Training Week 11: Final Language Interview, Saying Goodbye,
    Sworn In As Volunteers.. 171

21. Service Begins.. 181

22. Working Projects.. 197

23. Primary Project Introduction: La Empresa Creativa.................. 198

24. Los Pipitos and Handicap International............................ 199

25. Enter the Shady Bunch... 206

26. Los Pipitos Continued.. 208

27. Kathryn's First Top Ten List..................................... 213

28. English Classes.. 214

29. Stove Project.. 231

30. Whitewater Rafting... 235

31. Habitat For Humanity... 245

32. Kathryn "Quits".. 253

33. Kathryn's Second Top Ten List.................................... 257

34. Kathryn's April Fools' Joke...................................... 258

35. Community Banks.. 261

36. La Empresa Creativa: Our Primary Project......................... 276

37. Medevac.. 284

38. Sense of Smell in Health Care.................................... 288

39. Almost Back to School, but Not Quite............................. 290

40. Banana Truck... 291

41. Our First Full Year of Teaching Begins........................... 298

42. A Little More Fun.. 309

43. Kathryn's Women's Group.. 312

44. Kathryn Loses It... 315

45. The Shady Bunch.. 317

46. Visitors... 330

47. Operation Air Lift... 337

48. Close Of Service... 343

49. Final Thoughts and the Road Ahead................................ 344

Acknowledgements

First, a gracious thank you needs to be offered to my dear wife, Kathryn, for all of her patience and hard work to make this book a reality. If not for Kathryn's contribution to this writing project, the book never would have been able to be completed. I also want to say thank you to Kathryn for her inspiration, leadership, and love.

Kathryn and I needed a lot of support and assistance to have the opportunity to serve in the Peace Corps. We would like to humbly thank the following people for their significant help and great love: Grace and Jack Starr, Tom and Lois Chinnock, Sue Henry and John McClanahan, Angel Burgos, Kerry Reichs, Brian McNeil, Adam Cramer, Geoff Maron, Christelle LaPolice and Lee Boyle, Ryan Morris and Aimee Eden, Kelly Bauer and Jason Bennett, and Anita O'Shaughnessy. I also thank all present and returned Peace Corps Volunteers for their service, devotion, and sacrifice.

I dedicate this book to five people:

- Ambassador Jack Hood Vaughn, the second worldwide Peace Corps Director behind Sargent Shriver. Ambassador Jack Hood Vaughn is no longer with us, but he was an amazing man, an inspiration to many, and a great American. During his visit with Kathryn and me in Nicaragua, we were truly honored to engage him in some of our Peace Corps experience. He is dearly missed.
- Tom Chinnock, Kathryn's father. Tom's legacy of love and family commitment remains strong.
- Jack Starr, my father. The positive example he set is a guiding force in my life.
- Isabella Summer Starr and Serena Autumn Starr, my daughters. I hope that one day they consider service with the Peace Corps or other community volunteerism.

To all who read and hopefully enjoy this book, please consider suggesting *A Couple in the Corps* to someone you know, as a portion of the profit will go to benefit communities in Nicaragua. By simply suggesting *A Couple in the Corps* to others, you contribute to grassroots discussion and action to benefit humanity. Kathryn and I hope you like the adventure of *A Couple in the Corps*.

Preface

A Couple in the Corps is a book about a couple's experience while serving as Volunteers for the Peace Corps in Nicaragua.

This book was written to memorialize our journey, to provide insight about another culture, and to help shed light on what the experience might be like for those who have interest in serving with the Peace Corps. Prior to our arrival in Nicaragua, Kathryn and I did not know what to expect from training, nor did we know what to expect from our service. Therefore, in this book, I had the specific intention to depict the three-month training program in a chronological manner, whereas the story of our twenty-four month service is more fluid in relation to time; anecdotal scenarios as well as technical information are included throughout the story. The goal of this writing was to portray a broad-based picture of the country of Nicaragua and the Peace Corps experience from one Volunteer couple's perspective. However, setting prior expectations of general Peace Corps service is not recommended, as each Volunteer's experiences unfold on an individual basis. Further, all countries and cultures are different. Peace Corps operations are also unique on a country-to-country basis and each sector presents distinctive challenges.

Names have been changed where appropriate.

1
Peace Corps

"The best and most beautiful things in the world cannot be seen or even touched. They must be felt within the heart."
–Helen Keller

My wife and I chose to serve as a couple in the exciting and important work being accomplished by the Peace Corps; our relationship and lives are greatly improved as a result. The following is the story of a Peace Corps journey from the couple's perspective.

In 1960, Senator John F. Kennedy spoke at the University of Michigan and challenged students to serve their country in the cause of peace by living and working in developing countries. By Executive Order on March 1, 1961, President Kennedy established the Peace Corps to promote peace and friendship. The Peace Corps is staffed by Volunteers from the United States who live and work in developing communities around the globe. Peace Corps Volunteers presently work in sixty-five host countries and serve their communities in multiple sectors such as health care, agriculture, environment, and business development, among others.

The Peace Corps mission has three main goals:

1. Helping the people of interested countries to meet their need for trained men and women.
2. Helping promote a better understanding of Americans on the part of the peoples served.
3. Helping promote a better understanding of other peoples on the part of Americans.

Once accepted to serve, a Peace Corps applicant's worthwhile process to become a Volunteer begins with three months of intensive training in the country they are assigned. If a Peace Corps trainee successfully completes the rigorous three-month training program, they are sworn in as a Peace Corps Volunteer and begin their valuable service for a two-year duration. Total time served in the Peace Corps is twenty-seven months, unless an extension is granted. A Peace Corps Volunteer's service is generally filled with adventure and incredible challenges. Therefore, being a Peace Corps Volunteer can be one of the most spectacular life experiences an American could ever pursue.

2
Background On Who We Are

"It is one of the beautiful compensations of this life that no man can sincerely try to help another without helping himself."
–Ralph Waldo Emerson

I believe it is appropriate to have a little background about who we are to better understand our decision to enter the Peace Corps from an objective perspective. Changes happen in life's course, and sometimes fulfillment comes from following the disguised path that is laid before us; such was the case for Kathryn and me.

We feel we are decent human beings and good Americans. Some people called us crazy for joining the Peace Corps, but it was not the first time either of us heard that adjective to describe a part of who we are.

My name is Eric Starr. I have had the distinct pleasure of having my path in life cross with one of the most spectacular human beings who has ever walked this earth—my lovely wife, Kathryn Chinnock. What can I say, I love my gal. To be frank, she is an inspiration to me, and it is my goal in life to be like Kathryn.

Kathryn was thirty-three years old when the Peace Corps became a part of our lives. She has blonde hair and blue eyes, stands five-foot-four, and might be a hundred-five pounds soaking wet.

I'll use a few words to describe her, but I will let her story speak to who she is. Kathryn is independent above all else. She is intelligent, passionate and caring beyond my comprehension. She has an excellent sense of humor and is uniquely sensitive to the emotional energies of the people she encounters. Did I mention she is beautiful, tough as nails, and adventurous? Well, she is that, too.

Kathryn's story is explicitly interesting—not because she is an important person with a grand occupation—but because of the way she exists in the world. Being understanding, receptive, compassionate, and active is how we change the world into a better place. When I say "we," I am not just speaking about Kathryn and myself. I mean all of us, every person on the planet who wants and believes that the state of humanity and our attitudes towards each other can improve.

Throughout history, there are examples where important people have impacted the world on a grand scale. However, for the largest part it is we—collectively—whose combined energies and focused efforts can ameliorate the human condition. Kathryn is one of those folks who takes action to make life easier for other people.

Kathryn grew up in the Timberlake neighborhood of Barrington, Illinois. Her father, Tom, had his own real estate appraisal business. Her mother, Lois, taught high school English and worked as a substitute teacher while Kathryn was growing up, and then went back to work full-time after Kathryn left for college. At an early age, her parents instilled volunteerism in Kathryn through a variety of continuous community-service efforts. Kathryn and her two brothers, Tim and John, spent most of their summers as kids at Timberlake Beach, which is where we held our wedding ceremony.

Kathryn was a tomboy growing up. She was the first girl in the town of Barrington to register to play little league baseball. Like many women, she transformed herself from a tomboy and became a young lady, but she was always still interested in athletics. She excelled on softball and volleyball teams in high school and had a very active social calendar.

Kathryn attended Michigan State University and majored in International Relations with emphases in Sociology, Spanish, and Economics. She made good grades and when she graduated, Kathryn sent resumes to about a dozen schools in countries throughout Latin America. It took a few months, but finally someone called from a bilingual school in Cuernavaca, Mexico to ask if she could begin work as soon as possible. Kathryn packed two bags and left the United States the next week. Once in Mexico, she completely immersed herself in the Latino culture. She taught English and loved it.

Upon returning from Mexico, Kathryn moved to Washington, D.C. and began working for the Foreign Policy Group in October 1993. Her boss was a former U.S. Ambassador to Paraguay, and it was here that she acquired first-hand experience in international affairs. By the time she departed that firm in November 1999, Kathryn was the Ambassador's Chief of Staff and right-hand woman. She also had completed her Master's degree in Sociology at George Washington University during her tenure with the Foreign Policy Group.

Prior to our marriage, Kathryn traveled extensively in Latin America and lived in the Dominican Republic and Paraguay. Before she left for Paraguay, she expressed interest in being married to me. I was ready to marry her, but I did not appreciate the pressure. I said that when I was ready to be married, it would be me who would do the asking and that I would let her know when the time comes.

Kathryn paused, looked at me quite crossly and said, "That's fine big boy, but remember this—you may be the one doing the asking, but I will be the one saying 'yes' or 'no.'" I will let you ponder how my statement to Kathryn regarding marriage was going to come back and later haunt me.

I finally asked her to marry me on April 14, 1997 near the southern tip of South America in the Patagonia region of Chile. We were directly below Cerro Torres, a spectacular rock formation in Torres Del Paine National Park. The weather was dreadful with the wind blistering at about forty miles per hour accompanied by a horizontal, hard-driving cold rain. After the wind almost blew Kathryn off a cliff, we stopped in a small climbers' hut to get out of the weather. At that moment, I thought to myself that I could not ask for a more opportune place to ask the woman I love for her hand in marriage. I had pulled off the perfect surprise and I asked her to marry me. What did she do? Kathryn literally made me wait five minutes before she responded. The only sounds were the screaming of the wind outside and the rain pounding on the hut. I knelt in shock during those pressure-filled minutes. Kath finally said, "Yes" and then let me know that she felt so taken aback that she was not quite sure if I was being serious. Once she realized I was serious, she told me that she wanted to see me sweat a little. I ask you, is that tough love, or what? I deserved it.

We were married in 1998 outdoors at her neighborhood lake in Barrington, Illinois. We spent our honeymoon whitewater kayaking in western North Carolina and surf kayaking at the Outer Banks.

Kathryn wanted to continue pursuing her international interests. She always had a great fascination with the World Bank and wanted to understand more about how it functioned. She accepted a consultancy with the World Bank in 1998, working with the South Asia region. She juggled this consultant position while also working with the Foreign Policy Group. Once the contract job with the World Bank was completed, Kathryn pursued an opportunity at Johns Hopkins University.

She worked with the Center for Civil Society Studies on a research project that assessed the impact of the non-profit sector on a global scale.

On the weekends and a few weekday evenings during this period of time—while being employed with Johns Hopkins and occasionally with the Foreign Policy Group—Kathryn also worked as a whitewater kayaking instructor for an outdoor adventure company called Calleva. Even though her days were sometimes gruelingly long and exhausting, she never turned down an opportunity to work with people in a natural environment. She absolutely loved seeing adults light up like little kids when her students became hooked on kayaking. Kathryn has always been very active and unbelievably busy. She left Johns Hopkins to join the Peace Corps with me in May of 2004. Kathryn is a lovely lady who is highly competent and tough. I am really not biased at all.

My father, Jack Starr, was an Air Force Colonel, and my mother, Grace, often worked but was in charge of managing the home. I have an older sister named Margaret, who is an educator in Mississippi. My father was stern but fair and constantly encouraging. He rarely (if ever) allowed my sister or me to say the words "I can't." Jack Starr has had a major positive influence on my attitude toward life in so many ways. My father is my hero, and he definitely understands the concept of helping others. Jack Starr will go far out of his way to assist someone in need. My father's big heart is evident through community contributions, such as helping the elderly buy groceries and offering communion at nursing homes on Sundays. He also works for a community outreach program that helps families pay some of their utility bills, in addition to many other charitable endeavors. He is now retired and lives in Niceville, Florida. My father attends church on a daily basis.

One would think that because my father was a Colonel in the military, he would be the one you would not want to mess with in our family. Wrong. Don't play games with mom. I still often apologize to my mother for putting her through so much, as I was an incredibly active child. I even felt like I needed to apologize for going into the Peace Corps. The Peace Corps experience can be stressful for family members too.

I was thirty-six years old when the Peace Corps became a part of my life. I have brown hair (what's left of it) and brown eyes. I weigh two hundred and five pounds and am six-foot-one. I graduated from the University of Alabama with a degree in Commerce and Business Administration with a major in Finance. I would describe myself as reasonably intelligent with a good heart, an excellent sense of humor, a no-nonsense positive attitude, and a strong body developed by my outdoor activities.

I believe in acting on what I feel is right while also taking action on what I want out of life. I was deeply impacted by a book of motivational quotes that my father gave me during high school. The quote that I love the most is a bit selfish.

"It is one of the beautiful compensations of this life that no man can sincerely try to help another without helping himself."
–Ralph Waldo Emerson

I love the way the world recycles the good energies that we exert! No matter what you try to do for someone else, if your attitude and heart are in the right place, you will always win. I do not help others expecting something in return; however, how can we really receive anything worthwhile in life without first giving of ourselves? Working to benefit others is important. The result is an incredible human exchange of shared positive energy. This shared exchange can occur with any interaction, job, or volunteer service. If you are living honestly, have a smart plan, and you're working hard every day, positive results happen for all concerned. For me, that simple ideal is a way of life.

I have a profound appreciation for quality relationships. It is unlikely that any of us have achieved a worthwhile goal without developing a special relationship somewhere along the way that supported our successful endeavor. Kathryn and I are enthusiastically engaged with music and the arts. We have extended ourselves into many wonderful new relationships through attending creative performances.

We are both animal lovers and have an Australian Shepherd dog named Sam. Since Kathryn is such an animal lover, she joked with me frequently before going into the Peace Corps that she wanted to have a pet pig when we became settled in whatever country we were assigned. I always responded that bacon is a good thing to have around the house.

Like Kathryn, I have a sincere love for the outdoors and adventure. I have been a whitewater kayaking instructor for almost two decades. Kathryn and I regularly run experts-only level rapids and having this mutual passion fuels the fires of love for us all the more.

The activities that I have participated in are generally ones that could set your hair on fire. For example, I raced motorcycles and downhill mountain bikes for many years. I also worked on an offshore oil rig to help pay for college. Working offshore could quite literally set your hair on fire and that tough job taught me some valuable life lessons.

In August of 2001, I climbed the majority of Mount (Mt.) Rainier. I had never done any mountaineering before, and the idea seemed appealing. In a continuous twenty-four-hour push, I climbed from the bottom of the mountain to Ingram Flats and back. I climbed Rainier with close friends who are very experienced mountaineers, and the group moved up the mountain at an intense pace. Everyone who attempted the summit in our group succeeded except me.

The route up Mt. Rainier became sketchy once we climbed above ten thousand feet of elevation. Traversing almost vertical ice, moving through deep snow, and avoiding crevasses became part of the climbing challenges. The experienced team skillfully educated me about various climbing techniques, the dangers, and offered encouraging guidance when needed. However, prior to going to the mountain, I developed a strict set of my own safety rules. When one of those rules was violated, I turned around and descended the mountain safely. Mt. Rainier is incredibly beautiful, and I would like to return in the future with more than twenty-four hours in which to attain the summit of that spectacular mountain.

Immediately after safely climbing the majority of Mt. Rainier, another adventure began. I hopped on my bike and rode alone from Anacortes, Washington, across the North Cascade Mountains, to Sandpoint, Idaho. The bike trip was a very fun, four-hundred mile, week-long adventure.

Before joining the Peace Corps, I worked at Charles Schwab and Morgan Stanley as an Associate Vice President. Additionally, I worked as a kayaking instructor, ropes course instructor, and general outdoor guide for Calleva, in Darnestown, Maryland, which was the same adventure company that Kathryn worked with as well. The Calleva job was fabulous, as I helped people develop leadership- and character-enhancement skills through quality outdoor experiences. All of my previous jobs were very rewarding in their own ways and they were excellent precursors for our Peace Corps assignment.

Kathryn and I feel that we are people who love to experience life to the fullest from both professional and personal perspectives. We also strongly believe that the state of the human condition around the world can be improved. Thus, we wanted to place our lives in the service of others to help improve the quality of life for those less fortunate than us.

3
Why We Joined The Peace Corps

"People are generally better persuaded by the reasons which they have themselves discovered than by those which have come into the minds of others."
–Pascal

I still ask myself this question of why we joined the Peace Corps, even though the answers are known. Our correct decision to serve was not made lightly. First, it is important to recognize that, depending on individual circumstances, the total process could be almost four years from the time you begin your application to the time you have your life on track following your service. To demonstrate this idea, the medical overview and application process can take nine months to a year.

There are three months of training prior to the twenty-four months of actual service. Then, upon returning to the United States, you may need six months to comfortably adjust. That timeline estimate suggests almost four years of involvement with the Peace Corps in one form or another. Second, we are not talking about a single person just out of college with no obligations who can simply take off without reservations. Kathryn and I were a couple on successful career paths with significant responsibilities. With that said, I was definitely in search of another career direction.

We both had to fully commit to the Peace Corps endeavor for our own reasons; neither of us could have successfully completed the Peace Corps mission if our only reason for going was because our marriage partner wanted the experience. Serving in the Peace Corps is difficult, and even a solid relationship could easily be destroyed if "following your partner" was the only motivation for joining. In our story, the stars aligned themselves just right to bring together life's timing, desires, and career goals. Additionally, international events and other peoples' experiences contributed toward sending us on the Peace Corps journey.

I am privileged and blessed to have been born in the United States. I was raised in a great country by loving parents; we lived in decent middle-class neighborhoods with good schools. I received a fine education, and then I found challenging work that paid well. I have lived my life freely, making my own choices about who I want to be and how

I chose to get there. This is a privileged life—the life of an American in pursuit of the American dream. I am not wealthy, nor do I feel the need to be. Why? Because I am already rich. I have everything a man could ever ask for—a loving wife and family, beautiful supportive friends, a roof over my head, food on the table, good health with a strong mind and body, freedom, and a good community.

Understanding what all of that means in life is huge; it means that we are privileged. What responsibility comes with being privileged? For some people, it might mean absolutely zero—no responsibility at all, and that is fine. That's the freedom that Americans have earned. For me, however, the responsibility of privilege is helping people that are less fortunate, especially those who live in developing countries. It literally took decades for me to reach the point of being ready to fully commit to something like the Peace Corps.

You might wonder what happened in our lives to bring us to the decision of wanting to leave the comfort of the United States to live for two years in the second poorest country in the Western Hemisphere. When Kathryn was working at Johns Hopkins, she shared with me some of the experiences that a co-worker, Kelly Bauer, and her husband, Jason Bennett, had while serving with the Peace Corps in Uzbekistan. Kelly and Jason entered the Peace Corps as a married couple, and their service clearly impacted them very positively. Kathryn also told me that even though she had already lived and worked in other countries, she needed more international field experience to advance her career in a desired direction.

I also wanted international development experience, having realized that the career I had chosen in the financial industry was not a path that I wanted to continue. For the majority of my life, I followed international events and paid close attention to the severity of problems faced by people around the world with basic survival needs. The public and private sectors have many programs to assist with international development, and I wanted to pursue that work as a career.

Life-and-death experiences also moved us toward living our lives with more explicit meaning and purpose. Kathryn was diagnosed with Melanoma. It turned out to be manageable and not that much of a horrendous ordeal, but initially we had received some bad information from a doctor that led us to believe the situation was much more grave than originally thought. It turned out that the doctor had not read Kathryn's chart properly. That doctor had truly given us a scare!

Additionally, Kathryn and I both witnessed (and participated in the aftermath of) a pedestrian being struck by a car, which we believe eventually proved fatal. Sometime after that accident, I acted as the caregiver for a victim of a head-on motorcycle collision; the person I assisted died in my hands of severe head trauma. Further, I knew people who were killed in the terrorist attacks on September 11, 2001. Each of these life-and-death events impacted Kathryn and me in very profound ways that were challenging to process, both mentally and emotionally. These events altered our life perspectives.

One afternoon, my good friend Ryan Morris told me that we needed to get together for dinner soon because he and his wife, Aimee, were about to serve with the Peace Corps in Kazakhstan for two years. This news hit home hard for Kathryn and me. We were thrilled for our friends but saddened that they would be gone for two years. Although their dedication to their Peace Corps endeavor was evident, there had been no mention of their interest in serving prior to their announcement that they were leaving. Like us, Ryan and Aimee were mid-career professionals, and I was fascinated that people would potentially delay their career development to serve in the Peace Corps.

Aimee and Ryan communicated with us while they were serving in Kazakhstan, and we got involved in one of Aimee's Peace Corps projects by collecting eye glasses to send to her community. Kathryn and I were excited to help Aimee and her community in whatever way we were able. Ryan returned to the States during his service for a brief period. While he was home, we visited with him and learned much more about their experience in Kazakhstan. Plus, Ryan shared with us photos he had taken from the community where they worked, which enabled us to visualize their Peace Corps journey. By the time our friends' service in Kazakhstan had ended, Kathryn and I were having serious discussions about our own potential service in the Peace Corps.

Kelly and Jason, as well as Ryan and Aimee, communicated with us about their life experiences at exactly the right time to help put us on the path to the Peace Corps. Each couple was an outstanding beacon of leadership and influence for us. Clearly, Kathryn and I needed our own personal justifications to serve, but it was fantastic to witness and learn about the incredible possibilities of the Peace Corps experience from people that we knew.

Kathryn and I made a list of pros and cons for our possible service in the Peace Corps to help us better understand the problems and challenges we would face. Our brainstorming created the following rudimentary list of our Peace Corps "pros and cons":

Pros

- Place ourselves in a position to make a positive difference in people's lives.
- Receive a unique and rich cultural experience.
- Learn another language.
- Live in another country.
- Be American Ambassadors of good will in a foreign nation, which we felt was very important following the United States' invasion of Afghanistan.
- Learn what it felt like to face the problems associated with integrating into a new community as a minority and a foreigner.
- Potentially develop strong new relationships.
- Gain insight into what it is like to live in an impoverished nation.
- Learn the politics of another country.
- Gain valuable international development field experience at a grassroots level, which could benefit our careers.
- Travel.
- Have a big challenge and quite an adventure through the Volunteer experience.
- Spend more quality time with each other while doing something worthwhile.
- Possibly locate a river suitable for whitewater rafting to improve tourism for a community in the country in which we would be assigned.

After creating this list, Kathryn and I were very pleased with all of the splendid opportunities that being Volunteers would put in front of us. Next, we made a list of all the possible negative aspects associated with serving in the Peace Corps.

Cons

- We would have to leave our families and friends for over two years.
- We would lose the opportunity to make and save money for over two years. This lost income and savings would include maximum contributions to our retirement accounts. Losing the ability to save in our 401k/IRA for a two-year period, considering employer contributions and reasonable compounded returns, could cost us more than $100,000 by the time we retire in roughly 29 years.
- We might not be able to do any whitewater kayaking or other out door sports that we love, for over two years.
- We would have to consider what we would do with my long-time friend and loved one, Sam, my Australian Shepherd? Could we bring her, or would we have to leave her? I would never leave my dog!
- We could become victims of crime as it might not be safe in whatever country we were assigned.
- Kathryn's mother would not be happy to receive the news that we were leaving the United States for over two years. The mother-in-law wanted grandchildren.
- We would not be able to experience American entertainment, movies, plays, concerts, etc.
- We would not be able to consume food that we are normally accustomed to eating.
- We could possibly have to endure extreme personal hardships.
- We could possibly become sick and not receive medical care in a timely manner.
- We would have to pay for our things to be stored for two and a half years, which we estimated would cost about $2,000.
- We might hate the experience and have to come home early.
- We would have to make a decision to rent or sell our real estate.
- Following our service, we would have to start all over again to find housing, cars, jobs etc.
- Our marital relationship could be strained under new circumstances in a different culture.
- The experience could be very frustrating, sad, and lonely, which would take a toll on our mental well-being.

After making this rudimentary list, I had to take a step back and really think about my motivations for going. If we joined the Peace Corps, we would be giving up our current lives completely for over two years and would lose a lot of money. Not to mention that I would be making my mother-in-law furious, which could bring about unpleasant consequences. Although, maybe the mother-in-law being angry should be categorized as a positive…

Now that we had laid out our pros and cons of going overseas, we needed to consider the issues. To me, it seemed as though all the negatives were associated with the temporary loss of regular contact with family and friends, money, safety, health problems, and our personal enjoyment through our hobbies. It appeared to me that the negatives revolved around selfishness. Could I really give it all up for more than two years? Could Kathryn?

Again, we discussed our reasons for serving in the Peace Corps and narrowed the list into four main reasons:

1. We wanted to stop sitting on the sidelines and get involved to help make a positive impact in people's lives in a developing nation.
2. We wanted to be good-will Ambassadors for the United States at a time when world opinion of our country was very negative.
3. We wanted a rich and uniquely rewarding cultural experience.
4. We wanted to learn and understand more about grassroots interna tional development.

On the negative side, we found that there were five major reasons to reject the idea of serving in the Peace Corps:

1. Safety.
2. Being away from our family and friends.
3. Loss of money.
4. Not being able to participate in our favorite hobbies.
5. We would have to leave the comforts of the United States.

We came to the conclusion that each of the five negative points were legitimate reasons for staying home. However, our dedication and commitment to helping others, representing our country well, and the potential for cultural enrichment far outweighed the opportunity cost of remaining in the United States. We also speculated that acquiring Peace Corps experience might very well be a fantastic investment in our careers. Kathryn and I finally decided that we were going to pursue the Peace Corps journey. However, we also decided that we would make the decision twice.

The first decision was to commit to the idea and go through the application process. If we were accepted, we would make a second decision in the future, possibly as far off as one year[1]. It was not that we were taking the decision to apply lightly. If all went well with the application and placement process, we had made the commitment to serve. To complete the application is a long, tough process of roughly one year before you potentially receive your "invitation" to serve, which is another way of describing a job offer from the Peace Corps.

A lot can happen in one year in a married couple's lives, as well as in the world—especially post-911. There was also the possibility that we might not even be accepted, as the Peace Corps does not offer invitations to every applicant. In fact, some people have said receiving an invitation from the Peace Corps is an accomplishment in itself.

In January of 2003, Kathryn and I asked for applications and began the lengthy process. We had to provide essays about our motivations for joining the Peace Corps, our fingerprints, medical histories, and copies of our college transcripts, social security cards, and drivers' licenses. We had to have thorough physical and dental examinations. We had to provide three letters of recommendation—one from an employer, one from a friend, and one from someone who could speak about our previous volunteer experience in the United States in any capacity. After submitting resumes and completing a frustratingly detailed written application, we had interviews. The government apparently wanted to know our exact whereabouts for the last ten years. Applying to the Peace Corps was the most extensive and lengthy application process of our careers.

---

[1] The Peace Corps application process has been improved since we applied in 2003.

4
Placement Process

"One way to get the most out of life is to look upon it as an adventure."
–William Feather

The placement process happens once your application is accepted by the Peace Corps. One of the aspects of your application is selecting a region of the world where you would like to work. You may select first, second and third choices regarding areas of the world in which you would prefer to serve. Kathryn and I chose Latin America as our first choice. The Peace Corps seems to take your regional selection seriously and tries to accommodate your first preference, if at all possible.

By December of 2003, we had finally completed our medical examinations, and a Peace Corps staff person told us that we would probably be receiving an invitation to work in the Huaraz province of Peru. We immediately began researching the area. We were fascinated, but also a little nervous, as this was an area that had been used by a rebel organization called the Shining Path. Huaraz was extremely mountainous, poverty-stricken, and remote—just the kind of place that needed some assistance. Kathryn and I began to get very excited about doing our small part to help out where we could. However, the Peace Corps never called us back.

In January of 2004, we called the Peace Corps to receive an update on our assignment. As it turns out, the Peru assignment was taken away from us because of a red flag in Kathryn's medical history with Melanoma. Kathryn needed a dermatology exam every six months to make sure that she had no recurring health problem related to the Melanoma. Peace Corps had not yet designated an approved dermatologist in the Huaraz region, or even in Peru. This was a bit of a stretch for me to believe, but it was true. Peru had been taken away from us as an assignment, and there was nothing we could do about it.

Kathryn and I have always believed that things work out for the best, one way or another, so we were not too upset about being dismissed from Peru. The Peace Corps would eventually find a place where we could do our jobs and manage our healthcare at the same time. Once again, all we could do was wait and continue on with our lives until more news emerged.

Our Placement Officer, Ginny Michel, mentioned the possibility of us being assigned to Bolivia to work with water and environmental issues, so we began researching Bolivia. By March of 2004, we knew that we would likely be assigned to a Central American country, and it seemed that the possibilities were Costa Rica and Nicaragua. We would be working with youth wherever we were placed. When we heard that Nicaragua was a possibility, Kathryn and I once again did some fast and serious research. Up until that point, all we knew about Nicaragua was the Iran-Contra scandal and a little bit about the Sandinista rebellion. Unfortunately, none of our personal recollections regarding the country were positive. Whatever was going to happen, one thing was certain – we were acquiring quite an education from our research. We learned all kinds of interesting facts about multiple countries. The placement process was very exciting, and communicating with our Placement Officer was always interesting.

After our research, we were intrigued by the idea of going to Nicaragua. We learned that Nicaragua was the second poorest country in the Western Hemisphere, with an average per capita income of around $500 per year. Geologically, our research showed us that the country was incredibly beautiful, laden with many large lakes and volcanoes, and nestled between the Atlantic and Pacific Oceans. We imagined that it was not developed from a tourism perspective, and we liked the idea of being in a country that was less traveled.

From a recreational standpoint, there were some excellent surfing opportunities that we could pursue when we were not working. Not only that, Kathryn and I researched the whitewater of Nicaragua and found that no whitewater rivers had been discovered thus far. This was hard to believe since Honduras has whitewater to the north, and Costa Rica has great whitewater to the south. Geologically and geographically, Nicaragua was not that much different, so we believed that there was an outside possibility of kayaking a whitewater river that no one previously had ever descended. Should a decent river be located, it would bring a potential opportunity for new tourism. We still felt like these opportunities were long shots because almost all of the runnable rivers in the world have been discovered. If there was whitewater in Nicaragua, it seemed that someone should have found it by now. Maybe the civil wars had kept adventurers out. Then again, the more likely scenario was that there was no whitewater in Nicaragua. Nonetheless, we had interest in looking for ourselves.

In the first week of March 2004, we received a phone call from our Placement Officer, who said that an official invitation to work in the country of Nicaragua would be coming in the mail, and that we should begin to consider this assignment. We would be working to develop business skills with youth on the Pacific side of the country where Spanish is the prominent language. Kathryn and I then had to make some serious decisions about the course we were going to set for our lives over the next two years. The second and final decision to commit to joining the Peace Corps was upon us.

We discussed our reasons for serving again and determined that our commitment had not changed. Kathryn and I finally decided that we were going to pursue the Peace Corps journey, and we anxiously awaited the invitation packet.

However, when we received the invitation materials, we were confused. The invitation we received was not for what we were told we would be doing or where we would be living. It said that we would be working in youth development, but on the Atlantic Coast of Nicaragua. We knew there were significant differences between the Atlantic and the Pacific sides of Nicaragua. The prominent language in the Atlantic Coast region was not Spanish, but Miskito and Creole. In our research, we found that drug trade in the region affected the Atlantic Coast. We considered the safety issues and language differences and decided that we needed to have another conversation with Ginny Michel. Ginny explained that there were two programs going to Nicaragua at the same time – one in Small Business Development working with youth in the Pacific region and another in Youth Development on the Atlantic Coast. The invitation we received was the latter, not the former, as we had anticipated. Our enthusiasm immediately evaporated because Kathryn had hoped to use her knowledge of the Spanish language to acclimate into a community more easily and begin working immediately with the youth, rather than first spending a lot of time struggling to learn a new language. We seriously debated the decision whether to move forward with this program.

We consulted our former Peace Corps friends about our imminent decision. Ironically, they all conveyed that, even though being committed to Peace Corps means going anywhere they send you, it would probably be best for us to decline the invitation if we didn't have a good feeling about it and were not one hundred percent committed. This seemed to be good advice.

The more Kathryn considered the issues, the less she wanted to accept the invitation. I felt indifferent as to which region of Nicaragua we were assigned. However, respecting Kathryn's concerns was necessary because having the right scenario as a couple was critical to our success. Nonetheless, we were both worried that if we declined this invitation, we might lose our Peace Corps opportunity altogether.

In the meantime, Ginny Michel was out of the office for two weeks, which gave us plenty of time to ponder and debate our decision. When Ginny returned, we explained our concerns via the telephone. She surprised us by replying that "Peace Corps just wants to place Volunteers." We were not expecting that response, but finally Kathryn suggested that perhaps there had been some kind of mix-up regarding the program to which we had been assigned. Ginny asked us to hold for a moment. When Ginny came back on the line, she apologized and said we had been sent the wrong invitation. We felt so relieved! We accepted the invitation to serve on the Pacific side of Nicaragua without hesitation. We were going to Central America to help Nicaraguans.

There was much to accomplish in a very short time. First, we had to share this news with our parents—which was not easy—and then we had to sell our condominium, move our valuables into storage, set all of our other affairs in order, and resign from our jobs. We only had a few weeks before we departed, and the tasks overwhelmed us. Completing all necessary tasks in time would take us down to the last remaining minutes of being in the United States.

Two weeks before we departed for Nicaragua, our Placement Officer called and said she had received an important message from the Peace Corps office in Nicaragua. Kathryn and I, as well as another married couple in our training class, would have to be separated from each other during the three-month training period. Not only would Kathryn and I have to be apart during language classes, we would also be living with different host families that did not live in the same town. This news sent Kathryn and me into a tailspin of monumental proportion and forced us to ask ourselves many questions. The first and obvious question was, why would married couples have to live apart? Would our training towns be near each other? If not, would we be able to see each other at all during the three months? Could we deal with being separated in a foreign and possibly dangerous place? How would I get along without Kathryn there to help me understand what people were saying? The strongest thought I had was, "if I had wanted to enter the Peace Corps by myself, I would have. Kathryn and I joined the Peace Corps to share the experience together." Obviously the information about us having to live apart was very upsetting. We learned that separating married couples during training is not standard procedure for Peace Corps worldwide. However, Peace Corps Nicaragua implements this practice, which is highly unique.

As a couple, we quickly had to come to terms with being separated during training as we were scheduled to leave the United States in two weeks. In the end, Kathryn and I decided that we would only be apart for three months and we could survive anything for that time period. Although we were not very pleased about the idea of being apart, we began to prepare ourselves to not worry about what was going to happen and accept what needed to be done. The first stop on the Peace Corps journey to Nicaragua was the city of Miami for three days of orientation and training, which was aptly called "Staging."

5
Staging In Miami For Three Days
May 3–5, 2004
"If you make your job important, it is quite likely to return the favor."

We checked into the designated hotel, located the conference room for the Peace Corps, and registered. Kathryn and I were immediately given an abundance of general materials and a specific assignment. The assignment was interactive, similar to a game. We received a sheet of paper with twenty-eight statements. Each statement had been extracted from the individual resumes of the new Peace Corps trainees. The challenge – or assignment – was to match each of the twenty-eight statements to the correct trainee. What a great way to comfortably get to know your new co-workers! My first impression was that I had never been in a room before with such positive, like-minded people.

After we completed the assignment and before our actual training began, we had to complete an extraordinary amount of government paperwork. I believe this was, in and of itself, a test of the trainees' patience.

Following the paperwork bonanza, the Staging conversations began. Our Volunteer training class was called "Nica 35," which stands for the 35th group of Volunteers to serve in Nicaragua. Nica 35 consisted of two sectors—Small Business Development and Youth Development. The Small Business group would work and live on the Pacific side of Nicaragua, and the Youth Development group would live on the Caribbean side of Nicaragua.

During Staging sessions, we talked about safety, aspirations, concerns, and fears, and all of us were given an opportunity to be heard. The people in the room were amazing. We discussed the Peace Corps approach to development, watched a movie on the topic, and participated in a dozen interactive exercises. The excitement was palpable, as the group collectively appeared ready to leave the country to begin training.

That night, Kathryn and I became anxious about how much gear we brought. We had books and extra camping equipment, such as a water purifier. The challenges we would face for basic needs were not clear. We did not want to be caught unprepared, but we also didn't want to carry anything extra that would not be needed. Before we left Washington D.C., our Placement Officer told us that Peace Corps would allow us to carry eighty pounds of luggage per person. We had about two hundred and fifty pounds in total, obviously over the allotted amount, and we needed to reduce the weight and girth of our bags considerably. We spent that evening searching Miami for boxes and found a way to send the unnecessary items back home.

The second day of Staging, our group spoke about strategies to cope with unwanted attention. It was safe to assume that we would receive a plethora of looks while in Nicaragua, mostly because our appearance was simply different. The result can sometimes transform from a harmless "look" into harassment of American Volunteers. Dealing with any unwanted attention appropriately is helpful in not escalating the situation.

Our group conversed about risk management and the many forms of risk that a Volunteer may face. Risk to our health is the most important, so we discussed the need for taking Chloroquine tablets to prevent Malaria, as well as strategies for mitigating food- and waterborne illnesses. Additionally, we talked about managing stress and the possibility of crime, and how to deal with those situations should they arise.

Peace Corps policies were a pronounced part of the Staging process, which made a good test to see which trainees were interested in the nuts and bolts of the governmental wheel. Although we all listened, no one was overly enthusiastic and I even saw one or two folks beginning to nod off from time to time—an encouraging sign that we were all pretty normal people and bored to tears with procedures.

We also discussed, at length, crossing cultures, another important and very interesting topic. Then we reviewed logistics: when we would leave Miami, from where, in what type of vehicle, to where, etc. On the last night of training in Miami, many of the new trainees went out to have our last American meals, including our last American beers, candy, and desserts. We were becoming a cohesive group, understanding a little more about each other and what we planned to accomplish in the Peace Corps.

On Monday, May 5, we again packed our bags, checked out of the

hotel as a group at 5:30 a.m., and hopped on a bus for Miami International Airport. At the airport, Kathryn dropped the last of our bills in
the mailbox as I bought coffee for us. All necessary personal tasks to
successfully leave the United States with no lingering problems were
accomplished with little time to spare. We then boarded the plane and
left the country on American Airlines bound for Managua, Nicaragua.

I am proud of my country and its people for the respect and dignity that our diverse nation can portray to the international community. During the Staging event, I had very powerful feelings about how
pleased I was to be a part of this unique U.S. Government agency. I
thought about the twenty-eight people in our group from all walks of
life and different professions. Some of the folks had recently graduated college, and some had extensive business backgrounds. We were
all from different states, and despite our differences, we had something
very much in common—a genuine desire to try to help others. Collectively, we were determined to make a positive impact in an area of the
world that not many Americans knew much about.

The group would face very difficult challenges. The Peace Corps
experience would not go well for some us, I was sure, and the numbers
suggest that a few of us would not complete our tour. Yet, for now, we
were all going forward with a fierce will to survive the unknown and
have a successful service. If the Staging event in Miami was any indication of what our Peace Corps tour was going to be like, we were in for
a great life experience. Everyone in the Nica 35 class was an outstanding person who sacrificed much for the sake of helping others, and
they have made their country proud in putting forth the consideration
and effort necessary to pursue the Peace Corps. Nica 35 was about to
arrive "in country."

6
Arrival In Managua and Training For Three Days in Granada
May 5, 2004
"People forget how fast you did a job—but they remember how well you did it."
–Howard W. Newton

After waking up incredibly early in the morning to check out of the Miami hotel and jump on a bus to the airport, the Nica 35 group landed in Managua, Nicaragua at about 10:30 a.m. on May 5–Cinco de Mayo! Arriving in very foreign places can stir unique and excited emotions. The Managua airport caught my attention because not many people stood inside the baggage claim area, yet a lot of Nicaraguans stood just outside the baggage claim carousels looking in at us through a glass wall. As Nica 35 picked up our bags, I felt like we were in a fish bowl. At this point, safety concerned me and instantly I had to laugh at myself to relax. The emotions present when Kathryn and I arrived in Nicaragua will, in a humorous way, never be forgotten.

Kathryn and I discussed what our group would do next. The Peace Corps had instructed us that upon our arrival in Managua, we would travel to the city of Granada to have three days of training. I assumed there would be a Peace Corps representative at the airport to meet us. Even after we picked up our bags, there was no one around who looked like Peace Corps staff. I was about to become worried when a lady walked up out of nowhere and said, "You guys must be Kathryn and Eric." With a beautiful smile and great enthusiastic energy, she said, "Welcome to Nicaragua!" I could hardly believe it. Her greeting was incredibly comforting and I asked her how she knew who we were.

She turned out to be our Training Officer, Maura Lambeth. Maura knew that there were only two married couples in the Nica 35 training group, and she had seen Kathryn interacting with me so she made the correct assumption that we were married. I didn't ask her how she knew that we were not the other married couple because at that moment, I didn't care. I let my curiosity go and was content with the fact that Maura was obviously very observant, had her act together, and knew who we were. The Peace Corps logistical transportation plan functioned well.

Outside the airport, under a viciously hot sun, the Nica 35 group loaded all of our gear onto an old school bus until it almost burst. A second modern Peace Corps bus waited behind the school bus and quickly filled with trainees. When what we called the "pretty bus" became full, Kathryn and I realized that we would have to travel to Granada in the old yellow school bus packed with luggage. While in route from Managua to Granada, police officers armed with AK-47 rifles stopped our bus at a checkpoint. This interaction left me a bit unnerved as I was not used to police officers carrying automatic machine guns. However, they checked some paperwork and allowed us to continue on our way.

Nicaragua is a beautiful country, and my first thought was that tourism should increase exponentially in years to come. However, the poverty was immediately noticeable and quite disturbing, yet there was another issue that was troubling—the trash! It was everywhere beside the highways. I do not mean just a pile or two here or there—I mean trash could be seen in the fields, in front of homes, in the ditches, in and around businesses—it was everywhere! I wondered how the trash could possibly be so pervasive.

The Nica 35 group arrived at Hotel Granada at about noon. When we got off the old school bus, we noticed that the trainees who were exiting the modern bus had big smiles and looked much less sweaty than Kathryn and me. We heard that the bus everyone else was riding on had pleasant air conditioning and music playing. The school bus Kathryn and I rode on had neither air conditioning nor music. Sweat drenched us! Welcome to Nicaragua.

The trainee group unloaded baggage in assembly-line fashion from the bus into the hotel, illustrating that we had begun to work as a team. Unfortunately, I pulled a muscle in my back while moving bags through this assembly line. The injury did not appear to be serious, but there was definite pain.

Hotel Granada was nicer than Kathryn and I expected. The hotel utilized for training in Miami had far exceeded our expectations, especially knowing that we were about to embark on the Peace Corps experience in a developing country. Frankly, Hotel Granada did not seem to mesh with all the Peace Corps literature we had been reading to prepare ourselves for very minimal living conditions. Hotel Granada was a two-story, colonial-style, 46-room establishment, adorned with beautiful plants and flowers. Each room contained what we considered "luxuries," such as air-conditioning and hot showers.

Kathryn and I checked in and took the allotted half hour to freshen up before our day really began. We ate a surprisingly robust and tasty lunch and received our itinerary for the following three days in Granada. We then had briefings on our purpose for being in Nicaragua. Our Training Officer, Maura Lambeth, introduced the training staff, administrative staff, and a few current Volunteers who would help acquaint us with Nicaragua.

From 5 to 6 p.m., we had a medical procedure overview. Most of us had hardly gotten any sleep the night before, and we had all awoken by 5 that morning. Needless to say, our exhausted group appeared to have little concentration left.

We ate dinner and then had our first round of vaccinations, which were not very fun. Sure, I love to be poked with needles! Blood work had to be done, as well, and then the Peace Corps staff reviewed our medical histories. They also explained to us that Volunteer trainees are individuals who are training to become Peace Corps Volunteers. During training, Peace Corps staff is very consistent in not calling the trainees "Volunteers," but rather, they are addressed as "*aspirantes*" or "trainees" until the day they are sworn-in as actual "Volunteers." We were finished with our first day at about 9 p.m. and it did not take long for Kathryn and I to fall asleep.

The next day of training in Granada began with an introduction to Peace Corps Nicaragua and our Country Director, Jeff Freeman. Jeff is an outstanding human being and a legacy Peace Corps Volunteer. Jeff served as a Volunteer from 1981 through 1983 in Guatemala. I was in the 9th grade when he completed his service. This fact really hit home for me—I was in the presence of a man with serious experience. Before becoming the Peace Corps Country Director for Nicaragua, Jeff had been a Democracy Officer with USAID in La Paz, Bolivia. Mr. Freeman retained my full attention.

Nica 35 then met its Associate Peace Corps Director (APCD) for Small Business, Alberto Gonzalez, and the APCD for Youth Development. Each APCD offered presentations on development work in general, and on our respective project goals.

Afterward, we had our individual language interviews to see how well we could speak Spanish. These interviews were conducted entirely in Spanish, administered by people who did not speak English. This terrified me because I did not speak Spanish. People exited their meetings saying things like "Yeah, my interview went well. We talked about what had to be done to fix a stove." When I walked into the room, I tried to be as polite as possible to my interviewer. He sat across from me, pushed 'record' on a tape recorder, and then began speaking to me in Spanish. It might as well have been Pig Latin. I knew nothing! He realized this almost immediately and simplified his questioning. He asked me to tell him about my family. I knew the word for sister, brother, mom and dad, but I did not know how to connect any of the words. I felt like an idiot! Not only that, I felt like I had disrespected my interviewer. I was in his country to help his people, and I had not even bothered to learn the language before I arrived. He then asked if I could identify items in the room. I knew the table was green and that the language interview was a horrible experience.

When my language evaluation was later read to me (by Kathryn because the evaluation was written in Spanish), it said that I did not know a single word of the language. While I knew this was true, I became very upset. I again felt inadequate relative to the majority of trainees who could speak Spanish quite well. I also knew that I could not help anyone if I could not communicate properly. I just kept thinking, "How am I going to teach?" I had to walk away and calm down as I began to have thoughts that maybe it was a mistake to come here with no language skills. I had not studied Spanish before entering the country because we were not sure exactly where we would be assigned, I worked long hours, and our Placement Officer had told me that the language component would comprise a large part of the three-month training process.

Later, the Peace Corps staff asked us to relinquish our personal and Peace Corps passports. This request made us a little uncomfortable. What if something happened and we needed to leave the country immediately? Without our passports, we would not be able to leave. We complied although we recognized that for the moment, Peace Corps controlled our ability to travel outside of Nicaragua. Peace Corps ensured us that the passports would eventually be returned to us. The Peace Corps staff then strongly urged the Nica 35 group to turn over all of our U.S. cash and access to money—not only for safe keeping, but because we were supposed to be living at average income levels of Nicaraguans. We turned in our valuables to be placed in a safe in the Peace Corps office. We were not too keen on giving them all of our money, so Kathryn and I kept about $250 for unexpected emergencies.

The Volunteers posed for photos for official Peace Corps Identification Cards. Then another round of vaccine shots occurred for Rabies and Measles, Mumps and Rubella (MMR). Following these vaccinations, I had an epiphany that there is room in my life to enjoy only one type of shot, and that seldom-ingested fluid is called liquor!

After lunch, our group had a briefing on safety and security in Nicaragua, which summarily comes down to the fact that if you behave in a stupid manner in this country, you could suffer severe consequences. At that time, I was really paranoid about being safe. The Peace Corps does a fine job of giving you all the information you need to know about how to avoid becoming the victim of a crime, if at all possible.

At half past five, Maura Lambeth provided an engaging language program overview. Maura told us not to worry about our language skills as we would be taught to communicate regardless of our current language level. I thought that the Peace Corps language program must be some kind of miracle-working machine. The facilitators (Spanish instructors) would bring us up to the Peace Corps' minimum language standard; otherwise, depending on the circumstances, we could possibly be sent home instead of being sworn in as Volunteers. This news upset me again. I felt there was no way I could speak acceptable Spanish in three months, and the risk of being sent home appeared high because I might not be able to meet the minimum language requirement. Kathryn reassured me that all would be well—if I were sent home, it would only be two years and we could still see each other every once in a while.

Her statement caught me off guard. I said, "What the hell are you talking about?" She asked if it would be okay for her to stay should I be sent home. I thought she might be kidding, but I really could not tell for sure. Kathryn had pushed the right button inside of me, and fear transformed into determination. She knew I would learn Spanish. Funny girl! Tough love, don't you think?

On Friday, which was the third and final day of training in Granada, we began with something fun—a group picture. We then had a class on basic survival Spanish, as well as nonverbal communication. We were given a handout that told us how to understand different situations based on Nicaraguan body expressions. For example, when a Nicaraguan lowers their eyebrows and scrunches their nose at the same time very quickly, it means they do not understand what you just said to them. Also, Nicaraguans point with their lips. They will pucker their lips as if to kiss and then point them toward whatever they want you to see. The survival Spanish class taught us how to make sure we could eat, drink, and find a bathroom, and as far as I was concerned, this was enough to send us out into the world. I was ready to survive in this Spanish-speaking country.

After lunch, Nica 35 was introduced to our Small Business sector Technical Trainer, Josh Edwards, and we discussed our goals and expectations again. Over the course of the three-month training period, Josh spent quite a bit of time with our group. He was an outstanding guy and very professional. Josh was twenty-five years young, and he did an excellent job. He had many organized, unique learning activities for our group, such as taking us to a ropes course in a nature reserve so that we could learn team-building skills. In business, if you do not build a solid team, your business may have real problems. Kathryn and I were very impressed by the training program Josh put together for us.

On Friday afternoon, Maura Lambeth delivered some very exciting information to Nica 35—what cities we would be living in and who our host families would be for the next three months of training. Maura distributed host family dossiers that contained basic information, allowing Kathryn and me to learn that we would be living in towns about twenty minutes apart by bus. Knowing we could take a short bus ride to see one another, if needed, was a great relief for us. Kathryn would live in the town of Masatepe, and the town where I would reside was called Catarina.

In addition to the information contained in the host family dossier, Maura said that I would be living with a first-time host family. Continuing, she said that Kathryn's assigned host family had accommodated nine previous trainees, so they were very experienced as a host family. Luckily, a current Volunteer who had been selected by Peace Corps staff to come to Granada to welcome the Nica 35 training group to

Nicaragua had previously lived with Kathryn's host family as a trainee. The Volunteer kindly shared details about Kathryn's host family, house, and community. Kathryn now knew a great deal about her host family. My living situation was more of a mystery, but I felt I could deal with whatever came my way.

Following the host family orientation, the Nica 35 group received a great surprise. The hotel staff took us on a sunset boat tour of the islands of Lake Nicaragua. Our group also had a new topic to converse about—where everyone was going to live.

Some of the islands on beautiful Lake Nicaragua have picturesque single-family homes. This appeared to be an area where wealthy Nicaraguans vacation. Meanwhile, as the boats cruised slowly around the islands, we watched the waterfowl float and the local people fish. As the sun gently set, the aroma of the evening was fresh and clean, and the sky lit into brilliant shades of red, pink, and yellow. The serene backdrop for this splendid sunset cruise was the Mombacho volcano, which has erupted in the past. A legend of Mombacho is still told today about two forbidden lovers who took each other's lives. The male lover's death caused the volcano to erupt, and the female lover's body formed the present-day islands from the volcanic debris. There are many such fascinating legends in Nicaragua. After this special island cruise that offered a glimpse of the Nicaraguan natural environment, culture, and tourism, we returned to the hotel. We then had another fulfilling dinner and later congregated on the hotel balcony to watch life meander by in Central America.

On Saturday morning at seven o'clock, we packed our bags again, placed them in a corner of Hotel Granada with the other trainees' gear, and then had another survival Spanish class to ensure we would not have problems attaining the basic necessities of life. Kathryn and I knew that our orientation would be over very soon, and our three months of training were about to begin. It also meant that we, as a couple, were about to be separated. While Kathryn and I fully accepted being separated during three months of training, it did not mean we liked the idea.

7
History of Nicaragua

"History ... is indeed little more than the register of the crimes, follies, and misfortunes of mankind."
–Edward Gibbon

To understand how Nicaragua has come to its current state politically and economically, it is important to know about the cause and effect of past events that have developed the fascinating history of this country. The history of Nicaragua and its people is one of mystery and intrigue, repression and conspiracy, brutality and survival. Nicaragua has weathered the natural elements as well as allegedly corrupt governments, dictatorships, insurrections, and counter-rebellions, the likes of which other nations hope never to face.

The history of Nicaragua would necessitate a book within itself, so the history presented here will be recent and fairly narrow in scope. When speaking to the history of Nicaragua, it is also important to include the involvement of the United States, as our foreign policies with respect to Nicaragua have caused our countries to be forever linked. Another purpose for presenting a brief history of Nicaragua is to demonstrate how Nicaraguans might perceive the United States and its culture. Not only has the United States generated major change within the borders of Nicaragua, but also particular individual U.S. citizens helped mold stereotypes of Americans and played extensive roles in the politics of Nicaragua. One such individual was William Walker.

William Walker was a significant player in the history of Nicaragua during the middle nineteenth century. Mr. Walker was fanatically religious and a greedy racist who thought he could come to Nicaragua to create an empire. His zeal for power and riches were relentless. This American captured the attention of millions, and at one point, he was the focus of world news. In 1856, Walker had acquired enough power in Nicaragua to call for a presidential election; he announced his candidacy and then allegedly rigged the voting process in a manner that guaranteed his victory. On July 11, 1856, at the age of only thirty-three, Walker was inaugurated as President of Nicaragua. Further, the American Government officially recognized Walker's presidency.

Prior to venturing into Nicaragua, Walker became infatuated with the idea of Manifest Destiny, deciding that divine intervention would guide him to liberate Spanish-speaking nations from themselves and bring them into the comfortable arms of white rule. He tried his wares in Mexico first and was almost killed. Unfortunately for Nicaragua, he escaped Mexico with his life.

In 1854, Walker learned of a conflict in Nicaragua that, if handled correctly, could potentially give him the power he desired. There were Liberal and Conservative groups fighting each other in what could be considered a civil war. Neither group could achieve a decisive advantage in this war effort. Walker then worked a conspiracy with a Californian by the name of Byron Cole. Cole became an intermediary and made an agreement with a beleaguered Nicaraguan Liberal leader by the name of Francisco Castellón. The accord that Byron Cole helped orchestrate would bring Walker and his group of mercenaries to Nicaragua to lead pro-Liberal soldiers who were fighting for Castellón. If the war was won, Walker, the filibusterer and his soldiers would be awarded booty in the form of money and land. Walker began to recruit his soldiers in San Francisco, most of whom were from Kentucky and Tennessee. Walker called his group "The Immortals," and they set sail for Nicaragua. The Immortals were nothing more than ruffians, misfits and idealists, but they were committed to the job of liberating the country of Nicaragua and creating an empire for themselves.

After four months of strategic battle, Walker captured the capital city of Granada. Granada was a tactical gem in the heart of Central America and Walker made claims that he would soon control the entire isthmus. Walker now began to garner the attention of newspapers from around the globe.

After the victory in Granada, Walker initiated his rhetoric about taking control of the presidency. Once he became the President of Nicaragua in 1856, he made immediate and permanent enemies with many Nicaraguans and rulers from nearby countries who were paranoid about what this American's future plans might be. Walker made English the official language of Nicaragua and legalized slavery. The leaders of Central America were shocked at Walker's audacity, and it was not long before soldiers from Nicaragua, Costa Rica, Honduras, El Salvador and Guatemala converged upon Granada to rid Central America of this preposterous man. Walker and his boys put up a fight, but they could not deal with being greatly outnumbered by their opponent. Walker eventually surrendered, but first he had the city of Granada set on fire, which resulted in severe destruction.

William Walker had the nerve to try a second Nicaraguan campaign to recapture what had been taken from him. On the way back to Nicaragua, his situation changed for the worse when a British Navy Captain captured him and turned him over to the Honduran authorities. Walker was immediately tried, convicted, and then promptly executed by a firing squad on September 12, 1860.

At that time, many Nicaraguans incorrectly considered William Walker to be the epitome of what Americans were like. Walker solidified a mass sentiment of anti-Americanism in Central America, particularly in Nicaragua. Walker was an arrogant radical who brought a great deal of pain, suffering, and paranoia to Nicaragua.

The United States took a keen interest in Nicaragua during the mid-to-late nineteenth century. U.S. citizens on their way to the West Coast of California for the gold rush were traveling through Nicaragua to avoid the hostility of Indians and the harsh reality of crossing the mountains in the western United States. Sailing to Nicaragua, Americans would then travel up the Río San Juan and cross Lake Nicaragua. Once across the lake, they only needed to traverse a twelve-mile-wide finger of land to arrive at the Pacific Ocean. From there, these would-be miners sailed up the Pacific Coast to California to begin their foray into the adventure of fortune hunting.

Cornelius Vanderbilt created a successful transport company moving these Americans across Nicaragua. By the year 1887, there was much discussion about building a canal through the country of Nicaragua. However, Panama achieved a major economic coup to capture the construction of the Canal for its country.

In Nicaragua, a Liberal President by the name of Zelaya was in power from 1893 to 1909, and he became very disagreeable to the Americans as well as Conservatives within the country. Zelaya made a few decisions that negatively affected American businesses and other interests in Nicaragua, severely annoying U.S. President Taft. Conflict became inevitable. The United States remained on the sidelines to see how the Nicaraguan Conservatives would proceed. The Conservatives in Nicaragua joined forces with Juan J. Estrada leading their military effort. However, two Americans were captured by Zelaya's forces. Zelaya claimed the captured men were fighting for the Conservatives, and he had them shot. The execution of the two Americans infuriated the U.S. Government, which consequently severed diplomatic relations with Nicaragua. Zelaya resigned the presidency in 1909 and agreed to exile in favor of a new President, Dr. José Madriz, another Liberal. The United States, however, withheld recognition of President Madriz, causing problems for the Liberals. Military desertion began and Madriz's regime rapidly crumbled.

With yet another presidential vacancy, a power vacuum was gathering strength within the country. Two more Nicaraguans became President in the year 1910, and they both quickly lost power. Eventually, the Conservative military leader Juan J. Estrada, who earlier led the revolt against President Zelaya and the Madriz regime, swarmed in and took control of the government. The Conservative Estrada served as President of Nicaragua from 1910-1911, and his administration was recognized by the United States.

President Estrada, accepted loans from the United States under the foreign policy known as "Dollar Diplomacy," and he tried to correct the wrongs of President Zelaya's Liberal administration. The "Dollar Diplomacy" agreements that President Estrada accepted became a rallying cry for the Liberals who caused large-scale problems, and violence was again approaching. An American diplomat negotiated with all parties and was able to avoid bloodshed with the resignation of President Estrada in favor of another Conservative, a mining accountant named Adolfo Díaz. President Díaz was the leader of Nicaragua from 1911 to 1917, and his administration was able to offer marginal stability for the chaotic country.

Immediately prior to President Díaz, the country of Nicaragua was in extreme turmoil, evidenced by a three-year period of multiple uprisings and numerous Presidents. Many different countries, politicians, and businessmen were involved in Nicaragua, including the United States. Nicaragua was obviously struggling, and at the request of President Díaz, the U.S. Marines were deployed to protect American business interests in Nicaragua, as well as help stabilize the situation. However, perceived U.S. influence and intervention in Nicaraguan politics ignited an upheaval.

Benjamín Zeledón became particularly enraged by the policies of the Díaz administration and what he considered blatant political interference from the United States. Zeledón formed a group of like-minded Nicaraguans and created a military faction. The armed forces of Zeledón set up camp in an old mountaintop fortress called Coyotepe, near the city of Masaya. There are many tales about Coyotepe, none of which are pleasant to think about because they usually revolve around horror stories of torture during the Somoza and Sandinista eras. However, in 1912, when the Americans came to call at Coyotepe, another legend in Nicaraguan history unfolded—the story of the assault on Coyotepe, where Zeledón would not accept surrendering to the U.S. Marines as an option.

In the early morning of October 3, 1912 the U.S. Marines attacked Zeledón and the Coyotepe fortress in coordination with President Díaz's government forces. The power of the Conservative forces and the Americans quickly overwhelmed Zeledón's position. The assault lasted about an hour before Zeledón's men began retreating. The Marines and Conservative forces diligently pursued Zeledón and his men during their retreat. A day of isolated haphazard combat ensued. Zeledón was killed during the retreat. Yet how and where Zeledón actually died became the subject of a blistering debate. According to the Marine Corps Historical Reference Series, Zeledón's own men killed him when Zeledón tried to desert. Unofficial versions, other than the Marine Corps Historical Reference Series, say that Zeledón was captured in Catarina (my training town) and taken to Masaya where the U.S. Marines ordered his execution and his body was subsequently paraded through the municipality. Yet another unofficial version says that Zeledón's retreat was thwarted in a town called Diriomo and a heated battled followed with the Conservative military faction. According to this version, Zeledón was shot in the spine during the action and taken to Catarina, where he was pronounced dead on arrival. Despite these various accounts, what is not disputed is that a bullet struck Zeledón in the spine, and the wound took his life. However, everything else surrounding Zeledón's death is subject to debate—including when he was killed, where, how, and by whom.

When I asked Nicaraguans about their theory of what happened, many responded that Americans executed Zeledón and paraded his body through the streets of Masaya. These responses provide valuable insight into how Nicaraguans may perceive Americans based on U.S. involvement in their history.

It is also speculated that one of the witnesses to the Zeledón parade procession was another future legend in the history of Nicaragua, Augusto Céasar Sandino, who was allegedly infuriated by the parade. While Conservative Nicaragua had rid itself of the Liberal Zeledón, the new rebel, Sandino, would be more elusive and treacherous.

Sandino supposedly attended Zeledón's memorial and was beside himself with anger and frustration. Some years later in the mid-1920s, Sandino led an insurrection to rid Nicaragua of what he considered the tyranny and oppression of Conservative rule and American support. Sandino waged a seven-year rebellion and denied U.S. Marines of victory against his troops in the northern mountains. Ultimately, Sandino became a Nicaraguan legend.

Sandino's rebels consisted of mostly rural people who attacked any American installations they could find. One such target was the U.S. Marine post commanded by Captain Gilbert D. Hatfield near the town of Ocotal. Sandino wisely decided that the best way to operate against superior numbers and technology was to wage guerrilla warfare with hit-and-run tactics.

During the late evening of July 15, 1926, small groups of Sandino's men slipped into Ocotal. In the early morning hours of July 16, the Marines realized what was happening and began firing. Sandino's men then attacked Ocotal with full force. Three separate charges by Sandino were met with sufficient defense. Sandino then demanded that Hatfield surrender. When Captain Hatfield refused to surrender, Sandino strangely ordered his troops to fall back instead of making an expected all-out assault. However, Captain Hatfield had already called for support. While Sandino retreated out of the city, five American planes bombed the area for about an hour. Sandino escaped, but the town of Ocotal endured significant destruction.

The Marines searched the northwestern mountains for Sandino, but it was simply an impossible task. The rebels generally traveled in small groups and moved at night whenever possible. Respect and support from the local people allowed Sandino and his troops to survive.

With the approval of the Nicaraguan President, the Marines next tried to use a policy of re-concentration around the area of Ocotal. To reduce food sources for the rebels, the Marines ordered the local people to leave their farms and bring their property and cattle to an area protected by the U.S. military. Nevertheless, this policy did not work as the rebels lived off the land. Consequently, area residents suffered hardships, and thus, the Marines quietly abandoned the re-concentration effort.

The U.S. Government did not want its military to stay in Nicaragua forever. The 1932 elections had been protected, as well as American property and businesses. As a result, the United States began a process to support the Nicaraguan army (called the National Guard) so they could take on Sandino and maintain the country's stability on their own.

The U.S. economy faced serious problems in the 1932–1933 time frame, and American support was waning for the Nicaraguan effort. President Roosevelt withdrew U.S. troops from Nicaragua in 1933 following the inauguration of President Juan Bautista Sacasa.

When American troops pulled out of Nicaragua, an opportunity for peace with the Sacasa administration (1933–1936) became a real possibility for Sandino. Indeed, successful peace talks did occur in 1933. However, one man in particular felt threatened and irate by the withdrawal of American troops and the prospect of peace between Sandino and the current Nicaraguan administration. That man was General Anastasio Somoza García, who had been tasked with leading the Nicaraguan National Guard.

President Sacasa invited Sandino to Managua for talks of peace. On February 20, 1934, Sandino and a few of his commanders left the peace talks and the National Guard assassinated Augusto César Sandino. It is believed that Sandino and his commanders were almost immediately accosted in their automobile and driven to another location where they were all repeatedly shot.

Sandino's body was dispensed in great secrecy. One legend says that his body was dumped into the lava pool of the volcano in Masaya. Other myths indicate he was buried in Somoza's garden. People in Nicaragua generally believe Sandino courageously defied the United States and worked for the good of the common man. Eventually, Augusto César Sandino was unanimously named a "national hero" by Nicaragua's Congress.

Since Somoza led the Nicaraguan National Guard with the support of the United States, and Sandino gone, Somoza was able to intimidate his way to complete control of Nicaragua. Somoza muscled President Sacasa out of office with little resistance, and called for an election in 1936 appointing himself as the Liberal candidate. A landslide election followed in favor of Somoza. General Anastasio Somoza García became President of Nicaragua on January 1, 1937.

General Somoza ruled Nicaragua with brutality and oppression, using his power to acquire phenomenal wealth. He had his hand in almost every profitable business venture and leveraged support from the United States as a non-communist stronghold. President Franklin Roosevelt offered Somoza a lavish reception when he visited Washington, D.C. in 1939. The reception was quite the spectacle, complete with airplanes flying overhead and ceremonial guns. Roosevelt supposedly remarked that, "Somoza may be a son of a bitch, but he's our son of a bitch."

In 1944, Somoza announced his intention to remain in office for a third term. The announcement resulted in violent protests, as Nicaraguan law prohibited more than two terms. Somoza planned another way to maintain control by choosing a political ally named Leonardo Argüello to be his puppet. General Somoza directed a suspected fraudulent election, intending to wield power from behind the scenes until he could figure out a way to push Argüello aside, as he had previously done with Sacasa.

Argüello's general message during the inaugural address shocked Somoza. Argüello declared that his administration would be straightforward and independent of influence from other countries or individuals. It turned out that Argüello might have had plans of his own.

President Argüello eliminated press censorship and openly supported unions. He also called for Somoza and his military leaders to retire. General Somoza pursued a military coup almost immediately, and Argüello lasted only 26 days in office as the President of Nicaragua. Somoza subsequently controlled political power either directly or indirectly until the year 1956.

In 1956, Somoza traveled to the liberal city of León to be nominated for yet another Presidential term (a constitutional amendment had been passed to allow re-election). A grand party commemorated the festive occasion, and after Somoza danced with a beauty queen, a man stepped from the crowd firing a weapon multiple times at the President. Security forces immediately killed the assassin. However, the mission to kill Somoza had effectively done its damage—President Anastasio Somoza García died of his wounds a few days later on September 29, 1956.

The assassin, Rigoberto López Pérez, became an immediate hero for dissidents. Oddly enough, Rigoberto was a Liberal, like Somoza. Knowing he would not survive the mission, Rigoberto López Pérez wrote a note to his mother saying that killing President Somoza was his duty to Nicaragua.

Following the assassination, the country of Nicaragua was in great turmoil. The Nicaraguan Congress placed the assassinated President's son, Luis Somoza, into power. Luis Somoza led the country from 1956 until 1963, when a heart problem caused him to eventually relinquish direct control of Nicaragua. Trusted friends of the Somoza family maneuvered into the Presidency until Luis died of heart complications in 1967.

Elections were held and Luis Somoza's little brother, Anastasio "Tachito" Somoza, became President in May 1967. The Somoza family was so dominant that no political group, up to that point, could thwart its power. Tachito became the third Somoza to lead Nicaragua.

Tachito's regime jailed and tortured dissidents regularly. Learning well from his father and older brother, Tachito acquired a fortune beyond what his predecessors combined had amassed. Greed, repression, and brutality set the stage for a violent rebellion. However, before further violence could occur, Mother Nature wreaked havoc on Nicaragua with an incredible earthquake.

On December 23, 1972, a massive, 6.3 magnitude earthquake struck Nicaragua. Managua was almost completely destroyed, as the earthquake immediately leveled five square miles within the capital city. This geological event was a true human tragedy. Although estimates vary, it is thought that around ten thousand people were killed or injured, and fifty thousand families left homeless. The infrastructure of the capital city and surrounding areas had been devastated. With Managua as the centerpiece of business for the country, the earthquake decimated the nation's economy.

Even today there are dead areas in Managua, as rickety uninhabited buildings stand in ruins. Venturing through this tract of Managua is an unnerving experience, forcing the question of how and why this section of town was not rehabilitated. Part of the answer is that President Somoza led the reconstruction after being designated Chairman of the National Emergency Committee. As Chairman, Somoza controlled the relief and reconstruction effort, allowing him to use land, companies, and bank accounts of his choosing. Tachito tried to keep a positive image by making an offer that turned out to be a political mistake. He offered the highly respected Archbishop Miguel Obando y Bravo a position as vice-chairman of the Committee. Obando y Bravo, however, understood the character of Tachito. The Archbishop declined Tachito's offer and the rebuke was not received lightly, leading to future confrontations between the two men. The Archbishop himself was already in the beginning phases of secretly supporting a non-violent opposition to Somoza. In fact, this was one of the first public indications that the Catholic Church was about to cease its unquestioned support for the Government of Nicaragua.

Relief supplies poured into the country and were immediately sucked into a black hole of theft and backdoor deals. Those who were allied with the Somoza regime received some assistance, but everyone else was left to fend for themselves. The majority of the relief materials never even surfaced.

The earthquake was devastating enough, but the mysterious theft and ravaging of the relief supplies under Somoza's watch was the last straw for many Nicaraguans. The stage was set for another destructive blow to the country as a true rebellion was brewing.

The rebellion was slow to grow and was carefully orchestrated over years of secrecy. Many men were tortured and jailed or executed for being anti-Somoza. Speaking out against the Somoza family was very difficult, and censorship of the press was rigorously enforced. Miraculously, censorship of the press was drastically reduced, if not eliminated, when martial law was lifted in 1977.

Pedro Joaquín Chamorro—a previous classmate of Somoza—was willing to accept the risks associated with speaking about the injustices of the regime, and he did so relentlessly. Chamorro was the editor of the national newspaper, *La Prensa*. Somoza's book, *Nicaragua Betrayed*, portrays a genuine hatred between Somoza and Chamorro. In *Nicaragua Betrayed*, Somoza goes so far as to describe Chamorro as a dissident leader. Chamorro's reporters tried to publicly implicate Somoza in the theft of the earthquake relief supplies. Of course, Somoza was less than thrilled with Chamorro and the *La Prensa* newspaper.

Chamorro was an intellectual and a man of the people. He believed that a government should lift up and protect its people, as opposed to repressing and robbing them. His affront to Somoza made him famous in Nicaragua, and he stirred the anti-Somoza fervor wherever he went. Chamorro had to have known that eventually his high-profile and adamant opposition to Somoza would catch up with him, but he never tried to protect himself, nor did he compromise his antagonistic approach to confronting Somoza.

On January 10, 1978, Pedro Joaquín Chamorro was assassinated on his way to work. Chamorro had begun to eat away publicly at the Somoza regime, and the underbelly of revolution was seething with anticipation. Patience was necessary for the rebels, as anyone who got in the way of Somoza was thrown in jail or met the same fate as Chamorro. Nicaraguans were deeply distraught about the death of Chamorro, and large scale riots broke out around Managua and other cities. It took National Guardsmen roughly two weeks to bring order back to the country.

Somoza denied killing Chamorro and claimed that Chamorro's death was a murder-for-hire plot by a Cuban named Dr. Pedro Ramos. Shortly before Chamorro's murder, Dr. Ramos flew to Miami. The alleged killers were arrested, and following some intense interrogation, confessions occurred. The confessed murderers were tried, convicted, and thrown in prison. Even with the murderers in prison, Somoza could do nothing to dissuade public opinion that he had Chamorro killed. Dr. Ramos was never imprisoned for the conspiracy.

While Chamorro had publicly lambasted the Somoza regime through the press, the Sandinista movement had already been secretly working for years to develop a successful revolution. The Sandinistas were the eventual group to overthrow Somoza, but victory would come with a severe price tag.

The Sandinista rebellion began as an idea in the 1950s, inspired by the success of Fidel Castro and his communist vision. The Sandinista philosophy was based upon Marxism and was a pro-common man revolution. The Sandinistas also adopted Augusto Sandino's ideology of anti-imperialism, nationalism, and a real hatred for the United States. It should be remembered, however, that Augusto Sandino was assassinated in 1934 and had no living role in the Sandinista rebellion. Carlos Fonseca was the true founder of the Sandinista revolution, and he resurrected and brought Sandino's name and ideals to the Sandinista movement.

The idea of becoming wealthy at the cost of ordinary people infuriated the Sandinistas. In the eyes of dissidents, the Somoza regime was considered the epitome of greed, repression, and corruption. The Sandinistas realized early on that the only way to gain power in Nicaragua was to throw the current rulers out by force. The founders of the Sandinista rebellion took a blood oath and swore themselves to success or death—they would not cease their efforts until victory was achieved for the people.

The Sandinista Party (*Frente Sandinista de Liberación Nacional* or FSLN) was formally organized on July 23, 1961. Three men—Carlos Fonseca Amador, Silvio Mayorga, and Tomás Borge—had founded the FSLN, but only Tomás Borge would survive the insurrection. Daniel Ortega would later join the FSLN, eventually emerging as its leader and true figurehead. All of these men were dedicated revolutionaries.

In the early days, one had to be invited to become a Sandinista, as speaking out against Somoza could cost your life. One of its most respected recruits, Daniel Ortega, was responsible for spreading the Sandinista word in and around Managua. There were bank robberies and other crimes committed to support the movement, and the Sandinistas were quickly becoming a serious threat to Somoza.

Carlos Fonseca and Silvio Mayorga were both killed during combat in the northern mountains, but the rebellion did not falter. Tomás Borge and Daniel Ortega were steadfast in their pursuit of the revolution, and many Nicaraguans who were fed up with Somoza and his National Guard began to listen and follow.

The dissidents trained in Cuba and sought help from outside Nicaragua, such as Palestine, Russia, and North Korea. Organization was taking shape and membership was growing. However, the revolution was slow to develop since many of its members were captured by Somoza's underground information network. The arrest of several important Sandinistas began to take its toll on the group. After working relentlessly to regain strength, the rebels wanted to strike hard into the heart of the Somoza regime and free their imprisoned colleagues.

They did so on December 27, 1974, with a brazen and shockingly successful assault on a Managua Christmas party. Those present at this holiday soiree included members of Somoza's family, the Nicaraguan Ambassador to the United States, as well as numerous other dignitaries. They were held captive for almost three days. When all was said and done, the Sandinistas were well-heeled with a one million dollar ransom paid by Somoza, and their revolutionary comrades were released from prison. Additionally, a Sandinista official communique was broadcasted over the radio and printed in the *La Prensa* newspaper. The rebels were even afforded safe passage to Cuba. The Sandinistas considered the operation a complete success.

The Christmas party assault also gave the FSLN a much-needed public boost, and the number of anti-Somoza recruits increased. Yet, the insurrection was still nowhere near a level that could oust Somoza. The fugitive Sandinistas began infiltrating back into Nicaragua from Cuba to reach the maturity phase of the rebellion. The Christmas party assault had been planned by Nicaragua's future Minister of the Interior, Tomás Borge, and one of the prisoners liberated during the assault was the future President of Nicaragua, Daniel Ortega. These two men were committed to each other and to the eventual overthrow of the Somoza regime.

Following such an embarrassing event that was so widely publicized, Somoza brought forth a plan of extermination for the Sandinistas and went after them with a vengeance in the mountainous northern departments of Nicaragua. Somoza focused his aggression in Estelí, Matagalpa, Jinotega, and Nueva Segovia. The human rights violations in these areas were appalling, which spurred international criticism of the Somoza regime.

In 1977, the Carter administration introduced a new human rights policy that made Nicaragua a top priority. U.S. military and economic assistance was drastically reduced to motivate the Somoza regime to improve the human rights situation. With support from the United States waning, the rebels and political adversaries grew stronger. The Somoza regime was losing its grip on power.

In the months following Chamorro's death in 1978, the country became paralyzed by riots, strikes, and general upheaval. The Sandinistas used these events to their advantage by recruiting heavily, stockpiling weapons, and organizing themselves for a final assault.

In August 1978, only eight months after Chamorro's assassination, the Sandinistas once again initiated a brazen assault. This time they seized the National Palace while the Nicaraguan Congress was in session. The rebels took 1,500 hostages and halted the governmental process dead in its tracks. The hostage crisis negotiations resulted in $500,000 in ransom money paid to the Sandinistas, the rebel "manifesto" printed in the Nicaraguan national newspapers, and more Sandinista prisoners released from jail. The rebels responsible for the National Palace assault also successfully negotiated their escape from Nicaragua by plane. President Somoza had been dealt another serious and very public defeat.

The political moderates of Nicaragua could not deny that the power of the Sandinistas had crested the tipping point. The overthrow of the Somoza regime appeared imminent, causing many moderates to join the Sandinista movement. Immediately following the Palace assault, a mass insurrection emerged with general strikes and attacks on the National Guard. The cities of Matagalpa, Estelí, León, Chinandega, and Masaya became battle zones. The slaughter was intense and Somoza dropped bombs on his own people—galvanizing the rebellion and fostering more support for the dissident cause.

The final onslaught on the forty-two-year rule of the Somoza family began in June 1979, and it was obvious that nothing less than complete surrender would be acceptable. In less than a month, the Sandinistas' offensive brought them control of the nation's major cities, the majority of the countryside, and over half of Managua. In an effort to arrest Sandinista progress, the National Guard really hammered Managua by summarily bombing its neighborhoods. Although the bombings killed many and set the city of Managua ablaze, the National Guard's effort was crushed. In the end, the National Guard controlled only a few key areas of the city.

The United States did not want the Sandinistas to control Nicaragua, but there was no doubt that they were already in control. Following the deaths of thousands of people from both sides, the Sandinistas had finally attained their goal of purging the country of the Somoza regime.

On July 17, 1979, President Anastasio Somoza DeBayle fled Nicaragua into exile. His original destination was Miami, Florida, and the entire senior command of the National Guard went with him. With no military leadership, it only took 24 hours for the National Guard to completely implode. Somoza eventually ended up living under the security and protection of Paraguay and would live roughly one year longer. On September 17, 1980, while driving on the streets of Asunción, Paraguay, Anastasio Somoza was assassinated by a rocket-propelled grenade fired at his vehicle. According to the Paraguayan press, forensics identified Somoza only through his feet because his body was so unrecognizable.

The Sandinistas had accomplished the worst of all possible scenarios for the United States—a complete Sandinista victory. On July 19, 1979 a new government was announced under a provisional junta led by thirty-five-year-old Daniel Ortega. Violetta Barrios de Chamorro, a political moderate and widow of Pedro Joaquín Chamorro, also served on the junta leadership team.

The Sandinistas inherited a country in ruins. Estimates vary, but indicate that around fifty thousand people were killed during the war and six hundred thousand were homeless. The country was $1.6 billion in debt, and the economic infrastructure of the country was devastated. Worse, Daniel Ortega had absolutely no experience running a government—he was a military man.

After the victorious rebellion, the United States offered an olive branch to the Sandinistas by reversing its outright hostility and initiating a cautiously receptive attitude. The Sandinistas were mistrustful of this tenuous new relationship with the United States. For one, how could they ever forgive the U.S. Government for the years of unwavering support of the Somoza regime before President Jimmy Carter began reducing aid due to Somoza's human rights abuses? Further, the Sandinistas were paranoid that the United States might support a counter-rebellion. As it turns out, their paranoia was justified as the U.S. did in fact support a counter-rebellion after President Carter left office.

In the meantime, the Sandinistas accepted aid, counsel, and general support from Russia and Cuba. The United States reached out to the new leaders of Nicaragua and offered money to assist in the post-war relief effort. However, a change in U.S. leadership ended our moderate policy towards the Sandinistas.

The U.S. policy toward Nicaragua reversed when Ronald Reagan was elected President in 1980. The Reagan administration held a deep mistrust of the Sandinistas, and Communist support to Nicaragua from Russia and Cuba threatened our national security. The American President feared that Nicaragua was destined to become a Communist state and thought it needed to be dealt with before the Marxist/Leninist philosophy took root in all of Central America.

Shortly after Reagan's inauguration in 1981, a covert operation was under way to support Nicaraguan exiles. These exiles consisted of mostly the same military officers who had previously commanded Nicaragua's National Guard. A revolution was going to happen all over again, but in reverse. This group of men were called the "Contras," which is short for counter-revolutionaries, and they planned a counter-rebellion. As with any revolution, it takes time to organize, locate man power, fund, and then execute all operations necessary to attain the desired result. Meanwhile, the citizens of Nicaragua suffered under the policies of the new Sandinista Government.

As the Sandinistas and Daniel Ortega were learning how to govern, life in Nicaragua was rapidly changing—and not necessarily in a positive direction. The new leaders were in a mad rush to implement policies and organize a functional government. The Sandinistas developed a basic platform that included the following (condensed here for simplicity's sake):

- Nationalization of property owned by the Somozas and their collaborators
- Land reforms
- Improved rural and urban working conditions
- Free unionization for all workers
- Controlled living costs, especially the basic necessities of food, clothing, and medicine
- Improved public services and housing conditions
- Free education through high school
- A national literacy campaign

- Nationalization and protection of natural resources, including mines
- Abolition of torture, political assassination, and the death penalty
- Equality for women
- Formation of a new army under FSLN leadership
- Pesticide controls
- Rainforest conservation
- Wildlife conservation
- Alternative energy programs

Two Sandinista platform ideas in particular had an intense impact on the people of Nicaragua—one of which was very negative and the other was extremely positive. The first platform idea offers a glimpse into what happens to a country when wage and price controls are implemented without having complete control over the supply of products being distributed or their true value. The second platform idea is the nationwide literacy campaign.

Wage and price controls were implemented by the Sandinista Government. Eventually almost every occupation in Nicaragua was given a title with a fixed salary. A majority of the products distributed by the government were also given a fixed price. With the government in control of product distribution, the Sandinistas felt they could control inflationary pricing. The common man would then be able to afford all of life's basic necessities. However, what happens in theory is not necessarily what occurs in reality.

The Sandinistas were surprised when food production fell at an alarming rate. What happened next is a simple matter of economics, human nature, and an eventual loss of confidence in the government.

When a product becomes more scarce and the demand for that good remains high, the natural result is that this merchandise becomes more valuable. It does not matter what price the government places on the item because the people decide the item's true value. This is a basic economics concept of supply, demand, and market forces. Thus, when the supply of mechanical parts, food, and other necessities became scarce in Nicaragua, their values went through the roof. Human nature characteristics of fear and greed facilitated successful black markets that became a part of Nicaragua's culture.

Nothing will create a backlash as fast as not providing your people with the basic necessities of life. Rumblings and complaining began about food lines, prices, and the lack of mechanical parts. The result was a loss of confidence in the government.

The Sandinistas also faced another insurmountable problem—they needed to use much of their available resources to confront the rapidly-evolving counter-rebellion. Instead of allocating money to fund useful projects to help their people, the Sandinistas were forced to buy materials of war to fend off the counter-insurrection. This diversion of funds had a devastating impact on the already dire economic situation.

Once again, the people of Nicaragua were dying by the thousands in this rebellion—the Contra war—and the Sandinistas were just as oppressive and brutal as the Somozas had been. The Sandinistas arrested suspected Contras, committed human atrocities, and censored *La Prensa* newspaper—at one point shutting down publication completely. The Sandinistas ultimately lost control of the government, but not before they did something positive.

One of the lasting positive legacies of the Sandinistas was the National Literacy Campaign. During one of my Spanish classes, my instructor, Angélica, mentioned that she had been a part of the Sandinista National Literacy Campaign when she was eighteen-years-old. Her story fascinated me. I asked if she would be willing to spend some time educating me about how the literacy campaign functioned, as well as what her role was in this massive countrywide effort. Seeing my intense interest in the history of her country, Angélica gladly shared her knowledge and four hours of her time after class one day. I will forever be grateful to her.

Angélica first explained that her boyfriend was killed during the Sandinista rebellion. He was taken from the town of San Juan del Oriente to the northern mountains to fight, and she never saw him again. Speaking about her boyfriend was still very upsetting for her even though decades have passed since his death. After due sympathies were offered on my part, I immediately tried to change the topic to the literacy campaign to relieve her of the emotional trauma of sharing this sad story from her life.

She walked to the blackboard and wrote down "Father Fernando Cardenal" and "March 1980." She explained that Father Cardenal had been entrusted to manage the National Literacy Campaign in March of

1980. This was a massive undertaking that Cuba had helped Nicaragua plan. Cuba had experience implementing the same strategy after Fidel Castro's successful rebellion. Cuba helped staff the Nicaraguan campaign by sending 1,200 teachers to assist. Other countries were also involved including Spain, Costa Rica, and the Dominican Republic. Angélica then wrote on the board that there were approximately sixty thousand teachers enlisted to eradicate illiteracy in Nicaragua. Pointing to her chest with the marker, she proudly said, "I was one of them." She told me that prior to the literacy campaign in 1979, fifty percent of the population in Nicaragua was functionally illiterate. Before I could express my shocked disbelief, she continued. She said the majority of the teachers were teenagers. Angélica had left home for an extended period of at least five months for the first time in her life. At the age of eighteen, she had packed a bag and traveled to the Atlantic Coast.

The Atlantic Coast generally consists of sparsely-populated jungle areas that are impoverished to the extreme. Angélica headed to this region with 150 other teachers. They took a bus as far as possible by land to the town of Rama, and then traveled the Río Escondido by boat to the town of Bluefields, where they began walking. After walking for almost three days, the group arrived in the region where they would be teaching. The collection of young teachers then split up, and Angélica was assigned to live with a family for the coming months.

These Atlantic Coast teachers were spread across a wide distance, and Angélica was left alone in a tiny community in the middle of the jungle. She helped the families with household chores during the day, taught in the evenings, and slept on a mud floor. Basic survival was difficult at best for the people in her isolated rural community, and the experience was an emotional challenge for Angélica. I asked her if she felt her time there was well spent, and she emphatically said, "Absolutely. The people could not read!" By the time she left her community, literacy was improved, and Angélica feels quite proud of that accomplishment. She told me, "When the Sandinista Literacy Campaign was over, the literacy rate jumped to about eighty-four percent. The program was a success." I thanked her for her time, and we said good night.

The National Literacy Campaign was a success and helped the Nicaraguan population begin to understand the importance of education. While the literacy campaign was going on, another effort was continuing outside of Nicaragua—the counter-rebellion against the Sandinistas.

The Contra rebellion could not have been successful without the support of the United States. In 1981, Ronald Reagan justly accused the Sandinistas of exporting Marxist/Leninist ideals and weapons to other Central American countries, namely El Salvador. The United States immediately took action against the Sandinistas because the administration felt that having a Communist state in Central America would not be a positive development.

President Reagan had undertaken two major actions. The first was beginning immediate support for exiled Nicaraguans in the hopes of starting a counter-revolution to successfully over throw the Sandinistas. The second action was to initiate a complete trade embargo. These two initiatives began another era of trouble for the ordinary people of Nicaragua.

Mechanical parts in Nicaragua became practically non-existent, which resulted in tractors, trucks and manufacturing equipment being left to rust with only minor problems. My neighbor told me that during this time period, all he needed was a tie rod for his truck, yet the vehicle sat stationary for almost two years because he was unable to locate the part. The trade embargo and the counter-rebellion successfully hindered Nicaragua from functioning.

The United States helped to finance, arm, and train the Contras, and it worked with foreign governments to allow the insurrection to use Central American territories to base the operations. The Contras used Honduras to the north and Costa Rica to the south for their invasion into Nicaragua. Once the United States began a system of support for the counter-rebellion, the Soviet Union and Cuba began sending more war materials to support the Sandinistas, and the vicious circle of violence continued. Before the insurrection was over, there were ten thousand Contras facing seventy-five thousand Nicaraguan government troops, and blood was being spilled at an alarming rate. Ambush and guerilla war tactics were utilized by the Contras, and the common people of Nicaragua suffered severely.

In 1982 , the U.S. House of Representatives passed the Boland Amendment, which aimed to limit U.S. Government assistance to the

Contras. When this amendment passed, the situation in Nicaragua and the United States became worse. The Boland amendment caused funding and materials for the Contras to be cut off for a brief time, creating shortages for that faction. As a result, these soldiers went into Nicaraguan communities and stole food, supplies, and other materials that they needed to survive. This made life more difficult and dangerous for the average Nicaraguan. In the United States, the Contras had the full support of the Reagan administration. American officials began to circumvent U.S. law, resulting in **the Iran-Contra Affair**.

What a lovely way to describe illegal activity, by using the word "affair." The basics of this scandal are fairly simple to describe using broad strokes. The intricacies, however, are immensely complex and only lead to more questions. Some questions will never be answered due to document destruction and national security protection orders by the Reagan administration. The following information was obtained from publicly-released documents by the Iran-Contra Independent Counsel summary report.

In short, the United States began illegally selling arms to Iran from October 1984 to October 1986. A percentage of the profits from the arms sales were then funneled to the Contras in Nicaragua. The Reagan administration had two main reasons for this course of action.

1. Supporting the Contras in the continuation of their war effort would rid Central America of the Communist-style Sandinista Government.
2. Selling arms to Iran would aid in the release of American hostages.

With one event, the whole covert operation began to collapse. On October 5, 1986, the Sandinistas shot down an American C-123 transport plane that was bringing supplies to the Contras. The Sandinistas hunted down and captured a surviving crew member named Eugene Hasenfus. Hasenfus admitted to working for the CIA, and this startling news was made public, offering indisputable proof that the U.S. Government was acting illegally in support of the Contras. All hell broke loose back in Washington with the revelation of a monumental scandal.

One month after Hasenfus was blown out of the sky in Nicaragua and U.S. support for the Contras was revealed, the other shoe dropped for the Reagan administration. On November 3, 1986, a Lebanese publication reported controversial U.S. sales of weapons to the country of Iran. The joining of these separate, but coordinated operations, was made public on November 25, 1986, when Attorney General Meese announced that Justice Department officials had discovered that some of the proceeds from the arms sales to Iran had been diverted to the Contras.

In Washington, bi-partisan battles went ballistic, leading to an Independent Counsel investigation. An operation of this magnitude cannot be pulled off without several key people involved. High-level CIA officials, State Department officials, members of the National Security Council, and individual private citizens were all implicated. In total, fourteen men were charged with criminal violations. All of the individuals charged were convicted except for one CIA official whose case was dismissed on the grounds of National Security and two officials who received unprecedented pre-trial pardons from President Bush just before he left office in 1992. Speculation had begun that President Bush might have been called as a witness in those trials.

The Independent Counsel's summary report said there was no credible evidence that President Reagan violated any criminal statutes. However, it did say that President Reagan set the stage for the illegal activities of others by encouraging and, in general terms, ordering support of the Contras during the period when funds for the Contras were cut off by the Boland Amendment, and in authorizing the sale of arms to Iran in contravention of the U.S. embargo on such sales. The President's disregard for laws enacted to limit presidential actions abroad, such as the Boland Amendment, the Arms Export Control Act, and the congressional notification requirements in covert-action laws, created a climate in which some of the government officers assigned to implement his policies felt emboldened to circumvent such laws.

In other words, President Reagan approved the operation without actually doing anything criminal. For example, the President gave a directive to keep the Contras alive "body and soul" during the Boland cut-off period. If you are a Marine Lieutenant Colonel working for the National Security Council and you received a ridiculously broad-ranging presidential directive, what kind of authority would you think you had for an operation to keep the Contras alive "body and soul?"

Marine Lieutenant Colonel Oliver North was the individual from the National Security Council held responsible for carrying out the President's directive, and he viewed the orders as an invitation to take whatever action was necessary. North offered an immunized testimony during the televised Iran-Contra hearings. For his part in the Iran-Contra scandal, North was convicted of altering and destroying documents, accepting an illegal gratuity, and aiding and abetting in the obstruction of Congress. His conviction was reversed on appeal. North worked with two other men, Richard Secord and Albert Hakim, to create the covert-action enterprise that received, managed, and distributed funds for the Contras. The Independent Counsel's summary report also concluded that the Iranian operations were carried out with the knowledge of Vice President George Bush.

Not much could be done by way of prosecutions with serious jail time as a consequence in the Iran-Contra Affair. The reason? Even though there were apparent violations of the Arms Export Control Act and the Boland Amendment, they are not criminal statutes and do not contain any enforcement provisions. Even if the Act and Amendment did have prosecutorial teeth, the cover-up would have impeded the chain of evidence and investigation. Almost all the charges and convictions associated with the Iran-Contra scandal were related to the cover-up. According to the Independent Counsel summary report, the highest officials within our government acted with blatant disrespect for U.S. law.

For roughly ten years during the Contra-revolution (1980-1990), the ordinary people of Nicaragua suffered. The Contra-rebellion occurred on the heels of many more such years of misery during the Sandinista revolt. Had the U.S. Government not supported the Contra rebels, the fate of average Nicaraguans may have been much different. So also might have been the fate of the United States had the Communist system of government truly taken ahold in all of Central America. President Reagan faced a difficult situation and very tough decisions were made. It is impossible to know what the outcome might have been if the President of the United States had acted differently.

Subsequent to the Iran-Contra meltdown and the scandalous aftermath, including congressional hearings, President Reagan asked Congress in 1987 for another $270 million for the Contras. The war in Nicaragua raged on, indeed intensifying. Young people were killing each other and the country was ripping itself apart. Was there ever going to be peace?

The economic environment in Nicaragua worsened until both the Contras and the Sandinistas realized that their situations needed to change. The Contras had only ten thousand men facing seventy-five thousand Sandinistas. Even though Contras' funding remained somewhat intact, the Contras knew that they were facing many more years of war before they could forcefully overthrow the Sandinistas. The Sandinistas' funding was drying up as Russia headed for bankruptcy and the Cold War was all but won by the United States. The U.S. trade embargo had also been effective; export prices were low, and the economy in Nicaragua disintegrated with inflation rates running as high as thirty-six thousand percent. Facing a serious financial situation and continuing bloodshed, there was no end in sight to the human tragedy. The Sandinistas and Contras finally agreed to peace talks. It took another two years after the Iran-Contra scandal to achieve meaningful peace.

On March 23, 1988, the Sandinistas and Contras finally agreed to end the fratricidal war that had devastated the country for nearly a decade. Subsequent agreements were later signed in February and August of 1989, but the road to lasting peace was hammered out. The country was going to attempt to mend the deep wounds of civil war and begin moving forward.

The year 1990 brought about a new era for Nicaragua, and presidential elections were held. In an internationally observed election, Sandinista leader Daniel Ortega was defeated by a liberal candidate from the National Opposition Union party, Violetta Barrios de Chamorro. The elections were peaceful, and Ortega relinquished control of the country. However, the Sandinistas retained significant control of the National Assembly, police force, and labor unions.

Under Chamorro, great strides were made toward consolidating democratic institutions, advancing national reconciliation, stabilizing the economy, privatizing state-owned enterprises, and reducing human rights violations. Any leader who takes control of a country following years of brutal civil war has their work cut out for them, and she did a respectable job of maintaining the peace and adopting a policy of inclusion. The people of Nicaragua began to pick themselves up and shake off the dust from a long and difficult historical road.

In 1996, another "first" came to fruition for Nicaragua. Right-wing Liberal Alliance Party candidate, Arnoldo Alemán, was elected President of Nicaragua. This historical event marked the first time in decades that two consecutive elections had produced a peaceful transfer of power between rival parties. The elections were deemed free, fair, and peaceful by the international community that was present to observe. Peace and the democratic process were taking root, and the Nicaraguan economy was continuing to gradually improve.

Alemán was in the middle of his presidential term working towards fulfilling his campaign promises when a horrible and tragic weather event eliminated almost everything that had been accomplished to lift the country of Nicaragua from the depths of economic hell. Hurricane Mitch descended upon Nicaragua in late October 1998.

8
Hurricane Mitch

"History...is a nightmare from which I am trying to wake."
–James Joyce, *Ulysses*

Nicaragua is a land of geologic wonder and beauty. Historically, the country has been impacted significantly by both earthquakes and hurricanes. In 1998, Hurricane Mitch bore down on Nicaragua, wreaking such devastation and loss that my neighbors in Estelí (a northern town where we served for two years) described life with time caveats such as "before Mitch" and "after Mitch," similar to how people in New Orleans describe time as "before Katrina" and "after Katrina." Our neighbors believe Nicaragua's climate drastically changed subsequent to Hurricane Mitch, becoming much more drought-ridden. Without question, Hurricane Mitch was a defining event in the recent history of Nicaragua.

Just when the country had begun to gain a slight economic foothold after the Sandinista revolution and the Contra counter-rebellion, Nicaragua yet again faced incredible human suffering and economic collapse. Hurricane Mitch caught Nicaraguans by surprise; the media downplayed the storm by saying that the path of the hurricane would only lightly brush the Atlantic Coast before moving north. The media was generally correct in what happened. However, the surprise for Nicaragua was the size and encompassing range of the storm. Hurricane Mitch occurred in late October 1998—at the conclusion of Nicaragua's rainy season.

According to the National Oceanic and Atmospheric Administration (NOAA), Hurricane Mitch was a unique and horrendous beast as it gathered energy and power from both the Atlantic and Pacific oceans. The extended feeder bands of Mitch spread across the entire expanse of Central America. It became a Saffir-Simpson Category V hurricane with sustained winds of between 150-170 miles per hour and peak winds of 157 knots (180 MPH). The eye of Mitch stalled just north of Honduras on the morning of October 28, 1998. Nicaragua would not escape the wrath of Mitch.

What destroyed Nicaragua, however, was not so much the wind, but the rain from the storm bands swirling away from the eye of the

hurricane. From satellite-derived estimates for the six-day period end-
ing on October 31, 1998, the National Climatic Data Center (NCDC)
stated that rain fell at a rate of about a foot a day and total rainfall in
some mountain areas reached approximately six feet over a seven day
period! These estimates of rainfall given by the NCDC are not considered unreasonable, given the tropical location and altitude of the
mountainous terrain. Further, this was a monster hurricane.

By October 27, heavy clouds worked their way over Nicaragua and
the bottom dropped out with a ferocity that Nicaraguans had never before seen. My Spanish professor in Estelí told me she literally thought
the end of the world had come. She cried in fear during the last two
days of the seven-day storm. Clearly this horrible time in her life left
her emotionally scarred.

The consistent and torrential rain from Mitch flooded paved roads
as the drainage systems were not designed to disperse so much water.
Dirt roads that make up the majority of Nicaragua's byways and neighborhood thoroughfares became virtually impassable. The rivers grew
exponentially over their normal flows and became apocalyptically massive. These rivers overran bridges and thundered through the countryside, collecting thousands of homes, trees, power lines and light poles,
trucks, farm equipment, animals, and human bodies. Debris fields of
violently-moving river water annihilated absolutely everything in their
path. The entire infrastructure in the northern mountains was rendered
almost useless, and all of the bridges between Managua and León were
destroyed, leaving that part of the country with no contact or access
to the rest of Nicaragua.

While the massive rivers were killing people and destroying much of
northern Nicaragua, many people in the south did not even realize their
nation was in the midst of a complete disaster. As an example, one of my
Spanish teachers told me that she actually conducted language classes in the
town of Catarina during the hurricane! The amazingly intense storm caused
power outages across the nation, and any news that would provide her with
information about the weather event became difficult to obtain. Although
the overall scenario was tragic, envisioning my dedicated Spanish teacher
and Peace Corps trainees dutifully attending language classes with no power
and torrential rain during the hurricane brought about mild amusement for
me—a classic example of serious commitment to getting a job done.

While Spanish classes continued in the southern city of Catarina, a truly hideous event unfolded in the northwestern Pacific region, in the Department of Chinandega. The crater of a dormant volcano named "Casita" filled with rainwater. Casita was a 650-meter-high composite volcano that was quite steep near the crater rim. As the crater filled with rain water, the support structure at the cone became overwhelmed. Shortly before eleven o'clock in the morning on October 30, a wall of the Casita volcano disintegrated, severing the top portion of the southwest sector, sending a debris-filled avalanche of mud, rock, and water over a mile-wide and nine feet high moving at an estimated speed of sixty miles per hour into the farming communities of El Porvenir and Rolando Rodríguez. The avalanche consumed everyone and everything in its path with near-perfect killing efficiency, eliminating thousands of people in only a few minutes as it traveled over four kilometers to the outskirts of a town called Posoltega. No one foresaw a disaster of this magnitude.

The aftermath was a hopeless situation with extreme emotional devastation. It was impossible to identify the majority of the victims. The poor survivors who did not get caught in the colossal avalanche had to resort to agonizing burning brigades, torching all of the mutilated corpses they could find in human pyres before disease could bring its gruesome element to the disaster. In a single moment, life for these people changed forever in a vicious and tragic way.

In March 2009, the U.S. President Bill Clinton and First Lady Hillary Clinton traveled to Nicaragua and helped dedicate the memorial park built for the thousands who lost their lives. The plaque they offered was a genuine gesture of American respect for the victims.

For survivors of the deadly Casita volcano landslide, life is unquestionably defined in terms of "before Hurricane Mitch" and what their lives are like now. During our service, Kathryn and I traveled two and a half hours from Estelí to Posoltega to better understand what happened. It was a moving and extremely humbling experience. We spoke with the Mayor of Posoltega and his staff about what occurred and how his constituents were continuing to recover. Despite the fact that about seven years had passed, it was clear that the people of Posoltega were still besieged with problems.

Before Mitch, the area destroyed by the avalanche had consisted of about seventy percent of the farm production for the municipality's inhabitants. Afterward, all of that once-usable land was condemned, and beans, corn and rice could no longer be cultivated. Many of the surviving farmers deserted the area, moving to Costa Rica to begin anew and leaving the horrible memories behind.

The remaining people who lived in the damaged farming communities of El Porvenir and Rolando Rodríguez eventually received relocation assistance in the form of housing within the town of Posoltega. However, at the time of our visit, the relocated farmers had not acquired job training to empower them to function in a business sector other than agriculture. Over eighty percent of Posoltega's roughly 15,000 residents were unemployed and their desperate state remained palpable.

The country of Nicaragua experienced financial ruin subsequent to Hurricane Mitch's destructive rampage. That season's crop was almost a complete loss and many factories were decimated, leaving thousands of people jobless. Electricity was not restored in some areas for months, and people who lost their homes lived in churches or schools. Mitch eliminated almost three-quarters of the country's infrastructure. The economy prior to Mitch, while teetering toward progress, had already been weak, and these new economic losses evaporated all hopes of post-war prosperity.

Scientists from NOAA declared Hurricane Mitch as the most deadly Western Hemisphere storm during the last two hundred years. There had not been a more deadly storm since "The Great Hurricane" of 1780.

How does a country recover and rebuild itself after such devastation? By coming together as a people, burying the dead, pulling themselves up by the bootstraps, and accepting help from anyone willing to offer assistance. However, yet another wound from Nicaragua's history destructively reopened following Hurricane Mitch.

Unfortunately, President Arnoldo Alemán did not work constructively with other political parties to lift Nicaragua from its perilous state. For example, he rebuked pleas for relief from the landslide-decimated Sandinista farming communities of El Porvenir and Rolando Rodríguez near the town of Posoltega. The Sandinista Mayor of Posoltega, Felicitas Zeledón, called President Alemán regularly for a forty-eight-hour period following the landslide, telling the President of the dire situation in her area. No assistance was provided. In fact, President Alemán called the Mayor of Posoltega "a crazy woman" during a press conference. Can you imagine what that must have felt like to the Sandinista party, not to mention the people of Posoltega? Alemán's reaction—and non-action—deepened divisions along political party lines.

Hurricane Mitch also prompted incredible greed. Much like Somoza after the 1972 Managua earthquake, it is speculated that Alemán either stole or profited significantly from the relief money that poured in from other countries. Later, President Alemán was imprisoned for his administration's corrupt practices. Although his imprisonment was not attributed solely to his activities during the relief effort for the hurricane, Alemán's actions during Nicaragua's time of great need were certainly motivation to bring him to justice.

Nicaraguans have shown that they are determined, tough, and unbreakable. After the Hurricane Mitch disaster, people began the slow process of rebuilding their lives and the infrastructure of the country. Bridges were eventually reconstructed in a more sturdy fashion, better health clinics were built, and factories were renovated with more modern technology. Time heals emotional scars, and the stage had been set once again for wide-ranging economic recovery. Following despair, a glimmer of optimism for a brighter future inspired the majority in Nicaragua. Even considering this newfound confidence, decades of improvements have still been necessary for this country to thrive financially. The history of Nicaragua further encouraged Kathryn and me to represent the United States well and impact our assigned community in a positive way.

9
Separation And Departure To Our Training Towns
"Progress always involves risk; you can't steal second and keep your foot on first."
–Frederic Wilcox

Following our orientation in Granada, the three-month training program began. Kathryn and I knew we would live in separate towns, and the suspense of how that would work out weighed heavily on our minds.

We had lunch and then a simple goodbye moment with each other in Granada. We rode in different vehicles to our new host families' homes in separate training towns. Nervous and excited energy flowed inside me. Many thoughts ran through my mind as we drove through the beautiful jungle countryside. I thought about all that Kathryn and I had done to arrive at this point. I wondered how Kathryn would get along with her new host family. I did not know what was facing me with respect to my host family, but I knew somehow that I would make it work. I started to think about what I would I say to my new host family? I could not say much of anything. I hoped they would be nice. I wondered if I would be able to help them in some way during my training. Would they help me with my Spanish? What would my living situation be like? I wondered what the financial situation was for my family. How would having to feed me affect them financially? (I later learned that the Peace Corps pays the host families an attractive sum by Nicaraguan standards.) I hoped my town would be safe. My last thought before I arrived at my host family's home was—"What a crazy adventure this is going to be!"

My first day on site turned out to be really interesting. Don Alfredo dropped me off in front of my new home. "Don" is a title in Nicaragua, not a name. It is kind of like saying he is a boss, so calling him "Don" shows respect. Don Alfredo was the boss of logistics for the Peace Corps. He was in charge of everything that had to do with moving anything—people, bags, materials, supplies—it did not matter what, Don Alfredo was the man.

Catarina, my training town, is about an hour south of Managua in the department of Masaya. My facilitator (Spanish professor) and I got out of the truck, and she introduced me to my new "host mother,"

Marisol Gómez. Marisol was twenty-eight years old and a spectacular woman. She was kind, considerate, and funny. She was a great mother and wife who worked ridiculously hard. After our introduction, my facilitator and my new "host mother" spoke for about fifteen minutes. Of course I could not say much, but the three of us sat in Marisol's living room and tried to get acquainted. Then my facilitator said we needed to go meet with my other site-mates and their host families so I could become familiar with where they lived ("site-mate" is a Peace Corps term for other "*aspirantes*" in the same training town.). The Peace Corps chose the host families for myself and my site-mates in Catarina well, as all of them seemed to be good, hardworking families.

After we located and spoke with the two other trainees in Catarina, Lee Hamilton and Hollis Bennet, we all walked together to the "Mirador"—a scenic overlook of the lagoon. My head spun from everything I saw. Jungle flowers were everywhere with an intoxicating sweet aroma. Local businesses had merchandise outside of their storefronts including handmade furniture, vibrant crafts, and artwork, as well as my wife's favorite—hammocks.

I could begin to see a great distance as we approached the Mirador, and then the land suddenly fell away precipitously, revealing incredible beauty. Beneath us was one of the most lovely sites I have ever seen—a pristine lake in the cone of a volcano a thousand feet below. I could see the city of Granada and Lake Nicaragua, fifteen to twenty miles away. The land, covered in lush jungle, surrounded the water in the crater of the volcano below, which looked iridescent blue from so far above. A pleasant breeze comforted us from the heat and Nicaraguans everywhere relaxed and had fun. Vendors sold candy and rented binoculars, and the general atmosphere of this small park was peaceful and serene.

We returned to my new home, and as I unpacked, I thought this was exactly the kind of place I would like to live for three months. Yes, the area was poverty-stricken, but the landscape was definitely resort quality.

My host mother, Marisol, was gracious and welcoming. I learned much later that many in her family lost their lives during the Sandinista Revolution. A statue and plaque next to the town park honored the fallen members of Marisol's family and the martyrs of Catarina.

Marisol had two sons. The youngest son, eight-year-old Diego, was a spitting image of his father. The eldest son, Pedro was nine years old. They loved to play and cause mischief, as would any young boys.

The patriarch of the family, Pedro Sr., was quite a man. Two of his attributes stood out immediately. One was his stature—the man is large! Pedro was about six feet tall and weighed around two hundred forty-five pounds. The second very noticeable attribute was that he is incredibly easy going. Pedro was thirty-one years old, and he worked his butt off. He owned an old school bus that he drove for public transportation. He left the house six days a week at 4:30 in the morning and did not return from work until about 8:30–9:00 at night.

I met Pedro when he came home from work that first night. I felt slightly awkward because all I really knew of Spanish was "hello," "how are you," and "I am happy to be here." I suppose this was sufficient, although I also wanted to let him know how excited I was to be in his country and his home, but I could not. He was genuinely cool and offered me something to drink by hand gestures—a juice of some sort. I accepted the beverage; however, that was the last time I accepted a drink without knowing what I was ingesting. Under the social pressure, it did not occur to me that what I was consuming could potentially make me very sick. Parasites and/or bacterial infections are nasty to deal with, and I could have easily contracted one or the other on my first night by accepting my host father's offer. Nonetheless, whatever that drink was, if I had been in the United States, I would have spewed that liquid all over the living room—it was a horrible tasting refreshment. However, I held it together and finished it to the last drop. We said good night, and I went to bed.

I thought about how great my day had been and how much I already missed my wife. I considered the possibility that I might have made myself sick with that drink, but it was already done. I could not worry now, so I quickly got over it. Before I fell asleep, I whispered good night to Kathryn from afar.

My first full day in town was a Sunday. When I woke up, Marisol offered me fruit and bread. I drank my own water, as the stories I had heard about drinking bacteria-infested water terrified me. As I ate breakfast, my little host brothers began asking me questions. Although the tone of voice indicated that they were asking questions, I had no idea what they were saying to me.

The Peace Corps had given all *aspirantes* a small Spanish survival book on what to do and say in a conversation where you have absolutely no idea what is being said. I remembered two things—first, nod your head "yes," and second, say "*sí, hombre,*" which means "yeah, man." I perceived this as a perfect opportunity to try out my survival skills, so I did what the book had suggested. The boys freaked out! I could not tell what they said, but they seemed happy—yet up to something. From their excitement, I surmised that I had volunteered myself for an activity. It turns out that I had volunteered to go with them to a local baseball game, but I had no idea where we were headed when we left the house. I resolved to take things as they come. I mean, how much trouble could these boys cause?

Since we brought along an old, worn-out soccer ball, I thought we might be going to play *fútbol* (soccer). Nope, the soccer ball occupied our time by kicking it back and forth while we lazily walked down the street. As I played with the kids, I also noticed a few things about the town. Some people in Catarina lived in plastic shacks made with cardboard while other homes consisted of wood. The more solid homes were constructed with cinder blocks or brick, and the roofs consisted of tin or zinc. The jungle landscape also grabbed my attention, as I noted beautiful and unfamiliar plant life.

As we ambled through town, it seemed as though everyone stared at me. It felt as if a freak show had arrived, and I was it! Further, I began to suspect that Nicaraguans didn't think much of fences, or perhaps, could not afford to build them. Horses walked in the streets. Goats roamed freely, cruising around from yard to yard grazing where they pleased. Roosters and hens were ubiquitous, and starving mange-ridden dogs marched about like they were battle-hardened. I thought to myself, "*Damn this place is wide open!*" I imagined it being similar to the late 1800s to early 1900s in the United States.

After walking and playing for about a mile, we came to the termination of the concrete-tiled road. We suddenly walked on a dirt lane and came upon an open field. What the hell was this? It's a baseball game! The sight of a baseball game surprised me, and my brothers laughed at my reaction. I liked these kids already.

The field consisted of hard-packed dirt, a lot of rocks, and only a few sprigs of grass here and there. Tall palm trees that swayed in the breeze acted as boundary lines, and dense jungle surrounded the area. The bases looked like burlap sacks, and the teams were changing positions in between innings. Was that a horse grazing on the last four sprigs of grass in left field? It sure was—you gotta love that. The kids and I walked around the outfield, which also lacked a fence, and I began to get confused. I wondered if this was some sort of all-star game, because I could not tell who was on which team. Here is why—every single uniform was different on both teams. When I say different, I mean not even remotely resembling one another. The thing that is interesting is that they were all perfect uniforms right down to the leggings and spikes. They were very old uniforms, but perfect nonetheless. The first baseman was wearing a blue jersey, pin-striped pants, and a white hat. The second baseman had on a red jersey with plain white pants and a Cubs hat. The shortstop was sporting all white with a San Francisco Giants hat, and the third baseman was looking very colorful with a North Carolina blue jersey, gray pants, and a red hat. Individually, all the players looked great.

However, it was not an all-star game, but rather an ordinary game in the middle of their league's season. I learned that without a sponsor, the players lacked sufficient funds to buy cohesive uniforms, so they purchased used uniforms individually and equipment from wherever they could find it. Even if they had the money, there was not a company that produced uniforms in the area. What's more—and it was quite beautiful to witness—they all shared their gloves with one another. Nicaraguans have a very competitive spirit, but the salient point is that they unconditionally love the game of baseball. The U.S. Marine Corps introduced baseball to Nicaragua in the early twentieth century. During the time of our Peace Corps training, there were only two Nicaraguans playing Major League Baseball in the United States. In my opinion, the pro scouts from the States were missing out on some seriously talented ball players. The Nicas can play! I saw some dingers (home runs) that would make any American Major League Manager proud.

The horse that had been grazing in left field acquired a "friend" during the game, and so the two horses very slowly made their way to the infield, grazing as they moved. I thought for sure the horses would be shooed away by the players, but they were not. Then a batter hit a blistering ground ball into the gap between the third baseman and the shortstop. The ball shot like a lightning bolt straight beneath one horse's legs and spooked the animals. Dust flew up, both horses began bucking, and the shortstop dove to his right, stopping the ball. The shortstop then bounced off the hard-packed, almost gravel, playing field, threw a tight rope to the first baseman, and got the man out by a fraction of a second. I thought, "damn, Derek Jeter would have loved to see that play." What a challenge! Both teams screamed their approval of the shortstop's spectacular play, the horses bucked as they ran away, while my host brothers danced a fine little jig. I almost fell off my tree stump with laughter. The people of Nicaragua were quickly earning a special place in my heart.

The game ended by 11:30, and we headed towards home. The day had become murderously hot. As I sweated profusely, I could not help but think how interesting my first outing had been. When the day started, I had no idea what I would be doing, yet I told myself to just go and see what happens. It worked out great. For me, a lot of why I joined the Peace Corps was to think outside the box and have new cultural experiences. While the outing with my host brothers had been to watch an American-style game of baseball, the experience was indisputably Nicaraguan. I had reaped a pleasant reward.

Diego, little Pedro, and I returned home about noon. I struggled expressing to my "host mother" that I wanted to go to the *pulpería* (corner store) for a drink, and that I would return in ten minutes. While on my way home, I saw my host father and some of his friends in the back of an old Toyota pickup truck. I said "hi" to them, which was about all I could say. My father began speaking to me and motioning for me to hop into the truck. The only thing I could understand was laguna (lagoon). I had just told my host mother that I would be returning in ten minutes, but I really wanted to go with these guys to see what they were up to. I tried to explain that it would be rude of me to leave without the courtesy of telling Marisol where I would be, but the effort was a complete failure in communication. Finally, I stretched out both hands in front of me as if to say "*stop,*" and then I said "*five minutes, please.*" One of Pedro's friends then chimed in to say, "Tell me, I speak a little English." I explained as simply as possible, and he said, "no problem."

As I ran home, I wondered how I would explain to Marisol my intentions. I suddenly realized that I communicated best without talking. I walked in the door and found Marisol cleaning. I pointed to my chest with one hand and out the open door with the other. I put both hands together, intertwined my fingers and said, "Pedro." Marisol nodded her head "yes," so I turned and left. On my way back to the truck, I thought about how good I would become at charades and wondered if I could get by with only hand gestures for two years—probably not. When I got to the vehicle, the guys looked ready to roll. I jumped in the back of the truck, and off we went.

The fellow who spoke a little English told me that we were headed to the lagoon to go swimming. I thought, fantastic! A baseball game in the morning, and then swimming in the lagoon for the afternoon. Not bad for a first day.

Six of us filled the truck—two in the front and four in the back. My chest tightened as I thought that I may have stepped into something that I might regret as the driver swerved from one side of the road to the other. He would stay in the opposite lane of traffic for a long time and then swerve back into our lane right when another car was about to hit us head on. For a while, I thought he was playing a dangerous game of "chicken." Quickly he slammed on the brakes as we re-entered our lane and hit a massive pot hole—then another and another. When I looked out the back of the truck, I realized that our lane was pretty much nothing but giant pot holes, and that our driver was doing a superb job of missing them as he swerved back and forth.

As we drove through the countryside, I witnessed some extreme poverty. Cement shacks with tin or plastic roofs and dirt floors were surrounded by clothes hanging to dry on the lines outside. Latrines from these homes presented opportunities for flies to congregate, while barefoot kids played soccer using plastic bottles as their ball.

We finally came to a gate, and two of the guys jumped out and looked around suspiciously. They opened the gate, and we drove down a rough pathway to the lagoon. My host father explained to me very slowly, and with many hand gestures, that this was private property. They knew the owner well, but had not asked for his permission to access the property today because they thought he would be there to join our group. I had to have help understanding from Ernesto, who spoke only a little English.

The lagoon was absolutely spectacular! It is huge—possibly a mile in radius—and lined with palm trees and pristine beaches. The champagne-like water looked crystal clear and tasted salty to some degree. Feeling the brisk wind and trying to comprehend how the lagoon had been a crater of an ancient volcano, I watched three-foot waves rolling onto the beach.

Ernesto and his friend Domingo could not swim, so they put on their lifejackets—if that is what you want to call them. They were more like belts of some sort with very little foam inside them. I would not want my life to depend on one. However, they did not seem concerned at all. They walked into the water and were happy floating and kicking about five feet from shore. I caught myself pondering how much I needed to lighten up.

As I walked into the lagoon, the depth almost immediately off the bank stunned me. The water came up to my neck just a few feet from shore with the bottom rapidly descending beneath me. After I asked about the depth of the lagoon, Ernesto and Pedro guessed that it could be one hundred fifty to two hundred meters. However, they qualified their response by saying that they were not sure because no one can swim that deep. Pedro and I dove to see how far down we could go, but we laughed out loud because nobody believed each other's reported distance unless mud was brought back from the bottom.

As the day continued, my new friends and I conversed, all of us genuinely wanting to learn more about each other's culture. They asked what kind of music I liked and wanted to know about Washington, D.C. At the time, I had no idea that Bob Marley was very popular in Nicaragua. It did not surprise me though, because Bob Marley is the man; but I wouldn't have guessed that Nicaraguans love his music.

While we were sitting on the beach, Ernesto pushed away some sand and started to wipe mud all over his face. I was thinking, "yeah, this guy has lost his mind!" Then Domingo wiped mud all over his face. I thought, "Now this is getting weird!" I looked at my host father—who was five years younger than I was—and asked, "what's up?" Pedro and Ernesto told me that the minerals in the volcanic mud are really healthy for skin. As Pedro smeared mud on himself, he explained that you put the wet mud on your face and then wait twenty to thirty minutes to allow the mud to dry and the minerals to sink into your pores.

After rinsing your face, your skin should feel ultra-smooth and great. I doubled-over with laughter. Not only did I have the opportunity to experience a spectacularly beautiful lagoon, but I was about to receive a hundred-dollar spa treatment to boot. I wiped mud all over my face just like the rest of them and thought, "so, this is a *'Nicaraguan spa.'*"

The six of us sat hanging out in one of the most beautiful places I had ever seen and laughing at each other because we all looked circus-style ridiculous with dried mud all over our faces. Astonishingly, my friends were right—when I washed away the volcanic mud, my face had never felt so smooth or clean. The Nicaraguan spa treatment was pretty sweet! After collecting some mud for their wives in the plastic bottles we had brought, we headed back to Catarina.

When we returned home, Marisol had dinner waiting for us. Kathryn had been worried about me and travelled by bus to Catarina earlier that afternoon to meet my host family. Kathryn left a note stating that she was sorry she missed me, but that she was happy to learn that I had gone to the lagoon with Pedro and his friends. Kathryn said she would see me soon, and that all was well with her host family. Her note and news made me very happy, as I had been extremely worried about Kathryn and her living situation.

Dinner with Marisol and Pedro consisted of rice and beans with plantains. I was quite hungry from the day's activities, so the meal tasted fantastic. I gratefully ate everything on my plate. As I finished, I said thanks to my host family for a wonderful first day and retreated to my room after an exhausting, but rewarding day.

My six-foot by nine-foot room contained a small night stand, a coat rack on the wall, and a bed only big enough for a child to sleep on—probably fit for little Pedro or Diego. The room held nothing else, nor was there space to hold another piece of furniture. Imagine placing a child's bed into a makeshift, walk-in closet, and that will give you an excellent idea of my living quarters.

It suddenly became clear to me that I had taken my little host brother's room. Pedro, Marisol, Pedro Jr., and Diego now slept in one room about fifteen feet away—their quarters not much bigger than mine. Although I often like to read as I fall asleep, my room did not have a light. I soon realized that at night, the only way to see around in my bedroom was to have the living room lights on. My room could still receive light from the living room since the plywood walls did not reach the tin ceiling. If someone was in the living room with the lights on, my bedroom would be fairly well lit. The sleeping arrangement required patience and consideration of others regarding light.

Two posters of Michael Jordan from an old Gatorade ad hung on one wall of my room. The wall next to my bed had a window with bars, but no glass. A beautiful papaya tree in the front yard posed a lovely view from my bedroom. The host family had simply sectioned off my bedroom from the living room with plywood and a door. My child-sized bed had a wooden headboard and a footboard. If I laid down on my back, my feet would extend past the end of the bed up to my Achilles tendon, with the footboard placing direct pressure on that tendon. If I laid on my stomach, my feet would dangle off the end of the bed with my toes pointing toward the floor and my ankles stretched across the footboard. I had to scrunch my legs up so my feet would not hit the footboard or hang over it. After a few minutes of rearranging my body, the bed became more tolerable. I realized that no matter how I slept, I often woke up because my feet had "fallen asleep."

The Peace Corps issued all the *aspirantes* a mosquito net and required us to sleep beneath it at all times because it would increase our comfort and reduce cases of Malaria and Dengue Fever. Before I went to bed, I had not had time to nail holes in the walls to put the net up, and mosquitoes were wreaking havoc on me. I pulled the net over my entire body like a blanket and tried to go to sleep with it covering my face. However, pulling the net over me only trapped mosquitos beneath the net with me! I hunted the blood thirsty critters only by sound, clapping at their buzz, as the lights had already gone out. Laughing at the predicament, I hunted and clapped until the annoying buzzing ceased beneath the net.

I thought about how much I missed my wife—it had only been one day. I fell asleep thinking how lucky I have been all my life and thanking God for all of his many blessings. I asked for the strength, resolve, and intelligence to be able to help my Nicaraguan friends. I softly said "I love you" and "good night" to my wife, who slept beneath the same moon only a couple of towns away, and then I fell fast asleep.

10
Training Week 1
Training Begins, A Period of Adjustment
"Small opportunities are often the beginning of great enterprises."
–Demosthenes

The first week of training started out with a bang. At 4:30 in the morning (or as I like to call it—the middle of the night!), I awoke to a horrifically loud noise. The roof rattled, and I began to panic. The hair on the back of my neck stood straight up, and I felt goose bumps all over. For a moment, I was definitely fearful. I bolted upright in bed, confused and with a mosquito net hanging off my body. I swiped at the net as if I had walked into a spider web and could not get it out of my face or see around me. It was very dark. I thought, "earthquake!" However, I quickly found mental awareness and realized my host father had started his old diesel school bus parked in the driveway, with its tail pipe about three feet outside my window.

I had no idea that my host father began his work days at 4:30. I felt like going outside and saying, "It's 4:30 in the morning, what the hell are you doing?" Common sense prevailed, and I decided to try to go back to sleep. However, it was impossible! A diesel bus is extremely loud to begin with, but the horrible fumes were also blowing right through my glassless window. After about ten minutes of engine warm-up, Pedro's bus pulled out of the driveway. Finally, I could get some more sleep.

Not five minutes later, I awoke to what sounded as if fifty alarm clocks were going off. Every rooster in town crowed—some as near as my front yard, and others far off in the distance. God bless'em, they are vociferous little birds. At that moment, I was thinking I would like to have chicken for breakfast! After about ten minutes of what I call "the full-on rooster salute," the dogs began barking. Damn it! How many dogs could there be in this town? Just when I thought all the noise was about to go away and I could go back to sleep, some lady walked right up to my window, practically sticks her head inside my room and yells in Spanish, "Bread here, how about some bread? Got your bread here."

Realizing that sleeping was impossible, I laughed and gave up trying. Then deciding to do something productive, I climbed out from under the mosquito net, dressed, and started on a run.

It was about 5:30 in the morning now and quite bright outside, as the sun had come up around 5. As I jogged through the central park, I noticed the beautiful church with the sun rising directly above the tattered bell towers. The architecture was incredible. Large shade trees, a huge concrete slide, and a basketball court in disrepair surrounded the church. The colorful park had jungle flowers of various genealogies everywhere.

As I jumped back out onto the cobblestone streets of Catarina, I realized that the town's two main businesses were *artesanias* (handmade art shops) and *jardíns* (garden centers). The owners of these businesses prepared for the day by watering their plants, hanging their multicolored wind chimes, and putting out their hand-crafted vases. Other vendors in the streets offered fruit, eggs, and bread from large baskets carried on their heads. They called out in loud voices what was for sale, much like the lady that had stuck her head in my window a few minutes ago yelling that she had bread to sell. It seemed quite convenient that you could have someone deliver fresh bread to your front door first thing in the morning.

I must have been quite the spectacle, as I received looks of bewilderment and curiosity from the local town folk while making my way to the Mirador. The Mirador has a stunning view, especially at sunrise. Alone, I looked due east standing atop the crater of an ancient volcano, and gazed upon a vast jungle with the lagoon laid out a thousand feet below. The massive volcano towering above me, Mombacho, had its uppermost crown nestled in a cloud. I could see in the distance the city of Granada and Lake Nicaragua, which made me realize charming truth in the statement typically used to describe this country: Nicaragua—the land of lakes and volcanoes.

With no one around, the serene environment felt peaceful and motionless. The feeling could only be received from viewing an enchanted sunrise in a strange and wonderful place. What a spectacular sight! As I ran back towards the house, I knew that I was definitely in for quite an experience here in Nicaragua.

Upon returning home, I slept for about a half hour before pulling myself from bed at 7. I wanted to shower, but I understood we had no run-

ning water and did not know how to ask about the process. I went outside
to a fifty five gallon barrel, and using a plastic bowl that was brought from
the States, I scooped out about a cup and a half of water. Then I carefully walked to the bathroom with the little bowl, grabbing a shaving kit
and towel along the way. Considering how much water had been drawn, I
thought this was going to be interesting because I needed to shave, wash
my face and brush my teeth with only a cup and a half of water. I recognized that I could wash my face first, because that is what I wanted to do
most. However, if I washed my face first, I would have to brush my teeth
and rinse my mouth with soapy water. I could shave first, but then I would
have to brush my teeth and wash my face in the same dirty water. I decided the best approach was to first brush my teeth and rinse my mouth.
I could subsequently wash my face because clean water was not needed
for shaving. A simple process to manage basic hygiene requirements had
been established, using a minimal amount of a precious resource—water.
In the States, just by turning the tap, water abundantly comes forth to be
used in any manner desired. The bathroom experience in Nicaragua is
unique. I learned how comically different bathroom life can be.

I had to use the restroom. Unfortunately—"number two." At this
point, I began to notice my environment, which included only a light
blue plastic curtain for a bathroom door that was not wide enough to
cover the entrance. The blue plastic left four to six inches of open air
on both sides. I worried about someone walking by or walking in on
me, and would have preferred to sit in peace.

We had electricity in the house, but I was told by the Peace Corps
not to use the lights if I didn't need to because power was expensive
and I should conserve whenever possible. I could see reasonably well,
so I did not turn on the bathroom light.

My eyes left the bathroom entrance and shot to the roof, which
was not attached to the walls as a six inch gap existed between the two.
I came to the problematic realization that there would be no possibility of a sound or odor-proof bathroom, much less a fan. Oh boy, this
could be embarrassing. Yet, "it" had to be done.

Suddenly, I heard footsteps coming my way. I thought surely they
would knock on the wall or say something before entering. Nope! My
nine-year-old host brother yanked the curtain open and boldly walked
into the bathroom.

There I sat in all of my glory on the toilet with a very red face and my shorts around my ankles. All I could say was, "Good morning." Little Pedro said something in Spanish and walked out roaring with laughter. I completed my business, which was not very quiet or odorless.

I remembered that I had been instructed not to put paper in the toilet as the septic system wouldn't be able to function properly, and could overflow. I wrapped my wipe with another piece of paper like it was a fine gift and tossed the package in the trash can. I stood up, about to flush, and recalled that the house had no running water. If I flushed, no water could return into the commode. As I looked to my left and found a bucket of water, I considered how this resource might be utilized, possibly for bathing or flushing, maybe both. I poured about half of it into the toilet and the commode flushed—a forced flush, and it worked perfectly.

I realize that for some people "a forced flush" may be common knowledge, but for me the thought of putting your paper in the garbage can and then pouring a bucket of water into the toilet was a completely foreign idea. This procedure was everyday life for Nicaraguans, and my family had it good. Most Nicaraguans either have a latrine or an outhouse—inside plumbing of any kind is an absolute luxury.

When I walked out of the bathroom, both my host brothers were sniggering and whispering to one another. By the time I got to the middle of the living room, I realized that it smelled like the bathroom because there was no door and the walls were not attached to the ceiling. There was nothing to keep the odor contained. I was completely embarrassed but also laughed at the situation. Wow, I never considered that going to the bathroom would present such a unique challenge.

Following my first bathroom experience with a family in Nicaragua, I decided two things—one, I was going to be in the bathroom as little as possible, and two, I should speak with someone in my family about how to let people know the loo is occupied. But how? I could not speak Spanish. The second item would have to wait a while. I laughed again and dressed for the day.

Breakfast consisted of black beans with rice, a piece of bread, and a *Nalgene* bottle of water. I rarely ate beans in the States and had never had them for breakfast. However, I was genuinely happy to have the food. I realized my host family might be struggling financially, but were trying to take good care of me. I ate all of my breakfast and thanked Marisol.

The Peace Corps' recruiters had told me not to worry about my Spanish level because the training program would teach me to speak the language, and that by the end of the three-month training period, I would be able to get along fairly well. I guess I had it in my head that some kind of miracle would happen during those three months, and I would come out the other side speaking Spanish.

The first week of Spanish classes were held in my home and started on Monday morning at 8 with my two site-mates from Catarina, Hollis Bennet and Lee Hamilton, the other Peace Corps trainees who were at the same language level. When our Spanish facilitator walked into the house, she spoke no English whatsoever. Hollis and Lee appeared as confused as I was, looking at each other with bewilderment. The three trainees immediately began discussing how we were going to learn Spanish from someone who does not speak English. During the little pow-wow, our facilitator stated, "Please no English." We respected her wishes, and class began in silence.

Our facilitator was Arabella Orihuela, a very relaxed and easy going forty-year-old woman. She lived in Managua and commuted an hour every day to our training town. Her husband was a school principal in Managua, and they had two children. Arabella had a spectacular attitude and a wonderful sense of compassion. Her patience rose above and beyond what you would normally expect from a teacher—at least any teacher I had ever had.

To get to know each other better, the class began with Lee, Hollis, and I trying to present personal information to the group. It occurred to me during this first class how difficult learning Spanish would be. No miracle chip could be implanted into my brain. Learning a new language was going to be a long and arduous process. In this first class, the facilitator taught us how to introduce one another and some basic common courtesies.

We had an hour break for lunch, which, in my host family's house, consisted of beans and rice with fried plantains and a piece of bread. I began to consider how monotonous eating beans and rice would become, but ate every bite, and offered gratitude to my host mother.

In the afternoon, our class had to go out into the city and talk to people. The Peace Corps called this session "applied Spanish." I am a very positive-minded person, but my first response to the idea was, "No way!" But we did it. We found about ten children in the park and Arabella waved them over and said we would like to speak with them. I learned something through this experience that would bring me a great deal of happiness in Nicaragua—the kids love to speak with *gringos*. I introduced Lee, Hollis, and myself to the children. We asked the kids how old they were and how many family members they had. We then told them where we were from and how old we were. Once this personal information was shared, we did not have anything else to say. We were done with our conversation, yet the kids were by no means finished with us. The ten or so children followed us out of the park and down the street as if we were comical prey. The kids waited very patiently to have a good laugh. Our three-person Spanish class found a man walking by who looked to be another perfect victim for our torturous language skills. Under the watchful eyes of these children, Arabella approached the new victim, explained that we were learning Spanish and asked if we could speak with him for a few moments. At least that is what it looked like she was saying, but I had no idea. She could have been saying, "Excuse me, would you like to have a good laugh at these Americans who are trying to learn Spanish?" The reason I say this is that every time we approached anyone, they would always smile to the point of almost laughing before we began to speak with them in Spanish.

The ten kids from the park surrounded us and laid in wait for the *gringos* to begin speaking. We asked the man the exact questions that we had asked the children earlier, and of course the kids wailed with laughter. Our class appreciated the humor too, and we thanked the man for his time and patience. I loved the experience!

"Applied Spanish" became one of my favorite activities because meeting people in the community is important, and laughter is good for everyone. However, the applied Spanish process is difficult in the beginning because one is definitely out of a comfort zone. I learned that I had to be bold and without shame. Embarrassing moments occurred frequently, and people looked at us with any number of expressions—from blank stares to fits of laughter. Our first day of class ended at three in the afternoon, we said goodbye and went our separate ways.

There are four main aspects to the Peace Corps language program: 1. Four hours of in-class study daily; 2. Applied Spanish and cultural understanding for two hours daily; 3. Community assignments outside of class hours; and 4. Host family-immersion in the language. The idea is that you will learn much faster if you are completely surrounded by Spanish.

Peace Corps training also has a technical element, in which it provides instruction in the specialty areas. Since Kathryn and I would be working in Small Business Development, we needed to know a particular financial vocabulary and the business culture of Nicaragua, in addition to having a complete command of the business class subject matter associated with our primary project.

Our first assignment outside of class hours required mapping our entire community and noting the different businesses in our towns. In addition, we walked into these businesses and introduced ourselves to the owners, explaining to them who we were and what we were doing. We practiced the introduction in our best Spanish, but once we introduced ourselves to the owners, a flood of other questions immediately followed—and of course, we only knew a very limited amount of Spanish. Thankfully, not a single business owner was rude to us, but rather, they were all very accepting of, and patient with, our language levels. This amazed me because in the States, we would have certainly encountered someone who would not have had time to speak with us.

Catarina is a fairly small town of roughly 2,400 people, and by the end of the week, we had been to each part of the city. Not only did I get to know Catarina well, but these cultural and technical projects were completed with my training town site-mates, so I also came to know them quite well.

One of my site-mates was 26-year-old Lee Hamilton—a great guy and quite a character. Lee was an Italian-American with jet black hair, brown eyes, and a physical build that says he likes to eat and drink well, but will also exercise once in a while. He is from New Orleans and graduated from Tulane University. Before entering the Peace Corps, Lee held a sales job until he grew bored with it and decided to travel. He went to Turkey, Nepal, India, Singapore, Thailand, Australia, and New Zealand. He had an air of experience, but more importantly, he had a noticeable mystique of mischievousness in his eyes. The man was just plain funny. Lee was adventurous by nature and found the sight of dogs having sex hilarious to the point that whenever seen, which was quite often in Catarina, he pointed out the activity. Lee was an absolute blast to have as a site-mate as he loved to have fun with people, particularly concerning his Spanish. For example, if someone asked Lee a question and he did not understand what was asked, the situation would elicit a response from Lee in Spanish such as "Yeah, I have two brothers." Then he would shrug his shoulders and laugh. Lee simply said anything that came to mind if he did not understand. The one I enjoyed most, was when his host father asked Lee where he had been all day. Lee responded with "I love chicken!" The whole house erupted with laughter—and there were twenty-seven people living in Lee's house. His host family had five generations living under one roof, and they have had fourteen Peace Corps trainees live with them throughout the years.

Lee had so many host brothers that they came close to populating an entire soccer team and were a force to be reckoned with in the community league. Lee joined his host brothers' soccer team, which was hysterical because while Lee played soccer well, he was not an outstanding athlete. The league Lee played in had serious talent. However, Lee deserved well-earned respect for playing soccer with his host brothers because he knew all eyes would be watching for even the slightest mistake. I supported Lee and his team by attending almost every game. Clearly Lee's host brothers enjoyed playing soccer with him and it was a great way for Lee to be accepted, not only by his host family, but also by the people of the community.

Lee's host family loved him and tried to set him up with single Nicaraguan women so often that Lee came to Spanish class and told us about his "problem." Our facilitator, Arabella, adored the juicy gossip and convulsed with laughter. After one young woman had been making his dinner and washing his clothes for two days, Lee finally mentioned to his host family that he was not looking for a girlfriend. His host mom said that was fine. However, that same afternoon his host brother, Miguel, asked Lee if he wanted to visit with his grandmother in another part of the house. Lee agreed. When they arrived at the grandmother's section of the home, the young woman who had been washing Lee's clothes and cooking for him was sitting next to the grandmother. This very pleasant young woman happened to be an employee of the grandmother. Lee's host brother, Miguel, left the room smiling and Lee respectfully sat in the parlor and visited with the ladies. It had been a complete set-up, and Lee was blindsided quite effectively. Hollis, Arabella, and I laughed our heads off. Arabella said that Lee was "Like a bull being put out to stud." Lee received the nickname "*El Toro*" (the bull) immediately. How could he deny the name? Like any good natured person, Lee accepted the healthy joking in great stride. I had become a huge fan of Lee Hamilton!

There was a running of the bulls in my wife's training town of Masatepe soon thereafter. The *aspirantes* who wanted to watch the event met in Masatepe and walked down to the park where most of the action would be—or so we were told. Little did we know that some of the most exciting action of the day would be with one of our trainees.

Lee showed up late in Masatepe for the running of the bulls. He knew we were going to meet in the park, so he started meandering through town, unaware that the running of the bulls had already begun. As he walked through town, a bunch of Nicaraguans began yelling at him; however, Lee thought they were just teasing the *gringo* again, so he ignored them and continued on his way. After a sustained vocal assault toward our friend, Lee finally turned to see what everyone was yelling about and found himself nearly face-to-face with a charging bull. Lee freaked out and started running for his life down the street while the Nicaraguans yelled delightedly about the *gringo's* decision to participate in the running of the bulls. After a twenty-yard dash of terror with the bull within feet of him, Lee busted a move that would have made any NFL running back proud. Lee's move confused the bull, the crowd cheered, and Lee narrowly escaped being gored. This event solidified Lee's nickname of "*El Toro*" forever. Lee was not in a humorous mood to take a bow when the Nicaraguans offered their due applause. The running of the bulls was an entertaining and unique cultural experience that I am sure Lee will never forget.

Lee, quite a hysterical human being, was also a very concerned and caring man with a deep respect for others and their culture. I thoroughly enjoyed his company as my site-mate.

Hollis Bennet was my other site-mate in Catarina. Hollis was one half of the other married couple in our training group. Hollis was from South Dakota, but he moved to Minneapolis, Minnesota, where he and his wife Christi lived before coming to Nicaragua. Hollis was an information technology professional for the Fortune 500 company, 3M, prior to joining the Peace Corps. Hollis was tall, maybe six-foot-two, with dark hair in a shaven military-style cut. He had prominent blue eyes and an excellent sense of humor. In addition to being physically fit, he was thoughtful, well-mannered, and somewhat quiet. Hollis seemed young at heart and loved skateboarding. He knew a lot about bicycles, so he and I had many pleasant conversations about Nicaraguan bikes—most of which were pretty sweet and well-maintained.

On Hollis' first night with his new host family in Nicaragua, his host brother, a fantastic guy named Manuel, wanted to play bingo in a town about twenty minutes away called Masaya. When they arrived, Hollis was astonished at the large number of bingo players. The building held about five hundred people and the place was slam-packed. These folks take their bingo as seriously as my mom does in the States. In between the last two games (the last game being the jackpot), there was a dance competition for all of the kids under ten years old. When the announcer called for the competition, about fifty children bum-rushed the stage, and Hollis said they were throwing down like he had never seen. The winner of the dance competition received a giant *piñata*, which is a great prize!

The bingo jackpot was still yet to come, and the prize was serious—a female goat. Manuel was very excited about the possibility of winning, as he owns a farm but has only one male goat. This was high stakes bingo—obviously he could grow his farm with a female goat. Hollis said that you could feel the tension in the room as the announcer called the numbers. You can believe it, out of five hundred people, Manuel won the jackpot! He screamed "Bingo!" and ran to the stage to collect his prize.

After the initial excitement, Hollis asked how they were going to get the goat home. Manuel laughed and said they would take the goat home the same way they arrived in Masaya—by taxi. They went outside and caught a cab with two other people already in the taxi, one of whom was pregnant. Manuel and the goat rode in the back seat with the pregnant woman and her friend, while Hollis rode up front. What a fun cab ride—four people and goat! The goat brayed in Hollis' ear the whole way home, and Manuel was all smiles. Hollis said the goat needed a name, so Manuel and Hollis agreed they would call the goat "Jackpot."

Manuel gave all the credit for winning Jackpot to Hollis for bringing him good luck. The next morning, when Hollis and Manuel told me what happened, we laughed so hard that the neighbors came out to see what the fuss was about. Hollis and Manuel shared their story with the neighbors, and it was even funnier because the neighbors wanted Hollis to go play bingo with them. Good luck is hard to come by in Nicaragua, and if the *gringo* was bringing good luck, the neighbors wanted in on the party! My site-mates were fantastic guys, and I enjoyed spending three months with them.

Our first week of training was in full swing, and I was already beginning to feel the wear and tear of not being around my wife. I missed Kathryn terribly! Every Wednesday our entire training group would be together for a technical lesson. This meant that Kathryn and I could see each other on Wednesday afternoons. I could not wait to see her smile and visit with my buddy!

The first technical lesson was held at a restaurant about ten minutes away from Catarina, and I had been looking forward to it since arriving at my training town for two reasons—the principal one being that I wanted to see Kathryn, and the second was that I had great interest in learning how Nicaragua became so financially distraught. I immediately began looking for my buddy, but she had not arrived yet. When she did, we gave each other a big hug and separated from the group for about five minutes to talk. I asked about her family and she reassured me that they took good care of her and that the household was actually quite social. We both shared a little about our living situations, and then Peace Corps staff called us to convene our session about the economic history of Nicaragua.

An economics professor from Managua provided us a fascinating lecture. A few statistics absolutely floored me, such as the distribution of income in Nicaragua. At the time, seventeen percent of the Nicaraguan population made less than $215 annually. Thirty-one percent of the population made less than $405 annually, and fifty-two percent of the population made $1,200 or more. Eighty percent of the population was employed with eleven percent working part-time, and around nine percent were unemployed. However, "unemployed" was a very loose term. For instance, tens of thousands of people in Nicaragua sell goods in the street. The Nicaraguan Statistical Office considers these street vendors as 'employed', but they are clearly not making an average wage and are consequently, extremely impoverished. The lecture discussed the economic development of Central America in general, and Nicaragua in particular.

The professor covered many topics that impacted Nicaragua's economy including but not limited to, allegedly corrupt governments such as the Alemán administration, the Sandinista-Contra war, and natural disasters. Every time Nicaragua showed signs of dramatic economic improvement, something would happen to negate any positive traction and set the country back another fifteen years. For example, when Nicaragua began to mend itself economically after the Sandinista-Contra war, Hurricane Mitch struck and destroyed much of the country's infrastructure. Such devastation is hard to overcome, and being a poor nation creates more obstacles to the recovery process.

I felt for the Nicaraguans because they are tough and have had incredible man-made and natural disaster misfortunes forced upon them. The technical training lecture served its purpose well by giving all the Small Business trainees a look at what the country has faced historically.

The lecture ended and all the *aspirantes* hung around talking about their new training towns, host families, and living conditions. I was only able to speak with Kathryn for a few more minutes, and then we had to head back to our training towns. This did not seem fair—I wanted to spend more time with my wife and was really interested to learn more about her host family.

Upon returning home, I played basketball in the park with my host brothers. I have always enjoyed playing basketball, but this particular outing cost me dearly. As I went in for a lay-up jumping for the basket, my host brother played good defense and stepped in front of me. Little Pedro and I got tangled up, my feet and legs went above my head, and I came down full-force on the concrete, landing entirely on my lower back and hip. The impact was severe. I knew immediately that some kind of damage had been done to my back, but I could not tell exactly what at that moment. I could still walk, but only with a considerable amount of pain. The discomfort could be dealt with as long as I could function physically.

I was nervous because I had also pulled a muscle in my back lifting luggage from the buses the very first day in Nicaragua. That pulled muscle did not seem like any big deal at the time, but after this impact, the pain was super intense in the exact same spot.

I told my little host brothers that I had to stop playing for the day, and I limped home. After we had dinner, I studied Spanish for an hour and then said good night to the family. I went to bed thinking I would be fine and fell asleep pretty quickly.

On Thursday, we had Spanish class in the morning from eight to noon, ate lunch, and then had an extremely difficult afternoon session of applied Spanish. We went to a *muebleria* (furniture factory) and interviewed the owner to learn about his market and the challenges he faces as a business owner in Nicaragua. This might not be so challenging in English, but with only a few days of Spanish class, I found the task of interviewing someone to be nightmarishly tough. We also walked around town and interviewed several small business owners. After each interview, we discussed what we had learned and laughed about the mistakes we made. Again, we were not allowed to speak any English during class, so these commentaries in Spanish subsequent to the interviews were also quite humorous. Our torture finally ended for the day at three in the afternoon when class was dismissed. I say "torture" because the interviews, although very interesting, were also extremely challenging. On a positive note, I would say that my class was definitely learning Spanish quickly, and we all had good attitudes in the face of such daunting tasks.

After I returned home and let my brain vegetate for twenty minutes, my little host brothers asked me to play basketball. Their other ball had popped and they had somehow "acquired" a new ball, so to speak. I looked at the "new" basketball and giggled to myself inside. The ball could not possibly bounce and it looked frayed to the point that I was scared to even try it lest it disintegrate. How do you say "no" to your little host brothers? My back hurt, but I could function physically and thought that moving a little might be helpful. Besides, this was why I joined the Peace Corps—to have interactions such as playing with my host brothers.

Back in the States, my work day would have been gaining intensity at three o'clock in the afternoon, with a long way to go before quitting time. Here in Nicaragua, however, the day technically concluded at three, although daily work assignments still had to be completed following class hours.

I went to the park to play basketball with my eight- and nine-year-old host brothers and felt great about spending time with them. Our basketball games would usually turn into games of soccer or really fun games of tag. By the time our new games commenced, other children always wanted to join.

That afternoon, we played a half-court game of basketball with so many kids that it turned into a game of every-man-for-themselves—there were thirty or so kids of various ages going nuts! I was overwhelmed with laughter because at one point I had at least three or four children hanging off one of my legs as I dragged them around the court toward the basket, with other kids pulling my arms in different directions until I was forced to drop the ball.

I also constantly tried to learn Spanish from the children. I asked them to be patient and repeat what they said so that comprehension could occur. I found myself looking forward to the afternoon, as Spanish could be learned and new little friends were made in the process. Fun transcends any language, and laughter is easy to understand. I have always been able to play well with others, especially children. I was having the time of my life. In the middle of those games, I would think of my wife and how beautiful she is to me, and of how thankful I am for the wonderful blessings of life.

There were other benefits to playing in the park. I learned that I could become good friends with adults in the community through playing with their children; and it proved much easier to break the ice when meeting the adults. The "bottom-up" approach worked—meet the kids first, then the adults. Walking around town, I saw children who I knew in front of their homes, and I would ask them to introduce me to their parents. It was not long before I could walk through town saying "hello" to my new friends and have kids walking with me. The experience I had hoped for was coming to life.

On Friday, Lee, Hollis and I (the Catarina boys) planned to travel to Managua for meetings and another round of vaccinations. I awoke at 4:30 in the morning to my host father firing up his bus again. The 4:30 wakeup call had begun to seem a little more normal, and the frustration of being awakened at that hour was more than countered by the admiration I had for Pedro's determination to make a living for his family. I knew the roosters' crowing would not be far behind when he left the driveway. As a matter of fact, I started to think that Pedro's bus was the very thing that woke the roosters and stirred them to crow. I began believing that the roosters were upset about being woken by a loud bus at 4:30 in the morning. Thus, the roosters decided that, if they could not sleep, nobody else would either. Of course this was a citywide conspiracy and so all the roosters in the city would begin to crow. This is the kind of thought process one goes through after being woken up regularly in the middle of the night by a loud bus! I knew it was ludicrous to think that the roosters could be upset and therefore crow, but it made me laugh, and I was delirious at that point, so I did not care that I was having odd thoughts.

After waking, I went for a run to the lagoon to watch the sunrise. I could run with my injured back. I just kept thinking that with proper rest and a light exercise program, the damage that had occurred could be overcome. However, down deep I could tell, but did not want to admit, that I had seriously hurt myself. The run was enjoyable until I tried to stretch at the Mirador. While stretching, a vicious pain shot down my leg. I struggled to ignore the discomfort and focused on the beautiful surroundings. Instead of running, I walked back to the house because the back pain was so intense. Nonetheless, preparing to face the day with a great attitude seemed natural after witnessing that glorious sunrise.

When I returned home, I stayed the hell away from the bathroom as I was still shell-shocked from my last adventure there. I had a dry shave in my room and went to the breakfast table sweaty. After eating beans and rice for breakfast, I dashed out the door to meet Hollis and Lee for the day's festivities.

Arabella arrived in our town at about ten minutes before 8 to head for Managua with us. The funny thing is that Arabella was from Managua, so she endured the hour-long trip to Catarina only to immediately return to Managua while making sure that her new, non-Spanish-speaking ducklings would not have any problems finding their way to the training session. As we walked to the bus stop, we practiced asking what the fare to Managua would be in Spanish and made sure that all of our valuables were put away such as our watches, sunglasses, etc. Arabella taught us the safety basics that would keep us from being targets of crime. They were easy things to do, but many people do not think about them. She suggested that we not show anything of value that could be snatched off of our bodies. For Lee, she explained that could be a purse, and we all laughed. Arabella also taught us to plan ahead and not carry large bills to pay for the bus fare because people might see how much change we received and target us for robbery. She taught us to keep our money in our front pockets, to pay attention to our pockets when people bumped into us, and to keep a close eye on each other. All of this preparation did not make me feel any more comfortable about my safety. As a matter of fact, I was quite nervous.

When we arrived in Managua, we exited the bus one block short of the actual terminal. Arabella told us that she did not like the bus terminal called Huembes (pronounced, *whim-base*) because it had the potential to be dangerous; and that was where our bus was headed. We jumped off the bus at a place called Quetzal, and then we learned how to safely catch a cab. Under his breath, Hollis said, "Hopefully a cab without a goat."

When a cab stopped, we first checked the license plate to ensure that the car was a registered taxi. Registered taxis have very distinct red license plates. Next, we looked for the driver's registration with photo, which is supposed to be prominently displayed on the passenger side of the car. If the driver's picture did not match the driver, we were instructed to say "no, thank you" and step away from the taxi. Arabella told us of stories where people looking for cabs jumped into cars that were not actually taxis at all, only to be robbed soon thereafter by criminals. She also told us that thieves steal legitimately registered taxis and pick up unsuspecting people to rob them. So we also needed to match the cab driver's photo on the registration to the driver. Arabella further explained that we had to ask how much the ride would cost before we got in the cab. Volunteers have had problems when they arrived at their destination only to have the cab driver say that they owed an absurd amount of money. Additionally, we needed to clarify if the fare quoted to us was in dollars or córdobas because Volunteers have been quoted prices that sounded reasonable in córdobas, only to find out at their destination that the fare quote was in American dollars, which would be outrageously expensive!

We learned how to negotiate for our fare, as many cab drivers would overstate the cost to try to get the most out of their passengers. To be fair, we typically found that the majority of cab drivers seemed to be pleasant, honest, hard-working people. Yet we were prepared for a bad apple that we could run into every now and then. I appreciated all of the safety and travel information. I learned some valuable tips that could help to avoid an uncomfortable situation, and I was very grateful to Arabella.

The Peace Corps is serious about our safety, and our facilitators prepared us well for different contingencies. The only problem with all this good information was that it made me very nervous. By the time Arabella finished our lesson, I was expecting people to jump out from the shadows at every corner to rob me. I became paranoid of every cab driver and everyone else for that matter because my guard was up all the time. The reality is that relative to other major Central American cities, Managua is generally safe as long as you act like you have some sense. Arabella did an excellent job of educating us.

We took a cab to the office, and I must say it was an eye-opening ride. At almost every red light, people surrounded the cars and walked into the lanes of traffic trying to sell all kinds of items, beg for money, or wash car windshields. Arabella warned us to be mindful of our backpacks and to put them on the floorboards, as people could walk up and snatch the packs through an open car window. Most of the folks appeared only to be trying to make a living, but every now and then, I would have a weird feeling about someone walking by the car.

I really felt for the people we watched and thought about how difficult it must be to earn a living vending in the streets. The street vendors impressed me the most in that they were all willing to work and do what was necessary to make a living. Their toughness, tenacity, and enduring persistence to live inspired me. The trip from Catarina to the Peace Corps office in Managua took an hour and ten minutes total, so we arrived at the office at about 9:30 a.m.

At the office, we received vaccinations for Rabies II and IPV Polio. That was great fun! I always thanked the medical staff for working to keep us healthy.

At 1:00 that afternoon, we received an interesting regional security briefing from American Embassy security staff, who told us which parts of the country were potentially still dangerous and why. We were informed as to where Volunteers were allowed to travel and what areas of the country we were forbidden to enter. For example, much of the northeast section of Nicaragua, otherwise known as the R.A.A.N. (The Autonomous Region of the North Atlantic), is an area that is sparsely populated with very little—if any—law enforcement. For safety reasons, we were warned that Volunteers were restricted from traveling to the R.A.A.N. However, it did not really matter to us right then because as *aspirantes*, we could not leave our training towns until we were sworn in as Volunteers. The security staff also told us that San Juan del Sur, a beach resort on the Pacific southwest side of Nicaragua, was the most dangerous place in all of Nicaragua for Peace Corps Volunteers. Why? Because San Juan del Sur is the most common destination for vacationing Volunteers. There were people in San Juan who target *gringos* for crime, and Volunteers could become prime targets when drinking and relaxing. The Embassy security staff shared with us that Volunteers had been beaten and robbed there. They provided suggestions as to how to stay safe if we visited San Juan del Sur, such as, not going out drinking late at night, or if that occurs, take a cab back to the hotel or walk in large groups, if possible. Although visiting San Juan del Sur was not prohibited, we received a stern warning to be very careful while in that area.

The United States Embassy security staff was very competent and allowed the *aspirantes* to freely ask questions. They made it clear to all of us that our safety was always their number one priority and that they would do whatever they could to help us be free of crime for our two-year tour of duty.

After the Regional Security meeting, we met with our APCD (Associate Peace Corps Director), Alberto Gonzalez. Alberto was in charge of the Small Business Development program, and he gave a presentation about the Nicaraguan business culture. Alberto, a Nicaraguan and capable leader, provided us some insight into how the Nicaraguan business mind works.

Alberto gave us the standard caveat that everyone in the Nicaraguan business environment does not think alike, and that it would be foolish to stereotype or use absolutes. Nonetheless, his presentation provided some general insights about Nicaraguan small businesses. He told us that in general, Nicaraguans believed that having access to money or credit was the most important requirement for starting a business whereas having good, creative ideas was a distant second on the list of necessities. Nicaraguan businesses tend to be individually or family-owned and limited in size because people usually hire family members as needed. Alberto conveyed that from a business perspective, small Nicaraguan businesses generally have little respect for other people and distrust individuals from outside the family. Bad customer service and breaches of contracts are common. Planning for the future is limited since it is not deemed important. In addition, earnings from these businesses, if any, are spent instead of being reinvested in the business.

Our job was to help change general business practices, which would be challenging considering this cultural mindset. Alberto indicated that he would like to see ownership of businesses go beyond the family and that jobs should be for those who have the best qualifications, not just for a family member who might want or need a job. We were challenged to facilitate teamwork, responsibility, and respect for others. He wanted us to teach that working toward a quality product or service is best and that a prosperous future for a business requires proper planning. Reinvesting earnings for future expansion and job growth in this country would be a requisite in the years to come. He outlined his goals for us:

1. Work with our Nicaraguan counterparts to create sustainable, small business classes in high schools.
2. Develop basic business skills for high school students.
3. If possible, work directly with micro-business owners to enhance their management capabilities.

We were then told that teaching in high schools would be our primary project. The colossal goal of creating sustainable business classes was going to be a significant challenge.

Alberto ended his presentation by thanking us for our willingness to come to Nicaragua to improve opportunities for his people. He said that he very much looked forward to seeing the progress that we would help bring to his country. With that, our meetings concluded, and our next adventure was about to begin—traveling back to our training towns.

We left the office as a group at about 4:30 and traveled in a new, white Peace Corps bus that could transport about twenty-five people. The bus had a lot of glass and turned out to be quite the target for children wanting to wash the windows when we stopped at traffic lights. Don Alfredo waived the children away from the bus, but they continued trying. Our windows received a cleaning at almost every stoplight, and the kids expected payment for their work. I sat directly behind Don Alfredo in the first row of seats while another female facilitator, Camilla, sat on the passenger side up front. She harassed Don Alfredo to pay the kids. "They need the money," she said. Don Alfredo allowed Camilla to give the children a córdoba or two, and then we moved on to the next light where our windows were cleaned again. I loved the fact that these kids were actually aggressive in trying to make some money. I understood that with their work venue as the street, they were exposed to a lot of dangers, and they were a bit of a nuisance, but I appreciated such determination.

The facilitators instructed us to take off all jewelry, watches, sunglasses, or anything of value that could be snatched as we were heading to the Huembes bus station—the place that Arabella had made us avoid that very morning. When we were informed of our destination, I became very concerned about what might be in store for us.

I lost track of time as we moved through Managua. The windows on the bus were up, music played, the AC was on, and the ride was very comfortable. Outside, however, the day was still murderously hot and humid. I found myself drifting away, looking out the window, and thinking about how difficult normal life must be for the average Nicaraguan. People shuffling around in the bus brought me back to reality.

As we arrived at Huembes, the *aspirantes* gathered their backpacks and belongings and prepared to depart the bus. The bus station outside had a carnival-like atmosphere as people were everywhere, selling anything and everything. Huembes had the feel of a truly insane place with little to no order. Some people were running to destinations unknown, while others watched our bus very closely as we pulled into the station. Dirty children with no shoes or shirts played games or picked up garbage to inspect whether or not it could be useful to them. Policemen observed the general area with a low profile.

People from every walk of life occupied the bus station—businessmen, students, average people, and possibly a few criminals as well. The energy of the place amazed me! While passengers were coming and going as fast as they could move, the vendors aggressively pressured anyone they could come in contact with to buy some of their goods. People on top of buses pulled down baskets of vegetables and other items. The Nica 35 group anticipated splitting up to go in different directions to each of our *pueblos*, which meant that we would all be taking different buses in separate small clusters of about three people.

When Don Alfredo opened the doors of the bus, the *aspirantes* dashed to get to our buses as quickly as we could. Since we were *gringos* and dressed in business casual, we must have been quite the spectacle. Vendors, cab drivers, and beggars immediately bombarded us from all directions. One guy forcefully grabbed my arm and I almost decked him before I realized he was just asking me where I was going in order to help me find the right bus—for a price. I lost Kathryn for a few moments when a cab driver grabbed her arm, and then an actual cab almost ran them both over. The place was chaotic. Forty or so buses were lined up in their respective bays, and I tried to find the correct bus, while looking for Kathryn at the same time. Finally, I saw the bus we needed, and headed there straight away. I had spotted Kathryn briefly and knew she could handle herself, as this was not her first rodeo.

As I approached the bus we needed, ridiculously loud music played and a few scary-looking drunks danced around our means of transportation. One guy appeared to be an angry drunk, as he sort of danced and made martial arts moves at the same time. The man was completely oblivious as to who he might punch when someone walked by him.

I could see Kathryn moving toward the bus and kept my eye on her as she made her way. In the meantime, I had said, "No, thank you" and politely shook my index finger at no less than ten people within thirty seconds. When Kathryn was close enough to see me, I boarded the bus to get a seat so that we could ride together near the front of the bus. When she joined me, we both looked at each other and laughed. How crazy was that!? I looked out the window of the bus where the mad drunk was still dancing/shadow-boxing, and then vendors began boarding the bus. They walked onto the bus with baskets on their heads, yelling out whatever it was that they were selling. The vendors continuously announced their product in a very particular, repetitive, vocal cadence as they walked down the bus aisle, such as *"maní, maní, maní, maní con chile, chicle,"* or *"agua, agua, agua,"* or *"pollo caliente, caliente pollo, gaseosas."* The cadence was consistent in terms of three. Once the vendors completed walking down the aisle of the bus, they continued through the bus by jumping out the back door emergency exit.

A steady procession of these vendors moved through our bus and then made their way to the next bus and repeated the process. The vendors varied in ages from six-years old to a few who looked to be at least eighty. People with disabilities crawled through the bus begging for córdobas, which broke my heart. Then a child, who was no more than ten-years old placed a piece of paper in Kathryn's lap. It read, "Help me, please. I would like to continue my studies and go to school. But if I go to school, I can't eat. Give me money, please, before I have to start robbing people." The note was disturbing. I did not give the child money, as a threat was attached to the statement. When the child came back through the aisle, he called me "cheap" and disappeared into the crowd.

I looked through the window to see where that child had gone. Outside the bus, our drunk, shadow-boxing dancer was doubled over with blood pouring from his hand. To his right, I saw a jagged piece of tin with blood all over it, and deduced that he had punched the tin, hurting himself rather badly. I considered getting off the bus to help him, but thought that could be dangerous. I decided to observe for a minute or two and see how he handled the situation. If the man could do nothing for himself, or no one else helped him, I would eventually assist. From the bus, I watched him stand there and bleed. Finally, a woman came out of her storefront and offered the man a towel which he wrapped around his hand. I looked behind me and saw that Lee and Hollis had also made it onto the bus, and the driver fired up the engine to leave. About eight vendors remained on the bus. While we headed toward the exit of the bus station, the vendors jumped out the emergency exit, one by one, with the bus in motion.

After departing Huembes, I could not help but contemplate what we had experienced. Huembes is quite a place. I made a note to self—Huembes was an interesting bus terminal, and we should only go back there when absolutely necessary.

Upon departure, the bus was full with everyone seated. However, not more than a block away, the bus pulled over and picked up five more passengers. In three more blocks, we picked up another ten people. Another two blocks, and we picked up five or so more. People now lined the aisle of the bus. At this point, I began to notice the person helping the bus driver, who is called a *"cobrador."* The guy looked to be about eighteen- or nineteen- years old and wore an old Atlanta Braves baseball hat, torn jeans, and a greasy gray t-shirt. He looked lean and very strong. As the bus moved down the road, the *cobrador* hung out the door and yelled to people on the street to see if they needed to get on the bus. He did this by calling out the cities where the bus was traveling. Again, I heard a very rhythmic, particular vocal cadence in bursts of three. For example, he would yell out, "Masaya, Masaya, Masaya!" If Masaya was a town where someone wanted to travel, the person on the street waved at the bus and the driver would slam on the brakes, pulling over for them. The funny thing was that the bus was already packed—or so I thought. Amazingly, the bus continued to stop about every two or three blocks to pile in more people.

Slowly, but surely, no room whatsoever remained, as sixty to seventy people stood packed in the aisle of an ordinary school bus. Yet, the *cobrador* still tried to attract more passengers! Shockingly, the *cobrador* maneuvered toward the middle of the bus while hanging on the outside of the bus by grabbing ahold of the windows as we traveled at 40 miles per hour down the highway! Then he stuck his head in the bus window and asked people to move toward the middle so he and other potential passengers could get on the bus. People tried to move but could not. The second there was enough room, the *cobrador* called for the driver to stop and pick up another person. Once back in the bus, the *cobrador* turned his butt to the new passenger and pushed pretty hard to pack in all he could. He then climbed on top of the bus and rode up there for a while. Whenever the bus stopped to let passengers exit, the *cobrador* climbed down with a basket full of something and jumped back on the bus by grasping a window and whistling loud as hell for the bus driver to keep going. The bus never stopped more than a few seconds.

The *cobrador* came inside and collected money. All I could think was, "How the hell is he going to make his way down the aisle?" He pushed people. As gently as possible, the *cobrador* pushed someone until they gave way so he could stand in one spot and collect money from the ten people in each row. Then he pushed his way on to the next row. It was absolutely incredible! I had never seen anything like this before. There must have been a hundred and forty people on the bus, and the *cobrador* had a bead on all of them. He knew where they were going and called by whistle only for the bus to stop when the passengers needed to exit. He knew what they had on top of the bus and which basket belonged to whom, never mixing them up. I would equate this to a waiter taking care of an entire restaurant and not missing a single order or offering bad service. This young man worked his tail off!

With the blistering sun now setting, we had a reprieve from the unbearable heat as we were now only sweating, instead of sweating profusely. Nonetheless, thick humidity still existed making everyone on the bus absolutely miserable. I could not imagine what it must be like to stand up and ride so crammed for an hour in this humid climate. I had a seat, with my own space, although people pushed in from the packed aisle and made that comfort zone smaller and smaller. Soon, a lady's stomach hung right in my face—literally an inch away. I offered to give her my seat, but she did not accept—probably because she was experienced enough to know that if we changed positions, my junk would have been in her face. This bus ride was no joke; there was no escape and no relief. If an accident occurred, a nightmare scenario would immediately unfold.

About fifteen minutes from our destination, I thought I had seen everything, when the *cobrador* stood up in the front of the bus and climbed on the exit stairway railing. He then yelled something. At first, I thought he was making an announcement. When I asked Kathryn what he was doing, she said he was preaching. Sure enough, this young man stood there above all the passengers and offered a sermon with conviction like I had never heard before. He was a fire-breathing evangelist of the first degree. I asked Kathryn to translate some of his statements. To sum it up, he talked about his people needing to work for what they receive and that God would reward them well for their effort. This young *cobrador* was motivated and inspired.

As we approached the town of Masatepe, Kathryn and I tried to respectfully push our way through the aisle to get into a position for exiting. When we escaped the bus, I shared in my best Spanish with the young *cobrador* that he was a good man. He shook my hand firmly and looked me in the eyes as only few men I have known could and we made a connection. The *cobrador* had a strong leadership quality. Smiling, he said, "*Adios, gringo*" and climbed the ladder to the roof. As the bus rolled down the highway almost out of sight in the setting sun, the kid stood on top of the bus and offered Kathryn and me a prominent goodbye wave.

As we walked away, I reflected on and admired what the Nicaraguan people do to maintain life. Most—if not all—of the people on the bus commuted regularly to Managua and lived at least an hour away. Those folks endure an intense daily commute. As we walked, the town seemed noticeably quiet and the late evening air felt warm and humid, but with a gentle breeze. The stars began to show themselves, and the sweet aroma from the jungle flowers was delightful. Kathryn and I held hands and slowly walked three blocks to her new home. In anticipation of meeting Kathryn's host family, I had a great deal of excitement twirling in my head. I was quite nervous as I could only understand a little Spanish. I was concerned about my ability to have a social interaction with her family, but everything worked out fine.

Before leaving Catarina, I had mentioned to my host mother, Marisol, on Friday morning that I would not be returning home that night because I would stay with my wife in Masatepe. Marisol understood and said that she and Pedro planned to go to the lagoon on Sunday with the boys and a few friends for a barbecue. She asked if Kathryn and I would like to join them. I said that we would love to go and that we would be back in Catarina Saturday afternoon.

Kathryn's host family was phenomenal. She lived with a single mother by the name of Natalia, and six children—three girls and three boys. The boys were Jamiel, age nineteen; Timoteo, age seventeen; and Matías, age nine. The girls were Mariana, age twenty-four; Isabella, age twenty-one; and Juana, otherwise known as "Juanita," age fifteen.

Jamiel, the oldest son, was a pleasure to be around. He traveled

Look

three times a week to study economics at a university in Managua. Matías (pronounced *Ma-tee-as*), the nine-year-old boy, was not actually an immediate family member. He stayed with the family during the weekdays so he could go to school. We heard that his father had been abusive and his mother struggled to take care of him financially. Kathryn's "host mother," Natalia, was a friend of that family, so she accepted the responsibility for Matías and took him in full-time during the week so that he could attend school. Timoteo (pronounced *Tim-o-tay-o*) the second boy, was a quiet, yet confident young man who loved to play soccer with Matías all the time. An aunt named Vida lived next door with a newborn girl named Serena, and the two of them always visited at Kathryn's house. Natalia's daughters took care of Serena as if she were their own, so it seemed that Serena basically had four mothers. The child was never without attention, and it was beautiful to watch.

Natalia is a truly remarkable woman. She was a single mother and how she managed to keep a roof over their heads and meals on the table bewildered me. The money that the Peace Corps paid Natalia for taking care of *aspirantes* might have been helpful, but regardless, she managed to take care of her family.

Natalia had been a host mother to nine previous trainees. She had experience with Americans and had been through everything that comes with having a foreigner living in Nicaragua—the illnesses, such as parasites, and the loneliness or homesickness that many *aspirantes* have while in training. Natalia had been through it all, and I felt like Kathryn could not have been placed in a more ideal situation.

Natalia was a seamstress who worked all hours of the day and night. She completely earned my trust and respect. Not only did Natalia provide for the family financially, but she clearly was a fantastic mother. She had incredible energy. At forty five-years old, Natalia was a vibrant woman and kind to an extent that was difficult to compare. Natalia's Spanish sounded quite clear and she corrected us without criticism when we made language mistakes. We greatly appreciated her assistance.

I walked in that Friday evening at dinner time. I thought it somewhat strange that all the boys were already eating, while the girls were socializing with the newest client for Natalia's sewing business. A local woman, who had commissioned Natalia to make something pretty for a special occasion, had come over to check on the progress of her new dress.

Then I started to notice a pattern. The boys ate first and washed their plates, and then the girls had a turn to eat. I realized they did not have enough plates for the entire family to eat at once, and the utensils were made of plastic. However, by eating in shifts, Natalia's family had enough kitchenware to accommodate their household needs and everyone seemed happy.

I met the family and could immediately tell that Kathryn would be right at home in this household. Natalia's children embraced Kathryn, and it was easy to see that they had already bonded. The girls made a fuss over me, as they had heard so much about me from Kathryn. I did the best I could to communicate. Isabella speaks English, but she did not while we were in her home, as she realized that speaking our language would not help us adapt. Everyone was incredibly kind and hospitable.

The family consisted of beautiful people. The girls were independent, charming, and gorgeous. The boys of the household were well-behaved, respectful, intelligent, good-humored, athletic, and handsome. Each person did their part to help around the house while Natalia worked to make the money. The girls said they wanted to give me a tour of the house. Who was I to say no?

Natalia had turned her garage into a seamstress shop with different kinds of material piled all the way to the ceiling. She had one small work station with a sewing machine and two or three rocking chairs to accommodate customers or family members who wanted to socialize while she worked.

The house, a typical Nicaraguan home with a tin roof, was painted yellow on the outside with black bars on all the windows. The house shared walls with the two houses on either side. The front door was made of heavy iron and painted black with three locks. I loved seeing that sturdy door and the bars on the windows, as I knew I would not have to worry about someone breaking into the home. To break in, a criminal would have to go through the roof, which was possible, but not likely.

Entering the home, the living room was off to the right with five rocking chairs lined against yellow walls and a twenty-inch television on a small table. The décor included prominently displayed religious artifacts, such as paintings of the Virgin Mary and the Last Supper. The living room opened into the garage/sewing room, and this was the most active area of the house. People could sit with Natalia in the sewing room and still be able to converse with others in the living room. Doors from the back of the living room led you to an outside walkway.

Three bedrooms lined up along the left wall of the outdoor walkway. Each of these rooms had a window looking out to an open patio, where a rooster stood tied to a pole and six clothes lines ran in different directions.

At the end of the outside corridor, a covered but open work area contained four items—a sink, stove, bathroom, and an adobe oven. The sink, called a *pila* (pronounced, *pee-la*), was a work zone in and of itself. Typical *pilas* are made of concrete, weigh roughly five hundred pounds, and are about six feet long with a horizontal scrub board for washing clothes and two ten-gallon concrete spaces for storing water to rinse the clothes and dishes. A garden hose attached to the *pila* provided running water.

To the right of the *pila* sat an adobe oven that resembled an igloo made of mud. I loved the way the oven looked, and all I could think of was brick-oven pizzas. A four burner stove and a wooden cupboard with pots, pans, and dishes stood to the left side of the *pila*. Directly behind the stove was a bathroom that had been sectioned off with plywood and contained a latrine box made of wood. Directly beside the latrine box, a garden hose ran up the wall to create a shower. The roof was four feet higher than the bathroom door, which made the loo an open-air environment. At least Kathryn could lock the plywood door and not have to worry about someone pulling open a plastic curtain, and the shower seemed to be secure and private.

After the house tour, we went into Kathryn's room, which had belonged to Isabella. This meant the girls of the host family had to double up or someone slept at the grandparent's house around the corner.

Kathryn's bedroom, about twelve feet by twenty feet, was much larger than my Harry Potter cupboard in Catarina. Kath's room, sparsely furnished, consisted of one twin bed with a mosquito net, one small desk, a chair, and a wood furnishing of some sort that could be used as a makeshift closet. Then it hit me! One twin bed for a married couple—not only in Kathryn's home, but in my host family's home as well. I knew that sleeping with my wife on a twin bed might not be very pleasant, as she has a jumpy leg and is a restless sleeper. We would have to live with what we had been offered. What else could we do? Complain to the Peace Corps that this was an unacceptable sleeping arrangement? Not bloody likely! There was no way I would ever complain—not to the Peace Corps, not to the host family, and not to my wife. My bed in Catarina was even worse because it was made for a child—and with two people in it?! I was not going to have a decent night's sleep for three months! All I could think was "be positive, and get used to it."

Following my shock about the sleeping situation and the ten-second mental acceptance process, Kathryn told me that the girls of the house participated in a folkloric dance group. The ladies had practice that evening by the park, and we were invited to watch. Of course we would go. After dinner, Kathryn and I walked through the town to see the girls practice.

Masatepe is a very relaxed and friendly town; we felt safe walking at night. Upon arriving at the park, its large size amazed me, and I recognized the location as a centerpiece for town life. People were everywhere in and around the well-lit park. Kids were playing on the swings, and teenagers were doing what teenagers do—hanging out. There were adults visiting with each other on park benches, some playing chess. Vendors sold cookies, chewing gum, peanuts, and blow pops.

As life in Central America unfolded before us, I began to notice a consistency with respect to the design of each town I visited. In every town, by every park, was a very large church, and Masatepe was no different. The park, a square block in size and painted colorfully in pastels that complimented the jungle plant life, was also cultural, emphasizing several statues and plaques commemorating different historically-significant events.

The beautiful church beside the park had massive and intricately detailed doors and two bell towers that stood a hundred feet high. Masatepe's church was twice the size of the church in Catarina, which was impressive in and of itself. The Masatepe church's aesthetics, architecture, and artwork mesmerized Kathryn and me. We sat for a few minutes holding hands and observed this place of worship in all of its glory. We discussed the underdeveloped Nicaraguan tourist industry, understanding that in a few more years this great country would no longer be a secret. That would be fine with me, because there would be more opportunity for employment with an increase of tourist money pumping through the economy.

Kathryn and I lost track of time admiring the church, and continued our walk to find the folkloric dance group's practice site. When we arrived at the correct place—which seemed to be some sort of community center—traditional Nicaraguan music wafted through the building and out into the street. We located the dancers at the community center's small, but lovely, concrete amphitheater. Kathryn's host sisters were practicing folkloric dances with about fifteen other men and women. We found the dances very entertaining and culturally interesting. Children also participated in the dance process and it looked like great fun. The kids were unbelievably cute.

Kathryn told me that in a week or two the group would be performing for a festival in Masatepe, and asked if I would like to attend. While I fully support the arts, a dance-recital-activity is usually not my cup of tea, and my wife knows this all too well. I decided that I would share the experience with Kathryn, as she loves this sort of event. Besides, I had already seen what would be performed by the dance group at the festival, and it captured my heart. Yet, I would never let Kathryn know that I was as excited as she was for the coming performance. Why? Because I could earn "good husband bonus points" for attending the event with a positive attitude. Naturally, I said "yes" to her invitation.

As I sat beside her grinning, Kathryn told me that Natalia had made all the costumes for the dance group. The women's dresses were beautifully elaborate, and the men were planning to wear different masks, each a work of art. I could not wait to see the costumes and I wondered if the masks would be similar to those I had seen in Mardi Gras parades of years past. I would have to wait and see.

When the dance practice was over and we started walking home, we ran into two Peace Corps *aspirantes*, William Protti and Leslie Nolen, who were also training in Masatepe with Kathryn. We shared some good laughs about the safety instruction that brought about a level of paranoia, and we discussed how lucky we were to be living in Central America. Our little group continued toward home together, as the *aspirantes* of Masatepe lived within a few blocks of each other. Arriving at Kathryn's house, we said "goodnight" to them, and went to our room.

Sleeping on a twin bed with two people is difficult at best, but the lumpy mattress provided by Kathryn's host family made it more challenging. I suppose this could be construed as a complaint, but it's really not. I am only saying that the bed was not the coziest one I had ever slept on. The reality was that Kathryn's bed was more comfortable than mine in Catarina because it was long enough that my feet did not hang off the end. Examining the pillows revealed two towels stuffed in the pillow case. They were not quite the feather pillows I had become accustomed to in the States, but they did the trick nonetheless.

The last day of the first full week of training had been a fine day. I fell asleep thinking about how much I love my wife, how motivated we were to make good things happen, and what adventure tomorrow might bring. We did not have to wait until morning to be delivered more excitement.

Kathryn and I were happy to be together again and the house was eerily quiet as we peacefully slept. Quiet, that is, until we awoke to a shockingly loud scream coming from where Isabella was sleeping, accompanied by a crashing thud against the wall. Brief yelling followed the initial scream and then all became eerily quiet again. I immediately asked Kathryn if I should go to check on Isabella to ensure that all was well. Kathryn said, "No, let's wait a few minutes and see if we hear anything else." Not a peep came from Isabella's room.

The next day, Kathryn asked Isabella what happened in her room the night before as we heard yelling and then a crashing noise, like a baseball being thrown into the wall. Isabella laughed hysterically and dramatically explained that a mouse had fallen from the rafters of the home and landed on her chest in the middle of the night. Isabella had screamed with fear, but at the same time, reacted quickly by grabbing the mouse with her bare hand before it could escape and violently threw the vermin against the wall, killing it instantly. We laughed really hard with Isabella at the random event. With respect and good humor, Kathryn and I discussed the fact that anything can happen in

Nicaragua and that it would be a serious mistake for anyone to mess with Isabella. We also began to appreciate other benefits of sleeping beneath the mosquito net.

Earlier that morning, I awoke on my side with my back flush against the wall and my left arm very much asleep with pins and needles beneath Kathryn's head. Kathryn lay on her back with both arms and legs sprawled as if she was sleeping in a king size bed with her mouth wide open. I took a moment to appreciate the sleeping beauty, and then gently tried to remove my arm from underneath her head, which might as well have been a ten-pound rock. Kathryn woke up briefly and was none too happy about being disturbed at six in the morning.

For me, six o'clock was sleeping in, as I had been awakened at 4:30 every morning for the past week by my old man's bus. I did my best to be sweet and gave her a kiss on the cheek, which almost cost me my teeth. Kathryn is not what I would call a morning person. I gave her another kiss, said that I loved her and good morning, and then crawled out from underneath the mosquito net.

William Protti had promised to come over and offer the two of us a yoga lesson Saturday morning at 8. After two hours of writing about what we had experienced that week, I heard William knock on the door at eight o'clock sharp.

William looked very serious with his yoga mat ready to go. We just needed some space to exercise. Kathryn's host sister, Isabella, wanted to join us, and the four of us walked to the back of the home near the adobe oven. We laid out our towels, and William placed his mat. Breathing deeply was very relaxing, and having only had one previous yoga class, I enjoyed the activity.

William effectively gave instruction in both Spanish and English to guide us into different yoga positions. Before I knew it, I had wrapped myself up like a pretzel and felt quite uncomfortable. I am about as flexible as an iron rod, and yoga quickly became difficult for me.

My back had been jammed up since taking a pretty good spill on the basketball court while playing with my host brothers in the previous week. I thought that yoga would help me work out the kinks, but I only felt more pain. I stopped twenty minutes into the lesson. Talk about feeling like a wimp.

Did I mention that William Protti was a handsome, athletic guy?

Was I jealous? You bet I was! I wanted to continue the yoga lesson and show my attractive wife that I could do anything this kid could do. The truth was that I could not finish the class. I left the area feeling incompetent and I could not bear the sight of the three of them breathing deeply and placing their bodies in contorted positions. As I walked away, I could not help but think how good yoga must be for our bodies—yet I was in no position that morning to strain my back more than it already had been. I wanted breakfast.

Splendid! More beans and rice—but this time with eggs and bread. The breakfast had been cooked by the lovely Mariana, and the food was remarkably tolerable. Kathryn and I were both becoming accustomed to the beans and rice for almost every meal and we were thankful to have the food.

The arrangement between the Peace Corps and the host families was that the host families were to provide safe housing, prepare all meals, and wash clothes for the *aspirantes*. The host families did not, however, have to wash the socks and underwear of the trainees. I instantly decided this was a great rule.

Mariana's responsibilities for the household were to cook and wash the clothes. As I watched her washing clothes, I realized that doing this chore is physically exhausting. Washing clothes by hand is a difficult process that can make the knuckles of even the veterans bleed. The scrub board in the sink is made of concrete sharp enough to cut you if you run the back side of your hand across it quickly.

I felt like I needed to help Mariana as she had just cooked breakfast for us. I walked over and asked her if I could wash the clothes, and she started laughing. I really did not know what to make of this humor. Did she think I was incapable of washing clothes? Why did she giggle when I offered to help? Kathryn overheard our conversation and said that men don't do laundry in Nicaragua, and that I was a joker for suggesting such a thing. Mariana did not think twice about my offer of help; she honestly thought it was funny.

Kathryn told Mariana that I helped do the laundry and cook back in the States. Mariana continued to laugh, and then she asked if I wore a skirt as well. Of course, I had not caught on to what she had said because I did not know much Spanish. When my wife doubled over with laughter, I became very suspicious and asked Kathryn to translate. The skirt comment had pushed Kathryn's funny bone, and they both had a good laugh at my expense. Okay girls, let's not get carried away. I told Mariana that Kathryn and I shared the work responsibilities of our home.

While continuing to wash the clothes, Mariana said I needed to teach her boyfriend that working in the home was acceptable behavior for a man. Kathryn nodded her head "yes" affirmatively and said that maybe Eric would do just that when his Spanish improved a little more, and Tomás could get to know him better. We all agreed that this would be a good way to approach Tomás with such a new idea. I had learned a good cultural lesson about washing clothes and cooking being jobs for women only, in this country. Hmm? Maybe I should have told Kathryn that I was going to adopt this aspect of Nicaraguan culture when we returned to the States. As I pondered the idea, I knew that I would never be able to get away with it; so I quickly buried the idea, before it buried me.

After breakfast, Kathryn and I walked through town to an internet café where I called my parents for the first time since we had arrived in Nicaragua. I let them know that I was safe, where I was living, and shared with them the contact methods should an emergency arise at home. My folks sounded well and the conversation was brief. Kathryn decided to email her parents because her mother was still having a hard time with our decision to serve in the Peace Corps.

We walked back to Kathryn's house and told Natalia that we would be staying in Catarina Saturday night. Kathryn and I loaded our backpacks and headed to the bus stop.

The bus stop in Masatepe was like many others in the smaller cities of Nicaragua. Bicycle taxis were coming and going and lined up on the corner, waiting for clients to exit buses. Vendors stationed on both sides of the main highway were trying to sell convenience items like candy, cookies, peanuts, cigarettes, and juices. I found how juice was sold quite interesting because it was not provided to customers in cups or bottles, but in plastic bags tied in a knot. The Nicas would bite off the corner of the plastic bag and suck the juice through the small hole.

These "*refrescos*" scared me to death and I refused to drink them because my site-mates, Hollis and Lee, had already become violently ill, possibly from drinking juices made from water of questionable quality. Yet, I thoroughly enjoyed watching these vendors at work. It was

Saturday and school was out, so many of these vendors were children.

Kathryn and I hopped on a bus for Catarina and sat together watching the rolling countryside fly by. There were a lot of interesting sights between Catarina and Masatepe, but one place in particular caught my full attention—the community of Niquinohomo (pronounced more or less, *nicky-no-moh*). I thought about its historical significance as we rode through the town. A large statue of Augusto César Sandino stood by the roadside, an amazing memorial to the legend of Sandino, who was born in Niquinohomo. It was fascinating to see Sandino's statue and the memorabilia surrounding the historical monument. The bus roared on by, and in another ten minutes we reached Catarina.

When we arrived in Catarina, a few things needed to be done before we could spend the night together comfortably. Primarily, I needed to put up my mosquito net. I knew that my wife would not want to sleep with a net laid over her body, and I had to admit that the net was quite a nuisance for the week that I slept with it draped on top of me. During my first week, I had been too busy to deal with locating a hammer, nails, and rope. With Kathryn here now, there was no avoiding the obvious—the net had to go up. The bus dropped us off at the entrance of Catarina and we began walking through town to my house.

We were about three blocks from the bus stop when we saw a guy named Guillermo walking in the middle of the street. Every afternoon he brought bamboo baskets that he made in the morning to the bus stop to be delivered to other towns.

I had made it a point to introduce myself to Guillermo earlier in the week because the guy was so amazing. What grabbed my attention was that the bamboo baskets Guillermo carried were large, possibly four feet in diameter; and, he usually had twenty of them stacked on top of his head. The stack of baskets was probably twenty-five feet tall. They were piled so high on his head that he could only walk underneath electrical lines in certain places.

When I first saw him my thought was, "oh, this guy has got to be kidding, it's a one man circus!" Guillermo walked from one side of the street to the other venturing under the electrical lines at their highest points, and even then, he only cleared the power lines by a few inches with his baskets. He had the walk to the bus stop down to a science and knew exactly where he needed to go relative to these electrical lines.

What also made me chuckle was that Guillermo did not care if there was a car behind him. He often had a train of eight to ten cars slowly following him. The people driving the cars who had to wait for this man walking in the street appeared perfectly content watching him work. The car drivers' patience was either due to great respect for his talent, or they were scared to have the baskets fall onto their vehicles. Either way, I never heard any horns blown, and no one hurried Guillermo by driving close behind him. I thought about how this man would make someone in the States absolutely nuts! However, in Nicaragua, everyone waited from a distance and moved through town at Guillermo's pace. What else could drivers do? Once Guillermo arrived on main street, everyone had to wait because his crossings of that street were random, and the baskets always looked like they were falling. Guillermo guided the baskets by leaning his body just a little until the whole pile on his head moved in the direction of his lean. He would catch up to the leaning stack of baskets by running back underneath the load before they all fell off his head and spilled in the street. The baskets had to be heavy, because Guillermo had no neck; and the grimace on his face looked to say, "I am buckling beneath these heavy baskets, and I could lose the whole pile at any second." However, I never saw him lose a load, and he always made it to the bus stop.

Once he reached the bus stop, all the cars that had been waiting for him could pass. Guillermo would drop the baskets perfectly to the ground by bending his knees and giving a hard thrust upward as if jumping. He then simply walked out from underneath them and guided the falling baskets to the ground with his hands. Guillermo would wave to each car and say "thank you for waiting." It was a celebration for everyone. He had made it to the bus stop successfully, and the waiting drivers could speed away.

By the end of my first week, I had seen Guillermo and his balancing-basket-circus act five or six times. One of those occasions, I followed him all the way to the bus stop to learn where he was headed, what he was up to, and how he got the baskets to the ground without disaster. Kathryn, however, had yet to see Guillermo; when she did see him struggling down the street, it stopped her dead in her tracks. Kathryn said, "Check this guy out, he's incredible." I responded, "Yeah, watch him as he goes back and forth across the street avoiding the power lines. His strength and talent are remarkable."

We sat on the corner and watched the one-man carnival until he disappeared out of sight down by the bus stop. I told Kathryn that we could visit Guillermo's basket fabrication site before she returned to Masatepe. Seeing this man strip a bamboo tree with a machete was as awesome as watching him carry his baskets to the bus stop. Guillermo was a professional.

When we arrived at my home, we began planning how to put up the mosquito net. I wondered if my family had any tools. If not, how did they section off my bed room from the living room with plywood and a door? It was not likely that they paid someone else to do the minor home renovation. I asked Marisol, and she gave us all the materials necessary to put up the net, an easy task, which was completed in ten minutes. We could then go play.

Kathryn wanted to walk to the Mirador to enjoy the view of the lagoon. I could not argue, as it is a beautiful place. I told Marisol where we were headed. Catarina is a pretty town with gardens and flowers everywhere. It could very well be the best landscaped town I have ever seen. As we walked through the city toward the Mirador, the kids I had been playing with in the park the week before came up and asked us to play. Adults were saying "hello," and of course, I introduced Kathryn to everyone I could. This little walk turned out to be quite the social event.

Hollis Bennet's host family's home was situated in a prime location across the street from the central park and on the way to the Mirador. Hollis was not home as he had gone to Niquinohomo to stay with his wife, who was not feeling well. Kathryn and I visited with his host family for about a half hour. We sat on their porch and watched all the activity in the park while still maintaining a pleasant conversation. What could be better for a Saturday afternoon in Central America?

On the way to the Mirador, Kathryn and I did something else that I would have to call "street shopping." I would normally say "window shopping," but there are no windows in the shops. Actually, there are plenty of windows – just none with glass. Many of the products were out in front of the stores. Gorgeous handmade jewelry and intricately detailed pottery were ridiculously inexpensive. Kathryn particularly loved the large, brilliantly-colored vases with sunflowers painted on them.

Normally, shopping of any kind for me is a quick in-and-out process, and it is safe to say that I generally do not enjoy window shopping. Yet, these products fascinated me. Everything was handmade—the jewelry, the pottery, hammocks, and the furniture; it blew me away. The craftsmanship was simply unbelievable regarding the designs and elaborate detail. Each piece of furniture was expressly unique, with a wide variety of styles and arrangements. The best part was that all of these items filled the storefronts, which makes Catarina a seriously colorful and artistic town. Not only is it an artistic haven, but in between the shops, lovely garden stores with beautiful flowers also lined the streets. All of these attributes make Catarina an outstanding place to visit or live, and I felt very lucky to have it as my training town.

The lagoon is a natural wonder, and such beauty attracts tourists to the Mirador. On a Saturday afternoon, Catarina is generally bustling with people. I knew, however, that prices go up on the weekends due to the incoming tourists, so I was not going to buy anything. If Kathryn really liked something, she could pick it out and then I could come back during the week when the town was much slower and prices were lower. The Peace Corps now provided us a small stipend each week, comparable to a local Nicaraguan wage. We needed to be frugal with our spending.

We made our way to the Mirador and enjoyed the atmosphere, the weather, and the people. My host mother owned a restaurant within twenty yards of the overlook and we visited with her sisters, who were working at the establishment. The afternoon felt very relaxed, and the stress of the world was completely gone; it seemed like we were on vacation—except we lived here!

We left the Mirador at about dark and returned home. While walking back, we ran into my host brothers, Pedro and Diego. They wanted us to come to the park and play basketball with them. We said that we would play after we ate dinner because we had been so busy that day we forgot to have lunch. When we arrived at my house, dinner was ready, which made me extremely happy because I have been told that I can become rather unpleasant when I am really hungry—and I was famished. Kathryn is like a food camel; she can go long periods of time with no food.

We had beans and rice again, but this time I also had fried chicken.

My host mother knew that Kathryn was a vegetarian and had made the necessary arrangements to accommodate her nutritional needs. I did not pay much attention to what Kathryn ate for dinner as I turned my full attention to the fried chicken. I devoured the bird and cleaned the bones with a conviction that made my wife laugh. Marisol told me there was another chicken out back, and that if I wanted, I could have more in a half hour. This comment stopped my monster momentum and forced me to think about the poor bird I had just crushed. Kathryn looked at me as if to say, "What do you think? You murderer. Want to kill another?" I then thought about the roosters that were waking me up every morning and asked Marisol if I could eat one of those. Marisol laughed and so did Kathryn. As I licked my fingers grinning, I decided I had done enough damage to the animal kingdom for one evening and complimented Marisol several times on how great dinner had been.

Lee Hamilton came by the house immediately after dinner and asked if we wanted to head to the park. Why not? My host brothers were already there waiting on us. Kathryn and I thanked Marisol again for dinner and left with Lee.

When we arrived at the park, the children's great energy was compelling. We played basketball for a little while, and as usual, the game turned to other activities—only this time we played American games. We played Rover-Red-Rover, Red Light-Green Light, Sharks and Minnows, and tag. The group of kids grew quite large and all had a great time. I love to listen to a playground full of children laughing and screaming, and that night brought an exceptional amount of noise, filling my heart with joy.

After I was sufficiently worn out and could not play anymore, I sat next to the basketball court and watched the kids play with Kathryn and Lee. The crowd thinned out a little more, with only about five kids remaining: four girls and a boy around the age of seven. We asked them to teach us a game or a song. The girls immediately began singing, clapping, and chanting a fantastically rhythmic tune that was group-oriented, but with each person having a chance to participate individually.

It went something like, "Kathryn robbed some bread from the store in San Juan."

Kathryn would then have to answer, "Who, me?"

And the group responded robustly, "Yeah, you!"

Kathryn would then have to defend herself saying, "I didn't do it."

The group would then sing together, "Then, who?"

Now free of the crime, Kathryn could call out a name and accuse any person in the group of the robbery, and the song would start over.

In Spanish, it went like this: "*Kathryn robó pan en la tienda de San Juan.*"

"*Quién, yo?*"

"*Sí, tú!*"

"*Yo no fui!*"

"*Entonces, quién?*"

"*Miguel!*"

And the song would start again.

These little people ripped out my heart and held it in their hands. Their smiles, spirit, and innocence inspired me. At around 9:30 p.m., their mothers came over and watched as we played. Kathryn and I introduced ourselves, and a pleasant conversation ensued. Why were we in Nicaragua? Did we work for a religious organization? How long would we be here? Where were we from, and what was it like there? Did we like Catarina and Nicaragua? The questions were continuous. Kathryn and I patiently responded to all of the inquiries and asked about their families and lives in Catarina. We left after agreeing to meet the kids in the park again soon to play more. As we departed, Kathryn, Lee, and I conversed about how much fun that little outing had been. We concurred that playing in the park with the children was something worth pursuing again in the future.

Kathryn and I arrived at home and went to my room. Because of the small size of the room, we realized that we had to take turns managing our personal needs. Kathryn grabbed her toothbrush, lotions, and whatever else she used for her ritual of getting ready for bed, while I waited outside. When we finally climbed into bed, I again ended up against the wall laying on my side, while she had all the room. We said good night to each other, and while Kathryn read a book with a flashlight, I prayed for the intellectual capacity to absorb the Spanish language rapidly and for the ability to make a positive impact while in Nicaragua. I fell asleep thinking about all the wonderful opportunities I had been offered in life and how lucky I was to be born an American.

I woke up early on Sunday like every other day in Catarina—to the roosters crowing and dogs barking. Only this time there was another disturbance that was impossible for me to sleep through—the sound of fireworks at 5:30 in the morning, and a lot of them! The fireworks were bottle rockets of some sort, but they sounded much more powerful. I could hear the swoosh of the rockets taking off, but the explosion was not the small crack that I was accustomed to hearing in the States. This sound was more like a twelve-gauge shotgun discharge with a big booming resonance. I laughed thinking, "This place is insane! Fireworks at sunrise on a Sunday morning? Where would this happen in the States?" I then grasped the fact that I was not in the States and this was what went on in Nicaragua. I pulled my arm—again full of pins and needles—from underneath my wife's head and crawled over her and out from beneath the mosquito net.

I achieved my goal of writing in my journal at the kitchen table for an hour, but it came at a cost. Mosquitoes chewed me to pieces and I scratched myself silly. Marisol was up and running at 6 a.m., doing laundry and making breakfast. Kathryn woke up and joined us for breakfast at 7.

Marisol had cut some fresh pineapple, mangos, and bananas. I requested fruit for breakfast as it was inexpensive and I preferred fruit over beans and rice. I had been having fresh fruit for breakfast each morning since the previous Wednesday and was sure Kathryn would enjoy it too. Every morning, I had been telling Marisol how much I liked the fruit and thanked her for breakfast.

As usual, I said in Spanish, "*Mucho gusto fruta y gracias por la comida.*" Translation?

"Nice to meet you fruit, and thank you for the food."

I should have said, "*Me gusta mucho la fruta,*" which translates to, "I like fruit a lot."

Kathryn began to giggle. I asked her what was amusing, and she then started laughing to the point that she almost spit up her coffee. She was in a fit of convulsive laughter.

I again asked Kathryn, "What the hell is so funny?" She said that I had basically introduced myself to the fruit, as if I was meeting a person for the first time.

I thought, "Oh, no—this should be amusing for everyone else but me." Marisol was straight-faced and had not cracked a smile. Kathryn, always an instigator, asked Marisol if she had heard what I said. There was no such thing as damage control for me because I did not know enough Spanish to stop the rapidly evolving situation.

Marisol said, "Oh yes, he's been saying that every morning. I just thought it was something you Americans said to your food." I had no idea what Marisol had said, but I could tell from Kathryn's response, it didn't go in my favor.

Kathryn howled with laughter and said, "No, Marisol, he's just not saying what he wanted to say correctly."

Marisol said she had thought saying "Nice to meet you fruit" was pretty strange. Yet, she did not want to laugh at me. Marisol then asked Kathryn if it was okay to laugh at me?

Kathryn responded, "Why not? I've been laughing at him for years." With that comment from the instigator, both ladies had quite a cackle at my expense. I laughed as well because anyone who introduces them self to their fruit has got to be a goofball. I played it off, but in reality I was a little embarrassed.

Then both Kathryn and Marisol offered me a Spanish lesson. I obviously needed the information, and I never introduced myself to my food again. Coming into the Peace Corps, I knew that I would say things in Spanish that were not correct and would unintentionally be funny. I had not, however, expected that this situation would cause me a feeling of embarrassment. From that moment on, Marisol would always put food in front of me and say, *"Mucho gusto beans and rice,"* or *"Mucho gusto pollo."* She grilled me incessantly about introducing myself to the food. It was funny, what could I do? The food jokes were an especially nice way for Marisol and me to laugh together and bond.

Kathryn loved my minor hiccups with the new language, and the worst part was that we both knew there would be more to come. I learned to have thicker skin and accept it, because for me, these types of language mistakes could not be avoided. I also knew Kathryn was not trying to be mean, and as far as I am concerned, a healthy laugh is positive energy.

After breakfast, Kathryn and I studied Spanish while we waited on Pedro's friends, Dennis (pronounced, *den-ee*') and his fiancé, Sylvia. When they arrived at the house, we began packing the back of a small Toyota pickup with eight plastic chairs, a cooler, the food, and a grill.

The grill caught my attention because it was a quintessential Nicaraguan homemade gizmo from an old car rim. To demonstrate the idea, visualize putting a car rim (without the tire) in a horizontal position, add some legs to it, and you've got yourself a grill. It was fabulously creative. The charcoal lays burning in the wheel, a screen sits over the top, and then the food is placed on the screen to cook. The legs of the grill consisted of three-foot strips of rebar (iron) welded in place to hold the car rim horizontal. This was a perfect grill! My friends were amazingly resourceful.

I thought about calling someone in marketing at NASCAR to tell them I had a great new way to recycle the wheels from race car teams. We could take all the old wheels discarded by the NASCAR teams and build grills out of them and call it, "The Official Grill of NASCAR."

"Gentlemen, start your engines," I laughed to myself as Dennis fired up his old truck to leave. Eight of us and one dog piled in Dennis' rig, with five people crammed in the back, plus the barbecue gear.

We left Catarina and headed for the lagoon. It seemed ironic to have to leave Catarina to arrive at the lagoon, as Catarina rested at the top of the old volcano's crater. Yet we had to drive twenty minutes outside of town down a winding road to get there. We went to the same private property as our previous visit. The lagoon did not let us down this time either as it was stunningly spectacular to be there.

As we arrived, a double rainbow hovered over the lagoon, and I could not help but think "This just gets better and better." Kind of like my relationship with Kathryn. We ran to the beach after unloading the barbecue gear and jumped in the water to swim. Kathryn and I asked if we could help get things started regarding the food, but we were told in no uncertain terms that they could easily handle the menial preparations.

Kathryn and I are water fanatics. We love to swim in it or be near it enjoying the sun. We love the water in a boat or with a goat, we love the water Sam I am. You get the point – water is a major part of our lives. Whether it's a lake, river, ocean, creek etc., we are always mystified by water's ability to relax us and take our cares away. Visiting this gorgeous lagoon was an exceptionally special treat.

Pedro and Dennis were trying to start the fire for the grill. It was like watching the three stooges, only there were two of them. Pedro was putting firewood in the grill to light. Dennis took a paper towel that was supposed to be starter fuel for the fire, twisted it up, then stuck the paper towel in Pedro's ear. They were funny to watch and playfully slapped each other around as only good friends would do.

The weather was great with just the right amount of sun and not too many clouds. Marisol and Sylvia sat in chairs beneath a lovely palm tree, engaged in what looked to be a pleasant conversation, while the boys kicked a ball back and forth. I thought this day was shaping up quite nicely—my wife, my host family, new friends, new country, great weather, a spectacular place to play, in addition to a good batch of food on the way. Yep, it was going be a sweet day!

Kathryn is five-foot-four inches tall, and about that same distance from shore, she had to swim as the lagoon dropped off quickly and water rose over her head. This shocked her, and she asked why the lagoon became so deep so rapidly? I did not know, and we discussed the swift descent of the lagoon floor as being highly unique.

It was so nice to be able to spend some time having fun with my wife again. I had missed her over the last week, and we lovingly embraced each other in the water.

Then Kathryn said, "You swim pretty well, Eric. Why don't you tell Pedro to check out how good your butterfly stroke is." I thought she was being serious, and she was. I said, "Give me a break, Kathryn. You know I don't say things like that." Kath said, "No, it's fine. Really, you can say things like that here in Nicaragua."

That made me think it was some kind of cultural thing as opposed to bragging. I asked if it would seem odd to talk about my swimming talent being that some of their family did not even know how to swim. I told her that I thought the idea was ridiculous, and I was not really comfortable with what she was asking of me. That kind of statement is not even close to being my style. "Besides," I said, "I don't know how to say that in Spanish."

Kathryn told me convincingly, "Oh no, they will think it's funny. Just put your feet together, roll over onto your back, and do the dolphin kick and say this: '*Mira Pedro, puedo nadar como una sirena.*'"

I reluctantly said, "Okay, why not?" I rolled over on my back, started kicking like a dolphin, and said to Pedro what Kathryn had stated. I had completely forgotten that I was supposed to be doing the butterfly stroke instead of lying on my back kicking like a dolphin.

The translation? "Look Pedro, I can swim like a mermaid!"

I had no idea what I was saying and had trusted Kathryn not to embarrass me. Pedro and Dennis about wet their pants laughing.

I looked at Kathryn knowing that the response from Pedro and Dennis was not from me saying I swim well. Kathryn had set me up, and I was the goat! I asked Kathryn what she had me say.

Laughing hysterically, Kath stated, "I had you say that you swim like a mermaid."

Great! Thanks a lot, Kathryn—now my host father is going to be calling me a mermaid. My little host brothers were now laughing. Marisol and Sylvia were laughing. At that point I said to myself, "Just go with it, it's funny, who cares?" I laughed and started swimming like a mermaid right over to Kathryn. I grabbed her and gave her a good dunking. When she came up laughing, I asked if she saw any mermaids down there. Then I gave the funny girl another good dunking. Of course she came up laughing even harder. Next time, my guard would be up and there would be no more of these shenanigans, or of trusting Kathryn regarding translations. Make no mistake, Kathryn has a hysterical personality.

When the sun began to set, Kathryn and I packed the truck with the wheel grill, chairs, and the cooler. However, there was something missing—our driver, Dennis. He and my host father, Pedro, remained swimming in the lagoon, which made leaving a bit difficult. Marisol and the rest of us were ready to depart, but once Pedro and Dennis went in the water, they were not going to leave until they decided it was time. They kept yelling for me to come back into the water to show them how to swim like a mermaid. We all laughed as I offered Kathryn an evil eye, with a hint of humor in the form of a simultaneous grin. It took about a half hour, but the boys finally came around and we left the lagoon. The day had been a complete success.

Kathryn and I were forming the relationships we wanted with our host families, and their generosity, kindness, and patience was never-ending. We stopped on the way home at a scenic overlook and took some photos of the lagoon from the rim. It was beautiful! When we returned home, we helped to unload the truck and Kathryn packed her things.

After Kathryn said goodbye to my host family, I walked her to the bus stop and sent her on the way back to Masatepe. We had an excellent day together and Kathryn's leaving made me sad.

I studied Spanish, had a fun dinner with my host family, and then went to my "Harry Potter" closet to get some rest and ponder life in Central America. My back had been hurting all day, and right before nodding off to sleep, I grimaced with extreme pain. This unfolding health saga began to concern me. However, as I drifted off to sleep, high hopes and achievable expectations eased through my mind regarding future work in our communities.

11
Training Week 2
Spanish Classes and Animal Brutality

"Unless you try to do something beyond what you have already mastered, you will never grow."
–Ronald E. Osborn

The next day during Spanish class, our facilitator told us that we would be heading to Catarina's high school to introduce ourselves— our first experience in a classroom environment. The objective was to walk into a class that we would eventually teach and offer some personal information, which is what we had been practicing. Then we would observe the class.

Lee, Hollis and I, along with two Spanish professors, walked a mile to the school in sweltering heat. Seriously, it was so hot I could feel myself cooking on the inside! I felt pretty nervous about our activity for the day, but all went well. In the classroom, we offered our names and where we were from. Then we stated that we planned to teach a few classes in creativity and team-building in a few weeks, and that we would be using some different teaching styles. However, for now, we were only going to observe class, and we thanked the teachers for allowing us that opportunity. The kids received us well and with genuine excitement.

Nicaraguan schools are not what I would consider very conducive to learning. The school where we observed class was a completely open-air environment—which means that, while the school had walls, there were more windows than walls, and all the windows were barred like a jail, with no glass. The kids spoke at will, and many children stood outside the classroom looking in through the bars, talking to the children attending classes. Pieces of paper randomly flew, and the class was ridiculously noisy and without order. The students packed the classroom, but many kids did not have notebooks, and some children sat on the floor as there were not a sufficient number of desks. Hollis, Lee, and I observed fourth year students, which in the States would be the equivalent to juniors in high school. The teacher had possession of the only text book in the classroom. The temperature inside the classroom easily exceeded a hundred degrees, and no fan existed.

The teacher did her best to speak over the children. As you can imagine, this was a futile effort. Her voice could barely be heard, much less understood. I expected the learning environment to be difficult, but I wondered how these children could learn anything. If there was a classroom like this in the States, heads would roll for sure. I definitely realized that in order to be effective teaching in Nicaragua, we would have to set some ground rules and implement discipline. Our objective of our first classroom experience had been achieved and appeared to be a success.

That evening after dinner, while Pedro and I were trying to converse outside his house, a lady walked up holding an object in her hands with a stray-looking dog following her. Since the woman asked Pedro a question, I assumed she wanted to sell something. Pedro told the woman that he did not know if the family needed the product she had, but he gave her permission to enter the house and ask his wife. The lady walked into the home, and Pedro and I resumed our conversation.

The next thing I knew, all hell broke loose inside the house. The stray dog had somehow slipped past Pedro and gone into the home. Pedro and Marisol have a cute little dog named Tattoo who looks like a mixed mutt Cocker Spaniel. He was black in color and a bit testy from time to time. With the stray dog in the house, Tattoo went nuts, and the dogs began a ferocious fight. Women and children began screaming, and complete chaos ensued. Seeing what was happening, Pedro ran to his bus, pulled out a three-foot length of 2x4 wood, and ran back into the house where the dog fight was still in full rage. Pedro raised the 2x4 above his head with both hands and came down on that stray dog with one crushing blow across its back. I heard a distinctly loud crack, and could not tell if the impact had broken the stray dog's back or the 2x4. The stray yelped loudly in pain and fear, receiving an additional swift kick in the back-side from Pedro as it staggered out the door. The home momentarily became strangely silent.

I said nothing and stood dumbfounded in quiet disbelief. I had never experienced anything like that before. I had seen plenty of dog fights, but had never witnessed one broken up in that manner. I checked Pedro's 2x4, which had no damage. I suspected that the animal would soon perish.

The next day during applied Spanish class, I saw this stray dog on the streets of Catarina. It looked injured and did not move. I told my facilitator as best I could what happened the previous night. The facilitator reaffirmed what I gauged from my host family the night before by stating that it was the dog's fault for entering the house and he deserved what he got. I walked closely to the animal to have a positive interaction, but the dog snarled at me severely without moving his head. I let him be, hoping that his back was not broken, or worse. Remember, Pedro was very strong, and weighed about two hundred and forty pounds. I would be shocked if the dog did not die within a few days, and in fact, I never saw the little guy again. A brutal reality in Nicaragua is that dogs are beasts of burden, and no sympathy would be offered to a street-dwelling animal. I had witnessed a rough lesson about Nicaragua. It would not be the last.

12
Training Week 3
Language Humor, Learning About Dengue Fever and Malaria

"Live your life each day as you would climb a mountain. An occasional glance toward the summit keeps the goal in mind, but many beautiful scenes are to be observed from each new vantage point. Climb slowly, steadily, enjoying each passing moment; and the view from the summit will serve as a fitting climax for the journey."
–Harold V. Melchert

The third week of language training, similar to previous weeks, included class from 8 a.m. until noon, with conversational Spanish and business-specific vocabulary. Applied Spanish was from 1:00–3:00 p.m., practicing on the streets with local people what we had learned from the morning class. The Catarina boys were becoming much more efficient with the Spanish language. Our group, accustomed to the training routine, began having a lot of fun with our facilitators because we could now speak some Spanish.

One slip of the tongue from Lee, however, had him confusing the word for "year," which in Spanish is *"año,"* with the word for "anus," which is *"ano."* Without the tilde (the squiggly line above the n), the word is pronounced slightly different and has a completely different meaning. Lee kept saying things in Spanish like, "This anus was great!" Finally, Arabella stopped Lee to explain his mistake and what *"ano"* actually meant. An awkward moment passed as she patiently provided descriptive, yet socially-delicate hand gestures to get her point across. Once Arabella's message got through to all of us, Hollis and I fried Lee good for making an *"ano"* of himself in front of our professor. We knew to expect language mistakes and we all laughed, including Arabella.

On Wednesday we were scheduled for another training session with the Nica 35 Small Business group, which also meant that I would be able to visit with Kathryn. The session plan included a medically-related lesson about Dengue Fever and Malaria. I did not want to experience either infectious disease. However, there was a distinct possibility of contracting both in Nicaragua. We heard that we would learn exactly what happens to our bodies when we contract Malaria or Dengue Fever and how best to prevent infection.

The Peace Corps Medical staff first introduced us to Malaria, which is a serious parasitic infection transmitted to people through the bite of an infected female Anopheles mosquito. These mosquitoes bite at night from dusk until dawn. Parasites enter the body through the bite, migrate to the liver, and then enter the blood stream, infecting the red blood cells. From there, they multiply in the red blood cells, and the cells will then rupture within forty-eight to seventy-two hours, infecting more red blood cells and worsening the symptoms. This is one reason that Malaria symptoms occur in cycles of forty-eight to seventy-two hours. If the person who is bitten has taken the proper dosage of Chloroquine, an anti-Malaria medication, the symptoms should be less intense. Medication prevents transmission of the parasites in the bloodstream and eventually ends the course of the disease.

High humidity increases mosquito life-spans, and seasonal outbreaks of Malaria often occur around the rainy season. The rainy season in Nicaragua starts in mid-May, which brings high humidity.

We learned that Nicaragua had a high risk of Malaria throughout the country, and according to the Nicaraguan Health Ministry (MINSA), Nicaragua currently was experiencing the highest incidence of Malaria in the last twenty years. GREAT!

What are the symptoms of Malaria? The symptoms depend on the degree of immunity and prophylaxis. A person infected with Malaria will experience high fever, shaking, chills, and profuse sweats. They will also feel very tired, but then these symptoms will disappear. However, these episodes will re-occur every forty-eight hours, and in between, the person will feel relatively well. If left untreated, Malaria can cause anemia, kidney failure, coma and death. We recognized that we may very well have Malaria to look forward to during our service.

How would we prevent Malaria? The primary prevention tip indicated that we should be very careful from dusk to dawn. Cover up with light- or bright-colored, long-sleeved shirts, long pants, and socks. The Peace Corps staff also required us to sleep underneath mosquito nets. Further, they encouraged us to use citronella candles or mosquito coils that burn like incense. They also highly recommended that we use insect repellent and remove all sources of standing water in the immediate vicinity of our homes.

My first thought was, "fantastic, Kathryn and I can manage all of the above except for the very last suggestion." How would we remove all sources of standing water in and around our homes? For goodness sakes, I have five huge barrels of standing water right outside my back door that my family uses for household needs. Clearly those barrels of water made a mosquito haven, not to mention a few old tires holding water. Plus, a ditch along the side of our house always had dirty stagnant water in it that could easily breed large numbers of mosquitoes.

I could imagine the conversation—"Um...Marisol, I have a problem. All the standing water around your home is a serious health risk for your family and myself, and therefore must be removed." No way! I decided I could not say anything to Marisol. Kathryn would also not mention any of this to Natalia.

I would have to cover up from dusk until dawn. One thing was certain—no one could avoid mosquitoes. Thus far, every day and every night I had been chewed on thoroughly by those pesky little vectors of disease.

The Peace Corps required another prevention method, taking a drug called Chloroquine, which actually does not prevent Malaria but can reduce the severity of the symptoms and eliminate the infection much faster. Staff instructed us to take this drug weekly for our entire two-year service, and then for a month following our return to the States. *Aspirantes* immediately began grumbling, as rumor had it that Chloroquine could be harmful to our health if taken for long periods of time.

Diagnosis of Malaria relies on the identification of parasites in a blood smear and treatment consists of a higher dosage of Chloroquine under close medical supervision, or Doxycycline. By the end of this lesson, I was concerned about contracting Malaria.

The next topic addressed Dengue Fever, which Nicaraguans call the "Bone Crusher"—a wonderfully descriptive nickname for a very nasty viral infection. Like Malaria, mosquitoes also transmit Dengue Fever. The virus occurs chiefly in tropical regions around the world. Epidemic transmission is usually seasonal, happening during or shortly following the rainy season.

Outbreaks of Dengue have occurred with increasing frequency in recent years in most countries of the tropics. The risk is greatest in Central and South America, with lesser occurrence in Chile, Paraguay, and Argentina. High risk exists in Mexico, all of Africa, and the Caribbean, with the exception of Cuba and the Cayman islands.

As with Malaria, transmission of Dengue Fever is via a female mosquito, although of a different variety known as the Aedes mosquito. These nasty little ladies are most active during the day and have been found throughout the entire country of Nicaragua. Breeding grounds include water storage jars or barrels, flower pots, tin cans, discarded tires, sinks with water, and water accumulated from slow drainage in the streets or ditches. Basically, anywhere that water can sit, a mosquito can breed. Further, one single mosquito may infect every member of a household. Oh, this is just too good to be true! Say it ain't so.

The symptoms of Dengue Fever consist of very high fever, severe headaches (especially retro-orbital or behind the eyes), muscle and joint aches, severe back pain, nasty skin rashes, swollen lymph glands, and an extreme loss of energy. No wonder the Nicaraguans call this viral infection the "Bone Crusher." This beast creates severe pain and makes life absolutely miserable for the recipient.

Prevention of Dengue Fever, again, requires removal of potential mosquito breeding grounds and immediately eliminating any pools of water, which Kathryn and I knew could not be done around our homes. I planned to cover myself well with light- or bright-colored clothes, use a mosquito net, put insect repellent on exposed skin, screen my windows, burn citronella candles or mosquito coils—basically the exact same strategy as to prevent Malaria.

Then it hit me. The female Aedes mosquitoes that transmit Dengue are most active during the day. Therefore, at any point during a twenty-four hour period, we could be in danger of contracting either Malaria or Dengue. Malaria mosquitoes are most active from dusk until dawn, and then the next shift takes over and Dengue mosquitoes roam around during the day. Oh, this is just GREAT!

The diagnosis for Dengue Fever is not a sure thing and is mainly symptomatic. Is there a treatment? The information presented stated, "Bed rest, bed rest, bed rest, and bed rest! Tons of fluids! Tylenol for the headache and fever, and Ibuprofen for the pain." The translation in terms of the way I felt at that moment was, "Not a damn thing you can do about it!"

I had perceived becoming seriously ill while serving as a Volunteer as one of the severe disadvantages that Kathryn and I had listed as a distinct possibility when we were considering joining the Peace Corps. Now it was a definite reality, and I was concerned.

The best action to take was to not worry about it and to pay attention to prevention methods. I wanted to suggest to Kathryn that we wear long sleeves and pants all the time. However, a voice inside my head started screaming, "Are you crazy? It's 100 degrees every day. We will not suffocate ourselves for two years. The Nicaraguans survive these infections, we can too." I suppose the little voice had a point. For Kathryn and me, wearing long sleeves and long pants was not realistic. A sudden humorous vision came about of me wearing a mosquito net suit while teaching a high school class, with the kids laughing hysterically. The ridiculousness of the "net suit" humor drove home the point that we were going to live like Nicaraguans, and if infected, we would deal with the situation.

Kathryn and I spent about an hour together after the technical medical session, and it was a great pleasure to see her smile. The rest of the third week consisted of Spanish classes and more vaccinations, followed by an entertaining visit to the old market that looks like a castle, in the town of Masaya.

13
Training Week 4
Applied Spanish, Middle of the Night "Wake Up" Call,
Learning About Volunteer Sexual Assault

*"Quality is never an accident; it is always the result of high intention,
sincere effort, intelligent direction and skillful execution;
it represents the wise choice of many alternatives."*
–Willa A. Foster

The fourth week of training had the Catarina boys interviewing people around town to learn more about the economic culture of Nicaragua. We visited many different types of businesses. We would eventually have to give a presentation to the Nica 35 group about what we learned in our interviews and what our plan of action might be to resolve some of the problems. The bottom line, generally speaking, was that almost every business struggled for mere existence. Transportation emerged as a serious issue; none of the merchants had cars or trucks to bring products from Managua to Catarina or to open new markets in other towns. Accounting systems either did not exist, or they relied on an "I just know accounting" system. This type of system means the merchants do not write down any financial activity—they keep a record in their heads. Making change for customers would be a pervasive problem for everyone, and customer service was abysmal. As a small business trainee, I began to see many challenges with our job. Making small strides would be the name of the game by working within the Nicaraguan cultural structure.

On Wednesday, during the fourth week of training, Nica 35 met again as a group and discussed the small business classes that we planned to teach and how we would help guide our students to choose a product for their businesses. One of the main goals of our small business classes was to assist our students with starting a micro-business. We strived to equip them with the skills to think creatively about what types of products would actually be feasible. It was an interesting discussion, but I quickly learned that these businesses would be on a micro scale—almost equivalent to lemonade stands for kids in the States. However, there would be value in that our students would be learning the importance of accounting for their costs. Many people who I spoke with in Nicaragua thought that if you have revenue of $1, your profit is also $1. Obviously this perception was not a good situation.

During this fourth week, Kathryn and I finally figured out that we could spend the night together on Wednesdays in either Catarina or Masatepe. We could then wake up early and take a bus back to the other training town by the time Spanish class would start. Kathryn decided that she wanted to stay with me in Catarina on this particular Wednesday night. We traveled by bus back to Catarina to visit with Hollis Bennet's host family and watched WWF wrestling on TV with them. We found it pretty entertaining to see a sixty-year-old Nicaraguan man with no teeth really enjoy wrestling on TV. The father of this family, Manuel, would ask us constantly if it was real or not, and he would laugh hysterically when someone was body-slammed. We greatly appreciated Manuel's friendship.

Kathryn and I went to bed early as she had to wake at about 6 a.m. to make it back to Masatepe in time for Spanish class. Around midnight while we were sound asleep, a woman came running up to my house screaming for Marisol to come outside. We only heard yelling, with Pedro's name and bus peppered throughout the dialogue. I assumed that there was trouble and Marisol was needed. I pounced out of bed along with Kathryn. Immediately, I grabbed the first aid kit, a pocket knife, and a headlamp. We ran down the street about four blocks and found two buses in the middle of the road. I saw Pedro with grease and dirt all over his white t-shirt and his bus had a headlight knocked out. There was some other damage to his bus in the front end, and Pedro was engaged in a very heated conversation with another man, who was clearly the owner of the other bus. The police, thank goodness, had already arrived, and all five of the cops carried Russian-made AK-47s. Pedro looked like he may have been fighting. I loved this guy! Nothing like an accident in a huge old yellow school bus, and an argument in the middle of the street at midnight to keep life interesting in Nicaragua. About fifty people had gathered in the street, all of them in bed clothes. I asked a few people what happened, and nobody could tell me. I did not want to bother Pedro because he was talking to the police and Marisol at the same time. After about a half-hour of sitting on the curb with Kathryn, Marisol came over and said that all was well and that we should go home. She, however, would stay behind with Pedro. Kathryn and I followed her directions and retreated home.

The next morning I inquired about what happened, and Marisol told me, although it was hard to understand. Apparently, the owner of the other bus had hit Pedro's bus while Pedro was driving home and then the other driver tried to flee the scene. Pedro basically caught up to the other bus driver and blocked him with his bus in the middle of the road until the cops got there to straighten things out. On top of all the excitement, I thought the best part about this particular morning was Kathryn receiving the full impact of Pedro cranking his bus right outside of my window at 4:30 in the morning. This time Kathryn shot upright in bed out of panic, not me, and I laughed and laughed as she struggled to comprehend the noise and fumes from the bus.

She said, "You have got to be kidding me!" She could not believe that Pedro did this every day. I was quite proud of Pedro for his diligence about getting to work on time, especially after being up so late the previous night.

On Thursday, we learned that each Peace Corps trainee would be traveling away from their training towns on Saturday to visit with an actual Volunteer in that Volunteer's site (city, town, or community). This meant that Kathryn and I would be traveling around Nicaragua alone for the first time. The idea made me nervous, but I looked forward to the adventure.

On Friday, Nica 35 met again for a training session focused on the topic of sexual assault and rape. Our Country Director, Jeff Freeman, and the Peace Corps Regional Security Officer for the entire Latin American region presented us this information, which we all took very seriously. Sexual assault and rape happens to American Volunteers worldwide, and we learned about the statistics of those attacks. Understanding that it is never a woman's fault for being raped, we were provided some precautions that may help women recognize some vulnerabilities. We were told in no uncertain terms to be very careful and to always be aware of our surroundings. Jeff Freeman specifically said, "Just because a beach looks deserted, it doesn't mean there aren't people around. We should always remember that we are living in a third-world country and have our guard up at all times." The message emphasized that we should use good common sense.

We also learned what to do should an attack occur—who we contact, where we go, when the Peace Corps should be notified, and what the support process would be from the Peace Corps. Based on the serious nature of the topic and the tone of the presentation, it was obvious to me that Volunteer rape had definitely occurred in Nicaragua. The Peace Corps was doing everything it could to prevent this terrible crime, while at the same time, preparing Volunteers in the event sexual assault or rape happens.

The presentations of our Country Director and Regional Security Officer were educational, compassionate, intelligent, and most importantly, useful. Sadly, just as our three-month training came to an end, a woman from Nica 35 was raped. Subsequently, the Peace Corps medically-evacuated her to the United States. This disturbing situation drove home the fact that being a Peace Corps Volunteer in a third-world country is not something to be taken lightly and can be life-fulfilling or potentially devastating.

The Peace Corps staff brought some relief from such a serious topic by also informing us about which cities each trainee would be traveling to for their Volunteer visit over the weekend. We also received quite a preparation class for this Volunteer visit, complete with homework assignments regarding the cities we would be traveling to and the work that the Volunteers were doing at those sites. Our facilitators provided us with comprehensive packets full of valuable information on how to travel to the different cities safely, as well as how to contact the different Volunteers, where to stay, and how much we should be paying for all of the above. Kathryn and I were headed to Sandinista territory—the city of Estelí, Nicaragua in the northwestern mountains of the country.

Kathryn and I huddled over the reports and scoured them for information. All of the trainees were truly excited. The Nica 35 group asked each other questions about where everybody else was going to travel. A few trainees received some tough places to visit due to difficult methods of transportation. One trainee had to travel to a river town called El Castillo, which involved a ten-hour bus trip and then a three-hour boat ride. He was heading out to the jungle on the Río San Juan and was in for a real adventure.

After receiving and discussing our Volunteer visit preparation reports, we had only one more *charla* (lesson) remaining for the day, which was on gender and development. We would receive a series of *charlas* on that subject matter during our service. Kathryn and I viewed gender and development as a very important topic and quite necessary for successful projects to exist on a sustainable basis. To effectively approach or work within a community, a Volunteer has to clearly understand the division of labor between the different genders. If a Volunteer initiates a project in a community without understanding gender and development within that culture, failure could occur in short order.

Two current Volunteers provided the *charla* on gender and development, and they were both very knowledgeable about the subject and hardened with legitimate field experience. After discussing the matter, Kathryn and I agreed that this day of training had been particularly enlightening.

We left the training being very excited regarding our upcoming travel and the opportunity to learn about different projects managed by the Volunteers in Estelí. Our Volunteer visit would be with another married couple who lived in Estelí. I spent the night with Kathryn in Masatepe, and we woke up Saturday morning bright and early to make sure we could make all of our bus connections to the mountainous northwestern part of the country.

We caught a bus from Masatepe to Managua; the end destination for this leg of the trip was Huembes—that crazy terminal we had encountered earlier in our training. We then had to take a taxi across Managua to another bus station called Mayoreo. Being that we had to take a cab anyway, Kathryn and I thought it best to try and avoid Huembes altogether if possible. We got off the first bus before Huembes at a place called Quetzal, which was close to Huembes, but a block or two away and much less hectic. We then took a cab across the city to the Mayoreo bus station. Mayoreo was so much calmer than Huembes, it's not even comparable. Kathryn and I were very happy to not be harassed. We then had a decision to make—do we take a *ruta* or an *expresso?*

There were generally three types of buses in Nicaragua. One was called an *expresso* (express). These were usually big school buses, but they could also be what we called a "pretty bus," which was more upscale than a school bus. However, a few *expresso* buses were really nice and had TVs—although the TVs never worked. After leaving the city of Managua, *expresso* buses generally only stopped once or twice on route to their destination. We were told these buses were the preferred choice if you want to get somewhere as fast as possible and be reasonably comfortable. The *expressos* were the most expensive form of public transportation in Nicaragua.

Another type of bus was called a *micro-bus*. The *micro-bus* was usually very uncomfortable, as they packed in as many people as humanly possible. These *micro-buses* were not actually buses at all—they were minivans that had been converted to carry about eight more people. Imagine an average minivan in the States, and then picture up to seventeen people crammed into it, with no air conditioning, in ninety- to a hundred-degree heat and the windows down. That's a *micro-bus* experience—tough traveling.

The last type of bus in Nicaragua was called a "*ruta*" (route or ordinary). *Ruta* buses were always old school buses or worse, and they could be a nightmare to travel on if you were in a hurry, as they were consistently packed with about one hundred seventy people. *Rutas* traveled unbelievably slowly as they stopped for anyone at any time. They usually wouldn't travel more than a mile or two without picking someone up, and can stop as many as eight or nine times in one mile. These buses carried anything that can be hauled on top of the bus, and it usually would take a long time to transfer the packages from the top of the bus to the ground, or vice-versa. *Ruta* buses carried goats, pigs, chickens, etc. on top of the vehicle and would stop at the whim of the driver for as long as the driver needed to do his errands in the different towns. If a trip would normally take three hours on an *expresso*, you could tack on at least another two-and-a-half hours on a *ruta*. *Rutas* were the least expensive form of transportation in Nicaragua and the most uncomfortable.

All of this was on my mind when Kathryn and I arrived at the Mayoreo bus station because we had to decide what kind of transportation to use. The decision was made a little easier for us because *micro-buses* were not even an option leaving from Mayoreo. We knew we did not want to take a *ruta*, but if there were no *expressos* available, we would be forced to travel slowly. Luckily, we found a normal *expresso* heading to Estelí, and it left almost as soon as we arrived at the terminal. This trip looked good already.

When we boarded the *expresso,* we *looked* around the bus and saw at least three other Peace Corps trainees from Nica 35 who were heading to the northwest mountains of Nicaragua as well. They would transfer buses again before arriving in Estelí.

We moved through Managua, and I was again shocked by the poverty and inspired at the same time by the determination of Nicaraguans to survive under difficult circumstances. Once outside the city of Managua, the bus cruised along at about fifty miles an hour on the Pan-American Highway through majestic farmland. After an hour of travel, our bus began to lumber and wind its way into the mountains. Leaving the flat farmland behind us, we entered a much more rugged and rustic region of the country. The mountains were green and lush, thick with large trees, and the *campo* (farm) houses dotted the countryside. "Gorgeous" is the only way to describe Nicaragua's landscape.

Once into the higher elevations, Kathryn and I practically broke our necks trying to look out the bus windows to see down into the various mountain ravines for whitewater rivers. We were already scouting for the first descent down a river untouched by kayaks that we had talked about before joining the Peace Corps. This trip provided us an opportunity to research different riverbeds, but nothing revealed itself. We began to realize that finding a first descent in Nicaragua was not going to be easy. If there was any whitewater to be opened up in this country, it would probably be remote and challenging to locate.

As the bus made its way into Estelí, Kathryn and I were thrilled to find a nice-sized town nestled in the mountains. It kind of reminded me of a third-world Boulder, Colorado. The bus pulled into the south terminal, called Cotran Sur. However, our travel report told us that we needed to go to Cotran Norte, the northern bus station in Estelí.

Kathryn told me, "This is the south terminal. I don't understand why we are here because we need the northern terminal."

I said, "Well, ask the guy if the bus will be going to Cotran Norte when they leave Cotran Sur."

Kath asked, and we were told "no," that this was the end of the line. I got a little upset because Kath had asked the same man when we boarded in Managua, if this bus would go to Cotran Norte and his answer had been "yes." Now they told us that the bus does not go to Cotran Norte. I motioned for this person to come back and speak with us again. I told him in my best Spanish that he had originally told us the bus would take us to Cotran Norte, and that we need to go to Cotran Norte so they should take us there.

The guy looked at me like I was crazy. He walked to the front of the bus, talked to the driver, and then came back to me and said, "okay."

I thought, "Wow! It worked! My Spanish is getting better."

All other passengers had exited the bus. Kathryn and I sat all alone as the bus departed Cotran Sur, travelled north for exactly two blocks, and then pulled into Cotran Norte. Ugh. I felt like such an idiot!

The driver said, "Here we are—Cotran Norte."

I said, "Thank you very much," and Kathryn and I got off the bus while the driver laughed.

Once off the bus, we also laughed with the bus driver and waved goodbye to him. We had just talked them into going an extra two blocks for the *gringos*. However, the scenario, while embarrassing and humorous, also demonstrated to us that Nicaraguans were willing to go out of their way to help tourists, which was exactly what we were at the moment.

Walking out of Cotran Norte, we knew that we needed to meet the Volunteers at their home, which should be close by. We only had to walk a few blocks to the west from the terminal.

When we arrived at the home of Erin and Mike Gerba, we were quite surprised to find a little party. Several Volunteers who worked in the surrounding areas of Estelí had come to town. Even better, the great Erin and Mike Gerba had prepared food that Americans were accustomed to eating. They had made pasta salad, brownies, hot dogs, and hamburgers—it was heaven! I did not even know you could make that sort of food in Nicaragua. All we had been eating in our training towns was pretty much rice and beans, chicken, and some sort of mystery meat. It was in that moment of eating their wonderful food that I realized living in Nicaragua would be much easier if we could consume food that we were more used to eating.

I cannot emphasize strongly enough how uncomfortable, at least for me, eating Nicaraguan food could be over long periods of time. I liked beans and rice and chicken, but every day? It gets old fast! Try eating beans and rice three meals a day and see how long it takes before you find yourself dreaming of a basic plate of spaghetti or a standard hamburger. I'll tell you how long it took me to start dreaming for other food—about one week.

I now knew that we had access to American food somewhere in this country, and I began to quiz Erin and Mike about which markets and stores had the food I desired. Without question, I thanked Erin and Mike at least ten times for cooking. The *fiesta* lasted through lunch, and afterwards, the other Volunteers left for their respective sites (small towns) around Estelí. We began our formal Volunteer visit by having a discussion with Erin and Mike about their projects. Kathryn and I had a great deal to learn within a short period of time, as we had to be back in our training towns by Wednesday of the next week.

14
Training Week 5
Volunteer Visit, Folkloric Dance, Adventurous Hike
"God does not command us to do great things,
only little things with great love."
–Mother Teresa

Our goal for the first part of week number 5 was to successful-ly complete our Volunteer visit. As trainees, we had a laundry list of questions to ask the Volunteers as our homework. In all, there were two pages of assignments and activities to accomplish during this time spent with active Volunteers. As an example of our many assignments, we had to write a report accurately describing the primary project of the host Volunteer, including what their successes and challenges had been thus far. We had to identify the key elements that facilitated posi-tive results or ascertain what impeded the achievement of the Volun-teer's goals. We also had to include all activities during the visit, such as meeting the Volunteer's counterpart. The term "counterpart" is used in reference to a Nicaraguan who has been identified to work with a Volunteer on projects. We had to visit the Volunteer's schools, observe their classes, and write about what we had learned. We had to visit the local police station and speak with them about various different safety issues, and if time permitted, we were to speak with the Mayor about the town. These were only the first few assignments that we were tasked to complete while in Estelí.

Mike and Erin undoubtedly worked hard in Estelí, and one thing became absolutely crystal clear—the majority of our time and ener-gy, as Volunteers, would be dedicated to teaching business classes to fourth- and fifth-year (junior and senior high school) students. Other projects could be initiated, but there would not be a lot of time during the week to work on them.

Kathryn and I accomplished everything on our assignment list and we thoroughly enjoyed our visit with Mike and Erin. Wednesday morn-ing rolled around, and Kath and I headed out of Estelí back to our training towns. We departed with a different perspective about Volun-teer life. If we could survive training, life would be a little easier on us, as we could have more freedom to develop our own projects and eat as we pleased. Most importantly, Kathryn and I would live together under one roof.

Now in the middle of the fifth week of training, Nica 35 used all of Wednesday to travel back to our training towns. Then we needed to write our reports.

During Thursday morning's Spanish class, each trainee presented Volunteer visit reports to their classmates. I learned about two other towns in Nicaragua that Hollis and Lee had traveled to, and I heard about the projects of the Volunteers living in those towns. I presented my report as well and told my group how much Kathryn and I loved Estelí.

On Friday, Nica 35 traveled about twenty minutes to San Marcos for our group technical training sessions. Our first *charla* of the day provided suggestions about how to deal with students regarding money and the conflicts that can arise from starting micro-businesses. The second *charla* was from our teaching manual, and we learned how to effectively give lessons on simple accounting to our students.

The last group session on Friday consisted of the "Volunteer Site Forum," which was held to discuss all the different potential site possibilities for Nica 35. This was a scary meeting for Kathryn and me because we were told that El Castillo and San Carlos were potential locations for a couple, and there were only two couples in Nica 35. El Castillo is 13 to 15 hours from any sizeable community, and San Carlos was not much better. We did not want to live that far away from modern conveniences, but would do so if necessary.

We spoke with the other couple in Nica 35, Christi and Hollis Bennet, and it was obvious they did not want to work in those towns either. There were only two other site possibilities for couples—Estelí and León. When we found out that Estelí was a site possibility for a couple, Kathryn and I were immediately charged with energy and excitement. We thought Estelí would be a fantastic place to live and work for two years. Kathryn and I spoke more with Christi and Hollis, and we told them that we loved Estelí. They said that was great as they wanted to live and work in León. Oh, how perfectly the world goes around.

Our entire group stirred with good energy about the Volunteer Site Forum. At least we now knew the possibilities. A strange thing about the Peace Corps was that they could really keep us in suspense, but

I suppose it's part of the process of being placed in a site. The Program Director had to match the trainees to the different sites, so the Director needed time to get to know the group before he could decide where to send Volunteers. Deciding where a trainee serves is not just pulling names out of a hat; there is a definite process to choosing who goes where.

Kathryn and I decided that our chances of having Estelí as our site were pretty good since Hollis and Christi wanted León, and none of us wanted El Castillo. We didn't think that there was anything in particular wrong with the community of El Castillo other than it's fifteen hours away from the nearest decent-sized town.

For all the other trainees, it was a free-for-all mentality. No one knew much more than they did the day before, except that the cities mentioned were now site possibilities. Everyone tried to lay claim to one town or another, and it made me laugh listening to trainees discuss why they thought they should be the one chosen for a particular site. For example, while the trainees were clamoring for their desired sites, I overheard "My Spanish is better than yours," or "I am more experienced with remote areas than you are."

Nonetheless, everyone left training that day in good spirits, and the weekend was upon us. The Nica 35 group made plans to meet Sunday morning in Catarina for all those who wanted to hike from the top of the Mirador in Catarina down to the lagoon.

Friday night Kathryn and I laid pretty low in Masatepe. We ate dinner and then went to the internet café to call home and send some emails out to our friends. We fell asleep by about 11:00 p.m. At around 2:00 a.m., we were awakened by a loud explosion type of sound. We both sat upright with a little fear and said to each other, "What the hell was that?" We finally concluded that a papaya tree that hung over the house had dropped its fruit, and the fruit had landed on the tin roof with a loud boom. Imagine someone dropping a ten pound rock on a tin roof right above your head at two o'clock in the morning while you are sleeping. It's an unnerving experience. Good ole' Nicaragua.

Saturday night was Kathryn's host sisters' folkloric dance presentation in Masatepe, and the event had everyone in the house preparing for the occasion. I helped the boys of the house shine shoes, while the girls made jewelry, selected ribbons for their hair, and tried on their presentation wardrobe. The next thing I knew, the girls had put Kathryn in one of their folkloric dresses. When Kathryn walked out of Isabella's room and I saw her in one of those brightly-colored, beautifully-detailed, flowing Spanish-style dresses, I could not believe my eyes. She looked incredible! A little out of place, but nonetheless, lovely. The girls of the house ran around Kathryn fussing over the dress and telling her how beautiful she was. Kathryn enjoyed the attention.

I immediately jumped out of the rocking chair and ran to grab the camera. Kathryn walked outside in the sunlight, and I snapped a few photos of her in the folkloric dress. Everyone in the house appreciated the moment with smiles all around. The girls of the house then decided it would be fun to have Kathryn try on all the different dresses. For the next forty-five minutes, Kathryn, indeed became the center of attention as she tried on at least six or seven different dresses, complete with matching ribbons for her hair and jewelry. Each dress was a customized, handmade work of art.

Once Kathryn's parade of dresses ended, it was time to leave for the presentation. We wished the girls well as they departed carrying their costumes. Everyone who remained in the house changed into their best clothes for the evening's festivities.

As we walked through town, it was easy to determine who was attending the dance presentation and who was not, as people really dressed up for this event. Natalia was famous on this particular evening, as she had made many of the dresses for the dance group. She greeted a lot of different people as we continued through town, and I felt like we were part of an entourage walking with the Mayor. Of course, having two Americans by her side added to the social occasion for Natalia, and Kathryn and I enjoyed the opportunity to meet new people.

When we arrived at the small, open-air amphitheater, we found seats reserved for all of us toward the front. The family, along with Kathryn and me, took up a whole row of plastic chairs. As the dancers entered the stage, the lights dimmed, the crowd quieted, the music began, and I felt like I was on a very special date with my wife at the Kennedy Center in Washington, D.C. for a true cultural event. Knowing the incredible performers further enhanced our appreciation of the festivities. Kathryn's host sisters and the entire dance group were talented, graceful, and very elegant in their beautifully-flowing, Latino-style dresses. They were all professional-caliber entertainers.

The dance presentation was a huge success, and Kathryn and I were thrilled to have been invited. We spoke with the girls after the event and congratulated them on a job well done and shared with them how much we loved their dancing. Everywhere we looked people were happy, and the other dancers laughed and told stories about different things that happened during the presentation. The families of the performers were elated for their loved ones.

I had just thought that the evening was a complete success when fireworks started going off above us. Everyone loved it and screamed in a final celebration. Joining the Peace Corps proved to be quite a good decision on this particular evening. However, I knew that there would be rough days ahead.

Sunday was another great day as many Nica 35 trainees met in Catarina to hike down to the lagoon. Standing at the top of the Mirador provides a view of the lagoon a thousand to fifteen-hundred feet below, with lush jungle guarding the entire area. However, a trail does exist that traverses along the edge of the Mirador, and then descends through the jungle, culminating at the lagoon.

I had no chance of participating in this activity, as my back hurt, and hiking that steep ravine would do nothing to help the situation. I planned to visit with Hollis Bennet's host brother, who lived next to the park, while Kathryn joined the hikers.

I naturally assumed that the group going on the hike would ask for directions, find the trail, and descend to the lagoon together. I am not sure why, but apparently the group split up into small factions. Each hiking party headed out in completely different directions, yet there was only one legitimate trail down to the water. Somebody was in for a tough day. I was completely oblivious to this situation as I went to hang out with Manuel.

At about 5:30 that evening, Manuel and I started to get a little worried, as no one had returned. We talked about the trail to the lagoon, and he told me it should not be that difficult. What we did not understand was that no one from the group had started their hike using the proper path. They all began on small trails and ended up bushwhacking their way down to the water through the jungle. About twenty minutes before dark, the group—almost as a whole—came walking through town from the Mirador. Manuel and I went out to the street to greet them and inquire about how the day had gone.

Everyone was laughing, so my initial impression was that the adventure must have turned out okay. Kathryn told me that different people became tired of waiting for the entire group to arrive at the top of the overlook and decided to go down separately. The prevailing idea was that everyone would eventually end up at the same place—the lagoon. However, this did not happen. Kathryn's group picked a trail and hiked almost to the bottom only to be completely shut off by a hundred-foot cliff. Her group turned around and climbed all the way back to the top, but not before one of them almost inadvertently grabbed a snake wrapped around a tree limb. Once again at the top, only then did they ask directions for the trail. They found the correct path, and arrived at the lagoon expecting to see the others, but no one else appeared. Kathryn's small group decided to go for a swim and then hike out. The other *aspirantes* were not seen until the end of the day.

A few of the trainees, who were not in Kathryn's group, told me later that they literally had to do some rock climbing and worked their way down very slowly and cautiously. Every trainee had gone swimming in the lagoon, but in different places and at various times. One group decided they did not want to climb back up the way they came down and found a road to walk on. Eventually those people hitched a ride back to Catarina. Kathryn and the group she hiked with were the only ones to actually use the official trail to the lagoon and back. Indeed, somebody had a tough day. We were just happy a search party was not necessary and that everyone had a fine adventure.

15
Training Week 6
Routine, Unique Businessman, Language Exam
"All things are difficult before they are easy."
–John Norley

Week six of training started out as usual with Spanish classes in the morning and applied Spanish in the afternoons. On Wednesday, the Nica 35 class went to meet a unique businessman just outside of Catarina. I call him "unique" because he was successful and actually trained his employees to eventually compete against him. Don Emerson was his name, and his company made beautiful, custom-designed furniture. The Nica 35 group toured his facility and spoke with him for approximately an hour about how the business started, his accounting system, and the manner in which he exported products to other countries. We appreciated the informative tour, and the employees seemed to be very loyal as they knew that Don Emerson was helping them to begin their own business ventures.

Our language proficiency exam that tells the Peace Corps how we are progressing with Spanish was scheduled for Thursday. I woke up that day very nervous, and some of the other trainees did not help me with the situation as they exited their interviews filled with anger and frustration. One particular trainee literally threw a fit, cussing and yelling about how terribly he had performed. For me this was almost comical because the guy was a perfectionist, and I felt quite sure that he had done very well.

The language interview was tough. I did not really feel like I did a good job, but what could I do about it? I had been studying as hard as I could and learning rapidly, but since I did not know more than a few words of Spanish upon arrival in the country, six weeks of study would not make me fluent. I hoped to have progressed two proficiency levels from where I had started. Kathryn came out of her interview feeling like she could have done much better as well. We would receive language exam results the following week.

On Friday, Nica 35 met in the central park of San Marcos and a Peace Corps bus carried us to our weekly technical classes. During the session, we discussed feasibility studies, break even points, and writing business plans. Week six was busy and very informative, yet it had a feeling of being quite settled into a routine. I appreciated the feeling of routine as up to that point of training, our lives had been constantly changing. The six-week mark offered a relief from travel and stress, and I noted it as the week that I began to feel at home in a new country.

16
Training Week 7
Teaching, Health Issue, Mystery Solved, Site Placement

*"Make no little plans; They have no magic to stir people's blood
and probably themselves will not be realized. Make big plans;
aim high in hope and work, remembering that a noble,
logical diagram once recorded will not die."*
–Daniel H. Burnham

Week seven was also routine, except that this week required the Catarina boys to teach a class. I felt relieved knowing that we were going to teach the class together. Hollis, Lee, and I planned meticulously all week, and each person had a responsibility to teach a section of the overall lesson. We rehearsed the *charla* in front of our Spanish teacher, and she corrected our Spanish when needed. We were prepared from the language perspective and our lesson plan was solid. We would be teaching the concept of how to work together in larger groups.

We wanted to make the lesson fun and impart the concept in a manner completely different from typical Nicaraguan teaching methods. We planned different scenes that the kids would have to act out in groups. We would explain the scene to them, and then each group would have five minutes to plan how they were going to act it out in front of the entire class. One scenario involved a bus that crashed when the driver had a heart attack because he almost hit a horse that crossed in front of his vehicle. This was a scene that could actually happen in Nicaragua, and we thought that the kids would be eager to take on the task. We planned four different scenes for about sixty-five kids.

The class went over quite well; the kids certainly learned about group dynamics and had a fun time in the process. One thing became clear—they had never had a class like ours in their entire educational career. Lee, Hollis, and I left the school pleased with the results, and our Spanish teachers gave us some constructive criticism following the class. The Catarina boys began to believe that we would actually be able to teach effectively; all we needed to do was plan and practice.

During the seventh week of training, some serious issues came to the forefront. One was that Lee and Hollis had not been healthy since they had arrived at their training families' homes in the first week, which meant that they had been sick for seven weeks! Lee had acquired a parasite on the first night with his host family. The little critter inside Lee's stomach was wreaking havoc on him. He had to travel to Managua several times for treatment, but nothing seemed to work. I really felt for Lee when he would be talking to me and then all of a sudden double over from pain, grab his stomach, and run to the bathroom. I witnessed these episodes frequently.

A severe stomach ailment afflicted Hollis as well – so much so that while engaged in conversation, he would jump out of his seat without a word and run to the latrine. Nothing needed to be said—obviously Hollis was very ill. While this situation could very easily be made fun of, I could not make jokes when someone was clearly in pain. Hollis ran to the bathroom so often that his host family gave him the nickname "*El Corredor*" (the runner). That was funny! Sometimes the name really fit, and for Hollis there was no escaping it. He also had to travel to Managua several times for treatment. Hollis had good days and bad days, but his pain continued.

The health situation for Hollis and Lee heightened my paranoia of what I ate and drank. I was so ridiculously careful that I would always ask if something I was about to drink was made with purified water. If there was not a response confirming purified water, or the person didn't know, the refreshment would not be consumed. We had been warned in training that not accepting a beverage offered to you could be offensive, but I didn't care if I had to offend someone or not. I always explained that I had a weak stomach. People generally understood, and being offensive was avoided due to my weak stomach, not their bad water. Lee and Hollis, however, could not bring themselves to say "no"—or didn't care—and as a result, became ill.

The seventh week brought an extremely problematic health issue to the forefront for me. As if dodging stomach bombs was not enough, my back pain increased significantly. I could tell something was seriously wrong and that I had hurt myself in a way that could not be fixed with stretching and light exercise. I constantly felt severe pain—enough that I recognized my Peace Corps service might be in jeopardy and that I had to speak with Kathryn about the situation.

I described to Kath the pain I endured, and we discussed the fact that Peace Corps might send me back to the States for treatment. If I had to return to the States during training, Peace Corps would probably medically separate me and my service would be over because I would miss at least a quarter of the training process. Endangering our service was not desirable. We decided that I would tell the Peace Corps that I had pulled a muscle and it was causing pain. For all I knew, the source of discomfort may have been a pulled muscle. I reflected on the fact that I had hurt my back lifting bags onto the bus the first day in-country, but I had also hurt myself from a fall playing basketball. The injury seemed like a lot more than a pulled muscle.

The Peace Corps provided Ibuprofen and a few other instructions to help the situation. I knew, however, that this health problem would not vanish on its own and that I needed to be extremely careful. The crazy thing was that all physical activity could be accomplished—walking, running, lifting, jumping, etc. Anything could be done, it just hurt. The strategy I pursued included stretching twice a day and generally taking it easy.

The seventh week consisted of many significant events. On Wednesday, we had plans to meet with our Program Director to talk about our site placement; on Thursday, we would receive the results from our language interview; and on Friday, we would be informed of our final site placement.

Kathryn and I met with the Small Business Program Director, Alberto Gonzales, separately on Wednesday and discussed the different possibilities for site placement. Kath and I agreed that we did not want to live 13 to 15 hours from civilization for a myriad of reasons. The thought of isolation did not appeal to us. When we spoke with Alberto, we both shared with him how much we loved Estelí and that we did not want to live for two years in a remote community, if it wasn't necessary. We mentioned the fact that Hollis and Christi wanted to live in León and that left just one other city available to couples—Estelí. If Alberto decided that he wanted us to work in Río San Juan or El Castillo, we would not have a choice and would be separated from practically all civilization for two years. Alberto understood our concerns completely, and he wanted us to live where we felt we would be most effective and comfortable. Alberto did not tell us that we would be assigned to Estelí as our permanent site; he said that he would "consider the issues" and that we would find out the final decision on Friday.

Thursday brought technical training sessions for our small business classes that focused on budgets and capitalization, accounting, and marketing plans. In the afternoon we received our language interview results. Kathryn had done well, she progressed nicely and was now considered an advanced speaker. I had not achieved my goal of jumping two levels. However, Hollis and Lee had brought themselves up to their goals of intermediate-level speakers. I knew I had to step up my studying quite a bit because I had to be speaking at an intermediate-middle level by the time training ended—or my service was over! Yes, I was worried; but Kathryn did not seem the least bit concerned, and offered to help me when she could.

Friday proved to be a great day, an embarrassing day, and an enlightening day. However, it started out horribly. For the first seven weeks of training, I had tried to avoid the bathroom as much as humanly possible by only using the restroom when my family was out of the house for privacy's sake. Pedro left the house at 4:30 in the morning like always, and Marisol was gone by 6 a.m. to Managua to buy food for her restaurant. Diego and little Pedro were gone to school by 7:30 a.m. That left the house empty except for me until 8 a.m. and I thought it would be safe to use the restroom with everyone gone.

The Peace Corps had stressed that electricity was expensive and that we should conserve energy whenever possible. Consequently, I did not turn on the lights in the house or in the bathroom, thinking I could eliminate some energy costs for the family. However, one morning when the sun was out and the inside lights were not necessary, I was using the restroom—sitting down with quite a load. Suddenly, I heard a noise in the house and froze in wretched terror. There was nothing I could do! Then I remembered, "oh no... no, no, no!! The neighbors!!" The neighbors used my host family's bathroom because they didn't have one. Sure enough, I heard fast approaching footsteps. Before I could move or say anything, the plastic curtain covering the doorway of the bathroom was ripped open, and there stood my next door neighbor's beautiful little nine-year old girl, Lenora. I could do nothing but sit there with my drawers around my ankles in horrified embarrassment, and poor little Lenora, bless her, looked traumatized.

"Disculpe!" ("sorry," or "excuse me, it's my fault"), she screamed with her hands over her mouth and eyes as she ran out of the house.

Demoralized, my face dropped and rested in my hands with a cheek in each palm. I thought, "How is that beautiful little girl ever going to recover from the trauma of seeing a grown man sitting on the toilet?! How am I ever going to face her again?"

Agh, I haven't felt that embarrassed in a long time, and one thing was certain—I would find out how to let people know someone was in the bathroom!! I could yell out *"ocupado"* (occupied) if I heard some-one coming, but that seemed embarrassing too. Surely there must be a way to signal that the bathroom was in use. That was the embarrassing part of my Friday, and the question of the bathroom "signal" would have to be resolved quickly!

When Marisol returned home that evening, the first thing I did was ask her how people know if the bathroom is occupied.

Marisol said, "Easy, turn on the lights."

Tight lipped at first, I nodded and said, "thanks."

This was the enlightening part of my Friday. Had I thought about it seven weeks ago, I could have saved myself not only an extreme amount of discomfort waiting to use the bathroom, but also the day's embarrassing humiliation if I had only asked the appropriate question my very first day! And yet, I could not have asked at that time because I didn't know enough Spanish. My strategy to avoid the bathroom de-layed the need for the question to be asked. The other lesson I experi-enced that day was that I should not always follow Peace Corps' advice to the letter, and that different situations merit some interpretation. Yes, electricity may be expensive; but you need to let people know that the bathroom is occupied if you want to maintain your privacy. I felt like an idiot. Live and learn.

The great part about Friday entailed Kathryn and I learning that our permanent site placement would be Estelí, Nicaragua. Fantastic project opportunities existed in Estelí, and we would be able to remain in contact with our families and friends. We would also be working in the northern mountains where the climate is much cooler. Knowing that we would live in Estelí for two years was very exciting news!

One of our biggest concerns before we entered the Peace Corps was where would we be posted for our service. We had many ques-tions: Would we be safe? Are there communication capabilities, such as phone and internet within 10 miles? Would there be good opportunities for our project(s) to succeed? The city or community where Volunteers are placed can potentially impact the quality of their service. For example, some Volunteers who lived on the east coast of Nicaragua during our training were exposed to increased safety issues.

17
Training Week 8
Trainee Assault, Counterpart Day, Site Visit

"The credit belongs to the person who is actually in the arena, whose face is marred by dust and sweat and blood; who strives valiantly; who errs and comes short again and again, who knows the great enthusiasms, the great devotions, and spends himself or herself in a worthy cause; who at the best, knows the triumph of high achievement; and who, at the worst, if he or she fails, at least fails while daring greatly, so that their place shall never be with those cold and timid souls who know neither victory nor defeat."
–Theodore Roosevelt

Throughout week eight, the Small Business Sector trainees learned more about safety issues in Nicaragua. Nica 35, as a whole, was comprised of two sectors: Youth Development on the Atlantic Coast of Nicaragua, and Small Business Development on the west coast, which was my group. Communication with the Youth Group trainees on the Atlantic Coast region did not really exist because the areas are remote.

During week eight, we had heard that a person from the Youth Sector on the Atlantic Coast had been raped. We later received information confirming that a trainee from Nica 35 had been raped by her host brother. This was an especially delicate situation because Peace Corps had been responsible for placing this person in a potentially dangerous home. The facts were not shared, which made jumping to inaccurate conclusions, based on the limited information we had, difficult to avoid. Nonetheless, the news of rape was extremely disturbing for everyone, and many questions needed to be addressed by Peace Corps leadership.

Recognizing the sensitivities of this occurrence, a Volunteer told us that the victim was physically okay, but that she was having to deal with the mental and emotional trauma of being assaulted. Kathryn and I knew the victim to be a very strong person, but we learned she would be sent back to the States for counseling. The troubling realization of safety concerns hit home hard for everyone, as it was now a reality. The training group on the Atlantic Coast struggled with serious problems, and they had become a little edgy.

Nicaragua's Country Director, Jeff Freeman, immediately flew to the Atlantic Coast to listen to everyone's concerns and to reassure them that the Peace Corps' absolute, number-one priority was the trainees' and Volunteers' safety. Mr. Freeman told them what the Peace Corps had already done about the situation, what would be pursued in the future regarding prosecution, as well as what steps were being taken to make sure this type of situation did not happen again. However, the fact remained that no matter what Peace Corps did to ensure security, no one on the planet can guarantee your safety.

Jeff's assurances regarding Peace Corps' security policy were not good enough for two trainees, and they early terminated the training program. Jeff Freeman is a stand-up guy, a great leader, and an experienced, highly competent professional; however, he could not guarantee a person's safety. How could he? How could anyone?

There are many legitimate reasons to terminate your service, and safety is at the top of the list. My sense was that there were no hard feelings from the Nica 35 Small Business Sector regarding the early terminations. We were all dealing with our own safety issues from a mental perspective, and everyone could understand why these two trainees early terminated.

Kathryn and I knew when we started this adventure that some people would not finish their service, and that it still could very well be us! During our orientation in Granada, Kathryn and I discussed that we had no intention of "persevering" during our time in the Peace Corps. If one of us felt we needed to leave for whatever reason, or we decided we could no longer contribute to our community in a positive way, we would leave as a couple.

Within eight weeks, Peace Corps had returned four *aspirantes* to the States—three early terminations plus the person who was sexually assaulted, although she would eventually return to Nicaragua. As mentioned previously, where the Peace Corps sends a Volunteer can potentially impact his or her service, depending on the circumstances. For the most part, Volunteers have to work wherever Peace Corps assigns them. Sometimes, through no fault of the trainee/Volunteer, people have to make very difficult personal decisions about whether they feel safe enough to continue with their service. If a person does not feel safe, the next action is simple— pack your bags and go home. Everyone felt badly for all of the *aspirantes* who had to return to the States due to various different circumstances.

Up to this point, Kathryn and I had been incredibly lucky to have lived with and learned from two great host families, as well as two outstanding communities in Catarina and Masatepe. We had received the news that we would be living and working in Estelí for the next two years. We had visited Estelí already and felt like we could get along pretty well there, and for the most part, we felt safe. The pieces of the adventurous puzzle seemed to be falling into place nicely for us.

Most of week eight was filled with worry and concern for the *aspirantes* on the Atlantic Coast, but our training continued. Spanish classes occurred as scheduled on Monday and Tuesday. Wednesday's sessions included a substantial amount of information about working with counterparts in our communities. The Peace Corps requires that the host school in each site select a "counterpart" to work with the respective Volunteer in that community. The purpose of having a counterpart is to offer the Volunteer support in his or her efforts, and to provide an opportunity for sustainability.

On Thursday, our Training Director, Maura Lambeth, traveled to all of the training cities to visit with the *aspirantes* and gauge how things were going. Maura wanted to listen to any concerns regarding living situations or anything that might be considered a problem.

When Maura came to Catarina, we walked to the park and sat on a bench in the shade. I spoke with Maura regarding my language level, and she assured me that I would be fine. Maura said that Peace Corps would provide everything I needed to be successful. We talked about my host family, and I shared with her that Kathryn and I could not be more pleased with our living situations, even though Peace Corps had placed us with different host families and in separate towns. I walked away feeling very positive about the conversation.

The previous day, Peace Corps presented a mountain of information about working with counterparts because Friday was "Counterpart Day." When Friday rolled around, the Catarina boys traveled to Managua together, which was always an adventure in and of itself. The counterparts from all over the country also traveled to Managua on Friday to meet and begin relationships with the new Volunteers. Following a full day of working with our counterparts, we then stayed the night in Managua at the Hotel Ticomo.

Since we planned to teach small business classes in two schools, we had been assigned two counterparts. One counterpart, the Director of the Instituto Guillermo Cano (La Nexa), which was a school where Kathryn and I planned to teach, did not attend the event because she had already been working with Erin and Mike Gerba in Estelí and knew what needed to be done from her perspective. We would also be able to meet with our counterpart over the weekend as we had a site visit scheduled for Saturday through Wednesday of the next week. Our other counterpart, who was the Director from Instituto Nacional, the other school in which we would also be teaching, did not attend the event. Nonetheless, we participated in all of the training sessions with counterparts from around the country and learned more about how best to use the resources available to us in our communities.

Saturday morning, trainees left for visits to the sites in which they had been assigned to work during their service. Kathryn and I traveled to Estelí for our site visit. We were both very excited for several reasons. One, we could be together for multiple days; and two, we could get away from our training towns and eat something other than beans and rice. I'm telling you, eating beans and rice after just one week with my host family exhausted me. Now in the eighth week of training, I wanted food that I was accustomed to eating. Finally, we could also really check out Estelí in a more detailed way. We would now have a full five days to get to know our new home.

The Gerbas graciously offered us their house to stay in while they were away for Saturday night. They went to their "*despedida*" (going away party) in San Juan del Sur—a beach town in the southwestern part of the country. The Volunteers in their small business group had planned a farewell party on Saturday night because they would all be leaving the country for good in a few more days, and they wanted to say goodbye to each other. The Gerbas would be back in Estelí by Sunday afternoon.

Kathryn and I had to remind ourselves that Sunday was actually the 4th of July! It's a huge celebration in the States, but here in Nicaragua, we had nothing planned. Nor could we, as we were supposed to be working.

The first item on our agenda consisted of securing a place to live in Estelí for our two years of service after our swearing-in as Volunteers. We had to find a house to rent and make the arrangements. This was not supposed to be an issue for us because we discussed renting the house where the Gerbas lived.

We felt very fortunate on this account, as most other Volunteers had to go into their communities and locate a place to live and negotiate a rental agreement, and we had heard this could be a very time-consuming and difficult task to achieve. In fact, some Volunteers did not have a place to live and had to build a home, such was the case of our friend who lived in a small rural community outside of Estelí.

However, the Gerbas resided in a home rented from their neighbors. We perceived it as a good situation from a safety perspective because the neighbors lived on one side of the Gerbas home and owned a convenience store on the other side of the rented space. The Gerbas shared a wall on both sides with the Arrieta family, sandwiched in-between the family and their business. This meant that a neighbor would always be around to look out for us or the house if we were not at home. We liked the idea of being surrounded by a Nicaraguan family from a social and safety perspective, yet we also had some privacy.

On Sunday, Kath and I began the long laundry list of items that needed to be accomplished during our site visit. While walking around Estelí, I noticed a guy on the corner who was openly shaking a huge wad of money at me. When I say huge, I mean that the wad of cash looked at least four inches thick. Once we had walked past the man, curiosity got the best of me. I asked Kathryn if she had seen the guy and if she knew what was going on with him.

Kathryn replied "No, I didn't really check him out very closely." He seemed harmless enough, so I said I wanted to go back and talk to him.

When I walked up to him, he said only, "*Cuántos?*" ('how much?'). After that, I learned that he exchanged money—córdobas for dollars—and that he is called a "coyote." I said "no," I did not need to exchange any money, I only wanted to speak with him. He was friendly, and I shared with him that we would be living in Estelí for two years. I guessed that he had more than $1000 in his hand, which was an extraordinary amount of money in Nicaragua, especially to be flashing it around. I asked him if he felt safe having all that money. He said he was not concerned at all, and then he walked over to a car that pulled up to the curb to transact some business.

While the "coyote" was away, his friend who had stood next to us sarcastically said, "Yeah, it's safe." He then said, "When the coyote walks back over here, check out his limp. He was shot on this very corner not more than six weeks ago."

I said, "Alrighty then, I guess we're through here. You have a nice day." And off we walked.

The list of things to accomplish during this site visit was extensive. First, we needed to address safety and logistics in case of an emergency. We walked to the police station to introduce ourselves to the Chief of Police and let him know our purpose in town, and where we planned to live. We also wanted to request his phone number in case anything happened. We then walked to the bus stations, Cotran Norte and Cotran Sur, to copy down the schedules of bus arrivals and departures, to and from what cities, and what type of buses (*rutas, expressos,* or *micro-buses*). We wrote all this down because we anticipated traveling a fair amount, and it made sense to be organized for general mobility and emergencies. We would then be able to plan our travel logistics properly in the future without having to go to the bus terminal and wait hours for the correct bus. After that, we walked to the military base for two reasons. One was that we had been told the military base was a likely spot for a helicopter to pick up Volunteers during an emergency. For obvious reasons, I thought it would be good to know its exact location. The second reason was that we needed to find a hotel directly across the street from this military base, as it would be the emergency rendezvous point for all the Volunteers in the department of Estelí.

We walked everywhere, and by late afternoon, I felt plumb tuckered out. That night we ate a fabulous pasta dinner, which we very much appreciated due to the simple fact that it was not beans and rice. Kathryn and I were not the type of people to critique meals. However, if I had eaten that particular pasta dinner in the States, I would not have been very impressed; yet here in Nicaragua, it was as if we were eating like royalty!

18
Training Week 9
Site Visit, Negotiating Rent, Surfboard Deal, Baseball Arrives

"Accept the challenges, so that you may feel the exhilaration of victory."
–General George S. Patton

I woke up on Monday thinking about anything but work. My back was killing me! I could hardly walk, and I was sure that the previous day's exercise moving around Estelí had not been helpful. The Gerbas had returned home Sunday night, and I asked them Monday morning if they knew of any chiropractors or physical therapists in Estelí. They told me about a natural wellness center called Cecalli (say-call-ee), located just outside of town. Kathryn and I traveled there by taxi to see if I could find any kind of relief from the pain. After several hours and a consultation, I received an acupuncture treatment for 5 dollars. I felt better afterwards, but was still hurt. The natural wellness center also suggested I take an anti-inflammatory called *"cola de caballo,"* which translated to "horse's tail." I started calling it "horse's ass," because the concoction tasted horrible.

Later that afternoon, we observed the Gerbas giving a lesson on household budgeting to some young folks with disabilities at an organization called Los Pipitos. Los Pipitos was a non-profit organization, primarily French-funded, that offered help to people with disabilities and their families all over Nicaragua. The Gerbas' side project entailed working with Los Pipitos giving classes on different topics and offering assistance where they could. The Gerbas' presentation seemed very informative and useful. In addition, it demonstrated to us some of the challenges we would encounter teaching. After the lesson at Los Pipitos, we rode a bus with them to a high school, La Nexa, to observe their business classes, which we would be taking over after the Gerbas' departure from the country in a few short weeks.

The Gerbas taught class for an hour and a half. We immediately noticed some difficulties in teaching, especially because of the challenges in maintaining a disciplined classroom. Kath and I planned to take over this exact class in the middle of the school year, and I could tell our work would be cut out for us.

By the time class finished and we had dinner (Chinese!), our day had pretty much ended. We talked with the Gerbas until bedtime about negotiating with the neighbors for rent. They indicated that the family planned to raise the rent and that it could be a very touchy subject. We recognized that the situation might go either way as to whether or not we would actually live in the Gerbas' home. One of the main reasons that Kathryn and I really wanted to live in that particular home was because Erin and Mike told us that they had never had a problem regarding security. Erin and Mike lived in another home in Estelí for a brief time and almost immediately experienced a robbery.

I liked the idea of the neighbors being attached on both sides of the house, but I knew we had to live within a monthly stipend that the Peace Corps provided. The stipend was not a great deal of money because it was meant to emulate living like an average Nicaraguan. If the neighbors put the rent out of our reach, we would have to look for another place to live. The Gerbas were paying $100 per month, including electricity, and they suggested we pay the same amount. It had been a busy day and tomorrow would be as well.

Tuesday we met briefly with our counterpart, Marta Perez, the Director of La Nexa, the downtown high school. She was always inundated with minor emergencies and distractions. Marta seemed to be interested in a sustainable business class for her school, but at that time, the budget did not have money available to pay another teacher to continue with the class. It became apparent that the reason the school needed another Volunteer was to fill in until they could find a teacher willing to do more work with no extra pay or until the school's budget had enough money to hire a teacher. We knew the school would not locate someone who was willing to work without pay; the region was just too poor and most of the teachers already worked at multiple schools.

From a technical standpoint, Marta would be our official counterpart at La Nexa according to the Peace Corps; but the Gerbas shared with us that we would unofficially be working on a daily basis with the school's accountant, Ruben Dormus Centeno. During our visit, we met him as well. Ruben was an extremely pleasant fellow, twenty-eight years old, intelligent, thin, and energetic. He seemed genuinely pleased to meet us, and we had been told by the Gerbas that Ruben was a good guy. They suggested that if we had any problems or needed anything, we speak with Ruben first; if the issue could not be resolved, we could go with Ruben and talk to Marta.

After meeting our counterparts, the Gerbas suggested that we walk toward the center of town and visit the "Casa de Cultura" (House of Culture) and the Sandinista museum called, "Heroes and Martyrs." We followed their suggestion and learned more fascinating facts about the Sandinista revolution and the Sandinista-Contra War. The museum was run by the mothers of soldiers who died in those two conflicts, and bullet holes—big ones—littered the building. The outside of the structure had never been renovated, which added to the intensity of the museum. We also found the Casa de Cultura to be quite unique with frequent community activities offered and traditional artwork displayed.

When we joined the Gerbas that afternoon in class, we felt fairly discouraged by their students' lack of general business knowledge. By the time a student reaches high school, they should at least have some idea of what a marketing slogan is and why it is necessary. Clearly, that was not the case here, and the Gerbas had started at square one by presenting basic marketing concepts in the most rudimentary form. To us, this scenario exemplified why small business classes were needed in Nicaragua.

That evening, while having dinner with the Gerbas, we further discussed rent negotiations. Afterward, Kathryn and I walked next door to begin the conversation with the neighbors and find out exactly what they wanted for their monthly rent.

Kathryn and I had met Santiago and Valentina Arrieta on our previous Volunteer visit during week five of training. The Arrietas were a very nice couple in their late forties with six children—three boys and three girls. When we started our service, the youngest child was five years old, and the oldest son was twenty-five. One of their sons, Aurelio, was married with children; and his family lived in the same home. In total, the Arrietas had 11 people living under one roof.

We exchanged pleasantries with Valentina and Santiago, but we all knew why we were there and when we expressed that we would like to rent their home, they seemed very happy. However, when we asked them how much they wanted for the rent, they said, "one hundred fifty dollars per month, and not in córdobas."

When we calculated what we would have to pay them in córdobas, we were shocked that they had significantly raised the rent. Furthermore, we recognized that due to the devaluation of the córdoba relative to the dollar, our rent would actually increase slightly on a monthly basis if we agreed to their terms. Peace Corps Volunteers in Nicaragua are not paid in American dollars; we were paid in the local currency, córdobas, and our stipend was a fixed córdoba amount. This meant that if we paid the Arrietas in the dollar terms that they wanted, we would be losing in two ways every month—once because of the devaluation of the córdoba to the dollar and then again because we would have to pay to exchange our córdobas for dollars every month. This did not even consider that it would be a huge pain in the rump to make that dollar/córdoba exchange on a regular basis. The news regarding rent did not make us very happy.

I brought to their attention that the Gerbas only paid an equivalent of $100 per month in córdobas, including electricity. The Arrietas emphasized that the cost of electricity had risen considerably and that $150 per month was fair to cover their own costs. Kathryn and I could not decide if they were being truthful or trying to take advantage of us. We finally made an arrangement to pay for our first month only, which would be $125. We wanted time to investigate the housing market a little more carefully during our first month living in Estelí, and then decide if the home would be worth what the family was asking. We knew that a buck-fifty was expensive, and we would be paying much of our entire monthly income on rent. The amount of rent being requested remained within an acceptable household debt level for us; however, that percentage of rent to total income, would increase over a two-year period due to córdoba currency devaluation and exchange fees. We also had the feeling that we were being asked to pay more than the fair market value of the home.

We made our agreement for the first month, and that was good enough to get our foot in the door, so to speak. We were not thrilled with the situation, but we felt like we could eventually either keep the rent at a $125 per month or find somewhere else safe to live for a lesser amount. We planned to do some research and think about it a little more.

When we came back to the Gerbas' place and shared with them the new rental terms, Mike and Erin looked at each other in shock much like Kath and I had. They said we would be able to work something out with the family and to be patient. I thought that was good advice, but I had hoped to button everything up before we returned to our training towns. I guess that part would have to wait.

In the meantime, other issues needed to be addressed. Once a trainee swears in as a Peace Corps Volunteer, they receive a settling-in allowance. That allowance is supposed to enable the Volunteer to buy all the basics to live, such as a bed, sheets, refrigerator, stove, plates, utensils, pots, pans, glasses, etc. The Gerbas already had all of these things in their home, and they planned to either give them away or sell them. I was in the frame of mind to buy everything they had to make things easy on both them and us. We could walk right into a fully furnished home and immediately focus on work. Most Volunteers would have to spend a week or two, or sometimes much longer, getting settled. Kath and I negotiated with the Arrietas that evening, and then we spoke with the Gerbas about a price for furniture and other useful items in their home. They quoted us a number for it all, and we accepted without argument, mostly because we knew that we would not have to run around town trying to find the right products at a decent price.

During that process, the Gerbas also helped Kathryn and I make an arrangement to purchase a surfboard; we became very excited—our first surfboard! One of the positive personal aspects about coming to Nicaragua was that we were going to have the opportunity to learn how to surf! That deal went something like this—the Gerbas said another Volunteer named Jake, who lived in Condega (the next town to the north of Estelí, about 45 minutes away by bus) wanted to buy a surfboard from a Volunteer named Ian, who lived in the southern part of Nicaragua. Ian had a short board that he was trying to sell before he left the country. Jake wanted to buy Ian's short board because Jake's girlfriend could not break through the waves with the long board that Jake owned. The deal was that if Jake could buy Ian's board for $125, Jake would then sell his long board to us for the same price. We agreed to the deal and trusted that the long board we were buying would be in fairly decent shape. Everyone walked away happy. Ian sold his board before he had to leave the country. Jake and his girlfriend got to buy a manageable short board for themselves, and Kathryn and I acquired Jake's long board. Not only were we going to be living and working in a place that we thought we would enjoy, but we were almost finished with training, so learning how to surf would not be too far off on the time horizon. The thought of surfing excited us!

On Wednesday, we joined the Gerbas in a meeting at a non-profit organization called Handicap International. Mike Gerba had helped some youth with disabilities from Los Pipitos write a business plan. The youth from Los Pipitos already ran a small-scale food bar. The purpose of our meeting was to evaluate if the business plan adequately justified a loan from Handicap International for a stove that would help the youth expand their product line, and thus improve their bottom line.

Mike had chosen to work with Handicap International as another side project. Handicap International provides micro-credit financing to assist people with disabilities in Nicaragua. In this case, the youth from Los Pipitos had a business plan, Handicap International had a financing program, and Mike made the connection between the two.

By the end of the meeting, the youth's business plan had been approved for a loan, and Kathryn and I soon realized that we had our first work assignment before we even lived in Estelí. After the youth from Los Pipitos had been approved for their loan, Mike informally suggested to the Handicap International loan committee that Kathryn and I could train the youth group to use the stove safely and that we could also teach them how to make some unique items like soy burgers, pizza, and different types of breads that they could sell. Mike suggested that we could help them because he was about to leave the country, and we would be moving to Estelí to begin working. Kathryn and I had already talked about side projects to get involved with, and this looked to be a very useful and positive endeavor. The loan committee agreed. Mike walked out of that meeting feeling pretty good. His idea of helping those kids would have the needed support, and we felt energized about our first work opportunity outside of our primary project. It had been a productive morning.

We ate lunch with the Gerbas, gave them cash for their basic household items that we considered settling-in necessities, and prepared to return to our training towns. While we were packing up to split, we heard someone at the door. The Gerbas said it was their "street kids." Curious, I went to the door with Mike and Erin to speak with the youngsters. As the Gerbas correctly predicted, two children, one boy and one girl, stood in front of us outside of the Gerbas' enclosed patio. The girl, Perla, looked about nine years old, and the boy, Marlon, about six. They were both very cute yet obviously impoverished.

Erin immediately asked Perla, "Why aren't you in school?" Perla made up some excuse, but Erin gave me a look that indicated she highly doubted what Perla had just told her. The Gerbas introduced us to the kids, but then said that the kids could not come in to play because Kathryn and I were visiting. I instantly thought, "wow, they let "street kids' into their home to play?"

After the children left, Erin and Mike explained that the kids had become quite special to them and that they would let the little people in to draw, watch TV, or generally just to hang out. The Gerbas said that the kids would not steal anything; they were good kids, just very poor. Mike and Erin also informed us that the kids would probably stop by to visit us following the Gerbas departure from the country.

Kathryn and I love children, so we did not anticipate any issues considering the Gerbas said the children wouldn't steal and were decent, pretty fun, little people. We also learned that these kids comprised only a small part of a larger family. However, the older kids were much more problematic and not allowed to enter the home. The Gerbas said we shouldn't worry about the older boys because they know they are not allowed to visit. With that, we finished packing and thanked the Gerbas profusely for all their generosity, time, and assistance. We headed to the bus station to return to our training towns.

Kathryn and I talked all the way to Managua about how much we liked Estelí, the bad rent situation, our new project, the two organizations (Los Pipitos and Handicap International) that we would now be working with, and the street kids. Once we arrived in Managua and changed buses to head farther south, our conversation switched to our host families, our training town site-mates, their future sites, our Spanish levels, and what else we had to do to finish out the rest of the week.

The hardest part was saying goodbye to Kathryn. We had been together again for the last five days, and I had enjoyed being able to spend time with her. When the bus stopped in Catarina around 5:30 that evening, Kathryn had to continue traveling to Masatepe.

Being separated from Kathryn was awful; but we recognized that it was what we signed up for. I hugged her, kissed her, and told her how much she was loved, and that I would see her on Friday, just two short days away.

Walking from the bus stop to my host family's home was lonely, but for no more than five minutes. The second after arriving at the house, I became occupied with Spanish and trying to communicate with the family about how the trip to Estelí had been. I shared with them that Kathryn and I would be living in Estelí for the next two years. The family agreed that we had been very lucky to be assigned to work and live in such a great town.

The rest of the evening was spent preparing reports in Spanish for class the next day. We had to write about everything that had been accomplished during our site visit in Estelí. Although the task would not be difficult to complete in English, writing the report in Spanish took several hours to finish.

Thursday brought about a little surprise when all of my site-mates gathered at Hollis' home for class. First, there were two new facilitators (Spanish teachers) present. Everyone exchanged greetings and talked a bit about all of our different sites and how excited we were about our new future homes. Then one of the facilitators informed me that I would have private Spanish classes from now until the end of training, meaning that I would no longer be attending class with Lee and Hollis. The Peace Corps felt that having personal attention would increase my language ability considerably. After the language personnel reviewed the mid-term interviews again, and I spoke with Maura Lambeth concerning my Spanish level, Maura decided it best that I receive some individual attention.

I did not feel like my Spanish was horrible, but I could tell that Lee and Hollis were picking up the language a little faster. I had shared that fact with Maura during our conversation in the park. She wisely decided that this new approach would enhance my language skills. I kind of felt like the slow kid on the short bus, but quickly determined that this was necessary, and that I should be pleased about receiving the needed assistance to prepare for service.

That Thursday morning, the new facilitator, Angélica, told me that class would be held in my home every day from now until the end of training and that we should head on over there and get started. The four-hour morning class was tough because there was no one else present to deflect attention. I had to speak all the time, which was really my problem. I had not been speaking enough. I had mostly been listening, studying Spanish from a book, and only talking in class when spoken to. Quite honestly, listening and studying from a book is simply not enough. You have to talk, and talk a lot. In the private classroom scenario speaking was required, and Angélica corrected me all morning long.

During the afternoon, applied Spanish felt even harder because we conversed with people in the community, and Angélica stood there, correcting my mistakes. By the end of Thursday, Angélica had become enemy number one! Of course, I kept this frustration in perspective. Obviously, her job was to correct when necessary and my job was to learn, but that doesn't mean the situation did not try the patience of both parties. Only two weeks of training remained, and the personal pressure to learn the language increased significantly.

Hollis and Lee came over after dinner to check in and hear about my class. All I could give them was one word—brutal! They agreed. Not having me in class also meant that they also received more attention, and their day had been pretty tough as well. We also concurred that our facilitators had ratcheted up the intensity of class and that the material was becoming much more advanced. This was good and bad—good in that we were learning more, bad in that classes had become more difficult for everyone.

Lee chimed in with, "only two more weeks. We can do this!"

Friday, another busy day, consisted of everyone from Nica 35 traveling to San Marcos for our weekly group technical session. Fridays always made me really happy because Kathryn and I could see each other again, even if only to sit together in meetings. The day started at 8 a.m. with what Peace Corps calls a "site visit procession."

Basically, the "site visit procession" consisted of nothing more than having each aspiring Volunteer provide a brief presentation about their site visit. The trainees spoke a little regarding their future site community so that other *aspirantes* could learn more about that town and the country. The trainees talked about what they did during their visit and what they learned. This was a useful process because everyone understood more about different individual situations and some of the challenges encountered.

For instance, Brandi Mathews' permanent site placement was Somoto, a town to the north of Estelí. When Brandi arrived in Somoto, she learned that she had no counterpart, school director, or teacher to work with. The director of her school had been identified as Brandi's counterpart, but she had left her job during the previous week. The director was supposed to have arranged for a teacher to work with Brandi, but that arrangement had not been made. Not only that, but the director had not spoken with anyone else in the school about Brandi's visit. When Brandi showed up to meet with the director, no one knew who Brandi was or why she was at the school. Brandi had to explain to the sub-director about the Peace Corps and that she was supposed to be working in their school. Overall, Brandi did not have a very productive site visit. Somoto also wasn't a very big town, and Brandi did not have a place to stay because no previous Volunteers were living in that city. She tried to locate her previous counterpart, but she had left town to visit family in another part of the country. Stranded, Brandi had to find a *hospedaje* (small hostel), which required some searching.

After hearing about all the problems Brandi had encountered during her site visit, Maura Lambeth still found something positive to say, "but you liked the food, right?" Everyone laughed. With a big smile, Maura told Brandi not to worry and that Peace Corps would begin working on the problem immediately. The site visit procession was really informative and interesting. A few aspiring Volunteers had been extremely lucky with their site visits and placements, which included Kathryn and me. However, a few unlucky *aspirantes* had difficult situations that needed to be dealt with as soon as they arrived in their new sites.

Next up, Peace Corps gave a presentation about alcohol awareness for safety and health purposes. The message consisted of how sober individuals are obviously more capable of making better judgments than those who are inebriated. Most Volunteers drink responsibly, but there are always a few who lack some self-control while drinking. When that situation occurs, Volunteers lose proper judgment, making them more vulnerable and safety problems can arise.

Sometimes a Volunteer's mental health can suffer. Volunteers are exposed to tough work environments and difficult living situations, and sadness often results. Faced with tough conditions, some people may drink more to escape or relieve stress, thus potentially damaging their overall health. Peace Corps made a convincing argument to be very careful with alcohol consumption.

The last business of the day consisted of presentations from various *aspirantes* on businesses in their training towns. At the start of training, we all picked a particular business sector (e.g., service, production, etc.) and then selected a type of business within that sector to interview, such as small businesses that sell hand-crafted furniture. We then interviewed multiple businesses within that category. Conducting the interviews enabled *aspirantes* to learn more about small businesses in Nicaragua, practice their Spanish, meet more people in their training towns, and improve their overall understanding of a community's challenges and needs. We all then offered formal presentations to the group about our findings from this community research.

In a nutshell, the overall results from the group's research had several common themes—accounting systems basically did not exist; small business owners had little to no access to short-term credit; businesses generally did not plan for the future; and a majority of businesses were family-owned with no outside employees. The *aspirantes'* presentations sounded eerily similar to Alberto's presentation at the beginning of our training program that outlined standard business practices within Nicaragua. While we had not easily gathered the information for our research, clearly we had all learned a great deal about various business sectors and our communities as a whole.

Before the *aspirantes* left San Marcos for the weekend, we received something wonderful—mail! When Kathryn and I checked to see if we had anything, a package had arrived from my parents that we had been waiting on since the second week of training. This fair-sized parcel contained a couple of baseballs, a bat, and two gloves for my host brothers, Pedro and Diego.

I had asked my father to check around the house for any sporting equipment he could donate to my host family. My dad could not find anything around the house, so he went to the local thrift store and bought some items. He told me via email that he had found some baseball gear that looked almost brand new. When Kathryn and I opened the package, I was shocked that everything looked absolutely brand new and wondered if my father had gone to a sporting goods store. I was super psyched because Christmas was about to come for my host brothers in July.

Kathryn and I left San Marcos and traveled by bus about twenty-five minutes to my training town, Catarina. When we arrived, I told Diego and Pedro that we had something special for them. They came over to check out the package, and I told them there was something inside for them and that they could open the box. When they opened it and saw the baseball equipment, they sat speechless for about five seconds. Their eyes lit up! They looked at each other first, then they asked if the baseball equipment was for me.

I said, "No! The bat, baseballs, and gloves are for you!"

They grabbed the gloves and freaked out! I mean they went absolutely nuts screaming and dancing around; it was crazy. They said "thank you" and asked if we could play now. Why not? We played a little baseball in our front patio area. Witnessing the boys opening that package and then playing ball with them was a memorable experience that I was happy to share with Kathryn. My host brothers were only eight and nine years old, and had never received any gifts like that before. Happy children are a joy to be around, and on this particular afternoon, Diego and Pedro appeared to be on cloud nine. Simply put, we all had a blast! My father's gifts were greatly appreciated.

Kathryn and I spent most of Saturday studying Spanish together. We took a break at about one o'clock and walked down the street discussing the fact that we only had two full weeks left of training. We found a comfortable spot in the shade on the corner and sat down on the curb to watch life in Central America meander slowly by. About fifteen seconds after we sat down, a group of young boys who appeared about twelve years old walked around the corner. When we looked up, one of the boys caught sight of Kathryn's blue eyes and became fixated on them. Unable to stop staring at her while he continued to walk past us, the poor lad slammed into a telephone pole! This kid was walking at a pretty fast clip, and bam! He really hit it hard. Kathryn and I could not help but laugh; however even worse, his group of friends let that pitiful little boy have it with both barrels. The small crowd was a full block and a half away and we could still hear his friends giving the kid a hard time.

Meanwhile, we laughed and laughed about that child slamming into the pole until Kathryn put her hand near her face and realized that something smelled rather foul. We had probably been sitting on the curb where someone or something had taken a piss. Not only her hand, but our shorts, had a acquired a rather strong odor, and we immediately got up and walked away in disgust.

We started to learn that is typical life in Central America—one minute you're doubled over laughing, and the next minute you're appalled. The crazy thing is that it only takes a split-second to go from one end of the spectrum to the other. We suddenly recognized that we had just walked into a telephone pole of our own.

On Sunday, Kathryn and a group of *aspirantes* met in the central park of Masaya to climb a volcano just outside of the city called Volcán Masaya, one of the most active volcanoes in the country. Kathryn had wanted to hike to the top of it since our first few days in Nicaragua. I could not go on this adventure for two reasons—one, my back was still killing me, and a hike like that would undoubtedly put me in the hospital; and two, I needed to study Spanish.

When Kathryn came by Catarina that afternoon, she said the hiking trip had been tough but quite fun. She suggested that when my back was better, I absolutely had to get up there and check it out. I did not feel very happy at that moment. Not only was I frustrated with my Spanish, but I couldn't get around to check out all the cool adventures that Nicaragua had to offer. I had to keep telling myself that my back would get better and training would be over soon, and then I could go have some active adventures. The truth is, I was kidding myself about my back because it was not going to heal on its own.

Kathryn left Catarina about five o'clock that day for Masatepe, and once again I did not want to say goodbye. However, the upcoming week's training schedule inspired me because it looked like we had a ton of group activities scheduled, with minimal Spanish class time. That meant that I could be with Kathryn a fair amount during the week. Yes!

19
Training Week 10
Personal Spanish Classes, Community Bank Priority,
Coping with Stress

"The highest reward for a person's toil is not what they get for it,
but what they become by it."
–John Ruskin

Week ten started with Spanish class. On this particular week, Olivia showed up in Catarina as my new facilitator, and she walked into the house highly motivated. Olivia informed me that we would no longer have applied Spanish in the afternoons this week, so therefore, we needed to make the most of our morning classes. Then it hit me like a ton of bricks – if we were not having applied Spanish for the rest of this week, that meant applied Spanish was over with completely because in week eleven, we would be busy with other matters, including being sworn in as Volunteers! I felt a rush of excitement, as I had completed a very difficult part of training. Olivia also told me that this was the last week of Spanish class. Training was coming to a close fast, but I still had a lot of work to do to prepare for my final language interview. Olivia made the learning process fun and interesting, but every minute of the four-hour class was extremely challenging!

In the afternoons during week ten, trainees had the option of attending various seminars and presentations at the Peace Corps office in Managua. For example, an organization called the UN Industrial Development Initiative offered the *aspirantes* a presentation on the challenges facing small industries in Nicaragua. We could attend another presentation called "The Export Market and Nicaragua's Future." "Community Banks" was another seminar topic; Kathryn had a keen interest in learning about micro-finance options, so we attended that fascinating seminar. Kathryn subsequently decided that starting a community bank in Estelí would be her top priority outside of our primary project, and I completely agreed.

During the tenth week of training, time stood still in the mornings during Spanish class and blew by in the afternoons with the presentations in Managua. The Catarina boys returned home together every evening that week, and we studied our Spanish as a group and played with the kids in the park during breaks.

The worldwide Director of the Peace Corps also happened to visit Nicaragua during week ten, so all of the trainees got to hear from our fearless leader, Gaddi Vasquez. The position of The Peace Corps Director is a politically-appointed position. The Director and his vision for the Peace Corps going forward were very impressive. I could only imagine that his job had to be a nightmare, especially post 9-11. Security for Volunteers was his number one priority, and Mr. Vasquez had implemented a number of various innovations to help improve safety for Volunteers around the globe. I felt quite confident that the Peace Corps was in good hands after listening to our Director speak. He seemed to be a very motivated, competent, high-quality leader.

On Friday, everyone from Nica 35 traveled to San Marcos for our last group meeting and technical session. The topics covered medical policies and coping with stress, in addition to classroom management and sustainable development.

The session on coping with stress entailed splitting up into small groups to talk about different situations that create tension for people. It is absolutely amazing to me how some situations really put people on edge, while other folks faced with the exact same scenarios would not think twice about it. I shared with my group that my communication skills here in Nicaragua have created a great deal of stress for me. A few people in my group agreed with me and felt the same way, but others were completely comfortable with their language skills. Conversely, I was completely comfortable handling drunks in the street who liked to harass people, while those same street drunks sent others in my discussion group running. Not only did the drunks affect them in the moment they were harassed, but these *aspirantes* found themselves stressing out about the situation hours afterward.

We were all unique in so many ways, and listening to everyone from my group speak about their stressors really helped me to understand different strategies people used to relieve stress. Reducing stress is serious business for Peace Corps Volunteers because if you cannot be cool while you are out there in those communities working by yourself, you could have serious safety issues or quickly blow a mental gasket. I was pleased to see that Peace Corps staff recognized how stressful a Volunteer's life can be and that they were implementing sessions like this to help them deal with that stress.

At the end of week ten, all of the *aspirantes* had to turn their journals over to our Head Trainer, Josh Edwards, before we left San Marcos. Josh had made keeping training journals mandatory—not personal journals, but business journals. These business journals could be useful to us when we were out in the communities working. He wanted to read them before we were sworn in as Volunteers and then return them to us, giving some feedback so they would be more useful to us in the field. I thought it was a great idea and looked forward to hearing what Josh had to say about my work thoughts as a trainee. With that Friday's technical session completed, week ten ended and we were free to do what we wanted over the weekend.

Kathryn and I went to Masatepe to spend the weekend with her host family. Her host sisters' folkloric dance group was performing in Granada at the central park on Friday night, and we had been invited to attend the performance. We had a fabulous evening, and like the dance presentation we had seen previously, Kathryn's host sisters and their group danced elegantly and were a joy to watch.

Saturday and Sunday we laid pretty low in Masatepe, and Kathryn helped me study Spanish in preparation for my final language interview scheduled for the early part of the following week. Training was coming to a close rapidly, and I still had to achieve the language level of Intermediate-Mid to be sworn in as a Volunteer. If I did not hit that mark, the Peace Corps could send me home. That just could not happen, so I continued to study like a madman.

Kathryn and I were about to enter our last week of training. I could not stand the anticipation of being out on our own working and living together as a couple. I was incredibly motivated and excited.

I needed to share some good news and hear a friendly voice, so I called my family to tell them about what a hit the baseball equipment had been. Further, I shared with my mother and father that training was almost finished and that up until now, everything had been amazingly smooth for us. They were happy to hear from me and genuinely thrilled that my host brothers loved their baseball gifts. What a great way to start the last week of such a special experience—by speaking to my family and being able to share the news that all was well and that we had pretty much made it through the training process. I was fired up and ready to tackle my last significant hurdle—the language interview.

20
Training Week 11
Final Language Interview, Saying Goodbye,
Sworn In As Volunteers
"I always entertain great hopes."
–Robert Frost

The last week of training blasted off by getting together with Olivia for Spanish class. Our goal was to organize a self-study program so that I could continue to advance with the language after training had ended. We thought about many different ways to keep me on an increasing learning curve, and I documented my action plan.

That Monday night I had to pack up all of my belongings because everyone from Nica 35 would travel to Managua and stay there for the rest of the week after our final language interviews on Tuesday morning. Subsequent to being sworn in on Friday, we would all have to leave for our sites early Saturday morning. This meant that I was leaving Catarina and my host family for quite a long time. I felt sad, but had to accept the fact that we were moving forward.

Kathryn and I could always return to visit. I talked with Marisol, Diego, little Pedro, and Papa Pedro about coming to Managua for the swearing-in ceremony on Friday, and they said they would be there. I then spoke with them about having to leave for good. We said our goodbyes that night because everyone would go in a hundred different directions by 6 o'clock the next morning. This was a difficult moment for me; I had lived with these wonderful people for three months, and they had taken excellent care of me as well as my wife when she visited. I felt like I had become a part of their family. I loved my host family, and I could tell that they had taken to me pretty strongly as well. The best way to describe it is that we had formed a strong bond that would last forever in my heart. We had a group hug and then said good night and goodbye for now. I hated saying goodbye and silently vowed that I would be back to visit my host family soon.

Tuesday arrived—first on the morning agenda was the final language interview. I felt as ready as I would ever be, but I still had to calm the nerves. The Catarina boys—Lee, Hollis and myself, who had started training just eleven short weeks ago at an almost non-existent

Spanish level—were about to demonstrate that we were now able to communicate at a level acceptable to be Peace Corps Volunteers.

Joaquin, my facilitator for the interview, said hello as I sat down, asked if I was ready, turned the tape recorder on, and we began our conversation. Joaquin was reasonably pleasant to be around and he had been the facilitator who gave me the original language interview in Granada, back when we initially arrived in Nicaragua. No matter what, this final interview had to be an improvement over the first one. At least Joaquin would know that I had worked very hard to learn how to speak and understand his language.

When I finished the interview, I thanked Joaquin for the time he had spent with me. I felt okay about our conversation and the final interview, but some doubt remained in my mind as to whether or not I had achieved the goal of Intermediate-Mid. I would have to wait a few more days to receive the interview results, as the facilitators had to evaluate the transcripts.

In the afternoon on Tuesday, the Catarina boys traveled to Managua. We left our bags and belongings in our training town because the Peace Corps did not want us moving around Managua with a lot of luggage. Don Alfredo would go to all of our host families' homes and put our bags in his truck to take them to Managua for us. We would then find our belongings at the Hotel Europeo.

As the Catarina boys cruised down the highway in the bus, we celebrated the completion of language training. What a great sense of accomplishment! We had all worked hard and stayed focused, doing what was necessary to be successful. Several *aspirantes* did not have to worry about their language because they came to Nicaragua with an advanced skill level. According to our entrance language interviews, Kathryn had landed in the country already speaking at an Intermediate-Mid level; she had nothing to worry about from that perspective. For the Catarina boys, however, learning the language was a constant struggle and a difficult task to accomplish.

When we arrived at the Peace Corps office in Managua, I spoke with Kathryn about her final interview and she indicated that it had gone pretty well. She asked about mine, and I said that we would have to wait and see, but I felt like I had probably achieved the needed level. Kathryn was immediately encouraging saying, "of course you made it, you speak and understand Spanish well."

I asked her if she was okay after saying goodbye to her host family. She welled up fast, and I knew I had asked the wrong question. She gently hugged me and said, "It was really difficult to say goodbye to my host family."

I knew it would be; it was hard for me too. I guess maybe I should not have even asked her, as I already knew the answer. Kathryn and Mariana had become especially good friends. Kathryn said that she was looking forward to seeing her host family again as they would be attending our swearing-in ceremony on Friday.

That afternoon, Nica 35 had a technical session about bridging the divide between training and actual service, which is quite a divide to bridge. Volunteers face numerous problems almost immediately after the swearing-in ceremony. Most of those issues have to do with settling into their sites and finding what is necessary to live, like safe homes to rent in their communities, while at the same time starting to work in a foreign place. This technical session dealt with those matters and provided useful information. All of the Nica 35 aspirantes stayed at the Hotel Europeo from that night until the end of the week.

Wednesday, the Nica 35 group traveled across Managua to what is officially known as the Casa Grande (big house), to meet with the Ambassador of the United States to Nicaragua. The United States received this lovely mansion as a gift during the Somoza dictatorship. The house, beautifully designed with the highest quality craftsmanship, resides on top of a large hill overlooking the city of Managua and offers stunning views.

The *aspirantes* took a few moments to look around, overwhelmed at the display of wealth with respect to this mansion. Nica 35 had spent the past three months living with average Nicaraguans, who live in homes that typically have tin roofs and are...well, let's just say they are not the Casa Grande.

At nine that morning, we had a meeting to review the Peace Corps handbook. Oh, the pain and boredom of official government drudgery! At 11 a.m., the Honorable Ambassador Barbara Moore arrived and congratulated our group on a job well done in completing the training program. Ambassador Moore spoke with us about the actions of the United States' mission, including economic assistance, to improve relations with Nicaragua. After Ambassador Moore finished her presentation, we had an opportunity to ask questions. I was interested in learning about what actions the United States was taking to advance our diplomatic relations with Nicaragua, but the overall message provided by the Ambassador was rather unimpressive, although Ambassador Moore was very professional and seemed to be quite effective in her diplomatic role. Considering that the United States' relationship with Nicaragua was still tenuous, I had to be satisfied with the fact that the United States continues to work in good-faith, and as long as we are in the game, there is still hope for everyone involved. I could only imagine how challenging it must be to work with the Nicaraguan Government.

Subsequent to Ambassador Moore's departure that day, Nica 35 had a session about our Emergency Action Plan for all of Peace Corps Nicaragua, and what would be expected of us as Volunteers in the event of a full-blown emergency. Basically, if notified of an emergency, we were expected to travel to certain accessible rendezvous points around the country. If we could arrive at those points around the country, we could be evacuated. The action plan had many more components, but that was pretty much it in a nutshell.

To celebrate the completion of training, Kathryn and I went out for a decent Mexican dinner at a place called Santa Fe, and it was awesome! We called it an early night because we still had a full day scheduled for Thursday.

We started Thursday with a final medical presentation, and Peace Corps provided every *aspirante* with a thorough first aid kit to take with us to our sites. Staff guided us through each article in the kit, including how to use a few of the different items. This was no ordinary first aid kit, and I hoped we never needed to use it!

Later, Peace Corps walked us through the swearing-in ceremony preparations. Then the results of our final language evaluations arrived! This was it! Would I have to go home, or did I hit the mark of Intermediate-Mid? I could not stand the suspense, so I asked Kathryn to read the results to me. She gave a drum roll and then said, "and the winner is," as she opened the envelope.

I had done it! I attained the goal! Kathryn and I calmly but excitedly celebrated the results. I wanted to go running through the building screaming "I did it! I did it!", but that probably would not have been very appropriate. Kathryn's results indicated that she achieved the level of Advanced-Low, which was great because after her first language interview, Kathryn had tested out at Intermediate-Mid. Kathryn had significantly improved her language skills as well. We were both incredibly happy with the results of the language interviews! Everything had come together nicely in the last day of training—a fitting end to the program.

Two more sessions remained in the day, one of which was about banking. Everyone needed to understand the córdoba checking accounts and dollar savings accounts that had been opened for us. We all knew we would only receive a modest stipend to cover our basic expenses, but we did need money to survive. The dollar savings account would hold our travel allowances—again, not much money—$24 per month to be exact. Yet we still had to have the information about access and management of the financial accounts.

Our last session of the day ended our pre-service training! This presentation was given to us by Maura Lambeth, the first person Kathryn and I had met when we entered Nicaragua. Maura congratulated all of us on getting through training and talked with us about our future service. She read a few of the aspiration statements that trainees had written during the Peace Corps application process. It is reasonable to say that very few of us had even thought about our aspiration statements during training. By reading from a few selected applications, Maura poignantly reminded us of what had originally driven each *aspirante* to pursue becoming a Peace Corps Volunteer. Kathryn's aspiration statement happened to be among the few that were shared with the group. Maura had intentionally brought us all full circle, and after her presentation the emotions of our group ran high. From the moment I met Maura, I knew she was a special lady. She once again proved herself to be an effective leader.

That night the party started, and most of Nica 35 hung out by the hotel pool, and celebrated the fact that we had pretty much finished training. However, as was the case most of our time in Nicaragua, we could not be too happy or ride too high for long.

An *aspirante* from the Atlantic Coast Youth Group, Alice Britton, shared with Kathryn and me that she planned to early terminate her service the following day. I cannot begin to tell you what kind of shock wave that sent through us. The news from Alice did not make any sense.

I asked Alice to clarify what I thought I heard, "so you endured three months of a really difficult training process to early terminate your service on the day that you are to be sworn in as a Volunteer?"

She replied, "Yes," but there was obviously a good reason.

I sat down and thought, "this I have to hear." Someone had to have died in her family or something. I could not possibly think of a reason to make an *aspirante* want to leave the country on the day they are to be sworn in! Again, it did not make sense.

Alice, who trained on the Atlantic Coast, began to explain that she was sent to Puerto Cabezas, a large-sized city in the northern department of the Atlantic Coast, for her site visit. Peace Corps then informed her that Puerto Cabezas was where Alice would be permanently placed. During the site visit, Alice felt very threatened and did not think that she would be safe living in that community. She came back from her site visit in Puerto Cabezas and shared her feelings with the Peace Corps on the safety issue. She requested to be changed to a different site. Peace Corps would not offer her another site. Alice did not feel comfortable about her living situation in Puerto Cabezas, so she felt that she had no other choice but to tender her resignation and early terminate her service.

I did not know what to say. Neither Kathryn nor I spoke for a few moments, and Alice sat there nodding as if to say "yep, can you believe that?!" It's not as if Alice didn't ask for another site. She wanted to work on the east coast of Nicaragua; she just did not feel she could be safe in Puerto Cabezas. I had not been to the east coast of Nicaragua, but I had lived in this country long enough to know that region can be dangerous. Two women with the Peace Corps had already been raped on the Atlantic Coast. Alice might have been overreacting about the whole safety thing, but I highly doubted it. Alice seemed to be a woman in tune with her instincts, and you can never go against your gut in that situation. Unfortunately, the Peace Corps let her go.

Alice was completely fluent in Spanish, had earned her Master's Degree in social work, and had actually been working as a social worker before joining the Peace Corps. I personally could not figure it out and felt that she was a major loss, not only to Peace Corps, but to the vulnerable communities she potentially could have served. All I know is that we lost a potentially great Volunteer and that we were very sad to see her leave. There may have been other reasons for not accommodating Alice from the Peace Corps side of the story, but we never heard them. I had only listened to one side of the equation, and I was not about to ask Peace Corps staff about what had occurred.

Subsequently, just a few days after our swearing-in ceremony and Alice Britton's early termination, we found out that the Peace Corps summarily eliminated the entire Atlantic Coast Volunteer program due to safety concerns. Consequently, every Volunteer from the Atlantic Coast region was reassigned to another city or town on the Pacific side of Nicaragua. Eliminating the Volunteer program on the Atlantic Coast by the Peace Corps left Kathryn and me with plenty of questions that we would continue to think about during our service.

Friday, July 23 finally arrived and was a great day for Nica 35—the day that Peace Corps swore us in as Volunteers, putting our lives as *aspirantes* behind us forever. Training to become a Volunteer is filled with difficult challenges—trainees have to be completely dedicated to endure the process, and mental toughness was needed to be successful. For some *aspirantes*, unique circumstances had terminated their service before it even got started. I knew it would be that way before we landed in Nicaragua. Luck, fate—whatever you want to call it—does sometimes help determine how difficult an *aspirante*'s life will be, and safety is included in that scenario.

I was thrilled that Kathryn and I had made it through the process relatively unscathed from a physical and emotional standpoint. However, many of the *aspirantes* about to be sworn in lived with serious stomach ailments for the entire three-month period. As an example, Lee Hamilton, was constantly sick. The majority of *aspirantes* had been ill or damaged in some way, at least once, during our regimented program. I was no exception; hurting my back had definitely made training much more difficult. A Volunteer/*aspirante*'s life includes a lot of walking. It hurt to walk, so I felt consistent pain throughout the three-month period. For Kathryn and me, complaining or whining was not acceptable, and the *aspirantes* learned to deal with situations that they would normally never come across in the States simply because of living in a completely different culture. Coupling illnesses and pain with an intense learning environment along with safety stressors, whether they are real or perceived, creates quite a training cocktail that is difficult to finish. Not to mention that on a personal note for Kathryn and me, as a married couple, we had been away from each other for much of that three-month time frame. Training was tough and we achieved success. The individuals of Nica 35 earned the right to become Volunteers and were about to be sworn in.

We traveled once more as a training group to the "Casa Grande," the location of the swearing-in ceremony. All of the host families attended the event, and Kathryn's host sisters showed up bearing gifts. The family Kathryn lived with were professional seamstresses, and they had secretly been making Kathryn a traditional Nicaraguan dress to wear for this event. When the ladies revealed their tailor-made, all white, intricately-detailed, handcrafted garment to Kathryn, it was difficult to stop the flow of emotions from everyone. The tears followed, as well as wonderful, loving hugs.

Kathryn then ran to the bathroom with the girls to quickly change before the ceremony started. She looked beautiful in her new white dress that had embroidered flowers on it, and we both again felt very humbled by the kind thoughts and generosity of our host families. We took photos with everyone from both of our host families, and it was a very festive occasion.

The ceremony itself was really nice, and included some encouraging words from the U.S. Ambassador and the Peace Corps Country Director. We sang the national anthems of both the United States and Nicaragua. When the time came to take our oath, all the *aspirantes* stood and spoke the following aloud, first in Spanish, and then in English:

> In the name of God and for the understanding and friendship among people and Nations, I solemnly promise to work with dedication and enthusiasm in the tasks that are assigned to me, during two years, or during the time that I may stay in the country. I promise to strive to secure bonds of affection and solidarity with the Nicaraguan people through mutual respect and sincere vocation of service.
>
> For God, for Country, for Peace.

A sense of humility overwhelmed Kathryn and me now that we had the opportunity to follow through with the promises we had just sworn to uphold. It felt spectacular to be an American, and to have this opportunity to serve as a Peace Corps Volunteer in Nicaragua. Immediately following the end of the ceremony, Kathryn and I hugged each other and celebrated a personal moment together.

We again took photos, this time with our Country Director, Training Director, Facilitators, the Catarina boys, our host families, and anyone else I could get my hands on, including all the other Volunteers. The swearing-in ceremony had been a grand celebration of the culmination of a difficult journey. We looked toward the future with great hope that we would be able to make good things happen while living in our communities over the next two years.

That night the party really started. Everyone hung out again by the hotel pool, but this time there was a much more celebratory feel to the group. We were all Volunteers now and looking to relax and have some fun. I do not think I let my guard down for the entire three months of training until after the swearing-in ceremony. I relaxed that evening and had a good time. Kathryn and I celebrated knowing that our adventure was actually just beginning. All of the new Volunteers said their goodbyes to each other that night because early the next day everyone would depart for their site cities.

On Saturday, July 24, Kathryn and I arranged to catch a ride to Estelí with Brandi Mathews. Her host brother planned to drive Brandi north of Estelí to the town of Somoto, and they would drop us off on their way. We were grateful to have the ride, as we did not want to take a cab or have to deal with the bus stations of Managua while loaded down with a couple of very large duffel bags. Kathryn and I put our bags in the back of the pickup and settled in with them for the three-hour trip north. I loved riding in the back of the truck, except while going through Managua. I kept thinking someone would try to snatch a duffel out of the back of the truck at a stop light, so I guarded them closely as the people selling items on the street or beggars approached the vehicle.

On our way out of Managua, we stopped at a traffic light where on the opposite side of the highway, a fatal accident had occurred. The poor man was laid out on the scorching hot pavement as people stood over him making the sign of the cross. It was a sobering moment.

Our truck moved north along the Pan-American Highway. Riding in the back of the pickup truck reminded me of my childhood days in Mississippi, when my grandfather would drive us to town. Except for a little rain on the way, the trip to Estelí was beautiful; Kathryn and I were happy.

21
Service Begins

"In life you can never be too kind or too fair; everyone you meet is carrying a heavy load. When you go through your day expressing kindness and courtesy to all you meet, you leave behind a feeling of warmth and good cheer, and you help alleviate the burdens everyone is struggling with."
–Brian Tracy

Our near-term goals in Estelí were to unpack and settle into our new home, get to know the community better, schedule some appointments with our counterparts so that we could begin working as soon as possible, have some kind of treatment done to relieve the pain for my back, and to take a weekend vacation at the beach. We also needed to arrange for a family member to come to Nicaragua.

The community where Kathryn and I planned to live for the next two years was a very interesting city. Estelí, known as *El Diamante de las Segovias* (The Diamond of the Segovias), had a population of approximately 215,000 people, and the majority of economic wealth derived from agriculture. The area was internationally known for great cigar production, as well as nature preserves and impressive waterfalls.

A short twelve-kilometer trip outside the city leads to a protected area roughly fifteen hundred meters above sea level, called Tisey-Estanzuela. The scenic overlook of Tisey presents a spectacular view all the way to the Gulf of Fonseca on a clear day. The Tisey area offers lodging, camping, horseback riding, and hiking, in addition to various cheeses that are made by hand. Near Tisey is also one of the highest waterfalls in the country of Nicaragua called Estanzuela. Another Nature Reserve called the Miraflor, located on the east side of Estelí has interesting tours, excellent views, and various waterfalls. All of which add up to a spectacular display of nature immediately surrounding our new home.

The Pan-American Highway runs straight through Estelí, which brings an element of a bustling truck-stop town. This major thoroughfare is lined with restaurants, bars, gas stations, bus stations, hotels, and other convenience-oriented businesses, as well as a military base. Kathryn and I were very excited to work in Estelí, as we envisioned plenty of project opportunities and great places to explore.

When we arrived at our new home, we unloaded our bags from the truck and opened our home/office for business. Not much time passed before the street children, who we called, "the Shady Bunch," showed up to welcome us to town. We called the street children "the Shady Bunch" in the positive spirit of the Brady Bunch, as we were about to theoretically adopt an entire family. The Shady Bunch even welcomed us before our neighbors had a chance to say hello. Marlon (age 6), la Perla (age 9), and Miguel (age 11) wanted to come into our home and visit. We still were not completely comfortable with letting them in, but Erin and Mike Gerba said they would not steal and were generally okay to have around, so we let them in.

It only took two minutes before things went completely out of control. We had already started to unpack, and the Shady Bunch, offering to help, rummaged through everything. They were yelling "look at this" back and forth to each other as they took things out of our bags. It was pandemonium! Kathryn and I looked at each other and did not need to say a word; it was understood. The children had to instantly stop what they were doing. I blew the whistle, so to speak, and laid down the law, but gently. The Shady Bunch would have to leave until we were unpacked, and then we would consider a visit. Marlon asked if they could come back in five minutes? I loved that kid already. He was funny and full of great little-kid energy.

While Kathryn and I unpacked, I started to develop a mental plan to help these children in some way. We had the ability to choose any side projects we wanted as long as we continued to work our primary project of teaching business classes in the schools. I would have to be around the children long enough to identify what talents and interests they possessed, and then plan an activity of some sort; but what could a family of three street kids under the age of 12 accomplish? That would come later.

The first order of business was to get settled, and the second priority was to figure out how to bring our family member, Sam, from the United States down to Nicaragua to live with us. Who was Sam? Sam, short for Samantha, was our 11-year-old female Australian Shepherd (black-tri) dog. Sam had been with me since she was a tiny fur ball that fit in the palm of my hand. When Kathryn and I agreed to join the Peace Corps, we recognized that we had to include Sam. We planned to complete three months of training without having Sam in Nicaragua with us. Once our service began, we would bring her down as soon as reasonably possible.

While in training, we needed to live with our host families and could not expect them to also host a dog. Plus, having Sam could potentially cause problems or be a distraction. However, once we completed training and were working in our assigned site city, we would be living alone. Three months seemed like an eternity to be away from Sam. Up to that point, our dog had never spent a day in any kennel. We always took her everywhere we went or had her in the excellent care of a close friend. Sam had been staying with long-time friends during our three months of training, and I missed her as a father would miss his daughter. Now with training over, we could put some brain power and situational luck into play to rendezvous with my little buddy. We would have to utilize a specialized service to enable Sam to fly on an airplane without us.

The service cost a lot, but our obligation was with Sam, not our bank account. We knew what had to be accomplished to have success in transporting Sam before we left the United States, and now we began taking the necessary steps to get the job done. Our long-time friend, Angel, ran around Washington, D.C., visiting different offices to acquire an array of stamps, seals, and certifications that were necessary for Sam to fly to Nicaragua. Angel indicated that his part of the mission had a green light. Now we had to make sure that the weather would cooperate and not be too hot for the airlines to let her fly in the belly of the plane.

Meanwhile, after experiencing three months of challenging training with no break, we were ready for a weekend vacation, and we needed a serving of fun to prepare us for the upcoming challenges. However, before the vacation could happen, we sought some help for my back. It was still giving me problems as a result of a fall during the first few days of training. From the type of pain I felt, I could tell a simple process would not be sufficient to get me patched up. We decided to start with chiropractic care. All things in all good time—settling in, Sam, health, vacation, with work mixed in. None of these items would be completed overnight.

After unpacking, we walked to the mercado up the street for sustenance and inadvertently stumbled across a gallon of chocolate ice cream. Holy guacamole batman, that was a huge score! I had not seen chocolate ice cream in what seemed like forever, and the weather was sweltering hot. Kathryn—who would not normally partake in a gallon of the icy goodness—was as excited as I was. We decided to hold the food shopping for later and instead, bought the gallon of ice cream and grabbed a couple of extra plastic spoons for our friends outside. We had accumulated a small following of street kids as we walked to the store, but these children were not the Shady Bunch. I asked the vagabond crew of kids if they knew Marlon, Perla and Miguel, and the group knew the Shady Bunch well.

Kathryn and I sat on the steps of the Mercado at sunset with the street kids, and we all dug into the quickly-melting gallon of goodness—a huge celebration for everyone. We were settling into our new home and had met some new little friends. In addition, they appeared thrilled that the *gringos* willingly shared the ice cream that was so incredibly rare for them. Everyone was happy during our indulgence. However, following the fiesta, Kathryn and I had stomach aches that resulted in our aversion of ice cream that lasted for months. A standing theme had occurred that remained throughout our service – you could never be too high or too low for very long. Yes, the celebration was great, but we paid for it dearly in stomach ailments. One high, one low, and a few lessons learned. This experience resulted in our never eating a gallon of ice cream again in one sitting. In fact, it took a long time before we even wanted ice cream.

From a project standpoint, Kathryn and I felt incredibly lucky in that we had a very workable site with plenty of positive activities that we could potentially pursue. We still had to purchase some basics to get the household up and running, but for the most part, we moved into an established situation. This established living arrangement provided us an advantage in moving forward quickly toward working on our projects, instead of having to focus on home preparation. Most Volunteers could spend a week or two, or maybe even a month or so, trying to accumulate all of the basic necessities.

Estelí was a hub city for the Volunteers in the northern part of the country, known as the Segovias, and our city is where Volunteers from the region would come to buy supplies. Kathryn and I witnessed a few

Volunteers loading small mattresses onto bus roofs, and they had to purchase kitchen equipment like small one- or two-top gas stoves, plus all of the other basics to live even a meager life style. Most Volunteers would not have electricity for two years, and some would have to construct their own latrines. For a few Volunteers, including our friend Jami, one-room cinderblock homes had to be built so they would have a place to live in their community. Settling into our new home did not seem necessarily easy, even considering that we had a bed and a basic kitchen set up; but it certainly was not a major challenge. We endured these mundane tasks while also making contacts and scheduling future meetings with our counterparts in the two high schools, as well as meetings with Los Pipitos and Handicap International. We also noted some potential projects while walking around town.

We were making some progress on the near-term goals, but the list of things to do had a number of remaining items, including Sam, my back, vacation, and work, yet not necessarily in that order. The Sam plan was in play already, and so was work, with scheduled meetings filling up our calendar. I did not want to alarm the Peace Corps regarding my health and did not contact them. Instead, we walked to an internet café and searched for chiropractors in Nicaragua. We finally found one—three hours away in Masaya. Nonetheless, it did not matter if the practice was ten hours away, I had to have someone knowledgeable to examine what might be going on with my back. Extreme pain occurred when I stood or walked, and Peace Corps Volunteers spend a ton of time on their feet.

Kathryn and I walked to Coltran Sur and boarded a bus to Masaya. Following three and a half hours on the bus, we arrived in Masaya and found the chiropractor's office. During this appointment, he indicated that I would be okay after some manipulation and physical therapy. The chiropractor brought about some pain relief, and I felt genuine comfort to hear him say that a full recovery would occur with the right treatment. I had become nervous and concerned that I had seriously hurt myself. I could do any physical activity, it just hurt like hell to do it.

When we exited the chiropractor's office, Kathryn and I experienced quite a shock to see thousands of people on bicycles riding down the street waving Sandinista flags. At the time, we did not realize that Sandinista supporters had gathered in Masaya to celebrate Independence Day. We recognized that this situation might not be good for us because transportation would be difficult to obtain and our safety might be compromised, based on the fact that a lot of blood had been spilled during the Sandinista Revolution. The Iran-Contra affair during the counter-revolution was against the Sandinistas and was supported by the United States—we were *gringos*! Kathryn and I thought we should exit Masaya as fast as we could move.

While we were walking to the bus terminal, a group of very drunk Sandinistas blocked our way on the sidewalk in front of the Central Park of Masaya. We tried to go around, but one of the guys kept moving in front of us.

Finally, he said to me, "That is a nice backpack you have."

I said, "Thanks, excuse us, please."

We tried to walk past them once again, only to have our way blocked. Meanwhile, chaos engulfed us. Hundreds of lined up buses slowly passed by with people hanging out the windows yelling and celebrating; bus drivers consistently kept their horns blowing; *bombas* or the super charged bottle rockets exploded frequently; and Sandinista flags waved constantly in every conceivable direction.

The trouble-maker blocked our path once again and said, "Why don't I take the backpack from you?"

At this point, I knew there was going to be a problem. Unless a weapon was shown, there was no way I was going to give this guy and his friends my backpack. I knew that we could take off running; but Latinos might view that as being cowardly, and so I decided that the best way to handle this was to call the guy's bluff—but in a funny way. If the bluff did not work, we would run like hell—with my backpack. I grinned as big as I could and started laughing and then quickly got right in his face and said, "You can try."

The next few moments were extremely tense as the trouble-maker was trying to decide what to do with the rather large *gringo* in his face. Right when I thought all hell was about to break loose, Kathryn and I heard my name called loudly from just a few feet away. I ever-so-carefully glanced to see who had been calling my name without really taking my eye off the guy in front of me and noticed it was my host brother-in-law, Javier, and practically my entire neighborhood of guy friends from the town of Catarina. They were all big-time Sandinistas.

Javier knew I was having a problem and said to the trouble-maker, "He's with us, man." The trouble-maker and his friends looked at the pickup loaded to the brim with about twelve of my friends, and the confrontational odds, as well as the situation, changed for the better immediately. Javier was one of those guys that looked like he would rip you limb from limb even though he was a big teddy bear.

The trouble-maker turned and said to Javier, "We were just joking around with the *gringos*. Let's party!"

The next thing you know, I was invited to ride on top of the trouble-maker's bus with all of his Sandinista friends. I considered it an invitation for a positive cultural exchange and accepted, but taking this action also made us later question whether it would be against Peace Corps regulations. Volunteers were not allowed to participate in politics in their host countries. The press was certainly covering this popular event. If a random photo had been taken of the pale-faced *gringo* sitting on top of that bus during the celebration, and a Peace Corps authority saw the photo in the paper, it is quite possible that I would have received a ticket to ride all the way back to the States.

I remained on top of the bus with my new friends long enough to show appreciation of their generous offer, and then said goodbye, hopped down, and thanked Javier and his friends for the love. Then Kathryn and I quickly boogied out of town.

The theme of not being too high or too low for very long was still in play. One low (a bad back)—one high (the chiropractor relieves some pain and tells me recovery is possible); one low (the trouble-maker)—one high (my host brother randomly appears). Another high was the positive cultural exchange with the trouble-maker, and then we were out of town with a few more lessons learned. The lessons? Pay attention to the calendar for big events in Nicaragua, as you can find yourself in trouble quickly under the wrong scenario. Also, try to have a peaceful plan to avoid trouble when it shows up, while still saving face for the American people in the eyes of the Nicaraguans. Culturally, saving face is a big deal in Nicaragua, and I was going to play by their rules. Had we run or given up my backpack, those Sandinistas potentially would have told everyone within their sphere of influence about what a coward the *gringo* had been, facilitating negative perceptions toward Americans. As it eventually turned out, the Sandinistas likely walked away from this encounter with a better view of Americans based on what had transpired. If anything was to be said by those particular Sandinistas—if they could even remember the encounter after their drunken stupor wore off—I would expect they had something positive to say. Although I was in the Peace Corps and wanted no part of physical altercations, I was not going to run from anybody or give up anything unless absolutely necessary. So far so good!

Kathryn and I were now making significant progress toward meeting our immediate goals. We had unpacked, researched our community to some degree, and made contact with our counterparts, as well as taken care of health concerns for the near-term. The only items remaining on our to do list for the immediate future included a weekend vacation and orchestrating Sam's arrival into the country.

We had arranged for Sam to be flown into Nicaragua within the first month of our service in Estelí. At this point, all we had to do was show up at the airport and make the grab. I was, however, highly concerned about what would happen to Sam while in transit because she would be flying from Dulles International to Miami International, changing planes in Miami, and then traveling to Nicaragua. There was plenty that could go wrong, and most of it was heat-oriented. Sam could only be flown if the temperature stayed below eighty-five degrees. If the temperature rose above eighty-five, Sam's health could be compromised, and she might even die from heat in the belly of the plane. The transportation service had stated that if the temperature was not appropriate, the dog could not travel and no refunds would be offered. The way we would work this system was that Angel would show up at the airport with Sam, and if the weather was not cooperating, we would have to pay to change the ticket to another day and start all over again. Luck would play a major part in this scheme, as late August was already upon us.

Another Volunteer working in the area of Estelí, Beatrice Burkes, needed some supplies and stayed the night in our home. During conversation that evening, she told us that she had a dog too, but had purchased it in Nicaragua. Her Volunteer service would end within a few weeks; however, she would not be able to take her dog back to the States. Beatrice said that there was a previous Peace Corps Volunteer in San Juan del Sur who planned to adopt her dog. She also mentioned that he was traveling to the States in the very near future. I immediately had an idea to help bring Sam down to Nicaragua, but it was a long shot. I told Kathryn that we had put off our weekend vacation plans long enough and we needed to head down to San Juan del Sur.

San Juan del Sur is a spectacular beach town. It has not been spoiled by full-scale development, and yet there are a few four- or five-star resorts in the area. You can eat just about any type of food, and many of the beaches are pristine with great waves. The people in San Juan del Sur seem incredibly laid back, friendly, and make you feel right at home. Kathryn and I were about to travel to a place that would be a safe haven for mental sanity and emotional relief whenever life became tough as a Volunteer.

We had arranged to purchase a surfboard because one of the benefits of working in a country like Nicaragua is that you can learn to surf during your own free time. Kathryn and I are water fanatics—always have been—and the thought of learning to surf was very attractive. The deal for our surfboard was dependent on another deal with another Volunteer. The Volunteer who had our surfboard, Jake Bradbury, was to purchase a shortboard from another Volunteer who I did not know. If that deal went through, then Kathryn and I would be able to buy Jake's longboard.

Jake lived in Condega, a small town about thirty minutes to the north of Estelí. He would come to Estelí from time to time to resupply, and we had made contact with him about the surfboard transfer. Jake traveled down to Estelí and we had lunch with him. He said it looked good to complete the surfboard transactions and that he was supposed to finish his end of the deal in the very near future. Jake was a great guy from Seattle, Washington, and I really enjoyed spending time with him. Plus, he already had experience with surfing around San Juan del Sur. I proposed the idea of going down to San Juan together, and he said that he and his girlfriend were going down that very weekend with Christi and Hollis Bennet. Hollis was my training site-mate, and we had a great relationship. After consulting with Kathryn, we all agreed to have a couples' weekend at the beach. Everyone traveled from different places, so we decided to meet at a bar called Ricardo's on the beach and then figure out where to stay.

Kathryn and I had agreed that while working in our site, we would

sustain ourselves at the pay rate of an average Nicaraguan based on resources provided by the Peace Corps. During our own time away from
the watchful eye of our community, we would splurge a little so that
we could indulge in a nice meal and a decent place to stay from time to
time. These extra "frills" would come out of our own pocket.

Everyone met at Ricardo's Friday evening. We peacefully watched
the spectacular sunset slowly drift away into the Pacific ocean. Then we
had to decide where to stay. I proposed a decent hotel with air conditioning because, with the exception of a night or two during training in
Managua, we had not had access to A/C since we left the States, over
four months ago. Hollis and Christi did not argue—they resided in the
hottest department of Nicaragua in the city of León. In that department, volunteers had been known to strip down completely, throw
cold water on their concrete floors, and lay down on the cool concrete
just to have relief from the blistering heat. A/C would be a welcome
luxury for them too. Jake graciously agreed, and we walked a block or
two away from the beach front and found a quaint hotel for twenty
bucks a night with no A/C, and twenty-five bucks with A/C. We took
the upgraded room and felt like royalty.

I almost could not sleep for the blissful thought of spending time
on a pristine beach and surfing great waves. The next morning after we woke up, we walked to the local market and ate a spectacular,
almost-American breakfast with no beans or rice. Over breakfast, we
discussed what beach to surf. Jake mentioned a nice deserted beach
not too far from town with great waves; but he also clearly expressed
some concern about safety issues, as he and two other girls had been
robbed at knife point at that very same beach. I immediately took a
pass on visiting the deserted location and suggested we visit a less
secluded place that had good waves and a refreshment stand of some
sort. Jake had solid experience in the area and knew the perfect match
for what I had described. We would travel to Majagual, an eco-resort
thirty minutes away by car-taxi and forty-five minutes by boat-taxi.

I stopped Jake and asked, "Can you get to this place by boat cruising up or down the coast?"

Jake answered, "Yes," and we all agreed to this method of traveling.
Within twenty minutes, we boarded the six-person boat taxi.

The trip north up the coast was heavenly. The views were unbelievable, and the breeze gently blew the humid, salty air just enough to almost feel cool. There were rocky shorelines and lush jungle hillsides that lined the coast, waves breaking, empty beaches with palm trees swaying, and fish jumping. With surfboards in tow, everyone on the boat was smiling and incredibly happy.

About a mile from Majagual, I saw a spectacular one hundred-foot high, crescent-moon rock outcropping, and I pointed it out to everyone. Jake said that Majagual was just around the corner from that landmark. The prominent rock outcropping was a dazzling testament to the beauty of the Nicaraguan shorelines.

We arrived at Majagual and found an almost beatnik-type place with one large, open-air, grass-hut cabana, complete with a restaurant and bar. Hammocks swayed, parrots and monkeys roamed the premises, and an interesting international clientele of surfers and backpackers hung around. I instantly knew that I had landed at my home away from home. The place was owned by a very welcoming Aussie. We checked in and then walked about a mile down the beach to a place called Maderas. Majagual was a great location to stay, but that small bay usually had limited surfing conditions.

Before we departed Majagual for Maderas Beach, I had struck up a conversation with a Californian male surfer and a German female surfer, who also planned to walk to the same location where we were going. I learned that the waves were pretty big and that if I wanted to make it out through the break with my longboard, I would have to enter the water from between two particular sets of rocks. I asked if we could walk over with them so they could show me the spot to paddle out. As we walked down the beach, I shared with them that this was my first time surfing.

They both looked at each other with some shock as if to say, "today is not the day for you to learn to surf." But I also shared with them very respectfully, that I was a strong swimmer and a whitewater kayak instructor/class V boater. Taking beat-downs was not unusual for me. They laughed and said that I could expect a beat-down.

I felt almost unnerved by the time we arrived at the point of entering the water. The waves appeared just as the Californian and German had described, which is to say, BIG! I immediately recognized that I would not be able to duck dive the longboard through the spin-cycle backwash of these waves. Meaning that for each attempt to surf a wave, I would have to ride it—or swim—all the way to the beach. Then I would have to get out of the water and walk two hundred yards back to the rocks that broke up the waves enough to allow me to paddle past the break and into the lineup. That was a lot of work.

The waves were clearly well overhead with a heavy swell, and I stood watching for a while to determine if I could handle what rolled in before me. Kathryn asked if I would be okay.

I returned her question, smiling, "well, what's the worst that could happen?"

She laughed and started in on me with the obvious, "you could get yourself killed."

Kathryn's comment made me giggle, and I responded chuckling with truthful sarcasm, "Life is about accurate judgment and good decision-making. I am clearly about to make a bad decision based on poor judgment." I kissed Kathryn on the cheek, said "I love you," and glided onto my board into the Pacific Ocean for my first-ever surf session.

The session did not last long. It was tough paddling out between the rocks, which was supposed to be the "easy route." I paddled as hard as I could to get past the breaking waves and then started down the beach two hundred yards toward Maderas, where other surfers were lined up. The paddle was vigorous and exciting, and I could feel the power of the ocean as the heavy waves rolled beneath my board.

Once in front of Maderas, I needed to rest for at least twenty minutes to settle my nerves and let my muscles recuperate. I sat out past the break for what seemed to be a long time. I relaxed watching the other surfers. Specifically, I observed how they caught the waves. I studied what directional angles they utilized to catch them, where on the cycle of the wave they would try to stand, their body positioning – everything I could think of to assist me with this effort.

Finally, the German girl paddled over to within 40 yards of me and yelled with a thick accent, "You are on da outside."

I heard her, but did not say anything.

Again she said, "You are on da outside!"

I could tell she expected a response. Not at all embarrassed about being a rookie surfer or bashful about trying new things, I finally said, "Okay, thanks. I have heard what you said, but what does it mean?!"

She laughed and said that I was sitting beyond the breaking waves and would never catch one from that far out. I laughed and said, "Yeah, I'm just observing things right now. I'll get in there in a minute."

She could see my nervousness. The German laughed and paddled back into the lineup. After sufficient rest and observation, I gathered my nerve, committed myself to going for it, and paddled into the line-up. The German girl was on my right and the Californian on my left. A nice set of waves rolled in. I let the first one pass and went after the second one as hard as I could. The wave built underneath and lifted me about eight feet, and all of a sudden, I was racing down the face of the wave still on my stomach. Everything was happening so fast, but yet in dream-like slow motion. I was about to pop up on my board to stand when a large lightning fast blur came from my left. The Californian had caught the wave too, and he was shredding down the wave from left to right. He ripped right across the tail end of my board and his fins smacked my ankle. He and I went for a couple of ugly rolls in the spin-cycle, and we both came up hoping not to find another wave crashing on us. No such luck—a second wave broke. It crested and slammed down onto us with sufficient force for me to think that maybe going surfing had not been such a good idea. When the Californian and I finally returned to the surface through the good graces of mother nature, we looked out and found a third breaking wave coming at us. We dove back underwater to minimize impact. When I had dreamt of surfing, receiving beat-downs and surfacing three times in two minutes was not exactly what I had in mind. I was learning the skill of holding my breath the hard way.

Finally, the waves subsided, and the Californian said not to worry about what had happened and that I should come back out.

"What happened?" I asked.

He said, "You took the wave from me. I was on the inside of you, and you still caught the wave."

I didn't necessarily mind putting myself in danger based on my lack of experience. However, I definitely did not want to put someone else in a hazardous situation, and I had just caused an accident. Neither one of us were injured or deterred from surfing. However, it seemed appropriate to return some other time, when there was a smaller swell that would be more conducive for learning. I said to the Californian, "thanks for being cool about what happened." I paddled toward the beach and had fun with easy waves closer to shore.

Kathryn was concerned about the "crash," but after she learned all was well, she started laughing hysterically and sarcastically commented about the new kid out there tearing up the surf. Without a doubt, the waves had beaten me down and humbled me, but I had also learned some quick lessons. By the end of the weekend, I had actually caught a few of those large, overhead waves and rode them until they dispersed. Kathryn decided the waves at Maderas were a little big for her, so she pursued surfing in the bay at Majagual and became very efficient. Surfing hooked me, and it netted Kathryn too. Being avid kayakers, we had been feeling like fish out of water, but surfing completely refreshed us and satisfied our water bug desires. We had a spectacular weekend adventure with super-fun people in a beautiful environment. We hoped to return to Majagual in the future.

From Majagual, we traveled back to San Juan del Sur and prepared for the five-hour trip to Estelí. Before leaving San Juan del Sur, I had one errand to run. I had to track down Beatrice Burke's friend, John Crompton, who had committed to adopting Beatrice's dog. This guy was traveling to the States soon, and I wanted to talk to him about the possibility of attaching Sam, our dog, to his plane ticket because flights to Nicaragua usually went through Miami or Houston. I was hopeful that Sam could at least have someone to speak on her behalf if an issue arose. When I tracked him down, not only did he say he was going to the States, but even better, he was flying to Virginia. Hallelujah! He also did not hesitate to offer tagging Sam to his ticket, helping her get on the plane in Virginia, and looking out for her as best he could in Miami. We had found an angel in disguise in John Crompton. He was leaving San Juan del Sur on Monday and would return the next week. All the pieces were falling into place to get our family back together again. Now all we needed was good luck with cooler weather.

Operation "Airlift Sammy" had a green light. Immediately following our trip to the beach, we called Angel Burgos, who had taken care of all the paperwork and shots needed for our dog to travel to Nicaragua. He indicated that Sam was ready for transport and that he would take her to the airport the next day. We gave John Crompton's contact information to Angel so that John could attach Sam's name to his ticket when he arrived at the airport, and then John and Sam could fly on the same planes to Nicaragua. The plan for operation "Airlift Sammy" was set. Kathryn and I rode a bus from Estelí to Managua and were dropped off at the airport. I will never know how all of this worked out, but that afternoon Sam arrived in Managua with John Crompton. We hugged Sam tightly, thanked John profusely, and then walked with our dog out to the Pan-American Highway. When the "pretty bus" stopped for us, I carried Sam on board, and she sat in my lap for the journey back to Estelí.

Sam, a relatively normal American dog, was healthy but slightly overweight due to the fact that she was beyond the age of regular exercise. She was eleven years old, stiff with arthritis already, and did not exercise much, other than her daily walks. Quite frankly, with Sam arriving in Nicaragua at eleven years old, Kathryn and I did not plan ahead for her return to the States. I'll leave it at that.

Sam adjusted well to her new community. However, the community had a difficult time adjusting to Sam. Nicaraguans in general did not know what to think about her or understand what kind of animal she was. She was certainly heavier and generally had a lot more fur than other dogs in Nicaragua. Sometimes, when we walked down a crowded street, people who saw her would react in shock. Mothers would pick up their children and dash out of proximity from Sam. Literally waves of humanity crossed the street to walk on the other side because they could not identify Sam's animal type. They also could have thought she was a danger in general. When someone was brave enough to get close to her, they would ask, "what is it, a small bear?"

We would say, "No, she is only a dog with lots of hair."

As time passed, people became used to seeing her and recognized how gentle she was. After that, everyone wanted to pet her. Sam was lots of fun, and people in the neighborhood began accepting her.

The dogs in the community and in the country in general, were another story and never got used to Sam. For almost our entire service, I carried a stick with me to keep the neighborhood dogs from attacking Sam. At one point, when Kathryn and I visited my host family in Catarina, five dogs ganged up on Sam and fortunately my host brothers helped to protect her from being eaten alive by street-thug dogs. The scene was intense and an aggressive encounter. Four people—myself, Kathryn, Pedro and Diego—all chased away a pack of dogs that charged Sam from every direction, in multiple waves, as we walked through town. This protective battle persisted for half an hour. Finally, some other Nicaraguans got involved, and we all successfully chased the blood-thirsty street-thugs away.

Our near-term goals in Estelí had been to unpack and settle into our new home, get to know the community better, schedule some appointments with our counterparts so that we could begin working as soon as possible, have some kind of treatment done to relieve the pain for my back, and take a weekend vacation at the beach. We had also needed to arrange for a family member, Sam, to come to Nicaragua. All of our near-term goals had now been completed, and we felt ready for the next phase. Sam was back in our daily lives, and a ton of challenging work needed attention.

22
Working Projects

"I am only one, but still I am one. I cannot do everything,
but still I can do something;
and because I cannot do everything,
I will not refuse to do something that I can do."
–Helen Keller

A Peace Corps Volunteer can pursue different types of projects during their service—a primary project, which is assigned by the Peace Corps, and secondary or side projects, which are developed by the Volunteer based on community needs. Different development sectors within the Peace Corps, such as Agriculture, Health, or Environment, may allow the Volunteer to facilitate their own primary project, depending on community needs. However, for Volunteers in the Small Business sector working in Nicaragua, Peace Corps determined the primary project plan.

Outside of the primary project focus, each Volunteer had the luxury of choosing whatever side projects they wanted to pursue. Some Volunteers even chose not to develop secondary projects. Kathryn and I wanted to immerse ourselves completely in development work in as many different aspects as possible. Therefore, we viewed our side projects to be as important as our primary project.

23
Primary Project Introduction
La Empresa Creativa
"Constant dripping hollows out a stone."
–Lucretius

Our primary project required teaching business classes called, *"La Empresa Creativa"* (The Creative Business), in two local high schools, La Nexa and Instituto Nacional. Kathryn and I had scheduled meetings at both La Nexa and Nacional high schools before our trip to the beach in order to better understand the schools' expectations, including the type of involvement we should expect from the Directors of the two schools and our counterparts. We felt comfortable at all levels of participation and interest during our meetings. However, we knew before starting the business classes that the main sustainability issue would be school funding to support a teacher to lead the classes once our service ended. Without proper funding from the schools to pay a teacher, long term continuation of the business course seemed highly unlikely. How could a teacher continuously work for free?

The Volunteers who worked in Estelí before us, Mike and Erin Gerba, also taught business classes as their primary project. They taught only at La Nexa and had experienced this problematic sustainability issue during their service. Despite the Gerbas teaching business classes and training a teacher, no educators were presently available to manage the class. Therefore, Kathryn and I planned to continue teaching the business classes until either proper funding could be provided by the school to pay a teacher, or a teacher volunteered their time. Neither option seemed likely when our service began. We also planned to begin a new program at the other high school, Nacional. The end-goal of the Peace Corps Small Business Development project was to have the *La Empresa Creativa* class incorporated into the national curriculum throughout Nicaragua by the Ministry of Education. If the national goal could be achieved, then teachers would be paid to lead the classes on a permanent basis. Our fearless Associate Program Country Director, Alberto Gonzalez, worked to accomplish that mission.

24
Los Pipitos and Handicap International
"Knowing is not enough; we must apply.
Willing is not enough; we must do."
–Johann Wolfgang von Goethe

While preparing for the school year to begin, Kathryn and I seamlessly pursued a side project working with Los Pipitos to complete Mike and Erin Gerba's previous work. Los Pipitos serves children with disabilities and their families. The gradual growth of this organization has been steady from its inception in 1987 and is a fantastic example of grassroots development.

In 1987, a woman in Managua gave birth to twins, both with Down Syndrome. The mother and her family decided to create Los Pipitos, an association of parents who have children with disabilities. The news regarding this type of an organization traveled quickly throughout the country because nothing like Los Pipitos had ever existed in Central America. Today, Los Pipitos remains a major voice for the rights of people with disabilities in the country. Now over twelve hundred families benefit from Los Pipitos, and presently Los Pipitos centers can be found in most rural and urban towns of Nicaragua. Los Pipitos coordinates with governmental and non-governmental institutions, the media, and the population of Nicaragua to raise awareness about integrating persons with disabilities into society. Los Pipitos does not receive any government funds, and relies on donations, as well as the selfless work of local Nicaraguan volunteers.

Our involvement with Los Pipitos offered a natural connection to Handicap International, the independent international aid organization that works to address poverty, social exclusion, conflict, and disaster mitigation. The organization assists people with disabilities and vulnerable populations through awareness-raising and responding to their essential needs in order to improve their living conditions and promote their dignity and fundamental rights. Handicap International and Los Pipitos were separate but complimentary entities, with a shared goal of improving the life situations of people with disabilities in Nicaragua.

Our side project at Los Pipitos was directly associated with Handicap International. In order to help families affected by disabilities,

Handicap International loaned money to groups and individuals to assist them with business opportunities. Mike Gerba had worked with a small group of youth with disabilities who had a small food bar at Los Pipitos. Mike had assisted the group in creating a business plan and applying for a loan with Handicap International to expand the enterprise. Handicap International approved a loan for the Los Pipitos group to purchase a gas stove and oven for the business.

Kathryn and I envisioned our work with this side project as following through with the Los Pipitos group to ensure that the kitchen was safely operable with the new equipment that could produce a more varied menu capable of producing a profit. Easier said than done.

We met with Handicap International to discuss development of the Los Pipitos project and the scope of needed support and training. By the time our meeting ended, Handicap International had also proposed the idea of using our assistance to support their departmental (regional) loan project, which had a near-term deadline to distribute funds to beneficiaries.

If we accepted the Handicap International suggestion to assist with loans in the region, we would have three projects up and running almost immediately. But the question was—could we handle the scheduling and work load? After detailing the business class schedules for two schools and the time needed to assist Los Pipitos, we decided we could take on the Handicap International regional loan project as well.

The Handicap International project would be short-term as the funding for these loans would expire by the end of December 2004, and it was a use-it-or-lose- it proposition. Becoming involved with this project was a good deal for us because we could evaluate the community of Estelí more effectively, while simultaneously facilitating loans for Handicap International. By December, we would have an excellent idea of project design development in our community, and the work initiated by the Gerbas could be successfully closed-out. Completion of the Los Pipitos project would make the Gerbas happy, as they would know their side project was successful and finished with no loose ends. The Gerbas had helped Kathryn and me a great deal with getting to know the community and settling into our home, and they offered us exceptional advice. We were pleased to not only be helping the youth of Los Pipitos, but also assisting the Gerbas finish what they had started.

Two basic types of loans could be distributed within the community affected by disabilities—group loans and individual loans. Our first responsibilities working with Handicap International included identifying groups and individuals with business ideas. Second, we were to help those people develop business plans sufficient to receive loans, and third, we needed to assist with business implementation once the loans were distributed. At first glance, the responsibilities that Kathryn and I agreed to accept appeared straightforward and simple enough. However, we soon learned that these basic tasks would present significant challenges.

The first challenge occurred while working with the groups that had been identified. We needed to help them develop their business ideas, consider market opportunities, and contemplate the strengths and weaknesses of the group. Therefore, we needed to recognize the severity and types of disabilities of the people who might receive a loan.

Making loans to groups could potentially maximize the strengths and minimize the weaknesses of people with varying degrees of disability. There were some extreme cases including severe physical limitations, as well as hearing, sight, and mental-capacity issues. The disabilities were so serious that there was no way the individual could ever achieve independence or contribute to a business endeavor. That fact caused the families with disabilities to be involved in the businesses too. This would mitigate the disability issue, but the loans would go to the families, as opposed to facilitating independence for the individuals with disabilities. Kathryn and I still supported the group loan idea because these families had no capacity whatsoever to pay for health care for their loved ones, not to mention the lack of available technology to assist the people with disabilities in overcoming their physical limitations, such as wheel chairs, hearing aids, seeing-eye dogs, etc. The families also had limited employment options because they had to provide full-time care to their family members with disabilities. If these small loans and micro-businesses could function, the families could potentially coordinate work schedules so that proper care could be provided. Additionally, the families might be able to generate income, while simultaneously attending to the needs of the individuals with disabilities. Group sizes ranged from as small as two families to as large as four or five families.

The Handicap International loan project was regional in scope, so the entire Department (state) of Estelí was included in the search for groups and individuals. Handicap International identified San Juan de Limay and Pueblo Nuevo as possible areas to search for loan candidates. Kathryn and I made contact with two other small business Volunteers in those towns to see if they had interest in working with Handicap International on a short term project. We recruited John Briggs in San Juan de Limay and Stephen Pope from Pueblo Nuevo.

Stephen and John are great guys to work with and were a welcome addition to the effort. Kathryn traveled to San Juan de Limay and Pueblo Nuevo with the Director of Handicap International to meet with Stephen and John to discuss the goals and specifics of the project.

The Handicap International regional plan had the same objectives and goals as the one in Estelí. John and Stephen agreed to work with Handicap International to locate different groups, facilitate community needs assessments and business ideas, and then assist groups with business plan development. The key, however, was that each group had to make the decision on what type of business to operate.

Shortly thereafter, John Briggs worked with a group in San Juan de Limay to complete a market study, which determined that there would be a viable business opportunity for fresh fish not only in his town, but in surrounding areas as well. With John's facilitation, the members of the group began to develop a business plan. During these group meetings, however, John learned that none of these families liked each other. In fact, deep resentment existed among some of the members of his group, and everyone had different ideas of how the business should function. It became apparent that there was no way the group of families in San Juan de Limay would be able to work together. Before John could make any significant headway in planning for the business, this project was over from the group perspective. The participants would not compromise or be at all flexible. John indicated that he had never experienced anything like it.

Kathryn and I experienced a similar situation in Estelí. While not quite as intense as what John witnessed in San Juan de Limay, the conflicts among participants were significant enough to discourage us from continuing down the path of group loans. Stephen Pope had the same problem in Pueblo Nuevo.

We were all somewhat bewildered as it seemed like a good opportunity to receive capital to start potentially profitable small business ventures that could provide income to multiple financially-impoverished families. Yet these groups in San Juan de Limay, Estelí, and Pueblo Nuevo could not rise above their personal differences in order to have a chance at success. John met with the Handicap International staff and us to figure out different ways to bring these groups together, and we tried them all. Some of the families involved had issues with other families for various reasons, including historical Sandinista versus Contra war participation. In addition, some participants expressed a lack of willingness to work with others who had more severe disabilities because their contributions to the business would likely be minimal compared to those who would have to shoulder more of the work and responsibilities. There were issues within these groups far beyond our ability to understand or deal with, other than to know the project's goals could not be achieved from a group perspective. Handicap International staff pursued additional meetings with these groups, but the Nicaraguans were unable to overcome their differences.

We also tried to locate other families who were dealing with disability issues and different combinations of multiple families were put together, but to no avail. The only other option was to assist these people individually, which was what we ultimately recommended to Handicap International. However, this meant much smaller funding amounts would be available for micro-enterprises, resulting in significantly reduced revenue streams and minimal income.

Individual loans were distributed, and micro-businesses were initiated in San Juan de Limay, Pueblo Nuevo, and Estelí that included examples such as knitting, raising chickens, and baking bread. Following the loan distributions, Handicap International told us that the organization was hopeful the loans would be paid back, but it did not necessarily expect that to happen. Nonetheless, we provided basic business training to some of the loan recipients to equip them with necessary skills to successfully run their micro-businesses.

The end result of the Handicap International project was, in my opinion, marginally successful with respect to improving the financial quality of life for the families affected by disabilities. Some loans were distributed—and that was a positive—but not on the scale that we had originally envisioned. However, the project also helped to develop relationships and facilitate quality cultural exchanges between Americans and Nicaraguans. All of the Peace Corps Volunteers involved learned valuable lessons that we could carry forward to pursue future projects. In addition, the loan recipients received business training to assist with their new endeavors.

Oddly enough, during the same timeframe that everyone was having problems with their Handicap International groups, Kathryn and I were working in Estelí with a group of youth with disabilities at Los Pipitos with no conflicts whatsoever. However, the demographic makeup of the Handicap International groups and the Los Pipitos group that we worked with was different in that no family members were involved with the Los Pipitos youth group. The food bar operation was run by the youth themselves without parental influence or guidance. Additionally, the disabilities of the Los Pipitos youth were not so extreme as to render them dependent upon others for basic functionality.

The Los Pipitos group received its loan from Handicap International just before Kathryn and I arrived in Estelí to start working. Mike Gerba's last order of business with this project before he left the country was to help purchase the stove and make sure it was installed properly. Our side project with Los Pipitos was to follow through on Mike and Erin's efforts to help these youth expand their product line, make sure the kitchen operated safely, and to ensure that pricing of the products generated a profit. Expanding the product line was going to be an interesting process because generally speaking, Nicaraguan food is based on the staples of beans and rice plus a meat of some sort. The product line expansion was going to be Kathryn's mission, and I volunteered to work as her assistant.

We visited Los Pipitos to meet the youth we would be working with, and we loved both the organization and them. Los Pipitos had created an excellent environment for learning and development, and the youth were very pleasant to be around, ranging in ages between fourteen to nineteen years old. They appeared eager to get started and had a great little snack bar already operating. Six youth participated in the group project. Each individual worked the snack bar at different times depending upon their schedules, but it was agreed that any profit would be distributed equally. This was a solid working group that was interested in learning to run a business and being independent.

Kathryn and I started with brainstorming sessions about what items and resources were available and what we thought Nicaraguans might enjoy eating. We recognized that we could not propose the group make key lime pie, for example, when some of the materials to make that dessert were not available in Nicaragua. However, we had access to plenty of other items, such as bananas, which were readily available and inexpensive. After researching the process to make banana bread, it looked as though this product was a distinct possibility. We then considered the complexity to produce the new product. If the recipes were too complicated, the kids would become frustrated, make mistakes, and lose money. Banana bread did not require a complex process to produce. The ingredients were readily available, inexpensive, and thus affordable to the clientele and profitable for the business.

Kathryn and I had a two-burner stove and a small oven in our home that could accommodate a six-by-six inch baking pan. We decided it would be best to initiate product-testing at home first, in order to determine the edibility of the item. We then needed to implement a small market study to reveal whether or not Nicaraguans would eat banana bread and at what price point they would purchase the product. I helped Kathryn prepare the banana bread one afternoon, and it turned out to be easy enough to make.

25
Enter the Shady Bunch
"You miss 100% of the shots you don't take."
–Wayne Gretzky

The following Saturday, the Shady Bunch (the street kids) came by our house for a visit. We let them in our home and decided that it would be a good time to try out the banana bread recipe as an activity that we could do with the children. Together we baked banana bread for the first time, and it was hysterical! Kathryn and I asked Marlon (age 6), Perla (age 9) and Miguel (age 11) for chopped up bananas to put in the bowl to mix, but the bananas kept disappearing.

Kath would say, "Now where did those bananas go?" and the kids would have their mouths completely crammed with bananas, but would shrug their shoulders as if to say they had no idea what she was talking about.

I would give Marlon fifty cents and send him next door to our neighbor's *pulpería* (convenience store) to purchase more bananas. I knew how many bananas fifty cents would buy, but Marlon would always come back with less than he was supposed to and a look on his face that said we were buying very tasty bananas. Not to mention that our neighbor, Valentina, who owned the *pulpería* would come over and very surreptitiously mention that the kid had eaten some bananas.

I would be super sarcastic and say, "No, are you sure?"

Valentina would laugh and say, "Just wanted you to know," and then walk back to the *pulpería.*

The Shady Bunch gorged themselves to the maximum on bananas intended for the banana bread. They were loving life. Next, we added the other ingredients for the bread and the mixing began. Before we knew it, flour covered the floor of our house. The Shady crew would roll out some dough and then clap their hands to the music we had playing. Puffs of flour clouds would billow in our one-room home. These clouds would drift to the floor, and the kids would walk/dance around the house barefoot, leaving behind evidence of little feet everywhere!

We had a real mess on our hands, but it was fun. Everyone was working, eating, laughing, and having a real good time. Kath and I knew we were getting ripped off by the Shady Bunch; they were eating us out of house and home with these bananas, but it was so funny and they were so cute that we went along with the game, encouraging more shenanigans.

By the time the afternoon was over, a couple of things were very clear. Banana bread could easily be made; the Shady Bunch even had a handle on how to do it by day's end. The bread was inexpensive to produce, and it looked as though we had a good suggestion for product expansion at the Los Pipitos snack bar. Then the idea came to me. If the Shady Bunch could make the banana bread – as they had just proven they were capable, with supervision—we could start a micro-business with them and teach some valuable lessons, while potentially improving their situation.

I shared the idea with Kathryn, and she was in on the plan one hundred percent. The kids had been fun to have around that afternoon, and while they were very messy, it had been a productive activity and our home was a safe place for them. Besides, the Shady Bunch were in such dire straits financially that we decided it could not hurt to try the micro-business even though they had so many problems and were still very young. It felt good knowing that they at least had something to eat before they left our home that day. Stay tuned for more tales on the Shady Bunch.

26
Los Pipitos Continued
"Try not to become a man of success but a man of value."
–Albert Einstein

The next food item to test was based on my own selfish wants—homemade pizza. Kathryn and I agreed that vegetarian pizza was the best choice. Finding pepperoni, sausage, ham, or meat of any quality to put on a pizza would be very challenging in Estelí. Therefore, we surmised that it would be best to keep it simple and inexpensive. Fortunately, the pizza turned out great. We then moved on to experimenting with potato salad, donuts, veggie soy burgers, and brownies, all of which tasted fantastic. The Los Pipitos project was really good for me because I was able to eat food that was a little more normal to me than *gallo pinto* (a mixture of rice and beans). However, on any given day in the States, you would be hard pressed to have me eat a veggie soy burger. Regardless, they were really tasty and seemed like they would be profitable.

The process to identify which items could be successfully added to the Los Pipitos snack bar menu took a few weeks. We ran into some challenges, but for the most part, the youth at Los Pipitos liked trying the recipes, and they were capable of producing the items. However, one young lady did have an issue with our potato salad recipe. She was mentally challenged, but not significantly. I do not know what her exact disability was, but Kathryn and I knew she had a tendency to either really focus on the task at hand, or drift away. For whatever reason, this young lady insisted that carrots go into the potato salad, but the insistence came about very slowly yet grew with intensity. We began to make the dish, while the girl pulled a carrot out of the refrigerator and asked us if she should chop up the carrot for the potato salad. When we explained that the recipe did not include a carrot, she put it back in the refrigerator. However, a couple of minutes later, we noticed that she was chopping a carrot. I thought she might be working on something else, recognizing that from time to time distractions are normal. Kath and I did not think much of the carrot until she had finished chopping and said, "And now we add the carrots?"

I looked at Kathryn to respond, and Kathryn looked at me, and the girl looked at both of us. Neither Kathryn or I knew what to say, and following an almost uncomfortable silence, Kathryn said something to the effect of, "Well, let's look at the recipe and see if we should put carrots in the potato salad now."

At that point, I smiled because I knew this was going to be a situation. If we put carrots in the potato salad, the dish would be altered from the recipe forever because the one thing we knew for certain was that change did not come easily for these youth. They seemed most comfortable within a routine or pattern, and if carrots were added to the dish now, they would always go into the dish. Kathryn thought reviewing the recipe with the young lady would demonstrate that carrots were not intended to be included in potato salad. I then tried to explain that carrots would be a good addition to coleslaw, which Nicaraguans sort of know about, but not potato salad. However, what the recipe said or what Kathryn or I or anyone else had to say about the recipe did not matter to this girl. Carrots were going into the potato salad, and no one could do anything to stop the carrot train from departing its track. She dumped the carrots in the bowl, and Kathryn and I went with it, adding the carrots to the line item costs of producing the dish.

Later Kathryn and I laughed with appreciation of the girl's intense focus. The girl would not let go of the fact that carrots belonged in potato salad, even though she had never eaten potato salad. We respected her determination and also envisioned all potato salad in Nicaragua containing carrots. One thing we had learned about Nicaragua was that if a new product does well in the market, the Nicaraguan population will copy that product extremely quickly. We predicted that if the potato salad dish became a hit, travelers to the country, will more than likely find that Nicaraguan potato salad is made with carrots.

At this point, the Los Pipitos group had veggie pizza, potato salad (with carrots), donuts, banana bread, brownies, and veggie soy burgers added to their menu, and the youth seemed to be happy with the results. We did not want to inundate the children with too many menu items. The end-goal was to help the snack bar be an efficient and profitable operation.

Our goals when we started the project were to assist the group with expanding their product line, facilitate safe operation of their kitchen, and ensure that the new products were priced correctly to generate a small profit. We felt that the project was a success as the goals were achieved and we had developed solid new relationships. Kathryn and I thoroughly enjoyed working with the youth and the organization of Los Pipitos. We were pleased with the outcomes of our work and learned more about how to cultivate true ownership of a project among the actual beneficiaries. In other words, we were learning how to put the project into the hands of the recipients in such a manner that they felt that they owned not only the process, but also the positive results. Cultivating ownership of the projects among the recipients, from the planning phase to completion, was going to be a common theme of our service and critical to the success of our efforts.

Kathryn clearly became the chef and I was her assistant. The Los Pipitos pizza experiment had been a success. However, we had also experimented with the item at home. Yet, making the pizza and using the oven in our home was still a new process for us.

We soon recognized that an additional bonus of the Los Pipitos project was that neighborhood families could benefit from varied, healthier eating, if Kathryn and I could get them to accept some of the recipes. One Saturday, Kathryn invited several neighborhood ladies to our home for a cooking lesson on the art of making vegetarian pizza. As Kathryn's critical assistant, I was there to set an example that a man could also cook in the kitchen, serve others food, and clean afterwards. All of the aforementioned man assignments were completely new ideas to the neighborhood women—in fact, they were shocked. There were six ladies plus Kathryn and me in our small, one-room living space. Everything started out great and the ladies were having fun cutting vegetables with me, while Kathryn was busy with the important stuff—making the dough. Everyone seemed intent on learning how to make pizza. After the dough was made and all the veggies prepared, it was time to put the masterpiece together and let it cook.

The cooking festivities were supposed to only last about an hour or possibly two at the most. Yet we found ourselves sitting around for three-and-a-half hours trying to figure out why the dough would not rise. Something had gone terribly wrong. Worse, our front door was open to let air in the home, and the guys from the neighborhood and people who happened to be walking by the house stared into our home to watch the *gringa* cook. I am not sure, but I think a wager might have even been instigated between the guys to see if the pizza would turn out correctly following the first indication that something was not going well. I quietly slipped out to the porch to see if I could get in on the action.

I watched Kathryn scour the recipe to see what she might have missed. The end result was that the temperature of the water that had been mixed with the yeast had been raised to a point that the yeast was killed and the dough ruined. Kathryn was not a baker and did not know yeast; her first couple of times having success making pizza must have been pure luck. Everyone had a good laugh because the *gringa* offered instruction about how to make pizza, and it turned out to be a cooking disaster. Pizza did come out of the oven, but I tried it, and it was horrible! The Nicaraguan women were very kind—they insisted that the pizza was fine and that they would try to make it in their own homes. However, the looks on their faces when they bit into the pizza were priceless. They had a look of pure torture. Kathryn was embarrassed, her confidence in her ability to cook was shot, and I could not stop laughing in a lovingly twisted, yet supportive, kind of way. It took so long for the pizza to come out of the oven that the neighborhood guys who were making wagers could not wait around long enough to find out the result. All bets were called off. Would the pizza be good or not? None of the guys could wait that long.

However, progress had been made that day regarding our neighbors. First, it did not matter what that pizza tasted like, we had certainly made some friends. Never had the ladies from the neighborhood been invited to such an event, and never had they seen a man willing to help in the kitchen. We felt these were huge successes. Not to mention that we had a really fun afternoon with the neighbors. Kathryn would eventually come to redeem herself with regards to her cooking ability in the eyes of the neighborhood kitchen pros. Yet, we always seemed to find ourselves in the scenario of two steps forward and one step back. Or in the next case, just two steps back.

Our oven was problematic. Both Kathryn and I had a hard time operating this important kitchen utility, which was not much bigger than an "Easy-Bake" oven. The small, two-burner gas stove and oven required a propane tank to ignite the flames of the unit. I had replaced an empty propane tank with a new one, and Kathryn was ready to be the fearless chef once again. With a brand new tank, the pressure was quite high when Kathryn released the valve, and a lot of gas went into the oven before Kathryn could strike a match to ignite the fumes. When Kathryn was finally able to get a lit match into the oven, the oven was full of gas fumes and the result was an explosion in her face!

Imagine Wile E. Coyote blowing himself up in the cartoons. I reacted quickly and looked up to see Kathryn standing there in shock—not moving—with a blown out match still in her hand. Some of Kathryn's hair was slightly burnt, and her eyebrows and lashes were completely singed. The explosion was so loud that the neighbors came over to see what had happened. Additionally, the neighborhood guys, who could see into our home through the open door, were making comments to the effect that the *gringa* was cooking again. After recognizing that Kathryn was not injured, I laughed so hard that I could not breathe.

Later, I had this image tattooed in my head of Kathryn standing there like a statue, holding that blown out match with her eyebrows singed. Make no mistake, the situation was hysterical, and I abused Kathryn to no end with, "Wile E. Coyote, superrrr gennnius." However, the neighbors made a point to come over and give both Kathryn and me very clear instructions about how to operate the propane tank safely. No matter how carefully we tried to follow our neighbors' instructions to the letter, the stove always produced a minor explosion when ignited. The stove was dangerous, and we treated it with respect and a healthy amount of humor.

Kathryn eventually made brownies for the neighborhood ladies. Following their spectacular response to such a delicious desert, the ladies viewed Kathryn as a culinary genius, even though we caused a minor explosion every time we fired up the griddle; I mean oven.

27
Kathryn's First Top Ten List
"Nothing great was ever achieved without enthusiasm."
–Ralph Waldo Emerson

After a couple of months of living on our own in Estelí, Kathryn created the following top-ten list of "Signs that we are adapting well to the Nicaraguan culture:"

10. Cleaning the house twice a day has become a regular occurrence and a necessity to keep the dust clear (Eric's job).
9. We are no longer shocked when the lights and water shut off.
8. We wash our clothes with the cycles of the sun so our clothes can actually dry.
7. At night, we sleep with a blanket because the temperature has dropped below eighty degrees.
6. Our feet have permanent dirt and tan lines that match our sandals.
5. We find ourselves ironing underwear, t-shirts, and pillowcases.
4. We ask, "How much did this cost?" for everything and to everyone.
3. We are no longer the first people at every meeting because we have learned to show up late, which is actually "on time."
2. We have learned to toss the nastiest of toilet paper in the trash can and not think twice about it.

And the #1 "sign" that we are adapting well to the Nicaraguan culture is…drum roll please…

1. Kathryn regularly leaves the house with her zipper down… and it no longer bothers her.

28
English Classes
"Life is a succession of lessons which must be lived to be understood."
–Ralph Waldo Emerson

Kathryn and I became fast friends with a neighborhood family that lived reasonably close to us. The patriarch of the family, Ricardo, and I became very close buddies. Ricardo was a quality human being, and I enjoyed his company very much. He was funny, caring, and tough as nails. After settling into our home, I put the word out that I would be teaching English classes for free in my home. Ricardo took an especially intense interest in attending class. Folks came by our home regularly to find out the details of the classes and when they would start. I had classes for neighborhood children, neighborhood adults, and a junior-high-aged girl from down the street. I also offered a conversational class for my counterpart from La Nexa that included a few other people. Before I could say "boo," there were five English classes up and running.

My goals of the English classes included the continuance of positive cultural exchanges with Nicaraguans and my integration into the neighborhood and community, as well as to provide a desired service.

It seemed that everyone in town wanted to *speak* English. The trick, however, was trying to encourage them to *learn* English. The neighborhood kids' class had seven participants, ranging in age from six to eleven. I taught the basics and the class was fun. However, the kids did not do the homework on a regular basis, which meant that each class entailed repeating previous material before new material could be presented. A review of earlier class material was something I planned to do, but not for the majority of the time. A few parents observed class from the porch. I was developing good relationships with the kids and their parents, which helped our reputation in the community and at the same time, improved our safety. I would play games and sing songs with the class to help with the learning process. Eventually progress was made, and the kids had exposure to some English. However, none of the children finished the class speaking the basics of English.

The classes for the older Nicaraguans were similar with respect to the completion of homework. After teaching vocabulary during class,

I generated assignments using those words for them to do at home. Yet, the next time the class would meet, people still did not know the vocabulary. I spent eighty percent of class time reviewing old material, and twenty percent moving forward. I guess progress was made, but it sure was slow.

The private lesson with the girl down the street only lasted a few months. At first, the classes seemed to be going well. The youngster was attending a private school and needed some extra help to keep up with her English lessons at school. I soon realized that all she wanted was for me to do her homework for her. She would literally put the lessons in front of me and ask for the answers. Worse, I would help her do the elementary-level English lessons, and she would return to me saying that her English teacher said the answers were wrong. I found this to be hysterical, but the young girl did not think it was funny. Apparently, the private school English teacher did not really know the subject she was teaching. This was bottom of the barrel basics—for example, "Jane saw Spot (run or ran)." Of course the answer was "run," but the English teacher would say that was incorrect. I wanted to go to the private school to work with the English teacher to improve her language skills, but I had enough on my plate already. Besides, a private school for the privileged of Estelí should be able to hire a decent English teacher.

The conversational English class with the adult Nicaraguans was much more serious. The students wanted to learn and would actually do their homework. They had some basic knowledge of the language, but their pronunciation was poor. My counterpart from La Nexa, Ruben Dormus, was a participant of the class with two other people. One student said he was going to attend the University of Iowa, but I never felt like he was telling the truth. I would ask him about enrollment at the University, and he would always dodge the question or give answers that did not fit. I was indifferent. As long as this guy was respectful of my time, I was willing to teach him. Ruben was the only one who really stuck with the class, and by assisting him with his English, he helped me with my Spanish. The conversational English class lasted for almost the entire two-year period of our time in Nicaragua.

Without my knowledge, the neighborhood adult conversational class turned out to be the one that had the most real-life impact. I slowly began to recognize why my neighbor from down the street took such a keen interest in learning English. Ricardo generally came to class prepared, did his homework, and eagerly accepted more material. In fact, he asked me questions about assignments or verb usage when I would go to his home for a visit.

One day Ricardo asked me if I knew how to swim.

I said, "Yes, I do know how to swim, and I love it."

He asked me if I could teach him how to swim because he had never learned. This did not surprise me, since a lot of Nicaraguans I had met did not know how to swim.

I said, "Sure, it would be my pleasure to teach you how to swim."

The next day we walked to the end of town with his sister and caught a bus to Estanzuela, a small community with a giant waterfall about twelve kilometers outside of Estelí.

If I was going to swim, it was going to be in a beautiful spot. Estanzuela is one of the most striking places I have ever seen, and the energy changes dramatically when you get down to the inner sanctum of this gorge. I always enjoyed feeling the power of the waterfall and the air temperature, which was refreshingly a few degrees cooler. Jungle foliage surrounded the waterfall and often unique birds flew above while butterflies danced around on the gentle breeze. The Estanzuela waterfall drops about seventy-five to eighty-five feet. As a kayaker, all I could dream about was paddling over the drop. However, with my back still hurt, running that waterfall seemed inconceivable.

When Ricardo and I arrived at Estanzuela, I immediately recognized Ricardo's hesitation to stand near the water, and I tried to get him to walk closer. He was terrified! I have been a ropes course instructor and a wilderness guide. In addition, I have several other qualifications indicating that I am pretty good at getting people to do things they would not normally try; but there was no coaxing Ricardo. After some time, he finally entered the water up to his knees, but no further.

I realized that he needed to warm up to the idea of swimming, so I encouraged him by saying, "Little by little, you can accomplish this goal of learning to swim. We will come back another day." In the meantime, I went for a swim and got as close to the pounding curtain of the waterfall as I could before being pushed back by the current.

That night I tried to think of ways to help Ricardo be more comfortable in the water based on available resources. I came up with the idea of using a car inner-tube as a flotation device. Lifejackets or any other types of flotation devices in Nicaragua do not exist, at least not in the Pacific northwest mountains near Estelí. I grabbed Ricardo the next day, and we walked to a car repair shop to purchase an inner-tube. While at the shop, I asked Ricardo why he wanted to learn how to swim as an adult if he was so nervous about the water. I reflected on his earlier response to my question about swimming, but he had only answered because it was something he had never learned.

Subsequent to seeing how scared Ricardo was of the water, I needed to hear a more detailed answer. Ricardo became quiet and looked away from me. This behavior I was not accustomed to from my friend.

I said, "Ricardo, what's going on? Why do you want to learn to swim?"

He finally asked me to sit down. Ricardo told me that he was struggling financially. He explained that he literally had trouble putting food on the table for his family, and no jobs were available. Ricardo then said he was thinking about using a "coyote" to take him to the United States where he thought he had a good-paying job waiting for him.

This information blew me away on so many levels. I put my hand on his back and said, "Let me think about this for a little while, and we can talk about it later." I did not want to scare him or let him know just how dangerous his potential trip would be, or to let him know that it bothered me that he admitted he was thinking about crossing the U.S. border undocumented. I didn't appreciate this knowledge of his intentions as I felt it put me in an uncomfortable situation. However, he had become my friend, someone who helped keep Kathryn and me safe by watching out for us while we were in his city. He offered us unquestioned friendship, and he had confided in me.

Looking back, I should have seen it coming. I knew he was in dire straits financially, but it seemed as though that was the case for everyone. I should have known he was trying to learn how to swim to save his own life when he got to the Rio Grande at the U.S. border. What Ricardo did not know was that the Rio Grande is generally a shallow river and he would be able to find a spot to cross pretty easily, depending on what time of year he traveled.

It all fell into place—the English classes, the swimming lessons—

he had been theoretically using my instruction to help him get into the United States. I questioned our friendship and what it really meant. Any way you look at it, he was a friend and he and his family were still helping us significantly and I was not going to leave Ricardo hanging. As a matter of fact, my level of respect for him increased dramatically. Ricardo was a family man, tried and true. He loved his wife and adored his children. Yet he was willing to risk his life and leave them behind so that he could provide at least the basic necessities to live healthily, such as sufficient food for his children.

Many Nicaraguans had asked Kathryn and me about going to the United States to make more money. We routinely responded by painting a more realistic picture of life in the United States by demonstrating that the cost of living was high. Stating that a burger could easily cost $5 often made people pause or generated shocked reactions.

Despite the stereotype "bleeding heart," I was not a bleeding heart, but I became one pretty quickly. I understood Ricardo's situation, yet I had many internal debates running through my mind. The immigration border issue was now staring me in the face, and I could not deny that the situation seriously challenged my sense of right and wrong as a United States citizen. I tend to over-think things, but there were questions I asked myself that related only to my situation. Considering that Ricardo's trip was not certain, could I be considered a traitor for helping someone learn to speak English and swim if I knew they "might" use those skills to cross our border illegally? Could my assistance to Ricardo be considered immigration fraud? Would it be against U.S. law to help Ricardo while in Nicaragua? What law would I be breaking? What was the penalty? What would happen to our friendship if I stopped giving him English classes and said "no" to teaching him how to swim? How would his family treat us if I took action on the aforementioned denials of assistance? Would my wife and I still be safe in the community? Would our house be robbed when left unattended? My thoughts almost bordered paranoia.

I had many questions, but I did know that Ricardo was my friend and if Ricardo's family hadn't been looking out for us, our home would have already been robbed. There is no question about that. Someone had previously jumped over our back wall, but they ran off because Ricardo's family saw the would-be crooks trying to get into our home and came running from down the street to stop them. What would I do about Ricardo? This question returned to me over and over again. I never informed Kathryn of my conversation with Ricardo about going to the States. She had enough on her mind, and I did not want her to worry. I must have been quite pensive, because for three or four days following the Ricardo conversation, Kathryn would ask, "What are you thinking about?"

My response? "Oh, nothing much."

I had two options—I could help Ricardo or not. I have always thought about issues as either right or wrong, without much consideration for the gray area. However, I considered a third option of trying to talk him out of going based on the risks associated with traveling to and entering the States illegally using a coyote. I wanted to make sure he understood what he was getting into. In the end, I wish I had not decided to take that course of action. I learned way too much about the human suffering and associated risks of multiple trans-border crossings from Latin America to the United States. It became clear to me that I was the one who really did not understand the intensity and level of risk related to such a daunting endeavor. Ricardo would have to cross the Honduran, Guatemalan, Mexican and finally U.S. borders. This would be a perilous trip, without question. He would also have to walk for several days, trekking roughly sixty miles through Mexico to get to the U.S. border, depending on where the truck dropped them off.

Ricardo never said he was going to go to the States for certain. He only said he would think about the risks and our discussion of him not going. I realized Ricardo could not be talked out of going on the night before he actually left for the United States.

Ricardo and I enjoyed ourselves hanging out at the waterfall and I taught him how to swim as best as I could using the car inner-tube. We had purchased a valve-stem puller so that he could let all the air out of the inner-tube and stuff it in his backpack. When we arrived at the river in Estelí, it seemed like the valve-stem puller might be a small tool that could be used when he arrived at the Rio Grande. All he would have to do was blow up the tube and screw in the valve stem, and he would be ready to swim. I even designed some flippers for him out of a couple of hardback, three-ring-binder notebooks and some duct tape to help speed him along in the water and offer more stability. He only needed to travel fifty yards at the most, and we experimented with the system several times. Trust me when I say the guy could get in that inner-tube with those flippers and haul butt. He was swimming for his freedom, his family, and his own life. How fast would anyone be able to swim? In the end, I decided that all I was doing was teaching someone about water safety and offering a basic English class. If that got me in trouble, then so be it. The whole time I questioned if he would really leave his family and Estelí.

Of the many things that troubled me about Ricardo's potential journey, one particular aspect was eating away at me. If he did not make it to the United States and was unable to pay $5000 back to the coyote for any reason, his parents' home would be taken by the coyote as collateral. While I was very curious, I did not ask about the details, such as when Ricardo had to pay the coyote or how he planned to acquire the money. It was a big risk because the coyote would put everyone in his family out of a place to live if Ricardo could not pay. These were enormous stakes for Ricardo and his family, and failure was not an option.

Ricardo had learned enough English for the bare necessities of life. He had become an accomplished swimmer with his inner-tube, even though I knew the probability that he would need to swim on his journey was minimal. Ricardo finally came over to my home and told me that he actually planned to leave soon. I asked him when, and he said probably the next day.

When the time came for him to leave, the sadness was overwhelming, as everyone knew they might not ever see Ricardo again. Even if he was successful, at a bare minimum he would not see his family for five years. His children would almost be teenagers by that point. His family threw a going-away party. We of course had a great time, but the uneasiness of the situation hung over the party like a dark cloud. From time to time, everyone exposed their disconnect from the party and their faces displayed deep thoughts concerning what was about to transpire. Poor Kathryn had no idea what was going on until it was clear that Ricardo was going to leave, and the news was hard on her. Kathryn was extremely aware that this type of smuggling (voluntary) into other countries could easily turn into human trafficking (involuntary), and she was devastated.

Kathryn and I hugged everyone dearly, as if they were our own family. I hugged my friend Ricardo and told him that when I returned to the States, I would come find him and visit to make sure he was okay. Then we said "good night." Ricardo would depart sometime during the hours of darkness, but he would not say when.

The next day was absolutely horrible! I actually tried to avoid anyone in Ricardo's family because the situation was so heartbreaking. With time, however, the pain of Ricardo's absence began to loosen its grip on us all, and we waited patiently to hear that he had successfully made his way into the United States. The trip was supposed to take a little over a week, depending on how things went.

After three weeks had passed and no one had heard a word from Ricardo, we were all coming unwound. The women were so worried they could barely speak, and while Ricardo's father tried to be positive about the situation, you could tell his heart was breaking. Quite frankly, so was mine.

In the middle of the night, sometime during the fourth week, Kathryn and I woke up to Ricardo's mother banging on our door and yelling for us to wake up. Ricardo was on the phone and needed our help. We shot bolt upright from bed, ran down the street to their home half-dressed and grabbed the phone. After hearing Ricardo's voice with some relief, I understood that he was at a bus station in Orlando, Florida. When the bus stopped, Ricardo had exited to get something to eat. When he returned, the bus had already departed without him.

Naturally, Ricardo was very scared because he had very little money and had traveled completely alone. Who would he ask for help? Would the police catch him? I told him to calm down, and let's think about it for a minute. I asked if he still had his ticket. He replied "yes," and I asked him where he was going. Ricardo told me the name of the city further south in Florida, and I told him to go inside the station and ask for an agent that spoke Spanish. He could tell the agent what happened, and they should be able to put him on the next bus heading to his destination. I asked if he was okay. He said "yes," but that it had been a really tough trip. As long as we got the word that he was okay, everyone sighed relief. Ricardo's uncle was supposed to pick him up at the final destination, and he should have a job soon thereafter. We asked that he call us once he arrived safely in south Florida.

Everyone was thrilled to hear from Ricardo and that he had made it to the States and continued to make progress toward completing his journey. Once I heard that his uncle planned to pick him up, I knew he would be okay. He just needed to have the agent help him get back on a bus heading south. I felt pretty comfortable that he would be able to successfully speak with an agent, and that they would take care of him. The family thanked us for helping Ricardo, and we all tried to go back to sleep.

Two days later, Ricardo called his family in Nicaragua after getting some much needed rest. He said that his journey was over, he had reached his destination, and he was safe. This news thrilled us! We all hugged each other, happy to learn of his safe arrival. We still had no idea what his living situation was, but the first major hurdle had been crossed. At least the family could breathe again.

Over the next few weeks, Kathryn and I heard from the family that Ricardo was struggling severely and that he lived with sixteen people in a three-bedroom home. He was working, sometimes sporadically, but his boss was not paying him. This was terrible news. We worried that Ricardo might be in trouble. I understood that despicable things like that happen to undocumented immigrants in the United States, and that is awful, but this was my friend, and it was now very personal. The only way to determine the severity of the situation was to go see for myself. Kathryn and I told the family that we would fly through Miami on our way back to the States for Christmas. We could then travel by car from Miami to check on their son. Kathryn and I felt pretty nervous about what we would find—not to mention that Christmas was still a few months away. Ricardo could potentially be in serious trouble by that time. Fortunately, before leaving Nicaragua, we heard that Ricardo's situation might be improving.

We could not work it out to check on Ricardo as soon as we arrived in the United States. We had to back-end the reconnaissance operation on the way out of the States. We would fly from Chicago to Miami, landing sometime around midnight. We would then rent a car and drive three hours north to where Ricardo lived to check on his situation. Returning to Miami International after seeing Ricardo concerned us because we had booked an 8 a.m. flight to Tegucigalpa, Honduras. If all went well, we would arrive barely under the two hour minimum required for international departures. From Honduras, we would catch a bus back to Estelí. The trip would be a logistical feat to pull off. It also meant that we would be awake for twenty-four hours or more. We hoped to catch some sleep on the plane to Tegucigalpa.

While standing in the very extended security line at Chicago's O'Hare Airport, an older Latina female happened to be waiting right behind us. No other Latinos stood in our line of at least a hundred people except for this woman. She randomly asked in Spanish if we knew how to speak Spanish. I responded that I understood the basics and asked what she needed. She wanted help getting through the security checkpoint, as she worried that she would not understand what security personnel might say to her. She appeared very decent-hearted, and there was something in her voice that made us feel very relaxed. Kathryn and I did not hesitate assisting her with security and told her not to worry. We introduced ourselves and learned that her name was Carmen Lobo and she was traveling to Honduras. As it happened, she was traveling on the same flight as us to Miami, arriving at midnight, and then catching the same 8 a.m. flight to Tegucigalpa the next day. I thought it was a very strange coincidence that she was the only Latino person in the security line, yet she was right there with us, needing help, and she had tickets to our same destination. Something was brewing here, but I did not know what. I just accepted the fact that strange things happen in life and that sometimes you have to go with the direction of the river.

We helped Carmen Lobo through security, which was very easy because they asked her no questions and I did not have to say a word. We really liked Carmen. Ms. Lobo had a wonderful attitude and seemed serenely energetic. While walking through O'Hare with Carmen Lobo to our gate, we passed through an area of major construction—a large open space of about three thousand square feet with nothing but a completely smooth concrete floor and exactly one orange construction cone. Kathryn was so engaged in conversation with Carmen Lobo that Kathryn walked right into the orange cone, tripped, and splayed herself out—full body, face first sliding across the concrete airport floor.

Carmen and I were shocked by what just happened, but as we rushed to help Kathryn and make sure she was okay, we heard a business guy in a suit walk by and say out loud to all of us, "Oh, where is my camera when I need it! That was hysterical." The man never stopped to see if Kath was okay and kept on walking. Normally, I would have wanted to hurt someone like that, but Kath was okay and it was hysterical. Somehow Kathryn tripped on the only obstacle that existed in an area with an incredible amount of open space. Plus, the tone in the business guy's voice was so sarcastic that we all started to laugh, and before we knew it, hardly any of us could talk because we were laughing so hard. Thus, the bond with Carmen Lobo had been sealed.

Carmen asked if we could help change her tickets so that she could sit close to us. Of course we complied with her request. We not only changed the seat for the trip to Miami, but also for the 8 a.m. flight the next day to Tegucigalpa. While en route to Florida, we asked where she would spend the night in Miami after arriving so late. Ms. Lobo smiled and said that she had family there who would pick her up and return her to the airport the next morning. Ms. Lobo then asked us the same question. I told her the truth—that we were going to rent a car and drive north for three hours to check on a neighbor from Nicaragua who had traveled to the States undocumented and may be in trouble, and then we would return to the airport to fly to Honduras. We received a couple of "Dios mios" (my God), which would be something equivalent to "for heaven's sake" in English. When she asked about Ricardo's problems, I shared with her that we had initially heard that he was living in a three-bedroom house with sixteen other people and was working but not being paid regularly. This made Ms. Lobo angry. She asked how far it was from the Miami airport to Ricardo, and then she began calculating all that had to be done before our flight for Honduras departed. She offered to hold the plane for us until we arrived. We all laughed at the prospect of little Carmen Lobo holding up a huge 747 by standing in front of it with her back to the wheels, digging in her heels, and not allowing the plane to move until the *gringos* boarded. The visual of that scene cracked me up.

We landed in Miami right on time and said goodbye for now to Carmen Lobo. We hustled to get the rental car. This little operation would go down to the wire from the very second we arrived in Miami. The car company upgraded us to a larger vehicle—a nice convertible! I was not going to argue—if we had to suffer on a long overnight drive, we might as well go in style. Nonetheless, we thought we would enjoy the change of climate from the Chicago cold to the Miami heat. The convertible's top came down and operation "Midnight Maneuvers" was underway.

Three hours later, about 3 a.m., we pulled into a blue-collar neighborhood and rolled silently into the driveway of the address we had for Ricardo. I had no idea if we were in the right place, but Ricardo was supposed to be expecting us. I knocked gently on the door, and Ricardo opened it after about thirty seconds. I cannot express how fantastic it was to see my friend standing there before us. Kathryn and I both hugged him, and then we walked to the car so as not to wake the others in the home with our conversation.

Ricardo's situation had improved dramatically in the months that followed the initial conversation in which everyone thought he was not getting paid and had no money for food. He looked healthy and had a halfway decent roof over his head. He was working, and he told us that he was now getting paid by his boss and that things were much better. The sixteen people living in the home had been reduced to eight, and that number would be lowered again sometime soon. Ricardo was working as a roofer and was making a respectable $8 per hour. In Nicaragua, $8 an hour was a fortune! For many people there, especially in the countryside, two or three dollars a day was a good wage that would make them happy. The bottom line was that Ricardo was not in dire straits and his situation appeared tolerable.

We gave him a stack of photos that we had taken of his entire family. As he looked at the pictures, he could not speak and was quietly fighting back tears. After a couple of minutes, Ricardo handed me $1000 in cash and asked that I take it to his family. For a moment, I stood in shock feeling responsible for that kind of money. He also asked if we would take a few items back for him. He expressed how this would be his only chance to send things home to his family because sending packages was too expensive by mail.

Ricardo was correct about the cost of mailing packages. My dad paid $100 to send a baseball and a couple of gloves to my host brothers. We again did not hesitate to help, and I envisioned being able to throw a few extra items into my carryon backpack. Ricardo also asked if we could take some things back for the uncle who had been helping him in the States. I knew we had been "had" at that point, but I did not care because it was Christmas. Ricardo and his uncle wanted their families to benefit from their living and working in the United States. We agreed, and Ricardo said he would be right back.

When Ricardo reappeared from behind the home carrying a monster suitcase, Kathryn and I stood in disbelief, as the luggage was almost as big as me. He also had another suitcase, of a more normal size. As we put the two suitcases in the car, he said that his uncle lived a few blocks away and asked if we would drive there to pick up his items. Ricardo got in the car and we drove to the uncle's home.

Ricardo knocked on a window, and in a minute or two, the uncle came out of the home with one oversized suitcase and one regular-sized suitcase. If we took this luggage, it meant that now Kathryn and I would have to carry back two huge suitcases, plus the other two normal suitcases, plus our own bags, which were also significant in size and number.

I fully realized at this point that there was no way we could manage carrying all of these bags and that we might encounter serious trouble trying to transfer all this stuff from the airport to the bus station in Tegucigalpa, Honduras, which we had never before visited. In addition, Tegucigalpa is not exactly the safest city in the world, and I was sure that Kathryn and I would be quite a spectacle trying to manage all of this luggage. I could easily envision a scenario of a group of people in Tegucigalpa engaging us to ask if they could help, and while we were distracted with all these people around us, the bags would quickly and discretely disappear. Plus, I had $1000 in cash in my hands to carry for Ricardo. I informed both Ricardo and the uncle about the possible problematic scenario, and they agreed it might be tricky to transfer from the airport to the bus station. However, they said that they had faith in us even though I specifically warned them that we could potentially be robbed of everything. We also worried that the bags could be robbed/lost while in the hands of customs agents and airlines. They understood the risks and still wanted us to try.

Kathryn and I agreed to help them after I asked about the contents of the suitcases, because the last thing we needed was trouble with a customs agent regarding bags that were not actually mine. I had no issues with the items, as they consisted of toys and gifts for their families. However, we struggled to make everything fit and moved our seats up to carry half of the luggage in the back seat of the convertible.

We said our goodbyes quickly because we had a long trip back to the airport. The hug that Ricardo gave me was intense. I could feel his appreciation for all we were doing for him, and he started to cry. I told him not to worry, that we would be back, and that I would let his family know that he was doing reasonably well. I knew we had a tough trip in front of us and I was mentally preparing myself to defend everything we had, which was a lot!

We arrived back at Miami International at about 6:30 a.m., returned the rental car, and struggled to get all the luggage to the check-in counter. The attendant behind the counter said she could not guarantee that the bags would even make it to the plane because we were late. I was not going to think about what would happen if the bags didn't make the plane. I then expected the attendant to tell me I owed her five hundred bucks for the extra, overweight/oversized luggage, but to our relief, she said, "okay you're all set," and handed us the baggage receipts.

We quickly moved through the airport and arrived at the gate just as passengers were boarding. We looked for Carmen Lobo, but she was nowhere to be found. Kathryn and I thought maybe she was already on the plane or standing in front of the wheels to make sure we got on board before the plane could move. We boarded the plane, and Carmen Lobo still was nowhere to be found. She was supposed to be sitting next to us. Just as the flight attendant was about to seal the cabin door, Carmen Lobo banged on the door and was let onto the plane. She came down the aisle and was happy to see us waiting on her. I helped her with her overhead bags, and we settled in for the flight to Honduras.

Kathryn and I were exhausted from being up for over twenty-four hours, and we drifted off into dreamland. We woke up when the flight attendant asked if we wanted breakfast or something to drink. Carmen Lobo then inquired about what happened with Ricardo and if he was okay. We shared with her everything that had happened. Ricardo was doing quite well, in my opinion. I also told Carmen that I was totally paranoid that we were going to be robbed in Tegucigalpa because there was no way I could handle all this luggage. She agreed that we had a problem, but she said not to worry. In that moment everything came together as to why we had met Carmen Lobo in Chicago. She was our angel in disguise! She reached across the aisle from her seat and tapped on the arm of a gentleman sitting there. I had no idea she even knew the man, as she did not greet him when she initially sat down for the flight. Ms. Lobo introduced us to him and said to the man, "When we land, you are going to get your truck and assist these people in loading all of their baggage onto your truck. Then you are going to personally escort them to the bus station, not leaving them until the bus pulls away from the station and they are on their way to Nicaragua."

The man said two words, "*Sí, Señora.*"

I could not believe what I had just witnessed. This lady must carry some serious clout. I had never asked Carmen Lobo what she did for a living, and at that point, I understood that she clearly had earned respect in her community. Carmen Lobo then said to us that she had appreciated our helping her through security in Chicago and that we were very good people to be helping others in the manner that we were. She then said that when we land in Tegucigalpa, we would be in her town. She would take care of us, and we had nothing to worry about. "Guardian angel" was the only way I could think of Carmen Lobo. If it had not been for her, I am sure that we would have had some serious issues trying to get to that bus station. Even with the assistance, we still had to dodge through an aggressive crowd of people trying to get us into their taxis. We hugged Carmen Lobo and abundantly thanked her for the help. She was one of the nicest ladies I have ever met.

Kathryn and I made it through Tegucigalpa and out of Honduras without any major issues, thanks to Carmen Lobo. In fact, the first leg of our bus journey was unexpectedly enjoyable. Since we had arrived at the bus station well in advance of our departure time, we had our pick of the seats, and it was a double-decker, "fancy" bus. We sat in the upper deck front seats with our legs kicked up, as we observed spectacular views of Honduras. We thought we would be cruising all the way back to Nicaragua in comfort and style. However, our comfortable tour of Honduras came to an abrupt end when we had to switch to another smaller bus that would take us into Nicaragua. We were late to the game this time and got stuck in the last row with people sitting rather closely on both sides of us with no view outside of the bus. Welcome back to Nicaragua.

After a lengthy border crossing and a couple more hours of travel, we arrived in Estelí by seven that night. Road-weary and exhausted, we caught a taxi through Estelí, with bags in laps, on the roof, in the back seat, and filling the trunk. We got everything inside the house, crashed onto the bed like a couple of bricks, and fell fast asleep. Operation "Midnight Maneuvers" had been a success. We looked forward to sharing with the family that Ricardo's situation had improved and that we returned bearing gifts from him.

The fact of the matter was that I never knew for sure that Ricardo would actually travel to the States. Even though I spoke with him about not making the journey, Ricardo never said definitively that he was going. In the end, Ricardo did leave for the States, and Carmen Lobo helped us help Ricardo. Without question, it was as if Kathryn and I had inadvertently earned some acceptance and respect in the neighborhood that consequently made us feel safer in Estelí knowing that Ricardo's family, and the neighborhood in general, would watch out for Kathryn and me for the rest of our service in Nicaragua. The scenario was similar to us being "made men" if we were "wise guys" back in the States. No one could touch us without serious problems from the neighborhood. The neighborhood knew what we had done for one of their own, and we had earned complete respect.

I asked other Peace Corps Volunteers about undocumented people leaving Nicaragua for the States, and each Volunteer knew of someone or had a friend of a friend from their communities that had left for the States. Undocumented immigration is a problem that is not going to go away. Far too many people depend on the U.S. economy to keep their families financially afloat in Latin America and other nations. The U.S. economy also depends largely upon the undocumented immigrants' abilities to work in our country. The United States Government needs to facilitate improved laws to allow the U.S. economy to continue benefiting from immigrants' hard-working services. And the new laws should permit immigrants themselves to be able to benefit from their hard work—legally!

Were my original goals for the English classes met? The English classes that I taught were educational to the people that participated in them. By teaching these classes, I integrated further into my community and was looked upon as a leader and a respectable American. The experience of teaching English as a Peace Corps Volunteer in Nicaragua led me down a path that I never imagined possible. At the end of the day, I became a better person from that particular project endeavor; goals achieved.

29
Stove Project
"I failed my way to success."
—Thomas Edison

The main goal of the stove project was to improve health through reduced smoke in the kitchen because "black lung" is a pervasive problem in Nicaragua. Imagine cooking over a camp fire in your kitchen three meals a day, every day of the year. You will then have an idea of what preparing meals is like for at least half of Nicaragua's population. Eventually, the person doing the cooking—which is usually the matron of the home or the teenaged children—will have lung problems from exposure to continuous smoke. Aside from reducing smoke, newly-constructed stoves also increase wood-burning efficiency, thereby lowering the operating cost of the stove and further improving the environment through less deforestation. These all seemed like worthy issues to address. Could the goals be attained? I viewed this project as an interesting endeavor because I had no idea how to make a stove.

There was a *fritanga* (street-side restaurant) very close to our home, and I loved to stop in for lunch and get a skewer of pork and *gallo pinto* for fifteen córdobas, which is about the equivalent of one U.S. dollar. I had several pleasant conversations with the owner of the *fritanga*, Danica. Eventually, I began to ask her about the business she was running.

Danica had converted some space in her home that typically is a living room into an area where customers could sit down and eat in a comfortable setting away from the blistering heat. She had two locations for cooking. One was a small grill on the sidewalk outside her front door. The other location was the family's stove in the back of the home. On the stove they cooked *gallo pinto* and other side-order items like tortillas. I had heard from other Volunteers about stove projects that really made a difference in people's lives.

I was curious what Danica's kitchen looked like, so I asked if I could take a brief tour of her facilities. Danica was thrilled to show me around and was incredibly kind. When I saw how the family restaurant operation was running in the back of the home, I felt pretty sure I could be of assistance.

I had no idea how to make a stove, but I knew some Volunteers that had been successful with that type of project. I inquired with a guy named Doug Hurt the next time he passed through town. Doug, who worked outside of Estelí in the *campo* (farmlands), had the stove construction experience that I needed.

Doug traveled to Estelí frequently, and I enjoyed his company and also learned a lot from him about farming in general, the *campo* life, and agricultural projects in his community. I asked Doug if he would teach me how to make an efficient wood-burning stove by actually constructing it with me at Danica's restaurant. I knew he liked to have lunch at Danica's when he came through town. Having Doug on-site during construction would provide me a wealth of knowledge regarding stoves that I would not otherwise be able to obtain. Plus, he would be able to help me avoid unnecessary mistakes. Doug would stay in our home while he was in town working with me. Once the first stove was built, I would have the experience to continue making stoves in my community. Peace Corps-Nicaragua encouraged collaboration between Agricultural Volunteers and Business Volunteers, and here was a perfect opportunity to make that happen to facilitate positive change.

Doug came to Estelí prepared. He had a couple different kinds of dirt in fifty pound sacks for the clay mixture. I wanted to spend as little money as possible to build this stove, which would increase the likelihood that this project could be replicated elsewhere in the community. We also needed bricks, but instead of having Danica go to the hardware store to purchase the bricks, I walked the streets of Estelí searching for material. If the bricks I found sat in front of someone's home, I would knock on the door, introduce myself, tell the folks my intention of building a stove, and ask them if they minded me taking the brick. People loved it! Here was a *gringo* scrounging for scrap materials. I carried a large sack that not only looked really heavy, it was heavy. I made sure all the bricks that I collected were whole and looked relatively new. The stove project also needed rebar and concrete as well as other materials such as wood and screws.

When I proposed the stove idea to Danica, we agreed to build the stove, but she would have to pay for the materials. Danica decided to purchase the supplies and move forward with the project. We scavenged for the majority of the materials, which made the stove less expensive. The items Danica had to buy included screws, concrete, and a stove pipe.

Building the stove required tough manual labor, and it took almost a full week to construct. When finished, we took some photos and felt like we had accomplished something that could be replicated elsewhere in the community. Danica was very pleased. I returned two days later to buy lunch and check on the stove. Danica said there was a problem. I went to the kitchen area, and sure enough, the stove looked like it was falling apart. Huge cracks in the clay ran up the stove. If something was not done quickly to correct the problem, the stove would completely fall apart. I contacted Doug immediately and he came to town with more mud/hay and dirt filler. We worked for another whole day to patch up the stove, and we told Danica that we would monitor the stove on a daily basis to ensure that the issue was resolved.

The next day I returned for lunch and to check on the stove. Again, it looked like the thing was falling apart. At this point, I became quite nervous that we had taken down Danica's original stove and replaced it with something that was not going to function. That would not be a positive development, and I had no idea what the solution might be. I contacted Doug again, and he returned to Estelí that day. He was not concerned and basically indicated that it was a materials issue and that we only needed to get the clay mixture correct. I had the utmost confidence in Doug, which calmed my nerves considerably. From the initial construction to the clay "mixture" corrections, the project took three weeks to complete.

I always assessed our projects by asking, were the initial goals achieved? In this case, yes and no. A stove was successfully financed and constructed. The health of Danica's family would also be improved as the new stove pipe guided smoke out of the home and through the roof. The stove would certainly help Danica save money by purchasing less wood. In addition, because Danica would not need as much wood to operate her business, the environment would benefit. The benefits were improved health, lower expenses, and less environmental resources used.

However, the impact of this stove project turned out to be of no apparent significance for the community. Nonetheless, Danica's family's health would be improved through less exposure to smoke within the home, and I felt we gained and/or strengthened relationships within the community. Yet, one of my specific desires for this project had been to spread this great idea and replicate it to have a more extensive impact on the community. If many of these stoves had been built, it would have had a greater reduction in the amount of wood usage for fuel, resulting in less damage to the environment. We had hoped this project would have been larger scale, but unfortunately, because the construction process was not more efficient and required Doug's assistance, I could not construct a stove without the risk of it falling apart on me. I would have to rely on Doug's experience for the proper clay "mixture." The bottom line was that I still could not properly build a stove on my own and Doug had work responsibilities in his own community. I could not keep asking him to take that much time away from his own endeavors. Danica, however, was happy with the result. Nevertheless, the stove project came to an end with my desire for greater community impact not being fulfilled.

30

Whitewater Rafting

"You cannot dream yourself into a character:
you must hammer and forge yourself into one."
–Henry D. Thoreau

One of our initial goals when entering the Peace Corps included possibly finding a whitewater river and working with the community to open up economic opportunities in the form of a rafting business—not for Kathryn and me, but for local Nicaraguans. The whitewater industry has proven to be quite profitable around the world, and theoretically Nicaragua would be no different if a suitable river could be located and utilized on a consistent basis. Costa Rica has great whitewater, and Honduras has some whitewater, as does Guatemala. Nicaragua has basically the same geographical attributes and elevation changes as the above-mentioned countries. The weather patterns are somewhat similar, and I did not feel like it was out of the realm of possibility that an acceptable whitewater river existed in Nicaragua. Yet tourism based on rivers had not been developed in Nicaragua. We speculated that perhaps people did not feel secure traveling to and exploring Nicaragua due to the brutal reputation the country had earned during its civil war. Then again, maybe no whitewater existed. Either way, Kathryn and I decided to find out for ourselves.

From the moment we set foot in the country, we looked anywhere and everywhere for a decent river. We studied maps and asked local people for their thoughts on the subject. The general consensus was that if a good whitewater river existed, it would be in the Pacific northwest region of the country, right where Kathryn and I lived for our service.

While we traveled via bus, taxi, or walking around, we inquired about rivers. Nothing interested us until Kathryn and I took a trip farther northwest to a town called San Juan de Limay to visit with our Volunteer friend, John Briggs. About twenty minutes north of Estelí on the Pan-American Highway, Kathryn and I spotted what looked to be whitewater in a canyon well below the highway. We marked the spot from the bus and noted that we should return to explore the area. When we asked the locals what river was down below, we learned that it was the Río Estelí. It looked good from a thousand feet above the river, which meant that the water was more than likely pretty rough. Additionally, when we arrived in San Juan de Limay, we asked John Briggs about the rivers and he said with certainty that he had seen whitewater in the area. Would it be ideal for a whitewater rafting business? John did not know, but he promised to show us the river.

Half of San Juan de Limay had been completely destroyed by a river during Hurricane Mitch. The fact that half of the town was destroyed by a river does not offer an indication of regularly flowing whitewater, but it does suggest that the area's watershed is significant. With many tributaries flowing in, it was possible to have a consistently-flowing whitewater river.

Once John guided us to the river where the whitewater began, I could see how the river would be epic to kayak in a flood, but only for small sections. In my mind, the short run would not serve to support an actual business.

To explore the river, we had brought car inner-tubes with us to float through the rapids. We soon found that we were not alone at the river as a group of boys about 12 or 13 years old swam at the river too, totally naked. I did not think much of it until Kathryn had run the rapid in her inner-tube and walked back to the top for another turn. The boys surrounded her and asked if they could use the inner-tube. I suddenly realized that these boys appeared closer to the age of men than boys. Kathryn was cool about it and let them use the inner-tube, but I watched them like a hawk. If anything disrespectful occurred, we would have had a problem. Kathryn laughed out loud and the boys loved using the inner-tube so much that they would not leave Kathryn alone, although I could not tell if it was because she had an inner-tube or because she was an attractive *gringa*. Either way, I eventually asked that Kathryn come down river to where John and I stood, and that the inner-tubing for the boys come to an end. We all chuckled as we climbed onto our tubes to continue down the river. We had a magnificent day.

I asked John if he had interest in exploring other areas of the region with us to see what whitewater existed, and if he wanted to join our little expedition to research the Río Estelí. He reacted immediately and wanted in on the game. Following a good rain, Kathryn and I found time away from work on a Saturday and we invited John to stay with us in Estelí. We were going to take inner-tubes down into the canyon outside of town to see what we could find. John showed up in Estelí, we grabbed our inner-tubes, and headed to the Pan-American Highway.

Our plan consisted of hitchhiking to the spot we had previously marked from the bus on the Pan-American highway and then somehow hike down into the canyon to access the river. The three of us left our house, and as we walked to the Pan-American Highway, we were intercepted by our gaggle of street kids. The Shady Bunch was full of energy, as always, and we welcomed the opportunity to spend time with them. While we played, we put our thumbs out at a traffic light to hitch a ride. Usually we only have to wait a minute or two before a vehicle stops, yet on this day, no one offered us a ride. I finally realized that no one picked us up because everybody thought the street kids were coming with us. Why would they think that? Marlon was on my shoulders swinging his body wildly from side to side while my thumb was out. I finally told the kids that we needed to catch a ride and that we would play later.

The Shady Bunch went on their way, and we continued trying to hitch a ride. During the next cycle of the traffic light, a pickup truck slowed to let us climb in the back. John, Kathryn, and I, plus our three inner-tubes, filled the back of the pickup completely. Kathryn and John sat in the far back of the truck by the tailgate, the inner-tubes filled the middle section of the truck bed, and I sat close to the cab. At the edge of town, the truck stopped at a gas station. The owner of the vehicle walked inside, but I had not even noticed what the guy looked like. As Kathryn and John were completely engaged in conversation, I waited contently and silently contemplated the fun, as well as the potential problems that we might encounter in the canyon. I had the basic materials for survival, but not much more than that. Should anything bad happen while we were in that gorge, life could get pretty unbearable quickly.

In the meantime, a guy walked out of the store straight to the bed of the pickup truck where I sat, which immediately snapped me out of envisioning our trip ahead. He leaned on the side of the vehicle to speak with me. I had been distracted as we had pulled into the gas station and had not seen our driver, so I assumed this was the man who had picked us up.

I said to the guy, "Hey, thanks a lot for giving us a ride."

The man responded, "*a la orden*," which is similar to saying, "at your service." Kathryn and John caught my eye because they started cracking up hysterically. I looked over to see what all the hubbub was about. John and Kathryn laughed so hard they could barely get the words out to say, "He's not our driver!" As they laughed even harder, I took a closer look at the guy who had perched on the cab of the truck to speak with me. He proceeded to push himself away from the side of the truck, stand up, and then begin to wobble and stumble, trying not to fall. He staggered about ten feet away from us until he hit the ground face first. Bam! And that was it—he was passed out cold as a wedge, drunk out of his mind. Oh my, Kathryn and John shook speechless, their laughter uncontrollable at this point. They were howling!

I said, "Well, thank goodness he's not our driver. Look at him, he's drunker than Cooter Brown."

At that point, our actual driver walked up to the truck and asked if we were ready to leave.

I said, "Yes, and thank you so much for the ride."
Kathryn waved her arm at me as if to applaud saying, "Yes, he's our real driver!"

I responded sarcastically, "You think you're so funny!" And off we went.

As we flew down the Pan-American Highway at about eighty miles an hour, I enjoyed the gorgeous day, which was not too hot. The wind blew all around us in the truck as we continued the adventure to explore a beautiful jungle canyon with my life partner and good friend. I felt about as free and happy as I ever have been in my life. However, I noticed John looking around confused with outstretched arms, as if to see if it was raining outside.

Over the top of the inner tubes situated between us, I yelled back to him, "John, what's wrong?"

John says, "I don't get it. We have a gorgeous day outside, and I feel like it's raining."

I hated to say it, but I recognized what was occurring and said,

"That's because the driver is spitting on you!" I started to laugh.

John said, "What are you talking about?"

I yelled, "The driver has chewing tobacco in his mouth, and he's spitting out the window. His tobacco juice is splattering on you!"

When Kathryn heard that explanation, she howled with laughter.

I said, "Watch."

Sure enough, another minute went by and the driver spit out the window. John reacted by saying, "Yeah, that's what it is alright." The problem was that he could not dodge the spit because the inner-tubes had him locked in place, and we were moving at a high rate of speed down the road. Any adjustment of the inner-tubes might send one flying out of the truck.

John said, "I'll just keep my mouth closed and wash off at the river."

I sat in the back of the truck with nothing to do but laugh and watch the driver from time to time hock a big spit out his window. Poor John could only sit with his hat across his face trying to protect himself, and Kathryn and I were in a painful state of hilarity! John could do nothing.

We suddenly saw the random path we wanted to take down into the canyon from the highway, banged on the side of the truck bed, and jumped out of the truck with our tubes when it stopped. We profusely thanked our driver as he drove off, quickly disappearing in the distance along the Pan-American highway. We found the path about a hundred meters away and agreed that it would be a good place to start. A few minutes later, we approached a man and woman who stood outside a house not too far from the road. We inquired about the river, who owned the land, and if we would need permission to walk down into the canyon.

The man pointed to a nearby trail to the river and affirmed that we did not need permission to access the Río Estelí. They did warn us that the river current was very strong, which really got me psyched for the adventure ahead. The trail had a lot of switchbacks and was pretty steep, but not ridiculous. We walked toward the inner sanctum of the gorge, taking about forty-five minutes to an hour to find relative flat ground at the bottom of the canyon.

We stumbled across an old cow trail running parallel with the river and followed it upstream until we came to a wire fence/gate. The gate looked old and seemed to be locked, but I did not study it. I decided that we had to climb over the fence. I threw my inner-tube over the wire and asked Kathryn for her inner-tube, and she gave it to me. I tossed it over the fence with mine, and then I grabbed John's tube from him and tossed it over with the others. I readied myself and then tried to hop-step over the fence, leaping into the air. Unfortunately when I landed, I fell into a rather large and disgusting mud hole on the other side. Realizing that there was nothing I could do about it, I bounced up with my entire backside soaking wet and muddy and exclaimed, "Well, I guess that's one way to do it."

Kathryn and John had stood unusually silent while I had been in motion. Finally, after witnessing my messy fall, Kathryn suddenly responded, "Or you could just open the gate." And with that she whipped out her index finger like it was a switch blade knife and effortlessly pushed the gate open with her finger. Kathryn casually walked through the gate as if she was a fashion model on a New York runway. I watched speechless and devastated. I also realized quickly that I would not soon live this moment down. John followed Kathryn through the gate as if he were Kathryn's designer, and they both cracked up, laughing and almost inaudibly saying that they could not understand for the life of them why I had asked for the inner-tubes.

I said, "Let's just keep moving funny people, shall we?"

John said, "And I'm supposed to trust you to be my guide in the wilderness after that?!"

Kathryn had trouble controlling her laughter. Boy, I felt embarrassed and recognized that John had a point.

After another twenty minutes or so hiking on the cow trail, we finally arrived at the river. Thus far the trip had gone rather easily—minus the gate crossing. As we approached the river, Kathryn and I were stoked! The river looked big, and a rapid upstream of us definitely appeared to be advanced-difficulty, experts-only whitewater (Class V). I knew we would not go anywhere near that one with an inner-tube, and I grew highly concerned about floating into a big rapid farther downstream after observing the beast up river from us. However, the rapid immediately in front of us looked to be a solid intermediate difficulty (Class III/IV), and certainly doable in a raft. Floating this rapid in an inner-tube was going to be an exciting ride. I wanted to scout the huge rapid upstream of us, but the vegetation was intensely thick. We decided to explore downstream for now and planned to come back again another day to closely observe the monster rapid upstream.

I expressed the plan that I would go first to see how rough the first rapid might be, and if I had problems, John and Kathryn would stay on the bank. I planned to cross the river on the inner-tube and end up downstream on the river right side in a calm eddy near the bank. I jumped out into the river on my tube, and the ride was on! The rapids almost threw me off the tube three or four times, and I constantly swam with my hands and kicked hard with my feet. I slammed into and bounced off a few rocks like a pinball and finally made it to an eddy across the river about fifty yards from the bottom of the rapid. I surprisingly made it into the eddy that I had aimed for, and from there, I could signal back to Kathryn and John. If I had traveled any farther downstream, I would not have been able to see them.

Now I had a decision to make. The question remained, could Kathryn and John make it through the rapid without hurting themselves? I knew the odds were pretty good that they would get tossed out of their tubes, because quite frankly, I was super lucky to have stayed in mine. Would the river be kind to them once they were exposed to the river swimming without their tubes, or would they be exposed to real danger? I had bounced off a few rocks and had checked out the riverbed pretty well and determined that the rocks did not seem jagged. They were well rounded, almost smooth. Should the others have to swim without their tubes, I decided the river would be kind enough to them. They might get skinned up a bit—maybe a few bumps and bruises, but nothing indicated that a severe accident would occur. Another risk might be a broken bone from an awkward impact on a rock. I determined that a broken bone—while difficult to deal with from this location—would be manageable, but that was not likely to occur. I signaled with my hands for them to go ahead, as I was too far downstream for them to hear me even if I yelled at the top of my lungs. I had to trust they were up for the challenge. Kathryn was next to go.

She entered the water and started swimming the tube toward the middle of the river. Almost immediately, she bounced out of her flotation. She struggled to get back on the tube, but it was no use; the river's strong current already had her, and she was rocking and rolling, trying to hang onto her flotation. She was swimming and kicking and pushing off rocks, and in general, managing her situation pretty well. The last fifty yards of the rapid was a big flush of water, like something a fire hydrant would blow out. I waved at Kathryn as she swam through this last jet of water, and she looked at me like I was supposed to do something. What could I do? Throw her a rope we did not have? Jump in my non-existent kayak and pick her up? No, she had to swim this one out, and that was all there was to it. She blew out the bottom of the rapid and came to a stop in a calm eddy. She remained there for a moment or two, catching her breath, and then yelled out, "Whooo hoo!!!" I knew she was fine, and my insides glowed with love for her. That was my gal. That woman is full-blown hard-core to the bone! I definitely married the right girl! Kathryn was jacked with adrenaline.

I gave John the go-ahead, and he jumped out into the river even after witnessing Kathryn's rather difficult swim. Poor John was upside-down almost immediately. This situation could cause a problem. He held on to the inner-tube, and he was still upside-down with his feet literally in the air. Then Kathryn and I could see his feet rising and falling, which probably meant that he was bashing his face on the rocks on the bottom of the river. I became very nervous as we watched his feet bob up and down, but there was nothing we could do. He was on the train, and once you are on that train, you are on your own. All of us understood that unfortunate fact before we even left Estelí.

Finally, John straightened himself out, popped his head up, and pointed his feet downstream. He bounced into rocks and pushed off of them while Kathryn and I jumped in the river to meet him downstream when he finished the rapid. A bloody miracle! He barely had a scratch or a bruise, but John definitely said his face was brushing the rocks on the bottom of the river. I had been correct about how smooth the rocks in the riverbed were. If I had been wrong about that fact, John's face may have been mangled. I was shocked there was not more bruising.

Kathryn and I decided to let John name the rapid since we were more than likely the first people from the States to run it. If you are the first to run a rapid, you get to name it. John decided to name the rapid "*Cara en las piedras, piernas en el aire*" or "Face in the Rocks, Legs in the

Air." Kathryn and I laughed and thought the name to be fitting of the experience.

We moved on down the river together and found the rapids to be small for several miles until we came to a bridge that looked to be a perfect take-out spot. We asked the locals about the river's water levels at various times of the year. By the time we were done with our research, we determined that the Río Estelí would not be appropriate for a whitewater rafting business. The river was beautiful, but the water quality was not very good, the rapids were not consistent, and the water level was very high at that moment relative to normal flows. If the rapids were not consistent at a high water level, they would theoretically not even exist at normal flows. Nonetheless, Kathryn and I agreed that we would come back to the Río Estelí to scout upstream next time and return in the future inspecting the river during different water levels.

When the next burst of rain came to the Pacific northwest mountains, Kathryn and I headed back to the Río Estelí without our friend John Briggs. Same deal—we hitched out of town and walked into the canyon at the same spot. We had to cross the river once again to scout the big Class V rapid upstream. We made it across successfully and very carefully hiked upstream through incredibly thick jungle vegetation to where we could have a decent view point. It was indeed impressive—a solid Class V rapid.

I brought a video camera with me this time so that I could document the rapid and study it later to determine where the hazards were and which lines to run. While videotaping the rapid, I felt like my left shoulder was itching. I asked Kathryn to check my right shoulder without stopping the video tape. She brushed my shoulder and did not say anything. I thanked her and continued to focus on what I was doing. In another thirty seconds I felt the itch again, and this time I stopped videotaping to look at my left shoulder. I am so thankful I did because a scorpion about the size of my HAND sat on my shoulder staring me right in the face with stinger up! My instinct was to instantly swipe at the creature with my right hand before it could sting me. I sent the six-inch scorpion flying about ten yards off into the vegetation, and then I felt the goose bumps run down my neck and my arms. I had remained calm, but I had also been stunned with fear. It was a close call, and I had damn near pissed myself.

Kathryn had seen the scorpion sail through the air and she circled me to ensure there wasn't another one. Then, I immediately checked her. She repeatedly asked me if I was sure I had not been stung. Being stung by a scorpion is something you would notice. I was confident I had not been stung, but I had definitely been incredibly scared for a moment. That critter was huge! We were both a bit shaken. I don't want to think about what would have happened if that scorpion had stung me in the neck or face. It reminded us that the jungle is no joke and we needed to be careful!

Kathryn and I moved farther upstream. The rapids again did not appear to hold any more consistency with higher elevation, and our exploration of the river as a whitewater tourism destination came to a disappointing end. We had concluded that the Río Estelí did not have what was needed to support a whitewater rafting business.

While the end goal was not attained as far as the Río Estelí was concerned, Kathryn and I, as well as John Briggs, certainly cherished our time in the gorge and immensely enjoyed tubing the river. We returned to the river a few times with our inner tubes on really hot days after good rains. We always had a phenomenal time on the river, and we have dear memories of the time we spent in that remote canyon. Yet, after searching the country as best we could, while at the same time not breaking Peace Corps rules regarding where we could travel, we exhausted our whitewater river potentials for a rafting business. I will say that Kathryn and I located and explored a potential first-decent for kayakers of an awesome creek outside of Matagalpa, complete with seventy-foot waterfalls, but I am keeping that one a secret for a future date. Other than that amazing creek (not for rafting), we were not able to find a single river in the country of Nicaragua that could be considered viable for a whitewater rafting company. However, we had a marvelous time during the search, and we loved our interactions with local Nicaraguans who we met along the way.

31
Habitat For Humanity
"A willing helper does not wait until he is asked."
–Danish Proverb

The goals of working with Habitat for Humanity were similar to those of all of our other Peace Corps projects. By constructing homes in this case, we wanted to improve the lives of others, develop new relationships, facilitate cross-cultural understanding, provide leadership within the community, portray the United States and the Peace Corps in a positive light, and have fun.

Working with Habitat for Humanity was fantastic! Kathryn and I initiated the effort through another Peace Corps Volunteer named Kerry Goodspeed, who referred us to the Habitat organization. Habitat was in need of translators, organizers, and general laborers, all of which were within the realm of capabilities that Kathryn and I had to offer.

We contacted the Habitat Project Manager in Estelí and learned that Habitat had an upcoming project planned in the town of San Ramón, located in the Department of Matagalpa. Kathryn and I were excited to work in another community, which would give us an opportunity to expand our familiarity with the country.

For this project, Habitat asked us to help translate and assist a rather large religious group from North Carolina that served as a sister church to a Nicaraguan church in San Ramón. The North Carolina group had raised a considerable amount of money to contribute to the construction of six new homes in San Ramón. The project was scheduled for the week of Semana Santa (Easter Week), which meant that we would not have classes to teach and had the time available to volunteer in this capacity.

Habitat constructs or rehabilitates homes, and the owners pay for the work being done in the same manner as a standard mortgage. However, the financial terms of these arrangements are manageable for the families, which is similar to how Habitat's operation runs in the States.

The monetary donation to Habitat from the North Carolina group supported the project through the purchase of materials. In addition, the North Carolina group volunteered their time, which usually meant that they took time off from their regular jobs to travel to Nicaragua and work in the brutal Central American heat by providing manual labor in an effort to improve the lives of Nicaraguans. I was in awe of their dedication because it was hard work, which was not for the mentally fragile or physically weak. In addition, many of these fine people from North Carolina were not young and had to pace themselves.

Kathryn and I caught a bus from Estelí at about 5:30 a.m. to Matagalpa and then caught another bus to San Ramón. We showed up in that town at about 8 a.m. and walked to the center of the small community. In the middle of the town, as in most Nicaraguan towns, stood a lovely church that was directly next to a central park. However, as Kathryn and I walked to our meeting with the Habitat organizers, we discussed how the church was run-down and in dire need of a paint job.

We learned later that week from a member of the North Carolina church group that a US$10,000 donation had been provided specifically to paint that San Ramón church, and enough time had passed to have that task completed. As I walked by the home of the preacher for this church, I took note that oddly enough, his home was in immaculate condition, perfectly painted with a white picket-fence circling the house and a new Toyota Hilux truck parked in the driveway. The woman from North Carolina had expressed disappointment and frustration that the church remained in disrepair, while the preacher's home had evidently been completely renovated. Welcome to Nicaragua. Let's be fair—there are also church scandals and theft in the United States. Yet this fine person from North Carolina looked to be in shock, whereas it did not surprise Kathryn and me in the least that it appeared there was a possibility that the Nicaraguan preacher had used the donation to fix his own home and maybe even buy a truck.

I may seem insensitive to this possible scandal or jumping to conclusions with respect to graft. Another example of a preacher taking money in Nicaragua was indeed a fact. A dental brigade from the United States came to a town near Estelí to offer free dental service. Yet the people seeking those services had to sign up for dental appointments through the local preacher. We learned that, without the knowledge of the dentists, the preacher was charging people from his own community for the dental appointments. Graft happens, and I'll leave it at that.

From a construction process and labor perspective, the Habitat project clearly demonstrated that building a home in Nicaragua is nowhere near the same as in the United States. First of all, we never saw any power tools whatsoever —no electric saws, nail guns, drills, cement mixers, jack hammers, backhoes, or other tractor machinery. This means that all work activity was accomplished by hand. The time it would take to complete a construction task in Nicaragua was likely four times as long as what it would be in the United States, and the rate of labor exhaustion was exponentially higher due to extreme heat and maximum effort.

During the Habitat project, I spent two days digging a hole for an outhouse! I worked with the local people to break the tough rock-laden ground, and the only tools we had to open the earth were a crowbar-type device or a square-toe shovel. We did not even have a pickaxe. Kathryn came to check on the house that I was working on and took photos of me with my arms around my new friends standing in that outhouse hole, knowing what it would be filled with in a few days. We laughed hysterically!

While what I consider "convenience tools" were not accessible, later a welding machine and a grinder became available to attach the beams for the roofs. However, we cringed watching the men weld because of their job-site work habits. The men wore welding masks on their heads—but no one would actually use the masks to protect their eyes.

During the welding process, the intense light that is distributed from the strike of the welding stick to metal can cause blindness over a long period of time. Workers should use protective eye wear with a thick UV shield to prevent permanent eyesight damage. In San Ramón, while attaching the beams of the roofs, the men welded and looked directly into the light that was being emitted. It is similar to looking at the sun for an extended period of time. I thought that maybe I was just not seeing things clearly at first or maybe there was a special "welding situation" that required an uncovered eye to complete the job. Yet the longer I observed, the more clear it became that these men were destroying their own eyesight. Worse, they had the proper protective equipment in their possession.

I did not want to be bossy and tell somebody what to do, so I inquired with one of the North Carolina folks if they had noticed the safety hazards related to the welding. I was told absolutely "yes," and the welders had been instructed to cover their eyes during these work activities because it could seriously damage their eyes. For whatever reason, these men would not protect themselves, and it was tough to watch.

The welds also needed to be cleaned with a metal grinder to take off what is known as the "slag." A face mask is required to operate a grinder because chunks of metal and sparks fly everywhere. However, here again, these guys used grinders with no face masks. Every once in a while, the men would jerk their heads away from the grinder, which basically meant they had just been hit in the face with a piece of metal. I spoke with more people about this safety hazard, but they explained that the men who were working this machinery understood their risks. If I had been the project manager, that job site would have been shut down instantly. Yet, Nicaragua, was a completely different scenario. I kept my mouth shut.

We learned a lot and came to have a greater appreciation for machinery. We mixed all the cement by hand. I am not sure if people are aware of how much concrete goes into building a brick home, including the slab for the floor, but it's a lot. Mixing cement in Central American heat will wear you down! Rock, sand, cement, and water—then MIX! This was heavy labor that took a toll on me, and I am not a small guy or unaccustomed to hard labor. I could only imagine how the sixty- to seventy-year-old women and men from North Carolina were feeling. They earned my complete respect.

We hand-cut all the rebar for the foundations of the house and the columns. We tied the rebar together with metal wire. The dull hacksaw blades required more time and effort to complete the assembly process. Absolutely everything was done by hand.

Constructing the homes took at least five days. During that time, we found the accommodations for Habitat's volunteers interesting. Kathryn and I stayed in a dorm-style hostel on the "girls only" side. Habitat told me I should sleep there—on the girls' side! Kathryn and I laughed and laughed because a big group of fifteen or so high school girls from Managua that had volunteered to provide labor for the project stayed in the same dorm as me. Velcro comes to mind when I think about how close I stayed to Kathryn while residing in the dormitory. I found the situation to be strange. I was told all the other beds for project volunteers were taken. I believed it, because Kathryn and I had to sleep together on a single bunk bed for five days. By the end of the five days, the girls from Managua had sort of adopted me as their team mascot. We joked about my presence, and they clearly had a fantastic volunteer experience.

At the end of the week, after the new homes had been pretty much completed, Habitat arranged a ceremonial party where the Mayor of San Ramón spoke to the volunteers and the recipient families. Kathryn and I felt the ceremony was a very uplifting experience and we appreciated the positive emotional reaction of the home beneficiaries.

I did not join the Peace Corps for a "thank you," but I had not really understood how good it would feel when a "thank you" did actually come our way. Kathryn and I had experienced what I would consider to be a "Peace Corps moment." It is the realization that something special that we had been involved with was accomplished.

The ceremony to end the project was amazing as all the people that worked on the project gathered to celebrate the accomplishment of a task to improve the lives of others. The magic of bringing people together for the right reasons, with the right resources, at the right time, with the right project idea was incredible! We commended Habitat for Humanity for their good work. Kathryn and I enjoyed the manual labor in the hot Central American heat so much that we volunteered again for another Habitat for Humanity project in Estelí.

Kathryn and I asked to be included in more Habitat projects in the Pacific northwestern part of the country. Within another month or so, Habitat asked us to help translate for a group of Canadians who had volunteered to build four homes in Estelí. We felt thrilled to have the opportunity to work with Habitat again. This time, the group of volunteers was much smaller. The San Ramón project had probably thirty people working on various different homes. The Habitat project in Estelí would have only ten volunteers plus Kathryn and me. Three people at each job site would do the manual labor as requested by the Habitat foreman. Our job was to translate the job tasks between the Canadians and the Habitat foremen. The Canadians really impressed us. These second-generation Canadians spoke English perfectly and were of mostly Chinese descent whose families had migrated to Canada for improved opportunities. We enjoyed being around them and they all worked incredibly hard. Like the volunteers from North Carolina, the Canadians made a large cash donation to purchase materials and came to Nicaragua on their vacation time.

Kathryn and I spent a week with the Canadians, working alongside them and throwing our sweat-equity into the homes. The Nicaraguan families worked right beside us as well, and we experienced an awesome three-way cultural exchange. Canadians, Nicaraguans, and Americans all laughed with each other and about one another's culture and peculiar ways.

At the end of the week, Kathryn and I had so much fun with the Canadians that we decided to join them on Friday for a night on the town to celebrate the accomplished work. Kathryn and I typically did not venture far from home after dark for safety reasons. I am sure nothing would probably have happened to us, but why take the chance if we did not have to? This particular Friday night, we met the Canadians at a disco, but the disco was pretty tame and the only thing going on was Karaoke. The Karaoke was painful to watch and to listen to, yet we were all thoroughly entertained by the lack of talent.

I noticed the amusement of our Canadian friends waning, and apparently Kathryn did too. I knew it was eventually coming, and Kathryn finally got around to harassing me to sing a tune. I brushed her off, blew her off, and begged her to stop until I finally realized she was not going to leave me alone until I gave the Americans a bad name for singing horribly. I asked for the song book and selected Harry Belefonte's Day-o Banana Boat Song. The song was so much fun in the movie *Beetlejuice* that I knew that whatever happened, the result would be fun. No matter how badly I sang, people would still have a great time.

I told the Canadians that I would only sing if they gave me their full support. They all agreed, and Kathryn was laughing hard before I even ripped the first note. I started into the tune, and the whole table stood up and began to dance. Some people were doing the twist, some were doing the Pulp Fiction John Travolta peace sign across the eyes, some were doing the submarine where you hold your nose and wiggle down to the floor. Then they would chime in to back me up at the appropriate time, "Day-o, day-o, daylight come and me want to go home." When the song ended, the whole bar was going nuts with laughter and applause! It was a great moment—definitely one of my best performances. Wait a minute—it was my *only* performance, but it worked. Oh my, how we laughed!

We attended a Habitat closing ceremony with all of the volunteers. Kathryn and I translated some of the sentiments that were shared between the Canadians and Nicaraguans who had worked together on the homes. Habitat even presented Kathryn and me with certificates of thanks—only my certificate said my name was "Erick de Cimmock," which implied that I was Kathryn's husband/property. Some of the Canadians found that pretty funny too—not just because she owned me, but because our names were also misspelled. We did not care; we were very grateful for the thought and consideration. We loved the Canadians and wished them well. They were all excellent, very caring human beings, and we were honored to have spent time with them.

During the Habitat project, Kathryn and I developed relationships with the Nicaraguan families that were constructing homes. A few weeks after the completion of the project, Kathryn and I wanted to go visit with those families to say hello and bring them a small, token housewarming gift. Everyone seemed to be very happy with their new accommodations.

There was one family in particular that had a household composed of a husband and wife, three daughters and one son. When we approached the home, the nine-year-old son was out front crying. Kathryn put her arm around him and asked what was wrong. The child said that his father had died. Kathryn hugged him, and so did I. His father was a good man who was incredibly pleased that the family finally had decent living arrangements. He had gone through a lot to be selected by Habitat for Humanity and worked very hard for his new home. His strength had been failing while we had worked on the house. At the time, he shared with us how much he appreciated the help of the volunteers and that he wished he could have physically helped more. Now the man was gone, and the family was in shambles. The father had died a few days earlier, but the emotion was clearly still raw and intense. Kathryn and I sat with the family for a while and then went home feeling an immense sadness but hoped that the father had felt some peace seeing his family living in their new home.

Our Habitat for Humanity projects were very successful and fulfilled all of our desires relative to our goals regarding Peace Corps and why we came to Nicaragua. In addition, the extensive press on the projects made the communities of both San Ramón and Estelí fully aware of the projects going on in their towns and what organizations had participated. The Peace Corps and Americans certainly received a fantastic bang for the buck with those Habitat for Humanity projects in terms of good press and community awareness. Habitat for Humanity Nicaragua rocks!

32
Kathryn "Quits"
"Who indeed can harm you if you are committed deeply to doing what is right?"
–Peter the Apostle

Living in Nicaragua can cause a significant amount of stress on Peace Corps Volunteers. Stress comes in many forms and may be caused by a variety of triggers—feeling homesick, personal safety concerns, no access to decent "American" food, social issues, lack of proper exercise—you name it, and it can cause stress in Nicaragua. Even good things like having a birthday party with a cake can cause stress. Why? Because other people might see the cake and their faces show sadness because they cannot afford one themselves. As another example, Kathryn and I went to the local grocery store and bought macaroni and cheese, which I was super excited about because it was difficult to find in Nicaragua. When we paid for the item, the clerk said something to the effect of, "How delicious, I wish I could eat that." It was Kraft macaroni and cheese from a box for goodness sake, but buying it caused me stress because I recognized that someone else wished they could afford to eat like I was. Guilt was my stressor in this scenario.

Exercise has always been a critical part of Kathryn's happiness. Physical exertion makes her feel good and helps her sleep well. In Nicaragua, safety concerns, limited free time, and the lack of cultural acceptance restricted Kathryn's ability to exercise. Once we moved to Estelí, I noticed that Kathryn began to become unbelievably moody. Through husband-and-wife communication, we finally narrowed this issue down to the fact that she was not getting enough exercise. Kathryn then initiated a running regimen in the mornings. This seemed to resolve the matter for about a week.

One day after her morning run, Kathryn came through the door, burst into tears, and yelled out, "I'm done! I quit!! I'm going home!!!" She then went into a verbal tirade that would make a sailor blush. It was a serious stressful situation, and I recognized it as such immediately. Kathryn does not behave like that for no good reason. I asked her to sit with me and explain what was happening. She conveyed that she was being verbally abused when she ran and that she did not understand why she was still sticking out here instead of blending in after several months of living in this town. Why did people not recognize her as more than a visitor and know not to treat her like a foreigner? In her training town, she had the advantage of walking with her "host sisters" who automatically afforded her acceptance and status. But here on her own, she was an outsider and this incident was the last straw to break the camel's back.

I said, "What do you mean, abused?" I told her that I had never heard anyone say anything negative to her in the streets of Nicaragua, ever. Unfortunately, my apparent disbelief seemed to incite Kathryn even more and she said, "That's because you are with me and you are a big guy. No man would ever say anything to me when you're around. When I go out on the street by myself, I receive constant 'catcalls.'"

I asked what was being said, and Kathryn said everyone started out by hissing and calling her "Chela" or "Chelita," which is kind of like saying "white girl" or "little white girl." Then she explained that the chanting would sometimes proceed to more hissing and other unmentionable commentary. Our language facilitators during training had told us that these terms "Chela" or "Chelita," and the masculine version, "Chele," in general were not intended to be offensive when directed toward *gringos*. Yet, every time I heard the word, which was often, I always felt awkward and completely understood Kathryn getting upset about being peppered with this slang while in the streets. Nonetheless, I asked her if she really wanted to go home because of a couple of silly men after all we had sacrificed to be here. Kat said that "no," she did not want to go home, but she was sick of putting up with these ridiculous men. Certainly catcalls exist in the United States and women everywhere must deal with this unwanted attention, but here in Nicaragua this situation was apparently exponentially more intense.

I proposed that I walk behind her incognito to witness the street behavior. "Operation Katcall" was about to begin. The next day as we left the house, I followed Kat from a distance to observe this behavior. Sure enough, guys called out and definitely made Kathryn feel uncomfortable.

When we retreated home, we talked about the situation. Kathryn seemed to think she needed some "Nica jeans" to help her "fit in" better. I indulged her in this venture and joined her to buy some "Nica jeans," which basically were stretchy jeans that fit tightly. Shopping is therapeutic for ladies, and with the danger of potentially terminating our service on the line, I was not about to interfere with a small spending spree. If anything, I thought the "Nica jeans" might make the situation worse because my wife is a beautiful woman, and tight jeans would draw more attention. I was thinking an ankle length burlap sack, a baseball cap, and a pirate patch for her new wardrobe, but I knew that would not fly.

I thought long and hard about her situation and began to realize why Kathryn was struggling. She wanted to fit in and be treated like an average Nicaraguan, so we talked about that, despite our living like many Nicaraguans, she was never going to "blend in" like she wanted. Recognizing this, I encouraged her to embrace the fact that we were different from Nicaraguans and there was nothing we could do about it. "Nica jeans" would not change that fact. I emphasized that we should not hide our differences, but embrace them and utilize those differences to learn from each other.

I also decided that the best way to work through this matter was with humor. I told Kath that I had another plan that should take care of the problem. I called my dad and asked him to order a Michigan State jersey with "Chelita" as the name on the back in big letters. A few weeks later the jersey arrived, and I presented it to Kathryn. The long jersey looked like a dress on her, which was perfect. I then suggested that she walk down the street normally, and when the guys call her "Chela," she should immediately go over to them and angrily tell them that her name was not "Chela," but "Chelita!" They needed to get the name straight! She would then turn around and point to the name "Chelita" on the back of the jersey, tell them to have a good day with a smile, and quickly walk away.

To try this strategy, I followed Kathryn out of the house and kept my distance. The first guy she passed by who normally harassed her from his porch immediately started in on her, saying "Hey Chela" and hissing at her. Kathryn stopped, casually walked over to the guy—right up to the steps of his porch, which actually seemed to scare him—and said, "My name is not 'Chela', it's 'Chelita,' understand?!" And then she turned quickly, pointed to the name on the back of the jersey, smiled, and quickly walked away.

The guy cracked up with laughter! He laughed hysterically and said something to the effect of, "*es buena gente, chelita,*" which translates to, "You're good people, little white girl!" And so Kathryn walked/ jogged/ran throughout the town. Everyone seem to appreciate the humor. Sidewalk merchants laughed, and people in general talked about "Chelita." By the time Kathryn came home, she seemed happy as she could be, and the guys around town stopped harassing her. At least the men who knew her understood not to mess with her. Kathryn is plenty tough with a great sense of humor, and now our community was getting to know her as I did. Operation "Katcall" came to a successful end with one of the best tools a Peace Corps Volunteer could use in their community—the very sharp and efficient tool called a sense of humor.

33
Kathryn's Second Top Ten List
"A light heart lives long."
–William Shakespeare

After several months of living in Estelí, Kathryn created the following top ten signs that we are further adapting to Nicaraguan culture:

10. We no longer swim far from shore for fear the lake will suck us down or that the monster beneath the surface will get us. (We have learned from some Nicaraguans that this could happen).
9. We no longer go barefoot on the cold ground, drink something cold when we are cooking, or take showers after ironing for fear of getting sick or permanently disabled.
8. We are pleasantly surprised to catch a "pretty bus," which is basically a slight upgrade from an old U.S. school bus.
7. We are no longer shocked to look out the bus window and see a pair of shoes at eye level with someone in them as we are cruising down the highway at sixty miles-per-hour.
6. We are no longer surprised to see security guards with shotguns in front of every decent restaurant or business, and all banks.
5. We are no longer alarmed to see a herd of cows cruising down Main Street.
4. We only mix rice with beans in the evening (not at lunchtime).
3. We no longer plan for a quick trip to the bank (there is no such thing).
2. We no longer expect an uneventful bus ride—that is to say a bus ride where no one throws up on you or shits their pants (due to parasites in their stomachs or having motion sickness), there are no flat tires, no major break downs, or no one gets run over. All of the above have happened. There is no such thing as an uneventful bus ride in Nicaragua.
1. We just wave when people call us "WHITEY" (Chele/Chela) and "LITTLE WHITEY" (Chelita)!

34
Kathryn's April Fools' Joke
"Happiness is not a state to arrive at, but a manner of traveling."
—Margaret Lee Runbeck

On any given day, I walked my dog briefly a couple of times. During one particular outing, I felt almost accosted by the female custodian of the school across the street from our home. Sam, my dog, liked to use the bathroom on a small spot of grass, located across the dirt road from our house and outside of school property. The female custodian shook her broom at me and told me to take my dog elsewhere to use the bathroom; she pointed out that she had kids walking through the area.

The custodian's suggestion to go to another location of course made sense on the surface. However, while the space just inside of the fence on school property was quite clean and free of trash and general debris, the area outside of the fence off school property, was terribly littered with trash and poop from neighborhood dogs. Waste was everywhere. I found it a bit comical that the custodian did not want my dog utilizing the area when it was clearly already in shambles.

With that said, I wanted to keep people in the neighborhood happy, and I certainly did not want to cause any problems with a school that was directly across the street from my home.

I asked the custodian, "Where would you prefer I walk my dog?"

She pointed to a place down the hill at the end of the block where Sam could go in peace. I agreed. I took the dog to the suggested area, and all seemed to be well. I came home and shared with Kathryn that we could no longer allow Sam to use the bathroom on the small spot of grass across the street. We now had to go to the bottom of the hill at the end of the block. I also told her why we had to make this change.

Kathryn reacted by laughing and said, "Really? With all the trash and neighborhood dogs roaming through that area, the lady picked you and Sam to prohibit use of that public location?"

I responded, "yes" and shrugged my shoulders as if to say, "welcome to Nicaragua." While it's fun to poke fun, the custodian had a point, and I did not want to contribute to the problem. I was fine with what was suggested, and so was Kathryn. We just found it odd.

A few weeks went by of following this new dog-walking routine.

One morning at about 7:00 a.m., Kathryn returned home from exercising and opened the curtain to our room and said, "Eric wake up, you are not going to believe this!"

The heat registered 95 degrees outside already and the noisy city buses running directly outside our house sent dust into our home through the rafters that were not attached to the roof. Dirt slowly sifted down onto me in bed through our mosquito net while I tried to sleep. In addition, I was sweating profusely and in general, just plain tired. Groggy, I said, "What is it, what's going on?"

Kathryn said, "Do you remember the custodian lady from the school that said we couldn't let Sam use the bathroom across the street?"

I responded, "yes," still trying to orient myself to the fact that the day was about to begin with a problem of some sort.

Kathryn continued, "Well, I took Sam to the bottom of the hill like the lady suggested, and while Sam was relieving herself, the lady came running from within school property to the fence and began yelling at me from behind the fence."

"Yelling at you? About what?"

Kathryn said, "The lady was screaming that Sam could not go to the bathroom there either."

As I shook my head, fully becoming awake, I said, "That's where the lady suggested we go!"

Kathryn said, "That's not all. After she yelled at me for a minute, Sam started to go poop and the lady freaked out and began climbing the eight-foot chain link fence in her skirt carrying a broom."

"What?!" That seemed a bit far-fetched, but it crossed my mind that weird things happen in Nicaragua.

Kathryn continued, "And after climbing the fence in her skirt with the broom, she ran over and hit Sam with that broom in mid-poop."

I was sitting up at this point, but had not even gotten out of bed yet and was shocked! In a tone of fiery anger, I said, "Kathryn, you're telling me this woman hit my dog with her broom for using the bathroom in a place that she suggested?!"

"Yes!"

I came flying out from under the mosquito net, threw on my pants, and was putting on my shirt as I walked out the door barefooted (which

I never do). This woman was about to learn that she could never hit my dog again without severe consequences. Kathryn suddenly jumped in front of me in the middle of the dirt road and says, "And that's not all!"

"You have got to be kidding, there's more?!"

"After she hit Sam with the broom, I grabbed the leash and started running back up the hill toward the house, but the lady was still yelling and chasing me with the broom over her head, as if she might hit me!"

"That's it!!" I said, and began charging across the street toward the school with Kathryn trying to hold me back a little.

Kathryn continued, "Yeah, so she was chasing us up the hill, and finally I got tired of her nonsense and turned around and yelled!"

At this point Kathryn stood on her tip toes, got right square in my face, literally two inches from me. Then she yelled, "I finally turned around and screamed at the lady—'April FOOLS!'"

I shook my head to let her words swirl around my furious brain, and then I yelled back at Kathryn, "April FOOLS?! You're yelling 'APRIL FOOLS,' at me?!! AT ME?!!!"

Kathryn's face broke into an enormous smile. Then in a super-calm, cool, and sarcastic voice she said, "Yep." And left me in the street to digest her devious joke while she walked back inside our home clapping and laughing hysterically. Standing stunned and motionless in the road, I contemplated just how badly she had burned me. I have no idea how long I remained in that spot before a truck horn brought me back to reality. The truck had stopped about three feet away, and the driver looked as if the biggest idiot on the planet was blocking the street. Quite frankly, his perception was not wrong. I quickly retreated home and began the healing process. I remained in shock, as a victim of this brutal humorous attack that utilized the most sensitive and vulnerable of subjects—my dog, Sam. Damn that woman! Without question, this situation required revenge.

Normally I would say the circumstances of being in Nicaragua caused Kathryn to act in such a sick and twisted way, but the truth be told, she has been getting me like this for years! You would think I'd learn. Every year we have been together she has successfully pranked me on April Fools' Day.

35
Community Banks
*"Let me tell you the secret that has led me to my goal.
My strength lies solely in my tenacity."*
–Louis Pasteur

In my mind, the community bank project was without question our most effective project while working in Nicaragua. It was also our personal top priority from the very beginning of our service, even though the community banks were considered to be a "side project" by the Peace Corps. We viewed this financial project as our highest priority because we recognized that adults could potentially benefit immediately, which would help their children, and the community impact might be long-lasting.

Kathryn had spoken of micro-finance projects and how much she had interest in them for many years while working at both the World Bank and Johns Hopkins University. When we decided to enter the Peace Corps, she commented that one of her first goals was to start a community bank or become involved with micro-finance in some way. From everything I had read, the endeavor seemed to have promise for benefiting a community, so I always supported Kathryn's interest in this effort.

Our three-month, regimented Peace Corps training program exposed us directly to different community bank models and processes that had success in some communities and other countries. After learning more about community banking projects, I was overwhelmed with enthusiasm for their potential. Kathryn and I both became determined and planned diligently to get one up and running in Estelí.

The banking model that we chose to study and potentially implement had been used with the Peace Corps in Ecuador, but we had to adjust some of the basic tenets in order to have long-term success in the Nicaraguan culture. We began to realize first-hand that the absolute keys to success included trust among the bank members and ownership of the banks by Nicaraguans. Outside intervention in these programs could jeopardize their sustainability. We definitely had a solid challenge on our hands.

What is a community bank? A community bank can come to fruition in many different forms. Some banking models, like the Grameen bank model, require money and continual technical assistance from outside the community to be successful, and others do not. What attracted us most to the banking system that we wanted to establish was that it was a true grassroots micro-finance development project. Why? All of the resources to start the bank came from within the community, and the money stayed within the community. In addition, once the bank was up and running, the community did not need outside technical help because they would have formed and managed it on their own. Therefore, the bank would be completely self-sustainable, and the community itself would benefit from the project over the long-term. Quite simply, our community bank model targeted a group of like-minded people working together and had three basic common goals:

1. To cultivate a habit of savings;
2. To provide access to short term credit; and
3. To increase their savings through interest earned.

At the end of each calendar year, the banks are liquidated and started again so that people can benefit from their savings and additional members can join.

Kathryn and I recognized and had to consider that trust among the banks' members was crucial to success. If members did not have confidence that other members would repay their loans, a run on the bank could occur and would fail rather quickly. Therefore, selecting the right group of people was mission critical. Yet who could we approach, and how would we—as *gringos*—convince them that starting a bank would benefit them?

What we did first was observe our community in action and think about different units that might work well together. We considered a multitude of groups, starting with large families. Families were generally like-minded and trust commonly existed. However, Nicaraguan families often had one income source, such as from a particular business or one breadwinner. The distribution of cash ended up skewed toward the head of the household. For that reason, using a family as a model banking group did not seem plausible and was swiftly put to rest.

However, consideration of the family-group selection process shed some light on another aspect of the bank, which was that each bank member had to have some type of income stream in order to make regular contributions to the bank in the form of savings. As obvious as that may sound, we were hoping to assist very poor people, but to have the bank be truly grassroots, the resources for the bank had to come from the community bank members themselves. No one outside the bank, including Kathryn and I, would loan money to start the bank. The Nicaraguan bank participants would save money that would then be available for loans to each other, and outsiders would not enter the picture financially. Our job was to facilitate the organization and structure of the bank, and Nicaraguans would own and run it. Thus, in order to participate in a bank, a member had to have consistent income. The stable income requirement presented another challenge—what types of people have jobs with consistent income in Nicaragua? The country is very poor!

The legitimate or recognized national banks of Nicaragua have strict financial standards for someone to open a checking account, and receiving a loan is difficult because approval depends on income level and credit history. Access to any type of credit is problematic in Nicaragua. Private-sector businesses, such as electronics retailers and even some banks, charge outrageous interest rates that can be as high as fifty percent on basic retail loans. The high rates placed many loan recipients into a position in which they could almost never pay back their debt. The reason for high interest rate credit is that financial stability within Nicaragua is fundamentally volatile, and many people default on their loans. Therefore, banks and individual businesses usually charge higher interest to maintain profitability. This common practice of high interest rate loans suggested an obvious need for access to reasonable credit in Nicaragua.

One of our basic rules for pursuing any project was to ask ourselves the simple question, *what is our community's need for this project?* In the case of access to credit, the community's need seemed severe.

We continued trying to find an appropriate group to start a bank. Not only did we want to find the right group, but we also hoped to find one with comparable groups in other areas of Estelí so that we could replicate the banking model. The idea being that if the first bank was successful, we could start other banks within Estelí.

We decided to approach merchants who sold vegetables in stalls next to each other in the town's market. They seemed to be like-minded with similar business activities, and they had income that was probably relatively stable. However, after talking to about twenty-five different vendors and making personal observations, we found that no one trusted anyone in this particular market, and each vendor thought that everyone else would default on their loans. In fact, we learned that there had been some confrontations between the merchants that bordered on small-time violence. Clearly the merchants were not a viable option.

After we tried a few other groups with no success, Kathryn and I grew impatient and even somewhat frustrated. We had been hopeful for success after speaking with a Director of a small school/day care for the children of working mothers. We met with the Director at length to explain the concept of the community bank and how it would work detailing the actual processes. We explained how participants would have to regularly contribute in the form of savings in order for the bank to function. Following our discussion, the Director offered to gather a group of women whose children attended the center.

We returned to the center a couple of days later as scheduled, very excited about the possibility of starting a community bank with a group of working mothers. We sat in a circle of chairs with the women and Director while we explained the entire bank concept and process to the group. The women sat quietly, yet attentively. When we asked if they would be interested in participating in this type of bank, the Director spoke before anyone else could answer and said, "These women have no money. They are so poor that they cannot save a single peso. If they save a peso for the bank, then they won't be able to have a cup of coffee that day." Kathryn and I were stunned. Not only did it seem humiliating to the women to have someone make the decision for them not to participate, they were also explicitly reminded by a person of authority of how poor they were. Moreover, we could not understand why the Director did not express this dilemma to us two days earlier when we had thoroughly explained to her how the bank worked. Disheartened, we thanked everyone for their time and left.

On our walk home, we tried to figure out what happened. Did we not explain the bank well two days ago? Did the Director not understand? After many questions, the most reasonable conclusion we could ascertain was that although we felt pretty confident we had conveyed the bank concept sufficiently, the Director must have thought that we would ultimately show up with funds to provide the women or center. The center existed on outside funding, and thus, perhaps the common expectation was that we would have financial resources to offer. This was not the first or the last time in Nicaragua that we faced what we thought was an expectation of providing monetary funds.

The challenge of finding an appropriate group for a bank had been daunting thus far, and we discussed the situation with several other Volunteers to receive their input and ideas. We learned that no community banks had been initiated by Volunteers in larger cities. Any successes at all with community banks in Nicaragua had been in small communities.

Nonetheless, we found a Volunteer that had a bank up and running in her community, and we traveled there by bus to observe a meeting and to interview the bank members to learn anything new to help us form a group in Estelí. The community was indeed very small; everyone knew each and every person within the community, and the bank members seemed especially close. Trust was quite evident among the members, and during our interviews, the participants expressed how the bank had been very beneficial to the community. Learning of the community benefits made us more determined to find an appropriate group in Estelí.

Back in Estelí, Kathryn and I typically "team-taught" during our business classes at the La Nexa high school as part of our primary Peace Corps project because about sixty students regularly attended our classes. One day, while Kathryn stood at the front of the classroom presenting material to the students, an extremely noisy accumulation of people gathered directly outside of our room. The classrooms in Nicaragua are open-air, meaning there is no glass in the windows—only bars so that there is a barrier, but air can easily flow. However, any activity that occurs outside the classroom can easily be seen and heard from inside.

I became distracted by the boisterous group of people outside, and I was surprised to see that the noise originated from several teachers. If this had been a bunch of kids, I would have immediately walked outside and asked them to either move along or be quiet and respect the learning environment. However, I had no intention of telling a group of teachers to move along or be quiet. Their lack of respect for the classroom environment disturbed me though because they had to know how disruptive their noisy conversation was to learning. They were either oblivious to this fact or did not care. I became more angry as the noise elevated so much that Kathryn looked over at me as if to say, "Can't you do something about that?"

I sat to contemplate my options, and then I began to closely observe the teachers interacting. They obviously shared good friendships and were fully engaged in discussing something they had each experienced. I thought to myself that they all generally deal with similar problems every day. By nature of occupation, they were a like-minded group. Then it hit me like a ton of bricks—the teachers were responsible, had steady jobs, and had some semblance of income stability since their paychecks were paid by the government. Then it hit me like another ton of bricks that the solution to our quest had been right in front of us this whole time—the teachers could potentially be a functional group for a community bank. It could be like a teachers' credit union in the United States. Kathryn and I had been overlooking the obvious!

A group of teachers would be perfect for a community bank—not to mention that Estelí had multiple schools. Should a bank work for one group of teachers, theoretically it could work for many groups. I became very excited about this possibility and immediately shared my thoughts with Kathryn after class. We both agreed that this could be the ideal scenario. We next needed to figure out how to approach the teachers very tactfully so as to have the Nicaraguans take interest in and assume ownership of the project.

Following some lengthy discussions about how to successfully sell the idea of a community bank to the teachers, we decided the best approach would be to drip the idea onto our counterpart at the other high school where we taught, Instituto Nacional. We pondered trying the community bank first at La Nexa, but some of the teachers already participated in some sort of credit program going on there, and we did not want to interfere.

Our counterpart at Instituto Nacional, Felipe, was a stellar individual. We loved working with him and spending time with him, and we had great rapport with him. We often visited each other's homes. One night, Kathryn and I had dinner with Felipe at our house and started talking about community banks. We made very subtle suggestions that a bank might work well at Instituto Nacional. Before long, Felipe said something to the effect that he thought a bank would work well at Nacional and that he would speak with the Directora (Director) of the school about organizing a bank with the teachers. BAM! The seed was planted, and it had become his idea to introduce it to the school where he worked. All we did was put some information out there for him to grasp. Felipe became our communicator of the idea and he completely understood the concepts. He transitioned from seeing how it would work well at the school to introducing the idea to the Directora. The scenario could not have worked out better. Taking this approach put the initial action entirely in the hands of a Nicaraguan to sell the idea. We would only help organize the bank. We did not need to have permission from the Directora; however, we did want to have her, as a person of authority, to allow the space to bring the bank to the attention of the teachers. The idea would then not only be coming from a Nicaraguan, it would also have the consideration of a supervisor.

Felipe did an excellent job of selling the bank concept to the Directora, and in turn, the Directora supported the idea by providing us the opportunity to present the bank concept to the interested teachers at the school, outside of classroom hours. In the meantime, Felipe discussed the bank idea with several teachers, and he said that some of them showed definite interest. He did warn us, however, that we had a challenge to overcome because a bank scheme in the recent past had not gone over well with some of the teachers.

During the first scheduled meeting with the teachers, Felipe introduced us and the community bank project briefly. We described the three main goals of the bank. We also communicated our roles as Peace Corp Volunteers and stated very clearly that we would have no place in the bank as investors, and that the pool of money to be loaned would have to come from them. Our only responsibility would be to help them establish the accounting system and the basic guidelines for the bank. The participants would decide the rules of the bank and how it would function based on various options that Kathryn and I would present. The members would own the bank and they would operate it free of outside influence, although we would certainly be available to assist if any problems arose.

The purpose of that first meeting had been to introduce the general idea and gauge the teachers' interest to determine if it was worthwhile to further pursue. At that point, we only asked if there was enough interest to have another meeting to explain the details and answer additional questions. In order to make this determination, we requested that everyone write either "yes" or "no" on a piece of paper that they put into a box on their way out the door, and we would look at the responses later. We thanked everyone for their time. We had run the idea of voting by slips of paper in a box through Felipe because we thought that the process would allow us to accurately gauge the general interest of the group, and it would avoid Nicaraguans feeling like they might offend us if they chose to say "no". Plus, it would allow them to privately vote without judgment or persuasion from other teachers. We did not want to contribute to any arguments or embarrassment among the teachers, which could potentially ensue if there had been any tension about others in the room not being able to pay their debts. We needed to ensure trust among the members.

The vote was almost unanimous in favor of another meeting among the approximately thirty teachers who taught classes in the school's afternoon session. The affirmative vote indicated those teachers had faith that loans would be repaid.

Prior to another meeting with the teachers, Kathryn and I knew that the bank would need a cash box with locks and keys, so we decided to help facilitate that process. We visited one of Estelí's many cigar factories to ask for an empty wooden cigar box. The management seemed surprised at our request for an *empty* box, but ultimately handed us one. After securing three different sets of locks on the box, it was ready for use.

When the teachers met again, we presented the participants with the box that would hold the community bank's money. We demonstrated how three bank officers would each be responsible for one lock, and they would not share keys. With separate locks, no one person would have access to the money, and all three bank officers would have to be present together to open the cash box. This practice would ensure transparency and accountability. We explained the details of how the bank would function and listed some of the rules that would need to be established. Everyone was still on board with the idea, and the teachers voted to appoint four bank officers: President, Treasurer, Secretary, and Sargent of Arms.

Later that week, we invited the four elected officers over to our house for dinner to discuss and establish the specific rules of the bank. As a guide, we provided examples of the rules set in other banks, but we reminded them that they needed to determine rules that would function best for their own bank. The context of this new community bank was quite different from that of other community banks in the country because those savings organizations had income sources that were varied. In this community bank, the participating teachers received their monthly salaries on the same day and had similar income levels, so the bank officers determined rules that were relevant and reasonable to this specific group.

By the next meeting at the school, the bank officers had already presented the rules to the other bank members, which had been slightly tweaked and approved by all participants. The teachers began saving money and the bank initiated loan distributions.

The key aspects of the community banks included a banking system that used basic accounting, and it was transparent, trustworthy, and efficient. The following provides some important points of how the bank functioned:

- The bank members determined the amount of savings, the maximum loan available, and the terms of repayment. In this case, the teachers earned about $80/month in salary, so the teachers decided that each of them could save one hundred córdobas a month, which at that time, would have been the equivalent of about $6.50/month.
- Everyone had to save the same amount of money at the same time. In this bank, since the teachers were paid monthly, they would all make their deposits on the day following payday, once a month. The deposit consistency kept the accounting very simple, and everyone knew exactly what was expected of them.
- The maximum loan amount was one thousand córdobas or about $65. Whatever amount was available in the savings pool was the amount available to loan to the participants. The members had to establish a maximum loan amount because there would always be

people who needed a lot of money, but one person could literally destroy the bank should they not be able to repay their debt. Plus, without a maximum loan amount, if one person had a gigantic loan, there might not be sufficient cash to support other members' credit needs.

- The bank only collected savings and distributed loans during a single year; there would be no withdrawal of savings until liquidation of the bank at the end of the year occurred. If some one had an absolute emergency or decided to leave the bank for whatever reason, they could have their deposits returned to them with no interest.
- No one had to take a loan if they did not need it. However, theoretically there would never be any cash in the box, as all the money would be loaned out and in the hands of the members. Plus, loans are how the bank made money through the interest earned.
- The terms stated that payment in full, plus ten percent interest, was due within thirty days.
- The bank would be initiated with a fixed number of members, and to keep the accounting simple and straight-forward, no new entrants would be allowed to join during the year.
- At the end of the year, the bank would be liquidated, and all who participated would receive their savings, plus an equal share of the bank's interest earned throughout the year. Subsequently, the bank would start planning for the next year's process.
- New members could be added to the system for the next year beginning in the month following the liquidation of the bank.

As we monitored the bank throughout the year as a "pilot," we discovered that the community bank could be used by the members similarly to how an American might use a credit card. We did some research on what the basic needs were in the community when a little extra cash was required to get through the month. The majority of extra expenditures that affected the teachers were related to health or education, such as buying medicine or school supplies. Kids got sick and although a doctor's visit required no expense to Nicaraguans, the patients or parents had to pay out-of-pocket for any medicine, often an unanticipated amount. Likewise, although primary and secondary education was legally free, associated costs, such as notebooks and transportation sometimes precluded children from attending or put the parents in a financial bind. Household repair comprised another common expense that usually revolved around protecting the home from weather, such as a sheet of tin to fix a leaky roof. Access to credit would definitely help improve these teachers' lives, and to top it off, each member would benefit through interest earned. Nonetheless, loan default risk is always involved, and for Nicaraguans without much disposable income, that risk was exceptionally high.

With the first bank now up and running, we planned to monitor this model bank, and if the results were positive, we would try to repeat the project at other schools in the community at the end of the year. In the meantime, Kathryn and I met a few teachers at the newly targeted schools so that we would not be complete strangers when we showed up later to present the idea of a bank. We recognized that teachers generally held more than one job, and thus often taught in more than one school. Due to this circumstance, teachers spread the word of the community bank's success faster than we ever imagined, They sold the idea for us.

With the exception of a few minor accounting questions, the first bank operated successfully with no major issues. Kathryn and I attended monthly bank meetings to offer support, but we did not interfere at all with how the meetings were conducted. We informally asked members about their perspectives on the bank, and the overwhelming response was very positive. We learned of parents being able to buy medicine for their sick children, repair homes, and purchase clothes, shoes, and basic school supplies. Everyone seemed happy with the process of saving and loaning money.

An unanticipated benefit was that our stature and relationship with the bank members continued to grow. Kathryn and I received an invitation to a party to celebrate the liquidation of the bank at the end of the year—an amazing experience. The bank was scheduled to liquidate at the end of the school year, which was very near to Christmas and before "summer break." Not only did everyone receive their money in the form of savings—not a common Nicaraguan practice—but they also received an equal portion of the income earned from the interest the bank had accrued. The calculated interest earned for each member was about 10% on their savings—an excellent rate. There had not been a single loan default all year! The bank members were thrilled, and so were we! Seeing Nicaraguans that happy was not a regular occurrence in our daily lives. In addition, during the party, the bank members gave thanks to a lot of people, including us for bringing the idea to their attention. What we appreciated so much about their "thanks" was that it confirmed that the community bank was their own and we had only introduced the idea—our goal had been achieved. Further, they expressed that they had never anticipated how the bank would bring them closer together as a group because they were able to support each other in times of need.

When Kathryn and I walked away from the bank liquidation party, Kathryn said to me, "I think we just had another Peace Corps moment." It was a wonderful feeling to have been of service, as facilitators, and the project looked to be sustainable.

While we were walking home from the bank liquidation party, still elated, yet baking in the Central American heat, a random street kid came up to us out of nowhere and said in very bad English, "Hey, fuck you, and give me one dollar!!"

I immediately and firmly asked that he go away and told him that what he said to us was very offensive. The kid moved on, but he definitely had popped our "happy" bubble in an instant. We continued for a few moments in silence before discussing what had happened and that such was the way of life in Nicaragua. We could never be too happy for very long; and yet, we were never very sad for too long either. The one constant we came to expect was that the ups and downs would be short-lived. Living in Nicaragua for us was consistently like riding an emotional roller coaster.

At about this time, Kathryn and I began our second year of service, and we had observed the first bank, as a pilot, for almost a full year. After the bank completed the annual cycle from initiation to liquidation, we knew for sure the banking model would work with the right group, and teachers appeared to be a functioning target market. We only had one year remaining to accomplish more.

In order to start additional community banks we believed the initial concept still needed to come from Nicaraguans. We kindly asked the

President of the first bank to present the idea and details of its operations to a new group of teachers at another school. If those teachers were in agreement, we would then help organize their bank. The President of the first bank instantly agreed, and within a week we stood in front of another group. This time it was the Ruben Dario Elementary School, across the street from our home. The President made our jobs easy by effectively explaining the concept and process of a community bank to the new group of teachers. Additionally, he sold them on the idea, based upon the positive personal experience that he and other teachers had while operating their bank over the past year. Before long, a community bank at the Ruben Dario Elementary School was up and running.

Much to our surprise, teachers who participated in the first community bank and worked at other schools had spread the word of success to their colleagues. We did not even have to approach additional schools because we were now being invited to present information about the community banks. We always tried to have the President of our first bank make the initial presentation because he was a sturdy character, an excellent salesman, and a very pleasant man. Before Kathryn and I could say, "Busy like popcorn on a skillet," we had SEVEN more community banks in operation. We were thrilled, but at the same time, we were somewhat nervous to see if the additional six banks would have positive results.

The Treasurer from the first bank at Instituto Nacional even started a savings program with the students in her class so that the class could have enough money at the end of the year to throw a party. Every student saved five córdobas per month, and the entire process was formally documented to help facilitate a habit of savings for the students as well. There were no loans involved with the students, only savings.

During our quarterly report to Peace Corps, we notified our Program Director of our progress. The Program Director asked us to deliver training sessions to current Volunteers in the country and to a newly-arriving group of business trainees. The hope was that others would be able to adopt the bank concept and put it to use in their own communities.

Community bank projects facilitated by Peace Corps Volunteers had some historical success in Nicaragua. However, success to that point had always been in very small communities. No other Volunteers had been able to, or had an interest in, initiating banks in a large community. Kathryn and I had broken new ground, and having seven banks in operation was pretty encouraging that others could reproduce the model in major cities around the country.

Relative to the population sizes of the metropolitan areas, our project imprint was still extremely minor. However, we were encouraged that teachers throughout the country might be able to benefit from these banks. All business Volunteers in Nicaragua had primary projects in schools, so the relationships with the teachers were baked in!

We looked for any opportunities to share the community bank idea. One weekend, as Kathryn and I tried hitching a ride back to Estelí from our monthly surfing trip in San Juan del Sur, a guy driving on the Pan-American Highway randomly offered a ride. He was a really nice fellow, and he asked if we were tourists and what we were doing in the country. We shared with him that we were Peace Corps Volunteers and told him a little about our projects. Of all the projects that we were tinkering around with, he said he really liked the idea of the community banks. He then said that he was the owner of a manufacturing plant, which was called a *fabrica* in the Zona Franca, an area that housed multiple manufacturing operations with tax incentives to employ large numbers of people. He happened to own the plant that manufactured Dickey's pants. He asked us if we thought the model we were using could be tailored to be effective with larger groups. We said we did not know, but that we would give it due thought. I asked how many people we were talking about, and he responded, "two thousand three-hundred."

I said, "Wow, that is a lot of employees."

The man continued by saying that he was always looking for ways to improve the lives of the people employed at his plant. Before he dropped us off for the next leg of our journey, he invited us to his plant to discuss the idea with his managers and financial team to see if we could develop something that would function. Kathryn and I readily agreed, and then he said, "Here, take these passes and show them at these casinos and get yourselves a nice meal. I own the casinos."

Two words for that luck—"Good Karma!" We thanked him for the opportunity, his kindness in offering us a ride, his willingness to help his employees, and for the free meals.

Kathryn and I considered the challenges with his request to start a community bank at his manufacturing plant and came up with some ideas to adjust the banking model. We traveled to Managua to speak with the Managers and Accountant at the plant. Sadly, in the end, we were unable to come to a workable solution, mostly because the company was already offering credit cards to employees who had been with the organization for a certain amount of time. Plus, we were due to return to the States within a month—so although this company seemed to be offering a lot of benefits to its employees already, we were not able to pursue offering a bank idea to other Zona Franca companies. Additionally, no Peace Corps Volunteers work in the immediate area of Managua, so it would have been tough for anyone else to initiate or carry on a project of that size. I still have difficulty seeing how it would have worked. What can I say, we tried.

Were our goals achieved regarding the community bank project? Yes, and then some. We offered people access to credit, we helped them establish a habit of savings, and enabled members of the bank to successfully realize more income through interest earned, even with currency inflation! Further, the empowerment factor was off the charts. The bank helped establish new relationships among teachers, and the project also helped establish our role as leaders within the schools and the community in general. Our goals were most definitely achieved!

36
La Empresa Creativa:
Our Primary Project

"Determine that the thing can and shall be done, and then we shall find the way."
–Abraham Lincoln

Our primary project was a lofty educational endeavor teaching high school students how to start their own businesses through a course that mirrored the Paul Coverdell-founded Junior Achievement program in the United States. The business course we taught called, *"La Empresa Creativa,"* was part of a national Peace Corps initiative to implement sustainable business classes in high schools all over the country.

As a small business Volunteer in Nicaragua, *La Empresa Creativa* was the primary project. The reasoning behind this national effort was that the unemployment rate in Nicaragua was very high, the economy was in shambles, and the ability of high school students to attend college was minimal. Therefore, as soon as students completed high school, they faced the extremely harsh realities of no employment, an unlikely possibility of obtaining a higher education, and a limited aptitude to initiate their own businesses. *La Empresa Creativa* was designed to help facilitate skill sets for those students so that upon high school graduation, the students would be able to initiate a micro-business and thus, possibly grow the entity into something that could sustain a household financially. Additionally, these classes would also teach the students valuable skills to help make them more employable for local businesses.

Kathryn and I received training on how to efficiently organize and lead these classes from the moment we began with Peace Corps Nicaragua. We were excited about the program and felt like we were prepared to face the challenges.

The project would help these students learn to think creatively in small groups about how to initiate businesses and then conduct market studies to determine the legitimate chance at success. Recognizing the importance of a solid market study before a business begins would help limit failures both within the class environment and hopefully in the future when their livelihoods depended on success. The following topics were specifically addressed in the *La Empresa Creativa* project:

- Creative thinking
- Introduction to business
- Business planning
- Market study
- Business expenses
- Budgets and capitalization
- Accounting
- Manufacturing
- Customer service
- Sales
- Reporting
- Cost benefit analysis
- Fixed and variable costs
- Personal household financial budgeting
- Critical decision-making
- Banking
- Occupations, businesses, institutions
- Risk management
- Economic cycles
- Interpreting economic indicators
- Public speaking, presentations, and a business competition between other schools.

There was a lot of material to cover, and the course included quizzes and tests like in a normal classroom scenario.

One unique aspect of this business class and project consisted of a local, regional and national competition. There was an intra-class competition to recognize the top four businesses at each participating school. The top four businesses from the intra-class events then competed at the regional level, and the best four businesses from the region then presented their businesses at a national competition to determine which school produced the most creative and potentially profitable enterprise.

The national competition, held in the capital city of Managua, awarded prizes to the winners and offered something great to have on the students' resumes. Prestige became a positive aspect as well because the Nicaraguan press covered the national event. Considering that most of these students had never traveled away from their communities, the thought of taking a trip to the capital city of Managua to present their businesses in a national competition was an exciting prospect.

How was the *La Empresa Creativa* class organized in terms of getting these micro-businesses up and running? The class divided up into small groups of no more than six students. Each group decided upon a business. Subsequently they planned, researched, financed, manufactured, accounted for, and sold their products. Each student had a specific area of responsibility for their group's business. At the end of the year, every student prepared an individual written report (similar to a term paper). All the group enterprises had to submit a written report and then deliver class presentations regarding their businesses and results. The written group business reports and the class presentations formed the basis of judging for the competition at the end of the school year.

The concept of these micro-businesses had to be "sold" so that they would be financed by resources from the community and families. The students put together a business plan and then conveyed that plan to potential investors. Some students managed to sell their ideas to people within the community, but most of the financing came from their families. Shares of each company were distributed to the individual investors, and the profits would likewise be returned according to the percentage of shares owned. The sizes of the businesses were very small—smaller than small—they were micro-businesses. The average business was initiated with minimal capital of no more than $20. Fortunately, $20 can go a long way in Nicaragua.

When Kathryn and I became Volunteers after completing our training program in late July of 2004, the previous Small Business Volunteers in Estelí, Erin and Mike Gerba, had just departed the country. This meant that we were taking over the Gerbas' *La Empresa Creativa* classes immediately upon our arrival. The Gerbas were teaching in one high school called La Nexa. Another high school had been added to our responsibilities, and so Kathryn and I taught at both La Nexa and Instituto Nacional.

In late August, we began teaching class right away at La Nexa, and we clearly saw the students excitement regarding their businesses. At that point midway through the school year, the national competition was not far away—November. The classes were active and moved at a brisk pace.

Our first class at La Nexa met three times a week in the evenings and had over sixty students. The classroom contained only fifty desks and chairs, so some kids sat on the floor, or two to a chair, which made classroom management challenging. Due to the high number of students, Kathryn and I decided to team-teach so that both of us would be in the classroom at the same time in order to offer more attention to the students and maintain better discipline. We also developed lesson plan consistency for all the classes that we led. Kathryn would teach one class, and I would support her. Then we would switch up, and I would teach a class with Kathryn supporting me.

The school system in Nicaragua was fascinating regarding the school calendar and the length of time that a student attends class on a daily basis. The schools in Estelí where we taught had various "sessions" during the day due to limited space and increasing student populations. Students attended class for a total of four hours per day. Following four hours of school, students would leave the premises and then another population of students would enter the school for a new session. There were three sessions—morning, afternoon, and evening. Every four hours there was a large flow of students coming and going from the building. Classes also occurred on Saturdays. Our class was generally held from 4:30-5:30p.m., which was outside regular school hours because *La Empresa Creativa* was considered an "elective" course.

The school year ran from the end of January to almost the end of November. However, while we lived in Nicaragua, school mostly began in February due to teachers' strikes over their low salaries, which was basically about $80/month. The school year was structured around typical harvest seasons, which were mostly November through January and considered their "summer" or "dry" season. The "winter" or "rainy" seasons were May through October.

We taught classes three times per week, and the students made solid progress with their businesses. Each student group sold enough shares of their companies to raise sufficient capital to purchase materials and begin manufacturing. Each company had various problems that were workable issues, and the majority of the students seemed to enjoy the financial activities in class because they learned about their own personal businesses.

In Nicaragua, classes could be generally cancelled for almost any reason, and one evening our class had to end early for a legitimate purpose—the electricity had been lost in all of Estelí. Ironically, instead of celebrating getting out of class early, our students were so engaged in the class activity that they continued on for as long as they could with no lights. To provide some illumination, I stood in the middle of the classroom with a lighter, which is a basic survival necessity in Nicaragua due to the electrical inconsistencies.

However, a female student then wanted to bump up the illumination a notch or two, by trying to ignite a torch made of notebook paper from my lighter. Kathryn and I both gasped as the student's wad of paper came alive with fire. The room immediately became fully lit, but in shock, I took the paper torch and stomped it out for fear of the fire getting out of control. However, after witnessing our reaction, the student gave Kathryn and me a peculiar look. We then noticed that using fire or a "paper torch" was in fact the standard operating procedure when the electricity went out in the school. We could easily see a significant fire burning in the library! Can you imagine setting any kind of fire in the library of a school in the United States? The experience seemed surreal and we noted this event as a big eye opener with respect to how different life was in Nicaragua.

As the school year progressed into the final month, the students' technical verbiage improved dramatically and so did their test scores. It was time to submit their individual and group written reports and to make their presentations for the intra-class competition to determine who would make it to the regional level. Only four businesses ended up in the regional competition in November—a t-shirt business, a newspaper, a bracelet/jewelry company, and an underwear business.

The intra-class competition was very educational, a little disturbing, and quite hilarious. The event was educational for everyone, myself and Kathryn included, as we learned first-hand what it meant for a Nicaraguan to give a public presentation. To help our students prepare for the competition, Kathryn and I provided an outline of the key elements of the student businesses. The presentations would have a time limit and would be judged on the overall idea of the business (its creativity); accounting (fixed costs, variable costs, and a budget); challenges faced and how they were overcome; profitability; manufacturing processes; students' roles and responsibilities; and quality of their visual displays. Each student would present information on their area of expertise within the business to allow everyone the chance to speak publicly. In the outline to their presentations, we proposed that they first introduce the business and acknowledge each student within the group. This is when Kathryn and I truly witnessed "fluff" in Nicaraguan presentations.

The first group to present was a business composed of all girls. The young ladies, clearly all very well-prepared personally to stand before a group of peers, walked confidently to the front of the class. At that time, Kathryn and I noticed they did not have any visual displays—no charts, no diagram of the company organization, nothing. We quietly acknowledged the issue between ourselves, decided to listen to what the students had to say, and then grill them on their business practices later to find out why they did not have visual displays. The visual graphics had been emphasized as critical elements to the success of their public presentations, and specific examples of our expectations had been provided.

The girls began by very eloquently thanking us for our hard work and for our leadership of the class. Kathryn and I smiled agreeing that their presentation was off to a good start. Then, an introduction of the corporate team occurred, and subsequently they thanked each member of the group for their contributions. Next, the team recognized the parents for their assistance and the principal for supporting the class. Following that, the group thanked the Mayor of Estelí for the work that had been done in the schools in general. The group recognized the Ministry of Education for bringing the class to their school. The group also sent out appreciation to the Peace Corps for their partnerships with the Ministry of Education and the school. The group gave special thanks to the President of the country. Finally, the librarian and janitors were thanked. By the time the young ladies finished offering their thanks, Kathryn sat amazed, while I was both furious and holding back laughter. They had used almost their entire presentation time as an introduction! The group spoke for about one minute concerning actual business material. The situation was shocking, and we thought we had failed in our ability to provide actionable instructions regarding their important presentation. While Kathryn and I thanked them for paying attention to who was actually involved and responsible for bringing this program into their class, we made it clear that a lengthy introduction was unnecessary and they needed to better prioritize their allotted time, not to mention the fact that there were no visual displays.

We thought about immediately terminating the intra-class competition at that point and beginning again with a demonstration of exactly what we expected to see and hear from the student's business presentations. We believed we had failed to properly describe what we were looking for in judging the businesses. However, we decided to give another group a chance to present. Much to our surprise, the next group's presentation was fabulous! They followed the outline we provided and had great visual displays. The business information they offered was accurate and easy to understand, each student participated, and they interacted with their audience. Those students presented a solid business.

After the first presentation, our reaction was shock; however, following the second presentation, we were elated that some students had learned valuable concepts. Obviously, the girls from the first group had not prepared. We offered the first group of young ladies another opportunity to present again in a later class because their grades depended on a successful presentation of the business, regardless of whether or not the business actually succeeded. At the end of the intra-class competition, we selected the top four businesses to compete in the regional event with schools from Condega and Pueblo Nuevo.

The regional event included Peace Corps Volunteers from other towns and the Directora of the school as judges. In the event of a tie, the Directora would make the final decision. Despite an entertaining and interesting competition, the final results of the regional event were disappointing for our school, as none of the businesses from our classes made it to the national competition.

The business competition was not only beneficial for the students to compete and speak publicly as experts on their very own enterprises, but it also delivered great media exposure for the Peace Corps project and its partnership with the Ministry of Education for implementing these business classes throughout the country.

The school year ended with a fantastic graduation ceremony, and of all things, a swimming party! Kathryn celebrated with the students, but was the only teacher to get in the water with them.

Were our goals for our first *La Empresa Creativa* class achieved in only four months of teaching? Most of our goals for that time-frame came to fruition. The children certainly learned what kind of effort and activities were needed to begin their own businesses, but our main goal of finding a teacher to take over the class had not been realized. However, time was on our side with respect to the issue of sustainability.

37

Medevac

"Fractures well cured make us more strong."
–Ralph Waldo Emerson

Unfortunately, I missed the memorable graduation events for our *La Empresa Creativa* class in the first year. I had to be medically evacuated (Peace Corps often uses the term "Medevac") to the United States for the back issues that had plagued me from pulling a muscle my first day in the country and then further injuring myself by falling while playing basketball with my host brothers during training. It turned out that I had herniated a disc, and I could not take the pain any more. After seven months, I needed serious help. Fortunately, while on "Medevac" status in Washington, D.C., the doctors from George Washington University Hospital Center treated the issue with an out-patient surgery, which led to an eventual complete recovery. The effective medical procedure allowed me to return to Nicaragua and finish my Peace Corps service. If the doctors had not been able to resolve the problem, my service would have ended. I am very grateful for the doctors' excellent medical care. I had been away from Nicaragua for two weeks, but it took much longer than two weeks to heal completely. However, the initial work had been done—the rest of the healing was up to me through physical therapy.

Shortly after my return, Kathryn also had to deal with medical issues in the States. While I had been in Washington, Kathryn went to the beach one weekend with some Volunteer friends. A few days after her beach trip, she became quite ill in the middle of the night in Estelí. Kathryn first knew she was sick when she laid in bed covered with 4 blankets and her thickest fleece clothing, while shaking violently from chills. It is cooler in the mountains of Estelí relative to other parts of the country, but not *that* cold. The chills were the first in a series of symptoms of her illness.

After about ten days of being sick, Kathryn thought her health was improving and traveled to the airport to greet me when I arrived from my Medevac leave of absence. Unfortunately, it was clear to me that Kathryn was still feeling very ill on the return bus to Estelí; she doubled over with stomach pain. By the time we arrived back in Estelí, we headed straight to the local hospital, as she had a fever of 104 degrees and punishing diarrhea. The Central American heat is difficult enough, but we were about to experience what it meant to be extremely sick and have to deal with the local health care system.

While waiting at the hospital for many hours into the middle of the night, Kathryn had to use the bathroom frequently. Being at the hospital actually seemed to exacerbate her condition, as there was no restroom available that she could easily use. Kathryn's pain appeared to increase. Someone occupied the only bathroom for an extended stay. When the occupant finally left, Kathryn entered and returned quite quickly. She informed a nurse that the bathroom was out of toilet paper, and the response shocked us. We discovered that the hospital provided no toilet paper in its own bathroom. Toilet paper, an obvious luxury, could be purchased in the little hospital store, if the store was open. However, at that hour of night, the store was closed. Finally, a very prepared woman, who knew what she was getting into, gave Kathryn some paper. My little buddy was incredibly ill. She lay down on a bench with her head in my lap and groaned in pain for hours. It broke my heart to see Kathryn in such a miserable condition.

All the while, we were witnessing some things that *gringos* do not get to see every day. A guy walked right by us who had cut his arm off with a machete. We also witnessed how expectant families are accommodated by the hospital—which is to say, they are not. A pregnant lady, who was clearly in labor, came into the hospital from the *campo* with her husband. The hospital admitted the pregnant woman and told the man that he could not stay with his wife. He was escorted out of the hospital and could not return until he was called. Since the couple lived in the *campo*, the husband had nowhere to stay in the city, so he slept on the ground at the parking lot of the hospital.

The hospital doctor finally attended to Kathryn and his only recommendation was for Kathryn to stay overnight to run some tests. Kathryn and I gave each other one look and politely exited the hospital. Staying overnight in the hospital was a scary proposition and we did not even consider it. After receiving basically no help from the hospital in Estelí, we traveled back to Managua by bus the next day to seek help from the Peace Corps doctors. A trip to the capital on a bus can be very unpleasant as there are no bathrooms on board. To some

Volunteers, it is a personal challenge to ride a bus at length with para-sites and not mess your pants. Kathryn was being put to the test.

Once in the capital, Kathryn took another series of exams that included blood work, and although it seemed she still had a bacterial infection, she did not have a severe blood infection, as was originally suspected. The results of additional tests would be ready in a few days, but the doctors thought that she may also have a parasite and pre-scribed Cipro. The Peace Corps typically prescribes Cipro to resolve most bacterial infections. Cipro is a strong medication, also known as the remedy for Anthrax. With medicine in hand, we returned to Estelí. Yet the symptoms did not go away. The pain was persistent for days, the diarrhea was a continuous problem, and a fever remained. Some-thing nasty was attacking Kathryn's system with brutal effects.

A few days later in Estelí, a Peace Corps doctor called Kathryn with the results of the tests. They indicated that she had acquired an amoeba, and a bacterial infection had wreaked havoc on her. However, the doctor explained that she did not know what kind of a bacterial infection. Whatever Kathryn had inside her seemed resistant to Cipro. Since we were soon traveling to the States for Christmas, Peace Corps said that we should call them for the latest results in a few days, which should help determine what medication would be needed. Following a week in the States, Kathryn called Peace Corps to learn that she had been living with E. coli. The doctor in Illinois had never treated E. coli before and had to do some research before prescribing medication that would eliminate it. Nonetheless, Kathryn still had more exams done via the Peace Corps when she arrived in Washington. She eventually made a complete recovery from a very serious illness. Peace Corps doctors took good care of Kathryn and me during times of need, and we were grateful to them for their highly professional care.

I did experience one minor health care incident, which was actually outside of Peace Corps' care, that I did not feel was very professional. In fact, it was downright ridiculous. I acquired a parasite during my last week of service and called the Peace Corps, who suggested that I seek a doctor in Estelí for a blood test. Fortunately, it did not take long to access a medical clinic in Estelí. As I sat in front of a doctor to explain my symptoms, the doctor opened his desk drawer, pulled out a regu-lar old thumb tack and said, "Hold out your thumb." I did not think he was going to prick me, but bam! He jammed that old tack into my thumb.

I screamed "Ouch, son of a bitch!" I do not normally curse, nor am I violent, but I almost punched him. Kathryn was three doors down the street from the doctor's office buying something at a store, and heard me yell. Alarmed, Kathryn came quickly to the clinic and asked me what happened.

As I told her, Kathryn rolled her eyes and responded with, "My husband, the wuss." The guy jammed that tack into my thumb so hard he hit bone! No sterilization or anything—but the doctor got his blood, and the test results revealed that I did have a parasite. No harm, no foul; but it was a very uncomfortable doctor's visit when I was already sick.

38
Sense of Smell in Health Care

"What we have to do ... is to find a way to celebrate our diversity and debate our differences without fracturing our communities."
–Hillary Rodham Clinton

Nicaraguan culture and health care sometimes produced scenarios that allowed Kathryn and me to truly celebrate diversity. A cultural trait of Nicaraguans is that they use their sense of smell to assist them with many different aspects of their lives. One of those uses of smell is to determine infection, and we learned that doctors commonly use the sense of smell to make their diagnoses.

Unfortunately, Kathryn had to have a root canal while in Nicaragua. Kathryn's tooth had been causing her increasing pain, so she traveled to Managua for dental care. The female dentist tried to ascertain the cause of the pain by sticking a needle into the root of the tooth and upon withdrawing it, held it to her nose taking a big whiff to determine that an infection was in fact present. The dentist then passed the sample on the dental instrument around the room for others to smell, confirming that the tooth was infected. They all undoubtedly concurred. Although this surprised Kathryn, she appreciated a different, more holistic approach to diagnosis.

Kathryn also had a relatively common occurrence for a female—a yeast infection, and she visited a local physician in Estelí. While Kathryn was in the stirrups being examined by a female physician, the doctor got really close in between Kathryn's legs—so close that the doctor's hair tickled her inner thighs. This "closeness" alone was enough to make Kathryn uncomfortable. However, after the female physician utilized a swab of some sort on the suspected "infected area," the doctor pulled away and stated that, as a matter of fact, Kathryn did indeed have a yeast infection. Then the doctor took a big whiff of the swab. While Kathryn was still squirming from witnessing the big sniff of the swab by the female physician, the doctor asked Kathryn if she wanted to smell the swab to confirm the doctor's opinion. She then put the swab up toward Kathryn's nose. While still in the stirrups, Kathryn kindly looked away and simply said, "No thank you, I'm sure you are correct."

I have always appreciated the sense of smell, but I had never heard of a physician taking a whiff of a swab that was just used on someone's crotch to diagnose a yeast infection. And then to actually put that swab up to the patient's nose??!! When Kathryn left the physician's office, she grabbed my arm and said, "Let's get out of here!" She then told me what transpired, and I could not walk because I was laughing so hard. It was a cultural difference in how infection was diagnosed, and the doctor was correct. However, that did not mean the experience was not funny—it was.

Both health care professionals had been accurate with their diagnoses. Those were cultural experiences to celebrate!

39

Almost Back to School, but Not Quite

"The most important trip you may take in life is meeting people half way."
–Henry Boyle

Our first full year of teaching business classes had been scheduled to begin on January 31, 2005. However, an ongoing nation-wide teachers' strike went unresolved for over three weeks. The strike, which we learned happened often during that time of year, had been initiated due to low teacher salaries. Educators in Nicaragua earn about twelve-hundred córdobas (or $80) per month, which calculates to less than $1000 per year. Most teachers needed a second or third job to survive.

At one point, the Nicaraguan Government declared the strike illegal and stopped paying the teachers completely, which made life especially hard on them. Kathryn and I could not turn our backs when a teacher we worked with, who supported his family on eighty dollars a month, asked us to borrow twelve bucks during the period of non-payment. Recognizing this was an unusual situation for educators and for our friend especially, we ponied up the $12. He hated having to ask for it, and we tried to make it as comfortable as possible. He promptly repaid the loan when the teachers' salaries were restored.

With the Nicaraguan Government deeply in debt, the International Monetary Fund (IMF) had a direct say in the budgetary affairs of the country. What we heard was that the IMF approved the increase in the education sector's budget, and consequently, classes began, albeit quite late. However, during the strike, we focused our time on other projects because there was always work to accomplish. We also made a trip to the beach that was one to remember.

40
Banana Truck

"Often I feel I go to some distant region of the world to be reminded of who I really am....Stripped of your ordinary surroundings, your friends, your daily routines, your refrigerator full of your food, your closet full of your clothes, you are forced into direct experience. Such direct experience inevitably makes you aware of who it is that is having the experience. That's not always comfortable, but it is always invigorating."
–From *Travels* by Michael Crichton

After we had been in the country for quite a while, there was one thing we learned to do that assisted our comfort and increased our adventures significantly—hitchhiking. Many uncomfortable bus rides made it clear that we preferred an alternative to using the bus system in Nicaragua. We liked to travel to get out of town one weekend a month, so we hitchhiked whenever possible. We had asked other Volunteers and Nicaraguans plenty of questions about the subject of hitchhiking to help manage our risk, and we started with very small trips. Nicaraguans hitchhike all the time. We finally decided to graduate and hitchhike to San Juan del Sur to surf. The trip took over five hours of actual travel time with five separate legs, so depending upon how long it took us to catch rides, we really had no idea how long we would be on the road. We had been to the beach enough to observe the roadway activities to and from, and we felt comfortable with the effort that we were about to make.

Surfing had started to feel more natural. It's hard to keep us out of the water, so the beach was an obvious place for us to vacation. Traveling to San Juan del Sur was always an adventure and never the same trip twice. We preferred hitching rides, as there is nothing quite like cruising through the countryside of Nicaragua with the fresh air whistling around in the back of a pickup truck.

Our strategy to catch rides was to use Kathryn as bait. Who wouldn't stop for a blonde-haired, blue-eyed *gringa* looking for a ride? Kathryn would stand out on the Pan-American Highway and bring in the catch, while Sam (our dog) and I would try to either hide completely behind a bush or look occupied some distance away. Once the vehicle stopped to help Kathryn out, she would ask if we could come along too. When she received a "yes," Sam and I would come running and jump in the back of the truck. Kathryn often rode up front with the Nicaraguans, and Sam and I would get the fresh air in the back.

On the way down to the beach on this particular occasion, we caught a ride with an eighteen-wheeler headed to Costa Rica. The semi did not really stop to pick us up; it was more like the truck driver decided he would slow down enough to offer a ride. Kathryn stood on the side rails and asked if Sam and I could come too. She quickly waved us in as the truck kept slowly moving down the highway. I darted out from behind a tree about thirty yards away, carrying Samantha in my arms. At that time, Sam was a forty-five-pound dog and eleven years old. I ran alongside the truck and literally hoisted the dog eight feet up to Kathryn, who was already in the cab. Still running, I made sure Sam landed safely in the cab and then did the best I could to hang onto the truck with one arm, as it accelerated down the highway. I finally pulled myself up and into the cab. Once situated in the eighteen-wheeler, high-fives were thrown all around, including to Sam. Off to the beach we went!

We quickly observed that this trucker waited for no one and passed at will. Who would challenge an eighteen-wheeler in Nicaragua? Cars and bicyclists ran off the road left and right as they encountered our rig, and high-fives for our driver went around inside the truck—WE WERE HAULING!!!

Kathryn and I felt nervous about the ride for many reasons, but the one that kept getting my attention was that every five miles or so, the driver would reach for a gallon jug of water from his console and then dump a little on his head. Kathryn, who sat in the sleeper area of the rig with Sam—which I thought was hysterical—asked the trucker, "Why do you dump the water on your head?" The trucker responded that he had been driving since Guatemala, so he had been up for twenty-four hours, and that if he did not dump water on his head, he would fall asleep.

It's times like these that I hear my father's voice saying, "Son, this is not good. Bad decision, get out of the truck." I chose to watch the driver closely and help him out with a nudge if I saw him nodding off. It was incredible the way he would pass anywhere he wanted—going up a hill or around a corner—location did not matter. The second anyone saw him coming, they moved off the road.

Kathryn thought that engaging the driver in conversation might help keep him alert. However, the noise from the engine of the truck was exceedingly loud in the cab, which made conversation a struggle. Every time Kathryn tried to talk to the driver, he would lean way over so that he could hear her, but as he leaned, he would also pull on the steering wheel, which consequently made the truck swerve all over the road.

At that point, we decided it would probably be safer to limit our conversation, but we did learn a little about him and recognized that he was a good guy and a family man. He explained that he was trying to get this load home to Costa Rica so he could get paid and see his kids. He had a long unexpected delay crossing the border into Nicaragua on his way to Guatemala, and was trying to make up some time. The trucker dropped us off at a turnoff to the beach. To see Kathryn and Sam climbing out of that rig was a memorable sight. Kathryn handed Sam down to me and then carefully worked her way to the ground. Thank goodness the trucker decided to actually stop to let us off.

We then picked up a less eventful ride with a great couple from Idaho, who drove us into the town of San Juan del Sur. By the time the sun set, we were all eating dinner at our favorite restaurant on the beach. We offered many times to buy dinner for them in exchange for their generosity, but they insisted on separate checks. Kath and I enjoyed a glass of wine at dinner, Sam nibbled on some leftovers, and we all seemed quite happy.

The next morning we took a boat ride north along the coast to find our favorite surf spot. We had some great laughs with a lot of fun people that we met, enjoyed good food, and we slept in hammocks on the beach under the stars at a place called Majagual. During the early morning hours of the following day, the sounds of howler monkeys woke us up as they climbed in the trees above us. Kathryn and I took one last surf session before making our way back toward Estelí. We had a phenomenal weekend.

On the way back from the beach, our traveling good luck seemed to end. Sunday afternoons tend to be a time in which everyone travels, so the buses were slam-packed. After trying to hitch, but not receiving a ride, we caught a bus not too far from the beach. And although we had to stand, we originally felt like we had enough room, until we began stopping for what seemed like hundreds of more people to board the bus.

We had become used to this "togetherness." However, the dilemma this time was poor Sam, who was on the floor and continually having to move to avoid being stepped on. Kathryn became very concerned that Sam was eventually going to fall out the back door of the bus. The money collector would frequently swing open the emergency exit while going fifty miles per hour down the highway, and Sam's hind legs would dangle out the back door. Plus, I had to stand over Sam protecting her from the additional feet that entered the bus from the rear exit.

Finally, as even more people climbed into the bus, we said "ENOUGH!" The next time the bus stopped, we bailed. We disembarked in the middle of a perfect nowhere. We looked around, and the only visible structure was a little family farm. We tried hitching for a while, but because we stood on an open stretch of the Pan-American Highway where people drove by at high rates of speed, no one had any interest in slowing down to pick us up.

After about half an hour, a large, very colorful, banana truck passed by and stopped about a hundred yards up the road from where Sam, Kathryn and I were standing. We excitedly ran up to these angels of mercy, and before they could say anything to us, Kathryn said, "Thank you so much for the ride!" Then we quickly loaded ourselves up in the back of the truck—dog and all—to sit right on the bananas. One of the workers looked at us from underneath his giant straw hat as he remained silent, slowly swinging in a hammock above the bananas. We were not very comfortable, but we were happy that we had caught a ride.

The problem at this point was that instead of accelerating forward, the truck slowly began to back up. I thought, "What the hell—where are these guys going?" When the truck reached the front of the little farm, it cut its engine and the driver went up to the house. "what NEXT?" The workers took out some tools and started tinkering with the bolts on the wheels.

After about thirty minutes of sitting in the scorching midday sun, we tried to figure out a polite way of inquiring as to what was going on and when we would be moving again. Tact was important, especially since it seemed we had no other options. We soon realized that the driver had gone to the farm to visit and have lunch. We had seen two guys leave the farm earlier on a motorcycle, presumably to go to a store in some town—who knows where—to buy food to cook for lunch. As you can imagine, the passing time moved by in an unhurried fashion. However, we certainly did not want to create a presence that the *gringos* had somewhere to go, and we didn't think we would have any luck finding another ride. So we sat in the searing heat with the bananas slowly beginning to compress beneath us.

After at least two hours, the truck was about to leave the farm. Kathryn and I had sunk a good six inches into the bananas, creating a nice comfy seat customized to the shape of our butts. We questioned how the bruised bananas would impact their sales, but they did not seem to be too concerned. We giggled as we contemplated biting into the bruised part of a banana in the future. Consequently, we did not eat bananas for quite some time following this trip.

During this period of forced reflection in the blistering heat while stalled out on the side of the Pan-American Highway, it suddenly occurred to us that these guys had absolutely no intention at all of stopping to give the *gringos* a ride. Rather, their plan was to go to this little farm to eat lunch, and two *gringos* with a dog had suddenly jumped in the back of their banana truck. The poor guys apparently did not have the heart to tell us that we couldn't have a ride. Further, you can bet we were not about to get out of the truck. We had a ride!

At last, the driver reappeared and offered us some leftover chicken that he carried in his dirty hands (Nicaraguans are very generous). We thanked him for the offer but insisted that he share the food with his workers instead, which they ravenously accepted. Finally, the truck departed, heading in the right direction. At that point, we calculated that we would arrive in Managua at about sunset. Considering this, Kathryn and I decided to ride with them all the way into the capital and then catch a bus north to Estelí. Since it would be almost dark while trying to leave Managua, we thought a bus would be safer than trying to hitch the rest of the way home.

We knew it would be a "photo finish" because the last bus for Estelí departed Managua at 5:30p.m., and it would be an unfortunate scenario to be stuck in the capital at sundown. However, just before entering the city limits, two policemen on the side of the road stopped the banana truck to check the driver's papers, which cost us about ten minutes.

Within moments following the traffic stop, the truck had a flat tire.

Kathryn reported every turn of the lug nuts to me, as the sun and all hopes of us catching the last bus out of Managua continued to sink, along with our asses into the bananas. Thirty minutes later, the tire was repaired. We were finally moving into the capital city.

The banana truck crew dropped us off, and we thanked them incessantly. We offered to compensate them for the bananas that we squished by sitting on them, but they would not accept our money. Laughing, they said that there were thousands of bananas in the truck.

We immediately caught a cab and arrived at the terminal right as the last bus to Estelí was leaving. After finding a seat for the three of us to share, we sighed some relief that our trip was almost over, as it is usually an easy three-hour ride to Estelí from there. However, the bus we caught was a *"ruta"* not an *"expresso,"* so it stopped literally hundreds of times as it climbed into the mountains. In fact, we stopped at a town square long enough to watch part of a basketball game while the bus driver did a little grocery shopping.

One of the last towns where the bus stopped before we arrived in Estelí was having their *"Hípica,"* which is usually a week-long series of community celebrations. A Sunday event typically includes a full day of riding horses and drinking for the participants—one activity not being exclusive of the other.

A group of about fifteen young men boarded our bus in this town and filled the seats around us. They continued their party by sharing and throwing their rum and slapping each other as hard as they possibly could, which incited howling laughter. Then their attention turned to the *gringos*. Let me just say that after seven hours of miserable travel, Kathryn and I—and more than likely, Sam too—were past our point of being sociable or entertained. That did not stop the Nicaraguan youths.

After one of the guys threw enchiladas all over Kathryn and me, I counted their number and decided it best not to smack him in anger. Besides, I was in the *"Peace"* Corps. I decided the best defense was a good offense in this situation. As tired as I was, I joined the party, graciously accepted a shot of rum from their bottle, started laughing, and got in a few solid playful smacks to the back of one guy's head—hard enough to let them all know that they might not want to throw enchiladas toward Kathryn again. I then sarcastically yelled what my smacks on the back of this guy's head sounded like, i.e., "FWAP!," and all of his friends gave an approving howl of laughter. Boys will be boys, and they stopped throwing enchiladas all over the bus.

Following another hour or so of this continuous torture from kids partying on a bus at the end of eight full hours of travel, we finally arrived in Estelí. After walking a couple of blocks to our home, Kathryn and I—and Sam—fell asleep within moments of our return. In all of my years, that trip to and from San Juan del Sur sticks out as an "epic" adventure. It was an entertaining, unpredictable, roll-with-the-punches-style excursion in a developing nation. ¡Pura vida!

41
Our First Full Year of Teaching Begins

"A teacher affects eternity; he/she can never tell where their influence stops."
—Henry Brooks Adams

Following the three-week teachers' strike, the *La Empresa Creativa* class for 2005 began in February. It became clear that there was no teacher willing or available to participate regularly in the classes, and therefore, no one would continue the business course once we left the country. Kathryn and I spoke with our Associate Program Director of the Peace Corps, Alberto Gonzalez, about meeting with the Directoras of both schools to emphasize the importance of training a teacher to continue these classes. We had a good working relationship with Alberto, who provided us support when we needed it. Within a couple of days, he traveled to Estelí for the meetings with the Directoras.

The first meeting with one of the Directoras seemed to be going along well, and then Alberto pulled out a filtered French cigarette and lit it up in her office. To be fair, Alberto is a great guy and a classic Latino, in the sense that he is larger than life. At that moment, he was wearing a button down shirt with three of the top buttons undone and a long gold chain around his neck. When he lit up that cigarette, I almost cracked up laughing, and I felt like a kid in church trying not to giggle. He was not only smoking, but he was in an official meeting inside of the school in the Directora's office. Apparently smoking was accepted behavior.

What Alberto said during this meeting seemed to have been effective, because we were assured the participation of not only one teacher, but two! An educator would be available for all of our classes that year. The meetings at both schools had similar outcomes.

However, one of those two "teachers" at the first school turned out to be the librarian. Kathryn swears that early on in the school year, the librarian locked herself into a room so she would not have to teach. The librarian was a good lady, and when she did teach, she was competent. Yet, she also had her regular duties and responsibilities to fulfill, so this course was obviously an added burden. The secret to having the librarian teach was to stay after her constantly to get her into class, although that became exhausting for all of us.

The librarian was also responsible for turning in grades for her/ our class to the Directora. Kathryn and I graded the papers and tests for that class and taught most of the time too. We also recorded the grades and maintained all class records, subsequently providing the information to the librarian. And with a class of over sixty students, you have to know that a few children will cause problems, not show up for class, and fail. Kathryn and I were open to any method of helping a student learn in order to pass them. If a student did not do well on a test, we would figure out another way to determine their knowledge of the subject—for example, having them write papers, oral discussions etc. Yet a few kids still did not approach us, didn't care, and did nothing even after we approached them; so those particular students failed.

Kathryn and I turned in the grades for the first term of the year to the librarian. A day or so later we asked to have the grade book back so we could update the records, and Kathryn noticed that the grades had been changed! The librarian altered the grades and passed the students who had failed. Kathryn and I left without discussing the matter with the librarian; we needed to strategize on how to handle this scandal. We were frustrated and anxious to leave the school, but when we arrived at the doors to enter and exit the building, we became even more disturbed—the doors to the school were locked! No one could enter or leave the building until the "*muchacho*" with the keys arrived. The entrance and exit of the school was always controlled, presumably for the safety of the students. On this occasion, Kathryn would not have been upset if the door was forced open! The *muchacho* with the keys finally showed up to unlock the door, and we departed the school with a feeling of disgust.

Kathryn and I determined that speaking with the librarian without involving the Directora was the best way to proceed. When we had this conversation, the librarian was very matter-of-fact in saying that she changed the grades because she knew that the kids would be in severe trouble at home with their parents if they had a "failing" grade. My first reaction was that the children should be in trouble. The librarian explained that we did not understand the level to which the students would potentially suffer and that the parents might beat those kids or throw them out of the house, etc. We recognized that we were working inside a very different school system and culture, and instead of attacking it, we proposed a compromise. Kathryn and I suggested that we tell the children they failed, but that we would give them an option to do extra work to raise their grades. If they were not willing to do extra work now to make up for their previous lack of interest, we would insist that the failing grades remain.

When we spoke with the students, they cried and said that we could not fail them and that they would do anything to not take home a failing grade. Presumably, the kids knew that teachers would pass them through. I am not sure exactly what was going on, but they were not about to be passed through by us—they would have to work or accept their failing grades. And they did work and learn, but they were not happy about it. All the students who initially failed, passed as an end result, but not without stress for all concerned.

We made it clear to the librarian that we deemed it inappropriate to change grades and pass children through who were not meeting certain standards, especially without notifying us of her decision. We all made nice, but Kathryn and I were still shocked and furious about what had happened.

During the next term of school, while Kathryn and I administered an exam, we caught multiple students cheating. We had faced this issue in our previous class, but we could not necessarily catch and prove the matter. This time, the kids were so blatant that we had to take action. When we asked for each student who had been cheating to stay in their seats after the other kids left class, they knew trouble was brewing.

Kathryn and I confronted the six kids about cheating, and one of the guys reacted so strongly that he spat on the floor in front of me in a vibrant display of disrespect. Kathryn and I looked at each other in disbelief and asked that all the students leave the class immediately. We walked straight to the Directora's office and showed her the documented proof of cheating. She did not react until I explained how we had confronted them and informed her of the spitting incident. At that point, the Directora became livid! I had never seen such anger from her, and I was almost scared for the students. However, she did not care one bit about the cheating scandal; all she wanted was the name of the student who had disrespected Kathryn and me by spitting on the floor. That child was in big trouble.

The Directora never mentioned anything about the cheating or how the subject was dealt with under her administration. We left the meeting in confusion, but we failed the students for that exam and told them if we caught them cheating again, we would kick them out of the class. The Directora suspended the student who had spit on the floor, and he apologized to us upon his return.

The cheating incident propelled us to implement a discipline contract with the entire class. This written contract outlined how any misbehavior would require a meeting with the Directora on the first offense. A second offense would prompt a meeting with the student's parents, and the third discipline issue would trigger expulsion from class. The students and their parents had to sign the document. Everyone took this contract very seriously, which made it quite effective. The kids, terrified to take the letter home, did so and returned it with their parents' signatures. In some cases, although it was not requested or required, a copy of the parent's *cedula* (identity card) was attached. We did not have a great deal of trouble going forward. There were of course some issues to manage, but ridiculously poor behavior had been eliminated.

Although these stories may seem to provide a negative view toward our students, nothing could be farther from the truth. WE LOVED OUR CLASSES, and the absolute majority of students attended class eager to learn. Only a minority of students were involved in the behavior that caused us problems.

The second teacher, María Elena, who was assigned to our other class at La Nexa was dedicated and fantastic. She attended class while we taught, and subsequently followed up with questions, if needed. María Elena soon took over the class completely, and Kathryn and I transitioned into a supporting role. A class full of sixty kids is very difficult to manage, and so Kathryn and I worked very hard to keep this teacher moving forward, while we did most of the grunt work. I discussed with Kathryn how hard it would be to teach these classes on your own, and we decided that we should figure out a way to get María Elena some help. Plus, we knew that she taught in two other schools and had very full, exhausting days.

One day a student who had graduated from our previous year's class approached us on the street and mentioned how much our class had helped with her business studies at the university. She had been a very good student in our class and was from a somewhat affluent family, so college was not out of the question for her. We were thrilled to hear her say that our class had been useful, as we were never really sure how valuable the class was to the students. Then it dawned on me to seek a partnership between the local university and the high schools so that the college students could support the *La Empresa Creativa* teachers.

Prior to graduating, university students were required to fulfill a number of hours with community service, and assisting in the high schools would help satisfy that requirement. In addition, the university students would practice their business skills and leadership, the high school teachers would have the needed support, and the high school students would receive more individualized attention. This type of partnership would be a "win" all the way around. We approached the local university with this proposal, and the administration was excited about the opportunity to create this partnership and have their students work in the high schools. The partnership was also well received by the administrations of both high schools. Kathryn and I then informed our new Peace Corps supervisor, Christina Marco, of the concept so that she could suggest the idea to all of the Small Business Volunteers who needed help in the classroom. The idea worked for us.

To add to the *La Empresa Creativa* curriculum, Kathryn and I also invited good business role-models into our classes to speak with our students. The speakers were successful business owners from within the community who offered presentations on how their businesses were started, what challenges they faced, and what they needed as far as technical skills to achieve their goals. They also addressed what talents they looked for in their employees, as well as what was required from a planning perspective to remain profitable and competitive. These business owners provided real insights, and the students definitely learned a lot in hearing about successful entrepreneurship.

The students from our Instituto Nacional business class approached Kathryn and me about hosting a haunted house to raise money for their graduation party and asked that we help them plan it properly. This group project would operate like a business, and we readily accepted their request for assistance. The students came up with the haunted house idea all on their own, and we felt like this fundraiser would be a winner. Kathryn and I tagged along with a select group of students who presented the Directora with a formal letter of request to utilize the school property for the event. Some personal begging from the kids did not hurt either. The Directora gave permission to have the event at the school, which I thought was fantastic of her. However, the key rule from the Directora was that *only* students from Instituto Nacional could participate in the haunted house. I later learned that the rule limiting participation was an excellent example of the Directora's astute understanding of the problems that could occur should the doors to the haunted house be open to the public.

The students developed a business plan for the haunted house that was not difficult to operate. They needed a scary product, promotion, volunteers to help maintain discipline while the students were in line, and a few people to collect money.

The haunted house itself was nothing more than a classroom decorated with black plastic to form a maze, and the students hid in corners or reached out to grab kids for the "scare" effect. The entrance fee cost was five córdobas, and the line to enter wrapped halfway around the school; many kids went through the house twice. The event was a smashing success! The business had made a profit, the end-of-year party was funded, and the students divided the remaining money. The kids were all very proud of themselves. Kathryn and I were happy for them, and to our knowledge, no one had put on a haunted house in Estelí prior to this fundraiser.

We shared the students' haunted house fundraising idea with our friend, John Briggs in San Juan de Limay, and he thought his students would have a great learning experience by putting on a haunted house there too. He presented the idea, and the kids and the Directora of his school jumped all over it. However, John's school's haunted house did not limit participation to only students from that school, probably because San Juan de Limay was a much smaller community. The students used the school's largest space, the gym, to host the haunted house, and they aimed for a much bigger payday by actively promoting the event and allowing the public to attend.

Kathryn and I were very excited for John and his students as well as the whole community of San Juan de Limay—the event was the talk of the town. We told John that we would travel to his community to support it in various different aspects from an operations standpoint.

On the day of the event, we caught a bus headed north from Estelí for our three-hour trip. At the turnoff from the Pan-American highway to San Juan de Limay, Kathryn and I exited the interior of the bus and climbed on top for the ride over the mountains. Being inside the bus was ridiculously uncomfortable due to overcrowding. Riding on top of the bus was lots of fun and offered a feeling of freedom, as well as a better view of the landscape. We had ridden on top of buses to Limay plenty of times before and understood the dangers such as low-hanging trees, accidents, and bad weather.

The trip to Limay basically led us up and over a mountain range, which was beautiful. However, as we climbed further into the mountains, the higher elevations would usually produce rain that sometimes pounded us so hard, it felt like bees were stinging us. Kathryn and I would shiver with chills as we sat soaking wet while the bus continued to rumble up to the top of the major peak. Yet by the time we crested the peak and traveled a mile or so down the other side, the weather always broke and the sun came out. We would eventually arrive in Limay completely dry.

Going to Limay was never boring, and on this particular day, I suffered an injury. Traveling to Limay on top of a bus required constant dodging of low-hanging tree limbs in various areas. After about an hour of fairly consistent ducking, I failed to duck low enough on one occasion, and another Nicaraguan who was on top of the bus right beside of me decided to duck the same way I did. Neither of us ended up able to duck low enough to clear a hanging tree limb. The bus, moving at about thirty miles per hour, ran me into the limb clocking me right in the face. Yes, it hurt. Yes, I felt embarrassed. And yes, I started to bleed. Kathryn knew I had not ripped my face off and that I would heal, so the sick-and-twisted side of her personality came out and she began to wail with laughter. She tried to act as a concerned wife, but Kathryn absolutely could not hold back the giggles. I left the wound alone and let it bleed. I really did not care at that point. I was soaking wet from the mountain rain and had been hit in the face by a tree branch. I was not a happy camper.

We arrived in Limay and walked to John's home. When John greeted us at the door, he said, "Oh wow, Starr, that's good! Where did you get the fake blood for your costume?" Even worse, he was serious.

Kathryn could not stand up because she was laughing so hard, and then I had to hear about the tree limb incident through Kathryn's eyes. Everyone doubled-over with laughter—but me.

The time came to walk to the school, located at the edge of town, and get the haunted house show on the road. The whole town seemed to be walking that way with us. John said the students had been preparing all week and that the event was going to be fantastic. Two policemen stood present, which made me feel good about the safety of the cash-on-hand and the basic order of the event. However, I could not have been more wrong.

The line to enter the haunted house grew quite quickly and people became impatient. At that point, some pushing and shoving occurred from not only the kids, but also the adults. Soon, students and adults crammed the lines to an extreme, and a crowd-control problem rapidly developed. No matter how much the two policemen tried to keep people under control, the line kept pushing and there was a rush to get inside whenever the door to the haunted house opened. Eventually, the police could not control the crowd. Ultimately, fifty people bum-rushed the haunted house door when it opened, and the cops just walked away.

In that moment, way too many people had entered, and they completely destroyed all the decorations, the maze, and any hope of continuing. The event had made money up to that point, but the haunted house closed immediately and many people walked away disappointed. The students took it all in stride and seemed happy enough that they made money. The lesson learned was that crowd-control was critical to success, and nobody was able to understand to what degree the police would be needed. Even the cops had been shoved aside!

Toward the end of the 2005 school year, a rumor somehow ran through the grapevine in our classes that Kathryn and I were about to leave the country. In the middle of class one afternoon, our students presented us with several special gifts and expressed some very touching remarks.

Kath and I did not know what to think. My first gut instincts included, "What are they up to?" and "This is highly suspicious behavior," but the students were serious and really thought we had plans to leave soon. I almost did not have the heart to tell them that we still had another year teaching in their school.

We listened quietly to all they wanted to say, and when we finally told them that we were not leaving, Kath and I couldn't tell if they were going to kill us or hug us, so I quickly announced that we would give them all fifty extra points for the nice gifts and the thought. As you can imagine, the place immediately erupted with celebration as sixty kids jumped for joy. Then I had to tell them that I was joking, and that I could not give them fifty points. Kathryn announced, "You guys can kill him after class." They playfully bruised me up pretty well (even the girls were punching me), but I lived—no thanks to Kathryn.

As the 2005 school year was coming to a close, Kathryn and I prepared the students for the annual business competition. The competition at the close of the 2005 school year frustrated Kathryn and me for a second year in a row, as none of our classes' businesses won a place high enough in the regional competition to participate in the national *La Empresa Creativa* event.

The 2005 school year ended with a memorable graduation ceremony, and the students seemed to all be very excited about having completed high school. The students from Instituto Nacional used their haunted house funds to throw a fantastic graduation party on school grounds with food, drinks, and music. The La Nexa students also had their own graduation party, and we thoroughly enjoyed participating in all of the events.

That school year brought some major progress to the overall goal of having some impact and leaving behind sustainable business classes for La Nexa and Instituto Nacional. Now two classes at La Nexa had teachers assigned to the program. We knew the librarian probably would not actively participate in the class, but we also knew that María Elena had an excellent chance of continuing the class after we left the country. We had worked with her for almost the whole year. She was trained, competent—and even better—she had interest in the class.

At Instituto Nacional, the teacher assigned to the business class also served as the Treasurer for the community bank at the school. We had worked with her in the classroom during the year as well, and we were encouraged that the project at least had a chance at sustainability in both schools going forward into 2006.

The 2006 school year would be short for us because we started classes in early February, but our Peace Corps service would end in

July—twenty-seven months after our training started. From a project perspective, everything needed to be established early in 2006 so that we could feel comfortable knowing where the course stood by the time we left. Was the project going to be successful in establishing quality sustainable business classes at both schools? That was the two-dollar question. Meanwhile, during our entire service, the Associate Peace Corps Director for the Small Business Program had been advocating at the national level for the government to have all the schools across the country implement the *La Empresa Creativa* business course.

We had been training these teachers to take over the classes, and during the beginning of the 2006 school year, we planned to find out if the teachers would commit to leading the classes going forward. Our job in 2006 was to support the teachers while they actually led the classes.

The year started out great at Instituto Nacional as the community bank Treasurer, who had taken over our business class, was doing a wonderful job. At La Nexa, the second teacher, María Elena, turned out to be a highly-effective educator and the librarian was also making progress. All classes were taken over by Nicaraguan teachers, which was an incredible turn of events, considering where we had started.

We began the project in the schools with little chance of creating sustainable business classes because no teachers were available or interested. By the end of our service, teachers had been trained and there was interest in continuing the program. Having teachers assigned to lead our classes may have been the result of the Directoras' recognition that there was true value in business education for their students. The project seemed to be coming together nicely, and we still had a few months remaining to better prepare and help organize the teachers for their future classes. The lesson plans had already been designed for the teachers by us from the previous year of instructing the course, so all the new teachers had to do was follow the program. The project was working! Right at the end of our service, everything came together as well as we could have possibly expected. We had overcome a number of challenges during our service and were pleased that there had been some positive achievements, including increased business training opportunities for high school students.

Since our service concluded in July 2006, that school year ended early for us. The students from both high schools presented Kathryn and me with some very endearing going-away cards. The Directora of Instituto Nacional also gave Kathryn an elegant Nicaraguan dress. The end of our service was a very sad time for Kathryn and me, as neither of us wanted to stop working on our projects. We found ourselves saying "goodbye" to people in the schools and offering our contact information should they ever need help or want to say "hello". The only consolation was that we felt we had made a positive impact in the schools in which we worked, and our *La Empresa Creativa* project was functioning at a sustainable level—at least for now. In fact, María Elena, the teacher who continued working with our class at La Nexa, later contacted Kathryn and me to inform us that a business from her class won the *La Empresa* National Competition that year! We wished we could have celebrated that great success with the kids, but we had already returned to the States.

The *La Empresa Creativa* project was a very challenging and rewarding endeavor. In my opinion, it was a successful program, as the Ministry of Education eventually required implementation of the class for all schools nationwide in later years. This decision by the Ministry of Education meant that all high schools in the entire country had to assign teachers to the business classes. Available incoming Peace Corps Volunteers assisted with the training of these teachers.

The entire *La Empresa Creativa* project was uplifting for Kathryn and me personally, and it turned out to be sustainable. The project had worked on a national level and had been adopted by the Government of Nicaragua. Kathryn and I could not have been happier with this sustainability and that the main goals of our primary project had eventually been achieved.

42

A Little More Fun

"People rarely succeed unless they have fun in what they are doing."
–Dale Carnegie

The community of San Juan de Limay ("Limay") is considered a horse town. One usable dirt road led to that municipality from the Pan-American Highway, and it took three hours to arrive there by bus. Walking down the main street always made me think that we had been time-warped back to the late 1800s in the United States. Multiple horses typically stood tied up outside the general store, and life moved really slowly.

Around the time of the Limay haunted house, Kathryn and I became very interested in the idea of acquiring a horse. John Briggs, the Volunteer from Limay, already owned a tall, gorgeous, gray horse. Following a comment from Kathryn that she would love to have a horse someday, I said, "There's no time like the present." After John searched in nearby communities for us, Kathryn and I bought two horses for around a $100 each, which is about the cost of a day's rental in the United States. These horses provided a fabulous means to visit remote communities and explore the Pacific northwest mountains of Nicaragua.

My horse was white in color, so I named him "Chele," which means "Whitey." Oddly enough, I was called the same name, "Chele," quite often during our two-year service. I told people they could call my horse and me "Los Dos Cheles," or "The Two Whiteys."

Kathryn decided to name her horse "Barney," because for some reason she had been calling a dog down the street from us in Estelí "Barney." Here's the funny part—"Barney" was not the dog's real name! The dog's name was actually "Ranger," but Kathryn kept calling the dog "Barney" anyway. Why? Who knows? Kath apparently just liked the name "Barney." So when we purchased the horse, the poor critter was naturally going to be called....? That's right—"Barney." Go figure.

Poor Barney had a bad day when we purchased him. Kathryn says we "burned her horse." Other people call it "branding," which we were told was necessary. Kathryn said we "drove nails into Barney's feet." Other people would say we put shoes on him. Kath said we "had poor

Barney stuck with needles." Other people would say we gave him vita-min injections and parasite medication. Kathryn said we "cut Barney's mouth with knives and stuff like that." Other people would explain that the horse's mouth had a minor surgical procedure so that he could eat more effectively. By the time the day was over, Kathryn was giving poor Barney hugs and apologizing profusely for the "abuse." Other people would call it taking good care of your horse. The Vet certainly had a good day financially. Barney was a great horse with a strong, yet gentle spirit, and Kathryn loved him dearly. My horse, Chele, was a pretty sweet ride as well. Kathryn and I could not wait to explore the mountains by horseback.

A few weeks later, we decided to take a weekend camping trip with John Briggs on our horses. Kathryn's horse seemed to be growing up really fast and we quickly recognized that Barney started acting like an obnoxious teenager. After a long day of riding through a gorgeous mountainside, we found a camping spot beside a beautiful river. As I pitched our tent, Kathryn walked Barney up a distant hill to put him away for the night. Suddenly, I heard Kath scream loudly. Startled, I yelled up to see if she was okay, and Kathryn shouted back that the horse had bitten her hard—on the ass! I laughed, and she laughed too though it clearly hurt.

The next day, I shared what happened to Kathryn with an old man from the area. In front of Kathryn, the old man responded that he knew exactly why the horse had bit her in the ass. The old man con-tinued with an absolute straight face, "It's because you're fat!" I got another good laugh out of that comment! I generally like to share funny stories with others, because they will usually tell me a funny one in return. However, this time I was dismayed by the response from the old man, and so was Kathryn. It was hysterical! Kathryn was bitten in the behind because she had a fat backside. Yeah, Kathryn *loved* that comment (sarcasm).

The next night of the trip, we found a local family who had a fair-ly secure fenced-in-area where Barney and the other horses could stay. However, sometime during the middle of the night, Barney escaped by jumping over the gate. Barney's mischief created all kinds of problems because he managed to stir up other horses in the area, and they all start-ed howling like a bunch of coyotes! And they began running everywhere!

Sometime after our three-day trip, we loaned Barney to a Volunteer named JC Clark, who wanted to experience the mountains by horseback too. Kath was happy to offer Barney to him for this unique opportunity. JC ventured a day or two out into the wilderness with friends, and as he came upon a small community, all of a sudden, Barney freaked out and ran JC right into a Nicaraguan home! Barney literally ran into the house with JC somehow still on his back. JC said he found himself in the living room in the saddle with Barney going nuts! He said the kids in the house were screaming—which made Barney more frantic—and all hell broke loose until he was finally able to get the horse out of the home. JC was lucky on multiple fronts—one, Barney did not buck him off through the tin roof, so he actually did not get physically hurt; two, the man of the house did not pull a machete on him; and three, no one from the home was injured. Let's examine what exactly happened. JC rode into a strange community out in the middle of nowhere Nicaragua and then accidently ended up in someone's home with a horse. Personally, I think JC was lucky he did not have a serious conflict! The bottom line was that JC knew how to handle himself on a horse, but Barney had become borderline dangerous!

We loaned Barney to another Volunteer who was bucked off harshly, causing a knee injury. All of the Volunteers who had experiences with Barney finally came together in Estelí, and after a ton of laughter telling stories, everyone except Kathryn agreed to rename the horse "Beevis."

The horses provided a great way to distract our minds and hearts from the challenging work in Nicaragua, and we always looked forward to the opportunity to ride and spend time with our beloved Chele and Beevis. At the end of our service, I sold my horse to an incoming Volunteer who would live close to Limay, and Kathryn offered Barney to a deserving family.

43
Kathryn's Women's Group
"The better part of one's life consists of his friendships."
–Abraham Lincoln

Following Kathryn's episode of feeling verbally abused while jogging through the streets of Estelí, she looked to exercise indoors. Kath found a great gym that was about as classic a place to go work out as any you could find in the country. The fitness center was owned by a very pleasant, muscular man named Guido.

The walls of the gym had posters of women from the 80s with super-big hair, wearing skin-tight leotards or garter belts with thigh-high, laced hosiery. The gym equipment consisted of mostly free weights, and there was an aerobics room. Kathryn signed up for a membership and participated in aerobics classes religiously. Little did she know at the time that her membership at Guido's gym would positively and dramatically impact her service in the Peace Corps.

Kathryn met a woman at Guido's gym by the name of Carolina. Carolina was a Honduran with a personality that was larger than life. She and Kathryn immediately became fast friends. Carolina shared with Kathryn that she had friends who worked at a non-profit organization called Funhori (pronounced, *fu-nor-ee*). Funhori had different programs and services to assist at-risk youth who had been members of local "gangs." Carolina invited Kathryn to visit the organization and meet some of her colleagues, and to review the programs offered for the at-risk youth.

Kathryn came home that evening and proposed that we should consider training Carolina and Funhori's all-female staff of five ladies with the *La Empresa Creativa* program. They would then be able teach the at-risk youth from Funhori how to start micro-businesses. I thought Kathryn had a great idea, but felt like I had my hands full with various side projects and suggested that Kathryn take this one on by herself. And so she did.

Kathryn immediately began working two nights a week with the women at Funhori to train them to lead business classes with the at-risk youth. Additionally, Kathryn began teaching English classes for the Funhori ladies and some of their friends, and then she helped facilitate a community bank with them. A very strong bond between Kathryn and these ladies grew. Multiple projects were now up and running within this women's group.

Kathryn's classes with the Funhori ladies began late in the afternoon and finished well past dark. Walking around as a female alone in Estelí after dark, while probably safe enough, was not necessarily the best idea. The women of Funhori, all of them, would walk Kathryn down the Pan-American Highway into our neighborhood and safely to our front door. Because the women from Funhori lived close to each other, they would then walk themselves home. It never ceased to amaze me how much care these women took to look out for Kathryn. The relationships that developed between Kathryn and the Funhori women were very special to witness.

The women's group from Funhori threw quite a birthday bash for Kathryn at the end of July, 2005—complete with several balloons! It may not sound like a big deal, but trust me, it's HUGE! Birthday celebrations were not common in Nicaragua. In fact, some children did not even know their own birth dates. This birthday party clearly indicated that Kathryn had reached these women on a deep level, and that her classes with them had been well received.

After Kathryn had started the business classes with her women's group, one of the ladies started a reasonably successful *pulpería,* a small corner store. Another lady from the group started a small clothing business using money from the community bank as capital to fund the venture. It was not difficult to see that Kathryn was having a positive impact on these ladies' lives, and vice-versa. The women from Funhori were also teaching the at-risk youth the *La Empresa Creativa* program, but those kids were a tough bunch and progress was slow. In the course of their work with the non-governmental organization, the ladies also exposed Kathryn to areas that she would not have seen on her own but yet enriched her perspective, including visits to the Estelí jail and to the municipality's garbage dump where families picked through the trash.

Kathryn's personal and project experience with the ladies of Funhori was incredibly successful. When it came time for our service to end, the going-away celebration was bittersweet. The ladies surprised Kathryn by taking her to a local restaurant where they had reserved a private dining room. Each woman stood and gave a presentation of how Kathryn had entered their life and how special she was to each person. This display of affection for Kathryn almost made me cry, but there was no stopping the ladies—there was not a dry eye in the room. After all the crying ended, the ladies had a song piped in through the sound system for their own performance with lyrics tailored toward Kathryn. We all danced around laughing and had a great evening.

Kathryn waited until our very last day in the country to finish working with the ladies of Funhori, and I was proud of what she had accomplished with the women of that organization and their friends. Kathryn's goals for the Funhori women from a project standpoint were certainly successful, yet the personal relationships that had developed really highlighted the Peace Corps experience in a very positive way.

44
Kathryn Loses It
*"Life's challenges are not supposed to paralyze you,
they're supposed to help you discover who you are."*
–Bernice Johnson Reagon

After living in a country like Nicaragua for so long, different situations in general may begin to have an impact on you. I'll admit that toward the end of my service, I had my moments of when I saw anything of privilege, my first response was an indignant, "Well aren't they fancy!"

From time to time throughout our service, Kathryn and I had discussed how the Peace Corps seemed to initially adapt Volunteers to the living conditions of Nicaragua as slowly as possible. As soon as we completed training, we lived at about the average Nicaraguan income level, which was not much money. We had what we considered a few splurges, such as when Kathryn's dad slipped a ten dollar bill into an anniversary card for us and we went out to celebrate at a Chinese restaurant—all on the ten dollars. While waiting for that meal, our street kids found us and we felt compelled to explain how it was a very special occasion for us.

When you live at the poverty line for long periods of time, it gets to you when you see someone with something really nice, such as a fancy birthday cake. While there are cake shops in Nicaragua, you do not really see people carrying cakes around town all that often. Kathryn and I had been living at what seemed to be the poverty line for almost two full years. One afternoon we saw a lady in a nice dress standing on a corner holding a beautifully-decorated birthday cake. In a very serious manner, Kathryn turned to me and said, "What if I just walk over to that lady and knock that cake right out of her hand and stomp on it in the street?"

Quite honestly, I was in shock. I admit not being thrilled seeing the lady with the cake, but to want to knock it out of her hands and stomp on it in the street seemed pretty harsh. I then quickly tried to make a joke out of it saying very sarcastically, "Yeah the nerve of somebody trying to actually celebrate a birthday! Who the hell do those people think they are?!"

That snapped Kathryn out of it. We laughed about what she had said, but I began to see the wear and tear that Nicaragua was putting on her. The comment was completely out of Kathryn's natural character. Kathryn's normal response would have been something more along the lines of, "Oh look, someone's having a birthday. Isn't that great? Look how beautifully-decorated the cake is." Let's face it, Kathryn and I are not rich Americans, but we had certainly never lived the way we had been for almost two years. The poverty and the country were affecting us.

Another example of going nuts, or at least not acting as we normally would, was one day as we walked to school, a cab driver literally almost ran me over while I was crossing the street at a stop sign. The cab did not stop at all, and I quickly jumped out of the way. Relieved that I had not been run over, I waved at the cab driver and said, "Sorry, and thank you for not running me over. Have a nice day!" The cab driver had been completely at fault, and I was seriously apologizing and saying thanks for not running me over! Any other time, I would have been raising hell about almost being killed. Kathryn, surprised by this occurrence, brought it to my attention that my reaction was not normal. I agreed with her.

Kathryn only had one other episode of odd behavior toward the end of our service, and it was funny! As we walked down the street to the market to buy some vegetables, we noticed a guy working on a tall ladder in the very middle of the street trying to fix the electrical lines. He stood at the very top of the ladder about twenty feet off the ground.

Kathryn suddenly said to me, "What if I walk over there and knock the ladder out from underneath that guy? Do you think he would hang on the lines for a while screaming for help or would he fall? Either way, that guy will probably scream."

I said jokingly, "Kathryn, we have to get you out of this country quickly before you hurt someone."

We laughed, but again, I could tell that the lifestyle in Nicaragua had been slowly eating away at both of us. We were ready to return to life in the United States with family and friends, bathrooms with running water and toilet paper, air conditioning, access to any kind of food we wanted, and among other things, the financial opportunities that a decent economy offers.

45
The Shady Bunch
"Don't be sad that it ended, be happy that it happened."
–Dr. Seuss

The Shady Bunch, the group of four street kids that Kathryn and I took under our wing as soon as we arrived in Estelí, remained in our lives throughout most of our service. In the first few weeks we had started a banana bread business with the Shady Bunch that they aptly named *Panadería Pantástico*.

When I refer to these children as the Shady Bunch, I have nothing derogatory in mind about them; they were simply a tough crew, and in taking them under our wing, we were reminded of the Brady Bunch with the instant creation of a very large family. Thus, the origin of the "Shady Bunch" name. The Shady Bunch consisted of Marlon (6), La Perla (9), Miguel (11) and Juan (12). We generally welcomed the youngest three children into our house, but Juan was a very troublesome young man, who I did not appreciate having over, and neither did our neighbors. However, Kathryn and I cared for all of them dearly and liked providing a safe place for them to play and take a break from the streets.

Our first successful foray into making banana bread was an experiment to see what we could come up with for the snack bar menu at Los Pipitos. The Shady Bunch proved that with assistance, they were capable of making the bread, and this food item was very unique to the area. Thus, we decided to pursue the idea of a banana bread micro-business with them. Every Saturday the kids would come over to bake banana bread, and then we would all go out into the community to sell our wares.

The goal of the business first and foremost was to give the kids a safe place to go on Saturdays—our home. As well, we wanted to allow these children to achieve some self-respect and self-confidence. Other goals for the Shady Bunch included learning to work together, experiencing what it meant to earn a living, as opposed to begging for money/food, and understanding some basic business principles.

We taught them how to calculate the cost of their product and at what price they should sell their product to make a profit. We also had them write down what had happened financially at the end of the day.

The biggest financial lesson was how to save a percentage of their earnings. The end goal of the business was initially to save enough money for them to purchase their own little oven, so they could bake the bread themselves. The two main rules to continuing the business with us consisted of their not telling us lies, and they absolutely had to attend school during the week.

Kathryn led the manufacturing and packaging process, and everyone else worked as her support crew. We did whatever Kathryn asked. If Kathryn said to mash and mix, we snapped to and got the job done. If she said to run to the market and get a couple of eggs, we had a race to see who could get to the market first. We would bake a total of maybe five loaves of banana bread in a morning. I led the clean-up and sales.

Following the baking session, the floor would be covered with flour. The kids and I would sweep, mop, dust, and wipe down our one-room home to a nice shine. One thing was certain—making banana bread was a messy business. Once the house was clean, Kathryn was free to do as she pleased with the rest of her afternoon, while the kids and I hit the streets to sell the goods.

The very first day of the business, we all walked to a local *fritanga* (restaurant), and 6-year-old Marlon entered with me. I asked him to ex-plain to the owner of the business what we were doing. Marlon told the owner that he and his brother and sister had started a bread business with the *gringos* and wanted to know if he was interested in buying some banana bread. I asked the owner to try the bread before saying "no." He tried it and gave some to his mother who stood behind the counter. All she did was nod in approval, and the owner bought everything we had! Panadaría Pantástico had a new client and a great success on their first try! The owner handed me the money, and I immediately passed it to Marlon, which gave the owner of the restaurant a kick-in-the-pants smile. I told Marlon that we would take the money back to the house. We thanked the owner and his mother and left the restaurant.

When we departed the *fritanga*, the kids literally did cartwheels down the street. It was one of the happiest moments of all of my time in Nicaragua. The looks on these street kids' faces was of triumph, not defeat—hope, and not gloom—a true momentary state of bliss!

We returned home and discussed the financial activity of the day. We talked about the costs associated with making the bread, the sale price, and the profit. We then agreed to individually save ten percent of the profit to help them purchase an oven later. We put ten percent from each child in a piggy bank and then let them split the rest. The piggy bank would stay with Kathryn and me for safe-keeping. We wrote everything down in a notebook so that the Shady Bunch could learn how to account for their business, and they all understood what was happening. I asked them what they were going to do with the rest of the money they had just earned. They said they wanted to go buy food and asked if I would cook them eggs. For lunch, we had an egg party! This was a very encouraging first day.

To ensure that the Shady Bunch kids were continuing their education and holding up on their end of our agreement, Kathryn and I would randomly check up on them at their school and bring them snacks as a reward for their consistent attendance. We were always so pleased to see them at school, as we knew it was probably not easy for them to attend for a variety of reasons, but especially because they would lose some time available to earn money from the streets. Not surprisingly, we received a lot of attention from the other young kids at their school.

One time the Shady Bunch talked proudly about their little business as the other students saw the *gringos* giving them snacks. The other kids asked a lot of questions and were particularly awed that the *gringos* would let this Shady Bunch into their house. One little girl shockingly asked me, "You let them into your house to cook?!"

I responded with, "Not only do we let them in the house to cook, but we are friends, as well as business partners." You could see the tides immediately turn in favor of the Shady Bunch.

The Shady Bunch stuck out as disadvantaged children even in poor areas of Estelí. They were about the only ones without school uniforms, which seemed to highlight their differences even more, and they were often dirty or rough looking. On this particular occasion, the Shady Bunch's mother had walked them to school and took advantage of the *gringos'* presence. She said to the other fifteen or so students, "You see, we are all equal here." What their mother said made me feel like we were giving the Shady Bunch a much-needed confidence boost and heightened status with the other students, as the other kids surely did not have an opportunity to be in business with *gringos*.

As we walked away from the school, I turned to Kathryn and said, "I think we just had a Peace Corps moment."

Panadería Pantástico continued on the same path for a few months, and then Milton entered the scene. Milton was a three-year old boy, who was taken in by the Shady Bunch family. He was their cousin—cute as he could be and tough as nails!

One afternoon, as Kathryn and I walked up the street, we saw Milton boldly stick his hands into an outside café to ask the clients for food. The people, of course, could not resist the cute three-year old begging and gave him a piece of chicken. The child turned and ran down the street because he knew that his cousins were watching him. If Milton scored, they were going to take the food from him and make him beg for more. When the other kids caught up to him, Milton dropped his chicken on the ground, threw up his fists and started banging away on the bigger kids. It was hard to comprehend, but right there in front of us, was a three-year old kicking some older kids' asses so that he could eat! I liked Milton, and so I shooed away the trouble-makers and busted up the fracas. Milton then picked his chicken up off the street and started to eat it. Kathryn and I walked away discussing the disturbing nature of what we had just witnessed. It was a jungle out there, and these children were living in it with a pure survival mentality.

Milton joined the Panadaría Pantástico crew. Although he was too young to understand the business aspects of accounting, his natural ability as a salesman was an asset to get people to buy the bread quickly. He was a persistent little cuss. People would say "no" and keep walking. Milton would walk right along with them, tapping them on their arms or legs to tell them about the business that he and his cousins had started with the *gringos*. He would offer them a sample, and he was a tough kid to say "no" to.

The Shady Bunch would sometimes come over on Sundays, and Kathryn and I would walk with them to a local park several blocks away. Most kids who played in the park on Sunday wore their fanciest dresses or outfits. Little girls played nicely in their best dresses, and the little boys had their best shirts ironed to the hilt with sharp creases. Then entered our crew—no shoes, torn shirts, filthy from head to toe, and rowdy as hell. The other parents would look at us like, "Can't you control those kids?" Kathryn and I would always laugh because they were not our kids to control, but they were definitely with us.

One particular Sunday, Kathryn received the title of *"bruja,"* (witch). It is not exactly a title that you strive for in Nicaragua, but at times, it seemed to fit Kathryn well. Milton had begged for a *fresca* (drink) in a plastic bag and had received one from some kind soul. When he was finished drinking it, he threw the bag and straw across the park and hit a nicely-dressed little girl on a swing. Kathryn felt incredibly embarrassed and immediately asked that Milton apologize to the little girl, pick up his trash, and throw it away. His cousins also rallied around Milton to ask him to pick up the trash and throw it away. Milton looked right at Kathryn, said in a very indignant tone, "You throw it away," and walked off.

Milton then jumped up onto a large concrete tube about four feet off the ground and looked back at Kathryn, who was staring at him with a look that would kill. I suppose the look startled young Milton because he took another step, missed the concrete, fell flat on his face on the top of the concrete tube, bounced off of it, and fell four feet to the ground landing with a direct impact of his side onto a sharp curb.

Milton's fall truly scared me, but Kathryn never stopped giving the evil eye. All the other kids from the Shady Bunch laughed at Milton and said that Kathryn caused the fall by a spell that she cast upon him. The *bruja* had done it. Milton got up clearly in pain. He looked at Kathryn with serious bewilderment, but he never cried. If I had taken that fall, you would have had to call 9-11 and scrape me off the ground with a boom crane! But Milton was tough!

Following that day, he always minded Kathryn. If Kathryn asked Milton to do something, the child would do it with no questions asked. I always told Milton that you do not ever want to mess with a *bruja*. He consistently smiled at my comment, but with a look that said it was quite possible he believed Kathryn was a *bruja*.

On another occasion, the Shady Bunch was over at our house on a Sunday afternoon while Jami Duffy, a Volunteer from a nearby community, stopped by for a visit. The kids were coloring on the floor, and Jami, Kathryn and I were involved in a discussion about nothing in particular. I noticed that Marlon was balled up in the fetal position on the hammock; worse, I could swear that he was crying. I had seen this kid get hit in the head with rocks, beaten up on the street, and tossed around like a rag doll by his older siblings, but I had never seen him cry. Marlon does not cry.

I quickly walked over to the hammock and knelt beside him asking, "What's wrong? What happened?" I turned to say, "Kathryn, he's crying!"

Kathryn responded, "Oh my, it must be serious."

I kept asking what the problem was, and he finally rolled over and said his tooth was hurting really badly. Before Marlon said that, I was seriously thinking the kid could die. He never cries! The sore tooth made Marlon a little more human. My first thought was humorous relief—"Oh, so he does actually feel pain."

I asked Marlon if I could take a look, and sure enough, one of his back bottom molars had broken in half. I could actually see the exposed nerve. OUCH! I told him not to worry, and we would help him get better right away. I suddenly felt like an idiot because I had recently given him a lollipop as a special treat. I should have known that his teeth would be brittle because hygiene, especially any kind of dental care, in his family was limited, if not non-existent. At that moment, I felt like it was my fault that my little buddy, Marlon, was in such pain.

Kathryn, Jami and I quickly decided to find a dentist no matter the cost, but it was a Sunday afternoon. Not only would it be difficult to find a dentist, it would also be very difficult to find one who was open on a Sunday. We asked the neighbors for suggestions and headed to the downtown area. I was carrying Marlon in my arms, while Kathryn and Jami knocked on the doors of various dental offices. We also banged on the outside of pharmacies, which were typically closed on Sundays. At the third dentist's door, I put Marlon down and told the girls to bang harder. We were not going to be denied. I started pounding too. I yelled and pounded and yelled some more until finally, after about five minutes and a throbbing hand, a man appeared in the balcony above us to ask us what we needed. We explained, and he came downstairs to open the door, agreeing to treat Marlon. Jami, Kathryn and I, immediately felt relief that we had found someone to help the little guy.

We entered the dentist's office, which was not very impressive, and he asked Marlon to sit down on a 1960s looking dental chair. The dentist instructed Jami to hold the patient's head. After looking at the child's mouth for ten seconds, the dentist reached into a drawer. Then,

I kid you not, he pulled out construction pliers, stuck them in Marlon's mouth, and started pulling on the broken half-tooth that was left in Marlon's head. He offered no deadening agent, and he used nothing other than brute strength. Marlon screamed bloody murder and squirmed violently! Kathryn could not watch, and the dentist yelled to hold the kid down. He also yelled at Marlon to stop screaming! The scene was chaotic. The dentist pulled and pulled until finally the tooth popped out. At that instant, Marlon stopped crying. His painful ordeal had ended. I will never forget that dental experience and will always appreciate the care provided by my dentist in the States.

Kathryn and I often discuss how Marlon stopped crying the second that tooth came out, but we always marveled at the manner in which it was pulled. After the tooth was pulled, a fair amount of blood came out of the hole in Marlon's mouth. When we left the dentist's office after paying him five U.S. dollars for his services, Marlon spit blood all over the sidewalk for several blocks, until we stopped at a pharmacy to purchase some gauze to plug the hole.

Obviously, these children had become very special to Kathryn and me. I would walk around town with them on my shoulders, and one of them was always saying to me, "*para arriba*," which meant that they wanted to be put up on my shoulders. I would play with them on the patio of our home by piling all the kids on top of one another and then saying/singing a chant over and over. It went, "*juntos es mejor, no? Juntos es mejor!*" ('together is better, no? Together is better!'). The mosh pit of four (or more) children piled on top of one another was nothing but arms and legs and screaming laughter. When the play session had to end, I literally pulled each child out of the house as if they were a protester. We made it a game, and they would hold onto the metal bars of our patio as I dragged them outside of our front porch area, with their infectious laughter echoing through our house. No matter how much Kathryn and I pleaded for them to go outside and that it was time for Kathryn and me to get some work done, the kids would never let go of the bars. So I playfully pried their fingers loose, then they would drop to the ground and lay out on the floor. I would then grab them by the feet and pull them out of the patio. The kids would crack up with laughter! I would get one child out of the house, and another would run back in. We had good times together.

One afternoon when we were out and about with the kids, we randomly crossed paths with the mother of the Shady Bunch. She flat out told us to take them with us to the States. I thought I was hearing things, but she said it again. "Take my children with you to the States." We sort of played it off as a joke, but I could tell the lady was dead serious. Kathryn and I discussed the dire realities of what might be going on for this family, both at home and on the streets. At the same time, we had been conversing about having children of our own. The topic naturally moved toward adoption of the Shady Bunch, which really would put us in a Brady Bunch category. Marlon was the one child that we pondered adopting. Taking on so many children at once was not a realistic scenario for us. We had many discussions and conversations about the laundry list of issues that we would face by adopting Marlon, and while these discussions continued, the whole relationship with the kids started to unravel.

One Saturday, when the family came over to the house to bake bread, Marlon walked through the door and gave me a hug. He was soaking wet, and it was a beautiful day outside.

I asked him, "Marlon, why are you wet? It's a nice day outside."

He responded very directly that it had rained hard the night before and their roof leaked, so his clothes got wet. I checked the other kids, and they were all sopping wet too. I had always known they were poor and did not have a good living situation in a neighborhood on the outskirts of Estelí, but we had never visited their home to see just how bad it was. I then began to ask the children specific questions about their house because, if we were going to put a stove in their home, it must be secure enough to not damage the equipment and be locked up so that no one could steal it.

Kathryn and I asked for exact directions to where they lived and said we would be by for a visit sometime soon. I spoke to Kathryn about the potential issues with an unsecured home. We thought that maybe our first financial goal should be to get the family a new roof, instead of an oven, with the money that the kids were earning. We agreed to go check out the living situation of the Shady Bunch.

Kathryn and I woke up the next morning and traveled across Estelí to find the home of the Shady Bunch. The neighborhoods became worse and worse until the stares that we received from people on the streets became quite uncomfortable. When we arrived at the Shady Bunch's home, I was completely saddened. The roof was barely existent. There was no front door, nothing covered the windows, and sheets of plastic were used as one of the walls. We announced our presence, and the Shady Bunch came out to greet us. We were happy to see them, and they invited us into their home.

Kathryn and I walked inside and found a very small, one-room home with a dirt floor, one plastic chair, and one twin bed with a pile of clothes on it. We walked to the back of the house and found the Shady Bunch's mom working to boil water over an open fire with an old pot that had four tiny potatoes in it for breakfast. The Shady Bunch did not even have enough to eat, much less a place to securely manage a stove upon which this business idea depended.

Kathryn and I visited with the family for about an hour. We left the home saddened with how little they had—not only did their tin roof let rain in, but anyone could walk in and out of their home at any time. We discussed how we could help the family secure their dwelling enough for improved health and safety, as well as to eventually be able to keep a stove. The answer was that we would use the money the kids had saved for their stove to purchase building materials and secure their home. Once the home was protected, we could consider again the idea of purchasing a stove. However, the task of helping them to achieve basic safety and security seemed to be a daunting challenge on its own.

Kathryn has pointed to this visit as the saddest day she experienced during our service. She questioned how basic human rights of health, education, shelter, and security could so clearly fail to exist in this community, and these types of communities were pervasive throughout Nicaragua. We saw that basic human rights were obviously not being met—no running water, no food security, no access to health care, inadequate shelter, and perhaps worse of all, no personal security. The pledge of the international community to promote these rights and address extreme poverty, as outlined in the Millennium Development Goals, was completely lost in this area of Estelí.

After seeing how these kids were living, Kathryn and I decided to make an exception to our stance of only offering non-financial assistance to the projects we pursued because this was clearly a unique and dire situation. We had previously told the mom of the Shady Bunch "no" when she had asked for money for Milton's kindergarten graduation gown; we later learned from the kids that there was no graduation and Milton was not even in kindergarten. Although it was upsetting that she blatantly lied to us, we recognized that she was looking for whatever ways she could to help her family survive.

However, in this current situation, we determined that we would kick in a little of our own money to add to what the children had already saved in order to make the essential basic upgrades to their home as soon as possible. We talked to our neighbors who had an uncle that could manage the construction process and told him that we wanted four solid walls, a roof, and a door installed at the Shady Bunch home. By the time all the materials and labor were paid for, Kathryn and I had thrown in an extra $200 over and above the $60 the Shady Bunch had saved.

We proposed to the Shady Bunch the change in financial direction that we thought should be made to help them secure their house. If the Shady Bunch agreed, we would break open their piggy bank and put all of their saved money toward the effort. Once we accomplished better security, we could then consider again saving toward a stove. They instantly agreed, and we had a fun piggy bank-breaking ceremony. The kids looked at the cash in awe and were thrilled that they had saved a lot of money. We were happy to know their home would at least have four walls, a door, and a tin roof. We confirmed the construction deal with the neighbors' uncle, and within a few days, the Shady Bunch home had been renovated for basic security.

Our two primary rules when we started the banana bread business included the children attending school daily and not lying to us. We communicated the rules very clearly, and the kids understood them. About a month after the Shady Bunch home renovation and their mother's comment to "Take the kids to the States," different members of the Shady Bunch would randomly show up at our house during class hours. Kathryn and I always asked them why they were not in school, and they gave us various excuses. We did not have time to go check up on them as much as we had been able to previously because our projects were now fully operational and kept us quite busy. Plus, we wanted to believe they were telling the truth and that they were attending school regularly, as they had been in the prior school year.

On one particular occasion after the new school year had started about a month earlier, Kathryn and I were at home debating different ways to address an issue with one of our projects. Marlon arrived at our door when he clearly should have been in school. We asked why he was not in school, and he responded that he did not have school that day because the teacher had errands to run. I had heard every excuse in the book for not having class in Nicaragua, but running errands was a new one to us.

Kathryn quickly called his bluff. "Marlon, you know you are supposed to be in school, and you know you are not supposed to lie to us. Don't tell me your teacher cancelled a whole day of school so that she could run errands."

Marlon said that it was the truth. Neither one of us believed him.

Kathryn said, "Marlon, please don't lie to us. We know that you have school today, and if you tell me again that you don't have school because your teacher is running errands, I am going to the school right now to check to see if you are telling me the truth."

The situation quickly became very serious, and I could tell that Kathryn was starting to boil with anger. Marlon looked Kathryn straight into her eyes and insisted that he was telling the truth. Kathryn walked out the door and headed for the school. I followed, and Marlon left the house, but he did not come with us.

The Director of Marlon's school greeted us when we arrived; she was very familiar with who we were because during previous school years, we would check in with her about Marlon and the other kids and inquire how they were doing in school. When we asked her about Marlon on this occasion, she said she had not seen him or any of the other children for about a month. In fact, she continued, Marlon had not even been registered to attend classes that year, which had started a month ago. When that proverbial piece of straw was laid across the back of the burro, it broke the mule down. Kathryn and I terminated the Shady Bunch business.

Not only were Kathryn and I finished with the Shady Bunch business, it was also quite clear that we could not adopt Marlon. We thought we demonstrated to these kids that we were there for them and that we could be counted on and trusted. However, these children blatantly lied to us and violated our only two rules. Kathryn had an especially hard time dealing with the outright lying. They had distinctly taken advantage of our willingness to help them. Quite frankly, after we had spent almost two full years with these children, we were devastated when the School Director said that they had not attended school for a month—and were not even registered! The registration had been their mother's responsibility, and the kids could not be blamed. However, all of the children should have been able to tell us there was a problem with school and not lie to us. We would have explored options to help them had we been told. The situation was frustrating and laden with complex issues that we could not fully understand or deal with.

When the Shady Bunch returned to our home as a group on the following Saturday to work the bread business, Kathryn and I told them about our decision to stop making bread with them and why we had come to that conclusion. We shared with them that they were still welcome to come over to the house from time to time, but that they should not come back here every Saturday. We made them some eggs, and when they finished eating, we said we had to go run some errands. We all went our separate ways.

The kids did come back intermittently to visit, and they were festive occasions. However, life with them was never the same. One night, as Kathryn walked home with the women from the Funhori class, she had seen Perla, who would have only been 11 years old at that time. Perla stood at a gas station on the Pan-American Highway. The women from the Funhori organization expressed concern for the young girl, as that station attracted a transient, rough crowd and was known as a place where women prostituted themselves. Kathryn could hardly talk about it she was so upset, and I was so disturbed that I could not even think about it.

Juan, the eldest of the family, had been seen sniffing glue on the streets. For a short period of time, Kathryn saw Marlon at a *fritanga* where he was doing some kind of work for food. But after that, we did not see Marlon very often at all, and when we did, he was generally with his brother Miguel. Miguel actually seemed to be doing okay, and every once in a while we would see him with his shoe shine box or a box full of gum and candy to sell on the streets. Toward the very end of our service, we saw Marlon with a backpack and he said that an international organization was helping him to go to school.

Every time we saw the Shady Bunch it broke our hearts. And that is the way it ended for Kathryn and me. We were broken-hearted. Did it have to end that way? I believe cessation of business activities was the right action to take given the relationship that we had with these children. Our friendship with them remained in-tact, we just did not spend as much time together. Kathryn and I are certain that the kids learned some valuable lessons to carry forward with them in life.

Kathryn and I often discuss the Shady Bunch and wonder if these children are safe or if they are getting enough to eat. The reality is that the world is a tough place. Deep down, I believe the answer is "no." These kids are not safe. They are not getting enough to eat. They are not attending school, and our little friends are more than likely doomed to live a life of extreme poverty and suffering. However, we could always hope that life for them will improve. That is the story of the Shady Bunch.

46
Visitors
"Friendship is a single soul dwelling in two bodies."
—Aristotle

Kathryn and I had five special people visit us while we were in Nicaragua. These individuals who wanted to come and share some of our experiences were Rob Nelson, Maeve McKee, Ambassador Jack Hood Vaughn, who was the second worldwide Director of Peace Corps following Sergeant Shriver, Ambassador Joshua Lawson, and Bridget Kilgore.

Separately, we took Rob and Maeve, who were about our age or younger, to the beach, and we arranged for Maeve to go horseback riding with John Briggs in San Juan de Limay. We hitched rides everywhere and had a very special time with both Maeve and Rob. We are grateful to them for their visit.

Ambassador Jack Hood Vaughn, Ambassador Lawson, and Bridget Kilgore traveled together as a group. Kathryn previously worked with former U.S. Ambassador Lawson. Bridget Kilgore and Ambassador Lawson had both been previous clients of mine, and we remained friends following my departure from the financial industry. Kathryn and I considered them to be like family. We met Ambassador Jack Hood Vaughn for the first time during his visit, as he was a friend to Ambassador Lawson and Bridget Kilgore and had a distinct interest in Nicaragua and the Peace Corps. Ambassador Vaughn was present at the party when Nicaraguan President Somoza was assassinated in September of 1956.

The Ambassador group arrived in Nicaragua about two months before our service in the Peace Corps was completed. The general idea of their visit was that Kathryn and I would introduce the Ambassadors and Bridget to our host families in Catarina and Masatepe and show them our projects in Estelí. It was so nice to have Bridget and the Ambassadors demonstrate such genuine interest in how Kathryn and I had spent the last two years of our lives working to improve our communities.

As soon as the group arrived in the country, we departed the airport in a rental van, and headed into Managua for a courtesy call upon the U.S. Ambassador to Nicaragua at that time. As our van approached one of the first traffic lights, a group of street vendors worked the line of stopped cars, peddling a range of items. One guy walked up to our vehicle and started soaping up the front windshield, and I told him to stop. He continued, and then I saw a guy duck down by the left front tire of the van—I knew things were about to go downhill quickly. The scam was that one guy puts so much soap on the windshield that the people inside the vehicle cannot see out. Then another guy pops off the hub caps, blinker covers, and anything else they can get their hands on. I told everyone in the van that we were being scammed and vandalized. In the back seat, Mrs. Kilgore raised her walking cane to the man as he walked past her window. The thief kept moving, which was a good thing, but they had robbed us of some vehicle reflectors. Our visitors had not been in the country for more than twenty minutes and they had experienced a quasi-robbery. Nobody thought twice about the added excitement, and we continued to move through the city.

We arrived at the U.S. Embassy where we were invited in to meet with the U.S. Ambassador. I thought Kathryn and I would have to wait outside, but we were escorted into the Ambassador's office along with the visiting dignitaries. Kathryn and I were about to be put on the spot and had no idea it was coming.

But first, a reminder of how you never know who you are going to meet and what impact those encounters may have on future events. A few weeks before the Ambassadors' visit, Peace Corps had invited Kathryn and me to Managua to greet a new group of incoming Volunteer trainees at the airport and participate in their three-day orientation. We also conducted a training session on community bank projects for current Volunteers. The three days of training took place at the Camino Royale hotel, which also has a casino. I am not a gambler, but I do not mind watching other people throw their money away. So one evening after training ended for the day, I visited the casino. As I looked over the shoulder of another Volunteer playing the slot machines, someone kind of scratched me on my back. I turned around and found a man about a full foot shorter than I am standing in front of me.

I looked down and said, "Hi, how are you doing?"

The guy responded in English, "Great! My name is Chepito, and I was Santana's drummer."

I thought about what he said. I calculated the absurd odds of the situation and decided the man's statement could not be true. Politely, I responded, "Cool, that must have been lots of fun." And then I turned around to continue looking over the shoulder of the Volunteer playing slots.

The guy tapped me on my shoulder again and said, "No really, check it out." He gave me a business card with a picture of him and Santana taken at the Rock 'n' Roll Hall of Fame in Ohio.

I thought, "Well, I'll be damned. I guess I'm going to be talking with Chepito, Santana's drummer."

He asked, "What are you doing in my country?" I told him, and he responded, "That's great, want to come to my show tonight? I'm playing with some locals that are really good." I asked if I could bring my wife, and he said, "Sure, the more pussy, the better." Chepito's aforementioned statement further confirmed that he was, in fact, a rock 'n' roll drummer for Santana. Although the statement was shocking, I knew he was joking, so I kept a poker face and appeared unfazed. Grinning, I said I would be right back.

I returned to my hotel room and excitedly told Kathryn what was going on and that she had to get dressed and go see the show! She dressed and we followed Chepito's stretch limousine through the rough streets of Managua in our very own taxi. Chepito got us into the venue with passes and sent us to a sectioned-off area of the bar that was for the guests of the band.

While sitting in the guest area, a man asked me a very surprising question, "Hey gringo, why are you in my country?" I told him that I lived in Estelí and what I was doing in his country. We then proceeded to pleasantly engage in a conversation about Nicaraguan politics. As it turns out, the guy was the son of a previous Nicaraguan President.

The political situation in Nicaragua is complicated, and to fully comprehend the politics, you need to have an understanding of the country's history and power structure. After two years in Nicaragua, I had pretty much gotten a handle on the politics from the ground level, but I was not privy to who the money players were behind the scenes. I knew the businesses that were powerful, but did not know who owned them. By the time this guy finished talking with me, I had received a first-rate education in Nicaraguan politics. The rest of the evening was fantastic—Chepito tore it up on the drums, and couples danced amazingly to the music. Unfortunately, we could not stay late because of our work the next day.

Fast forward now three weeks later to our meeting at the U.S. Embassy with the then present U.S. Ambassador and our friends, Ambassador Jack Hood Vaughn, Ambassador Lawson, and Bridget Kilgore. Kathryn and I were only at this meeting because we were friends of people that were calling upon the current Ambassador. I did not think we would speak, ask questions, or participate in the meeting in any way, shape, or form, other than offering basic courtesies. Our anticipation of this meeting was that we would be present as wall-flowers only.

In the middle of the Ambassadors' very informal round table discussion, the acting U.S. Ambassador asked my general opinion on Nicaraguan politics because, as a Peace Corps Volunteer, I would understand the thoughts of the local people. Although we typically did not engage in political conversation, Kathryn and I often could not avoid it. Immediately I deferred the question to Kathryn and asked if she would like to respond. Kathryn said, "No, you go ahead." With a very broad brush, I laid out everything I knew about who was doing what, for whom, why, who was backing whom, why, and what their motives were for each aspect of my response. Additionally, I shared with the then serving U.S. Ambassador the general idea of how the communities that I had access to in Nicaragua were feeling about the upcoming election. I also shared with him quite frankly that people did not always like to see the U.S. Ambassador speaking in the news about Nicaraguan candidates or the election. Following two years of being in the country and hearing a lot of political talk during our hitch-hiking travels, I had finally put the entire political spectrum together in a broad context. Receiving a political education from a previous president's son didn't hurt either, and I never would have met the man had I not been training Peace Corps Volunteers in that particular casino hotel. Further, meeting Chepito, Santana's drummer, helped to facilitate the chain of events. At that moment, I was thinking that Hollywood could not make this kind of stuff up if they tried!

I knew my political information was organized and generally insightful. By the time I finished my comments, the then U.S. Ambassador said, "When you're done with the Peace Corps, if you would like a job here at the Embassy as a Political Analyst, we'd be happy to have you." Obviously the U.S. Government does not operate their human resources in quite that manner. However, the Ambassador's positive reception was a moment in life that I will never forget. Additionally, the random events that led to my brief presentation will certainly be remembered. My response to the Ambassador also likely carved out a pathway to a future job with Bridget Kilgore.

Subsequent to that meeting, the U.S. Embassy instructed us to follow a caravan on our way back to the hotel to avoid current protests and cars being burned in the streets. The next day we traveled north to Estelí.

When the Ambassador group arrived in Estelí, we wanted to show them where we lived and introduce them to our neighbors, so we stopped at our house. As I went to open the door of the van for Bridget Kilgore, I noticed our neighbor's dog, who I knew to be very aggressive, walking toward the vehicle. He started barking specifically at our guest, which made the situation extremely uncomfortable.

Throughout our time in Nicaragua, we consistently saw people scare dogs away by picking up a rock and throwing it at them. We did not condone the practice, but when I saw an aggressive dog charging Mrs. Kilgore, I picked up a rock in my hand—but I had no intention of actually hitting the dog. My plan was to simply throw the rock in its general direction, and the dog, based on his own life experiences, would instinctively know to move away. When I picked up the rock and turned to throw it, Ambassador Lawson yelled at me in a half-playful, half -serious manner, "Son, put that rock down! Have you gone native on us?" He knew that I love dogs and recognized how out-of-character this reaction was for me. He explained that "going native" was a term that the State Department used to describe someone who may have spent so much time in a particular country that they sympathized too greatly with the country of their service. It would then be time to re-locate that person to another post. I tried to explain that, "I , I, I , was just..."

The Ambassador shook his head and said, "No, drop the rock." It was a funny moment for me, because in the Peace Corps they wanted you to live like an average Nicaraguan, or more or less "go native." Apparently I had completely embraced that concept.

Later, our visiting Ambassador group met with our community

bank members and the ladies from Funhori. Our schools were visited and the dignitaries enjoyed speaking with teachers and students. They met our neighbors and even spent time with the Shady Bunch on the street. We felt honored to have these wonderful people take an interest in the projects that we had been working on for the past two years. Further, our community really appreciated the fact that retired U.S. diplomats would care enough to learn about their lives.

With only two months remaining before Kathryn and I were to leave the country, we had frantically tried to figure out how we were going to get our dog, Sam, back to the States. She was now 13 years old and it was almost summer time in Managua, so flying in the belly of an airplane was an unlikely (and scary) prospect. We raised the issue with Ambassador Lawson prior to the group's trip to Nicaragua. He let us know that Sam would receive the royal treatment and return to the States with the dignitaries on their private charter plane. I thought this was hysterical. Sam had been subjected to some tough living situations in Nicaragua, and now she was about to leave the country on a private plane. Kathryn and I got the exit paperwork for Sam in order quickly so she would be prepared to fly.

As we said goodbye to the Ambassador group at the Managua airport, we also had to say goodbye to Sam. We knelt down to say our fair well to Sam, and she turned, walking away, as if to say, "See ya suckers, I've put up with this abuse long enough. I'm outta here!" This had to have been one of the first times in thirteen years that my dog has had no interest whatsoever in saying goodbye. Even on a daily basis in Estelí, we could not leave the house without saying goodbye to Sam. Sam was ditching us! Kathryn and I looked at each other, shrugged our shoulders, and said to our departing guests, "I suppose she was just ready to go." We all laughed, hugged, and said our goodbyes, and Sam never even looked back.

Kathryn and I watched as Ambassador Lawson picked Sam up in his arms and carried her onto the plane. It was a surreal vision. I have no idea how it came about for Sam to leave the country like that, but we were thrilled to have friends willing to help us out. It would have been very difficult getting Sam back to the States without their assistance.

The people who came to visit us in Nicaragua will always hold a spot that is near and dear to our hearts. Ambassador Jack Hood

Vaughn, who was the second worldwide Director of the Peace Corps behind Sargent Shriver, actually took the time to write Kathryn and me a thank you note, which in part stated, "In a fairly long history with Peace Corps, I have seen few examples better than your achievements." We greatly appreciated the time spent with our guests while they were in Nicaragua.

47
Operation Air Lift
"How wonderful it is that nobody need wait a single moment before starting to improve the world."
–Anne Frank

The goal of Operation Air Lift was simple—donate some sporting equipment to the schools of Estelí. One of the interesting aspects of the Peace Corps adventure is cross-cultural involvement. Here are the players—a Volunteer, the international community in which the Volunteer works, and the home community of the Volunteer in the United States. As the third goal of the Peace Corps, Volunteers are encouraged to involve U.S. communities in order to further integrate the cross-cultural experience. Generally speaking, these American communities can also be immensely helpful to Volunteers in the field by becoming engaged in various projects. For example, early on in our service, Kathryn and I had identified a need for sporting equipment at every school we came across in Nicaragua.

Many communities in the United States have much more sporting equipment than needed. After watching Nicaraguan children play baseball with masking tape wadded up into a ball and a stick for a bat, we recognized that any old ball/sports equipment forgotten about in countless American garages could be a fantastic resource in Nicaragua.

During our training program when we first arrived in Nicaragua, I had asked my father to send me a couple of baseballs, old gloves, and a bat so that I could give them to my host brothers. When a package from my parents arrived and the kids opened it, the looks of pure bliss on their faces were literally priceless. However, sending that package to Nicaragua was not priceless. As a matter of fact, it was outrageously expensive. I think my Dad said it cost about a hundred bucks to send four balls, two gloves, one bat, and some chocolate brownies. There was also an import tax of some sort on the package once it arrived, which was not cheap for an average Nicaraguan.

After receiving that parcel from my father and seeing how much enjoyment the kids had with it, Kathryn and I began discussing finding a way to import sporting equipment to donate to schools, without incurring taxes or spending a fortune on shipping.

Once we arrived in Estelí and took a basic inventory of community needs, a lack of sporting equipment became an obvious issue to address. A teacher friend in Maryland had already offered to gather gently-used clothes and other items from her students to send to our community. However, we were cautious in accepting this offer because of the Nicaraguan custom taxes. We told her we would look into it.

We visited the Mayor's office in Estelí to introduce ourselves and discuss areas where our service might benefit the community. We proposed that one easy way for us to have immediate impact was to have a large shipment of sporting equipment from the communities where Kathryn and I lived in the United States sent to Nicaragua to benefit the Estelí schools. However, we raised the issue of the high shipping costs and the mysteriously expensive import taxes. We were assured by the Mayor's office that the tax could at least be addressed from their end, but that the shipping costs would have to be handled on our end. The Mayor's office was certainly on-board with trying to help out with this endeavor. The plan was to receive a "permission" from the Mayor of Estelí to allow the sporting equipment into the country without being taxed. Our responsibility was to collect the equipment and somehow get it shipped to Nicaragua.

Kathryn made contact with her home community through her parents. During our service, Kathryn returned to the United States to visit with her family. Her parents' neighbors had offered some used baseball equipment from the Little League in Wauconda, Illinois. Kathryn was thrilled to bring that back to Estelí and checked a large duffle bag with the equipment through the airlines, although it cost a substantial fee. Nonetheless, we were delighted to share the baseball equipment with various families and neighbors in Nicaragua.

Meanwhile, Kathryn had also talked with her parents' neighbor, who worked with American Airlines. This person also happened to be a volunteer with the American Airlines' Ambassador program that utilizes cargo space on planes to ship humanitarian goods and useful items to other countries free-of-charge. Very quickly, a plan came together.

It appeared that through the American Airlines Ambassador program, we could have free shipping if the equipment could be collected. Again, the woman from American Airlines was right on top of her game. Before long, there was a neighborhood community drive to collect sporting equipment to be shipped to Peace Corps Volunteers in Nicaragua for use in the local school system. The philanthropic drive was immensely successful, and there was a significant amount of gear collected.

We then waited on the permission from the Mayor's office to avoid the high customs taxes that would basically negate the benefits of this endeavor. We waited, we followed up, we waited, we followed up, and eventually we figured out that the Mayor's office did not have the power to provide us exemption. However, we were never actually told that permission would not be forthcoming, as this might cause embarrassment to the Mayor. We learned a cultural lesson that although Nicaraguans may genuinely want to help, they prefer to avoid saying "no" if at all possible. We eventually resigned ourselves to the fact that the Mayor's exemption was not going to happen.

We spoke with our American Airlines friend with all the sporting gear about the tax issue. She put us in contact with two volunteers from the American Airlines Ambassador program who planned to travel to Nicaragua with the equipment. They said that they would try to get the equipment into the country without having to pay the customs taxes. We had no idea how they would accomplish that, but if they were willing to try, we were willing to organize on our end.

Kathryn and I considered dividing up the equipment to distribute a few sporting items across multiple schools, but ultimately, we determined that there would be a greater impact by donating it all to one school. We thought, for example, that at a single school, an entire baseball team could be equipped with gloves, bats, and balls, versus multiple schools having a few items available. We then asked around about sporting programs, and the only school that was quite active in sports was one of the schools where Kathryn and I were teaching—Instituto Nacional.

We spoke with the Head Coach at Instituto Nacional. He was thrilled to hear about the potential donation, but then he became extremely concerned and said that he did not want to be responsible for the donated equipment. He explained that any decent equipment would walk off with the students and that there was no secure place at the school to put the gear. We were initially a bit disheartened in thinking that this equipment might not be welcomed here after all, and that it could actually create additional problems for the school.

We then decided that all of us should speak with the Directora of the school for her perspectives and to see what could be done. Eventually, we helped the school construct a big locker to secure the gear, and the only person who had the key would be the Directora since she remained at school throughout the entire day. Equipment would have to be checked out and returned in writing to ensure a manageable loss-prevention program.

Kathryn and I literally worked on the Airlift Operation for our entire service. It seemed like a simple idea—collect some stuff on one end, ship it, and then distribute it on the other end. Piece of cake, right? Not so! About one month before our service ended and following almost two full years of relatively continuous thought and follow-up, the American Airlines plane was in the air with the equipment.

The plan was to meet two female volunteers from the American Airlines Ambassador Program at the Managua airport. Kathryn's family's neighbor, who had helped to collect all the gear from her hometown of Barrington, Illinois, unfortunately, was not able to join the trip to Nicaragua. However, the two Volunteers who traveled to Nicaragua were dedicated and enthusiastic about the mission.

The American Airlines Ambassador Program also had contacts with an orphanage for girls just outside of Managua, and we made a plan to drop off/install mosquito nets and other items at the orphanage before proceeding to Estelí. We were told there was a significant amount of gear, and that a full-size pickup truck would probably be able to handle the load. Kathryn and I spoke with the Head Coach at Instituto Nacional, and he connected us with an Assistant Coach, who had a pickup truck and was willing to travel to Managua with us to help bring home the goods. Logistics were coming together, but the trick remained of getting around the import taxes at customs.

Early on the designated day, we rode with the Assistant Coach to the airport and waited with baited breath. At last we saw the Volunteers from the American Airlines Ambassador Program smiling and waving and giving us the thumbs up. The gear had made it through customs without having to pay taxes. I do not know exactly how the American Airlines crew pulled that off, but when I asked, I received a mumble and heard something to the effect that it was a close call. They also said that a letter that we had emailed them the day before, which had explained the purpose of the donations and included contact information for the school and orphanage, apparently helped significantly. We were thrilled that they had made it through customs without added fees and taxes.

We departed Managua with a pickup truck full of sporting gear and other items, and we rolled north along the Pan-American Highway. I rode in the back, Kathryn was up front with the Assistant Coach, and the ladies from American Airlines had rented a van to travel to the orphanage. Following our visit at the orphanage, these ladies from American Airlines would travel back to Managua to catch their return flight to the States.

The orphanage for girls was fantastic! We met the nuns who ran the organization as well as many of the girls who were living there. The orphanage was clean, well built, and a great looking facility. The girls were all incredibly well-mannered and somewhat shy, but they were extremely curious about our purpose for being there. When we pulled out princess mosquito nets in purple, pink, and blue with butterflies, fairies, and princesses all over them, the girls went nuts! The mosquito nets made each twin bed look incredibly special —as if a princess really might sleep there. We had to attach the nets to the ceiling using ladders, but the rest of the installation was pretty easy. We put up about forty fancy mosquito nets and then visited with the girls and played a few games with them. We also dropped off some clothing and other items with the nuns and said our goodbyes.

The Assistant Coach from Estelí, as well as Kathryn and I, thanked the ladies from the American Airlines Ambassador program for their incredible efforts and generosity. I settled into the back of the pickup truck for the three-hour trip north to Estelí. Meanwhile, up front, Kathryn engaged in a pleasant conversation with the Assistant Coach. I departed that orphanage with a feeling of deep gratification and looked forward to the next task in the journey.

When we arrived at Instituto Nacional, the Head Coach was there waiting for us. We inventoried and carefully put away all of the sporting equipment. It was a wonderful feeling to know this school was now hooked up! They received soccer balls, basketballs, basketball nets for the goals (only to be used for games to make them last longer), tennis balls and rackets, baseballs, enough baseball gloves to field a team, baseball bats, a complete set of catcher's gear, volleyballs, volleyball nets, and footballs. After locking down the gear, the Head Coach had a smile from ear to ear and shook our hands saying, "thank you."

The sporting equipment was a windfall for Instituto Nacional, and the Directora, coaches, and students were very excited about the ability to exercise and play with quality gear. Kathryn and I were pleased with the result and were humbly grateful to the community of Timberlake (Barrington/Wauconda, Illinois) and American Airlines for their willingness to partner up with us to make these donations.

After much persistence and patience, the goal of donating sporting equipment was finally achieved. We also felt that we had succeeded in facilitating involvement from the Timberlake community in a cross-cultural endeavor. Operation Air Lift was completed as the last item of business for our Peace Corps service. We visited Instituto Nacional to witness all the kids playing with the new equipment, which was incredibly fun and brought about a happy conclusion to the project, and our service.

48
Close of Service
"When our eyes see our hands doing the work of our hearts,
the circle of Creation is completed inside us, the doors of our souls fly open,
and love steps forth to heal everything in sight."
–Michael Bridge

The close of Peace Corps service was an interesting three-day process. The Nica 35 Small Business group convened at a resort on the Pacific southwest coast of Nicaragua that used to be a military flash point for both the Contras and the Sandinistas. The purpose of our time at this resort included: debriefing Peace Corps on our experience, completing exit interviews, discussing how the Peace Corps can assist Volunteers with future job searches, writing a summary of our accomplishments, and completing standard government paperwork, along with physical exams to ensure that we were all healthy before we returned to the States.

Maura Lambeth attended a close-of-service group session, and brought out all of the Volunteers' aspiration statements from our application process with the Peace Corps. Maura read a few of these, bringing some people to tears and others to applause. We all felt like it was a nice touch to bring the Volunteers full circle on their Peace Corps journey. The basis of my aspiration statement was: "to place my life in the service of others, and to work toward improving the quality of life for people within the community that I will serve. To immerse myself in a rewarding cross-cultural exchange and represent the United States in a positive light." I felt like my service had achieved each of those aspirations. Kathryn too had attained all of her aspirations, and together we felt a wonderful sense of accomplishment.

The close of service process was also a fantastic way to get together with Volunteer friends and share our experiences with each other. For example, one Volunteer from Kentucky had served in a river town in the remote area of Río San Juan, and no one had seen the guy for practically his entire two-year service. We enjoyed the opportunity to reconnect with all of the Volunteers in our group again and to reflect with them about the past two years. The end-of-service had arrived, and it was time to move forward, writing a new chapter of our lives.

49
Final Thoughts and the Road Ahead

"We should all be concerned about the future because we will have to spend the rest of our lives there."
–Charles F. Kettering

The Peace Corps experience, in the opinion of Kathryn and myself, was one of the best professional working experiences of our careers. The entire Peace Corps journey was absolutely worth the sacrifice. The range of individual problematic scenarios was taken to the far end of the spectrum, as well as the moments of extreme bliss. Never in our lives have we been so challenged or rewarded. In looking back at our list of "reasons to join the Peace Corps," our service fulfilled our aspirations and it was clear that the "pros" far outweighed the "cons." Of course, we had to endure some of those "cons" that we had identified, such as becoming sick and having to live without our family and friends, but we would not have gained the perspectives and insights that we acquired had we not become Volunteers.

The uniqueness of the Peace Corps experience cannot be attained with any other organization. Yes, the Peace Corps, as a U.S. Government agency, has its share of challenges. Each individual will have their own unique experience while serving. Some Peace Corps Volunteers encounter serious trouble during their service, and the experience has resulted in disaster for a few. For Kathryn and me, the journey was worth the risk. Personal security was a huge issue to overcome at first, but the Peace Corps provided appropriate training relative to the culture in which we lived, and we followed the advice and guidance of the Peace Corps security officers as closely as we could. Kathryn and I focused on safety issues at all times and had no incidents that rose to the level of serious concern.

On a professional level, we now have a first-hand knowledge of the reality, challenges, and probable solutions for international development projects in general, from the planning phase to facilitating solutions, to the close-out process. The key element toward sustaining any positive transformation is cultivating the desired change within the community and ownership of the project. At times, facilitating project ownership and desired change is an art form, as there is no one formula available to achieve success. Should a community not recognize the need to make a change, then there is no point in pursuing the project. If the community is also not able or willing to manage that change once implemented, then the project will not be sustainable. Community ownership, as well as management willingness and capability, are critical elements to long-term success. How those essential components of the complicated development puzzle are synergized offers the mysterious secret to success that only experience can provide.

On a personal level, we feel that we have a much greater recognition of the challenges that people face to survive, let alone, become educated or employed. That recognition leads to a permanent and positive quality of life perspective that is difficult to measure. The experience also benefited many aspects of our individual and marital character that has greatly enhanced our lives.

The relationship development made the experience of being a Peace Corps Volunteer in Nicaragua very special for a variety of reasons. We learned to listen more closely to our personal intuitions and trust ourselves more than we would have in our own comfortable environment. Being out of our comfort zones probably made us pay closer attention to our "gut" feelings, and surprisingly, we found that our first impressions of others were largely accurate. We were not making judgments, but rather, we were trying to stay safe. As a result, when we connected with others, the connection was genuine, positive, and solid.

The relationships that we developed while in the Peace Corps were nothing short of spectacular. Kathryn and I are now godparents to a little Nicaraguan girl, the daughter of one of Kathryn's host sisters. Both of our host families from training were amazing, and the families that watched out for us in Estelí were incredibly good to us.

In addition, as a couple in the Corps, our marital relationship noticeably evolved. Serving together brought us even closer, and in ways that are difficult to describe. The experiences were real and the emotions were raw; they pushed us to grow as individuals and as a couple. We learned more about our strengths and weaknesses and began to recognize how we could better support each other. Most of all, we learned how to address our weaknesses and bring the best out of each other. The love and support that we offered one another grew exponentially.

The future road ahead that Kathryn and I will take is unknown. We will face our imminent challenges with new and improved skill sets, and we expect to utilize our insights and experience to make positive changes happen. We appreciate life to the fullest extent and bask in the security of knowing that we live as citizens of one of the greatest countries in the world, the United States of America.

The third goal of the Peace Corps is to return to the United States and share our experiences of another culture with those in our community to promote better understanding. With this writing endeavor, Kathryn and I feel as though we will perpetually be working toward achieving the third goal. If considering service in the Peace Corps, we encourage the decision to take a journey of life experience beyond your wildest expectations. It could change your life and others in an incredibly positive way. By joining the ranks of the Peace Corps, we believe that you will be happy that you accepted the challenge. The country of Nicaragua and its people are amazing! We hope you enjoyed *A Couple in the Corps: A Peace Corps Journey from a Couple's Perspective.*

SOURCES

Adolfo Medal, Luis. "Nicaragua: Economic History," Peace Corps-Nicaragua Session, prepared by Arturo J. Solórzano, Small Business Development Program Manager Peace Corps-Nicaragua, May 2000, revised by Miguelito Lindhout, Master Trainer Peace Corps-Nicaragua, May 2002.

Berman, Joshua and Wood, Randy. *Moon Handbooks: Nicaragua* (first edition). Avalon Travel Publishing, January 2003.

Biographical Notes: Augusto C. Sandino 1895-1934, www.sandino.org, copyright 1992-2005.

Bolanos Geyer, Alejandro. *William Walker, The Gray-Eyed Man of Destiny*. 1991.

Executive Summary, Iran/Contra, Independent Counsel, Summary of Report, http://www.afn.org/~dks/i-c/a03-executive-summary.html

Fanny, Juda. "California Filibusters: A History of their Expeditions into Hispanic America." *The Grizzly Bear*, Vol. XXI, No. 4; Whole No.142 (February 1919). http://www.sfmuseum.org/hist1/walker.html.

Fletcher, Tom. "Mudslide on Casita Volcano," http://www.earth-foot.org/places/ni001b.htm

"Hurricane Mitch," *Wikipedia: the Free Encyclopedia*, http://en.wikipedia.org/wiki/Hurricane_Mitch

Instituto Nacional de Estudios Terrestres (INETER), "Las lluvias del siglo en Nicaragua." Managua, Nicaragua, 1998.

Kinzer, Stephen. *Blood of Brothers: Life and War in Nicaragua*, Putnam Publishing Group, 1991.

Kleinbach, Russell. "Nicaraguan Literacy Campaign: Its Democratic Essence," *Monthly Review*, July – August 1985: 75-84, http://faculty.philau.edu/kleinbachr/literacy.htm.

Leonardi, Richard. "Civilization, Nicaragua and Harper's Weekly: Reports from 1857-1860 on William Walker and Chontales" *Update Nicaragua Newsletter Archive*. August 30, 2003.

Minster, Christopher. "The Biography of William Walker: The Ultimate Yankee Imperialist," *Latin American History*, About.com. http://latinamericanhistory.about.com/od/historyofcentralamerica/a/wwalker_2.htm

Nalty, Bernard C. "The United States Marines in Nicaragua," *Marine Corps Historical Reference Series*. Historical Branch, G-3 Division, Headquarters, U.S. Marine Corps, Washington D.C., Reprinted 1968; Printed 1958; Revised 1961; Reprinted 1962; Reprinted 1968.

National Climatic Data Center, "Mitch: The Deadliest Atlantic Hurricane Since 1780." *Storm Review*, http://www.ncdc.noaa.gov/oa/reports/mitch/mitch.html

National Oceanic and Atmospheric Administration's (NOAA) National Environmental Satellite, Data and Information Service (NESDIS). *Hurricane Mitch Special Coverage: 10/22/1998 to 11/4/1998*. http://www.osei.noaa.gov/mitch.html

Peace Corps. "Mission." Accessed December 12, 2012. http://www.peacecorps.gov/about/mission/.

Pezzullo, Lawrence, and Ralph Pezzullo. "Chronology of the Nicaragua Revolution 1933-July 1979," *At the Fall of Somoza*, Pittsburgh, 1994.

"Sandinista." *Brainy Encyclopedia*. http://www.brainyencyclopedia.com/encyclopedia/s/sa/sandinista.html.

"Sandinista Revolution," Experience Nicaragua, http://library.think-quest.org/17749/lrevolution.html.

Schutz, Jorian Polis. "The Impact of the Sandinistas on Nicaragua," 1998, http://www.jorian.com/san.html.

Scott, Kevin. "Volcanic Landslides, Debris Avalanches and Debris Flows in Nicaragua Resulting from Hurricane Mitch," preliminary report of a USGS mission, USAID Managua, Nicaragua, January 1999.

Somoza, Anastasio with Cox, Jack. *Nicaragua Betrayed*. Western Islands,1980.

Vallance, J.W., Schilling, S.P., Devoli, G., Reid, M.E., Howell, M.M., and Brien, D.L. "United States Geological Survey Open-File Report 01-468: Lahar Hazards at Casita and San Cristóbal Volcanoes - Nicaragua," 2004.

"William Walker (filibuster)," *Wikipedia: the Free Encyclopedia*, http://en.wikipedia.org/wiki/William_Walker_(soldier)

"Walker's Expeditions," GlobalSecurity.org, http://www.globalsecurity.org/military/ops/walker.htm.

Walsh, Lawrence E. "Third Interim Report To Congress By Independent Counsel For Iran/Contra Matters," June 25, 1992, http://www.webcom.com/pinknoiz/covert/walsh3.html

Werner, Pat. "The Assault on Coyotepe, U.S. Marines Trounce Rebellious Liberals," *Nica News*. 1999. http://www.latinamericanstudies.org/nicaragua/coyotepe.htm

Woodhouse, Jennifer. "The Sandinista Revolution," *Hispanic Literature*, http://www.lclark.edu/~woodrich/WoodhouseSandinista.html

Fabrizio Blini

Mamma mia!

La figura della mamma come deterrente
nello sviluppo culturale, sociale ed economico
dell'Italia moderna

Series Editor
Lisa R. Tucci

Annotation by
Lisa R. Tucci
Elaine O'Reilly

THE ORIGINAL ITALIAN TEXT
WITH AN ITALIAN-ENGLISH GLOSSARY

LIN·GUAL·I·TY™
Cambridge

ISBN-13: 978-0-9795037-7-1
ISBN-10: 0-9795037-7-9

10 9 8 7 6 5 4 3 2 1

FOREWORD

Italy's mamma's boys, or *mammoni,* have long been endeared of and endured by generations of Italian women—the women who coddle them and the women who capture their hearts, begrudgingly tolerating them as husbands while spawning an entirely new generation of mamma's boys as they cuddle their bouncing *bambini.*

What is less known, or kept literally and figuratively under wraps, is the true effect on society of all this mothering, or smothering, as many foreign observers would suggest. Author Fabrizio Blini, a self-proclaimed *mammone,* offers a ruthless analysis of this most Mediterranean of epidemics. Beginning with his categorization of mammas, he supports his theories with corollaries and charts, all the while employing a wicked humor to depict the effect different types of mammas have on their offspring. As the original publishers Baldini, Castoldi & Dalai attest, the net result is a book that is "not a serious work, but rather, a dramatic one."

From a foreign observer's perspective, Blini's descriptions truly hit their mark. We have grown accustomed to seeing Italian children bundled up in layers upon layers of clothes on hot spring days and hearing their mammas call after them, "Don't run, don't go far, don't sweat!" If you find yourself married to an Italian man, you chuckle when he dons a scarf when the slightest breeze kicks in. It is less amusing, however, when you find him taking his laundry over to mamma's for washing and ironing, or when he compels you to invite mamma over every single Sunday evening so she can cook—and carefully inspect your domestic cleaning, which if not to her standard can illicit the *mal'occhio* curse. I once had a boyfriend whose mother washed, massaged, and manicured her son's feet each time we visited. They both proudly pointed out the benefits of this practice to me, the uninitiated foreigner. Suffice it to say, that relationship didn't quite work out.

What's most remarkable about this book, however, is that it was ever written in the first place, let alone by a *mammone*. Tackling *La Mamma* head-on is so taboo, it's surprising Blini hasn't been forced to hire bodyguards 24/7. There are probably new MADD chapters springing up across the Boot—not Mothers Against Drunk Driving, but Mammas Against Defamation of Domestic bliss. Of course, that would be their domestic bliss, not their offsprings'.

After 16 years of living in Italy, I was utterly shocked when Italy's minister of Economic Development actually cited the *mammone* pandemic as one of the direct causes of economic malaise in the country. Blini's book came out at the onset of the ensuing firestorm, offering a classic example of "art imitating life."

Foreigners rejoiced, the press reviled, mammas fumed, and the so-called *bamboccioni* simply stood by, totally immobile, unsure whether the minister was unclipping their wings, or whether they would be unceremoniously called out of their gilded cages and actually forced to take on such responsibilities as preparing a plate of pasta or making their own dental appointments.

As a manager of a business, I cannot count how many times I have fielded calls from mammas imploring me to hire their sons each time I have placed a job advertisement. I am not alone. My personal theory is businesses should ditch the kids and hire the multitasking mammas instead.

As you read this book, you will undoubtedly find yourself laughing out loud at the way mammas and their precious *bambini* are portrayed. I can assure you that while Blini uses hyperbole to make his points, nothing is exaggerated for effect. In fact, as Italy's divorce rate climbs, a new boomerang effect is exacerbating the problem: boy-men who finally leave the nest to start a family eventually return to rooms with tiny beds and soccer posters still pinned up on the walls. There they are treated to three square meals a day, 24-hour cleaning, and totally conditional love...the condition being that they stay put. Modern-day Italian homes look like curious natural history museums, where the specimens are frozen in time and place but continue to show signs of aging all the same.

Talk to a true *mammone* and he will argue fervently that his condition is a wonderful sign of family unity, that he takes responsibility in his own way (like deciding where to take mamma on vacation), and that he can have a perfectly healthy relationship with a woman without needing to move in together. But in an increasingly competitive world, it does not bode well for Italy, a country with one of the longest life expectancies on earth, that mammas are looking after their babies well into their 80s and middle-aged men are not venturing out of the comfort of their homes to be productive members of society. After all, even birds know to toss their chicks out of the nest so they can learn to fly.

Mamma mia! is a wake up call to a nation that is loving its kids if not to death, then certainly to petrification—or as Fabrizio Blini calls it, "mommyfication."

—Francesca Maggi, Blogger
Burnt by the Tuscan Sun, The True Story of Living in Italy
http://burntbythetuscansun.blogspot.com

deterrente deterrent, curb, means of prevention
sviluppo development

* *Glossed entries in the main text are highlighted in bold; in section titles and headlines, they are underscored.*

Fabrizio Blini

Mamma mia!

La figura della mamma come deterrente
nello sviluppo culturale, sociale ed economico
dell'Italia moderna

A mia mamma prima che si offenda

INDICE

PRE MAMAN, PRE MAMMON............................... 11

ASPETTI TEORICI DEL MAMMISMO 21
La questione ontologica.. 23
Il compromesso isterico 27
Utopia termodinamica della mamma 35
Cenni di sintomatologia del mammismo 41

ARCHETIPI DI MAMMA.. 53
Le principale tipologie di mamma 55
La Mamma Vittima detta Mamma Passiva o Mamma Karenina 59
La Mamma Totale o Mamma Imperatrice 69
La Mamma Iperprotettiva o Lupa Mammara 79
La Mammigna o Mammarmata................................ 87

COMPORTAMENTI TOPICI DELLA MAMMA................ 95
Agnosticismo temporale 97
Lo stato di pulizia 113
La strategia elettrodomestica 125
Apologia della canfora 139
La sindrome del sottovuoto 147
Simbolismo e minaccia dell'attività sartoriale 155

INFLUSSO DELLA MAMMA SULLA CULTURA MODERNA 165
L'embargo culturale della mamma 167

«All'inizio del cammin di nostra vita
mi ritrovai con una mamma oscura
che la madre mia era sparita.»
Dante Alighieri, 7 anni

PRE MAMAN, PRE MAMMON a play on *pre maman*, a French term connoting pregnancy. Here Blini uses *pre mammon* to mean "before becoming a mamma's boy (*mammone*)."

precede precedes
incinta pregnant

Dalla nascita in poi From birth onward
individuo sano e autonomo healthy, autonomous person
genitrice genetrix (*i.e.*, mother)
volontà del generato will/determination of the one born
nascituro unborn baby, future child
La scelta si rivela peraltro difficile However, the choice turns out to be a hard one
si opta per one opts for
di riserva spares, in reserve
il primo dovesse andare smarrito should the first one get lost
presidiato presided over, governed by
fenomeno phenomenon
tende a mantenere tends to keep
obiettivo objective, aim
impedire che il bruco si trasformi in farfalla to prevent/stop the caterpillar from turning into a butterfly
imperativo imperative, crucial
far abortire to abort

bisognosi di liberarsi needing to set themselves free
dall'eccesso di cure della mamma of mamma's excessive attentions
maglioncini lovingly hand-knit little sweaters
sberle slaps

PRE MAMAN, PRE MAMMON

La condizione di figlio **precede** di necessità quella di adulto. Quando una donna scopre di essere **incinta**, si dice che aspetta un figlio e non una persona, quindi, per almeno nove mesi si è solo figli. **Dalla nascita in poi**, la possibilità di rendere il figlio un **individuo sano e autonomo**, con un'identità precisa, dipende dalla maturità della **genitrice** e dalla **volontà del generato**, sempre che i genitori abbiano deciso il nome del **nascituro**. **La scelta si rivela peraltro difficile**, dato che di solito **si opta per** un primo nome più altri due o tre **di riserva**, forse nel caso in cui **il primo dovesse andare smarrito**.

Molto spesso, lo spazio che separa l'essere figlio dall'essere adulto è **presidiato** da un **fenomeno** che **tende a mantenere** distanti i due elementi.

Tale fenomeno è denominato *mamma*.

L'obiettivo esistenziale della mamma è **impedire che il bruco si trasformi in farfalla**: una volta nato il bambino è **imperativo far abortire** l'adulto che è in lui.

Dunque, la donna aspetta un figlio, il figlio non sa cosa lo aspetta.

In Italia, la percentuale di figli **bisognosi di liberarsi dall'eccesso di cure della mamma**, baci della mamma, gnocchi della mamma, **maglioncini** della mamma, **sberle** della

11

raccomandazioni advice, warnings, admonitions

valanga avalanche

cosparge spreads, sprinkles

escludendo quelli scappati di casa excluding those who ran away from home

si approssima it comes to roughly

tale libro this book

disagio diffuso widespread uneasiness

investe overwhelms, plagues

Nascosto Hidden

provoca it causes/brings about

si manifestano appear

tic nervosi…tifo calcistico the author lists all the possible disorders, from nervous ticks to gastritis, premature ejaculation, being slow-witted, and being a soccer fan

autoerotismo, erotismo in auto *another play on words: autoerotismo =* "masturbation," *erotismo in auto =* "making love in a car"

malessere malaise

fa sì che works in such a way that

incompiuta incomplete

l'anima the soul

incapace incapable

candore innocence

bonsanima bonsai + anima = "a miniature, warped soul"

La mancata evoluzione The arrested development

in concomitanza di tappe importanti simultaneously with important stages

ci si accorge one realizes

pensionati dell'infanzia childhood's retirees

che suggerisce from which comes

Mamma mia che gol!….Mamma mia che palle! The author lists some of the ways in which *Mamma mia!* is used as an exclamation, from *Mamma mia, what a goal!* to *Mamma mia, what a pain in the ass!* (*literally: palle =* "testicles")

É divenuta così It has thus reached the point of being

una locuzione abusata an over-used expression

prevalgono predominate

contempla allows for

si tratta di tutt'altra faccenda it's an entirely different matter

Svezia Sweden

mamma, **raccomandazioni** della mamma e dalla **valanga** di attenzioni che la mamma **cosparge** sulle loro vite, è piuttosto elevata: **escludendo quelli scappati di casa, si approssima** al 100%.

L'idea di scrivere **tale libro** nasce da un **disagio diffuso** che **investe** i figli a vari livelli. **Nascosto** nella stanza del subconscio, **provoca** infatti una serie di disturbi fisici che **si manifestano** giorno dopo giorno: **tic nervosi**, bulimia, gastriti, coliti, eiaculatio precox, comprendonio tardox, **tifo calcistico, autoerotismo, erotismo in auto.**

Questo **malessere fa sì che** la crescita personale resti **incompiuta** e che **l'anima, incapace** di conservare il **candore** dell'infanzia, si trasformi in una *bonsanima*.

La mancata evoluzione di presunti adulti in veri adulti si manifesta **in concomitanza di tappe importanti** della vita, come il quarantesimo compleanno, età in cui **ci si accorge** di avere 6 anni da ben 34 anni: dei **pensionati dell'infanzia.**

L'espressione **che suggerisce** il titolo del libro è emblematica, visto che la nostra è l'unica lingua in cui viene utilizzata, sempre: *Mamma mia che gol!*; *Mamma mia che casino!*; *Mamma mia che buono!*; *Mamma mia che incidente!*; *Mamma mia che pioggia!*; *Mamma mia che palle!*; *Oh, Mamma mia!* **È divenuta così una locuzione abusata** che pervade il linguaggio di ogni italiano.

In inglese e in francese **prevalgono** esclamazioni di natura religiosa: *Oh, my God!*; *Jesus!*; *Mon Dieu!*; Lo spagnolo **contempla** l'espressione *Madre*, ma la parola è appunto madre, non *mama* e, come vedremo, **si tratta di tutt'altra faccenda.**

Anche in **Svezia** dicono *Mamma mia!*, ma solo gli Abba.

modo di dire expression, way of saying

con quanto sta accadendo with what's going on

sintomo symptomatic

appare laddove non ha motivo di essere appears where it has no reason to be

si è insediata has installed herself

materia cerebrale brain matter

mammificato mamma-fied, a play on *mummificato* = "mummified"

mammismo mamma-ism, the quality of being a mamma's boy; a colloquial expression signifying a strong attachment to one's mother

sottostima underestimation

ne peggiora gli effetti worsens its effects

contagiati infected, contaminated

criptomammismo hidden mamma's-boy tendency

da diagnosticare to diagnose

non pensa affatto doesn't think in the slightest

si confonde one confuses/mistakes

affetto affection

essere affetto da being affected by, suffering from

reiterati repeated

i disturbi si cronicizzano the ailments become chronic

supera qualsiasi confine anagrafico exceeds any age limit whatsoever

richiamo appeal, allure

immunodeficiente lacking immunity

al limite solo deficiente ma immune mai or at least just mentally deficient, but never ever immune

non costituisce doesn't constitute, doesn't represent

ostacolo obstacle

possesso possession

denunciare denounce, condemn

duplice fine dual purpose

configurare to formulate

esame accurato careful/detailed investigation

disfunzioni dysfunctions

a carico that weigh on

residui residual traces

L'uso di questo **modo di dire** dimostra come in Italia la mamma sia costantemente presente, anche quando non ha alcuna relazione **con quanto sta accadendo, sintomo** di un pensiero che si è trasformato in idea fissa, subliminale e che **appare laddove non ha motivo di essere.**

La mamma **si è insediata** nella parte più grigia della **materia cerebrale** del Paese: il cervello degli italiani si è *mammificato.*

Il **mammismo** è un fenomeno nazionale grave e la **sottostima** del problema **ne peggiora gli effetti**. Il numero di adulti che non si sentono **contagiati** è elevato, tuttavia si tratta di casi di *criptomammismo*, semplici **da diagnosticare** ma difficili da risolvere, considerato che il soggetto **non pensa affatto** a curarsi: è la tipica situazione in cui **si confonde** *l'avere l'affetto di una madre* e *l'essere affetto da una mamma.*

Se **reiterati** nel tempo, **i disturbi si cronicizzano** e la forza di attrazione della mamma **supera qualsiasi confine anagrafico**: non esiste limite di età oltre il quale un adulto possa sentirsi immune dal suo **richiamo**, egli sarà sempre **immunodeficiente, al limite solo deficiente, ma immune mai.**

Anche la distanza **non costituisce** un **ostacolo**, perché il figlio sente la voce della mamma dentro di sé: il mammismo è una forma di **possesso** e il mammone è posseduto dalla mamma.

Oltre a **denunciare** un sistema ipocrita e *pathetically correct*, il teso ha un **duplice fine**:

- **configurare** il problema attraverso un **esame accurato**, descrivendo effetti e **disfunzioni a carico** del nostro sistema di vita;

- eliminare i **residui** delle overdosi da mamma ancora

circolanti circulating/in the system
**benché il tentativo di mettere in atto rimedi efficaci sia
  ostacolato** even though any attempt at carrying out effective
  remedies is blocked

tossicità toxicity, contamination

atroce appalling, atrocious

un'attrazione fetale a fetal attraction (as opposed to a fatal one)

indirizzato aimed at
poiché since, as
concorso di diversi fattori combination of various factors

destinatari recipients

inettitudine ineptitude
faccende domestiche household chores
igiene personale personal hygiene

subordinata subordinate
paritari between equals

prede più facili easier prey
sviluppo development
arredate decorated, furnished

Tuttavia Nevertheless
che si accingono a diventare who are about to become
nuore daughters-in-law

suocera mother-in-law
rende malfunzionante renders faulty

circolanti nei mammoni, **benché il tentativo di mettere in atto rimedi efficaci sia ostacolato** da resistenze quasi invincibili: la principale di queste forze si chiama sangue, la sua azione è tanto più potente quanto più elevato è il suo livello di **tossicità**, determinato da sostanze quali ragù, melanzane alla parmigiana, cotolette impanate, fritti misti e budini al cioccolato, che possono causare uno stato di dipendenza **atroce**.

È **un'attrazione fetale.**

Il libro è **indirizzato** principalmente ai figli, **poiché** più soggetti a diventare vittime delle mamme per il **concorso di diversi fattori**:

- i maschi sono **destinatari** di maggiori attenzioni, in quanto ritenuti più vulnerabili a causa della loro **inettitudine** nelle **faccende domestiche** e nella gestione dell'**igiene personale**;
- nei rapporti mamma-figlio, il maschio è sempre in posizione **subordinata**; mentre quelli mamma-figlia diventano presto **paritari**, nel rapporto mamma-figlio la mamma è sempre dominante;
- i giovani maschi sono **prede più facili**, perché il lento **sviluppo** psicofisico li confina a lungo in camerette **arredate** da Walt Disney.

Tuttavia, il testo può rivelarsi utile anche alle figlie e alle donne **che si accingono a diventare** mogli e **nuore**: il vantaggio in questo caso è doppio perché oltre a identificare il tipo di **suocera**, possono scoprire il difetto che **rende malfunzionante** il proprio uomo.

radici roots

non affondano are not embedded

qualunquismo indifferent and skeptical position (in English the term "whatever" is used to connote this attitude)

riconduce leads back to

colpe failings

insorga arises, crops up

accomuna have in common

giunta alla fine upon reaching the end

convenga will agree/admit

Concludendo, le **radici** di questo libro **non affondano** nel **qualunquismo** psicanalitico che **riconduce** alle **colpe** materne qualsiasi problema **insorga** nel figlio, ma esclusivamente nell'oggettività dei fatti. E basta osservare ciò che **accomuna** queste esperienze, l'identità tra il proprio vissuto e quello descritto, perché qualsiasi persona di sesso maschile, **giunta alla fine**, **convenga**: è tutto vero.

ASPETTI TEORICI DEL MAMMISMO

«Essere o non essere mamma, questo è il problema.»
Gertrude, regina di Danimarca e genitrice di Amleto

Nell'accezione comune It is widely thought
a ben vedere looking at it closely

allattato breast-fed
svezzato weaned
compiuto il suo dovere biologico fulfilled her biological duty
possano compiere il loro can fulfill theirs
sempre che ne abbiano voglia provided they have the desire to
comportamento behavior
fatta eccezione with the exception
scimpanzé chimpanzees
accomuna is shared with
esaurito once fully completed
cuccioli word used for most baby animals, *i.e.,* puppy, cub, etc.
si verifica takes place, occurs
allontanamento distancing, detachment
condurli lead them
reciproca estraneità mutual alienation
se non allo scontro if not outright confrontation
razza umana human race
distacco separation
si realizzi comes into his own, becomes a fulfilled independent
   adult
esprime expresses, conveys
in cambio in exchange
**al contrario accarezza in modo ossessivo il concetto di
   vicinanza** on the contrary, obsessively embraces the concept
   of closeness
non ammette she doesn't acknowledge/admit
non cede, non molla she doesn't give in, she doesn't let go
recidere il cordone ombelicale cutting the umbilical cord
protesi di se stessa extension of herself
alimenta feeds

LA QUESTIONE ONTOLOGICA
La differenza che distingue la madre dalla mamma

Nell'accezione comune, *madre* e *mamma* sono considerati sinonimi ma **a ben vedere** il loro senso viaggia in direzioni opposte.

Dopo aver protetto, **allattato, svezzato** e quindi **compiuto il suo dovere biologico,** la madre offre i propri figli alla vita, in modo che questi **possano compiere il loro, sempre che ne abbiano voglia.** Questo **comportamento – fatta eccezione** per gli **scimpanzé – accomuna** la maggior parte delle specie animali dove, **esaurito** il periodo dello sviluppo, la madre libera gli ex **cuccioli.** Dopo la nascita, **si verifica** un progressivo **allontanamento** tra madre e figli, che a volte può **condurli** alla **reciproca estraneità, se non allo scontro.**

Nella **razza umana,** la genitrice che comprende la necessità del **distacco** affinché il figlio **si realizzi** integralmente – la madre – **esprime** una forma di affetto sincera, disinteressata, che dà tutto senza decidere niente **in cambio.**

Il senso della madre è da dentro a fuori, da lei al mondo, da qui a là, da vicino a lontano.

La mamma **al contrario accarezza in modo ossessivo il concetto di vicinanza;** a differenza della madre, **non ammette** la possibilità di una separazione, **non cede, non molla,** invece di **recidere il cordone ombelicale** lo tira a sé, vive il figlio come una **protesi di se stessa:** il canale vitale che **alimenta** il

viene convertito in guinzaglio is turned into a [dog's] leash

impedisce prevents
di fortificarsi from growing strong
**debolezza perenne, una dipendenza inconscia, talvolta conscia
   o addirittura edipicamente sconcia** perpetual weakness, an
   unconscious dependence, sometimes conscious or downright
   shamelessly oedipal
ontologia ontology (the science or study of being)
tontologia science/study of stupidity (*tonto* = "stupid")

antepone replaces

Riconoscere Recognizing
colui che the one who

l'imbecille the imbecile

riscontrare to come across
miste mixed
entrambe le inclinazioni both tendencies
dando vita a giving rise to
piloro pylorus (opening from the stomach into the intestine)
raziocinio reason, common sense
affrontati di petto confronted head on (*literally:* chest-out
   confrontation)
spintonati dal furore driven by fury/passion
visceralmente legata viscerally tied, joined at the gut
comportamento di tipo sanguigno-addominale highly
   instinctive behavior (*literally:* blood and gut-driven behavior)
cannibalizza cannibalizes
anse dell'intestino intestinal loops
lo sublima sublimates it

rapporto **viene convertito in guinzaglio**.

Il senso della mamma è da dentro a dentro, da lei a lei, da qui a qui, da vicino a vicino.

Ciò va contro le leggi della natura, la quale non a caso è madre e non mamma.

L'eccessiva prossimità **impedisce** al figlio **di fortificarsi**, provocando in lui una **debolezza perenne, una dipendenza inconscia, talvolta conscia o addirittura edipicamente sconcia**.

È grazie all'**ontologia** della mamma che si può comprendere la *tontologia* del mammismo, cioè il disperato bisogno di protezione materna da parte di molte persone adulte, originato dalla genitrice che **antepone** il ruolo di mamma a quello di madre.

Riconoscere un adulto normale da uno mammone non è difficile: l'adulto è **colui che** costruisce una relazione matura con i propri genitori; il mammone è **l'imbecille** che insiste a chiamarli *la mia mamma e il mio papà*.

Nella maggior parte delle donne è quasi impossibile **riscontrare** una personalità totalmente mamma o totalmente madre, è più probabile trovare personalità **miste** in cui convivono **entrambe le inclinazioni dando vita a** tensioni opposte.

Nella madre il principale organo di conoscenza è l'occhio del cuore.

Nella mamma prevale invece il **piloro** dello stomaco: gli venti non sono mai valutati con **raziocinio** ma **affrontati di petto, spintonati dal furore**. La mamma è **visceralmente legata** ai figli ma mentalmente lontana da loro, e il suo **comportamento di tipo sanguigno-addominale cannibalizza** il rapporto nelle **anse dell'intestino**, mentre quello della madre **lo sublima** nell'intelletto.

IL COMPROMESSO ISTERICO The attempted compromise
between Italian right- and left-wing parties in the 1970s was
called *Il Compromesso Storico* (The Historic Compromise).
Here, the author substitutes the adjective *isterico,* making it
"The Hysterical Compromise."

ineluttabilità inevitability

istinto instinct
mantenimento dello statu quo maintaining the status quo
cuscini cushions
inesorabile relentless, implacable
suo malgrado to her dismay
ostinazione stubbornness, obstinacy
opporre una resistenza sufficiente put up any resistance
nonostante tutto in spite of everything
a rilento in slow motion
teneri tender
crescano i peli body hair grows
compaiano fenomeni mostruosi hideous phenomena appear
ciclo mestruale menstrual cycle
crudeltà insopportabile unbearable cruelty
strenuamente strenuously, doggedly
prerogative quali such privileges as
l'allacciamento delle scarpine the tying of shoe laces
pappabuona *baby talk:* yummy food
culetto santo sacred little tush

antipatia antipathy, dislike
dirottata rerouted, hijacked
ottenere un pareggio even the score
sconfitta dignitosa decorous/dignified defeat
disfatta assoluta total defeat
s'illude one eludes oneself
incurante *here:* oblivious to

IL COMPROMESSO ISTERICO
La resistenza della mamma davanti all'ineluttabilità dello sviluppo dei figli

L'**istinto** conservatore della mamma, che tende ossessivamente al **mantenimento dello statu quo** e della disposizione simmetrica dei **cuscini** sul divano, si scontra con l'**inesorabile** sviluppo biologico che, **suo malgrado**, investe la vita dei figli. Contro la forza della natura, neanche l'**ostinazione** della mamma può **opporre una resistenza sufficiente** ad arrestare il processo: i figli crescono **nonostante tutto**, ma lei cerca di farli crescere **a rilento**.

Ai suoi occhi, la brutalità con cui la natura permette che sui suoi **teneri** bambini **crescano i peli**, che cambi loro la voce o che **compaiano fenomeni mostruosi** come il **ciclo mestruale** e l'erezione, è una **crudeltà insopportabile** e alla mamma combatte **strenuamente** affinché non le vengano sottratte **prerogative quali l'allacciamento delle scarpine**, la preparazione della **pappabuona** o la pulizia del **culetto santo**.

Questa lotta tra mamma e madre natura – tra le quali esiste un rapporto di cordiale **antipatia**, almeno da parte della mamma – è **dirottata** dalla prima su un terreno in cui tenta di **ottenere un pareggio**, una **sconfitta dignitosa**, evitando la **disfatta assoluta**. Si tratta di un luogo di fantasia, dove **s'illude** di mantenere intatto il quadretto di famiglia; **incurante**

sapiente regia skillful direction (as in a movie)
alza il sipario raises the curtain (as in the theater)
apparenze outward appearances
mette in scena she stages
la stessa replica the same performance
girello baby walker
guadagnati gained, added
nasconde hides
comportamenti coatti compulsive behaviors

si piega, ma poi ti spezza [she] bends but then she breaks you, a
   play on the idiom *Si piega, ma non si spezza* = "It bends but it
   doesn't break"
provocano cause

si ostina she stubbornly insists

per restringerli in order to shrink them
atteggiamento attitude, approach
che ne deriva that follows as a result
conflittuale marked by conflict/strife
si verifica takes place, occurs
ponderale in terms of weight

antievolutivo anti-evolutionary
immerso immersed
spinta force

affoga drowns
scempi havoc, destruction
ne conseguono that follows as a result
oscilla fluctuates
rimprovero scolding
follia folly, madness
coccole cuddles
sbalzi umorali mood swings

dei cambiamenti, con **sapiente regia**, ogni giorno la mamma **alza il sipario** su una commedia delle **apparenze**, di cui **mette in scena** sempre **la stessa replica**, trattando i figli come se fossero ancora nel **girello**.

Dietro il sorriso da posa fotografica, che sembra esprimere la sua gioia per i centimetri **guadagnati** dai bambini, la mamma **nasconde** la difficile digestione della verità, all'origine di una serie di **comportamenti coatti**: il *compromesso isterico*.

La mamma **si piega, ma poi ti spezza**.

Nel suo subconscio, la crescita dei figli non è mai realmente accettata e i suoi tormenti **provocano** veri disastri. Il buon senso della mamma è un elemento puramente formale, poiché **si ostina** a definirli *i miei bambini* anche quando superano gli ottanta chilogrammi. E quando li osserva dicendo: *Guarda come sono grandi!*, avrebbe quasi voglia di lavarli in acqua calda **per restringerli**.

L'atteggiamento che ne deriva è sempre **conflittuale**: vuole far crescere i figli ma solo in apparenza. Infatti il loro sviluppo **si verifica** solo dal punto di vista fisico, soprattutto **ponderale**, e in modo inverso rispetto a quello mentale.

Principio antievolutivo di Archimede
Un bambino immerso in una mamma non riceve alcuna spinta uguale e contraria.

Corollario antievolutivo di Archimede
Un bambino immerso in una mamma affoga.

Gli **scempi** che **ne conseguono** sono molteplici e diffusi nella vita famigliare di tutti. Il barometro di questo clima *psicoillogico* **oscilla** tra la tempesta del **rimprovero** e la serena **follia** delle **coccole**: con rapidi **sbalzi umorali** la mamma

si accanisce becomes enraged

abbigliamento indecoroso unsuitable clothes

sciatteria sloppiness

pessime abitudini alimentari terrible eating habits

melense premure dopey, asinine acts of motherly love

ovetti sbattuti eggs beaten with sugar

irrimediabilmente cresciuto irretrievably all grown up

rimpiange mourns

rinfacciandogli la scortesia reproaching him for the disrespect

senza permesso without [her] permission

coniugati al passato conjugated in the past tense

Mi ubbidivi You did as you were told (*literally*: obeyed me)

raggiunge vette leopardiane reaches Leopardian heights
    (Giacomo Leopardi was a major 19th-century Italian poet)

cassetti, bauli drawers, trunks

riesuma she unearths

pupazzi orbi eyeless dolls

sebbene although

non si arrende mai she never gives in

nel tentativo di riappropriarsi in the attempt to retake possession

lancia la sfida she challenges (*literally*: launches a challenge)

fato fate, destiny

li ha strappati dalla culla tore them from their cradles

espedienti maneuvers, expedients

attacco al fegato [waging] an attack on the liver, *i.e.*, waging an
    attack by way of very rich food. Italians often complain of
    their livers being affected by rich food.

consueti usual, frequent

imprigionare imprison

arrosti domiciliare *in effect:* domiciled roasts, a play on *arresti*
    domiciliari = "house arrests"

un peccaminoso...per la gola a wicked means of entrapping her
    offspring, taking them by the throat (*gola* = "throat" or "gluttony")

indici di valutazione prime indicators

affidabili dependable

pericolosità danger

ciò vale this is the case

merenda snack time

costituiscono constitute

aggregazione famigliare family togetherness

lucchetto padlock

si accanisce sui figli per l'**abbigliamento indecoroso**, per la **sciatteria** nei confronti dell'ambiente domestico o per le **pessime abitudini alimentari**; allo stesso modo, si abbandona a **melense premure**, come la preparazione di **ovetti sbattuti** in quantità militari.

Davanti al figlio **irrimediabilmente cresciuto**, la mamma **rimpiange** continuamente la sua infanzia, **rinfacciandogli la scortesia** di essere diventato grande **senza permesso**. Tutti i complimenti sono **coniugati al passato**: *Eri così carino; Eri tanto bravo; Eri intelligentissimo; Mi volevi bene;* **Mi ubbidivi;** *Mi baciavi; Mi dicevi amore.*

Durante le crisi in cui la nostalgia **raggiunge vette leopardiane**, la mamma cerca di attraversare la porta del passato aprendo album, **cassetti, bauli** da cui **riesuma** foto, **pupazzi orbi**, scarpine di lana. Ma, **sebbene** disperata, **non si arrende mai** e, **nel tentativo di riappropriarsi** dei suoi bimbi, **lancia la sfida** al **fato** che **li ha strappati dalla culla**.

Tra i vari **espedienti**, l'**attacco al fegato** è uno dei più **consueti**. Piatto dopo piatto la mamma cerca d'**imprigionare** i figli dentro casa, legandoli al tavolo della cucina: gli *arrosti domiciliari*.

Nel passaggio da donna a mamma, il cibo perde la sua funzione primaria per diventare **un peccaminoso strumento che circuisce la prole prendendola per la gola**.

Le capacità culinarie della mamma sono uno degli **indici di valutazione** più **affidabili** per determinare il suo grado di **pericolosità; ciò vale** in particolare per la **merenda**. Se pranzo e cena **costituiscono** momenti di **aggregazione famigliare**, la merenda è un momento di confronto personale e uno spazio di assoluto dominio da parte della mamma. Dolce o salata, la merenda è il **lucchetto** per mezzo del quale chiude il figlio in casa, lasciandogli aperta solo la bocca.

Kinder e Ferrero   manufacturers of chocolate treats (most
   notably, Nutella)
esercita potere   exercises power

Quanto più   The more
abile   adept at
tanto più aumenteranno   the greater
abbandono del nido   leaving the nest
cedendo alle sue tentazioni   giving in to its temptations

di cuoca   as a cook

Prima legge di Kinder e Ferrero sulla dipendenza alimentare

La mamma esercita potere sui figli quanto più a lungo riesce a preparare loro la merenda.

Quanto più la mamma sarà **abile** nella preparazione della merenda, **tanto più aumenteranno** le possibilità che i figli continuino a procrastinare l'**abbandono del nido, cedendo alle sue tentazioni.**

Seconda legge di Kinder e Ferrero sulla qualità alimentare

Il potere della mamma è direttamente proporzionale alle sue capacità di cuoca.

insostenibilità   unsustainability

Lavoisier Antoine-Laurent de Lavoisier (1743–1794), French chemist and biologist, known as the father of modern chemistry, who first stated the law of conservation of mass
recita   says, dictates

la gassosa   fizzy drink
rutto   belching

La mamma è sempre la mamma   A common Italian expression exalting the role of the *mamma*

enunciato   enunciation, theorum

serbatoio   container, tank
si sposta   goes, moves

raggiungimento   reaching

scappano   they escape/run off
si scottano   they get burned
interagisca   interacts
subisce   it undergoes
innalzamento   rising
soglia di tolleranza   tolerance threshold

UTOPIA TERMODINAMICA DELLA MAMMA
Prove scientifiche dell'<u>insostenibilità</u> fisica della mamma

Il Principio di conservazione di **Lavoisier recita:** *In natura nulla si crea e nulla si distrugge, ma tutto si trasforma.* È a fondamento della Prima legge della termodinamica, che dimostra come il lavoro si trasformi in energia, l'acqua diventi vapore o **la gassosa** esploda in **rutto.**

Principio di conservazione della mamma
<u>La mamma è sempre la mamma.</u> E non si trasforma.

Il principio termico appena esposto permette di introdurre un'altra legge fondamentale: secondo l'**enunciato** di Clausius, *Non è possibile effettuare una trasformazione il cui unico risultato sia il passaggio di calore da un* **serbatoio** *freddo a uno caldo.*

Ciò significa che è sempre il calore che **si sposta** verso il freddo e mai il contrario, fino al **raggiungimento** dell'equilibrio termico. Quindi, poiché la temperatura di M (mamma) è superiore a quella di F (figlio), è sempre la mamma che va verso i figli, i quali hanno due alternative: o **scappano** o **si scottano.** Qualunque corpo **interagisca** con la mamma, **subisce** un **innalzamento** della temperatura che oltrepassa alla **soglia di tolleranza,** osservazione che spiega perché l'arrosto si bruci così spesso.

retta straight

le si attribuiscono they are attributed to her
appiccicosa, asfissiante, opprimente, assillante clinging,
  suffocating, oppressive, nagging

insorgenza onset
denuncia complains/protests about
assordante deafening
sudarelle, vampate, caldane sweating, outbursts of anger, hot
  flashes
stagioni più rigide colder months
spalancate thrown wide open

surriscaldamento overheating
scintilla scatenante initial spark
accadimenti happenings
calzini spaiati unpaired socks
tovaglia tablecloth

Legge della condotta genitoriale della mamma
La linea di condotta che separa M (mamma) da F (figlio) non è mai retta.

Il valore dei coefficienti mamma e madre dipende dalla velocità con cui aumenta lo spazio tra la donna genitrice (DG) e il figlio[1](F) nel tempo. Se la velocità di spostamento di F è uguale a zero, anche il valore dello spazio è uguale a zero e il coefficiente mamma è massimo: è la condizione di *mamma patologica* in forma severa (perciò **le si attribuiscono** particolari aggettivi: ***appiccicosa, asfissiante, opprimente, assillante***, o frasi come: *È molto attaccata ai figli*).

Terza legge della termodinamica della mamma
La temperatura media della mamma è sempre superiore alla soglia di tolleranza dei figli.

Grazie alla Terza legge è possibile motivare anche la continua **insorgenza** di quei fenomeni ipertermici che la mamma **denuncia** con **assordante** frequenza: **sudarelle, vampate, caldane**, geyser. Questi episodi si verificano anche nelle **stagioni più rigide**, periodo in cui la mamma adora tenere le finestre **spalancate**.

Il **surriscaldamento** della mamma ha una bassa soglia di attivazione, che trova la **scintilla scatenante** in **accadimenti** di apparente inoffensività: l'anniversario di matrimonio, il ritrovamento di **calzini spaiati**, il parcheggio, una macchia sulla **tovaglia**.

---

1. Per figlio si intende anche figlia

disconoscere le conquiste   disregard the accomplishments
rielaborandole   re-elaborating them
aleatorio   *here:* dubious

Moebius   August Ferdinand Möbius (1790–1868), German
mathematician best known for his Möbius strip, a two-
dimensional surface with only one side. Because of the
resemblance, the strip often is mistakenly believed to have been
the model for the infinity symbol.

la smonta   dismantles it
sacchetto del aspirapolvere   vacuum-cleaner bag

$M = C'\grave{E}^2$ Mamma = EXISTS (to the higher power)

Il pensiero integralista della mamma tende a **disconoscere le conquiste** del pensiero scientifico, **rielaborandole** in un relativismo molto **aleatorio**: per la mamma tutto è relativo, a lei.

Conclusione di Moebius
La mamma insegue i figli all'infinito.

Il suo favoloso castello dottrinale trova il colpo di genio nella riformulazione della Legge della Relatività: se per Einstein era $E=MC^2$, il dogmatismo della mamma **la smonta** e la cambia come il **sacchetto dell'aspirapolvere**, trasformando il relativo in assoluto e affermando la propria inevitabile eternità.

Legge della Relatività della Mamma
$$M = C'\grave{E}^2$$

CENNI DI SINTOMATOLOGIA   Excerpts of the symptoms
sciagura   catastrophe

essere incompiuto   unfinished being
involucro   outer casing, wrapping
dondola   rocks, sways
altalena   swing
sotto mentite spoglie   in disguise

di sana costituzione   in good health (*literally:* with a healthy
    constitution)
coppie cromosomiche   chromosome pairs
disgiunte   detached

avvinto   entwined

Polo   Mint candies described as "a hole surrounded by mint." The
    author describes mamma's boys as "a hole surrounded by a
    mamma."

diagnosi sollecita   thorough diagnosis
divario   gap
abissale   abysmal
coma edipico   Oedipal coma, a play on "Oedipus complex"

tuttavia   nevertheless
criptati   encoded

CENNI DI SINTOMATOLOGIA DEL MAMMISMO
Con particolare riferimento alla sciagura del collezionismo e del modellismo

Il mammone è un **essere incompiuto** di cui è cresciuto solo l'**involucro** ma non il contenuto. La sua vita **dondola** tra fantasia e realtà, sospesa su un'**altalena** che non è più in grado di sostenerlo; e l'adulto che tutti vedono in apparenza non è che un bimbo **sotto mentite spoglie**, testimonianza di un'infanzia passata e di una maturità in preoccupante ritardo.

Fisicamente, il mammone appare **di sana costituzione**: all'interno del suo patrimonio genetico tutte le **coppie cromosomiche** sono **disgiunte**, ma è l'intero patrimonio genetico che non riesce a separarsi dalla mamma, e le resta **avvinto**.

Legge di Polo
I mammoni sono un buco con la mamma intorno.

Una **diagnosi sollecita** diventa obbligatoria prima che il **divario** tra l'adulto che dovrebbe essere e il mammone che è diventi **abissale**, con il rischio di entrare in uno stato di irreversibilità: il *coma edipico*.

Esiste **tuttavia** una serie di sintomi che aiuta a valutare il grado di mammismo, alcuni evidenti, altri latenti, **criptati**.

a tempo indeterminato for an unspecified period of time
vacanze fisse regularly scheduled vacations

celibato sospetto suspiciously confirmed bachelorhood
tatuaggio tattoo
macaco macaque monkey

speleologia spelaeology, pot-holing
partecipazione a quiz taking part in TV quiz shows

meritano deserve
più attenta closer

l'atteggiamento irrazionale [his] irrational behavior
desiderio morboso morbid/pathological desire
mettono in risalto underscore, highlight
somiglianza similarity
similitudine resemblance
si prendono in esame one examines
pilastri emotivi emotional mainstays/pillars
eredità inheritance

possedere to possess

Hobby and Work publisher of magazines dealing with collectable
  items, bricolage, and DIY
si appiccica adheres, sticks

assorbiti absorbed, engaged

- Sintomi evidenti: coabitazione **a tempo indeterminato** con i genitori, **vacanze fisse** con i genitori, grado di istruttore nei boy scout, telefonate continue alla mamma, fotografie della mamma, **celibato sospetto, tatuaggio** *Amo Mamma*, masturbazione da **macaco**.

- Sintomi criptati: **speleologia, partecipazione a quiz**, collezionismo, modellismo.

Considerata la loro grande diffusione, collezionismo e modellismo **meritano** un'analisi **più attenta**.

La caratteristica principale del collezionista è la compulsività: **l'atteggiamento irrazionale** e il **desiderio morboso** nei confronti di un obiettivo specifico **mettono in risalto** la prima **somiglianza** tra mammismo e collezionismo.

La **similitudine** è ancora più evidente se **si prendono in esame** *possesso* e *conservazione*, **pilastri emotivi** sia del mammismo che del collezionismo. Questi due elementi sembrano un'**eredità** diretta della mamma che il mammone riceve e fa sua trasformandosi a sua volta in mamma: il collezionista è Norman Bates di *Psyco*.

La mamma vuole **possedere** e conservare il figlio; il figlio vuole possedere e conservare farfalle.

Sillogismo appiccicoso di Hobby and Work
Il francobollo si appiccica alla lettera, il mammone si appiccica al francobollo, la mamma si appiccica al mammone.

L'attenzione e il tempo del mammone sono **assorbiti** dal

soprattutto above all

con cui si strutturano with which are organized
sorprendente sincronia surprising synchronicity

sfogarsi give vent to his feelings, express himself
attirare a sé to surround himself with
attendibile sound, reliable

forme peggiori worst cases
pulsione incontrollabile uncontrollable impulse
sazietà satiety

ne vorrà un altro he will want another one
bramosia yearning, covetousness
irrisolta unresolved
rompipalle ball-breaking

represso repressed
via di fuga way of escape
alleggerisca la pressione takes the weight off, lightens the load

sesso sex

tentativo di incrementare la propria collezione, senza lasciare spazio a nessun'altra attività, **soprattutto** quelle sociali.

Anche la progressione **con cui si strutturano** mammismo e collezionismo mostra una **sorprendente sincronia**: più la mamma esercita un'attrazione sul figlio, più questo cercherà di **sfogarsi** su oggetti da **attirare a sé**. Mania del collezionista e crescita della collezione rappresentano un **attendibile** termometro del mammismo.

Prima legge di Christies
Il grado di mammismo cresce in modo direttamente proporzionale alla vastità della collezione.

Nelle **forme peggiori**, il desiderio di possedere l'oggetto diventa bulimico, una **pulsione incontrollabile** che non raggiunge mai la **sazietà**: il collezionista vuole uno specifico oggetto, ma poi **ne vorrà un altro** e un altro ancora, senza fine. Questa **bramosia** nasconde una costrizione emotiva, una condizione affettiva **irrisolta**, una mamma **rompipalle**.

La mamma ha un comportamento compulsivo nei confronti del figlio perché lo vuole tutto per lei. Il mammone **represso** cerca a sua volta una **via di fuga**, qualcosa che **alleggerisca la pressione**, e la trova nella collezione verso la quale si comporta come al mamma fa con lui.

Seconda legge di Christies
La grandezza della collezione del mammone è direttamente proporzionale alla distanza che separa il mammone dal <u>sesso</u>.

febbre fever

stroncata sul nascere cut off at the roots (*literally:* cut off at birth)

imponente extensive

è senza via di scampo has no way out

spacciato per adulto, anzi, un adulto spacciato passed off as an adult, actually, a severely damaged adult

incoraggiamento encouraging

agevolata da complici backed up by co-conspirators

asseconda il vizio goes along with the bad habit (*literally:* vice)

compagnuccio an old buddy

cretino esemplare perfect idiot (*literally:* cretin)

non unico not a one-of-a-kind

sedentarietà sedentary state, inactivity

predilige has a preference for

rimira compiaciuto he gazes admiringly

carezzandola con affetto affectionately caressing it

attrae attracts

distogliendolo distracting him, diverting his attention

ipermetrope hypermetrope, far-sighted

gravità seriousness

misurazione measurement

Più sale la **febbre** per la collezione, più cresce il mammismo, per questo la collezione deve essere **stroncata sul nascere**. Se la collezione diventa **imponente** e supera l'età della crescita per consolidarsi in età adulta, allora la mamma ha vinto: il figlio è suo. Il collezionista adulto **è senza via di scampo**, è un bambino **spacciato per adulto, anzi, un adulto spacciato**.

A volte, nell'**incoraggiamento** al collezionismo, la mamma è **agevolata da complici** a lei subordinati, come il papà che **asseconda il vizio** come un **compagnuccio** (con ogni probabilità è anch'egli un mammone), aiutandolo nella ricerca di monete, soldatini o francobolli.

Corollario di Christies
Il mammone è un cretino esemplare, ma purtroppo non unico.

L'attività del collezionismo evidenzia un altro triste aspetto: la **sedentarietà** in forma chiusa.

Il collezionista mammone **predilige** vivere dentro casa, nella sua stanza, dove **rimira compiaciuto** la collezione, **carezzandola con affetto** sotto lo sguardo compiaciuto della mamma.

La collezione è amica della mamma, perché costituisce un polo magnetico che **attrae** l'attenzione del mammone, **distogliendolo** dalla seduzione della vita.

Nella maggior parte dei casi, il collezionista mammone diventa **ipermetrope**.

La **gravità** del collezionismo ha un ulteriore parametro di **misurazione** nel valore dell'oggetto collezionato.

toglie takes away
ragione di esistenza reason for being

schede telefoniche phone cards
puffi smurfs
anomalia preoccupante worrisome anomaly/abnormality
disparate varied, disparate
lattine di birra beer cans
gonfiabili inflatable

terreno più fertile more fertile ground
trappola trap
atteggiamento air, way of being

accudire in bacheca place carefully in a display case
apposito raccoglitore suitable container

Hachette major French publisher of books and magazines
insorgenza an onset

Variante A variation
nocive harmful
rassegnata resigned, submissive
Per alcuni versi In some ways
inquietante unsettling, alarming
stanziale firmly established
venendo a mancare lo slancio della ricerca lacking the impulse
    of searching for [items]
impone forces

Terza legge di Christies

La gravità del collezionismo è inversamente proporzionale al valore degli oggetti collezionati.

La mancanza di valore oggettivo **toglie** alla collezione qualsiasi **ragione di esistenza**. Se la passione per i quadri antichi significa gusto per l'arte o ricchezza, una collezione di **schede telefoniche** o di **puffi** è solo il sintomo di un'**anomalia preoccupante**. La perversione del collezionismo assume le forme più **disparate**: bottiglie mignon, soldatini, **lattine di birra**, tappi di bottiglia, cappelli, bambole, bambole **gonfiabili**.

Il collezionismo trova **terreno più fertile** nelle famiglie con un figlio unico che, per mancanza di compagnia, cade più facilmente nella **trappola**. Verso di lui, la mamma avrà un **atteggiamento** ancora più pressante: i pezzi della collezione diventeranno tanti fratellini più piccoli, da **accudire in bacheca** o nell'**apposito raccoglitore**.

Legge di Hachette

La probabilità d'insorgenza di forme di collezionismo sono inversamente proporzionali al numero di figli.

Variante del collezionismo, con caratteristiche diverse ma altrettanto **nocive**, è il modellismo. Nel modellismo il comportamento compulsivo è meno impaziente e assume un'aria più **rassegnata**, seduta. **Per alcuni versi** questa attività è più **inquietante** perché ancora più **stanziale, venendo a mancare lo slancio della ricerca che impone** al collezionista di uscire.

accumulo accumulation
rivolge l'attenzione turns his attention
partorire to give birth to
gestazione gestation
affannose premure feverish attention
nascituro [yet] unborn baby (*here:* creation)
palese obvious
deliranti connotati frenzied features
voglia desire, wish
discutibile debatable
di fiammiferi made of matches

incolla glues together
custodendola guarding it
al riparo da tutto somewhere safe from everything
ostentarla fieramente proudly show it off

Invece di concentrarsi sull'**accumulo** di oggetti simili, il mammone modellista **rivolge l'attenzione** su un unico pezzo che lui stesso vuole **partorire** dopo una lunga **gestazione**, caratterizzata da **affannose premure** per il **nascituro**. Anche in questo caso, l'eredità della mamma è **palese** e assume i **deliranti connotati** della sindrome di Frankenstein: la **voglia** di mettere al mondo la creatura perfetta, ma che risulta esteticamente **discutibile** e priva di senso, come la Torre Eiffel **di fiammiferi**.

Il modellista **incolla** le parti dell'opera pezzo per pezzo, con precisione maniacale, **custodendola** gelosamente **al riparo da tutto** per poi **ostentarla fieramente** come il capolavoro della sua vita.

Fabrizio Blini

ninna nanna lullaby

ARCHETIPI DI MAMMA

«Ogni bimbo ha la sua mamma,
ogni bimbo ha il suo bel dramma.»
Prima ninna nanna di Johannes Brahms, 9 anni

si dispongono   are assorted

impedire lo sviluppo   to impede the development
fatta eccezione   with the exception of
altrettanto   equally
più consoni   most in line with

si distinguono   are recognizable
prevedono   count on

adottano   adopt
raggiro   *here:* bribery
si avvale di insidiosi tranelli   makes use of insidious traps
corrompe   corrupts
altrove   elsewhere
ricatto morale inocula   moral blackmail injects
sensi di colpa   pangs of guilt
scacco matto   checkmate

LE PRINCIPALI TIPOLOGIE DI MAMMA
Di mamma non ce n'è una sola

Le mamme si possono dividere in due tipologie generali – autoritarismo e permissivismo, attivismo e passività – nei quali le mamme **si dispongono** secondo le loro predisposizioni, perché se è vero che l'obiettivo finale della mamma è **impedire lo sviluppo** (**fatta eccezione** per le sue piantine di basilico), è **altrettanto** vero che esistono diversi percorsi per raggiungerlo e ogni mamma adotta i sistemi **più consoni** alla propria natura.

Le Mamme Autoritarie **si distinguono** per atteggiamenti inibitori che **prevedono** il comando diretto, il conflitto, o la tirannia che prende possesso della vita dei figli: Tu fai quello che dico io.

Le Mamme Permissive, al contrario, **adottano** la tecnica del **raggiro** che **si avvale di insidiosi tranelli**: la concessione **corrompe** la volontà dei figli, offrendo loro tutto quello che desiderano e annullando il bisogno di ricercarlo **altrove**; il **ricatto morale inocula** piccole dosi di **sensi di colpa**, immobilizzando la coscienza fino allo **scacco matto**.

Qualunque sia il tipo di mamma, ciascuna dichiara litanicamente il manifesto politico che la contraddistingue; frasi che la immortalano nella mente dei figli e che denotano un carattere e una particolare interpretazione del ruolo: *Io sono tua madre; Io ti ho messo al mondo, io ti ci levo; Io ti ho ti disfo* *slang:* I'll undo you

Senza entrare nel merito Without delving into it [the matter]
prenderemo in esame   let's take into consideration
rilevanti relevant

normotipi standard types

*fatto e io **ti disfo**; Metti a posto; Va' in camera tua; A casa ti do il resto; La prossima volta vedi; Te l'avevo detto; Sono nata prima di te; Quando non ci sarò più ve ne accorgerete; Se fai così la mamma piange; Con me non parli mai; Non mi dici mai niente; Sono sempre l'ultima a sapere le cose; Dillo alla mamma, cos'hai?; Questa casa non è un albergo; Mangia e stai zitto.*

E molte altre.

Senza entrare nel merito di una lista completa, **prenderemo in esame** alcune delle mamme principali, evidenziandone gli elementi costitutivi più **rilevanti**, in modo che ognuno possa valutare la composizione della propria mamma, confrontando le sue attitudini con le caratteristiche dei **normotipi**.

LE PRINCIPALI ARCHETIPI DI MAMME

Nome	Espressione	Amico Migliore	Figlio Ideale
Mamma Vittima o Mamma Passiva	Sa fai così la mamma piange!	il fazzoletto	il cotechino
Mamma Totale o Mamma Zarina	Ci penso io!	il cellulare	Piccolo Lord
Mamma Iperprotettiva o Lupa Mammara	Dammi la mano!	il defibrillatore	compreso l'airbag
Mammigna o Mammarmata	A casa ti do il resto!	il cric	il cucciolo di Sparring Partner

VITTIMA VICTIM
KARENINA a reference to Anna Karenina, the protagonist in the
    eponymous novel (1873–77) by Leo Tolstoy

l'esteta del dolore the aesthete of pain and suffering
sequela sequence
subite endured
pretesti pretenses
torti wrongs, grievances
immancabilmente unfailingly, unmistakably
colei the one whom
icona icon, emblematic figure
piagnone whiner, complainer
ingiusto unfair, unjust
insuccessi failures
commiserazione commiseration, sympathy

la mente inerta her dulled mind
Rai Uno the most conservative of the three government-run TV
    channels
Mammalinga a play on *casalinga* = "housewife"
votata al mantenimento della casa pledged to running the
    household
Salerno-Reggio Calabria a short stretch of highway in Italy's
    south that has been under construction for decades
scopa, grembiule o piumino broom, apron or feather duster
un gran da fare lots to do

agisce acts

LA MAMMA VITTIMA DETTA MAMMA PASSIVA O MAMMA KARENINA

La Mamma Vittima è **l'esteta del dolore.**

La sua vita è una lunga **sequela** di eventi da trasformare in sofferenza, di occasioni **subite**, di **pretesti** per inventare **torti**.

Che sono **immancabilmente** tuoi.

Questa è la mamma più diffusa, **colei** che ha originato l'**icona** dell'italiano **piagnone** che si lamenta del destino **ingiusto** e del governo ladro, accusando gli altri dei propri **insuccessi** e cercando **commiserazione** dove capita, preferibilmente da lei.

La Mamma Vittima attraversa le classificazioni socioculturali ma prevale nell'area mediterranea, specie in cucina, con **la mente inerte** su **Rai Uno**. È la mamma nazionalpopolare.

Nella maggior parte dei casi è di genere *Mammalinga:* devota alla famiglia, **votata al mantenimento della casa,** ministro della minestra. Con lei i lavori domestici sono sempre in corso – come sulla **Salerno–Reggio Calabria** – ed è raro vederla senza **scopa, grembiule o piumino.**

Nonostante abbia sempre **un gran da fare**, questa mamma è una maestra della resistenza passiva, fondamentale per il mantenimento dello statu quo: la Mamma Passiva **agisce** per impedire agli altri di agire.

il sospiro the sigh

puntaspilli pincushion
pretende requires, expects

espirazione exhalation
scarica unloads
patire endure
emanando emanating
diffonde she diffuses
Siete nati per soffrirmi You were born to put up with me, a play
    on *Siete nati per soffrire* = "You were born to suffer"
Guai a sincerarsi Trouble awaits you if you should so inquire
semmai or even
amaro embittered
intona intones
Ifigenia in Tauride *Iphigenia in Tauris*, a famous Greek tragedy in
    which Iphigenia is sacrificed to the goddess Artemis
a lanciarsi dalla rupe to throw herself off the cliff
espira exhales
espiano expiate, do penance

mezzo di relazione abituale usual means of relating [to others]
the lamento the moan/lament
dolosamente malcelato deceitfully ill-concealed
lagnoso, agonizzante whining, moribund

si annuvola gets gloomy, grows dark
cavia di laboratorio laboratory guinea pig
guaisce she whines
rivendica stakes his claim
non lo riconosce doesn't recognize it
contesa verbale verbal dispute
tace falls silent
lapide tombstone
con la propria foto with her picture [on it]. It is customary in
    Italy to place a photograph of the deceased on his or her
    tombstone.
epigrafe inscription, epitaph

La sua funzione neurovegetativa primaria è **il sospiro**: nella Mamma Karenina tutto sospira, il cuore, gli occhi, i capelli, il cuscino, le pentole, il **puntaspilli**. Non è un sospiro leggero, da innamorata, ma un sospiro grave che **pretende** attenzione.

Durante l'**espirazione**, la Mamma Vittima **scarica** la sofferenza che è costretta a **patire**, **emanando** un'aura di negatività attraverso la quale **diffonde** il senso della sua esistenza: *Siete nati per soffrirmi*.

Guai a sincerarsi del suo stato dopo un sospiro! La risposta sarà un altro sospiro – **semmai** seguito da un **amaro**, *Ah! Lo so io...* mentre alle sue spalle un coro da tragedia greca **intona** i canti funerei di *Ifigenia in Tauride* pronta **a lanciarsi dalla rupe**.

La mamma **espira,** i figli **espiano**.

La Mamma Vittima soffre, sempre, anche quando non ce n'è motivo, perché è mentalmente configurata per produrne uno inutile ogni sei ore.

Il suo **mezzo di relazione abituale** è **il lamento**, il dolore **dolosamente malcelato**: Mamma Karenina è affetta spesso da *Sindrome querulo lamentosa*, patologia che condiziona il suo modo di parlare con un tono **lagnoso, agonizzante**.

Quando il figlio vuole uscire con gli amici, la Mamma Vittima **si annuvola** e, con uno sguardo da **cavia di laboratorio, guaisce**: *No, ancora? Dove vai? Perché?*

Il figlio **rivendica** il diritto di vivere, la mamma **non lo riconosce**, segue una **contesa verbale** al termine della quale la mamma **tace**...lunga pausa alla Cechov – poi gli mostra una **lapide** in marmo bianco **con la propria foto** e un'**epigrafe**: *Fai come vuoi...*

stillicidio constant maddening repetition
sensi di colpa guilt feelings
avvelena poisons
intraprendenza initiative, enterprise

il morso the bite

Sostenendo Claiming
di peso a nessuno a burden to anyone
insopportabilmente pesante unbearably heavy
immolandosi carrying on like a sacrificial victim
Sdraiati pure sul divano Go ahead [and] lie on the sofa
sgabellino small wooden stool

rinunce deprivations, hardships
sovrappeso overweight
di nascosto in hiding, on the sly
penitenza penance, self-punishment
peccato sin
Meridione southern Italy
Mamma Cannone a very fat woman, also a reference to a human
    cannonball at the circus
indeboliti weakened
sferra più colpi di grazia wields more final blows
li accudisce she takes care of them
senza sosta tirelessly (*literally:* without a break)
seppellendo burying
molteplici strati multiple layers
Sono stufa di farvi da serva! I'm sick and tired of being your
    servant
frustrante frustrating
merenda midday snack
detentori holders [of the title]
Colpa dei Campioni Champions' Guilt, a play on *Coppa dei
    Campioni* = "Champions' Cup"

La tecnica del dolore le permette di allevare i figli con uno **stillicidio** di **sensi di colpa** che **avvelena** lo spirito d'**intraprendenza**, sempre sottomesso alla preoccupazione di non ferire la mamma pseudosofferente: *Se fai così la mamma piange!*; *Se te ne vai la mamma si ammala!*

L'effetto finale è immobilizzante, letale come **il morso** di un cobra.

In tutte le favole che racconta, la mamma della storia muore. E il figlio vero piange.

Sostenendo di non voler essere mai **di peso a nessuno**, la Mamma Vittima sa essere **insopportabilmente pesante**, **immolandosi** ad alta voce: *Sdraiati pure sul divano, io guardo la Tv su questo* **sgabellino**...; *Sono due anni che non mi compro un paio di scarpe, a te come stanno i mocassini nuovi?*; *Mangia pure la mia pasta se ti fa piacere...io non mangio... intanto non ho fame...*

Nonostante le continue **rinunce**, di solito la Mamma Vittima è in **sovrappeso**, poiché cerca consolazione del cibo **di nascosto**: **penitenza** pubblica, **peccato** privato. Nel **Meridione**, dove la versione bassa e grassa è più frequente, si trovano molti esemplari di *Mamma Cannone*.

Ai figli già **indeboliti** dal ricatto morale, la Mamma Vittima **sferra più colpi di grazia**: prima **li accudisce** amorevolmente **senza sosta** – pulisce, lava, stira, cucina – **seppellendo** i buoni proposti sotto **molteplici strati** di lasagne; poi li accusa di non fare niente – *Sono stufa di farvi da serva!* – condannandoli ad un'inattività **frustrante**. Il migliore amico del figlio della Mamma Vittima è la **merenda** della mamma.

I figli della Mamma Vittima sono i **detentori** della *Colpa dei Campioni*.

a raccogliere gathering up
punito punished
subdole vendette sneaky acts of revenge
oltranzista extremist
aria tombale tomblike atmosphere
di mummia ce n'è una sola you only have one mummy, a play
  on *Di mamma ce n'è una sola* = "You only have one mamma"
Altro connotato Another characteristic
permalosità touchiness
anticamera entranceway
fino alle lacrime to the point of tears
funge da umidificatore she doubles as a humidifier

fazzoletto handkerchief

mutande underpants

ha premura hastens
insonnia insomnia
condotta simulatrice simulated/fake behavior
colpita struck down
infermità micidiali deadly illnesses
lumino tiny night-light

estrema unzione last rites
si rianima comes back to life
resuscitare come back from the dead
ripassare la cera rewax the floors
fessure di verità glimmers of truth
scorgere l'inganno see through the deceit
il pertugio verso la salvezza an opening toward salvation

fessi foolish
bravi incapaci terrifically incapable [people]
innocui innocuous
civili invalidi invalid persons, a play on *invalidi civili* =
  "handicapped people"

Ogni entusiasmo è represso con risposte paralizzanti: *Mamma, quest'estate vorrei fare il giro dell'Olanda in bici!*

E io sto qui a raccogliere i calzini che lasci in giro!

Ogni tentativo di reazione è **punito** con **subdole vendette**, tra cui un silenzio **oltranzista** – *La strategia di Tutankhamon* — un vuoto che riempie la casa con un'**aria tombale: di mummia ce n'è una sola.**

Altro connotato esemplare di questa mamma è la **permalosità, anticamera** del vittimismo. Tutto ciò che non è in accordo con lei la offende e la fa stare male **fino alle lacrime.** La Mamma Vittima piange tanto che **funge da umidificatore.**

Il suo migliore amico è il **fazzoletto** che è sempre con lei, mano nella mano. Anche i figli ne devono avere sempre uno, indispensabile come le **mutande** e la *telefonata quando arrivi.*

La Mamma Vittima dorme poco e **ha premura** di fartelo notare perché la causa della sua **insonnia** sei tu.

Nella sua **condotta simulatrice**, la Mamma Vittima è periodicamente **colpita** da **infermità micidiali** che la costringono a letto, con la compagnia di un solo **lumino**: nessuno può o fare niente ma tutti devono essere a sua disposizione. Quando finalmente arriva il prete per l'**estrema unzione**, la mamma **si rianima** e gli intima di togliersi le scarpe, altrimenti dovrà **resuscitare** per **ripassare la cera.** Ed è proprio attraverso queste **fessure di verità** che i figli possono **scorgere l'inganno** e trovare **il pertugio verso la salvezza.**

I figli della Mamma Vittima sono tanti, una moltitudine assortita: grassi, **fessi**, depressi.

La mamma li educa in modo da farli diventare dei **bravi incapaci**, adulti impediti ma **innocui** che nella società si qualificano come *civili invalidi.*

cotechino large pork sausage usually eaten with lentils
paffuto e pacioso plump and placid
lenticchie lentils
incontinenza emotiva emotional incontinence
si piange addosso weeps self-indulgent tears
Morricone Ennio Morricone (b. 1928), Italian composer of very
    atmospheric film music

antepongono la mamma put their mamma before
complesso edipico Oedipal complex

ricorre al tritolo resorts to TNT
olimpionici Olympic champions
scopano they screw/get laid

Il figlio ideale è il **cotechino, paffuto e pacioso,** che se ne sta buono buono a giocare nella pentola con le **lenticchie.**

A questo tipo di mammone è individuabile per la sua **incontinenza emotiva**, alla minima contrarietà **si piange addosso**. A volte sono sufficienti poche note di un disco di **Morricone**.

I figli della Mamma vittima le telefonano tutte le sere.

I maschi **antepongono la mamma** a qualsiasi figura femminile, il loro **complesso edipico** è talmente difficile da rimuovere che la psicoanalisi **ricorre al tritolo**.

Molti diventano **olimpionici** del sesso, nel senso che **scopano** una volta ogni quattro anni.

debordante overflowing
la spinge drives her
non si accontenta mai is never satisfied with
strafare, disfare, rifare, sopraffare, trionfare   to overdo, to
    undo, to redo, to overpower, to triumph
iper hyper
eccedono exceed
imperare e imperversare   to reign and to rage

tradisce il timore della perdita   betrays [her] fear of loss
la perseguita e la stravolge   torments her and warps her
frastornante grueling
frenesia frenzy
rincorsa agli impegni running from one errand to another
abbondanti ritardi huge delays
caos chaos
strombazzante blaring

incontenibile uncontainable, overwhelming

LA MAMMA TOTALE O MAMMA IMPERATRICE

La Mamma Totale è la *Materpillar*.

La sua **debordante** personalità **la spinge** a invadere tutto ciò che confina con lei, soprattutto la vita dei figli.

Questa mamma **non si accontenta mai** di fare, ma vuole **strafare**, **disfare**, **rifare**, **sopraffare**, **trionfare**; il comune denominatore delle sue attività è il prefisso *iper* e tutte le sue manifestazioni **eccedono** il limite. La Mamma Totale vuole **imperare e imperversare** ovunque, per questo è nominata Mamma Imperatrice.

La tensione al comando della *Mamma Zarina* è massima perché comando significa controllo, l'unica condizione in cui trova pace. Questo atteggiamento bulimico **tradisce il timore della perdita,** l'ossessione che **la perseguita e la stravolge.**

Le immagini che introducono al meglio la **frastornante** Mamma Totale sono la **frenesia** del centro città, la **rincorsa agli impegni** che fuggono a bordo di **abbondanti ritardi**, il **caos** trafficato e **strombazzante**, il caos mentale, il caos. Ogni mattina la Mamma Totale si catapulta fuori dal letto e si prepara un bel caffè con l'idrogeno liquido, per poi dare inizio allo spasmo quotidiano. Grazie alla sua **incontenibile** vivacità, organizza la vita dei figli senza soluzione di continuità; la scuola, il doposcuola, lo sport, il pianoforte, le feste, le visite

mostre art exhibitions

zie aunts

zie mostre monstrous aunts

la riga the part [of the hair]

tattica tactic

pressing a tutto campo *soccer term:* exerting constant pressure on the opponent across the entire field; *cf.* full-court press

sommerge swamps, inundates (*literally:* submerges)

minzione urination, peeing

dirompente disruptive

stabilisce she establishes/decides on

ispeziona she inspects

lessare le orecchie to chew her ears off (*literally:* boil)

compiti homework

vigila keeps watch, supervises

si fa sotto pulls out all the stops

per concordare in order to arrange/agree on

consiglio d'istituto parent-teacher association

occupa l'edificio takes over the building (as students did during the 1968 student riots)

golpe coup

caccia il preside sacks/gets rid of the principal

come la grandine sta al vigneto as hail is to a vineyard

sfoggiare showing off

ipercinesi hyperkinesia: abnormally increased, uncontrollable, and usually purposeless muscular movement

esercizio commerciale retail outlet

chiacchiera chats

alle **mostre**, le visite alle **zie**, le visite alle **zie mostre**, per concludere con la scelta delle amicizie, dell'abbigliamento e del lato della testa su cui portare **la riga**.

Adottando la **tattica** del **pressing a tutto campo,** la Mamma Totale **sommerge** lo spazio e il tempo a disposizione dei figli, impedendo loro qualsiasi iniziativa, compresa la **minzione**: la mamma diventa *magma*.

Nel campo dell'istruzione scolastica è addirittura **dirompente**, diventando *mamma³*: nel periodo materna-elementare, **stabilisce** metodo d'insegnamento e tipo di scuola; poi **ispeziona** diversi istituti interrogando diverse maestre; infine sceglie l'insegnante a cui preferisce **lessare le orecchie** chiedendo ossessivamente del suo Pierpaolino: *È stato bravo?; È stato buono?; È intelligente?; Ha studiato?; Ha mangiato?; Ha pianto?; Ha chiesto di me?; Ha fatto la cacca?; Com'era la cacca?*

Durante i **compiti**, la Mamma Totale **vigila** sui figli aiutandoli a risolvere i problemi di matematica, senza che nessuno, purtroppo, li possa aiutare a risolvere quelli della mamma.

Quando i figli avanzano nella carriera scolastica, anche la mamma **si fa sotto**: decide il tipo di scuola superiore, poi decide l'istituto, poi parla coi professori **per concordare** il programma, poi diventa rappresentante di classe, poi entra nel **consiglio d'istituto**, poi **occupa l'edificio**, organizza un **golpe** e **caccia il preside**.

La Mamma Totale sta all'insegnamento **come la grandine sta al vigneto**.

Uno dei luoghi in cui preferisce **sfoggiare** la propria **ipercinesi** è il negozio. All'interno dell'**esercizio commerciale** la *Materpillar* si suddivide contemporaneamente in più esseri: una chiede, una tocca tutto, una prova, una **chiacchiera**, una

chiede lo sconto   asks for a discount
in perenne doppia fila   perpetually double-parked

la rende   renders her
più temuta   most feared
commessi   sales clerks

la fa assurgere   raises her to the highest position

restauro   restoration

vittoria corsara   predatory victory

manifestazioni dissociative   dissociative behaviors

con se stessa   with herself
ponendosi   asking herself
non tace mai   is never silent, never shuts up
sotto minaccia armata   when under fire
cazzate che spara a tutto spiano   b.s. that she fires off as fast as she
   can
incepparsi   stumbling
elevato   loud, raised
da comizio   as at a rally
le funzioni   devotional services
s'intromette dappertutto   she interferes in everything
rimedi più efficaci   most effective remedies
chiunque   anyone and everyone

in canna   ready to fire off
Vacci a nome mio   Go and mention my name

si lamenta, una **chiede lo sconto**, una esce a fumare una sigaretta o a spostare il Suv **in perenne doppia fila**. Nel negozio, la Mamma Totale riesce a lobotomizzare cinque persone con il solo uso della parola, proprietà che **la rende** la cliente **più temuta**: i **commessi** dei negozi di calzature fuggono appena la vedono.

Il suo esasperato egocentrismo **la fa assurgere** a centro gravitazionale del mondo e a considerare ogni evento in modo autoreferenziale:

- l'estinzione dell'emù: *Io una volta ho accarezzato otto emù!*;
- il **restauro** della *Tempesta* del Giorgione: *Io una volta avevo un Giorgione*;
- la **vittoria corsara** del Catanzaro sul difficile terreno di Bergamo: *Io una volta giocavo nel Catanzaro*.

Tale atteggiamento è causa di **manifestazioni dissociative**: durante le conversazioni, la Mamma Totale tende a ignorare l'interlocutore e a conversare **con se stessa**, **ponendosi** le domande e dandosi le risposte. La Mamma Totale **non tace mai**, neanche **sotto minaccia armata**, anzi, è lei a essere armata delle **cazzate che spara a tutto spiano**. La sua loquacità è da Guinness: riesce a pronunciare oltre cinquecento parole al minuto senza **incepparsi**.

Il tono di voce è sempre **elevato, da comizio**: in particolare al cinema, in chiesa durante **le funzioni** e ai funerali.

Lei sa tutto, commenta tutto, **s'intromette dappertutto**: conosce i medici più bravi, i posti migliori, i **rimedi più efficaci**. Frequenta personalmente **chiunque** e ha il consiglio giusto sempre **in canna**: *Il tuo pediatra non capisce niente, sai da chi devi andare?* ***Vacci a nome mio***.

si crogiola rejoices in, relishes
vanno fatte they should be done
scorrettamente incorrectly, badly

l'ansia del tempo che incalza the pressure of time marching on
gesti gestures, movements

cammina affrettatamente walks hurriedly along
arrancano trudge [behind]

vicini neighbors

fanno casino kick up a racket, make a mess
tranne il festeggiato except the person being fêted
subiscono have to endure
a sfinirsi to wear out
ad assumere un abito astenico to take on a disposition lacking
   in vitality, to wear a cloak of despair
cadenti slumped over
frangia dei capelli piangente bangs of stringy hair
abulici reluctant, downtrodden
in panne broken down
primeggiare be the best, be outstanding
soffici barboncini da concorso fluffy prize-winning poodles
campioncini da esibire specimens to show off

I discorsi si chiudono sempre con frasi definitive: *Ci penso io; Ci parlo io; Zitto, lascia fare a me,* oppure danno precise istruzioni: *Ora tu fai così, poi vai là e gli dici che...*

Il miglior amico della Mamma Totale è il cellulare.

La Mamma Totale **si crogiola** nei comportamenti spettacolari: fa le cose non perché **vanno fatte** ma per far vedere che le sa fare, per questo impara a parlare **scorrettamente** almeno quattro lingue.

I suoi abiti preferiti sono le alte uniformi militari reinterpretate da Chanel.

Dietro l'iperattività della Mamma Imperatrice non c'è solo la volontà di precludere ai figli ogni possibilità di fuga, ma anche **l'ansia del tempo che incalza.** I suoi **gesti** sono rapidi, nervosi e hanno sempre il fine di anticiparlo. La Mamma Totale si riconosce per strada perché è quella che **cammina affrettatamente** davanti ai bambini che **arrancano.**

La Mamma Totale preferisce che siano i figli a ospitare gli amici ed è un'autorità nell'organizzazione di feste per bambini, l'evento in cui diventa pirotecnica. Alle sue feste ci sono tutti: bambini, parenti, amici, **vicini.** Tutti urlano, tutti mangiano, tutti **fanno casino** e devastano la casa in allegria. Tutti si divertono **tranne il festeggiato**, perché la vera festeggiata è lei.

I figli che **subiscono** questo tipo di mamma hanno la propensione **a sfinirsi** rapidamente e **ad assumere un abito astenico**, con posture **cadenti** e **frangia dei capelli piangente**: sono passeggeri **abulici** di giornate **in panne.**

Il loro ruolo è sempre quello di attori *mai* protagonisti.

Da bimbi devono **primeggiare** per far fare bella figura alla mamma, come dei **soffici barboncini da concorso**, dei **campioncini da esibire.**

allevano they raise/produce
cretino prodigio idiot prodigy

si segnalano per are distinguished by
sfortunati unfortunate
acrobazie semantiche semantic acrobatics/somersaults

Da grandi As adults
apatici e antipatici apathetic and disagreeable

sostanze stupefacenti sintetiche synthetic drugs

a calci by force (*literally:* with kicks)
raccomandati those with an influential person behind them
    (*literally:* highly recommended*)*
prestanome the front man (*literally:* name lender)
superlavativi assoluti absolute super good-for-nothings, a play
    on *superlativi assoluti* = "absolute superlatives"

Il figlio ideale della Mamma Totale è il Piccolo Lordo o Shirley Temple, ma il più delle volte **allevano** un *cretino prodigio*.

I piccoli **si segnalano per** i nomi composti con prefissi come Pier, Gian, Carl, Anton o suffissi come Maria. Ai più **sfortunati** toccano **acrobazie semantiche** come Piergiancarlomaria, o il semplice e delizioso Mariomaria.

Da grandi diventano **apatici e antipatici**, la custodia vuota della loro stessa vita, naturalmente inclini all'uso di **sostanze stupefacenti sintetiche**.

I più sono introdotti nel mondo del lavoro **a calci**, come **raccomandati** o **prestanome**, contribuendo ad alzare la percentuale di *superlavativi assoluti*.

disgrazia misfortune
peggio the worst-case scenario

elevata all'ennesima *impotenza* raised to the nth impotence, a
  play on *elevata all'ennesima potenza* = "raised to the nth power"
***L'urlo* di Munch** *The Scream,* a famous painting by Norwegian
  painter Edvard Munch (1863–1944)

tremendo dreadful, terrible
sirene dell'allarme alarm bells
agire act
nulle null
carenze deficiencies

angosciante distressing, stressful
gita scolastica school field trip
rincaro dei cetrioli increase in the price of cucumbers

Atterrita Terrified
che ce l'hanno that have it in for

LA MAMMA IPERPROTETTIVA O LUPA MAMMARA

La Mamma Iperprotettiva è una fanatica della **disgrazia**, un'estremista del **peggio**: *Oddio!; Dov' è?; Cosa è successo?; Ti sei fatto male?*

Il volto di questa mamma è l'immagine della preoccupazione **elevata all'ennesima** *impotenza*. Prendete *L'urlo* di **Munch**, mettetegli i guanti per lavare i piatti, ed ecco la mamma Iperprotettiva.

La sua visione del mondo non si differenzia dalla visione di un thriller, sembra sempre che stia per succedere qualcosa di **tremendo**.

L'eterna paura della mamma Iperprotettiva fa suonare in continuazione le **sirene dell'allarme**, mentre le sue capacità di ordinare le idee e di **agire** con buon senso sono **nulle, carenze** che fanno di lei un aiuto inutile e la persona peggiore da avere accanto nei momenti di difficoltà.

Ogni novità ha un effetto **angosciante**: la **gita scolastica**, le previsioni del tempo, il **rincaro dei cetrioli**.

La Mamma Iperattiva cerca di proteggere i propri piccoli da tutto, soprattutto dalla crescita.

Atterrita dai virus **che ce l'hanno** in particolar modo con i suoi figli, la Mamma Iperprotettiva diventa maniaca della sterilizzazione: quando sono piccoli sterilizza tutto ciò che

calpestando l'ombra trampling the shadow
possiede she possesses
adesivo sticker

tazza della water toilet bowl
braccioli water wings
salvagente life preserver
raccomandazione command
assilla she torments
senza tregua ceaselessly, nonstop
monito admonition
amputarsele amputate them
legittima legitimizes, justifies
ammonimenti admonitions
disubbidito disobeyed
ha fatto un capitombolo fell head over heels

tutta d'un fiato all in one go

I divieti imposti The things forbidden
sudorazione sweating

nemica della corsa totally against running (*literally*: enemy of
    races)
ciò che è corrente any kind of current
fonte di sciagura [it is a] source of calamity
scosse shocks
affogamenti drownings

teorica person behind a theory

allertare alert, notify
forze dell'ordine police force

entra in contatto con loro, poi sterilizza anche loro.

Questa mamma cammina sempre **calpestando l'ombra** dei bambini e spesso anche i bambini. Su tutto ciò che **possiede** viene attaccato l'**adesivo** *Bebè a bordo*, compresi i cappotti.

Per lei le precauzioni non sono mai abbastanza: ai bambini è vietato sedersi sulla **tazza della water** in sua assenza, a meno che non abbiano i **braccioli** o il **salvagente**.

Dammi la mano è la **raccomandazione** con cui **assilla** i figli **senza tregua**, il **monito** che li marchia per sempre: Il mammone iperprotetto è quello che in pubblico, non avendo la mamma vicina, non sa mai dove mettere le mani. Alcuni vorrebbero **amputarsele** e lasciarle definitivamente alla mamma.

La Lupa Mammara **legittima** la propria ansia con continui **ammonimenti:** *Hai visto quel bambino che ha **disubbidito** alla mamma è poi **ha fatto un capitombolo** e gli è uscito il sangue dappertutto e gli devono tagliare le gambe?; Hai visto quel bambino che si è voluto togliere il cappellino e ha preso freddo e lo hanno portato all'ospedale? Vuoi andare all'ospedale?; Hai visto quel bambino che ha bevuto l'acqua fredda gelata **tutta d'un fiato** ed è morto?*

I divieti imposti sono innumerevoli, compreso quello permanente di **sudorazione**.

Non correre!! La Mamma Iperprotettiva è **nemica della corsa**, di ciò che corre e di **ciò che è corrente** perché **fonte di sciagura** certa: corrente d'aria per le malattie, corrente elettrica per le **scosse**, corrente marina per gli **affogamenti**, correnti di pensiero per le cattive idee.

La Mamma Iperprotettiva è la **teorica** del pensiero negativo: il ritorno da scuola con un ritardo superiore a minuti TRE è condizione sufficiente per **allertare** vicini, ospedali e **forze dell'ordine**.

lo accoglie   she greets him

lo maledice   she curses him
gocce di Tavor   tranquilizer drops
accenna   she starts alluding to
infartino   a mild heart attack

strati   layers
teca   display case, reliquary
turbe   nervous disorders
vacillante   trembling
in bilico sul cornicione della vita   precariously perched on life's
    cornice
cuccia   dog basket
indifesso   a play on *indifeso* = "defenseless"; *fesso* = "stupid"
domatici   domesticated

in molle abitudine   into a pathetic habit
tanto facile...quanto difficile   as easy...as it is difficult
intrufolarsi   to slip into

tepore   warmth
scomodo   uncomfortable
inquietante   disturbing

ansiogeno   pathologically anxious
contagio   contagion

Quando il figlio cresce ed esce di sera, lei lo aspetta sempre sveglia, nella finestra, in piedi: non dorme fino a quando non torna, e quando entra in casa **lo accoglie** con una frase di tre e poi una di cinque parole: *Dove sei stato? Tu mi vuoi vedere morta.* Poi **lo maledice** per tutte le lacrime e le **gocce di Tavor** che ha dovuto versare a causa sua. Infine **accenna** i sintomi di un **infartino**.

Il migliore amico della Mamma Iperprotettiva è il defibrillatore.

Per impedire che il mondo metta in pericolo il suo bambino, evita che ne faccia parte, nascondendolo in casa, sotto le coperte, **strati** multipli di vestiti o in una **teca**. Le sue **turbe** immobilizzano il *figlio coniglio* che si sente con le spalle al muro, **vacillante, in bilico sul cornicione della vita.**

I mammoni iperprotetti non sviluppano mai gli anticorpi necessari alla sopravvivenza al di fuori della **cuccia**; il loro aspetto *indifesso* li rende essenzialmente figli **domatici**, da salotto.

Da bambini, come tutti, desiderano dormire nel lettone con la mamma, ma l'invito frequente trasforma l'eccezione **in molle abitudine.** Per i figli della Mamma Iperprotettiva è **tanto facile intrufolarsi** nel lettone da piccoli **quanto difficile** uscirne da grandi: inconsciamente saranno sempre alla ricerca del **tepore** del lettone della mamma. Ogni altro letto avrà sempre qualcosa di **scomodo**, di **inquietante**.

Attento che cadi!; Attento, ti fai male!; Attento, scotta!; Attento, vai piano!; Attento alle macchine!

In otto casi su dieci, i bambini credono che il proprio nome sia *Attento!*

Il figlio ideale della Mamma Iperprotettiva ha l'airbag.

Il temperamento **ansiogeno**, che si trasmette per **contagio**

fobiche phobic

canottiera sleeveless undershirt, singlet
si incolla he stays glued
pesce pulitore small fish that keep whales' teeth clean
balena whale

per vendetta in revenge
inazione idleness
deperire precocemente prematurely waste away
li arrugginisce it makes them rusty
canizie prematurely grey hair
induce induces, drives
a fare ricorso to resort to
dopanti for doping
pompa del distributore gas pump
antigelo antifreeze
mitragliatrice machine gun

scalmanandosi working up a sweat
assistono stand on the sidelines
coetanei peers, children of the same age

inettitudine incompetence
rivelandosi proving themselves (*literally:* revealing)
alcunché a single thing
poiché since
posto fisso secure job (like that of a civil servant)
manichini mannequins
spugnette per francobolli sponges for wetting stamps
ipersudorazione copious sweating
zelo zeal
appendiabiti coatracks

diretto, provoca nel bambino sindromi **fobiche**: dorme sempre con la luce accesa per paura del buio, anche di giorno; fa il bagno e la doccia con la **canottiera**; fuori casa **si incolla** alla mamma ovunque vada, spontaneamente, come un **pesce pulitore** segue la **balena**.

Anche l'ipocondria è tipica dei figli iperprotetti nei quali si manifestano diverse patologie in forma isterica, forse **per vendetta**. L'inazione li fa **deperire precocemente, li arrugginisce** invecchiandoli prima del tempo. Spesso presentano alopecia o **canizie** e una fragilità organica leopardiana che **induce** la Mamma Iperprotettiva **a fare ricorso** all'abuso di farmaci, presenti in casa in quantità **dopanti**: Ogni due giorni fa ai bambini il pieno di sciroppo con la **pompa del distributore** – con **antigelo** – mentre le robuste somministrazioni di pillole avvengono per mezzo di **mitragliatrice** M60.

Nei giorni di sole, quando tutti i bambini giocano felici nei parchi **scalmanandosi** liberamente, questi **assistono** alle attività dei **coetanei** come bandiere senza vento.

Con il passare degli anni, i mammoni iperprotetti mostrano un'**inettitudine** generale, **rivelandosi** adulti inabili nel fare **alcunché poiché** alcunché può essere pericoloso.

Nel lavoro sono orientati a scegliere la sicurezza del **posto fisso** e diventano **manichini** nei grandi magazzini, calendari da tavolo, **spugnette per francobolli** grazie alla **ipersudorazione** delle mani; alcuni per **zelo** e ubbidienza diventano **appendiabiti** da ministero, così stanno sempre coperti come vuole la mamma.

arcigna strict
aspri e ruvidi harsh and rough
Mammarmata Armed Mamma
colpo blow, shot
sberla slap

affondano are rooted
campagne più arretrate backwaters (*literally:* most backward
  rural areas)
temprato hardened

selvatico savage, wild
regredisce regresses

la strada manesca the fist-wielding route
a colpire striking

gramigna weeds, couch grass
riesce ad attecchire manages to take root/thrive

Benché Although
squalificata disqualified, excluded

LA MAMMIGNA O MAMMARMATA

La Mammigna è il braccio violento della maternità.

Il neologismo Mammigna deriva dall'unione di *mamma* e *arcigna*, dati i suoi modi **aspri e ruvidi.**

È detta anche **Mammarmata** perché è sempre pronta a far esplodere il **colpo**, nel suo Dna è presente l'enzima della **sberla.**

Le radici di questa mamma **affondano** nel passato remoto delle **campagne più arretrate**, dove l'originaria *mamma mammut* conduceva una vita primitiva. Il suo vigore fisico, **temprato** dal duro lavoro nei campi, le dava un aspetto di maschia femminilità, inclusi talvolta i baffi.

Quando la Mammigna mostra il suo lato **selvatico**, il rapporto con i figli **regredisce** a un livello bestiale e l'inattitudine al dialogo la induce a scegliere sempre **la strada manesca** e **a colpire** ciò che non risponde alle sue attese: cose, persone, animali.

Tuttavia, il passaggio dalla società rurale a quella urbana ha tolto a molte Mammigne il terreno su cui crescere, dando inizio a una specie di mutazione: resistente come la **gramigna**, questo genere di mamma **riesce ad attecchire** anche sull'asfalto delle città.

Benché nascosta dietro un'apparenza di civiltà – e **squalificata** dalla pedagogia moderna – nel contesto urbano la

prosperare prosper, flourish

indole nature, character

perso il pelo ma non il vizio equivalent of a leopard not
  changing its spots
rozza crude
quando viene meno l'autocontrollo when she loses it
strepiti roaring
manrovesci backhands
roncolate blows with a heavy instrument
si traveste disguises herself
mammina endearing term for mamma
affiora emerges
ringhio snarl
temuta feared
nevrastenica temperamental, irritable
urlatrice screaming meanie

le logora i deboli nervi damages her fragile nerves

si mimetizza camouflages herself

li rovina she levels/flattens them

tirare ceffoni throwing punches
incontenibile uncontrollable
sfogarsi give vent to/release her anger
fa un capitombolo falls head over heels
disubbidisce he disobeys
lo sistema subito straightens him out
gli dà l'anticipo she gives him a first installment

Mammarmata continua a **prosperare** con un volto segreto, rivelando residui di animalità e il lato più isterico della sua **indole**.

Nella versione cittadina, la Mammigna ha **perso il pelo ma non il vizio** di alzare le mani: è meno **rozza** ma altrettanto brutale, e **quando viene meno l'autocontrollo**, la sua anima violenta emerge in modo sensibile con **strepiti, manrovesci** con anello, tirate di capelli, **roncolate**.

A volte la Mammigna **si traveste** da **mammina**, ma dietro il suo sorriso **affiora** presto il **ringhio**, peculiarità che la rende una specie fortemente **temuta** dai cani.

La Mammigna di città è la classica mamma **nevrastenica** e **urlatrice** che perde facilmente la pazienza: quando i problemi posti dai figli oltrepassano i limiti, li prende a calci, sia i problemi che i figli. La sua stabilità psichica è messa a dura prova dallo stress che **le logora i deboli nervi** e che trasforma lo sporadico raptus in un'abitudine.

Per far avvicinare i figli, la Mammigna **si mimetizza** dietro frasi pacifiche – *Vieni qui che non ti faccio niente!* – ma non appena arrivano a portata di mano, **li rovina** con una combinazione di colpi velocissimi, gridando come Bruce Lee.

Per questa mamma **tirare ceffoni** è un bisogno **incontenibile**, ogni negligenza dei figli è un buon pretesto per **sfogarsi**: il bambino corre e **fa un capitombolo**? Oppure **disubbidisce** e si fa male? La Mammarmata **lo sistema subito** – *Bravo! A casa ti do il resto!* – e intanto **gli dà l'anticipo**.

Per molti di loro, oltretutto, il motivo della punizione resta sempre sconosciuto, al termine di una sequenza standard di azioni:

- la mamma si avvicina con passo veloce che non lascia via di fuga;

l'occhio bianco e spalancato da squalo [her] white and
  wide-open, shark-like eye

sillabando syllabifying

scandita emphasized
fendente downward blow
va a segno hits its mark
giunta arriving
furia muta silent fury

esercitato practiced

incuria neglect
pretesa assenza di fastidi pretext of not being bothered
comportarsi behave
fedeli bestiole faithful little animals
intemperanze excesses

dalla cucina con furore *from the kitchen with fury,* a play on the
  title of a Bruce Lee movie, *Dalla cina con furore (Fist of Fury)*
si esibisce performs/shows off [her]
surgelati frozen foods
lotta fight, struggle

frasario phrasebook
ricorre la minaccia the threat is oft-repeated
a picchiare come un fabbro striking like a blacksmith
a tradimento underhandedly

Da boxe Boxing gloves

lividi bruises
sparsi sul corpo all over [his] body

- **l'occhio bianco e spalancato da squalo** indica che è fuori controllo;

- la mamma comincia a rimproverare il figlio **sillabando** le parole: *Qu-ante-vol-te-ti-ho-det-to-che-non-de-vi...*;

- ogni sillaba è **scandita** da un **fendente** a mano aperta che **va a segno**;

- **giunta** al *de-vi*, la mamma smette di parlare e si abbandona a una **furia muta**, lasciando incompleta la motivazione del suo gesto.

Il possesso **esercitato** dalla Mammigna è quello tipico della *madre-padrona* e il rapporto con i figli è caratterizzato dall'**incuria** perché in fondo non c'è una volontà precisa, né un obiettivo specifico, se non una **pretesa assenza di fastidi**. I bambini della Mammarmata devono **comportarsi** come **fedeli bestiole** e diventare il terminale delle sue **intemperanze**, lasciandosi colpire con il giornale bagnato.

All'interno della casa, la pericolosità della Mammarmata cresce dove si sente sicura e dove può armarsi di strumenti da offesa: ***dalla cucina con furore.***

La cucina è il ring in cui la Mammigna **si esibisce** nel lancio di coltelli, sedie, **surgelati**. Durante la **lotta**, può inseguire i figli intorno al tavolo per giorni interi, come Tom e Jerry.

Nel suo **frasario**, **ricorre la minaccia** *Conto fino a tre, poi vedi,* e al *tre* inizia **a picchiare come un fabbro**, a volte anche al *due*, **a tradimento**.

Come tutte le mamme, anche lei lava i piatti con i guanti. **Da boxe**.

I suoi figli non hanno il sangue blu, ma la pelle blu sì, per i **lividi sparsi sul corpo**. Al fenomeno dell'*imprinting*, comune

si scolpisce is carved
l'impronta the handprint
fanciullo youngster
alterandone i connotati distorting his features
attaccamento attachment
attacco attack
cric car-jack
agreste rural
cattività play on double meaning of *cattività* = "captivity or meanness"
golosi gluttonous
caccole snot balls
Il sudiciume si stratifica The filth becomes layered
serraglio menagerie, zoo
diseducati badly brought up
li sprona a intraprendere spurs them to embark upon
fuorilegge outlaw
al grado di manovalanza at the level of an unskilled laborer
Coloro Those who
volontà distruttrice destructive will/impulse

100% di *validità incivile* 100 percent uncivil validity, a play on 100% *invalido civile* = "[recognized by the government as] 100% handicapped"
Fernet Fernet-Branca, a bitter aromatic spirit taken to settle the stomach and help digestion
collerico choleric
scarsa tenuta nervosa poor control of [his] temper
avvia leads

invasati fanatical
di tirare pugni e calci to throw punches and kicks
ossessi madmen

Il mammone è segnato The mamma's boy is a marked man (also because he has so many bruises)

alle mamme di ogni specie, la Mammigna aggiunge il fenomeno dell'*impronting*: se il volto della madre **si scolpisce** indelebilmente nella mente del neonato, **l'impronta** della mano segna irrimediabilmente il volto del **fanciullo, alterandone i connotati.** L'**attaccamento** ai figli diventa semplicemente **attacco.**

Il miglior amico della Mammigna è il **cric.** La vista del cric provoca in lei eccitazione e un aumento della salivazione, come negli esperimenti condotti sui cani da Pavlov.

Nella versione **agreste**, i piccoli crescono in **cattività** e sono tra i più **golosi** mangiatori di **caccole. Il sudiciume si stratifica** sulla pelle dando loro un inconfondibile odore di **serraglio.**

La modalità con cui sono **diseducati, li sprona a intraprendere** la carriera di **fuorilegge** ma solo **al grado di manovalanza**, dato il basso quoziente intellettivo. **Coloro** che fanno propria la **volontà distruttrice** della mamma coltivano l'hobby del vandalismo.

Con il tempo, molti raggiungono il **100% di** *validità incivile* e diventano devoti del **Fernet.**

Il figlio ideale è il cucciolo di *Sparring Partner.*

Nella versione metropolitana, i bambini mostrano un temperamento **collerico**, facile agli attacchi isterici. La **scarsa tenuta nervosa** cerca compensazione nelle discipline orientali che **avvia** molti di loro alla meditazione e alla pratica di arti marziali. I più **invasati** abbandonano presto la meditazione e diventano cintura nera 12° dan, titolo che permette loro **di tirare pugni e calci** urlando come **ossessi**, proprio come fa la mamma.

Il mammone è segnato.

Fabrizio Blini

COMPORTAMENTI TOPICI DELLA MAMMA

«Così fan quasi tutte.»
Wolfgang Amadeus Mozart, 4 anni

fazzoletto di carta tissue paper

si astrae distances itself
forma intemporale timeless form
superamento counterbalance
Fa finta She pretends
rendersi insensibile rendering her unaware
scorrere dei granelli della clessidra running of the grains of sand in the hourglass
percepisce she perceives
sentore intimation
vaga e imprecisa vague and imprecise

mi rimpiangerete *here:* when I'm gone, you'll be sorry
Il ticchettio delle frettolose lancette è un monito The ticking of the scurrying hands [of a clock] is a warning bell
smesso ceased
rumore di fondo background noise
sovrastato drowned out
tiranno tyrant
despota despot
prevalere to prevail
frangiflutti breakwater
si oppone opposes, stands up to
fluire flowing by
trascinino carries off
si ancora she anchors herself
si aggrappa she clings
diga dam

AGNOSTICISMO TEMPORALE
Per la mamma, il tempo è solo un fazzoletto di carta

Non appena diventa genitrice, la neomammma si traduce dalla condizione umana a quella semidivina: la mente **si astrae** dalla realtà e il pensiero assume una **forma intemporale** alla ricerca di un **superamento** agnostico.

Fa finta che il tempo non esista.

La mamma suggestiona il proprio sistema molto nervoso, fino a **rendersi insensibile** allo **scorrere dei granelli della clessidra**. È per questo che **percepisce** solo un **sentore** di tempo, un'idea **vaga e imprecisa** che la porta a considerarlo solo per avverbi: *Vai* subito *a letto; Torna a casa* presto*; Andiamo* è tardi; Adesso *basta!;* Fra un po' *è pronto;* Dopo *facciamo i conti;* Prima *lavati le mani;* Un giorno ***mi rimpiangerete.***

Il ticchettio delle frettolose lancette è un monito a cui la mamma ha **smesso** di pensare, un **rumore di fondo** inascoltato, **sovrastato** dalla radio e dalla Tv perennemente accese.

Se nei secoli il tempo è stato considerato un **tiranno**, questo **despota** avrà un bel da fare per **prevalere** sulla mamma.

Come un **frangiflutti**, la mamma **si oppone** stoicamente al **fluire** degli istanti e, per evitare che le rapide giornate **trascinino** via lei e i suoi bambini, **si ancora** al mondo della loro infanzia, **si aggrappa** alle foto, alle abitudini e ai ricordi, accumula vestiti e oggetti, fino a costruire la sua **diga** immaginaria.

scandisce marks time
l'attesa che intercorre tra il trillo the time between the ringing

cottura cooking
somministrazioni administering [a dose of]

onomastici In addition to their birthdays, Italians also celebrate their name days, the feast days of the saints after whom they have been named.

parrucchiere hairdresser
affronta faces, deals with
prendendosi gioco di lui by making fun of it
detronizzandolo depriving it of its power (*literally*: dethroning it)
irridendolo mocking it

Legge di Tissot
Il tempo è una variabile relativa, soggetta al fattore mamma.

I meccanismi del cronometro le restano piacevolmente sconosciuti e così i momenti che **scandisce** in frazioni numeriche: Il secondo è **l'attesa che intercorre tra il trillo** del campanello e il momento in cui aprire la porta; il minuto è l'unità di misura che definisce la **cottura** della pasta; le ore sono spazi che separano le **somministrazioni** dello sciroppo; i giorni sono promemoria per non dimenticare quando cucinare il pesce e gli gnocchi o, nel migliore dei casi, dei contenitori per **onomastici** e compleanni.

Puntualizzazione di Longines
Il tempo è una variabile soggettiva, compresa tra lo zero e il quando lo dice la mamma.

La mamma cerca di evadere dal tempo in luoghi dove non permette che questo, né altri, possano disturbarla. Nelle fortezze sotto la sua giurisdizione, come la cucina, oppure nei distretti dove non ha autorità ma ha libertà d'azione, come il supermercato o il **parrucchiere**, la mamma **affronta** il tempo **prendendosi gioco di lui**, annullandolo, **detronizzandolo**, talvolta **irridendolo**.

Legge di Würstel
In cucina nulla si crea e nulla si distrugge, ma tutto si trasforma.

prende in pugno lo scettro holds in her fist the scepter
ribaltando i ruoli stabiliti overturning the established roles

pietanze dishes
data di scadenza expiration date
commestibili edible
oasi oasis
una pausa estranea al tempo a moment out of time
coperchio lid [of a pot]

viene steso e reso omogeneo rolled out and made even [like
    dough]
dolci a nastro ribbon-shaped cookies
borbotta spensierata mutters absentmindedly
pentole in ebollizione bubbling pots

interrompere la liturgia della pignatta to interrupt the liturgy of
    the saucepan
lo sforzo the effort
sradica uproots
costringendoli forcing them
all'infuori di lei other than hers
pietanza filosofale philosopher's dish of food, a play on *pietra
    filosofale* = "philosopher's stone" and *pietanza* = "dish of food"
faccia permanere keeps [them] stuck
riporli in una bacheca avvolti in una pellicola di Domopak put
    them back into a display case wrapped up in a sheet of
    Domopak plastic wrap

destrezza da prestigiatore conjurer's dexterity
artificiere bomb disposal expert
chirurgo surgeon
disinnescare defuse
intromissione intrusion
una faccenda a matter, an undertaking

La cucina

La cucina è lo spazio in cui la mamma **prende in pugno lo scettro** del tempo, **ribaltando i ruoli stabiliti** da leggi sovraumane. Qui è lei che decide l'inizio, la fine e la velocità degli eventi: quanto dura la preparazione dei pasti, quanto devono cuocere le **pietanze**, quando è ora di mangiare, oppure se i cibi hanno superato la **data di scadenza** e non sono più **commestibili**. Nell'**oasi** della cucina, la mamma afferma se stessa in **una pausa estranea al tempo**, che viene chiuso da un **coperchio** e reso invisibile da fumi e vapori. In questa astrazione, il presente **viene steso e reso omogeneo,** confuso nell'impasto della pizza e dei **dolci a nastro**, mentre la mamma **borbotta spensierata** con le **pentole in ebollizione,** le sue amiche di sempre.

La concentrazione posta nella preparazione dei cibi, durante la quale è blasfemo **interrompere la liturgia della pignatta**, evidenzia **lo sforzo** di ristabilire un ordine personale, rispetto al disordine del mondo che **sradica** i figli dalla tavola **costringendoli** a mangiare cibi **all'infuori di lei**.

Nel caleidoscopio di aromi, odori e spezie di cui si circonda, la mamma sembra un'alchimista alla ricerca della **pietanza filosofale** che **faccia permanere** i figli nell'età dell'oro, immuni al tempo, per poi **riporli in una bacheca avvolti in una pellicola di Domopak**.

In nessun luogo come in cucina, la mamma mostra una **destrezza da prestigiatore**, un sangue freddo da **artificiere**, un'onnipotenza da **chirurgo** quando c'è un pranzo da risolvere, una peperonata da **disinnescare**, un tacchino da salvare. Qualsiasi **intromissione** di cose, persone o animali è mal tollerata: in cucina è sempre **una faccenda** tra lei e il tempo,

divampa flares up

mezzogiorno di fuoco e fornelli *Mezzogiorno di fuoco* is the
Italian title of the famous Gary Cooper western *High Noon.*
Here the author adds *fornelli* = "burners."

sopportare to put up with

scatena triggers, sets off

frangente predicament

folle completely out of her mind

addirittura moreover

smagliante dazzling

rassicurante reassuring

confezioni packaging

peccati iperglucidici hyperglycemic sinful treats

ebbrezze drinks

detersivi detergents

regolata sul grado set to the degree [of temperature]

un duello che **divampa** in un **mezzogiorno di fuoco e fornelli**. In presenza della mamma, è meglio **sopportare** sete e fame pur di evitare l'ingresso in cucina, protetta da un sistema di allarme che **scatena** sirene infernali, incorporate nella mamma stessa. In quel **frangente** non deve essere disturbata – *Sto cucinando! Uscite immediatamente da qui!* – con le mani alzate, sarà meglio per voi.

Riflessione di McDonald's
Se la mucca è pazza, la mamma è folle.

Il supermercato

Il supermercato è uno dei luoghi che meglio annulla il senso della temporalità, perché nega **addirittura** l'esistenza della fine: niente può finire, altrimenti finisce il supermercato.

Qui lo scorrere del tempo è nascosto dietro la **smagliante** dimensione della novità: tutto è nuovo e sempre uguale a se stesso, nulla invecchia, nulla muore.

Allegro come un parco giochi, **rassicurante** come un ospedale, luminoso come una giornata di sole: il supermercato è un luogo amico per la mamma. La vivacità delle **confezioni** multicolori le offre una scelta illimitata, tanti piaceri e nessun dispiacere: cibi biologici, alimenti dietetici, **peccati iperglucidici**, **ebbrezze** alcoliche, **detersivi** ecologici, cosmetici prodigiosi.

Anche la temperatura è sempre la stessa, non troppo calda e non troppo fredda, inevitabilmente ideale, stabilmente **regolata sul grado** che assicura al meglio la conservazione.

scaffale shelf
subisce un'alterazione goes bad
rimpiazzato replaced
integra intact
come se nulla fosse accaduto as if nothing had happened
disgraziate appalling
disappunto disappointment
rievocando fantasmi assopiti nel solaio della coscienza
  stirring up dozing ghosts in the attic of the conscience
diffondendo spreading
lutto grief, mourning
offusca lo scintillio obfuscates the flashing
asettici corridoi aseptic aisles

L'incedere The solemn gait
regale, è in confezione regale regal, gift wrapped

belva feroce savage beast
arrecarle il minimo danno do her the slightest harm

imballaggi sigillati, barattoli stagni, chiusure salva freschezza
  sealed packages, tightly closed jars, sealed fresh enclosures
insinuarsi sneak in

frivola frivolous
irreverenza capricciosa mischievous lack of respect
atteggiamento beffardo mocking attitude
sottile piacere subtle pleasure

si sottopone undergoes

artificio della cosmesi magic of cosmetic art
protesa com'è aspiring as she is

Non appena un prodotto, e quindi l'equilibrio dello **scaffale**, **subisce un'alterazione**, viene subito **rimpiazzato** da un'altra scatola uguale ma **integra**, **come se nulla fosse accaduto**: il futuro del supermercato sembra non avere mai termine. Nelle **disgraziate** circostanze in cui la mamma scopre che il latte è terminato, il **disappunto** della scoperta va ben oltre l'impossibilità dell'acquisto, **rievocando fantasmi assopiti nel solaio della coscienza** e **diffondendo** un senso di **lutto**, una nuvola che **offusca lo scintillio** del neon.

Tra gli **asettici corridoi** del supermercato, la mamma avanza tranquilla, protetta da una totale assenza di pericoli. **L'incedere** trionfante con cui conduce il carrello alle casse è più che **regale**, **è in confezione regale**.

Nel supermercato, la mamma ha l'impressione di poter guardare negli occhi una **belva feroce**, senza che questa possa **arrecarle il minimo danno** poiché imprigionata in una gabbia. Del resto, in mezzo a **imballaggi sigillati**, **barattoli stagni**, **chiusure salva freschezza**, dove può **insinuarsi** il tempo?

Il parrucchiere

La dimensione **frivola** del parrucchiere invita la mamma a tirare fuori un'**irriverenza capricciosa**, un **atteggiamento beffardo** con cui prova un **sottile piacere** a ignorare il tempo, che in fondo è di genere maschile, e quindi deve aspettare.

Nel salone del parrucchiere, la mamma **si sottopone** a un trattamento che ha l'effetto di una *macchina del tempo*: Grazie all'**artificio della cosmesi**, effettua un acrobatico *salto vitale* all'indietro che la fa sembrare più giovane, **protesa com'è** nel tentativo di cancellare gli anni.

carro attrezzi tow truck
divieto di sosta a no-parking zone

la messa in piega hair set
messa domenicale Sunday mass
insostituibili inevitable
riviste di pettegolezzi gossip rags
masticate devoured (*literally:* chewed up)
sue simili her own kind
rotocalchi magazines
acritico uncritical
spiccata propensione remarkable tendency
a impicciarsi dei fatti altrui of minding other people's business
seppellito buried

irrespirabile unbreathable
phonosfera play on *phon* = "hairdryer" and *atmosfera* = "atmosphere"
depauperato impoverished
irriducibile voglia irresistible desire/urge
picchi heights
agevolato made easier
finzione phony

risuonano resonate
connotati characteristics
forcina hairpin
colpo di spazzola stroke of the hairbrush
asciugacapelli blow dryers
Erinni schiamazzanti Shrieking Furies
ordigni explosives
manicure (*French*) manicurist
artigli claws
stordito dazed
cotonata back combed

Dal parrucchiere il tempo non passa, e allora non gli resta che aspettare fuori dalla porta.

La mamma lo rimuove in fretta dalla mente, mentre il **carro attrezzi** rimuove in fretta la sua auto parcheggiata in **divieto di sosta**.

La mamma si abbandona alla lentezza del rituale celebrato con devozione dal coiffeur, vivendo **la messa in piega** come la **messa domenicale**: shampoo, taglio, piega, tinta e l'**insostituibili riviste di pettegolezzi**, **masticate** a bocca aperta in compagnia delle **sue simili**. I **rotocalchi**, così come le altre mamme, facilitano l'annullamento dell'etica a favore della cosmetica, stimolando un pensiero **acritico** ma sempre stigmatizzante, che esprime al meglio quella **spiccata propensione a impicciarsi dei fatti altrui**: Ogni personaggio viene giudicato, condannato e **seppellito**, proprio come il tempo, pagina dopo pagina.

Nell'**irrespirabile** *phonosfera* delle sale del parrucchiere, dal clima secco e **depauperato** di ogni riserva di ossigeno, **l'irriducibile voglia** di nascondere la verità raggiunge **picchi** di assoluto delirio. L'impegno è **agevolato** dal contesto, poiché tutto in quel luogo è **finzione**, a cominciare dai complimenti che le mamme si fanno l'una con l'altra, per finire con il nome dei coiffeur: i vari Antoine, René, Michel, Gabriel **risuonano** come un desiderio di fuga da tristi realtà sociali, alla ricerca di **connotati** esotici alla moda.

Tra una **forcina** e un **colpo di spazzola**, il tempo non solo è sovrasto dal rumore degli **asciugacapelli** e dalle urla di **Erinni schiamazzanti**, ma è anestetizzato chimicamente con **ordigni** a base di acetone che le '*manicure*' pennellano sui loro **artigli**. Il risultato di norma è il seguente: dopo un periodo che varia dalle quattro alle sei ore, il tempo esce dal parrucchiere leggermente **stordito**, la mamma **cotonata**.

con toni più accesi at a more fevered pitch
squillante esuberanza shrill exuberance
logorroiche long-winded
esonda spews out

assume sembianze takes the shape of
suocera insopportabile unbearable mother-in-law

ubicato situated
postazione confortevole comfortable setting
luogo di rifugio place of refuge

cornetta receiver
turbamenti e angosce troubled thoughts and anxieties
timbro della voce tone of voice
strilla shrieks
appeso al filo hangs by a thread, a play on *filo* = "thread" or "cord"

secreta secreted, given off

si ammorbidisce softens
complice a cui confidare an accomplice to whom one can
  confide

non si è accorta di niente she wasn't aware of anything
a oltranza outrageously
non colpevole not guilty

dall'altro capo del filo at the other end of the line

Il telefono

La fuga dal tempo si manifesta **con toni più accesi**, e in tutta la sua più **squillante esuberanza**, nelle **logorroiche** conversazioni che la mamma **esonda** al telefono, in cui l'argomento più ricorrente è il nulla, che **assume sembianze** di marito inutile, di figli incontrollabili, di **suocera insopportabile** o di menù serale.

L'interlocutore della mamma è sempre un'altra mamma, oppure la propria mamma, o una sorella, purché mamma.

Il telefono, **ubicato** nella casa in una **postazione confortevole**, rappresenta un **luogo di rifugio** e la telefonata esprime ad alta voce il bisogno di sostegno in un momento di difficoltà. Il sostegno si concretizza sia nella **cornetta** a cui la mamma si aggrappa, sia nell'interlocutore a cui lancia i suoi appelli, confessando **turbamenti e angosce**. Il **timbro della voce** indica il suo livello di disperazione: più la mamma **strilla**, più il suo equilibrio è **appeso al filo**.

Quando la proprietà sedativa **secreta** dall'apparecchio produce i suoi effetti, il tono della comunicazione **si ammorbidisce** e il telefono si trasforma nel **complice a cui confidare** indiscrezioni e pettegolezzi, perdendo altro tempo.

Al termine della telefonata, sembra risvegliarsi da un'amnesia, durante la quale **non si è accorta di niente**, e di fronte all'accusa di occupare il telefono **a oltranza**, si dichiara **non colpevole**: *Sarò stata al telefono cinque minuti, dieci al massimo.*

Considerando la quantità di parole pronunciate, nonché il volume della voce, e immaginando che altrettanto accada **dall'altro capo del filo**, è opportuno chiedersi: tra le due mamme, chi ascolta?

Proust Marcel Proust (1871–1922), French novelist whose monumental *Search for Lost Time* deals with "involuntary memory" and explores how the past and present can have a simultaneous existence

reami kingdoms
non è previsto isn't taken into account
attirare il suo sguardo capture her gaze
bugiardo liar
gli riserva she reserves for it
pericolante unstable
sveglia alarm clock

inutilità uselessness
congegno mechanism

Semmai If need be

sparsi e diffusi scattered and widespread
refrattarietà indifference to, disregard for
è solita ripetere she usually repeats

rivanga digs up

l'ultima ruota del carro the last one to be considered (*literally*: the last wheel on the wagon)

Adagio di Proust
La mamma è sempre alla ricerca del tempo perduto.

In questi piccoli **reami**, la mamma crea una dimensione parallela in cui il tempo **non è previsto**, e nemmeno i suoi simboli. L'unico orologio che riesce ad **attirare il suo sguardo**, ma non la sua attenzione, è quello **bugiardo** della cucina, altrimenti la considerazione che **gli riserva** è nulla. Ancora più critica e **pericolante** è la posizione della **sveglia**: se con l'orologio ha un rapporto di cordiale indifferenza, per lei la sveglia è inesistente. La sua **inutilità** è data dal **congegno** biologico di cui la mamma è dotata, allarme che le fa aprire gli occhi sempre molto prima dell'ora programmata sull'apparecchio.

Semmai è la mamma che avverte la sveglia che è ora di suonare.

Ma sono anche altri, **sparsi e diffusi**, gli esempi che dimostrano la sua **refrattarietà** al tempo, come la reiterazione delle stesse frasi: quando parla **è solita ripetere** le stesse cose, tornare sugli stessi argomenti, perché l'obiettivo è *non avanzare*. La mamma **rivanga** continuamente gli stessi concetti e gli stessi ricordi per evitare che il passato sia dimenticato, motivi che restano impressi come il primo giorno di scuola: *Perché quando parlo io non mi ascolta mai nessuno; Io in questa casa sono **l'ultima ruota del carro**; Tu sei come tuo padre; Te l'avevo detto; Alza i piedi quando cammini; Mi dài un bacio?*

Queste frasi dichiarano la precisa volontà di continuare a vivere e a rivivere quel momento, perché non intende muoversi da quel punto, perché non accetta che il tempo passi.

Eppure il tempo c'è.

vatti go

non esula is not beyond the reach
condizione di atemporalità state of timelessness
vi è compreso it's made up of
sporcizia dirt, filth
instaura establishes, sets up

domicilio coatto house arrest

ospite gradito a welcome guest
chiazze stains

illude deceives, deludes
Il candore di questi propositi The candor with which she
    undertakes
l'angelo del focolare the angel of the hearth
preposto intent on
spazzolone scrubbing brush
demone demon, devil
alle sette in punto un ululato sveglia di soprassalto interi stabili
    precisely at 7 o'clock, a howling suddenly jerks entire buildings
    out of bed
elettrodomestici household appliances
si spalancano are thrown wide open
***Volo del calabrone* di Rimskij** *Flight of the Bumblebee* by Nikolai
    Rimsky-Korsakov
tapparelle rolling shutters

LO STATO DI PULIZIA

«Pulisciti i piedi prima di entrare e vatti a lavare le mani!»

Anche l'ambiente domestico **non esula** dal principio di conservazione e dal mantenimento in una **condizione di atemporalità** di tutto ciò che **vi è compreso**. Per evitare **sporcizia** e deterioramento, la mamma **instaura** una forma di governo che prevede un continuo stato di pulizia e che costringe la famiglia a vivere in un **domicilio coatto**. Niente deve lasciare il segno, nulla deve cambiare, lo scorrere del tempo non è **ospite gradito**, soprattutto quando consente che le cose divengano altre cose, per non parlare poi delle **chiazze**, della polvere e dello sporco più sporco.

L'igiene della casa è sinonimo di una purezza originaria che **illude** la mamma di poter conservare tutto in uno stato primordiale. **Il candore di questi propositi** ha portato poeti e letterati a definirla *l'angelo del focolare,* un angelo **preposto** a difendere l'ordine a colpi di **spazzolone**. Ma se la mamma è l'angelo del focolare, è anche il **demone** di chi lo abita.

Come la sirena di un campo militare, ogni giorno **alle sette in punto un ululato sveglia di soprassalto interi stabili:** sono le turbine degli **elettrodomestici** delle forze di pulizia già in azione.

Le porte delle stanze **si spalancano** e la mamma entra al ritmo del *Volo del calabrone* di Rimskij. Su le **tapparelle**, i

a righe galeotte striped like a convict's
scaraventati thrown, flung
trascinati fuori dragged out

Vernel brand of fabric softener

diffonde a secchiate disperses in bucketfuls
palesa expresses

prima o poi sooner or later
esercitino wields, exerts
aspirapolvere vacuum cleaner

innocuo granello di polvere innocuous speck of dust
pelucco tiniest hair
peripezia *here:* acrobatics
precarietà precariousness
tergimania maniacal cleaning; *tergere* = "cleanse, purify"
strofinare wipe clean
a ridursi uno straccio wearing herself ragged
riflesso abbacinante shining/dazzling reflection
baratro vertiginoso vertiginous abyss

Henkel manufacturer of household detergents
tossicità toxicity
misurino dosatore little measuring cup

famigliari in pigiama **a righe galeotte** sono **scaraventati** giù dal letto e **trascinati fuori** dalle camere.

Utopia di Vernel
Tutto deve rimanere come nuovo.

L'ansia da controllo che la mamma **diffonde a secchiate** per tutta la casa è un'ossessione che **palesa** il suo turbamento, la spasmodica pulizia di ciò che è già pulito manifesta la paura del cambiamento. Sa che il mondo, **prima o poi**, suonerà alla porta e teme che le sue tentazioni **esercitino** sui figli un'attrazione maggiore di quella del suo **aspirapolvere** dodici cilindri.

Quando l'attenzione all'**innocuo granello di polvere** si fa maniacale, quando l'inseguimento del **pelucco** diventa **peripezia**, significa che la mamma cammina sul sottile filo della **precarietà** psichica. La *tergimania* costringe la mamma **strofinare** specchi e pavimenti fino **a ridursi uno straccio**, con il rischio di scoprire, nel **riflesso abbacinante** delle superfici da lei pulite, il **baratro vertiginoso** della verità.

peripezia = acrobatica / faticare così tanto...

Formula di Henkel
La tossicità della mamma si calcola con il misurino dosatore.

Formula concentrata di Henkel
Basta un misurino di mamma per sterilizzare fino a cinque figli.

impone imposes

mestieri domestici household chores

impietoso battipanni merciless rug-beater (once used in Italy for punishing children)

scopa di saggina broom made of twigs

ampliare il raggio d'azione *here:* expand [her] military operations

congegni devices, apparatus

solventi solvents, cleaning fluids

soffice tolleranza dell'ammorbidente soft leniency of fabric softener

appretto starch

varechina e trielina household bleach and trichloro-ethylene (used for removing greasy stains from clothes)

intimamente convinta utterly/profoundly convinced

depositaria repository

rimedio efficace effective way/means

macchie stains

tessuto fabric

Sia che intervenga in prima persona, sia che deleghi i mestieri a terzi Even when personally intervening or when delegating the job to a third party

l'olandesina the little Dutch girl, heroine of TV ads for detergents

zozzona dirty slut

Dash brand of detergent

onniscienza detersiva omniscience regarding household cleaning

colf short for *collaboratrice famigliare* = "domestic helper, cleaning lady"

insana *here:* unhealthy

diffida di lei she doesn't trust her

rendendola bersaglio di interminabili lamentele e caprio espiatorio per danni e sparizioni turning her into a target of endless complaints and a scapegoat for breakages and disappearances

pretende che fully expects that

lucido, come la sua follia a play on *lucido follia* = "obvious madness, plain folly"; *lucido* = "shiny, clear"

La deformazione mentale che **impone** lo stato di pulizia ha un'origine antica. Da sempre gli strumenti preposti ai **mestieri domestici** sono anche armi di offesa, basta pensare all'**impietoso battipanni** o alla dolorosa **scopa di saggina**. Tuttavia, l'evoluzione dell'industria domestica ha permesso alla mamma di **ampliare il raggio d'azione**, mettendo a sua disposizione **congegni** sempre più sofisticati e personalizzando i **solventi** in base alle necessità: la regola varia dalla **soffice tolleranza dell'ammorbidente**, alla repressione dell'**appretto**, fino alla violenza di **varechina e trielina**.

Ogni mamma è **intimamente convinta** di conoscere i metodi migliori per mantenere la casa perfetta, così come ogni mamma è **depositaria** dell'unico **rimedio efficace** per rimuovere le **macchie** più resistenti da qualsiasi **tessuto. Sia che intervenga in prima persona, sia che deleghi i mestieri a terzi,** nessuno meglio di lei sa cosa funziona davvero.

In confronto alla mamma, **l'olandesina** è una **zozzona**.

Contraddizione di D̲a̲s̲h̲ sull'unicità del pulito
Ogni mamma lava meglio di qualsiasi altra mamma.

La presunzione dell'**onniscienza detersiva** è spesso all'origine del conflitto con una figura chiave di molte case italiane: **la colf**.

Con la collaboratrice famigliare, la mamma ha un rapporto d'**insana** competizione: **diffida di lei** e la disapprova, **rendendola bersaglio di interminabili lamentele e caprio espiatorio per danni e sparizioni**.

Quando tutto è pulito, la mamma **pretende che** sia ancora più pulito, **lucido, come la sua follia**.

Sidol product for cleaning silver

codice mai redatto unwritten code

raccomandazioni, minacce warnings, threats

Non sbriciolate! Don't leave crumbs!

svuotamento complete emptying

si ubbidisce one obeys

senza opporre resistenza without putting up resistance

pervicace stubborn

bava di lumaca snail's trail

provvedimenti precautions

pattine *here*: special cloth slippers to be worn in the house that
    automatically shine up waxed floors (*literally*: skates)

angoscianti distressing

palla al piede ball and chain

il passo the footsteps

vi dimorano who live there

misera zattera frail raft

gorgo dell'anticamera whirlpool of the entrance hall

stretto del corridoio canal of the corridor

scatena l'uragano unleashes hurricane

soglia threshold

Porta di Brandeburgo Brandenburg Gate, site of a checkpoint at
    the Berlin Wall

Stasi East German secret police

Vapofamiglia a play on *Capofamiglia* = "head of the household"
    and *Vapo* = "brand of insect repellent"

redarguita reproached, scolded

aut aut ultimatum

non ammettono appello with no room for appeal

eventuale reclusione possible confinement

alloggi quarters

case circondariali euphemism for prisons

spolverare dusting

apparecchiare, sparecchiare setting the table, clearing the table

Legge di Sidol o dell'anticolf
Non è mai abbastanza brillante.

Le misure restrittive cambiano in funzione della virulenza del suo stato, e sono elencate in un **codice mai redatto** ma noto a tutti, poiché enunciato ogni giorno attraverso **raccomandazioni**, **minacce**, ultimatum: *Toglietevi le scarpe; Non sbriciolate!; Fermi! È bagnato!*

I comandi sono ripetuti fino allo **svuotamento** del loro senso razionale, per trasformarsi in ordini ipnotici a cui **si ubbidisce** per riflesso condizionato, **senza opporre resistenza**. L'eco delle frasi diventa indelebile nella mente di tutta la famiglia, **pervicace** come una **bava di lumaca**.

Tra i vari **provvedimenti**, le **pattine** rappresentano una delle restrizioni più **angoscianti** e metaforicamente più significative: la pattina è l'odiata **palla al piede** che trasforma la casa in una prigione, costringendo **il passo** dei poveretti che **vi dimorano**; è la **misera zattera** con cui affrontare il **gorgo dell'anticamera**, l'oceano del salotto e lo **stretto del corridoio**, sperando di non cadere mai nella disattenzione che **scatena l'uragano** mamma.

Il rientro a casa dei famigliari, o l'arrivo di qualche ospite, trasforma la **soglia** di casa nella **Porta di Brandeburgo** ai tempi della **Stasi**, un checkpoint dove le persone sono perquisite dalla *Vapofamiglia*. Ogni trasgressione è **redarguita** con **aut aut** che **non ammettono appello**: svuotamento delle tasche, pulizia delle mani, cambio di abiti, **eventuale reclusione** nei rispettivi **alloggi**.

Nelle **case circondariali**, i figli sono obbligati ad aiutare la mamma e impiegati nei lavori forzati: **spolverare**, pulire, **apparecchiare**, **sparecchiare**, mettere in ordine.

Vorwerk manufacturer of household appliances
aspirate sucked up; *aspirare* = "sucking action of a vacuum cleaner"

Vim type of cleansing powder

nemico giurato sworn enemy
la briciola the crumb
inconfutabile indisputable
sgretolamento falling to pieces
a scricchiolare dispettosamente to crunch spitefully
particelle particles
pronta a sparare ready to shoot
sfoderando drawing out, unsheathing
aspirabriciole Dustbuster™, crumb vacuum
cinturone holster-belt
si relaziona allo sporco relates to dirt
demenzialità madness, senselessness
aggravando aggravating
guanti in lattice latex gloves
grembiule al posto del mantello apron in place of a cape
le sembianze the persona
stermina i germi del lavello exterminates the germs in the sink
batteri bacteria
supervista super-vision
scansiona she scans
dalle piastrelle ai rubinetti from the tiles to the faucets
calcare lime deposits
smaschera she unmasks/exposes
individuando le sue tracce delittuose identifying their criminal
    tracks
maniglie handles
annichilirlo annihilate it
spruzzo chimico delle bombolette with a chemical spray from
    [her] aerosol cans
facendosi sistemare straightening itself out
bravo scolaretto well-behaved school boy

Legge di Vorwerk
Le aspirazioni dei figli sono aspirate dall'aspirazione della mamma.

Paradosso di Vim
La mamma ha sempre appena pulito.

Come Davide per Golia, il **nemico giurato** della mamma è **la briciola**, simbolo **inconfutabile** dello **sgretolamento** prodotto dagli anni, insolente presenza sul pavimento pronta **a scricchiolare dispettosamente** sotto le scarpe e a moltiplicarsi in **particelle** ancora più minuscole. Come uno sceriffo con la sua Colt, la mamma è sempre **pronta a sparare, sfoderando** i suoi **aspirabriciole** dal **cinturone**, in un duello che comincia all'alba e termina al tramonto.

Sola tra le mura di casa, la mamma **si relaziona allo sporco** attraverso un rapporto di fantasia che solo la **demenzialità** delle pubblicità dei detersivi riesce a rappresentare, **aggravando** il suo stato. Con i **guanti in lattice** rosa e il **grembiule al posto del mantello**, la mamma assume **le sembianze** di una supereroina, una *Wondermam* che **stermina i germi del lavello** e i **batteri** nel bagno. Con la sua **supervista, scansiona** una per una tutte le superfici del bagno, **dalle piastrelle ai rubinetti**, perseguitando il **calcare** fino alla totale estinzione. Come un abile detective, **smaschera** lo sporco grazie all'azione infallibile della pulizia scientifica, **individuando le sue tracce delittuose** su mobili, vetri e **maniglie**, per poi **annichilirlo** con lo **spruzzo chimico delle bombolette**.

Con la scopa in mano è *Mamy Poppins*, ai comandi della quale il disordine ritorna immediatamente in ordine, **facendosi sistemare** come un **bravo scolaretto**.

Fabrizio Blini

All'apice della smania At the climax of her frenzy
cosparge quintali di cera scatters tons of wax
sapientemente stesa, amorevolmente lucidata skillfully spread
out, lovingly burnished

fanciulle youthful

All'apice della smania, la mamma **cosparge quintali di cera** per tutta la casa: **sapientemente stesa, amorevolmente lucidata**, la cera è l'espediente con il quale trasforma l'abitazione nel *Museo della Cera*, sperando di immobilizzare i figli in statue eternamente **fanciulle**.

Legge di Spic & Span
Più la mamma incera, più la mamma c'è.

Alessandro Magno Alexander the Great
eserciti armies
Arrigo Sacchi former head coach of the Italian national soccer
    team and A.C. Milan
il trio di olandesi [his] three Dutch soccer players (who helped A.C.
    Milan win a European championship)
instancabili indefatigable

ardua impresa arduous/grueling undertaking
ronzio incessante incessant buzzing
api operaie worker bees
assiduo assiduous, tireless
Ape Mamma a play on *Ape regina* = "queen bee"

lo scarta she discards it
lo fa accomodare she settles it in/makes it comfortable

LA STRATEGIA ELETTRODOMESTICA
Non c'è mamma senza spina

Cosa sarebbero diventati **Alessandro Magno**, Giulio Cesare o Napoleone senza i rispettivi **eserciti**?

Cosa sarebbe diventato **Arrigo Sacchi** senza **il trio di olandesi**?

E cosa sarebbe la mamma senza il suo esercito d'**instancabili** elettrodomestici?

I piccoli e grandi elettrodomestici rappresentano i fedeli ufficiali che la sostengono nell'**ardua impresa** di distruggere la realtà. Il **ronzio incessante** dei loro motorini elettrici li rende simili ad **api operaie**, che lavorano in modo **assiduo** e diligente agli ordini dell'*Ape Mamma*.

Quando compra un elettrodomestico, la mamma non ha bisogno di leggere il libretto delle istruzioni perché parla la sua lingua: **lo scarta**, gli dà il benvenuto nella sua nuova casa, **lo fa accomodare** e poi gli spiega esattamente in cosa consiste la sua missione.

Legge di Braun
L'unità di misura della mamma è il kilowatt.

Ciascun apparecchio ha caratteristiche così sofisticate da renderlo specializzato per un particolare tipo di operazione,

da attacco e da difesa for offense or defense

l'apparato bellico the war apparatus

sperimenta she experiments
cavia guinea pig
micidiale *Sacher Bombe* lethal Sacher Bombs, from Sacher
   Torte, a rich chocolate cake that is the specialty of the Sacher
   Hotel in Vienna
esalta exalts, pays tribute to
condottiero mercenary troop leader
annichilisce la reattività cerebrale annihilates the mental
   aptitude
soggiogare il nemico overpowering the enemy
servizievoli obliging
subdoli sneaky
circuiscono coloro entrap those who

meschinamente a portata di dito meanly within a finger's reach
basta premere un interruttore all it takes is the push of a button
valletto valet
scappare escape, run away
trappole traps
camuffate disguised

appartare segregate

mangiatoia feeding trough
a puntare il tiro taking her aim
ad abbattere taking down, demolish

ma poiché l'elenco di tutti gli elettrodomestici con relativa funzione richiederebbe troppo tempo, sarà sufficiente dire che le macchine si dividono in due tipologie: **da attacco e da difesa.**

Per elettrodomestici da attacco, s'intende tutto **l'apparato bellico** localizzato nel laboratorio cucina e composto da strumenti con cui la mamma produce armi biochimiche dalla formula segretissima, che prima **sperimenta** sulla **cavia** marito e poi somministra ai figli: dalle minestre antiuomo, fino alla **micidiale** *Sacher Bombe*.

La multifunzionalità degli apparecchi **esalta** le capacità strategiche del **condottiero** mamma, non solo attraverso un bombardamento calorico che **annichilisce la reattività cerebrale** dei figli, ma dimostrandosi straordinariamente diabolica nel **soggiogare il nemico** senza combatterlo.

La praticità dei **servizievoli** elettrodomestici li trasforma in **subdoli** strumenti di corruzione che **circuiscono coloro** che ne fanno uso: la comodità della macchina per il caffè, che fa l'espresso come quello del bar, chiude il cerchio delle esperienze possibili all'interno della casa predisposta dalla mamma. In questo luogo armato di ogni possibile tecnologia, tutto è **meschinamente a portata di dito** e **basta premere un interruttore** per avere un **valletto** in grado di faticare per noi. Perché **scappare**?

La presenza di queste **trappole**, **camuffate** da aiutanti, offre lo spunto per chiarire il significato del termine *appartamento* associato all'idea di abitazione: è infatti preciso disegno della mamma *appartare* la vita dei figli dal mondo, per rinchiuderli nella **mangiatoia**.

Ma oltre **a puntare il tiro** contro i figli, la mamma utilizza questi corpi speciali anche per provare **ad abbattere** le fortezze

assalti assaults
ipercinesi polimorfa polymorphous hyperkinesia
sminuzzare chop up
irriconoscibile unrecognizable
centrifugare whip up in a centrifuge
melmoso sludgy
affettare slice up
si frappone comes between
impastare knead
sbriciolare crumble
sgradite unpleasant
frullare **le idee sovversive** blend up subversive ideas

dissertazione dissertation
frigorifero refrigerator
dal gelo marmoreo with the coldness of marble
un'opera imponente an impressive work
dalla sacralità tombale with the sacredness of a tomb
algido cold, icy

obitorio mortuary
ripiani shelves
ordinati scomparti orderly compartments

anestetizzando le ferite subite anesthetizing the wounds she has
suffered
maniere forti heavy-handed tactics

lo spirito più ardente the most passionate, fearless soul
brivido shudder

dei suoi nemici storici. Gli **assalti** delle truppe elettrodomestiche eseguono i comandi con armoniosa sinergia in un'**ipercinesi polimorfa**: *sminuzzare* la realtà così da renderla **irriconoscibile**; *centrifugare* il tempo al fine di ottenere un presente uniforme e **melmoso**; *affettare* tutto ciò che **si frappone** tra lei e i bambini; *impastare* la materia grigia dei figli con ingredienti accuratamente selezionati; *sbriciolare* le verità **sgradite**; *frullare* **le idee sovversive** fino a renderle incomprensibili.

Legge di Whirlpool
La mamma è apparecchio devastante.

Come accade in ogni casa che si rispetti, anche in questa **dissertazione** è dedicata una posizione privilegiata al **frigorifero**, uno dei migliori alleati della mamma.

Il frigorifero **dal gelo marmoreo** è il monumento domestico alla conservazione, **un'opera imponente dalla sacralità tombale**: bianco, **algido**, imperiale nelle sue forme squadrate.

Questo elettrodomestico è l'**obitorio** del tempo: sui **ripiani** e all'interno degli **ordinati scomparti** tutto si mantiene esattamente come desidera la mamma.

Il frigo le dà la possibilità di recuperare forze e sangue freddo, **anestetizzando le ferite subite** con la crioterapia, e quando stabilisce che è il momento di passare alle **maniere forti**, immobilizza nel freezer lo scorrere della vita a temperature polari, congelando ogni possibilità di reazione.

Davanti alla sua maestosità, qualsiasi nemico, anche **lo spirito più ardente**, non può evitare di provare un **brivido** di

incuta commands
timore fear
raccogliersi in preghiera one gathers together in prayer
profanazione desecration, profaning
dolore e sdegno sorrow and indignation
colpevole guilty party
scatena una rappresaglia impietosa triggers an unmerciful
   reprisal
lo sportello the door of the fridge
guastatori combat engineers
bollenti tentazioni fiery temptations

Kelvinator manufacturer of household appliances
pericolosità menace

Indesit manufacturer of household appliances

essere in grado di agire be able to act
ubicazione fissa fixed position
Ciò che accomuna That which they have in common
preposti in charge of
vale a dire in other words

ricognizioni quotidiane daily reconnaissance
agili agile
l'aspiraacari appliance for sucking up mites
l'aspirapiedidichiguardalativù appliance [concept] for cleaning
   the feet of people watching TV
pattugliano patrol
imprigionano imprison

terrore. Per questo la mamma ne vuole uno alto, grande, che **incuta** rispetto e **timore** come un totem, davanti al quale **raccogliersi in preghiera**.

La **profanazione** del frigorifero è vissuta con **dolore e sdegno**, e la scoperta del **colpevole scatena una rappresaglia impietosa**, soprattutto per chi si dimentica di chiudere **lo sportello**, lasciando libero accesso ai **guastatori**.

Chiudete subito il frigo!: l'igloo dove vivere felici, lontani dal mondo e dalle sue **bollenti tentazioni**.

Legge di Kelvinator
Il coefficiente di pericolosità della mamma è uguale al rapporto tra la grandezza della cucina e il volume del frigorifero.

Legge di Indesit
La capacità del freezer eleva il coefficiente di pericolosità della mamma al cubetto.

A differenza degli elettrodomestici d'attacco, gli elettrodomestici da difesa non hanno una posizione definita: alcuni di essi devono **essere in grado di agire** in tutta l'abitazione, mentre altri trovano un'**ubicazione fissa** in luoghi che variano da casa a casa, a seconda delle strategie. **Ciò che accomuna** questi elettrodomestici è la funzione cui sono **preposti**, **vale a dire** neutralizzare gli attacchi nemici.

Per difendere il proprio regno, la mamma effettua **ricognizioni quotidiane** con apparecchi **agili** che hanno l'obiettivo di catturare le impurità: l'aspirapolvere, l'aspirabriciole, **l'aspiraacari**, **l'aspirapiedidichiguardalativù pattugliano** la casa centimetro per centimetro e **imprigionano**

Folletto brand of vacuum cleaner (*literally:* Elf)
si fa molesta turns nasty
scherzi e burle tricks and teasing
manomettendo l'umore dei famigliari manhandling the mood of
   the family members

fatate under a spell

ricorrendo resorting to, falling back on
efferate cruel, sadistic
l'annientamento degli avversari the annihilation of adversaries
da lavaggio used for washing
la lavastoviglie, il vaporizzatore, lo sterilizzatore the
   dishwasher, the atomizer, the sterilizer
Kirby very expensive brand of vacuum cleaner, only sold door-to-
   door

attentatori che insidiano i suoi possedimenti terrorists who
   undermine her territory
corazzate battleships
stanziali solid, immovable
confacente appropriate
ripostiglio storeroom
fungere da vedetta act as a sentinel

svolgono compiti diversi carry out different tasks
lucidatrice floor-polisher
ferro da stiro iron
tozza squat, chunky
rozzamente medievale crudely medieval
schiacciante crushing, devastating
una piega play on *piega* = "crease" and "twist"
volto più spietato her most ruthless side (*literally:* face)
indumenti garments

il nemico, deportandolo fuori dai confini domestici, vivo o morto.

Se l'aspirapolvere è un *Folletto* – amico di generazioni di mamme – la pulizia **si fa molesta**. Qualsiasi momento è buono per fare **scherzi e burle**: il Folletto si accende quando si riposa, si ascolta la musica o si parla al telefono, **manomettendo l'umore dei famigliari**.

In compagnia dei Folletti le mamme non sono **fatate**, sono fatali.

Per la difesa del territorio, la mamma combatte **ricorrendo** alle armi di distruzione più **efferate** e **l'annientamento degli avversari** avviene per mezzo delle macchine **da lavaggio**: la lavatrice, **la lavastoviglie**, **il vaporizzatore**, **lo sterilizzatore**, il terribile *Kirby*.

L'ordine è: *non fare prigionieri*.

Lavatrice e lavastoviglie, caricate con detersivi chimici, soda o napalm, distruggono miliardi di virus, batteri e altri **attentatori che insidiano i suoi possedimenti**. Le dimensioni di queste **corazzate** le rendono **stanziali** e poiché la strategia di guerra varia da mamma a mamma, ciascuna trova la disposizione più **confacente** al piano di battaglia: la lavatrice può essere in cucina, in bagno, nel **ripostiglio** o sul terrazzo, dove può anche **fungere da vedetta**.

Alla guerra intrapresa dalla mamma, partecipano altri validi aiutanti che **svolgono compiti diversi** ma altrettanto decisivi: la **lucidatrice**, la spazzola lavavetri ma soprattutto il **ferro da stiro**. Quest'arma **tozza**, dall'aspetto **rozzamente medievale**, simboleggia al meglio il carattere repressivo della mamma e della sua forza **schiacciante**. Col ferro da stiro, la mamma dà alla lotta **una piega** irreversibile, mostrando il suo **volto più spietato**. Sotto i colpi del ferro, lenzuola, camicie, fazzoletti e **indumenti** passano dalla ribellione all'obbedienza: sedati, dominati e

privi lacking, deprived of
sgualcita crumpled

redenzione redemption
irrigiditi stiffened
abbondanti strati di appretto thick layers of starch
grucce coat hangers
l'ostentazione di una forza a show of strength
osare ribellarsi dare rebel against

consolidando firmly establishing/consolidating

si rivelano they prove to be
efficacissime extremely effective

disposti astutamente judiciously placed
rassicurante reassuring
focolare domestico hearth and home
comporta entails
vengono arginati are held in check
barricate innalzate barricades raised
Von Clausewitz Carl von Clausewitz (1780–1831), Prussian
    general and military strategist who advocated a policy of "total
    war"

infine reinseriti in una nuova vita, **privi** di quell'identità **sgualcita** che avevano assunto, sembrano arrivare direttamente dalla vetrina del negozio. Appena usciti dal trattamento di **redenzione** loro imposto, **irrigiditi** da **abbondanti strati di appretto**, gli abiti vengono immobilizzati sulle **grucce** come muti prigionieri, con **l'ostentazione di una forza** a cui nessuno deve più **osare ribellarsi**.

Legge di Mao
Pulirne uno per educarne cento.

Esiste anche un terzo tipo di apparecchi, quelli dell'ultima generazione: sono forze mercenarie, spesso di origine straniera, su cui la mamma non ha un potere diretto ma che agiscono a suo favore, **consolidando** il regime del non movimento. Le macchine in questione hanno nomi per lei impronunciabili, come Digital Video Player, decoder, HiFi, Playstation™, Gameboy™, Divx, Mp3 Player. La mamma non è in grado di metterle in funzione, né di comunicare con esse, tuttavia **si rivelano** comunque **efficacissime** per manipolare le menti dei figli, fino ad averne il controllo totale.

Ma la strategia di un vero esperto militare, quale la mamma è, non si limita al governo del suo esercito in azione, ma prevede altrettanto studio nel posizionamento e nella manutenzione delle forze a riposo. Uno dopo l'altro, **disposti astutamente** all'interno della casa, anche spenti gli elettrodomestici hanno un effetto **rassicurante** sulla mamma, proteggendo la sua idea di **focolare domestico**. I rischi e i pericoli che la vita **comporta vengono arginati** al di là delle **barricate innalzate** da Mamma **Von Clausewitz**.

spremiagrumi, minipimer, bollitori citrus fruit squeezers, handheld blenders, electric kettles

fanteria dagli inni ferrosi e assordanti infantry of metallic, deafening battle hymns
friggitrice electric fryer
sorvegliano survey
cima degli scaffali top of the shelves

tende curtains
paraventi screens
ripostigli closets
fortini inattaccabili little unassailable forts

Accatastati Lined up
erigono erect

presa di coscienza awareness
presa della corrente electric socket

Keplero Johannes Kepler (1571–1630), German astronomer who discovered three laws of planet motion

Gli elettrodomestici di pronto utilizzo, quali **spremiagrumi**, **minipimer**, **bollitori**, coltelli elettrici, aspirabriciole, stazionano sempre in prima linea, al fronte, dove è facile entrare in azione: è una **fanteria dagli inni ferrosi e assordanti**.

Le seconde linee – la **friggitrice**, la gelatiera, la yogurtiera – **sorvegliano** il campo da luoghi meno accessibili, ma dai quali si ha una visione migliore, come la **cima degli scaffali**.

Le scope elettriche e gli aspiratori attendono il momento di entrare in azione nascosti nell'ombra, dietro **tende**, **paraventi** o negli angoli bui dei **ripostigli**. Infine, le forze corazzate costituiscono dei **fortini inattaccabili**, posizionati sempre in punti strategici della casa.

Accatastati con pazienza, gli elettrodomestici **erigono** difese impenetrabili, all'interno delle quali vive un sistema di creature robot che gravita intorno al *deus ex mamma*: il principio generatore di tutte le macchine.

L'orbita di questi esseri non si allontana mai dalla mamma, la cui **presa di coscienza** della realtà non sarà mai importante quanto la **presa della corrente** elettrica.

Legge di Keplero
Il mondo gira intorno alla mamma.

CANFORA camphor
mezze stagioni intermediate seasons (spring, fall)
cambio di stagione change of season, *i.e.,* putting away winter
 clothes, taking out summer ones or vice versa

scandiscono lo scorrere dell'esistenza mark the rhythm of life's
 passing
dettandone tempi e modi dictating its cadences and customs
solstizi solstices
equinozi equinoxes
mondiali di calcio Soccer World Cup finals

riparo shelter

sconvolge upends
pregiudicando la sopravvivenza compromising the very survival

messe a soqquadro turned upside down
svaligiati burgled

paragonabili compared to

APOLOGIA DELLA CANFORA
Le mezze stagioni non ci sono più, ma il cambio di stagione è sempre lo stesso

La civiltà in cui viviamo è regolata da circostanze ed eventi che **scandiscono lo scorrere dell'esistenza, dettandone tempi e modi.** Alcuni sono di origine naturale come i **solstizi** e gli **equinozi**, altri sono di natura religiosa, come i **mondiali di calcio**.

Durante uno di questi periodi, la maggior parte degli esseri umani non mamma è obbligata ad abbandonare la propria abitazione, in cerca di un altro **riparo**: è una migrazione forzata, causata da un fenomeno definito cambio di stagione, che sui paralleli italiani si verifica due volte l'anno, all'inizio della primavera e dell'inverno.

Nel corso del cambio di stagione, la mamma **sconvolge** la vita domestica, rivoluzionando la casa e **pregiudicando la sopravvivenza** al suo interno. Tutte le stanze sono **messe a soqquadro**, sembra che gli armadi siano stati **svaligiati**, ogni diritto viene sospeso a tempo indeterminato, compreso quello di libero accesso al cassetto delle mutande.

Il cambio di stagione, che peraltro ricorda per durezza un altro periodo terribile conosciuto come *Pulizia militare di Pasqua*, autorizza la mamma all'applicazione di leggi speciali, **paragonabili** per intransigenza a quelle dei militari

cambogiani Cambodian
morbidezza delle polpette   tenderness of meatballs
durezza hardness
devastanti devastating
terremoti, maremoti earthquakes, tidal waves

uragani hurricanes
durata duration

ruspa excavator
si avvale resorts to
servitori asiatici Asian servants

Bernacca Edmondo Bernacca (1914–1993), general and
    much-beloved 1970's TV meteorologist
volge a bufera turns into a storm

sfollano are evacuated

bivaccano in rifugi di fortuna camp out in improvised shelters

subiscono le conseguenze peggiori suffer the worst effects

aleggia hovers

provvisorio disordine temporary mess

ordine perenne perpetual/everlasting order

cambogiani: con l'avvento del cambio di stagione, si passa dalla **morbidezza delle *polpette*** alla **durezza** di Pol Pot.

L'evento, che nelle forme più **devastanti** ricorda la furia di catastrofi atmosferiche come **terremoti**, **maremoti** e visita dei parenti, è conosciuto anche con il nome di *Tsumami*, ma ognuno di noi lo chiama con il nome della mamma che ne è responsabile: Caterina, Giovanna, Elsa, come per gli **uragani**.

La sua **durata** è variabile, normalmente compresa tra le 48 ore nelle forme meno violente e i 9 giorni nei casi più terrificanti. L'impatto e le modalità del cambio di stagione dipendono dal tipo di mamma: la Mammigna usa la **ruspa**, la Mamma Totale **si avvale** di **servitori asiatici** per soffocare la Rivolta dei Boxer e degli Slip, la Mamma Vittima si sacrifica facendo tutto da sé.

Legge di Bernacca
Quando inizia il cambio di stagione, la mamma volge a bufera.

Coloro che ne hanno la possibilità **sfollano** da parenti, da amici o si adattano alla formula del camping; altri, in mancanza di un posto amico, devono limitare al minimo la presenza dentro casa e **bivaccano in rifugi di fortuna**: bar, cinema, chiese, sale bingo.

Le persone che **subiscono le conseguenze peggiori** sono assistite da centri di igiene mentale.

Nella testa di ciascuno **aleggia** la stessa inquieta domanda: *perché?*

Perché il sacrificio del **provvisorio disordine** è una moneta che la mamma deve far pagare al fine di ristabilire un **ordine perenne**, il suo.

debitamente conservato duly put away
piegato, rinchiuso e benedetto folded, put away and blessed
regole liturgiche liturgical regulations
paramenti e oggetti sacri vestments and holy objects, *i.e.*
  accoutrements used in celebrating the mass
naftalina moth balls (naphthalene)
tarme moths
sconfiggono defeat

secreto secreted

li indossano wear them

qualora si ecceda nel dosaggio should one exceed the dosage

puzza stench
acre e pungente bitter and pungent

zaffate whiffs
aggrediscono attack

vale anche per also goes for

piastrine insecticide tablets
polveri powders
criminosa criminal

Eta Beta Eega Beeva (Walt Disney's highly evolved human from
  the future)

Durante il cambio di stagione, tutto cambia affinché nulla cambi: per essere **debitamente conservato**, ogni capo deve essere trattato, pulito, **piegato, rinchiuso e benedetto**.

Il cambio di stagione prevede **regole liturgiche** ben precise, con tanto di **paramenti e oggetti sacri**. Tra questi, i simboli magici per eccellenza sono la canfora e la **naftalina**, talismani che uccidono le **tarme** e **sconfiggono** il tempo, poiché contengono la forza divina che permise a Zeus di mandare in esilio Kronos sull'isola dei Beati. L'elisir di eterna giovinezza **secreto** dalla canfora mantiene gli indumenti inalterati nel tempo e, secondo la mamma, ha un potere miracoloso anche sui figli che **li indossano**. In verità, la canfora è solo una pianta con proprietà preventive che presenta anche rischi di tossicità **qualora si ecceda nel dosaggio**, fatto che si verifica puntualmente: la mamma ne mette così tanta che i vestiti stessi si rifiutano di restare chiusi negli armadi per la **puzza**.

Per la mamma, invece, l'odore **acre e pungente** emanato dai cristalli di canfora e dalle palline di naftalina equivale al profumo della vittoria, anche se le **zaffate** che **aggrediscono** chi apre gli armadi trasformano le camere da letto in camere a gas.

L'utilizzo indiscriminato di tali sostanze **vale anche per** altri prodotti: battericidi, insetticidi, fungicidi e tutte le armi chimiche diffuse in volumi industriali sul suolo domestico, sotto forma di **piastrine**, spray, **polveri** e solventi.

Quest'attività **criminosa** fa della mamma un corpo altamente tossico.

Legge di Eta Beta
L'unità di misura della tossicità della mamma è la pallina di naftalina.

pulizia neatness, arrangement
chiroteche liturgical gloves
inumati interred
officio sacro holy office

guerra santa holy war
redenzione redemption

a insaputa di tutti unbeknownst to anyone

Tarminator moth killer, a play on *tarme* = "moths" and "the Terminator"

La messa a posto è finita a play on *La messa è finita* = "The mass has ended" (pronouncement made at end of Catholic mass) and *messa a posto* = "putting things away"

Il modo in cui la mamma celebra il cambio di stagione ha tutte le caratteristiche del rito: la **pulizia** dei vestiti, l'uso delle **chiroteche**, la disposizione con cui vengono **inumati** nell'armadio. Non si tratta di un lavoro domestico ma di un **officio sacro**, durante il quale le mamme più devote si avvalgono dell'aiuto dei collaboratori più fedeli: *Pieghiamo insieme e diciamo, conservati o maglione…*

La preghiera del cambio di stagione sa elevarsi anche al senso di piccola **guerra santa**, battaglia necessaria per la **redenzione** degli abitanti della casa. La violenza silenziosa con cui la mamma si applica allo sterminio degli esseri infestanti, fa di lei un'eroina moderna, uno di quei personaggi che **a insaputa di tutti** salva il mondo da solo: *Tarminator*.

La messa a posto è finita, rientrate in casa.

SOTTOVUOTO   VACUUM PACKAGING

4 figli in padella   play on *4 Salti in Padella,* a brand name of
frozen, ready-made dishes; *salti* = "tossing rapidly over high
heat," *padella* = "frying pan"

conserve   homemade preserves

marroni   another word for *castagne* = "chestnuts," but it is also
used jokingly for "testicles"
chiunque le capiti a tiro   anyone who happens to be within range
febbrile   feverish
encomiabile   praiseworthy
sosta   rest
vasetto   jars
fico secco   dried fig
cremazione   cremation
feto   fetus
sotto spirito   preserved in liquor/spirits
dispensa   pantry
suole infiltrarsi ovunque   has the habit of creeping in everywhere
zerbino   doormat

consunzione   consumption
perseverare   persevere
custodisce   she harbors
impari   unequal, unfair
bollono pentoloni rimestati   huge, boiling pots are stirred
stipa credenze e cantine   crams kitchen cupboards and
basements
riserve alimentari   food reserves

LA SINDROME DEL SOTTOVUOTO
Sugo + Tupperware + freezer: 4 figli in padella

Uno dei sintomi dell'istinto conservatore della mamma è l'abitudine a fare marmellate e **conserve**: dall'arancia al pomodoro, dalle melanzane sott'olio alle cipolline sott'aceto, fino alla confettura di qualsiasi frutto, comprese le castagne del bosco e i **marroni** di **chiunque le capiti a tiro**.

Questa **febbrile** attività, peraltro **encomiabile** sotto l'aspetto gastronomico, non conosce **sosta** durante l'intero anno, poiché in ogni stagione la terra produce gustosi frutti da trasformare in **vasetto**.

L'imbalsamazione del **fico secco**, la **cremazione** dell'albicocca o il **feto** di mandarino **sotto spirito**, tutti riposti nelle catacombe della **dispensa**, non sono altro che atteggiamenti difensivi davanti all'aggressione del tempo che **suole infiltrarsi ovunque**, invadendo la vita della mamma. E magari senza neanche pulirsi i piedi sullo **zerbino**.

La costruzione di questi piccoli bunker di eternità, capaci di resistere alla **consunzione**, aiuta la mamma a **perseverare** nella sua opera: nella pace del sottovuoto, **custodisce** anche l'illusione della vittoria al termine di una lotta chiaramente **impari**.

In questo scenario di fuoco – su cui **bollono pentoloni rimestati** per giorni – la mamma **stipa credenze e cantine** con un esercito di **riserve alimentari**, ma l'avanzata del tempo

spietata merciless
qualche barattolo a few cans
controbattere wage a counterattack
scende in campo comes out onto the battlefield
attendenti orderlies
stagna airtight

effige icon
simbolo distintivo emblematic symbol

le gocce per il nonno grandpa's medicinal drops

tappo ermetico hermetic lid
mette in salvo rescues
imperituri everlasting, eternal
colpi delle lancette strikes of the clock's hands
faraoni pharaohs
sostentamento nei secoli centuries of sustenance
sopravvivenza survival
nell'aldilà in the hereafter

acquisisce acquires, takes on
non monetizzabile that cannot be assessed in monetary terms
Guai a perderne uno! Heaven help anyone who loses one!
amputarne [if you] amputate it
perdita irreparabile del coperchio irreparable loss of the lid
insostituibile irreplaceable

gioielli della corona crown jewels

immancabilmente si rovescia inevitably spills over

è **spietata** e non basta certo colpirlo con **qualche barattolo** per fermarlo: occorre intensificare l'azione e **controbattere** ogni giorno. Ed è proprio nella battaglia quotidiana che **scende in campo** uno dei fedelissimi **attendenti** della mamma, il *Tupperware*, l'alleato dalla sicurezza **stagna** con cui ha siglato il *Tappo d'Acciaio*.

Il Tupperware è l'**effige** gastronomica della conservazione, un **simbolo distintivo** di cui la mamma fa un uso indiscriminato, creando un pericoloso rapporto di dipendenza tra sé e l'oggetto. La funzione del contenitore sottovuoto è per lei vitale, come **le gocce per il nonno**, tanto che ha bisogno di saperlo sempre vicino a sé.

Sotto al **tappo ermetico** del Tupperware, la mamma **mette in salvo** momenti **imperituri**, destinati a resistere ai **colpi delle lancette**. Come ai **faraoni** erano offerti cibi per il **sostentamento nei secoli**, così la mamma nutre la propria idea di **sopravvivenza** con porzioni da consumare **nell'aldilà**: aldilà di qualche giorno, aldilà di un mese, aldilà del buon senso.

Il Tupperware è un semplice utensile che agli occhi della mamma **acquisisce** un valore eccezionale, **non monetizzabile** perché assolutamente necessario. **Guai a perderne uno!** Guai a trattarlo male o peggio ancora ad **amputarne** la struttura con la **perdita irreparabile del coperchio!** Ognuno di questi pezzi di plastica è unico e **insostituibile**, un gioiello di famiglia: se la Regina d'Inghilterra fosse stata Regina Mamma, probabilmente a Buckingham Palace i **gioielli della corona** sarebbero custoditi in sicurissimi Tupperware.

Il moltiplicarsi dei Tupperware nell'attività culinaria è la spia di un'ansia crescente, che **immancabilmente si rovescia** sulle fragili spalle dei figli.

riesce finalmente   at last manages
affrancandosi   freeing himself

iponutrizione   undernourishment
ritenendolo abbandonato a se stesso   certain he's not taking
   care of himself
a tutto gas   *here:* with all four burners going; *more commonly:*
   with the pedal to the metal
ripone e congela   puts [the food] in and freezes
affannosa staffetta   strenuous relay race
rimbalzare   bounding
elastico   elastic band

Trappola   Trap
spezzatino   beef stew

Ricatto   Blackmail
restituirmi   give me back

Pegno   Forfeit

Spia   Spy

Legge di Tupperware
Il grado di mamma è direttamente proporzionale al numero di Tupperware presenti nel frigorifero.

Quando un figlio **riesce finalmente** a conquistare la propria quasi indipendenza, **affrancandosi** dal suolo domestico, il Tupperware diventa per la mamma uno straordinario strumento *multitasking*. Fermamente convinta della sua **iponutrizione** e **ritenendolo abbandonato a se stesso**, la mamma cucina per lui **a tutto gas**: prepara, **ripone e congela** gli alimenti negli appositi contenitori, dando poi il via a un'**affannosa staffetta** che la vede **rimbalzare** da casa a casa come un **elastico**. In questo nuovo scenario, il Tupperware svolge diverse funzioni:

• **Trappola**: *Ti ho preparato lo **spezzatino**, il roastbeef, il tacchino in crosta e te li ho già divisi in porzioni nelle vaschette di alluminio, vieni a prenderli?*

• **Ricatto**: *Quando passi da me a **restituirmi** il Tupperware che mi serve?*

• **Pegno**: *Ti lascio il Tupperware a casa ma mi raccomando, riportamelo presto!*

• Scusa per telefonare: *Scusa, cercavo il Tupperware col tappo rosso, non è che ce l'hai tu?*

• **Spia**: *Tupperware, và a casa di mio figlio e dimmi tutto quello che fa.*

arginare restrain

azione surgelatrice freezing action

da baccalà *baccalà* = "dried cod," but the word is also used to mean "dumbo"

MAMMA MIA!

Quando la mamma arma la cucina con dozzine di Tupperware, vuole dire che è cominciata la Guerra Fredda ed è vitale per i figli riuscire ad **arginare** la sua **azione surgelatrice**, altrimenti il destino riserverà loro una vita **da baccalà**.

DIAGRAMMA DI TUPPERWARE

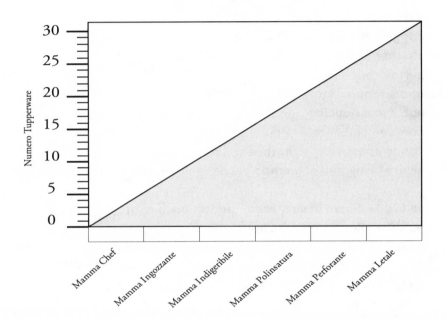

Fabrizio Blini

MINACCIA THREAT

SARTORIALE TAILORING, DRESSMAKING

sfodera i ferri unsheathes her knitting needles

dà filo da torcere she proves a hard nut to crack (*literally:* she gives you yarn to wind)

congetture assumptions

stringenti, serrate to the point, logical

parto childbirth

uno strappo a torn muscle

ago, filo e ricucirlo needle, thread and sew it up again

cordone ombelicale umbilical cord

con tempestività right then and there

sicuro ormeggio al grembo natale safe mooring to the mother's womb

vada alla deriva di se stesso finds himself adrift

posto di rilievo prominent place

dalla trama e dall'ordito of the weft and the warp

dal cucito e dal rammendo of sewing and mending

da gomitoli e rocchetti of balls of wool and spools of thread

indice sign, indication

tentativo attempt

indebitamente rovinato fittingly ruined/spoiled

sferruzzata knitted away

Krizia famous Italian fashion house

s'intersecano are interwoven

punti stitches

SIMBOLISMO E MINACCIA DELL'ATTIVITÀ SARTORIALE
Quando la mamma sfodera i ferri, dà filo da torcere

Sul piano logico, le **congetture** della mamma sono sempre **stringenti, serrate**: se il **parto** è causa di **uno strappo,** non bisogna fare altro che prendere **ago, filo e ricucirlo.**

Il taglio del **cordone ombelicale** è la genesi di un distacco da ridurre **con tempestività**, prima che il bambino, senza il **sicuro ormeggio al grembo natale, vada alla deriva di se stesso.**

A questo riguardo, merita un **posto di rilievo** il simbolismo di quel mondo contraddistinto **dalla trama e dall'ordito, dal cucito e dal rammendo, da gomitoli e rocchetti.**

L'attitudine all'arte sartoriale, che si esprime secondo diversi gradi d'intensità e di capacità, è un **indice** importante per la valutazione delle mamme. Il senso di questo lavoro domestico, altro non è che il **tentativo** di riparare ciò che madre natura ha **indebitamente rovinato**: la lunga sciarpa **sferruzzata** in silenzio non serve a proteggere dal freddo, ma assume il significato di un nuovo cordone ombelicale. Di lana.

Legge di Krizia
Dato un mammone, in esso s'intersecano continui, dolorosi e infiniti punti.

tagliata su misura made to measure

soccorso rescue, assistance

apposita sala, detta operatoria specific room, known as
operating theater
pronto intervento first aid
a seconda la gravità according to how serious it is

cuce e ricuce l'orlo della crisi di nervi *a clever play on words:*
sews and resews the hem (*orlo* also can mean "verge") of a
nervous breakdown

perizia expertise
l'apprendimento acquiring skill
tirocinio chirurgico surgical training
si esercita one practices
maneggia handles
con disinvoltura effortlessly
movenze gestures
bacchetta baton
leggiadria grace

soavità delicacy
poiché as
scaturisce springs
accorre she rushes in
imbastisce she bastes

sutura sutures

L'attività di sartoria offre una vasta gamma di applicazioni e ciascuna mamma può scegliere quella **tagliata su misura** per lei.

I lavori si dividono in due categorie principali: riparatorie e preventive.

Il **soccorso** sartoriale si prende cura di vestiti e di indumenti già esistenti ma gravemente feriti o danneggiati. Questo tipo di lavori si svolge in un'**apposita sala, detta operatoria**, e può avere i connotati del **pronto intervento**, dell'emergenza, **a seconda della gravità**.

Legge di Chanel
La mamma cuce e ricuce l'orlo della crisi di nervi.

Tra tutte le occupazioni sartoriali, il cucito è senz'altro la principale.

La **perizia** nel cucire rappresenta la condizione necessaria per **l'apprendimento** di qualsiasi altra attività tessile, un **tirocinio chirurgico** in cui **si esercita** la mano ferma e il sangue freddo. La vera mamma **maneggia** ago e filo **con disinvoltura**, con una grazia di **movenze** quasi musicale: l'ago segue evoluzioni morbide come la **bacchetta** di un direttore d'orchestra, dandole un'immagine di concertistica **leggiadria**. Ma è solo da un punto di vista estetico che la mamma riesce a dare questa sensazione di **soavità**, **poiché** il senso del cucito **scaturisce** da un'urgenza ben più tragica. La lesione del tessuto è uno strappo viscerale e per questo **accorre** con la valigetta del pronto soccorso: è sempre una lotta contro il tempo. I punti che **imbastisce** su maglie, camicie, pantaloni, o su qualsiasi altro indumento, sono disperati punti di **sutura** e la

resistenza oltranzista   radical/extreme resistance

orgogliosa   proud

usura   wear and tear

cucitura grezza   rough stitching

cocciutamente   stubbornly

esanimi   lifeless

accatasta quel che può   piles up whatever she can

breccia aperta   open breach

l'alluce trafigge come un ariete   [one's] big toe pierces like a
    battering ram

tempo incalza nel calzino   *here:* time socks the sock

toppa   patch

prostrazione   dejection

un danno   something so severely damaged

porre riparo   to put right

sconfitta lacerante   ripping (*i.e.,* agonizing) defeat

oltraggiosa   outrageous

vergognoso   shameful

lo ripudia con disprezzo   disowns him with contempt

Ostentando   Flaunting

la affronta con spavalderia   boldly confronts her

la sfida   he defies her

sistema omologante   homologizing system (that makes everyone
    the same)

radice   root

disagio   disquiet

rocchetti   spools

guardaroba   wardrobe

speranza che l'intervento riesca è sempre appesa a un filo.

Il rammendo è una forma di **resistenza oltranzista**, una protesta disperata ma **orgogliosa** contro l'**usura**. Con questa **cucitura grezza**, la mamma punta i piedi e, pur di non alzare bandiera bianca, tenta **cocciutamente** di far sopravvivere abiti ormai **esanimi**. Nel rammendo, la mamma **accatasta quel che può** davanti alla **breccia aperta** dal nemico, ma resta poco da fare quando **l'alluce trafigge come un ariete** una difesa ormai vulnerabile: il **tempo incalza nel calzino**.

Quando il rammendo non è più sufficiente, ecco l'azione disperata: la **toppa**.

La toppa è il simbolo della **prostrazione** della mamma, una medicazione insufficiente e malposta che tenta di fermare un'emorragia di verità. La toppa testimonia **un danno** a cui non è più possibile **porre riparo**, una **sconfitta lacerante**, seppure meno **oltraggiosa** di un buco evidente e **vergognoso**. Un figlio che esce di casa con i pantaloni strappati è insopportabilmente offensivo per la mamma, che **lo ripudia con disprezzo**: *Sembri il figlio di nessuno.*

Ostentando le ginocchia fuori dai jeans, questi **la affronta con spavalderia**, **la sfida**, manifestando la propria indipendenza.

I giovani dicono di combattere il **sistema omologante**, ma la **radice** del loro **disagio** ha un'origine più intima e individuale.

Legge di Lagerfeld
La pericolosità della mamma è direttamente proporzionale al numero di rocchetti di filo usati.

Se le operazioni di cucito e di rammendo sono il risultato di un'emergenza, la produzione di un nuovo **guardaroba** è il

imbastire to tack, to work out
accomodante accommodating
barlume flicker
la resa surrender
aver preso atto having taken note
ineluttabile unavoidable
affilatissime armi extremely sharp weapons
forbici, aghi, spilli, ferri scissors, needles, pins, knitting needles
ordisce e trama plots and plans
fogge styles
con rigore painstakingly
cartamodelli paper dress patterns
Burda…Rakam magazines for the home dressmaker
prende le misure *double meaning:* takes all the necessary
    precautions *or* takes the measurements
vero e proprio all out
girovita waistline
piano più articolato more complex plan
mira aims
confezionati sewn, made (for clothes)
costrittivi constricting
rinchiudere enclose
carcere prison
tutine rompers
l'abbottonatura fastening with buttons
camicie di forza straight jackets
lavoro a maglia knitting
impetuose impetuous
sfoggiano show off
destrezza dexterity, skill
moschettiere musketeer
dritto, rovescio, riso, treccia various types of stitches
punto e basta And that's that; a play on *punto* = "stitch"

acconsente he agrees
matassa skein
si ammanetta da solo handcuffs himself
s'ingarbuglia gets all tangled up

sintomo di una condizione meno instabile, in cui la mamma si sente più sicura di sé. La volontà di **imbastire** un confronto più **accomodante** con la realtà lascia intravedere un **barlume** di coscienza, ma non certo **la resa.** Dopo **aver preso atto** dell'**ineluttabile** crescita del figlio, la mamma sfodera le sue **affilatissime armi: forbici, aghi, spilli, ferri.** È grazie a questo genere di strumenti che **ordisce e trama** come un ufficiale in guerra, pianificando strategie di tutte le **fogge** e studiando **con rigore** i **cartamodelli** di **Burda** e i disegni militari di **Rakam.**

Al momento delle prove, la mamma **prende le misure** per poi realizzare l'attacco **vero e proprio.** L'immobilizzazione dei figli durante il calcolo di spalle e **girovita** – minacciati dagli spilli – è solo il preludio di un **piano più articolato** che **mira** a mettere il figlio nel sacco.

Gli abiti **confezionati** dalla mamma sono in genere piccoli e **costrittivi,** perché sono disegnati per **rinchiudere** e non per proteggere: l'obiettivo non è creare un modello perfetto, ma un piccolo **carcere** modello. Anche i pigiamini e le **tutine** dei bambini hanno l'**abbottonatura** dietro, come le **camicie di forza.**

Nel **lavoro a maglia,** le mamme più **impetuose,** come la Mamma Totale, **sfoggiano** tutta la propria abilità nel governo dei ferri, duellando con la **destrezza** di un **moschettiere** e mostrando di saper colpire con una grande varietà di punti: *dritto, rovescio, riso, treccia,* anche se il punto preferito è il *punto e basta.*

Nei casi più infelici, il mammone diventa persino complice della mamma, nonostante ne sia vittima. Quando **acconsente** a tenere la **matassa** con le braccia tese davanti a sé, immobili, il mammone **si ammanetta da solo.** E mentre la mamma conta le maglie, la vita del figlio **s'ingarbuglia.**

potenzia le forze avvalendosi dell'ausilio she builds up her
  forces through the assistance

fioca dim
torva grim

frangente instant

detenuti detainees
brivido metallico dello zip metallic chill of the zipper
furore della lotta heat of the struggle
cospirazione conspiracy
spara come un cecchino starts shooting off like a sniper
raffiche blasts, gunfire
Cavalcata delle Valchirie *Ride of the Valkyries*
gomitoli balls of wool
impigliati tangled
di che stoffa è fatta expression meaning "what she's made of"; a
  play on *stoffa* = "fabric"

Quando la mamma è stanca di combattere a mani nude, e vuole industrializzare l'attività bellica, **potenzia le forze avvalendosi dell'ausilio** della macchina da cucire.

La macchina da cucire è in grado di esplodere migliaia di colpi al minuto, esaltando il desiderio antipacifista della mamma.

Curva sul lavoro, con la sola compagnia di una luce sempre troppo **fioca**, la mamma trama con aria **torva**. L'apparente inoffensività della sua figura non deve muovere a compassione, poiché proprio in quel **frangente** sta approntando chissà quale disegno di vendetta o, nella migliore delle ipotesi, nuove uniformi per i piccoli **detenuti**, magari con il **brivido metallico dello zip**. Quando invece il **furore della lotta** non può essere contenuto nel segreto della **cospirazione**, la mamma **spara come un cecchino**, accompagnando le **raffiche** di punti con la *Cavalcata delle Valchirie*.

Fuggite, mettetevi al riparo! E soprattutto non restate lì a giocare con i **gomitoli**, potreste rimanervi **impigliati** per sempre. La mamma si mostra **di che stoffa è fatta**.

Aforisma di Singer
Madre santissima, mamma sartissima.

Fabrizio Blini

INFLUSSO DELLA MAMMA SULLA CULTURA
MODERNA

La mamma è l'oppio dei piccoli.
Karl Marx a 8 anni

favola fairytale

si consegna turns himself in
carnefice executioner
elogio dell'ergastolo ode to life imprisonment
traboccante overflowing
ha colmato la misura has gone too far
recitavano went (*literally:* recited)
proseguendo continuing on

l'ubiquità omnipresence
perniciosa deadly
accolte welcomed

forte di un'ascesa empowered by a rise
ostacoli obstacles
suggellato sealed, confirmed

L'EMBARGO CULTURALE DELLA MAMMA
«Ora la mamma ti racconta una bella favola…»

Mamma son tanto felice perché ritorno da te, la mia canzone
 ti dice che è il più bel giorno per me.
Mamma son tanto felice, viver lontano perché?
Mamma, solo per te la mia canzone vola!
Mamma, sarai con me tu non sarai più sola!
Quanto ti voglio bene, queste parole d'amore, che ti sospira il
 mio cuore, forse non s'usano più Mamma, ma la canzone
 mia più bella sei tu, sei tu la vita, e per la vita non ti lascio
 mai più…

La vittima che **si consegna** con felice incoscienza al **carnefice**! È questo il senso del testo di questa canzone, un **elogio dell'ergastolo**.

La cultura italiana, **traboccante** di lacrime versate dalle mamme per i figli e *viceversate* dai figli per le mamme, **ha colmato la misura**. A partire dai canti di guerra che **recitavano** – *Ho lasciato la mamma mia…* – **proseguendo** per il *Ciao Mama!* dei ciclisti del Giro d'Italia, **l'ubiquità** della mamma è diventata sempre più visibile e **perniciosa**: truppe di mamme hanno invaso ogni dominio culturale, **accolte** da cori festanti. In tutte le regioni, il mamma-pensiero ha assunto una forma devastante, **forte di un'ascesa** senza **ostacoli** e **suggellato**

ignari unaware

cinica e blasfema cynical and blasphemous

ingannevole misleading
accomuna associates

lasciapassare license, pass

spensierata carefree

incantato enchanted

in circolazione in circulation
sciropparsele a play on *sciroppare* = "making syrupy" and
  sciropparsi = "putting up with someone"

si sono insinuate have wormed their way
pensiero comune *here:* public mindset
il sostegno the backing

il culo a strisce a striped butt; a play on "stars and stripes"

è soggetta a is subject to

dalla gioia dei mammoni, **ignari** della propria dipendenza.

Date queste premesse, qualsiasi critica alla mamma era ed è ancora da ritenersi gratuitamente **cinica e blasfema**: l'italiano sopporta qualsiasi offesa, ma non toccategli la mamma.

L'**ingannevole** perfezione del *mamma-modello* ricorda il *Sogno americano* degli anni Cinquanta e la sua invadenza nella cultura **accomuna** la mamma alla Coca-Cola. Entrambe hanno avuto l'abilità di associare la propria immagine a una serie di valori positivi, garantendosi un **lasciapassare** universale.

La Coca-Cola porta con sé un mondo di sorrisi, di vita **spensierata**, di fresca gioventù e quando non è fisicamente presente come bevanda, è comunque presente la sua idea.

Allo stesso modo, il mondo **incantato** della mamma le assicura un favore indiscriminato, ma il suo operato e i suoi effetti non sempre sono salutari, basta vedere la quantità di mammoni **in circolazione**. Ma l'abitudine di **sciropparsele** dappertutto ha creato un'inevitabile disattenzione riguardo la loro reale sostanza.

Mamma e Coca-Cola **si sono insinuate** subliminalmente nel **pensiero comune**, conquistandolo, fino a diventare intoccabili. Ma considerando che la mamma non ha avuto **il sostegno** della multinazionale di Atlanta, come è arrivata a garantirsi il dominio culturale?

Illusione di Coke
La mamma ti fa vedere le stelle, poi ti fa il culo a strisce.

La crescita culturale **è soggetta a** due fattori principali; *sapere* ed *essere*.

Lo sviluppo del sapere The development of knowledge
nozioni ideas, notions
di fare proprio quanto appreso making what one has learned
    one's own
non si tratta solo di it's not just a question of

ostacolata obstructed
filtra filters

mistificatorie fraudulent
Ciò avviene This happens

abbia fatto tesoro sets great store by
Michel Foucault (1926–1984) French philosopher, historian, and
    public intellectual
Sorvegliare e punire *Oversee and Punish* (English title: *Discipline
    and Punish*)
prende in esame closely examines
stato di detenzione state of being detained
carceriere jailer
linea morbida softer approach
prevede calls for

mediante oculate concessioni by way of prudent concessions
autoritarie authoritarian

ambito longed-for

Lo sviluppo del sapere dipende dalla quantità di **nozioni** acquisite attraverso l'istruzione e l'esperienza; quello dell'essere dipende invece dalla capacità **di fare proprio quanto appreso**: **non si tratta solo di** capire ma anche di comprendere. La crescita, quindi, è il risultato della quantità di informazioni e della qualità con cui vengono elaborate.

Nel caso dei figli, la maturazione è **ostacolata** dal fattore mamma, che da una parte limita e **filtra** le informazioni, dall'altra condiziona le loro capacità intellettive con interpretazioni **mistificatorie**. **Ciò avviene** con qualsiasi tipo di mamma, poiché la differenza è solo formale: il fine comune è controllare lo sviluppo culturale e impedire l'autonomia dei figli.

Una parentesi.

Sotto questo aspetto, sembra quasi che la mamma **abbia fatto tesoro** dell'opera di **Michel Foucault** – *Sorvegliare e punire* – in cui il filosofo francese **prende in esame** l'istituzione della prigione. Lo **stato di detenzione**, condizione presa a modello dalla mamma, permette al **carceriere** di controllare il prigioniero, sia attraverso una **linea morbida** che si limita alla sorveglianza, sia attraverso una forma più repressiva che **prevede** la punizione. Anche in questo caso l'obiettivo condiviso è il controllo delle coscienze.

Se il permissivismo delle mamme più tolleranti è incline a *sorvegliare*, **mediante oculate concessioni**, l'intransigenza delle mamme **autoritarie** preferisce la repressione.

Questo sistema fondato sul controllo era alla base dell'opera riformatrice di Carlo Borromeo nella Chiesa cattolica del XVI secolo, che ha visto proprio in quel periodo l'introduzione della pratica della confessione, esercizio **ambito** da ogni

imposto imposed

agiscono per negazione e rifiuto operate by way of opposition
and refusal
cattiva compagnia [keeping] bad company
lettura sconveniente unseemly reading matter
atteggiamento behavior

ottenuto obtained
coercizione e la minaccia coercion and intimidation
sfinimento utter exhaustion
scomparsa dell'orco disappearance of the ogre
comparsa dell'orchite appearance of orchitis (inflammation of
the testicles)
in maiuscolo with capital letters
massimo comune denominatore greatest common denominator
divieto "not allowed" (no parking, no trespassing, etc.)

minata undermined

Ermete Hermes

è fulminante comes like a bolt of lightning

Sbrigati! *Hurry up! Get going!*
Sbrigatiste play on *brigatiste* = "members of the Red Brigades
terrorist group"

mamma ma **imposto** solo da quelle più autoritarie. Viene da domandarsi di nuovo: dato per certo che la mamma non si è ispirata a Foucault e a Borromeo, siamo certi che Foucault e Borromeo non si siano ispirati alla mamma?

Chiusa parentesi.

Le mamme più autoritarie **agiscono per negazione e rifiuto**: nessuna esperienza autonoma, nessuna **cattiva compagnia**, nessuna **lettura sconveniente**. Questo **atteggiamento** è paragonabile a sistemi dittatoriali quali il franchismo, il fascismo, lo stalinismo, il nazismo e appunto il mammismo. Quando il controllo non può essere **ottenuto** attraverso la **coercizione e la minaccia**, è raggiunto con la reiterazione e lo **sfinimento**: è il passaggio che vede la **scomparsa dell'orco** e la **comparsa dell'orchite**.

La risposta più frequente è NO, pronunciata **in maiuscolo**; la motivazione del NO è: perché NO; il **massimo comune denominatore** è il **divieto**; la tolleranza è zero. La negazione e la paura portano fisiologicamente all'immobilismo – *non uscire, non fare, non dire, non muoverti, non respirare* – e la sicurezza del figlio è **minata** affinché questo trovi serenità solo tra le sue braccia.

Legge della mamma di Ermete
Stai zitto!

La comunicazione **è fulminante**, la sintesi estrema è associata alla rapidità di formulazione. L'immediata obbedienza è una richiesta precisa e ogni ordine è completato da un terroristico *Sbrigati!*, motivo per cui queste mamme sono chiamate anche *Sbrigatiste*.

divise uniforms

dispotico despotic

si avvale di makes use of

subdoli shifty

preti donabbondiani Don Abbondio was the excessively accommodating priest in Manzoni's *The Betrothed.*

tate austroungariche Austro-Hungarian nannies

serventi a sonagli tattling servants, a play on *serpenti a sonagli* = "rattlesnakes"

fingendosi pretending to be

benestare approval

ottenere obtain

privazione accettata dal privato deprivation agreed to by the deprived

Cia CIA

ciorella *in effect:* sister in espionage; *Cia + sorella (sister)*

mira a indebolire aims to weaken

concedendo loro tutto granting them everything

pareti domestiche walls of the house

gabbia dorata gilded cage

insidie hidden dangers

lottare to struggle

ganglio vitale nerve center

voglia di scoprire curiosity

germogliare germinate

accecante blinding

scientemente ingrassata deliberately fattened up

fegato d'oca goose's liver

sazietà satiety

il senso dell'impegno sense of responsibility

castrati castrated

spogliati stripped

fatta eccezione except for

Sms "short message systems," *i.e.,* text messages

La vita dei figli delle mamme repressive è simile a quella del Gulag: la casa non prevede stanze ma celle, non libri ma manuali, non vestiti ma **divise**.

Nell'esercizio del comando **dispotico**, la mamma autoritaria **si avvale di** alcuni **subdoli** collaborazionisti: *preti donabbondiani, tate austroungariche, serventi a sonagli.*

L'azione di filtro culturale può essere esercitata anche in forme meno dolorose: **fingendosi** guida illuminata e maestra di vita, la mamma seleziona esperienze e informazioni cercando il **benestare** dei figli, così da **ottenere** una **privazione accettata dal privato**. È una vera azione di intelligence, ispirata dal modello **Cia**. E infatti la Cia è la *ciorella* della mamma.

In questi casi, l'embargo è mascherato dalla sua liberalità. La tattica usata dalla mamma permissiva **mira a indebolire** nei figli il desiderio di uscire di casa e dall'ambito materno, **concedendo loro tutto**: le **pareti domestiche** si trasformano in una **gabbia dorata**, un luogo senza difficoltà che diventa molto più attraente di un mondo pieno di **insidie**, dove è necessario **lottare**.

Il permissivismo è aconflittuale e agisce sul **ganglio vitale** della **voglia di scoprire**.

Il permissivismo non combatte le invasioni, non limita le informazioni, ma brucia il terreno su cui possono **germogliare**. La luce della libertà viene accesa in modo violento, tanto da renderla **accecante**; la vita dei figli è **scientemente ingrassata**, come un **fegato d'oca**, fino a superare il limite della **sazietà**. I giovani neuroni diventano obesi e non hanno voglia di fare mai niente, dimenticando presto **il senso dell'impegno** e della fatica. Come gatti **castrati**, i figli dell'iperconcessione stazionano intere giornate sul divano, **spogliati** di tutto, **fatta eccezione** per le puzzolenti scarpe da ginnastica, mentre i loro trigliceridi giocano alla Playstation o si inviano **Sms**.

sommerso submerged, *i.e.*, underground

l'oscura profondità its dark depths
aver partorito having given birth
non riesce a contenersi can't hold herself back
trascende transcends

esagerare, eccedere, dare i numeri, essere fuori di sé
   exaggerate, exceed, to lose it, be out of control

a trattenere to hold onto
grembo womb
inseguimento chase
iniziazione initiation
non la smette più she never stops

inculcare inculcate
fede religion
deroga exception
tifo calcistico being a soccer fan
poderoso alleato powerful ally
depauperazione impoverishment
sensibile sensitive, *i.e.,* capable of being perceived
è da ricondursi is harking back to

POTENZA RELIGIOSA DELLA MAMMA E DECADENZA DEL SENTIMENTO CATTOLICO
«In nome della Mamma, del Figlio e dello Spirito Santo...»

Il credo spirituale della mamma è *Mammology*.

Mammology è un movimento immenso e **sommerso**, un oceano di cui tutti vedono l'estesa superficie ma di cui nessuno conosce **l'oscura profondità**.

Dopo **aver partorito**, la donna che **non riesce a contenersi** nel ruolo di madre **trascende** in quello di mamma. Il senso della trascendenza della mamma non si riferisce ai significati positivamente transitivi del verbo trascendere – *superare, oltrepassare* (nel caso specifico se stessi) – ma a quelli negativamente intransitivi – *esagerare, eccedere, dare i numeri, essere fuori di sé.*

Nel momento in cui non riesce **a trattenere** il figlio nel suo **grembo**, comincia l'**inseguimento**: per la mamma il parto è una sorta di **iniziazione**, e quando la mamma inizia, **non la smette più**.

Sin dai primi mesi di vita, approfitta della vicinanza per **inculcare** ai piccoli il proprio catechismo e diventare la loro **fede**; l'unica **deroga** è concessa al **tifo calcistico, poderoso alleato** nella **depauperazione** dello spirito.

Il pensiero religioso è vissuto in modo autoreferenziale, e ogni manifestazione del mondo **sensibile è da ricondursi** all'unica entità generatrice: *Ella.*

accredita confers upon

voltaggio voltage
fulminandoli electrocuting them
promuove a proprio favore fosters for her own benefit

martirio martyrdom
petulante nagging
rinunce e sacrifici votivi self-deprivation and votive sacrifices
digiuni fasting
clausure cloistering
innalzarsi alla santità to raise themselves up to sainthood
mediante by means of
levitazione del ciambellone levitation of the doughnut
guarigione della bua per mezzo del bacino healing of a boo-boo
    by way of a little kiss
bastoncini di pesce fish sticks
autoascensione self-promoted ascension
piani dell'esistenza levels of existence
terrestre earthly
stadio sacrificale sacrificial stage
insopportabile insufferable
Mamma Celeste Heavenly Mother
inutili orpelli useless trappings
dolcificante artificial sweetener

educazione this word refers to both "education" and "child
    rearing"
decenni decades
sempre più fuori moda more and more out of date

Dalla Genesi della Mamma
«Il primo giorno Dio creò la luce, ma la mamma era in piedi da un'ora e aveva già fatto il caffè...»

La condizione di genitrice **accredita** la donna di una naturale devozione da parte dei figli: per i bambini la madre è la luce, il raggio luminoso che illumina l'esistenza. Peccato che la mamma esageri nel **voltaggio, fulminandoli** come filamenti di tungsteno.

Nel corso degli anni, la mamma **promuove a proprio favore** un processo di beatificazione, anche se con modalità diverse. Le Mamme Passive si gloriano nel **martirio**, attraverso la **petulante** annunciazione di **rinunce e sacrifici votivi: digiuni**, silenzi, **clausure**; le Mamme Attive scelgono di **innalzarsi alla santità mediante** i miracoli: la **levitazione del ciambellone**, la **guarigione della bua per mezzo del bacino**, la resurrezione del ciclamino, la moltiplicazione dei pani e dei **bastoncini di pesce.**

L'**autoascensione** permette alla mamma di attraversare diversi **piani dell'esistenza:** partendo dal piano **terrestre**, si eleva successivamente allo **stadio sacrificale** di *Moglie di marito* **insopportabile**, per poi realizzarsi nella figura di **Mamma Celeste** e infine accedere alla condizione illuminata di *Mahamma*, la grande anima, ma senza quegli **inutili orpelli** della nonviolenza e del digiuno, al limite prende il **dolcificante.**

Fino alla prima metà del XX secolo, l'**educazione** era deputata a tre istituzioni – famiglia, Chiesa e scuola – ma nei **decenni** a seguire, le ultime due sono diventate un costume sociale **sempre più fuori moda**. I Dieci Comandamenti delle

Mosè Moses
inoppugnabili incontrovertible

scolpiti sulle tavole benedette carved on the blessed tablets

vestale in vestaglia vestal virgin in her bathrobe
esterna interminabili prediche preaches interminable sermons

all'infuori di me before me

Pettinati Comb your hair

tavole di **Mosè**, sono stati sostituiti da regole meno sacre, ma altrettanto **inoppugnabili**: i *Dieci Comammamenti*.

Dai Comandamenti **scolpiti sulle tavole benedette**, si passa ai *Comammamenti* scolpiti sulle tavole della cucina: il pulpito da cui la **vestale in vestaglia esterna interminabili prediche**.

I COMAMMAMENTI

1. Non avrai altra mamma **all'infuori di me.**
2. Onora la mamma e dopo il papà.
3. Ricordati di santificare la mamma.
4. Pulisciti i piedi e lavati le mani.
5. Non allontanarti.
6. Non tornare tardi.
7. Non sudare.
8. **Pettinati.**
9. Non desiderare la mamma d'altri.
10. Non desiderare il ragù d'altri.

A volte Sometimes

cedere il passo to make way for
rassegnazione resignation
peli di differenza a hair's breadth, a play on *peli* = "hairs" and the fact that the boys have grown body hair (*i.e.,* have grown up)
si acquietano settle into
gerontocomio old folks' home
capolinea della terza età last stop of senior citizenship (*literally:* "the third age")

Nuocera play on *suocera* = "mother-in-law" and the verb *nuocere* = "to harm, damage"
nefasta triade evil triad
emisfero hemisphere
pacificamente peacefully
innocua e sovente harmless and frequently
plaid small soft woolen blanket
parole crociate crossword puzzles
dentieria instabile wobbly dentures
risorge is resurrected
taumaturgicamente miraculously
che sembravano scomparse seemed to have all but disappeared
supereroe superhero
calciatore gambizzato soccer player with a leg injury
Lazzaro Lazarus

LA NUOCERA
Resurrezione di un demone e genesi di un danno

A volte ritornano.

Poi ritornano più spesso.

Infine restano.

Quando l'illusione dell'eterna condizione di mamma sembra **cedere il passo** alla **rassegnazione**; quando tra coloro che erano i propri piccoli e quelli che sono i propri figli ci sono troppi **peli di differenza**; quando i processi intellettivi **si acquietano** sulla frequenza dei quiz televisivi; quando la porta del **gerontocomio** lascia intravedere il **capolinea della terza età**, ecco che il destino regala alla mamma una seconda giovinezza: nasce un nipote, rinasce una mamma, anzi, una *Nuocera*.

La Nuocera sintetizza la più **nefasta triade** femminile: la mamma, la nonna, la suocera.

Il suo antagonismo non trova alcuna corrispondenza nell'**emisfero** maschile, che resta **pacificamente** nonno, figura **innocua e sovente** accompagnata da **plaid**, **parole crociate**, **dentiera instabile** e pillole multicolori.

L'anziana che diventa Nuocera **risorge** a nuova mamma, riacquisendo **taumaturgicamente** le forze **che sembravano scomparse**: come un **supereroe** ferito che decide di tornare in azione, come un **calciatore gambizzato** e riabilitato dallo spray, come **Lazzaro**.

guarisce di colpo suddenly cures

ruggine delle artrosi rustiness of arthritis

raddrizza straightens up

i colpi della strega *in effect:* stiff backs (*literally:* the witch's blows [causing sudden onset of pain])

sconfigge il diabete overcomes diabetes

afferrandolo tra le mani grasping it in her hands

scartandolo con foga unwrapping it enthusiastically

ribadisce stresses

inamovibile irremovable

improvvise sudden

ben congegnato well contrived

sorda deaf

per stordire in order to stun

a giurare to swear

somiglianze resemblances, family likenesses

naso gobbo hooked nose

uguale-uguale exactly the same

spiccicato a quell'arpìa the spitting image of that hag

venefica malevolent

apparentate related

spietato ruthless

L'energia della mamma-nonna **guarisce di colpo** la **ruggine delle artrosi, raddrizza i colpi della strega** e **sconfigge il diabete.** La natalità del nipote è un dono del cielo e tale è la gioia che la neononna lo tratta proprio come pacchettino, **afferrandolo tra le mani** e **scartandolo con foga** per scoprirne la sorpresa.

Teorema della Nuocera
Dato un nipote, la Nuocera è tangente in ogni suo punto.

Qualora il nipote non si rendesse ancora conto di chi si trova davanti, la nonna **ribadisce** la sua **inamovibile** presenza con **improvvise** e incomprensibili esplosioni verbali: *Butibutibù!; CucciCucciCucci!; Tabatabataba!*

L'apparente nonsense di queste espressioni nasconde un *nonna-sense* **ben congegnato**: la Nuocera finge di essere **sorda** per tenere un tono di voce altissimo e **per stordire** il bambino da subito, rendendo inoffensivo ogni tentativo di ribellione, anche futuro.

La Nuocera è pronta **a giurare** che il nipote ha pronunciato come prima parola *nonna*, sottolineando che si riferiva a lei e non all'altra nonna, che invece chiama solo *brutta*.

Riguardo alle **somiglianze**, il nipote è sempre identico a lei quando era piccola, per la bellezza degli occhi e del sorriso, mentre il **naso gobbo** o le gambe corte provengono dall'altra famiglia. Stesso discorso vale per il carattere: quando dorme e mangia tranquillo, il bambino è *uguale-uguale* a lei; quando fa il demonio è **spiccicato a quell'arpìa** della *con-Nuocera*.

Se la mamma è sempre critica nei confronti delle altre mamme, la Nuocera è addirittura **venefica**: il confronto tra due Nuocere **apparentate** a uno stesso nipote è **spietato**, senza regole.

Lines   brand of disposable diaper

pannolone   adult-sized diaper

sfumature umorali   nuances of mood

tratti   characteristics
critica perenne   eternal criticism
nuore, generi   daughters-in-law, sons-in-law
gravi lacune nell'allevamento   serious gaps in their rearing

incontestabile   undeniable
inconfessata   unexpressed
turbare   to upset/disturb
Difficilmente contrastabile   It's difficult to counter

chiunque osi contraddirla   whosoever dares contradict her
cavallo di Troia   Trojan horse
recando doni   bearing gifts
per rivelarsi poi   to then reveal oneself
ferali   savage
Laocoonte   Laocoon, the mythological figure punished by Apollo
   for warning the Trojans not to accept the wooden horse
Timeo nonnas et dona ferentes   *pseudo Latin:* Beware of
   grandmas bearing gifts

allorché sgridati   as soon as they're scolded
scredita   she undermines

Legge di Grimm
Nessuno è in grado di contenere la Nuocera, nemmeno lo stomaco del lupo.

Legge di Lines
Niente è in grado di contenere la Nuocera, nemmeno il pannolone.

Le **sfumature umorali** della nonna si differenziano in base alle caratteristiche del precedente stato di mamma. Esistono comunque dei **tratti** comuni a tutte le Nuocere, come l'attitudine alla **critica perenne**, specialmente nei confronti dei parenti, e in particolare di **nuore, generi** e figli: tutti dimostrano **gravi lacune nell'allevamento**, nella nutrizione e nell'educazione dei bambini. Ai suoi tempi lei non faceva così, lei puliva meglio, lei cucinava meglio, lei educava meglio, lei era meglio, ma questa **incontestabile** verità deve rimanere **inconfessata** per non **turbare** la *pax familiare*.

Difficilmente contrastabile per via del rispetto che si porta all'età – e per il sorriso da *Nonna Lisa* che rende maleducato **chiunque osi contraddirla.**

Lo stratagemma del **cavallo di Troia** è una delle tecniche più diffuse: entrare in territorio nemico **recando doni** in segno di amicizia, **per rivelarsi poi** capaci di attacchi **ferali.**

Legge di Laocoonte
Timeo nonnas et dona ferentes.

La Nuocera difende i nipoti **allorché sgridati** dai genitori; **scredita** i genitori agli occhi dei figli; premia i bambini messi

incendia she torches
annoso impegno age-old commitment
Pur di compiacere Doing anything to please
attua she puts into effect
subdolo tradimento underhanded betrayal

acetone e carie acetone and cavities
baratta she barters
avari stingy
li pretende expects them [as a right]
guance irsute e pungenti hairy, prickly cheeks

Bahlsen manufacturer of chocolate cookies
vizi bad habits (*literally:* vices)

univoco unequivocal
si concretizza is accomplished
tramandate handed down
molestare annoying
presepe crèche
a scaldare i fornelli *here:* revving up the burners
bolide racing car
Toglietevi che scotta! Get out of the way, it's hot!
sfreccia she darts about
brodo bollente boiling hot broth
gli avanzi the leftovers
sfamare feed, relieve the hunger
Mozambico Mozambique
commensali diners
boccheggiano esanimi are gasping and lifeless
si lobotomizzano they numb their brains (*literally:* lobotomize
  themselves)

in punizione; **incendia** con una sola parola interi volumi di pedagogia, mandando in fumo l'**annoso impegno** di padri e madri. **Pur di compiacere** il nipote, **attua** qualsiasi forma di doppio gioco, qualsiasi **subdolo tradimento**.

La Nuocera è la principale causa di **acetone e carie**, per l'indiscriminata somministrazione di dolci che **baratta** in cambio di baci di cui spesso i nipoti sono **avari**, specie nei confronti di chi **li pretende** con petulanti richieste e con **guance irsute e pungenti**.

Legge di Bahlsen
La nonna è la mamma dei vizi.

L'evento in cui la Nuocera esprime al meglio la sua capacità distruttrice è il Natale, in particolare durante il pranzo. Con le dovute differenze di tradizione e di latitudine, l'intento delle Nuocere è comunque **univoco** e **si concretizza** nella preparazione delle specialità gastronomiche **tramandate** da generazioni. A partire dal giorno 8 dicembre, non appena finito di **molestare** la famiglia intenta nella preparazione dell'albero e del **presepe**, la Nuocera comincia **a scaldare i fornelli**, intorno ai quali raggiungerà, la mattina del 24, la velocità di 340 chilometri orari, come un **bolide** sull'anello di Indianapolis: *Toglietevi che scotta!* è il suo grido natalizio, mentre **sfreccia** portando quindici litri di **brodo bollente**.

La quantità di cibo prodotto e cucinato per una famiglia di dieci persone è tale che solo **gli avanzi** sono sufficienti a **sfamare** la popolazione del **Mozambico** per un mese. Al termine del pranzo di Natale, mentre i **commensali boccheggiano esanimi** sul divano, **si lobotomizzano** davanti

trionfa a capotavola   exults at the head of the table
raggiante   radiant, glowing
imperterrita   unperturbed
a spaccare noci   to crack open nuts

Cappucetto Rosso   Little Red Riding Hood

alla televisione, cercano di capire il funzionamento dei regali che hanno comprato o si gettano alla ricerca di una farmacia aperta per una dose di bicarbonato, la Nuocera **trionfa a capotavola**, **raggiante** come le luci dell'albero di Natale, continuando **imperterrita a spaccare noci** con aria trionfante: è arrivato il bambinello, ed è tutto suo.

Seconda legge di Grimm o legge di Cappucetto Rosso

Vince sempre la nonna.

rimbambiniscono render infantile

agevolata facilitated

affina she perfects
efficaci sinergie effective synergies
gode enjoys
speculare reciprocal

volentieri willingly
Narciso Narcissus
angola she angles
abbacinarli dazzle them
messi in onda broadcast

far scemare le facoltà mentali dumb down the mental faculties
scemi stupid idiots

impone enforces
atteggiamenti mimetici mimicking behaviorisms
catarsi catharsis
subìto surrendered to
ipnotizzano hypnotize

inerzia inertia

SINERGIA E COMPLEMENTARITÀ TRA MAMMA E TV
Come mamma e Tv <u>rimbambiniscono</u> i bambini

La paralisi da sofà, condizione in cui la mamma tenta di ridurre i figli, è **agevolata** da una serie di complici con cui **affina efficaci sinergie**. Tra questi, la televisione **gode** di un ruolo privilegiato, se non altro per una forma di cortesia, dato che anche la mamma ha sempre un posto privilegiato davanti alla Tv: il rapporto è **speculare**.

Lo schermo del televisore è la vetrina che la mamma guarda più **volentieri**, lo specchio che ammira come **Narciso** e che poi **angola** in direzione dei figli, in modo da **abbacinarli** e rendere loro difficile la visione della realtà.

Il programma ideato dalla mamma per i figli e quelli **messi in onda** sembrano realizzati dallo stesso regista: entrambi hanno come scopo quello di **far scemare le facoltà mentali** degli spettatori, fino a farli diventare **scemi**.

Sia la mamma che la Tv rappresentano per il bambino due esempi importantissimi: una è il modello educativo principale; l'altra trasmette e **impone** modelli sociali, stimolando **atteggiamenti mimetici** per i quali non c'è **catarsi**.

La Tv è un mezzo di comunicazione **subìto**, perché non richiede una partecipazione attiva: le immagini **ipnotizzano** i telespettatori riducendo l'attività cerebrale a uno stato di **inerzia**. Per questo i bambini, che sono i più indifesi, rappresentano il pubblico ideale, e la mamma è contenta di

resta in sosta remains parked
raggi roventi scorching rays

smarrendolo losing it

Grundig German manufacturer of television sets, radios, and other household appliances

L'assenza di stimoli The absence of stimuli

Rai Italian government-run radio and television networks

malinsesto play on *palinsesto* = "planning of radio and TV programs" and *male* = "evil"
di buon occhio in a good light
reputandola deeming it
foriera di pericoli harbinger of danger; *in effect:* precursor of worse things to come
sconce lewd
è lecito it is permissible
sceneggiati serials
accolti received, accepted
come una grazia as if they were a grace [from God]

vederli davanti alla Tv, sempre, anche quando è spenta.

Il televisore è un parcheggio desolato dove il cervello **resta in sosta** sotto a **raggi roventi**, ma se la sosta si prolunga eccessivamente, può succedere che il proprietario dimentichi il luogo in cui l'ha lasciato, **smarrendolo** per sempre.

Legge di Grundig
Il numero di Tv accese è sempre uguale al numero di bambini spenti.

L'assenza di stimoli fa della Tv una delle migliori amiche della mamma. I bambini con la bocca aperta davanti allo schermo sono una delle sue fotografie preferite, l'immagine del mondo ideale, con i figli che osservano lo scorrere della vita dalla finestra, senza prendervi parte.

Legge di Mamma Rai
Se l'audience della mamma sale, il quoziente intellettivo dei figli precipita.

Il *malinsesto* televisivo cambia da mamma a mamma.

Essendo inclini alla demonizzazione della novità e al divieto, le mamme più autoritarie non vedono la televisione **di buon occhio, reputandola foriera di pericoli**: le trasmissioni sono stupide, **sconce** e fanno piangere Gesù. L'opera di censura è costante ed **è lecito** guardare solo ciò che hanno preventivamente selezionato: gli **sceneggiati** sulla vita dei santi, mentre i documentari e le messe sono **accolti** dai bambini **come una grazia**.

cellulare cell phone
purché as long as
allarme inserito alarm which is set

schermo screen

Viceversa, le Mamme Permissive considerano la Tv la compagna perfetta che ogni figlio deve avere vicino: in camera da letto, in cucina, in bagno, sul computer, sul **cellulare**, **purché** non alzi mai la testa per vedere cosa c'è intorno. La televisione dà la tranquillità di un **allarme inserito**, finché è accesa nessuno può rubare i bambini.

Lo sviluppo dell'industria televisiva offre soluzioni tecnologiche sempre più diaboliche, come lo **schermo** al plasma, così denominato perché succhia il sangue dal cervello di chi lo guarda: un vampiro che dà alla vittima un brevissimo ma mortale piacere.

Io quel dottore non lo posso soffrire I can't stand that doctor, a
play on *soffrire* = "to suffer"

difetto di costituzione constitutional defect
vizia il rapporto spoils the relationship
paziente patient (both noun and adjective)

peraltro moreover
ruolo di comparsa role of an extra (as in films)
passano in secondo piano recede to the background

ammessi allowed
disturbi means both "ailment" and "disturbance"

Roche Swiss-based pharmaceutical and diagnostics giant

Supplica Supplication, Plea

fuori dalla portata out of reach

tuttavia however, in any case
bersaglio target

SINTOMI DI DIFFIDENZA CRONICA VERSO LA SCIENZA MEDICA
«Io quel dottore non lo posso soffrire!»

C'è un **difetto di costituzione** che **vizia il rapporto** tra mamma e medico, ed è l'incapacità della prima di comprendere il significato della parola *paziente*.

La mamma ha la prerogativa di essere sempre impaziente.

A parte la necessaria presenza del figlio, **peraltro** ridotto al **ruolo di comparsa** le cui condizioni di salute **passano in secondo piano**, la mamma è incondizionatamente la stella della scena: oltre alla malattia non sono **ammessi** altri **disturbi**, tanto meno il medico.

Avvertenza di Roche
Attenzione: non somministrare la mamma ai bambini al di sotto dei dodici anni.

Supplica di Roche
Attenzione: tenere i bambini fuori dalla portata della mamma.

Secondo la Mamma Classica, i medici non possono capire perché non conoscono a fondo il problema, **tuttavia** trova necessario consultarli per tre motivi: per avere un **bersaglio** su

sfogare l'ansia to unload her anxiety

bisogno animale animal urge/craving

esibirsi to show off

contraddirli contradicting them

iter process

scetticismo skepticism

espone le sue ridicole deduzioni expounds his ridiculous conclusions

da punta pointing (like a hunting dog)

bracco pronto a scattare verso la preda gun-dog ready to leap at the prey

tattica tactic

mira a far innervosire il medico aims at making the doctor ill at ease

a creare disagio at creating discomfort

cenni del capo nods

mimica del viso expression on her face

per spiegargli in order to explain to him

affidare entrust

vale a dire which means

colui he who

sostiene supports

intuito intuited

pallore pallor

colpo di tosse coughing attack

rossore redness, inflammation

bucio play on *bucio* = "asshole" and *bacio* = "kiss"

terapia treatment

ammette permit

del resto furthermore

ribadisce in continuazione she carries on reaffirming

pentola a pressione pressure cooker

tomo di ricette tome of recipes

convinta di serbare convinced of harboring

miscela alchemica alchemistic mixture

cui **sfogare l'ansia,** perché ha un **bisogno animale** di **esibirsi,** perché adora **contraddirli.**

Nell'**iter** diagnostico, la mamma decide di consultare più specialisti, sempre con **scetticismo.** Esiste anche una sua postura tipica mentre ascolta il medico che **espone le sue ridicole deduzioni:** è seduta, composta ma non rilassata, con la borsa appoggiata sulle ginocchia unite. È una posizione immobile ma di grande tensione fisica, quasi **da punta,** come un **bracco pronto a scattare verso la preda;** è una **tattica** che **mira a far innervosire il medico, a creare disagio.** L'espressione del volto è seria e attenta, accompagnata da brevi **cenni del capo,** che fingono di approvare quanto ascoltato. Poi, con il passare dei minuti, la **mimica del viso** cambia e un sorriso allunga lentamente gli angoli della bocca: sta aspettando che l'interlocutore finisca il suo stupido elenco di pensieri, **per spiegargli** la fisiologia del corpo umano.

Al termine delle visite, la mamma sceglie il medico a cui **affidare** il figlio, **vale a dire colui** che risponde esattamente ai suoi gusti, ma soprattutto quello che **sostiene** esattamente ciò che vuole sentirsi dire: la diagnosi che lei aveva **intuito** subito, sin dal primo **pallore,** dal primo **colpo di tosse** o da quello strano **rossore** nella zona perianale che controlla tutte le sere, un'affettuosa abitudine che chiama il *bucio* della buonanotte.

Durante la **terapia,** la mamma non **ammette** interferenze, **del resto ribadisce in continuazione** *È mio figlio!,* e lei sola sa come funziona, proprio come l'aspirapolvere e la **pentola a pressione.** Tra le pagine dell'immaginario **tomo di ricette** che conserva impresso nella memoria, la mamma è **convinta di serbare** il medicamento giusto, la pozione magica, una **miscela alchemica** che solo lei è in grado di amalgamare. È per questo che prova una felicità sotterranea quando la cura del «*dottore*»

Io apostrafo sempre in maniera virgolettata always putting it in
quotes

non sortisce doesn't produce

fallimento failure

battuta da Oscar line worthy of an Oscar

rosolia German measles

le oscura le luci del palco darkens her stage lighting

Lasonil ointment for bruises or sprains

(lo apostrofa sempre in maniera virgolettata) **non sortisce** gli effetti desiderati, per poter fare il suo ingresso in scena e certificare il suo **fallimento** con una **battuta da Oscar**: *Io l'avevo detto che non era **rosolia**...*

Il medico è vissuto dalla mamma come un antagonista che **le oscura le luci del palco**, e che va combattuto come la malattia, se non di più.

Assioma di Lasonil
La mamma è un trauma.

Osservazione di Poppins
Con un poco di zucchero la pillola va giù, la mamma no.

Fabrizio Blini

CONDIZIONAMENTO SOCIALE DELLA MAMMA

> *La mamma non vuole.*
> Edipo, 17 anni

PRODROMI WARNING SIGNS

Ringo Boys...Rinco Men play on *Ringo* cookies (like Oreos™) and truncated *rincoglioniti* = "super thick-headed"

inetti inept
politici bisticciano politicians quarrel
s'impantana screws up

collettività community

perdita di aderenza con la realtà loss of a grip on reality
dissociazione dell'individuo psychic dissociation of the individual

impatto sociale social impact
compromettendo l'integrità della prole compromising the integrity of the offspring
giovani promesse promising young men
riversa it spills out
giovani minacce menacing young men
classi dirigenti ruling classes

complesso overall system
complessati filled with hangups

PRODROMI DI SCHIZOFRENIA SOCIALE
Da piccoli Ringo Boys, da grandi Rinco Men

Un singolo mammone può sembrare comico, un insieme di mammoni è tragico.

Nel momento in cui diventano protagonisti della vita sociale, gli **inetti** mammoni privati costituiscono un grosso handicap pubblico: i **politici bisticciano**, la burocrazia **s'impantana**, il traffico si blocca.

Il mammone non riesce mai a inserirsi completamente nella **collettività**, perché una parte di lui è sempre assente, è con la mamma. E poiché la **perdita di aderenza con la realtà** e la **dissociazione dell'individuo** sono mali di grande attualità, è facile capire quale sia l'incidenza della mamma nel disastro dell'*egosistema* prima, e dell'intero sistema poi.

Il suo **impatto sociale** è una mina che esplode silenziosamente in ogni casa, **compromettendo l'integrità della prole**: invece di offrire alla nazione delle **giovani promesse**, **riversa** per le strade tante **giovani minacce**.

Il mammismo è diventato un fenomeno schizofrenico su scala nazionale: società di mammoni, **classi dirigenti** di mammoni, eserciti di mammoni, industrie di mammoni.

La disfunzione del **complesso** è il risultato di tanti individui **complessati**.

Engels Friedrich Engels (1820–1895), social philosopher and co-founder, with Karl Marx, of the Communist movement

avvenuti that have taken place
fascia d'età age bracket
dilatata extended
vanta boasts
mammolliti play on *rammollito* = "spineless"
arroccati safely sheltered
adesivi appiccicati stickers stuck
lettino a una piazza little single bed

inibisce she inhibits

stasi slump, standstill
la crescita zero zero birth rate
illudendosi fooling himself

spie dell'incedere signs of the advance
nel contempo at the same time
tintura hair dye
cinquantenne morettino cute dark-haired 50-year-old
arzillo biondino sprightly [old] blondish guy
truffatori swindlers
denuncia files a complaint against
truccare l'anagrafe to touch up the records
reticolo di rughe web of wrinkles
svela il patetico inganno exposes the pathetic deception

Legge di Engels
La madre è un bene privato, la mamma è un danno pubblico.

I cambiamenti sociali **avvenuti** negli ultimi anni evidenziano la gravità del problema: la **fascia d'età** in cui si vuole essere figli si è **dilatata** scandalosamente. L'Italia **vanta** una massa di ultratrentenni *mammolliti*, **arroccati** nella loro cameretta, con i poster dei calciatori alle pareti, gli **adesivi appiccicati** sulla finestra, il **lettino a una piazza,** desolata. È in questo senso che la mamma agisce come deterrente nello sviluppo del benessere della società, perché **inibisce** la crescita delle persone che ne dovrebbero essere il motore.

Anche la **stasi** demografica è un importante segnale dell'avanzata del mammismo: **la crescita zero** è figlia di figli che non vogliono diventare genitori. L'italiano invecchia **illudendosi** di restare giovane, quando al limite può sperare di essere giovanile. Ma ci sono altre **spie dell'incedere** del fenomeno, una delle più visibili, e **nel contempo** più ignorate, è la **tintura** per lui. Il **cinquantenne morettino**, l'**arzillo biondino** o l'anziano rosso fuoco, sono figure molto presenti nella società, **truffatori** che nessuno **denuncia**, quasi fosse normale **truccare l'anagrafe**, mentre un **reticolo di rughe svela il patetico inganno.**

Questa incapacità di prendere coscienza di sé, di andare avanti con serenità, annuncia il tramonto della giovinezza, ma non l'alba della saggezza: il futuro è grigio, come i capelli.

Legge di Perm and Colour
Il mammone ha cura dei propri capelli ma non di quello che c'è sotto.

Dercos brand of hair products
flaconcino vial

l'altisonanza the pomposity
doppiopetto blu dark blue double-breasted suit
amministratori delegati CEOs, managing directors

il governo ombra the shadow government
amorevoli onorevoli lovable honorables, a play on *onorevole*, the
 title given to members of Parliament
seggio-lone play on *seggio* = "seat in Parliament" and *seggiolone* =
 "high chair"
disegno politico political aspirations
avere ragione piuttosto che ragionare to be right rather than to
 think logically
Di conseguenza As a result
camaleontismo opportunism; *camaleonte* = "chameleon"
si fa a cuscinate one starts pillow fighting

Giulio Giulio Andreotti (b.1919), Italian statesman, seven-time
 prime minister, and senator for life
logora undermines

Legge di Dercos
L'unità di misura del mammone anziano è il flaconcino.

La mamma non è presidente, né generale, né guida importanti gruppi industriali, per scoprire il suo peso politico è necessario andare oltre le apparenze dell'ufficialità: è dietro **l'altisonanza** delle istituzioni, sotto il **doppiopetto blu** degli **amministratori delegati** che pulsa il vero potere, l'autorità che condiziona il loro volere.

È la *Mammocrazia*, **il governo ombra** che non abbandona mai gli **amorevoli onorevoli**, seduti sul *seggio-lone*.

La governante mamma non ha un **disegno politico**, né le interessa averne uno: preferisce **avere ragione piuttosto che ragionare**.

Di conseguenza, nella Cameretta dei Deputati e nella Cameretta del Senato domina l'instabilità, il disordine ideologico, il **camaleontismo**; l'emergenza diventa normalità e la norma diventa straordinaria; **si fa a cuscinate**.

Il welfare si trasforma in *malfare*.

Prima legge della Mammocrazia o legge di Giulio
La mamma logora chi ce l'ha.

Seconda legge della Mammocrazia
La mamma è la Presidentessa del Consiglio Sbagliato.

diplopazzia a play on *diplomazia* = "diplomacy" and *pazzia* = "craziness"

impervio percorso dialettico *here:* taking the impossible route of dialectics
di argomentare of debating
ottenere ragione getting your way
sei a corto di you run out of
aggredisci attack

imporsi make their weight felt
stimolatore elettrico per suini electric prod used for pigs

tanatosi thanatosis (posture suggestive of death)

uguaglianza equality
voto *sproporzionale* a play on *voto proporzionale* = "proportional vote" and *sproporzionale* = "disproportional, *i.e.*, antidemocratic"

altrui for everyone else

corporativo corporative

arbitro referee

La **diplopazzia**

La mamma evita sempre l'**impervio percorso dialettico** che la costringe a spiegare e motivare le sue azioni. Di fronte all'incapacità **di argomentare**, la mamma fa uso dello stratagemma 38 di *L'arte di* **ottenere ragione** di Schopenhauer: «*Quando* **sei a corto di** *argomenti,* **aggredisci,** *alza la voce, cerca la lite*». Soprattutto le Mamme Attive preferiscono **imporsi** e comandare con determinazione o con lo **stimolatore elettrico per suini**. Le Mamme Passive nascondono invece la propria forza, fingendosi deboli e disorientando il nemico: con il silenzio, il vittimismo o la **tanatosi**. Nel sistema politico della mamma, non è prevista alcuna forma di **uguaglianza**; per le decisioni importanti esiste un sistema di **voto** *sproporzionale*, perché la sua parola conta di più. In caso contrario, incrocia le braccia, proclamando lo sciopero della fame **altrui** e spingendo i famigliari nel tunnel dei cracker con la maionese.

Al dialogo, è preferito il monologo.

Tolleranza zero

La mamma è un animale asociale, senza alcuno spirito **corporativo**. Il suo individualismo le impedisce di stabilire un rapporto di collaborazione con la collettività, in particolare con le altre mamme, considerate come pericolose rivali e non come possibili alleate. La ricerca del confronto senza esclusione di colpi è vitale nella competizione tra di loro; ognuna è protagonista e **arbitro** allo stesso tempo, condizione che le rende tutte vincitrici, senza che sia riconosciuta l'esistenza di

una sola perdente one single loser

squisite delightful, refined

Sparlamento a play on *sparlare* = "speak ill of someone" and
    parlamento = "Parliament"

antipatia antipathy, dislike

estranei outsiders

riversandosi pouring out

Durbans brand of toothpaste

conigli rabbits

ubbidire he should obey

deputare delegate

al quale votarsi to whom one should place one's devotion

una sola perdente. Il confronto non è quasi mai diretto – faccia a faccia sono sempre **squisite** – ma si svolge per lo più in *Sparlamento*.

La paura e l'**antipatia** verso gli **estranei** aumentano con il tempo, **riversandosi** anche su parenti, amici e umanità varia.

Legge di <u>Durbans</u>
Mamma che sorride, morde.

Le generazioni di mammoni proliferate come **conigli** negli ultimi decenni, e poi trasformatesi in classi dirigenti, hanno quindi lasciato i fili del potere nelle mani dell'eroina della loro infanzia, diventandone dipendenti.

Il mammone è sempre alla ricerca della mamma a cui **ubbidire** e, nella vita sociopolitica, di un surrogato a cui **deputare** le proprie responsabilità.

Alle elezioni, più che pensare a un politico da votare, bisogna trovare un santo **al quale votarsi**.

prepotenza arrogance

Ufo Unidentified Flying Objects

madidi di sudore drenched with sweat
tentatrice tempting
lo nega she denies its existence

spalancando throwing wide open

per le palle by the balls
crampo cramp, spasm
emicranie migraine headaches

girone dei lussuriosi circle of lechers (as in Dante's Inferno)
che sale oscenamente that rises obscenely
fino al suo pianerottolo till it gets to her landing
si erge she rears up
erezione erection
già maggiorenni already of age
intossicati intoxicated
callose calloused
bandito a play on the two meanings of *bandito* = "banned" and
  "bandit"

Durex brand of condom

LATIN OVER
La prepotenza della mamma nell'impotenza dei figli

Il sesso non esiste, come non esistono gli **Ufo**, né gli zombie: è una fantasia inventata da menti degenerate per impressionare i bambini; è un brutto sogno che li fa svegliare **madidi di sudore** nel cuore della notte. La mamma teme la forza **tentatrice** del sesso e **lo nega**.

La scoperta della nuda verità da parte dei figli potrebbe esserle fatale, **spalancando** loro la via della fuga. Avere il controllo del sesso significa avere il controllo di tutto, per questo bisogna prenderlo a tutti i costi, **per le palle**.

L'erotismo è un **crampo** mentale che degenera in frequenti **emicranie**, assumendo le sembianze di un demone, un'entità appartenente al **girone dei lussuriosi che sale oscenamente fino al suo pianerottolo**. L'avversione con cui la mamma combatte la libertà sessuale ha qualcosa di eroico: **si erge** contro l'**erezione**, ultima disperata barriera a protezione della verginità dei piccoli, **già maggiorenni** e **intossicati** da masturbazioni **callose**.

A casa della mamma il sesso è **bandito**. E lei è lo sceriffo.

Equazione di Durex
La mamma sta al sesso, come Attila sta all'erba.

analfabeti sessuali   sexual illiterates
autodidatti   self-taught learners
scavandosi le occhiaie   carving out dark circles under the eyes
indefessi   play on *indefesi* = "defenseless" and *fessi* = "idiots"

Clitoride   Clitoris

pene   penis

trincea   entrenched
tese a ostacolare   set to hinder

placare   soothe
sudarelle   getting the hots, hot spells
sventolando un ampio ventaglio   waving a wide range (*literally*: fan)
castrazione cinica   play on *castrazione chimica* = "chemical castration" and *cinica* = "cynical"
cinte di castità   play on *cinta* = "circle of walls" and *cinto* = "belt"
condotta castigata   sober, decent behavior
sesso unico   play on *senso unico* = "one way"
morigerate attività formative   upright, formative activities
gruppi parrocchiali   parish clubs

crociata   crusade
pisellino   willy (baby talk for "penis")
peccaminosi   sinful
bigattino   silk-worm
Infernet   a play on *Inferno* = "Hell + Internet"
ammonisce   reprimands

Grazie alla diseducazione della mamma, sono cresciuti migliaia di **analfabeti sessuali** che tentano di recuperare le lezioni da **autodidatti, scavandosi le occhiaie** con full immersion nei pantaloni, o diventando clienti *indefessi* di peepshow e pornoshop.

Per molti italiani, **Clitoride** è un eroe secondario dell'Eneide; altri pensano che Vagina sia un nome femminile russo; ne esistono persino alcuni convinti che il **pene** non abbia l'osso!

L'avanguardista modello svedese che prevede semplici manuali d'istruzioni, come per i mobili dell'Ikea – che comporta eguale fatica ma una maggiore soddisfazione – è lontano.

A supporto di questa posizione di **trincea**, la mamma adotta una serie di soluzioni **tese a ostacolare** il corso degli eventi: il primo obiettivo è impedire la conoscenza del sesso.

Ogni mamma cerca di **placare** le frequenti **sudarelle, sventolando un ampio ventaglio** di possibilità che si differenziano in base alle tipologia di mamma: alcune fingono amicizia per poi operare una *castrazione cinica*; altre circondano i figli con insormontabili mura, **cinte di castità**.

La costrizione sessuale delle Mamme Proibizioniste impone una **condotta castigata**, lontana da pericolose promiscuità; l'educazione prevede scuole a *sesso unico*, con **morigerate attività formative** nei **gruppi parrocchiali**; la demonizzazione dell'altro sesso è continua, e tutto ciò che può stimolare il desiderio va cancellato. Le difficoltà incontrate dalla mamma nella **crociata** per la difesa del **pisellino** sono numerose: dai **peccaminosi** documentari sulla riproduzione del **bigattino**, fino alle bollenti linee erotiche e alle tentazioni di *Infernet*.

La mamma **ammonisce** e punisce, terrorizzando il sistema

ormonale hormonal
accorre con l'estintore rushes in with the fire extinguisher
letargo lethargy
melliflua gentle
mollezza tenderness
nell'oblio in forgetfulness
vieta forbid
coccole atte a dissuadere cuddles calculated to discourage
suscitare iperpudore bring about an extreme sense of prudery
facendo avvampare l'impaccio sul volto making his face blaze
    with embarrassment
avverte ovunque l'occhio vigile senses everywhere the watchful
    eye

perpetrato morbosamente perpetrated sickeningly
corteggiamento asfissiante suffocating courtship
da ostentare to be shown off
disinvoltura indifference
pedale del freno inibitorio inhibitory brake pedal

case chiuse brothels

Hatu brand of condom
preservativo condom

monti una guardia mounts guard
attentati terrorist attacks
ciuffo sul pube tuft of pubic hair

ipereccitati overexcited

ultras allo stadio violent football fans at the stadium
patta fabric covering the zipper

ormonale: ovunque si accenda l'infatuazione, la mamma **accorre con l'estintore**, o la spegne con le lacrime.

Il **letargo** sessuale dei figli può essere raggiunto anche in forma **melliflua**, attraverso la ricerca della **mollezza**, annullando il desiderio **nell'oblio**. La Mamma Permissiva non **vieta**, ma somministra ogni giorno tentazioni più morbide, **coccole atte a dissuadere** altre coccole. Baci e abbracci estranei devono **suscitare iperpudore**, **facendo avvampare l'impaccio sul volto** del mammone, che **avverte ovunque l'occhio vigile** della mamma.

Questa non perde occasione per dichiararsi, ricordandogli che lui è l'unico amore della sua vita. Il tentativo di dissuasione è **perpetrato morbosamente**, con un **corteggiamento asfissiante**: il figlio diventa un antimarito **da ostentare** durante le passeggiate, guardare ma non toccare.

Anche se fingendo **disinvoltura**, la mamma preme con forza sul **pedale del freno inibitorio**.

Le mamme moderne sono persino favorevoli alle **case chiuse**: le loro, con i figli dentro.

Legge di Hatu
La mamma è il preservativo del preservativo.

Nonostante la mamma **monti una guardia** militare, il pericolo di **attentati** cresce giorno dopo giorno, proporzionalmente al **ciuffo sul pube**. La natura si avvicina come una ladra, pronta a introdursi nella vita dei figli per rubare loro la verginità: cambia la voce, crescono protuberanze, gli ormoni **ipereccitati** sembrano **ultras allo stadio**. La situazione sta per esplodere, come i bottoni di una camicetta, come la **patta** dei pantaloni,

non implica la resa doesn't imply surrender

travolti dall'innamoramento bowled over by falling in love
cedono al piacere surrender to [its] bliss
si consuma is consummated
con l'accaduto with what has happened
sant'Irene Vergine e Martire Saint Irene Virgin and Martyr
approssimarsi al rogo che l'arse viva approaching the stake
where she is to be burned alive
macchiati della colpa stained with guilt
riacquistava regained
in ammollo soaking
ceci garbanzo beans, chickpeas

Giocasta Oedipus's mother
subita suffered

incellofanata wrapped in cellophane
pianta grassa succulent plant
pietose lamentable
si scorgono occur
sguardo gaze
quella *here:* that woman
Tomografia assiale computerizzata computerized axial
tomography
sorriso di circostanza smile suitable to the occasion
congegno che scansiona l'indesiderata device that scans the
undesirable
tintura dei capelli [her] dye job
la bassezza del culo how low-slung her butt is
gambe storte bowed legs
pugile boxer

ormai aperta ventiquattr'ore al giorno, come un selfservice. La mamma allora alza le difese, l'avanzata del nemico **non implica la resa.**

Nella maggior parte delle famiglie, i figli prima o poi sono **travolti dall'innamoramento** e **cedono al piacere:** la tragedia **si consuma.** La mamma cerca allora il coraggio per confrontarsi **con l'accaduto**, mascherando il volto con il sorriso di **sant'Irene Vergine e Martire** nell'atto di **approssimarsi al rogo che l'arse viva.** In realtà, vorrebbe immergere i figli **macchiati della colpa** nelle acque del fiume Kanathos, dove Afrodite bagnandosi **riacquistava** la verginità, e lasciarli **in ammollo** ventiquattr'ore, come i **ceci.**

Legge di Giocasta
L'atto sessuale praticato dai figli, è una violenza subita dalla mamma.

Per fortuna, sono rari i casi in cui la mamma riesce a conservare la verginità del figlio **incellofanata**, trasformandolo in un'inutile **pianta grassa.** Sono situazioni **pietose** che **si scorgono** occasionalmente in qualche sagrestia dell'umanità.

Sarebbe limitativo definire *sguardo* il modo in cui la mamma osserva *quella*, in occasione della prima visita: in realtà è una **Tomografia assiale computerizzata.**

Dietro un leonardesco **sorriso di circostanza**, la mamma nasconde un **congegno che scansiona l'indesiderata** dalla testa ai piedi: esamina la **tintura dei capelli, la bassezza del culo**, la bassezza del quoziente intellettivo, le **gambe storte**, il sorriso stupido, il cattivo gusto dell'abbigliamento, il nasino da **pugile.**

intrusa   intruder
di sopravvivere   of survival/surviving

soppesato   sized up
amabile   charming, gracious
occultato da   camouflaged as

penose   painful

per sottrarsi all'imbarazzo   in order to escape the awkwardness

un'occhiata   a look

calpestando   trampling

l'insidia   the threat

mentendo   lying
orgia   orgy

Mendelson   Felix Mendelssohn (1809–1847), German Romantic
   composer perhaps best known for his *Wedding March* (1842)

zona nuziale   wedding realm

confetti e bomboniere   In Italy, the bride and groom give out
   little gifts of candied almonds (*confetti*) in decorative sacks or
   containers (*bomboniere*) to their wedding guests.

L'analisi rivela i difetti in tempo reale, offrendo una diagnosi che non lascia all'**intrusa** alcuna speranza **di sopravvivere**. Almeno in casa sua.

Dopo aver **soppesato** con gli occhi la pericolosità dell'ospite, la mamma la sottopone a un **amabile** interrogatorio di terzo grado, **occultato da** false cortesie e biscottini con il tè. La riunione raggiunge una tensione tale che, durante le **penose** pause della conversazione, anche il divano tenta di fuggire **per sottrarsi all'imbarazzo**.

Se la mamma valuta il rischio elevato, si genera una rivalità elettrica che accende in lei **un'occhiata** piena di odio diretta alla sua avversaria, a dire: stai **calpestando** una proprietà privata che ho diritto di calpestare solo io.

Se **l'insidia** si mostra pericolosa la mamma passa all'azione.

La mamma risponde di nascosto al cellulare del figlio, **mentendo**: *Luca non è in casa, è andato a un'orgia, poi deve andare a dormire dalla sua ex, anzi, dal suo ex.*

In presenza di *quella*, non abbandona mai la coppia, ma si pianta nel mezzo, muta, con un implicito *Fate come se io non ci fossi.*

Legge di Mendelson
La salute del matrimonio è proporzionale alla distanza che intercorre tra gli sposi e le mamme.

Nel rapporto mamma-figlio, il sentimento *anti-Lei* raggiunge la massima intensità in **zona nuziale**. Il pericolo del matrimonio, con perdita del ruolo di femmina dominante, la rende intollerante ai suoi simboli: **confetti e bomboniere** sono aglio per la mamma-vampiro.

piange a dirotto weeps her heart out
spacciando un diluvio di tristezza passing off a flood of sorrow
per lacrime di commozione as tears of heartfelt emotion

colomba dove

abbarbicarsi put down roots
veementi vehement
gramigna weed
mammà term used, particularly in southern Italy, to emphasize
   the mamma
domarla tame/subdue her

incursioni postprandiali after-lunch raids
telefonate a raffica barrage of phone calls
agguati domenicali Sunday ambushes

L'esito della lotto The outcome of the battle

si opta he opts
timoroso frightened, worried

campeggia stands out
vistoso portafotografia flashy frame (for a photograph)
in divisa in uniform

vagheggia yearns for
illudendosi di conciliare persuading himself that he can
   reconcile
spaccato split

Condannata ad assistere alla cerimonia, la mamma **piange a dirotto, spacciando un diluvio di tristezza per lacrime di commozione**. Il fazzoletto che saluta la partenza per il viaggio di nozze ha l'innocenza di una **colomba**, ma è un minaccioso arrivederci: sa che torneranno e lei sarà lì ad aspettarli per tentare di **abbarbicarsi** a una vita che non è più sua e a una famiglia che non deve esserlo. Nelle forme più **veementi**, la mamma mostra la resistenza della **gramigna**, ottenendo il successo della convivenza: **mammà** va a vivere con gli sposi.

Nel caso in cui gli sposi riescano a **domarla**, tenendola a distanza, l'intimità dell'abitazione deve essere comunque protetta, perché anche lontana, la mamma sa come colpire: **incursioni postprandiali, telefonate a raffica, agguati domenicali,** competizione gastronomica con la nuora, corruzione della servitù.

La guerra non è ancora finita, e non finirà mai.

L'esito della lotta tra mamma e nuora dipende dalla virulenza con cui la prima ha contagiato il mammone. Nelle forme meno gravi, **si opta** per una soluzione compromissoria: pur essendosi dichiarato a un'altra donna, il figlio **timoroso** cerca d'includere la mamma nella nuova orbita sentimentale.

Quest'immagine **campeggia** sulla credenza di molti salotti italiani, incorniciata in un **vistoso portafotografie** argentato: nel ritratto più comune il figlio è al centro, spesso **in divisa**, e ai lati si vedono mamma e fidanzata, come i carabinieri di Pinocchio ma senza divisa (la mamma spesso sorride, la fidanzata qualche volta, lui mai). In questo caso, il mammone **vagheggia** una vita di coppia a tre, **illudendosi di conciliare** la felicità della fidanzata con la serenità della mamma. La verità è che egli è già **spaccato** in due, e le donne finiranno col

farlo a pezzi tearing him to pieces

duello all'ultimo sangue duel to the death (*literally*: last drop of
  blood)

trionfante triumphant

dall'aria dimessa looking unassuming/humble

podio podium

soppravvivenza survival

scarsissime extremely poor

infruttuosa futile

spacciando passing off

ipocrita hypocritical

scardinare la difesa unhinge, break down the defenses

si arricchisce is enhanced/augmented

anello ring

omomammone homosexual mamma's boy

nell'ombra *here:* underground

si traveste it's camouflaged

travestiti transvestites

assapora savors

farlo a pezzi perché il loro incontro è un **duello all'ultimo sangue** – del figlio.

La fotografia prevede uno sviluppo anche peggiore, con la mamma al centro, **trionfante**, tra i due sposi **dall'aria dimessa**. La situazione è più grave perché il danno si estende dal mammone alla coppia, appena fatta, ancora calda. Il sorriso della mamma testimonia il suo successo: non è una foto di famiglia ma la foto di un **podio**, dove lei è la vincitrice. Le possibilità di **sopravvivenza** per gli innamorati sono **scarsissime**, il destino è già inquadrato, sono già separati.

Quando la ricerca dell'altra metà si rivela **infruttuosa**, lo stato di mammismo peggiora con complicazioni che si amplificano nel tempo. Anche questa condizione è frequente ed è socialmente considerata tipica della modernità, **spacciando** una difficoltà relazionale per una conquista individuale: nel linguaggio **ipocrita** che contraddistingue i tempi, questi mammoni sono detti *single*.

Se nessuna donna ha le qualità per **scardinare la difesa** della mamma, è possibile che il mammone cerchi un maschio. La sua catena evolutiva **si arricchisce** allora di un nuovo **anello** – a volte anche di orecchini – maschio, uomo, mammone, *omomammone*. Questa condizione non sempre emerge alla luce del sole, ma resta **nell'ombra**, o **si traveste**, e per vederla chiaramente bisogna andare lungo i viali trafficati da altri **travestiti**. Nei casi di *outing*, al contrario, il mammone taglia definitivamente con l'eterosessualità e la mamma **assapora** la vittoria finale: è lei l'unica donna della sua vita. Nelle unioni omosessuali più felici, la mamma conserva il proprio bambino e ha addirittura la fortuna di trovarne un altro.

si acquieta settles down

mammagallino a play on *pappagallino* = "parakeet"
focosità fieriness, passion
fiammella tiny flame
polpastrelli fingertips

L'omomammone **si acquieta** al volere della mamma e accetta di vivere una condizione di dolce intimità, come un uccellino in gabbia, un *mammagallino*.

E così, la leggendaria **focosità** del latin lover italiano si riduce a una debole **fiammella**, che la mamma spegne tra i **polpastrelli**, come una candela.

Per il mammone è notte, si dorme.

mole bulk

sovrappeso overweight
al riguardo concerning it
fastidio annoyance

dieta dissociata a weight-loss program like the Scarsdale Diet
aborriti detested
sazia sated, satisfied

Galbani producer of cheeses and salami

impiastricciato smeared

goffi clumsy
divora quintali devours hundreds of kilos

IL PESO DELLA MAMMA NELL'OBESITÀ DEI FIGLI
Vuoi ancora un po' di carne? Vuoi ancora un po' di formaggio? Vuoi ancora un po' di pesce?

La **mole** del bambino è l'amore della mamma.

Ai suoi occhi, in nessun caso, il figlio è da considerare grasso e nemmeno **sovrappeso**, al limite robusto. Qualsiasi osservazione **al riguardo** è allontanata con **fastidio**, per mettere fine a una conversazione priva di sostanza e di peso. Idee vuote e argomenti futili, come la **dieta dissociata**, sono **aborriti** dalla mamma, dato che l'obiettivo non è dissociare la dieta ma dissociare i figli. La mamma non è mai **sazia** della fame dei bambini.

Legge di Galbani
Il volume del mammone è dato dalla mamma elevata all'ennesima pietanza.

L'obesità è amica della mamma e insieme danno vita a un'alleanza difficile da contrastare.

Il bambino clown, con il sorriso **impiastricciato** di cioccolata, indirizza il barometro della mamma sul sereno invariabile. I suoi movimenti **goffi** la rassicurano sull'impossibilità di fuga, e mentre lui **divora quintali** di carboidrati, lei se lo mangia con gli occhi.

puttino paffuto   plump little cherub
si fidelizza   becomes dependent

ciotola   bowl

chili   kilos

Anamnesi   Case history

Ingozzando   Fattening up, Stuffing [with food]
oche da cortile   farmyard geese

pende dalla parte   tilts towards
ignavi   sluggish
Obesame Mucho   *in effect:* Make me really obese, a play on the
    title of the Latin standard *Bésame Mucho* = "Kiss Me Lots"
sfama l'ingordigia   satisfies the greediness

Star   producer of ready-made pasta sauces
in bianco   play on the double meaning of *in bianco* = "pasta
    without tomato sauce" or "not getting laid"

omogeneizzato   homogenized; also used to connote commercially
    produced puréed baby food
secchiate di pappa   *baby talk:* bucketsful of baby food
seggiolone   high chair
braccati dal cucchiaio   hunted/pursued by the spoon
tentano di schivare   they try dodging

Il **puttino paffuto si fidelizza** alla mamma, trasformandosi giorno dopo giorno nella caricatura di Dumbo, incatenato alla cucina in attesa della prossima **ciotola**. La voglia di abbandonare il calore domestico diminuisce con l'aumento del peso: il mammismo cresce a **chili**.

Anamnesi di Lindt
I danni provocati dalle mamme sono direttamente proporzionali alla massa grassa dei figli.

Ingozzando i bambini come **oche da cortile**, la mamma accresce il proprio potere e i dati lo confermano: sempre più ragazzi hanno problemi di peso, il piatto della bilancia **pende dalla parte** della mamma, con i mammoni **ignavi** che cantano felici *Obesame Mucho*.

Nutrendosi del nutrimento dei figli, la mamma **sfama l'ingordigia** del proprio ego.

La disattenzione generale al riguardo è abilmente sfruttata dalla mamma che, padrona dalla cucina, alimenta il problema senza pensare minimamente a contenere le calorie. Le statistiche non solo sono ignorate, ma addirittura prese a torte in faccia.

Proporzione di Star
Più la mamma prepara il sugo, più i figli vanno in bianco.

Il pensiero della mamma si è **omogeneizzato** nell'infanzia dei figli e, attraverso **secchiate di pappa**, spera di bloccarli sul **seggiolone**. Sin dai primi anni, i bambini sono **braccati dal cucchiaio**, che **tentano di schivare** con rapidi movimenti del

tronco torso

capitolare give in

salvo poi vendicarsi col rigurgitino except of course taking their revenge by spitting up

imbocca spoon feeds

ricorrendo a vili ricatti resorting to craven blackmail

altrimenti lo licenziano or else he'll get fired

assimila assimilates

succo di colpa guilt extract, a play on *succo di polpa* = "juice from pulp"

Armeggiando Fussing around

cocente realtà bitter truth

De Cecco brand of pasta

compito task

spuntini, stuzzichini, frullatini snacks, nibbles, little fruit shakes

culoni fat buttocks

plagio moral subjugation

servizievole helpful

padroneggia keeps a tight rein on

viziandoli come foche overindulging them like seals

infatuarsi della rapitrice become infatuated with [his] kidnapper

Sto Colmo I'm Stuffed

tronco e della testa, ma alla fine devono **capitolare, salvo poi vendicarsi col rigurgitino**. La mamma **imbocca** i bambini **ricorrendo a vili ricatti**: – *Uno per la nonna se no muore; Uno per il papà* **altrimenti lo licenziano**; *Uno per lo zio oppure ti brucia i giocattoli* – e il mammone **assimila** per via orale il *succo di colpa*.

Armeggiando tra i fornelli, la mamma cerca le soluzioni per digerire la **cocente realtà**, ma l'utopia del progetto la conduce a un rapporto con il cibo sempre più inquieto.

Legge di De Cecco
L'ipernutrizione del figlio è necessaria al fabbisogno energetico della mamma.

Legge di Nestlé
Il grasso dei figli è composto da cellule di mamma.

Il **compito** della mamma è facilitato dalla ricchezza gastronomica, che mette a sua disposizione un arsenale devastante. La sua mano è sempre puntata alla gola del figlio armata di dolcini, panini, **spuntini, stuzzichini, frullatini** che finiscono tutti sui **culoni**.

Se la pressione alimentare riesce superare la soglia di resistenza, i figli diventano gradualmente vittime di **plagio**. La **servizievole** mamma **padroneggia** la situazione, **viziandoli come foche** allo zoo: è una sorta di Sindrome di Stoccolma che vede la vittima, benché costretta alla prigionia, **infatuarsi della rapitrice**, che ne ottiene l'amore grazie alla corruzione del cibo. Vista la quantità di piatti inflitti, più che *Sindrome di Stoccolma*, si direbbe *Sindrome di* **Sto Colmo**.

Barilla   producer of pasta, bread and cookies
ciccia   flabby tummies

virtuosismo   virtuosity, stroke of genius
sdraia   flattens

ferirsi   hurt themselves

costituisse   represented
alletta...allatta   a play on *alletta* = "confine to bed" and *allatta* =
   "breast-feed"
premurosa   overattentive, overindulging
ne annienta   destroys any of
pigrizia   laziness

Nesquik   instant chocolate drink

fucilante   like a sound of shots fired off
colpi ravvicinati   shots fired at close range

intrisa   filled
assonnati   sleepy

Legge di <u>Barilla</u>
Dove c'è mamma, c'è <u>ciccia</u>.

Tra tutti i vizi, la prima colazione a letto è un **virtuosismo** della mamma, un colpo di classe che **sdraia** l'avversario.

La mamma apprensiva, in particolare, timorosa che i figli possano **ferirsi** uscendo dal lettino, fa di tutto perché assumano il vizio di fare colazione sotto le coperte. È come se la colazione a letto **costituisse** un prolungamento del periodo di allattamento: più li **alletta**, più li **allatta**.

Ogni mattina la mamma **premurosa ne annienta** la volontà con l'aroma del caffelatte, trionfando sulla loro **pigrizia**.

Legge di <u>Nesquik</u>
La condizione di mammone è data dal rapporto tra colazioni in cucina e colazioni a letto.

La mamma è sempre preoccupata dell'iponutrizione del figlio: *Hai fame? Hai mangiato? Ti preparo qualcosa?*

Le domande sono formulate a gruppi di tre o multipli di tre, in modo rapido e meccanico. Il tono è **fucilante**, a ripetizione: non sono domande, sono **colpi ravvicinati** che non danno possibilità di reazione.

Ore otto del mattino circa. Quando la casa è ancora **intrisa** dell'aroma del caffè, e i figli **assonnati** hanno la guardia dello stomaco bassa, la mamma gioca d'anticipo puntando sul fattore sorpresa: *Cosa vuoi per cena? Torni per cena? Faccio il minestrone?*

frangente instance
astuzia cunning
ingoiare swallow
conato retching
mette al tappeto decks (*literally*: lays out on the carpet)
arrendendosi surrendering

Giovanni Rana founder and patriarch of the Rana Pasta Company

Buitoni manufacturer of pastas and ready-made sauces
fatto fuori taken out (as in "killed")

nido nest

treccia di bufala twisted buffalo-milk mozzarella cheese
L'esca The bait
loda sings the praises of
impareggiabili incomparable
autodafé auto-da-fé, ritual of public penance

comunità di recupero rehabilitation center

affannoso exhausting

il tragitto si tramuta the journey turns into
cordone [umbilical] cord
cannellone ombelicale play on *cordone ombelicale* = "umbilical
  cord" and *cannellone* = "baked pasta dish"

In questo **frangente**, la mamma mostra tutta la sua **astuzia**: nella terza domanda l'offerta del cibo prevede un piatto che sa non essere gradito, ma che vuole far **ingoiare** lo stesso. L'effetto **conato**, provocato dall'idea del cibo a quell'ora, **mette al tappeto** i figli, che accettano **arrendendosi** senza condizioni.

Legge di <u>Giovanni Rana</u>
Il mammone è fatto in casa.

Corollario di <u>Buitoni</u>
Il mammone fatto in casa è un uomo <u>fatto fuori</u>.

Quando il mammone riesce a lasciare il **nido**, la vera mamma riesce comunque a tenerlo legato: con uno spaghetto, una fila di salsicce, una **treccia di bufala**. **L'esca** è sempre appetitosa e la nostalgia dei piatti della mamma fa cadere il mammone in trappola. Il figlio che **loda** le ricette della genitrice cuoca, giudicandole **impareggiabili**, recita involontariamente un **autodafé** che tradisce un grande bisogno d'aiuto, un sostegno che è in grado di dargli solo una **comunità di recupero**.

Su questo punto molto debole, la mamma concentra gran parte dei propri sforzi per riattirare il figlio a sé, oppure per avvicinarsi a lui, proponendosi in un **affannoso** servizio di catering. Comportandosi come il dietologo della donna cannone, la mamma mette a punto un programma alimentare per i piccoli trentasettenni iponutriti: da una casa all'altra, **il tragitto si tramuta** in un lungo **cordone** di cibo, un infinito **cannellone ombelicale**.

Anche quando le distanze separano mamma e figlio in

Pomì brand of canned or puréed tomatoes

passato play on the double meaning of *passato* = "puréed" or "outdated"

diverrà will eventually become

terminali più ricorrenti most often the root cause

varca la soglia crosses the threshold

il dado è tratto the dice is thrown, a play on *dado* = "bouillon cube" or "dice"

Scavolini manufacturer of kitchen cabinets and furnishings

lunghe lontananze silenziose, la principale preoccupazione della mamma riguarda sempre il cibo. Il ritorno del figlio è sempre contraddistinto dalle stesse triplette di domande, come se il tempo non fosse mai passato, come se il bambino non fosse mai cresciuto: *Mangi abbastanza? Oggi hai mangiato? Ti cucino una bistecca con l'uovo?*

Legge di Campbell e Pomì
Il sugo di pomodoro della mamma non è mai passato.

Qualunque sia la strategia, il mammone svilupperà sempre un rapporto disequilibrato con il cibo, che **diverrà** uno dei **terminali più ricorrenti** delle sue ansie. Che ne abbia avuto in eccesso o in difetto, il suo atteggiamento sarà sempre viziato da un sentimento di amore e di odio. Quando la mamma **varca la soglia** della cucina, **il dado è tratto**.

Osservazione di Scavolini
La mamma è la più amata dalle cucine.

l'edificio concettuale theoretical construction
fondamenta inamovibili fixed/unshakable foundations
accidentata superficie stradale rough road surface

marciapiedi sidewalks

auspica l'avvento hopes for the coming
autoimmobilismo play on *automobilismo* = "driving, motor
    racing" and *immobilismo* = "inactivity"

intimano imply
Sitz!; Platz! *German*: orders for dogs to sit and stay (used often
    in Italy)

qualora si fosse inopinatamente verificato in case it should
    unexpectedly take place

è dettato dal timore is determined by the fear

INCOMPATIBILITÀ DELLA MAMMA CON IL PRINCIPIO DI MOTO
E di auto

Se l'**edificio concettuale** della mamma è costruito su **fondamenta inamovibili**, la sua posizione è ancora più statica sull'**accidentata superficie stradale**. Conservazione e immutabilità sono i punti fermi della sua vita e vuole che stiano fermi anche i figli lungo strade e **marciapiedi**.

Il futuro della mamma è antifuturista, il manifesto del mammismo **auspica l'avvento** dell'*autoimmobilismo*.

Il suo vocabolario è chiaro, a cominciare dal quinto Comammamento – *Non allontanarti* – tutte le più reiterate raccomandazioni **intimano** ai figli di non muoversi: *Fermo!; Stai lì!; Aspettami qui!; Dammi la mano;* **Sitz!; Platz!**

Altrettanto frequenti sono le frasi che tendono a ridurre il distacco, **qualora si fosse inopinatamente verificato**: *Vieni subito qui!*

L'imperativo *Non correre!* sembra motivato dalla preoccupazione per l'integrità dei figli, ma **è dettato dal timore** che possano fuggire: tutte le strade che portano lontano sono pericolose.

Variante del Rigoletto, poco allegra, non andante
La mamma è immobile.

Il concetto di moto, così antipatico alla mamma, non è ostacolato solo a parole, ma anche con azioni sistematiche.

In tenera età At a very early age
box playpen
carcere minorile juvenile home
stivaletto malese type of boot once used as a form of torture

l'avvertimento è di stampo mafioso it's a Mafia-like warning
gambizzati knee-capped
velleità vain ambitions
calza alla perfezione perfectly fits
celeberrimi notorious
occhietti buckles
cinghietta strap
piaghetta small sores

barbarie del guinzaglio the barbaric practices of the leash (for kids)

pattini, monopattini skates, scooters
assecondare give in to
avviandoli sending them off
iettatorio jinxed
capitombolo tumble
immancabile inevitable
spavento sia stato tale da togliere loro il vizio di riprovarci
  the scare was so bad as to extinguish the desire to try it again
parte il provvedimento di sequestro del mezzo the action for confiscation of the vehicle is set in motion

moto motorbike
Motorino small 50cc motorbike

In tenera età, i bimbi sono rinchiusi nella piccola Alcatraz del **box** o immobilizzati sulla torre del seggiolone; poi subiscono le scarpine correttive – come il **carcere minorile** – tortura ispirata allo **stivaletto malese**; quando gli scarponcini sono neri, **l'avvertimento è di stampo mafioso**: gli innocenti vengono **gambizzati** se manifesteranno ancora la **velleità** di allontanarsi; lo stesso discorso **calza alla perfezione** per i **celeberrimi** sandali con gli **occhietti**, modello estivo – da colonia penale – noto a generazioni di figli cresciuti, ma che ricordano il modo in cui la mamma stringeva loro la **cinghietta** sul dorso del piede, fino alla comparsa della **piaghetta**.

Censuriamo ma non dimentichiamo la **barbarie del guinzaglio**.

Quando i bimbi crescono, il mondo dell'infanzia e dell'adolescenza è caratterizzato dal divertimento a rotelle: **pattini**, **monopattini**, skateboard, biciclette costringono la mamma ad **assecondare** i loro desideri, **avviandoli** al gioco con uno **iettatorio** *Vai piano che cadi!* seguito da inevitabile caduta. Dopo il **capitombolo**, la mamma li rimprovera con l'**immancabile** *Te l'avevo detto!* nascondendo una segreta soddisfazione: spera che lo **spavento sia stato tale da togliere loro il vizio di riprovarci**. Nelle forme acute e punitive, **parte il provvedimento di sequestro del mezzo** con effetto immediato.

Legge di Rollerblade
Chi si ferma con la mamma è perduto.

L'avversione al concetto di moto si accende in tutto il suo fragore quando *moto* significa due ruote + motore.

Nella *Questione del Motorino*, la vita della mamma e quella

cedere il passo give the right of way
crocevia crossroads

fungono da ausiliari del traffico act as traffic cops

Benelli e Garelli manufacturers of motorbikes and *motorini*
incidente al motorino play on two meanings of *incidente:*
  "accident of" or "being directly related to" the *motorino*

trattative negotiations
**susseguirsi di rotture, riavvicinamenti, pianti, scioperi della
  fame, rappresaglie e rivendicazioni** succession of
  breakdowns, reconciliations, crying fits, hunger strikes,
  reprisals, and petitions
incatenandosi al cancello chaining themselves to the front gate
inattuabili unfeasible
investito assuming

investito e travolto run over and dragged

braccio di ferro arm wrestling, used figuratively to mean a final
  one-on-one trial of strength
garanzie guarantees

tregua armata armed truce

dei figli procedono in direzione contraria e si bloccano l'una davanti all'altra, senza che nessuno mostri l'intenzione di **cedere il passo**. La Questione del Motorino è un **crocevia** inevitabile, un problema che si presenta puntuale alla porta del garage al compimento del quattordicesimo anno di età di qualsiasi figlio, un caso nazionale.

Le forze in gioco nella Questione del Motorino sono opposte: i figli con il desiderio di conquista, le mamme con la paura della perdita, mentre i padri **fungono da ausiliari del traffico**.

In senso figurato, il motorino è sempre oggetto di scontro.

Legge di *Benelli e Garelli*
La linea di condotta della mamma è incidente al motorino.

Le **trattative** possono trascinarsi per mesi, con un **susseguirsi di rotture, riavvicinamenti, pianti, scioperi della fame, rappresaglie e rivendicazioni**. I figli minacciano di abbandonare lo studio oppure fanno ostruzionismo **incatenandosi al cancello** di casa; la mamma rilancia la proposta ciclistica o finge di arrendersi offrendo soluzioni **inattuabili**: *Ti compro il motorino però non lo usi*; il papà, **investito** del ruolo di moderatore, viene **investito e travolto** dalla situazione.

Il **braccio di ferro** ha un esito variabile, in funzione delle forze in gioco, ma spesso la mamma deve cedere, anche se ottiene numerose **garanzie**: la questione resta aperta, come in una **tregua armata**, il motorino può essere sequestrato, venduto o fatto esplodere da un momento all'altro.

tubo di scappamento   exhaust pipe; *here:* a means of escape
  (*scappare* = "escape")
mammitta   play on *marmitta* = "muffler"

Ducati   manufacturer of high-performance motorbikes
più vigile del vigile   more alert than the traffic policemen

Gli adolescenti cercano la libertà a bordo del motorino, ma non sanno che in fondo al **tubo di scappamento** c'è la *mammitta*.

Considerazione di Ducati
La mamma è più vigile del vigile.

dà i numeri is losing it (*literally:* gives off numbers)

facciamo i conti we'll get even

EFFETTI DELLA MAMMA SUL SISTEMA ECONOMICO

Mia mamma <u>dà i numeri</u>!
Pitagora, 11 anni

A casa <u>facciamo i conti</u>!
Mamma di Pitagora

Io confonde con she mixes/muddles it up with
Pippo Baudo popular TV personality and performer since the
    1970s
V secolo a.C. the fifth century B.C. (avanti-Christo)
strateghi del potere strategists of power, movers and shakers

indebolire to weaken

Sun-Tzu sixth-century-B.C. Chinese general, military strategist, and
    author of the highly influential *The Art of War*
Sconfiggere il nemico Defeat the enemy

va sempre assegno play on *assegno* = "check" and *a segno* = "on
    target"

Coin department store chain

agisca reacts
beni voluttuari nonessential/luxury items

DAL PROIBIZIONISMO ALL'IPERCONSUMISMO: IL MAMMOPOLIO
Dal supermarket al supermarketing

La mamma non conosce Sun-Tzu e, nel caso in cui ne abbia sentito parlare, **lo confonde con** il titolo di una vecchia canzone di **Pippo Baudo**. Tuttavia, alcuni suoi comportamenti sembrano ispirarsi al celebre trattato *L'arte della guerra*, scritto nel **V secolo a.C.** e diventato un libro di culto per gli **strateghi del potere**.

In quest'opera, si evidenzia come le possibilità di predominio sull'avversario siano tanto maggiori quanto più si riesce a **indebolire**, ma ancor meglio a controllare, la sua economia. Secondo il generale **Sun-Tzu**, non è necessario lottare: *Sconfiggere il nemico senza combattere è la massima abilità.*

Legge finanziaria della mamma
La mamma va sempre assegno.

Osservazione di Coin sull'acquisto paterno
Era meglio quell'altro.

Ma è soprattutto il mammone a subire una pressione costante: sia che **agisca** applicando l'embargo, sia che partecipi all'acquisto di **beni voluttuari**, la mamma soffoca le sue capacità, cercando di mantenere il controllo della spesa. Anche

mancia settimanale weekly allowance
pedinata followed, shadowed

presenziare all'acquisto be present at the purchasing
dissuaderlo dissuade him
cretinate idiocies

Ti hanno fregato di nuovo! They screwed you again!

spiccioli small change

Nell'attuale società In today's society
meno netta less clear-cut
si cimentano try their hand

sistema vestibolare tra gli scaffali system of organizing goods
    on the shelves
incorrano nell'errore keep on making the same mistake
reperimento finding, tracking down
ammorbidente fabric softener
ictus a stroke
depositaria del sapere domestico storehouse of household wisdom

avvisata forewarned

quando il figlio raggiunge la pseudoemancipazione grazie alla **mancia settimanale**, ogni sua iniziativa autonoma è **pedinata**.

La mamma cerca nell'ordine: A) d'impedire che effettui acquisti per conto suo; B) se non riesce nel punto A cerca di **presenziare all'acquisto**; C) se non riesce nel punto B cerca di **dissuaderlo** dal fare altre **cretinate** contestando l'acquisto fatto: *Ma che hai comprato?; Lo vedi che sbagli la misura?; Lo vedi che questo non è buono?; Lo vedi? **Ti hanno fregato di nuovo!***

Il potere economico della mamma cresce quindi secondo due direttrici: una indirizzata a controllare i grandi capitali, l'altra rivolta all'amministrazione degli **spiccioli**.

Equazione di Forbes
La mamma sta al denaro come il cartello «Attenti al cane» sta al cancello.

Nell'attuale società, si è registrato un aumento di single e una divisione **meno netta** dei ruoli all'interno della famiglia. Di conseguenza, persone diverse dalla mamma **si cimentano** con le spese ordinarie, ma pensare che questo cambiamento destabilizzi il suo potere è pura fantasia: in qualunque caso, è sempre la mamma ad avere l'ultima parola. L'incapacità di distinguere il sale grosso dal sale fino, o le disfunzioni del **sistema vestibolare tra gli scaffali** del supermercato, fanno in modo che i figli **incorrano nell'errore** di richiedere il suo aiuto (ancora oggi la scelta dello yogurt o il **reperimento** dell'**ammorbidente** è per molti causa di **ictus**).

La **depositaria del sapere domestico** si precipita subito, immancabilmente accompagnata dal rimprovero di non essere stata **avvisata** in tempo.

tesoriere   treasurer

Upim   chain of discount department stores
non fa sconti   doesn't mark down/give discounts; *in effect:* she
    doesn't take anything off

disagio   difficulty, uneasiness
surgelato   frozen foods
scioccante   harrowing, traumatic
scientemente architettata   skillfully orchestrated
conduce   leads, conducts

amplifica   intensifies, heightens
si distrae   is sidetracked
di soppiatto   sneakily
l'orecchio teso   [her] ear trained on

smarrito   lost and forlorn
soccorso   rescued
altoparlante   loudspeaker

accorrere   rush to the scene
per ricongiungersi   in order to be reunited
brutto spavento   nasty scare

lo sgrida   scolds him
sfuggito   slipped out

Legge tributaria   Fiscal law
una rata da pagare, senza estinzione del debito   [interest-only]
    installment to be paid, without ever paying off the debt

Ogni figlio è il tesoro della mamma perché la mamma sarà sempre il **tesoriere**.

Legge di Upim
La mamma non fa sconti.

Il **disagio** provato da alcuni adulti nel supermercato può essere originato dal *Trauma da* **surgelato**, un'esperienza **scioccante** vissuta da numerosi bambini, **scientemente architettata** dalla mamma stessa. Il piano è semplice: la mamma **conduce** il bambino in una zona in cui la concentrazione di clienti è maggiore, possibilmente vicino al banco dei surgelati perché il freddo **amplifica** la sensazione di paura. Non appena il bambino **si distrae**, lei si allontana **di soppiatto** per nascondersi dietro uno scaffale, dove attende con **l'orecchio teso** l'esplosione in lacrime del piccolo. Il minore, disperato e **smarrito**, è subito **soccorso** dai presenti e accompagnato alle casse da cui l'**altoparlante** diffonde il celebre annuncio: *Il bambino Lorenzo attende la mamma alla cassa otto.*

A quel punto, alla mamma non resta che **accorrere**, fingendosi preoccupata, **per ricongiungersi** al figlio che le ha fatto prendere un **brutto spavento**. A lei.

La diabolica mamma **lo sgrida**, facendolo sentire colpevole di essere **sfuggito** al suo controllo e ordinandogli di starle vicino, sempre. Da quel momento, nei supermercati il figlio si sentirà tranquillo solo in sua compagnia.

Legge tributaria della mamma
La mamma è una rata da pagare, senza estinzione del debito.

sostanzioso compenso substantial reward
completi gessati pin-striped suits
bretelle suspenders
straparlano talk and talk
flussi, listini fluctuations, price indices

borsellino play on *borsa* = "stock market" and *borsellino* = "purse"
oscilla oscillates
rincaro increase in the price
crollo collapse
cetriolo cucumber
non rendono più come una volta play on not earning as much *and* not being able to buy as many
contrattazioni bargaining
3X2 three for the price of two
mercati rionali local markets
chiude sempre la bilancia in attivo she always closes with a positive balance sheet
crollano slump, collapse
azioni play on *azioni* = "stocks/shares" and *azioni* = "actions"

improntato imprinted
latifondista borbonica reactionary large landowner
impone imposes
tassativi adamant
monito warning
dissipare waste
Scassaforte play on *cassaforte* = "strongbox" and *scassare* = "to wreck/smash"

La mamma si eleva in questo caso da semplice operatrice a consulente d'acquisto, un broker che vende la conoscenza del mercato, ricevendo un **sostanzioso compenso**: il potere.

Il cuore della finanza non è fatto di **completi gessati** e di **bretelle** indossati da manager che **straparlano** di trend, **flussi, listini** con un adrenalinico vocabolario anglomilanese. Il destino dei soldi è nelle mani di *Mamma Affari*.

Il **borsellino** di Mamma Affari **oscilla** tra il **rincaro** delle pere, il **crollo** dei fagiolini, il boom del **cetriolo** e la crescita dei pomodori, che **non rendono più come una volta**. Con abili **contrattazioni**, analisi attente del **3X2** e dei **mercati rionali, chiude sempre la bilancia in attivo**.

Più la mamma compra, più i figli pagano, con gli interessi.

Proporzione di Dow Jones
Se i figli crollano, le azioni della mamma salgono.

Anche nel mondo economico, si distinguono due modelli contrapposti: la *old economy* delle Mamme Autoritarie e la *new economy* propria di quelle più attuali. Il primo, **improntato** a una mentalità **latifondista borbonica**, fa assumere alla mamma un regime di austerity che **impone** una continua riduzione dei consumi. Gli ordini sono **tassativi** e il **monito** a non comprare, a non consumare, a non spendere, a non **dissipare** fa di questa mamma una *Scassaforte*.

La mamma della *new economy* è diversa e si mostra favorevole alla circolazione monetaria, purché sia lei a mantenerne il controllo.

Legge del mammopolio economico
È l'offerta che crea la domanda, è la mamma che crea l'offerta.

SPEREQUAZIONE, PSICOANALISI E FESTE IN MASCHERA
INEQUALITY, PSYCHOANALYSIS, AND COSTUME
PARTIES
lascia il segno leaves a scar, a play on Zorro's mark

noioso stilare boring to draw up

citarne una che trae mention one that garners
benefici e guadagni benefits and revenues

quintali di cachemire hundreds of tons of cashmere

spauriti frightened
professori di grido most fashionable specialists of the moment
    (in Italy, a specialist are referred to as *Professore*)

affidare entrust
quesiti demenziali insane queries

Bettelheim Bruno Bettelheim (1903–1990), Austrian-born
    American child psychologist and author

SPEREQUAZIONE, PSICOANALISI E FESTE IN MASCHERA
Come e perché il costume di Zorro lascia il segno

Sarebbe inutile e **noioso stilare** un elenco delle categorie professionali penalizzate o favorite dalla mamma, ma è il caso di **citarne una che trae** dal mammismo **benefici e guadagni** che vanno oltre i propri meriti: gli psicoanalisti.

Direttamente o indirettamente, la mamma ha reso centinaia di questi professionisti proprietari di ville e appartamenti, barche, auto sportive, **quintali di cachemire**.

Il successo sociale della terapia e il gusto di potersi esibire affermando: *Il mio analista mi ha detto che...* ha convinto molte mamme a trascinare poveri bimbi **spauriti** negli studi dei **professori di grido**, sicure di risolvere i problemi di cui sono la causa, e causandone molti altri.

È tipico della contraddizione di certe mamme provocare traumi per poi **affidare** al medico il compito di risolverli, ponendogli **quesiti demenziali**: *Dottore, mio figlio di quattro anni mi ha distrutto quattro cellulari, e pensare che gliene ho comprato uno nuovo anche la settimana scorsa! E poi lo chiamo tutte le sere alle nove per dargli la buonanotte! Che devo fare?*

Brutto affare per i piccoli, ottimi affari per il dottore.

Osservazione di Bettelheim
La mamma fa entrare i bambini in analisi, ma poi non li fa uscire.

pregiato ciliegio furniture made of high-quality cherry wood

adagiato comfortably settled
sfogliando leafing through
sbiadita faded

di colpo! all of a sudden!

musetto stravolto dalla vergogna little face stricken with shame
singhiozzante come *Cenerentola* sobbing like Cinderella
balbettante stammering
Tartagnan play on D'Artagnan (the fourth Musketeer) and
  tartagliare = "to stutter"

Turba Disturbance
l'imbarazzo patito the humiliation endured
nell'instaurazione in establishing

lieve o acuta slight or acute

si sente a disagio gets upset

isolandosi dal contesto removing himself from the situation
mitigata mitigated

Nell'iter psicoanalitico del mammone, superate le tappe freudiane delle fasi *orale, anale* e *genitale*, si arriva alla zona grigia che comprende i ricordi della fase *carnevale*.

Dopo decine di ore spese – e migliaia di euro guadagnate – in una stanza arredata con mobili di **pregiato ciliegio**, **adagiato** su una poltrona in morbida pelle di paziente, l'analista, **sfogliando** il subconscio pagina dopo pagina, trova la foto **sbiadita** di una festa in maschera: la seduta psicoanalitica si alza in piedi, **di colpo!**

Ecco apparire, ancora viva, l'immagine di un infante mascherato, con il **musetto stravolto dalla vergogna**, nelle sembianze del *Ragno Uomo*, **singhiozzante come *Cenerentola***, **balbettante** come *Tartagnan*.

È il ricordo del giorno in cui la mamma fece la festa al bambino.

Riportando al presente il ritratto del bimbo in costume, il medico individua la *Turba da festa in maschera*, uno shock che inibisce l'attività sociale del mammone, perché **l'imbarazzo patito** è causa di difficoltà **nell'instaurazione** di normali rapporti, anche in età adulta.

La Turba da festa in maschera si differenzia secondo due livelli di gravità, **lieve o acuta**, e la pericolosità del problema è proporzionale all'età.

<u>Turba lieve:</u> il bambino è stato invitato a una festa in cui tutti sono mascherati tranne lui; il piccolo **si sente a disagio** perché non riesce a essere parte del gruppo e del gioco, **isolandosi dal contesto**.

La forma di alienazione provocata dalla diversità è **mitigata** dal fatto che è comunque il bambino non mascherato a rientrare nella normalità, mentre gli altri, pur in maggioranza, sono in una condizione anormale.

conformi alla regola in keeping with the norm
comitiva group
viene deriso, schernito e umiliato he gets teased, mocked and humiliated
gli fanno la pipì addosso they pee on him
lo mordono they bite him

pianto incompreso a crying fit that goes completely misunderstood

esposizione al ridicolo exposure to ridicule
provocherà will cause
ai limiti dell'autismo bordering on autism
dalla mano sudato with sweaty hands
a fare figure di merda end up looking like a jerk

giace in un baule lying in a trunk

pagliacci del circo circus clowns
innocua coccinella innocuous ladybug
riecheggia resonates again and again
ripropone brings back again

<u>Turba acuta:</u> il bambino è l'unico a essersi mascherato, mentre tutti sono vestiti normalmente. In questa situazione, lui è l'eccezione mentre gli altri sono **conformi alla regola.** Il bambino subisce la propria diversità e la **comitiva,** perché appena fa il suo ingresso **viene deriso, schernito e umiliato:** se è un albero **gli fanno la pipì addosso,** se è un frutto **lo mordono,** se è un supereroe lo fanno volare dalla finestra. Quando la mamma torna a prenderlo e gli chiede sorridente: *Ti sei divertito?,* lui dà inizio a un **pianto incompreso** che può durare giorni, mesi, anni.

Da quel giorno, il timore dell'**esposizione al ridicolo** lo accompagnerà ovunque e **provocherà** problemi relazionali patologici, **ai limiti dell'autismo.** Nel passato dell'adulto **dalla mano sudata,** sempre pronto **a fare figure di merda** – soprattutto in occasione di feste e riunioni di amici – probabilmente c'è un piccolo costume da Zorro, mai dimenticato, che **giace in un baule.** E che continua a lasciare il segno.

Non c'è da sorprendersi se in circostanze insospettabili, certi adulti cominciano incomprensibilmente a piangere: all'ingresso dei **pagliacci del circo,** davanti a un film di pirati, all'arrivo di un'**innocua coccinella.** È il dramma che **riecheggia** dall'inconscio, che **ripropone** agli ex bambini la tragica maschera della loro infanzia.

Di fronte a questi mammoni, lo psicoanalista può fare poco, ma può guadagnare molto: i compensi saranno gestiti da sua moglie che li spenderà per suo figlio, magari comprandogli un bellissimo costume di carnevale.

ESCATOLOGICO ESCHATOLOGICAL (having to do with a
belief concerning death, the end of the world, or the ultimate
destiny of mankind)
chi si arrenderà prima who will be the first to give in

si agita whirls around

peccato originale original sin

capo del filo the start of the thread
infila is threaded
inesauribile inexhaustible
collana di contraddizioni play on the dual meaning of *collana* =
"series" or "necklace of contradictions"
antinomica antinomic (a law that contradicts itself)
delimitato dal controsenso circumscribed by contradictions
L'invariabilità The tenacity
congela freezes
perenne perpetual

Assioma Axiom
Findus manufacturer of frozen foods
data di scadenza expiration/expiry date

e tale quindi da non poter eliderlo and so it is this way so as not
to cancel each other out
si deduce one deducts

IL DUBBIO ESCATOLOGICO
Conclusioni: chi si arrenderà prima, l'uomo o la mammina?

La mamma **si agita** affinché niente e nessuno si muova.

La resistenza che oppone alla crescita dei figli costituisce il **peccato originale,** il vizio in base al quale giudica insostenibile qualsiasi forma di sviluppo.

L'assurdità di questo principio diventa il **capo del filo** su cui, perla dopo perla, **infila un'inesauribile collana di contraddizioni.**

La posizione esistenziale della mamma è sempre **antinomica** e le sue azioni non escono mai dal perimetro **delimitato dal controsenso. L'invariabilità** del suo comportamento **congela** ogni possibile soluzione al **perenne** contrasto tra mamma e buon senso.

Assioma di Findus
La mamma tende alla conservazione senza nessuna data di scadenza.

Nel rapporto fisico tra mamma e tempo, si è evidenziato come il fattore mamma M è sempre inferiore al valore del tempo T – altrimenti il mondo si fermerebbe – **e tale quindi da non poter eliderlo.** Viceversa, **si deduce** che T è maggiore di M e che T tende a ridurre M a zero, ma senza riuscirci in virtù

farla tacere to get her to keep quiet
al massimo at the most

di remare contro rowing against [the flow]

Allo stato attuale As things are now

sopraffare overwhelm
ridurla all'inerzia reduce her to inertia
3 periodico 3 as a recurring decimal
prezzemolo parsley

forza di volontà willpower

scatenato set off
esacerbato exacerbated

zavorra ballast, dead weight
L'incertezza The uncertainty

della Prima legge sulla termodinamica: *La mamma è sempre la mamma*, e non può essere eliminata, al limite è possibile **farla tacere** per quindici minuti, venti **al massimo**.

Ugualmente, è stato dimostrato come l'energia prodotta da M si trasformi tutta in calore e non in lavoro.

A questo punto, ci si domanda come andrà a finire. È qui che entra in gioco l'escatologia, la scienza del destino ultimo delle cose, chiedendo chi si stancherà prima: il tempo di andare avanti o la mamma **di remare contro**?

Allo stato attuale, il mondo si presenta come un sistema le cui caratteristiche sono: velocità, cambiamento e complessità, elementi che sembrerebbero poter **sopraffare** la mamma e **ridurla all'inerzia**, in realtà ciò non è possibile. La sua presenza non si può cancellare, è matematicamente indefinita come il **3 periodico** e insidiosa come il **prezzemolo** tra i denti.

Eppure, se con il tempo aumentano la velocità, le trasformazioni e lo sviluppo, è necessario che la mamma aumenti la propria capacità di resistere.

E così è.

Per spiegare la sua resistenza, bisogna considerare il valore del coefficiente di **forza di volontà**, che la mamma esprime in formato famiglia.

La mamma, non solo è sempre la mamma, ma *vuole* essere sempre la mamma.

Il conflitto **scatenato** dalla mamma nei confronti dello sviluppo biologico, ed **esacerbato** dai cambiamenti prodotti dalla modernità, pare non trovare un punto di risoluzione.

Il progresso è destinato a procedere a passo d'uomo, rallentato dalla **zavorra** mamma.

L'incertezza riguardo al rapporto tra mamma e mondo corrisponde all'indefinizione che risiede nel *Principio di*

Heisenberg Werner Heisenberg (1901–1976), Nobel prize-winning German physicist best known for his uncertainty principle: the more precisely the position of a particle is determined, the less precisely its momentum is known

sicurezza ingenua e sfrontata naïve and brazen confidence
senza accorgersene without even noticing
brasato pot roast

inossidabile figura rust-proof presence

Stanlio In Italian, the comedians Laurel and Hardy are called *Stanlio e Olio* (Stanley and Ollie)
D'altronde On the other hand
a riassumere who sums up
inquietanti rassicurazioni unnerving assurances
ribadisce impresses on, repeats

indeterminazione di **Heisenberg,** in base al quale non si può determinare con esattezza l'entità dei valori sviluppati dall'energia della mamma e dal tempo.

L'obiettivo della mamma è creare un'enclave esistenziale all'interno della vita stessa.

Nello spazio che separa il suo pensiero da ciò che le sta intorno, la mamma trova un limbo in cui riesce a dimenticare i rischi e i pericoli.

L'apparente assenza di minacce le dà una **sicurezza ingenua e sfrontata:** attraversa uragani e rivoluzioni **senza accorgersene,** poiché è sempre occupata nella preparazione del **brasato.** La mamma è immersa nella storia ma impermeabile agli eventi, la sua **inossidabile figura** resiste a qualsiasi catastrofe per il semplice fatto che non la nota come Mr. Magoo, che non capisce come **Stanlio,** che non l'aveva sentita a causa del rubinetto dell'acqua aperto.

D'altronde, è lei stessa **a riassumere** l'essenza del proprio pensiero nelle **inquietanti rassicurazioni** che **ribadisce** al figlio mammone: *Non ti preoccupare, la mamma è sempre qui con te.*

La mamma è un bene incurabile.

FABRIZIO BLINI

MAMMA MIA!

Grazie a Giovanna senza la quale questo libro non sarebbe mai nato, e grazie soprattutto ad Ambra senza la quale non sarebbe mai cresciuto e diventato un libro.

Mamma mia!

A Conversation with

Fabrizio Blini

author of

Mamma mia!

conducted by
Patrizia Todaro and Paola Goggioli

Recorded in December 2008
at Studio Colosseo, Rome

Transcribed and edited by
Lisa R. Tucci
Art & Media Communications, llc

pubblicitario ad man
trapiantato transplanted
saggio account, essay
edito published
carrellata round-up
castranti castrating
depotenziati unempowered

sviluppo development

iperprotettiva hyperprotective

chioccia the mother hen
badilate *here:* heaps, mounds
abbastanza comune fairly common

---

* *Numbers near the left-hand margins on the opposite pages denote*
corresponding track numbers on the interview CD.

① *Siamo con Fabrizio Blini,* **pubblicitario***, Milanese* **trapiantato** *a Roma, autore del* **saggio** *"Mamma mia!", che è anche il suo primo libro,* **edito** *da Baldini Castoldi e Dalai. E' una* **carrellata** *di tipiche figure di mamme, come si diceva una volta* **"castranti"** *e una parallela fila di figli un po'* **'depotenziati'.**

– *Fabrizio Blini, il sottotitolo del suo libro è* La figura della mamma come deterrente nello **sviluppo** culturale, sociale ed economico dell'Italia moderna. *Lei ha disegnato nel suo libro vari profili di mamma. Quale di questi corrisponda alla Sua madre?*

– Mia madre, mia mamma, anzi, non mia madre perché la differenza tra mamma e madre è fondamentale – mia mamma è una mamma **iperprotettiva** con tendenze vittimistiche. Quindi è una mamma che associa questo senso di essere **chioccia,** di essere protettiva con un'educazione fatta di **badilate** di sensi di colpa di cui ha nutrito sia me che mio fratello; ma vedo che il fenomeno è **abbastanza comune** in Italia.

② – *Che reazione ha avuto Sua madre quando ha visto il libro – lo ha letto?*

temendo fearing [the worst]

recitando citing

mettere le mani avanti *here:* cover myself (*literally:* put out my hands first)

ha fatto finta pretended

si è risentita it touched [a nerve]

argomento topic

Innanzitutto To start with

una volta per tutti once and for all

costituisca it becomes

catartica cathartic

talmente so

sotto gli occhi di tutti out in the open, obvious to all

affrontato faced it

– Mia madre lo ha letto. Io, **temendo** e conoscendo ovviamente mia mamma molto bene, le ho dedicato il libro, **recitando** precisamente *"A mia mamma, prima che si offenda"* in modo che ho tentato di **'mettere le mani avanti'** in questo modo. Lei **ha fatto finta** di essersi divertita, ne sono sicuro, perché da una parte ha riso, dall'altra ha capito o ha fatto finta di non capire perché quando...per esempio mi ha fatto la stessa domanda che mi ha fatta Lei all'inizio, chiedendomi, *"Ma...io, che mamma sarei di queste?"* E io gliel'ho detto, *"Guarda, secondo me, tu sei una Mamma Iperprotettiva con tendenze vittimistiche o anche una Mamma Vittima con tendenze iperprotettive, la cosa è più o meno la stessa."* E lei ha risposto, *"Io?"* Per cui ha fatto finta di non capire certe cose; certe cose proprio le ha rifiutate, però dice di essersi divertita, in verità sono certo che un po' **si è risentita** anche lei.

③ – *E' Direttore Creativo di un'agenzia di pubblicità, ed è al suo primo saggio di* **argomento** *sociologico. Dunque, da pubblicitario a scrittore, ci racconta com'è andata, per favore?*

– Ma i motivi per cui ho scritto questo libro sono tanti. **Innanzitutto** io ho una mamma. E allora, non potevo non scrivere, essendo italiano, di un argomento come 'il mammismo' che è un fenomeno che è sotto gli occhi di tutti ma che nessuno riconosce. Allora il motivo principale per cui ho scritto questo libro è mettere nero su bianco, codificare il mammismo **una volta per tutti** di modo che **costituisca** un punto di riferimento.

Diciamo che da una parte nasce per divertimento e anche con intenzione 'catartica' per quanto è possibile per cui di sublimazione del problema. E poi perché mi sembra un problema **talmente** evidente, talmente **sotto gli occhi di tutti**, ma che nessuno ha mai **affrontato** in maniera così, anche ironica. Per cui mi è sembrato opportuno scrivere il primo libro che mettesse su bianco il fenomeno del mammismo con

presupposto premise

invasività invasiveness
nei confronti del with regard to

concedono they concede

permeato permeated
affetto affection

non volere bene not be in love [with them]

sfaccettature sides, faces

presumibilmente presumably
non si evince one can't see it
sembrerebbe proprio di no it would seem truly not [the case]

una sorta di classificazione con termini anche scientifici che però scientifici non sono, ma così parafrasando un...un manuale vero e proprio.

❹ – *Allora, partiamo da questo* **presupposto***. Per esempio, ci fa qualche esempio delle tante mamme-tipo che Lei ha descritto nel suo libro?*

– Le mamme si dividono principalmente in due categorie: ci sono le mamme molto autoritarie e le mamme molto permissive. E tra le mamme molto autoritarie c'è una mamma che è veramente 'totale' nella sua **invasività nei confronti del** figlio; Quella che organizza qualsiasi...qualsiasi attività dallo sport alla scuola, alle lezioni di chitarra, alle visite alle zie, ecc. ecc. Invece ci sono le mamme più permissive, più tolleranti che sono quelle che danno al figlio qualsiasi concessione e gli **concedono** tutto quello che vuole purché lui resti lì con lei.

❺ – *C'è qualcuna di queste mamma che almeno Le sia un pochino simpatica?*

– Tutte mi sono simpatiche, perché poi il libro è anche **permeato** da un grande **affetto**. Poi la voglia di parlarne col sorriso sulle labbra è anche perché poi a queste mamme, non si può **non volere bene**. E che poi non c'è neanche, tra l'altro, una madre completamente madre e una mamma completamente mamma. Diciamo che ci sono delle percentuali che variano secondo le persone; così come anche i caratteri, sono varie **sfaccettature** molto spesso della stessa persona.

❻ – *Ma secondo Lei una mamma intermedia non esiste? Una che* **presumibilmente** *potrebbe così accompagnare passo passo nella crescita il proprio figlio? Dal libro* **non si evince** *ma* **sembrerebbe proprio di no.**

irriducibile unrepentant
genitrici genetrix *or* female parent

più conciliante more conciliatory
autoriferito self-centered

A proposito With regard to

equipararlo equate him

comparsa extra (as on a film set)

ha assunto [he] has taken on

di scorta spare, extra
barbuto bearded
pipa pipe
assomiglia [he] takes after, seems like

è frutto it is the result of

anch'egli insomma he too in short
Di conseguenza Consequently
mammificazione "mommyfication"
colpito struck

– Beh, anche guardandosi intorno sembrerebbe proprio di no, insomma. Considerando che ci sono ancora quarantenni che vivono a casa con la mamma...Mi sento di dire che la mamma è proprio un essere **irriducibile**. Ci sono sicuramente...non tutte le **genitrici** sono mamme. Ci sono le...le mamme più terribili come sono quelle descritte nel libro poi ci sono quelle che si avvicinano di più ad una figura di madre. La madre è una genitrice più...più attenta, **più conciliante** e con un ego meno **autoriferito** per cui fa qualcosa anche nell'interesse del figlio.

⑦ – *Ecco.* ***A proposito*** *di interesse dei figli, nel suo saggio Lei dedica giusto due righe alla figura del papà – lo dobbiamo chiamare papà e non padre per* ***equipararlo*** *alla mamma - Ma è veramente solo una* ***comparsa*** *nel nucleo famigliare, nell'educazione di un giovane?*

– Forse una comparsa è un po' troppo. Sicuramente nell'educazione dei figli, **ha assunto** un ruolo secondario. Non è un protagonista. E' diciamo, una...una figura di secondo piano, che molto spesso, invece di fare il papà fa il '*mammo*'; per cui diventa una mamma **di scorta** per i figli. Non è quel genitore **barbuto**, con la **pipa**, autoritario che c'era un tempo. Adesso è molto più conciliante e molto spesso **assomiglia** più alla mamma che al papà.

⑧ – *Quindi diciamo che* ***è frutto*** *di un'evoluzione storica questa...questo cambiamento della figura del papà?*

– Beh, sì probabilmente anche perché c'è stata una nonna che – il papà è figlio di una mamma – è figlio di una mamma **anch'egli insomma**. **Di conseguenza** il processo di ***mammificazione*** si è strutturato nel tempo attraverso varie generazioni e ha **colpito** anche tanti papà che alla fine si sono ritrovati ad essere mamme.

datato dated, deep-rooted
atavico atavistic

comportamento behavior, bearing

nazional-popolare emblematic of an entire nation

nutre feeds, nurtures
ricatti morali moral blackmail

in controluce backlit

sceneggiato played out, staged

Probabilmente c'è da dire una cosa: che il fenomeno ormai, come ho scritto nel libro, è molto **datato** cioè un fenomeno quasi **atavico** in Italia. Di conseguenza è probabile che questi mariti, questi uomini siano comunque figli di una mamma che c'è stata in precedenza...

Posso dire la mamma che sarei io...nel senso che qualora fosse un figlio perché poi il...il **comportamento** di mamma è spesso un comportamento proprio anche di molti uomini e quindi io sicuramente sarei un papà – una mamma – a secondo della punta di vista iperprotettivo...sicuramente.

⑨ – *Quindi rimane 'lei' l'archetipo: 'La Mamma' ...*

– La mamma. Assolutamente sì.

– *Ma, la mamma di cui Lei scrive è tipicamente italiana?*

– Sì. Sì, direi proprio di sì. C'è ne una su tutte...se io dovesse scegliere la mamma **nazional-popolare** per eccellenza, quella è la 'Mamma Vittima'. La 'Mamma Vittima' è quella che **nutre** i figli con chili e chili di sensi di colpa; con dei **ricatti morali.** È quella che quando il figlio vuole uscire, gli dice "*Vuoi uscire? Fai come vuoi...*" E' poi si mette in una posa molto drammatica sulla...**in controluce** davanti alla finestra e a aspettare che il figlio si decida di uscire...Ma il figlio non uscirà – mai.

⑩ – *E Lei è proprio sicuro che sia <u>solo</u> un fenomeno italiano questo?*

– No. La verità è che le mamme sono poi presenti in tutto il mondo. Gli italiani però hanno una tensione estetica maggiore per cui hanno modo di comportarsi più **sceneggiato**. E allora di fronte a questa evidenza che è così formale, sembra che siamo più mammoni degli altri.

codici estetici visual cues
gesticolando through gesticulation

bel daffare means of overdoing it

'bamboccioni' a term coined by Italy's economy minister to describe the country's "boy-men" and the problems they create for Italian society by not cutting the apron strings
ambito domestico domestic setting

promesse promising
minacce menacing

colpisce it strikes
pretestuosa [offering an] excuse/alibi

un rapporto paritario a more balanced relationship

Il rapporto madre-figlio, mamma-figlio, più esattamente, trovo che poi sia un fenomeno che non conosce confini ed è valutabile in...su scala internazionale. In Italia, il fenomeno ha dei **codici estetici** maggiori, per cui noi parliamo **gesticolando**, urliamo e di conseguenza riusciamo a sceneggiare il...il rapporto mamma-figlio in termini più visibili. Però anche all'estero, nelle mie esperienze straniere, c'è. Non è un patrimonio esclusivamente italiano. Noi forse lo facciamo un po' meglio, però anche le mamme straniere hanno il loro **bel daffare** per tenere i figli vicino.

Però in fondo, i mammoni ci sono anche in Svezia – non... non a caso gli Abba hanno scritto *'Mamma mia'*!

⑪ – *Senta, ma questa mamma avrà anche un effetto in qualche modo nella società, no? Questa mamma così 'castrante'. E soprattutto produrrà i famosi figli che recentemente... sono stati definiti 'bamboccioni'.*

– Diciamo che finché il mammone è nell'**ambito domestico**, per cui tra le mura di casa, il problema è privato. Nel momento in cui poi cresce, diventa un adulto, e...ed entra a far parte di un contesto sociale-pubblico, allora il problema diventa di tutti. E' per questo che la mamma, invece di offrire alla società tanti giovani **promesse**, offre alla società tanti giovani **minacce**.

⑫ – *Senta – ma il mammismo – il fenomeno del mammismo: chi è che **colpisce** prevalentemente, l'uomo o la donna? E' una domanda **pretestuosa**...*

– Io, ovviamente essendo anche un'opera autobiografica, credo che colpisca sicuramente più i maschi che le femmine. Perché in famiglia di solito il figlio è il preferito della mamma, la figlia è la preferita del papà. Di conseguenza la figlia arriva prima di avere **un rapporto paritario**, anche un rapporto

'il cocco'   the darling, the pet

a fondo   in depth

uno sguardo   a look
carnefice   executioner

velenosa   poisonous
ad affrancarsi   free himself
serrata   shut tight, confining
scappare   escape

allontanarsi   leave, distance oneself

nido materno   maternal nest

conflittuale con la mamma. Mentre invece il figlio resta sempre **'il cocco'** della mamma.

Però trovo e ho sempre visto intorno a me un carattere più forte nella...nella parte femminile. E quindi ho visto che... soprattutto con la mamma il rapporto di una ragazza che diventa adulta diventa un rapporto da donna a donna. Mentre da questo punto di vista trovo che il figlio sia sempre un po' penalizzato, nel senso che resta sempre un pochettino più il bambino della sua mamma. Comunque ci sono sicuramente tante e diffusi casi di mammismo al femminile. Questo... questo è certo.

⑬ – *Va da sé che quindi anche che Lei è o è stato un 'bamboccione', se la sua mamma è una mamma castrante, mi scusi.*

– Se io non fosse un bamboccione, non potrei conoscere il problema così da dentro, così **a fondo**. Per questo io non è che ho fatto un libro comico che ride di altri. E' più un tono umoristico per cui **uno sguardo** che osserva il mondo con gli occhi della vittima e non con gli occhi del **carnefice**.

– *Secondo lei c'è un antidoto contro questa mamma così* **velenosa***? Come fa un giovane* **ad affrancarsi** *da questa prigionia psicologica così* **serrata***?*

– Dalla prigionia psicologica si deve **scappare**. L'unica possibilità è una fuga. Bisogna tagliare il cordone ombelicale il prima possibile perché molto spesso si aspettano i trent'anni prima di andarsene da casa. Mentre invece creare una giusta distanza tra il figlio e la mamma, cioè **allontanarsi** piano piano, fare vacanze assieme, andare a vivere da soli il prima possibile nonostante le difficoltà, è sicuramente la soluzione migliore. Cioè creare uno spazio e non restare legati al tavolo della cucina dagli spaghetti della mamma. Per quanto sia difficile adesso...allontanarsi dal **nido materno** anche per

rottura clean break

occorre lo strappo one needs to break off (completely)

lotta durissima tough battle

le reazioni a caldo the immediate reactions to

si è offeso was offended [by it]
oltremisura above and beyond
denota denotes
un nervo scoperto a raw nerve
polemica matter, debate
scatenata set off

ha dato dei he called [them]

ultratrentenni over 30-somethings
se non addirittura if not even

condizione oggettive però ci dev'essere assolutamente anche una **rottura**, anche traumatica. Però i figli devono scappare, devono rinunciare ai tortellini, alle tagliatelle, alle comodità, alle camicie stirate...però se vogliono diventare degli adulti responsabili e autonomi devono allontanarsi dalla mamma al prima possibile. Però di fronte una mamma che tira a sé questo cordone ombelicale con tanta forza, **occorre lo strappo.**

(14) – *Però le sue mamme sembrerebbero non renderlo possibile, una presa di distanza di questo tipo.*

– E' una **lotta durissima**. È una lotta durissima. Per quello mentre una genitrice ideale lascia andare il figlio piano piano, cioè dà, offre al mondo il proprio figlio, la mamma tira questo cordone ombelicale a sé il più a lungo possibile.

– *Ci piacerebbe sentire da Lei quali sono state **le reazioni a caldo** al suo libro?*

– Ci sono state reazioni di vario tipo, allora: c'é chi **si è offeso** e quindi si è offeso anche **oltremisura**. Questa **denota** forse il fatto che il libro abbia toccato **un nervo scoperto** da parte di qualcuno e questo vale soprattutto per gli uomini.
Il libro è caduto in un momento storico particolare; che è stato quello della **polemica** dei '*bamboccioni*' **scatenata** da Padoa-Schioppa.

(15) – *Vorrei precisare per i nostri ascoltatori che Padoa-Schioppa è stato Ministro dell'Economia e la polemica è stata causata dal fatto che **ha dato dei** 'bamboccioni' ai giovani che oramai diventati quasi adulti, continuavano a stare in casa con le mamme anziché praticamente iniziare una vita per conto loro. In particolare, questa fascia di **ultratrentenni se non addirittura** quarantenni che continuano a convivere con i genitori.*

spaccato split

costume sociale social mores

Ciò non toglie That doesn't mean that
zoccolo ridge, barrier
sacrificio sacrifice

biancheria stirata ironed underwear
indolenza lethargy
fascia segment

vendetta revenge
catarsi catharsis

la mamma che è...è sempre la mamma popular Italian saying

Questa frase ha **spaccato** l'Italia un po' in due, nel senso che molti gli hanno dato ragione, altri si sono sentiti offesi. Ovviamente l'universo dei bamboccioni è fatto di tante...tante situazioni, tanti casi diversi. Diciamo che ci sono quelli che possono andare via da casa, ma non vogliono, e quelli che vogliono andare via da casa ma non possono. Perché sicuramente per tornare anche al discorso che riguarda gli altri paesi – all'estero c'è un **costume sociale** per cui è più facile andare via di casa. I ragazzi vanno a studiare nelle università che spesso non sono vicino...vicino a casa; hanno delle possibilità maggiori. Per un giovane italiano andare via da casa è sicuramente più difficile; gli affitti, le case sono...sono costose, non sono accessibili alla tasca, al portafoglio di...di molte persone. **Ciò non toglie** che ci sia però uno **zoccolo** duro – molto molto duro – di ultratrentenni che potrebbero, facendo anche un piccolo **sacrificio**, andare via da casa, ma invece restano con i genitori perché in fondo è più comodo avere la cena pronta, il pranzo pronto, la **biancheria stirata**...E quindi c'è un'**indolenza** sicuramente in una grande **fascia** di...di persone che fa sì che non...non ci si provi nemmeno a uscire di casa; sacrificarsi ma che si resti così con...con le tagliatelle della mamma.

⑯ – *Mi scusi, si tratta appunto di un pubblico femminile o di un pubblico maschile?*

– No, di un pubblico maschile. Il pubblico femminile è invece, soprattutto nelle generazioni più giovani non nelle generazioni più adulte, ha trovato nel libro una sorta di **vendetta**, una **catarsi**, un...un finalmente qualcuno che descriva alla perfezione i loro fidanzati, i loro mariti, i loro compagni che sono quelli che portano le camicie dalla mamma perché la mamma stira meglio, che vanno a mangiare a casa della mamma perché la mamma cucina meglio e che quindi impongono alle loro...alle loro donne, alle loro mogli, una continua comparazione con **la mamma che è...è sempre la mamma.**

conservare a sé keep for herself
contagio contagion, infection

ammette permit

sfogo release

Psyco The 1960 Alfred Hitchcock thriller is spelled without the "h" in Italian.

riversandolo [that] spills over
imbranata inept
goffaggine awkwardness

mancanza di prospettive lack of vision (for a positive future)
sfiducia distrust, uneasiness

impedisce she prevents

⑰ – *Lei traccia un parallelo tra mammismo e collezionismo. Di solito il collezionista Lei dice è sicuramente un mammone. E' l'esempio di una madre che tende a **conservare a sé** il figlio fa sì poi che il figlio tenda a conservare le cose. Ma come avviene questo **contagio**?*

– Beh, questo viene da uno stato di vicinanza veramente che non **ammette** soluzioni spaziali. Cioè, è un contatto, è una compagnia, una presenza quella della mamma nei confronti di questi figli che molto spesso sono figli unici. Perché il collezionista poi cerca uno **sfogo** anche perché non ha fratelli o sorelle con cui giocare. Per cui la vicinanza della madre è tale, il possesso della madre è tale che poi quasi per contagio viene assunto anche dal figlio. Ho scritto nel libro che poi si rischia di avere quasi delle figure alla Norman Bates di **Psyco** in cui poi il figlio in qualche modo diventa la mamma. E nel suo comportamento riflette questo…questo senso di possesso **riversandolo** su degli oggetti; per cui il collezionista è in effetti poi una persona che spesso si mostra un po' così **imbranata** nelle relazioni sociali, occhiali, un po' di…di **goffaggine** anche nella…comportamentale. E questa figura è una figura che mi sono molto divertito a scrivere per la verità perché trovavo fonte di grande divertimento.

⑱ – *Lei dice che la mamma è incompatibile con l'idea del progresso. Lei oramai è adulto. Ma che problemi individua per gli adolescenti di oggi?*

– Beh, per gli adolescenti di oggi sicuramente il problema non è solo la mamma, sia ben chiaro, perché oggi c'è una…una diffusa **mancanza di prospettive** soprattutto nelle classi più giovani per cui c'è un po' più di…di **sfiducia** verso…verso il futuro. Sicuramente la mamma resta comunque una componente, un deterrente come ho scritto nel libro che vorrebbe…cioé che **impedisce** un progresso, uno sviluppo,

pulcini baby chicks

lotta estrema fight to the bitter end

imbattibile unbeatable
combattività belligerence, fighting spirit
soccomberà will give in/subdue

accatastati piled up layer upon layer

si avventurano venture

assistenza medica healthcare system
Siccome Seeing that

degenza ospedaliera hospital stays

anche nei...nei propri figli. Ho scritto una cosa proprio relativa al tempo che il problema in fondo nasce dal fatto che la mamma vorrebbe che i figli restassero sempre piccoli, i suoi bambini. Per cui vederli crescere è inevitabilmente un dolore per...per delle genitrici così possessive. E quindi da questo punto di vista, è una...è un' anti-progressista la mamma perché vorrebbe fermare il tempo nel momento in cui lei è comunque la chioccia e avvicina a sé i suoi...i suoi **pulcini**.

⑲ – *Mi ci dica...in questa **lotta estrema**, alla fine, chi si salva l'uomo o la mamma?*

– La mamma. La mamma...La mamma è **imbattibile**. La mamma senza dubbio perché ha una **combattività** tale, ha una forza tale che è più probabile che **soccomberà** l'uomo.

L'uomo deve...deve lottare veramente molto per affrancarsi...ma ormai ci sono generazioni e generazioni di mammoni che si sono **accatastati** nel corso del tempo per cui hanno poca speranza.

⑳ – *Benissimo. Siamo arrivati alle conclusioni. Ci dica se sta lavorando a qualcosa di nuovo?*

– Sto lavorando ad un secondo libro che invece di famiglie, mamme e papà prende in esame gli ospedali. Quindi vuole essere un manuale di sopravvivenza per i malati italiani che **si avventurano** negli ospedali italiani.

E' un tema molto vivo in Italia, e non solo, noi ricordiamo anche il film di Michael Moore che ha fatto recentemente riguardo l'**assistenza medica** negli Stati Uniti. **Siccome** conosco molto bene diversi ospedali purtroppo per esperienze personali, pensavo di scrivere un manuale di **degenza ospedaliera**; ciòe come comportarsi in ospedali per soffrire il meno possibile.

a tutti gli effetti in every respect

di non capitarle mai sott'occhio   never to find myself within
eyeshot

㉑ – *Quindi giovani malati e malati invece* **a tutti gli effetti.** *Benissimo. Ci aspettiamo un...un prodotto almeno divertente e anche profondo come* Mamma mia! *Buon lavoro! Devo dire che come mamma spero* **di non capitarle mai sott'occhio** *in compagnia dei miei figli!*

Grazie mille. Grazie.

– Grazie a voi.